Praise For Dream Reachers II

"There are three kinds of people: those who make things happen, those who watch things happen, and those who wonder what happened. The stories in this book are guaranteed to inspire you to believe more deeply in your dreams and to motivate you to take the necessary actions to make those dreams come true. *Dream Reachers 2* is an inspirational book and a must-read for anyone who wants to make things happen in their own lives. It is guaranteed to be a runaway best-seller!"

- Darcy Donavan, *International Film & Television Actress, Recording Artist, Supermodel, Writer, Producer, Philanthropist and Entrepreneur*

"Betty Dravis and Chase Von know how to bring out inspirational stories from the people who are reaching for their dreams and living them! This is a true collector's book--a 'must' in every library!"

- Daniel L. Carter, author of *The Unwanted trilogy*

"Betty Dravis and Chase Von understand how important it is to *Dream Reachers* such as myself to continue to seek inspiration. In reading the stories they tenaciously collect and pencil, there's no mistaking that they have an endless love for people like me. Stories such as these will be passed on to generations, continuing to encourage and stimulate others in achieving their dreams. A heartfelt thanks to Betty and Chase."

- Norma Jean, *Actress and Comedienne*

"In this sequel to *Dream Reachers,* authors Betty Dravis and Chase Von again give us fascinating stories and interviews of men and women who had the perseverance to follow their passions and dreams. We meet an array of men and women in the arts, from filmmakers, writers, musicians and actors to world champion women boxers. We find out their challenges, sacrifices and determination to make their dreams come true. It is a very uplifting read, in a day when the world faces sometimes insurmountable challenges, to see how these talented men and women "stayed the mile" to make it happen. A definite good read for anyone who is pursuing a dream."

- Susan Alcott Jardine, author of *The Channel: Stories From L.A.*

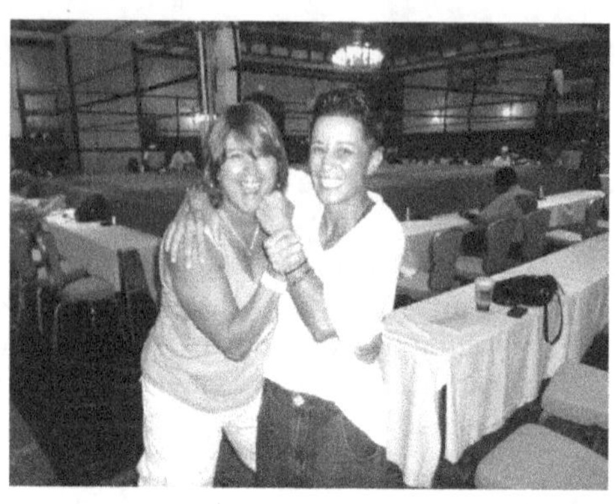

Mary Ann Lurie Owen and
Six Time World Champion Ada "Ace" Velez

"I like to think I've been a go-getter all my life, despite the many obstacles I have had to face. Consequently, I have also been drawn to those who 'go for the gold.' This book is full of such souls; more people I'd like to meet in the future. Kudos to you, Chase and Betty. *Dream Reachers II* rocks!"

- Mary Ann Lurie Owen, acclaimed *Sports Photographer,* author of *Extraordinary Women of the Ring*

"Dreams,
Like all other things
That hold true meaning
In this temporary existence
We partake in,
Increase in value
When shared."

by Chase Von
tlp
The Last Panther

Dream Reachers II

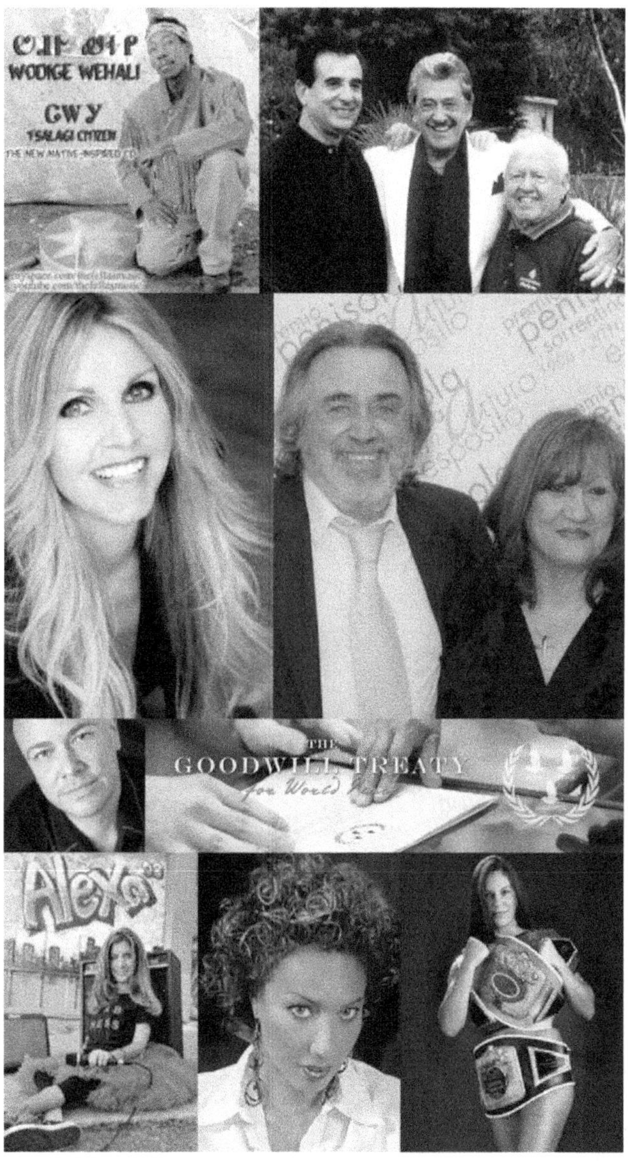

Only those who stretch to reach their dreams find themselves living them

VonChase Publishing Company

Contents

Other books by Betty Dravis

Nonfiction:
Dream Reachers Volume I

Fiction:
1106 Grand Boulevard
The Toonies Invade Silicon Valley
Millennium Babe: The Prophecy

Coming in May 2011:
1106 Grand Boulevard, E-book
The Toonies Invade Silicon Valley, E-book

Short Story Anthology:
Just Our Best Short Stories 2005
(includes three stories by Betty Dravis)

Other books by Chase Von

Nonfiction:
Dream Reachers Volume I

Poetry:
Your Chance to Hear the Last Panther Speak
Pink, Blue and Green

Note: Chase Von's interviews in this book were previously published in online website "Student Operated Press." Betty Dravis's interviews were previously published in online website "Dames of Dialogue."

A portion of the proceeds of this book will be donated to the Stem Cell Research Foundation and to the Breast Cancer Care Research Fund, causes that are dear to the hearts of the authors. In paying it forward, remember what Mark Twain once said: *"Kindness is a language which the deaf can hear and the blind can read."*

ISBN: *0-9823464-7-6*

LCCN: *2011927396*

Dream Reachers (Vol. 2) manufactured in the USA
An original publication by

Von Chase Publishing Company
P.O. Box 572
Winchester, CA 92596

Cover design by Chase Von, Betty Dravis and Daniel L. Carter
© May 2011

Cover photograph by cinematographer Mario Prado; Back cover photograph by Samantha Isom, NYC.

Authors: Betty Dravis, Chase Von
Editors: Betty Dravis, Chase Von

Parental advisory: this publication does include some adult content.

Dedication

This second collection of *Dream Reachers* interviews is dedicated to everyone who has ever had a dream, and that includes every man, woman and child on the planet. My dearest wish for you all is that you reach your dreams; even fulfilling a portion of them often makes a huge difference in lifestyle and attitude. We all have our dreams…

My writing is always dedicated to my children who are everything to me: my life, my loves. And Dream Reachers II is specifically dedicated to my dear friends and fellow bloggers on the popular website *Dames of Dialogue*: authors Christy Tillery French, Laurel Rain Snow, Caitlyn Hunter and blog founder Maggie Bishop. It is a pleasure working with these dedicated writers on a daily basis. Thanks for all your encouragement with my interviews and my books. Dames rule!

Betty Dravis

Doing the first Dream Reachers was an experience I don't think I will ever forget. The same holds true with Dream Reachers II and who knows? Perhaps there will be even more to come. I would, however, like to dedicate this current book to all the individuals in it, as well as my family and friends and everyone that takes the steps to make their own dreams a reality. I also dedicate this effort of love to my co-author Betty Dravis and to Judyth Piazza, the creator of the Student Operated Press. As anyone who has gotten anywhere will tell you, one thing often leads to another and meeting those two is what led to this series of books. Best wishes to all and it is my hope that you who seek your dreams will find encouragement to do so from the people in this book who are seeking and living theirs.

Chase Von

Special Thanks

Grateful acknowledgment to the following for permission to reprint photos and movie stills:

Artist Aynsley Nesbit, original art; K. Michael Crawford, original art and Special Olympics commissioned work; C. Robert Lee, copyrighted photography; Katherin Kovin Pacino, Claire Dodin and all the Dream Reachers for photos from their private collections; Talent Spotlight Magazine; Ennio Pontis, Italian producer, Director David Worth and Screenwriter Antonia Tosini for use of Between the Olive Trees (Tra Gli Uliva) movie poster; Eye in the Sky Entertainment; Nasser Entertainment; photographer Mary Ann Brown; photographer Sue Michelson, Soul Gallery; photographer Barry Slobin; Andre' Cohen Photography; Pacino Worldwide, Jackie Krudop and Iris Frank; Karianne Flaathen; Jessica Gilbert Angel photo courtesy of "Shadow"; Annette Ziegler; San Francisco 49ers Football Organization; Photographer Peter E. H. Riechof.

"I started with the firm conviction that
when I came to the end,
I wanted to be regretting the things
that I had done,
Not the things I hadn't."

--- Michael Caine (b 1933) English actor

Acknowledgements

Special thanks to everyone who helped create this book: all the talented Dream Reachers in both books; Director David Worth for writing the foreword; Italian Popera Sensation Romina Arena and author Daniel L. Carter for endless moral support; Linda Bulger for always "having Betty's back" and Judyth Piazza for "having Chase's back." ☺

For popular media events, we would also like to thank our network of fans and friends on Facebook, Dames of Dialogue, Student Operated Press, The American Perspective (Florida Radio), Al Cole of CBS Radio (Boston), Goodreads, The Next Cat, Amazon reviewers, etc. There are many more who have helped us. If we failed to list you, forgive the oversight... You know who you are, so take a bow.

Thanks for making a difference in our lives, thus enhancing the lives of all who read our inspiring book. In addition to urging our readers to go for your dreams, we also encourage you to repay kindness with kindness and make a difference in your own little corner of the world.

Most important, thanks to God for making the impossible possible. The glory is His because without Him we could accomplish nothing.

Betty Dravis & Chase Von

Charter Dream Reachers from Book One

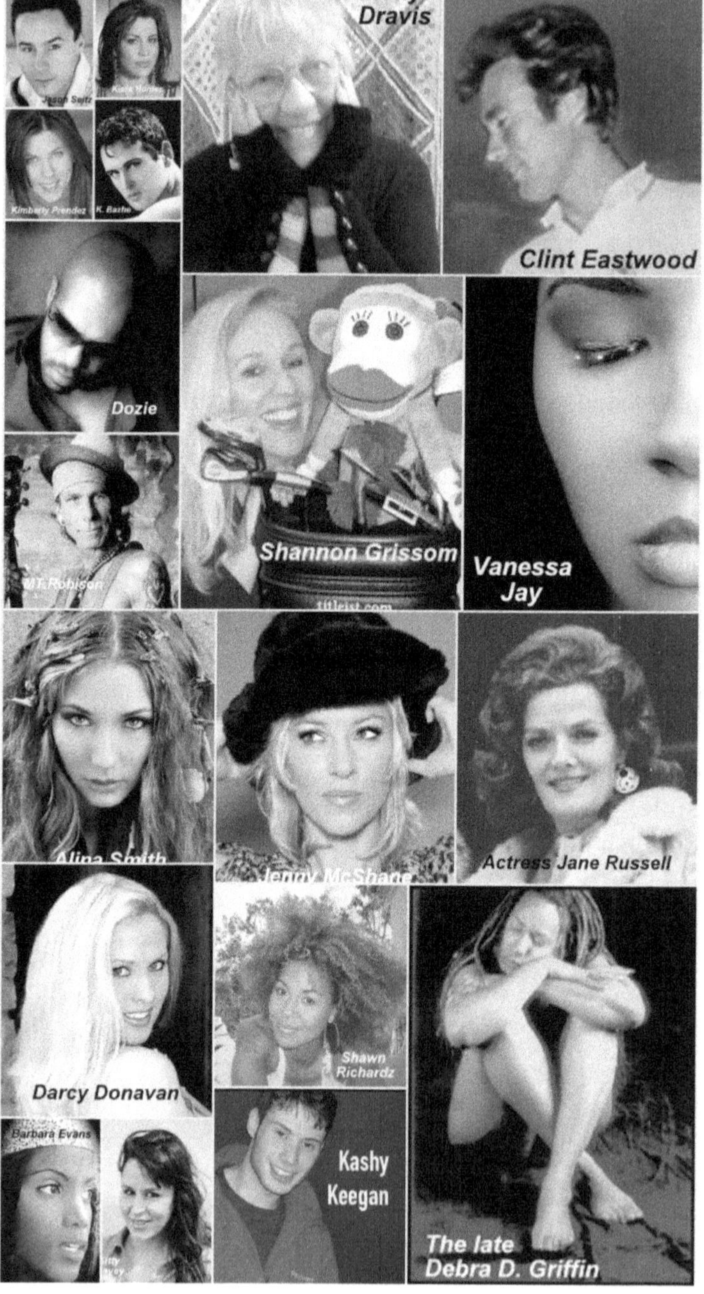

Charter Dream Reachers from Book One

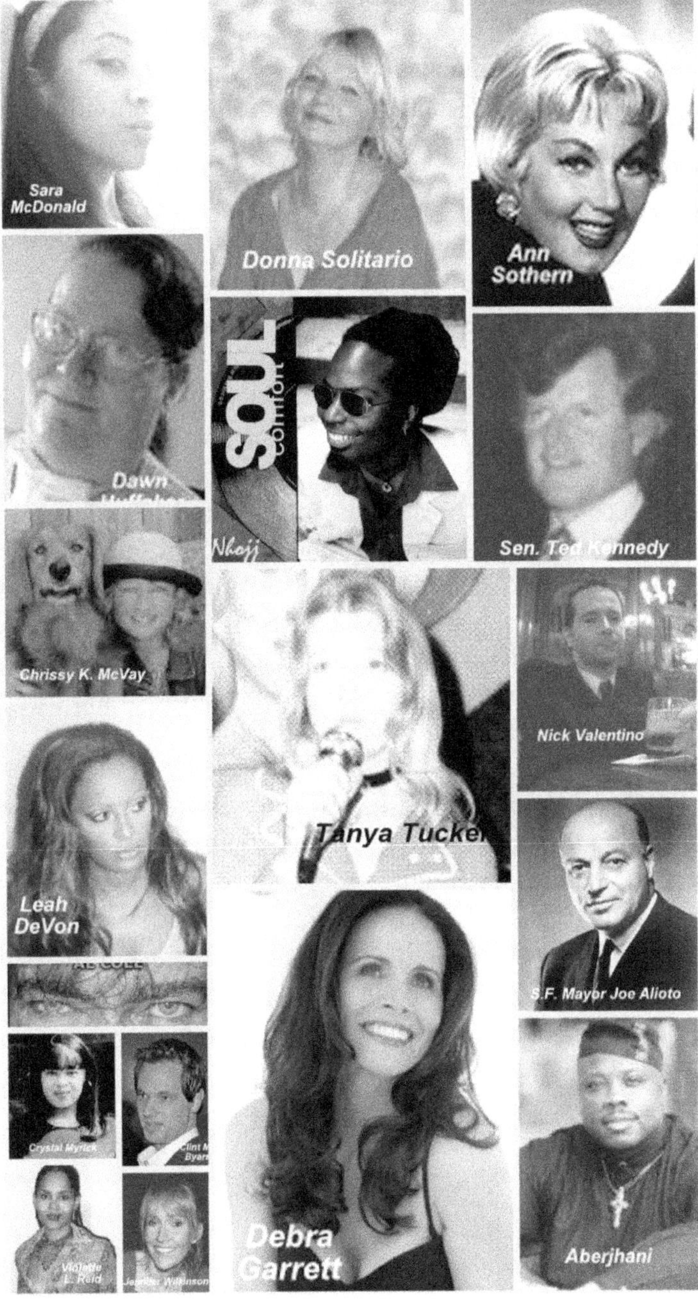

Foreword

I was overwhelmed and honored when Betty Dravis asked me to write the foreword for this new book that she did with Chase Von. Several of her interviewees are friends, acquaintances and colleagues and all of them are extraordinary individuals who have, through their insight, desire and perseverance, become DREAM REACHERS who have achieved greatness in their lives and work.

In an era when "self help" seems to be doled out by any and every "authority" with a laptop, this book offers an inspirational and refreshing alternative, by letting each reader discover for themselves the insights that led this outstanding collection of DREAM REACHERS to accomplish their goals.

Being successful can mean many things and in today's world that seems to emphasize corporate greed, it usually means being financially successful beyond all necessity and reason. Happily, the DREAM REACHERS in this book have a different perspective on success, and their insights and achievements into their own spiritual journey and in their service to the human condition speak volumes.

While making the classic film, *Rashomon*, Akira Kurosawa's great cinematographer, Kazuo Miyagawa, stated, "...Forget the expensive equipment, only a beautiful person can take beautiful pictures..." Something similar might be said for the authors and interviewees in this wonderful, insightful book... "Only a beautiful person can become a DREAM REACHER..."

David Worth

Director/DP/Author/Assistant Professor

Dream Reachers II

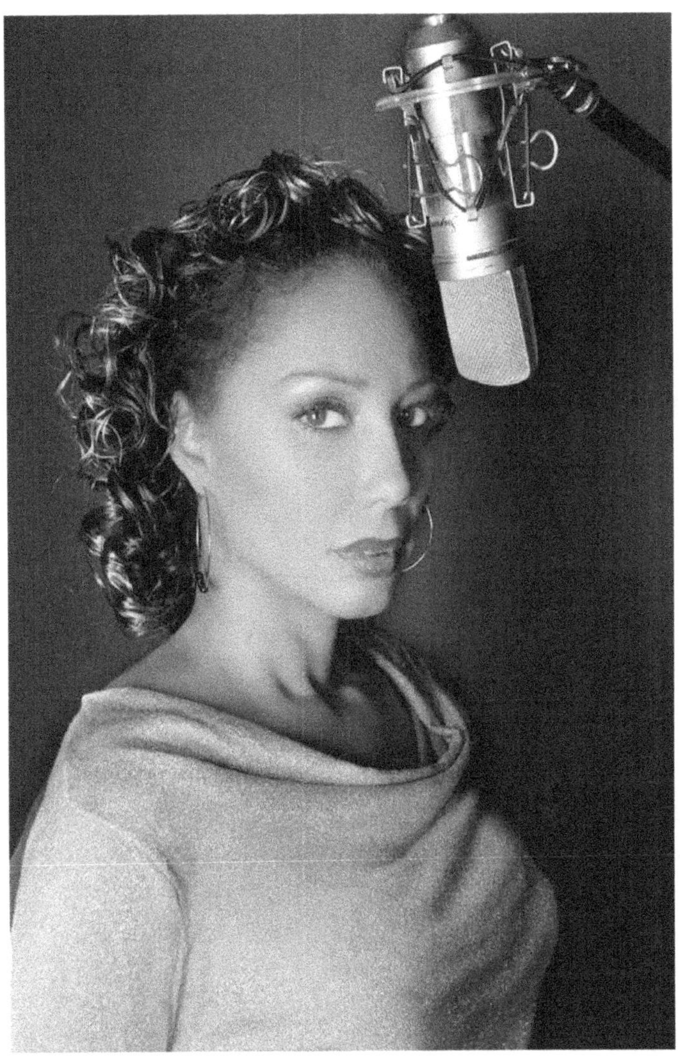

Joan Baker - Dream Reacher and "Voiceover Queen"

Only those who stretch to reach their dreams find themselves living them

Von Chase Publishing Company
http://www.bettydravis.com

Mindy & Kevin James Win 49ers Contest: Deluxe Super Bowl Trip

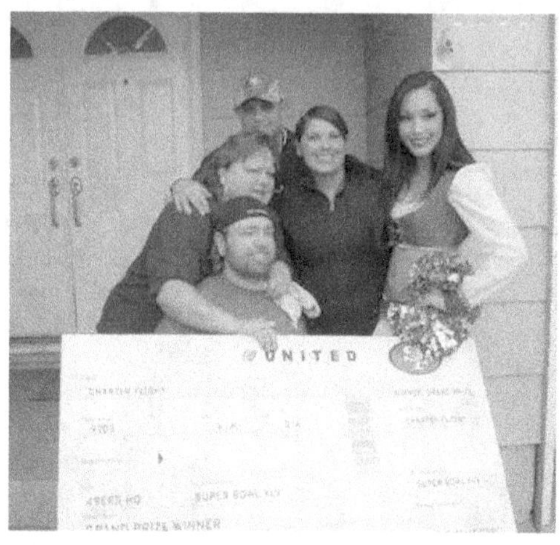

Dream of a Lifetime - Mindy, Kevin, Seth & Jessica James are pictured above with 49ers Cheerleader Carmen.

by Betty Dravis

There are dreams and there are DREAMS! Everyone has some kind of dream. Some dreams are small, like winning a spelling bee, singing with a local band or publishing a book for family members only. And some are large dreams: like being a famous rock star, an Oscar-winning actor or a best-selling author.

The people that Chase Von and I write about in our *Dream Reachers* books are, generally, those people who have reached their dreams through overcoming obstacles...no matter whether their dream be large or small.

Another kind of dream is a "once-in-a-lifetime dream" that lands in one's lap through sheer good luck! Well, that's what happened to my daughter Mindy James and her family. I wish to share their good fortune with you because it's an uplifting story.

When the Forty-Niners Football organization held a contest to award an all-expense-paid trip to the 2011 Super Bowl to three Season Ticket Holders, Mindy James told her ticket agent Dustin Albertson that winning would be a "dream come true."

So when she answered the door the following week and came face to face with him, 49ers VP of Tickets and Suites Jamie Brandt, Director of Marketing Ali Towle, 49ers Gold Rush Cheerleader Carmen and a camera crew, she was flabbergasted... *Stunned, really...*

James, a Realtor with Luxor Real Estate Group in Los Gatos, California, had this to say: "*The initial surprise was ultimately awesome. Kevin and my co-workers, Dennis and Sue Byron, kept it a secret and when I answered my front door, I was obviously in awe! After thirty years of marriage, there aren't many times Kevin has been able to keep a secret from me! It was so incredibly surprising to me because I had just entered the contest the week before and here at my front doorsteps were the 49ers crew, cheerleaders with balloons and a giant-sized airline ticket for Super Bowl XLV in Dallas Texas. Woo hoo!*"

It was an exhilarating, yet hilarious, moment…as the video posted on the Niners website shows. The other two winners were Carolyn Del Curto-Infante and Joe Wilson who were just as surprised.

To view the video on the Internet: http://tinyurl.com/5vyxr88. Mindy and Joe were chosen to document the trip and given special cameras. Since Mindy at one time announced for racing events, she was a natural; Joe did a great job also.

You can check their documented "Dream Trip" at: http://tinyurl.com/6cxufaf.

The prize included two tickets, round-trip transportation to Dallas on the 49ers charter plane and four nights at the Hyatt

Regency. Other passengers included 49ers President & CEO Jed York and rapper M.C. Hammer. York chatted with everyone on the plane, making them feel at home. Special thanks to Nikki Hawkins, 49ers Sr. Corporate Accounts Mgr. for coordinating the trip.

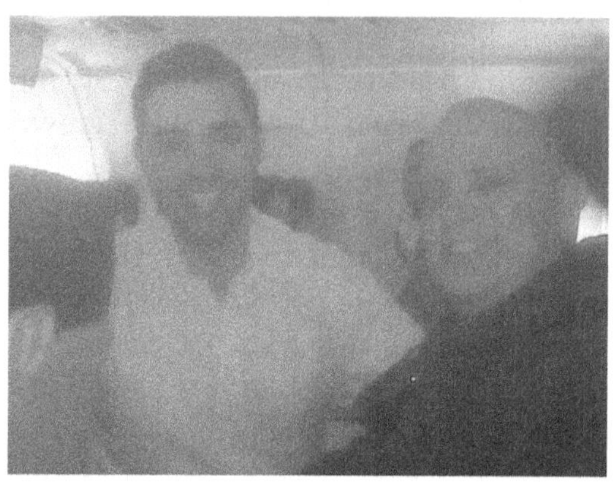

49ers President & CEO Jed York with Kevin James

Because of the NFC connection, the Bay Area fans rooted for the Packers and were delighted by Green Bay's victory. "My experience, all in all, was awesome," Mindy James told the *San Jose Mercury News.* "I just hope that next time we're at a Super Bowl, it's to watch the 49ers."

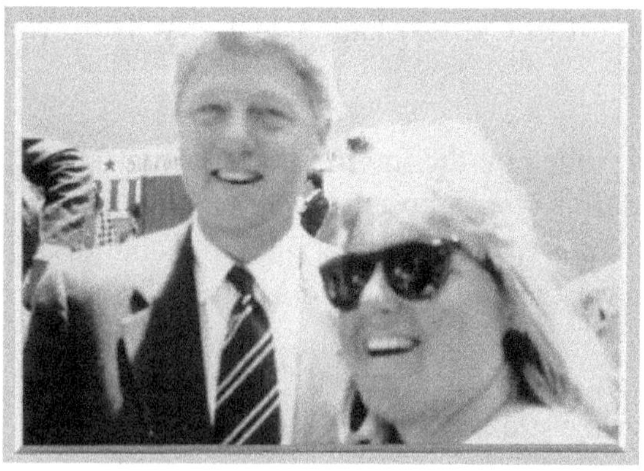

Mindy James with President Bill Clinton, taken during her news publishing career, before son Seth's tragic accident.

PART ONE

INTERVIEWS BY BETTY DRAVIS

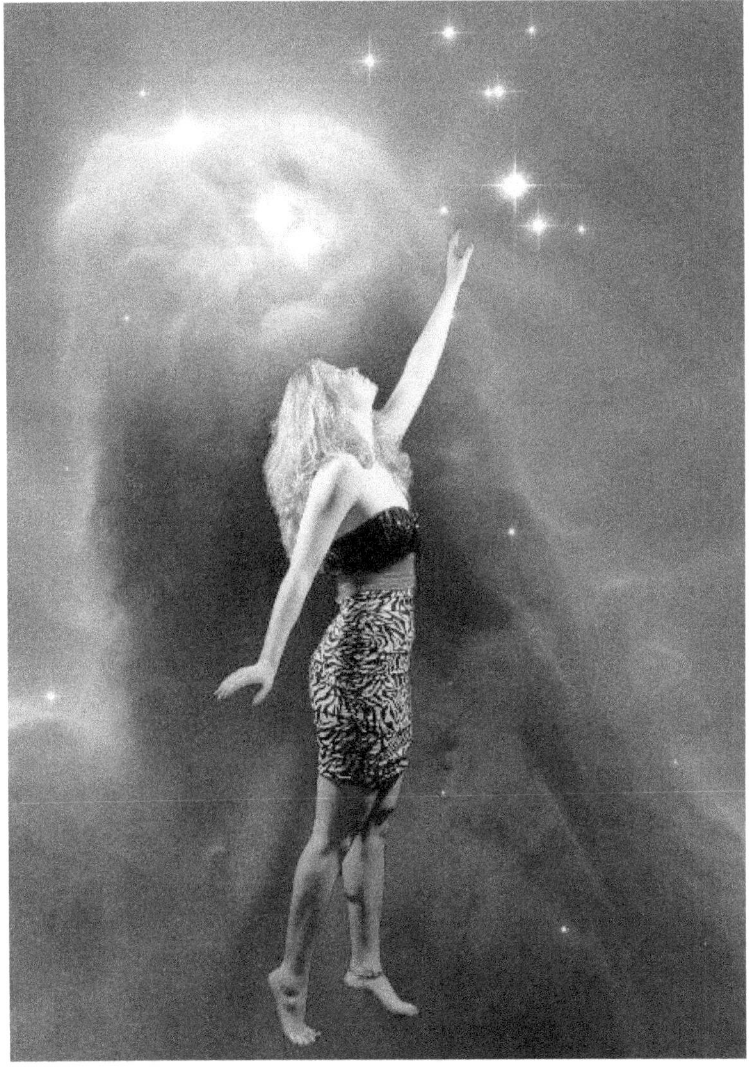

Gorgeous Actress/Singer Marissa Autumn Reaches for Her Dreams

Only those who stretch to reach their dreams find themselves living them

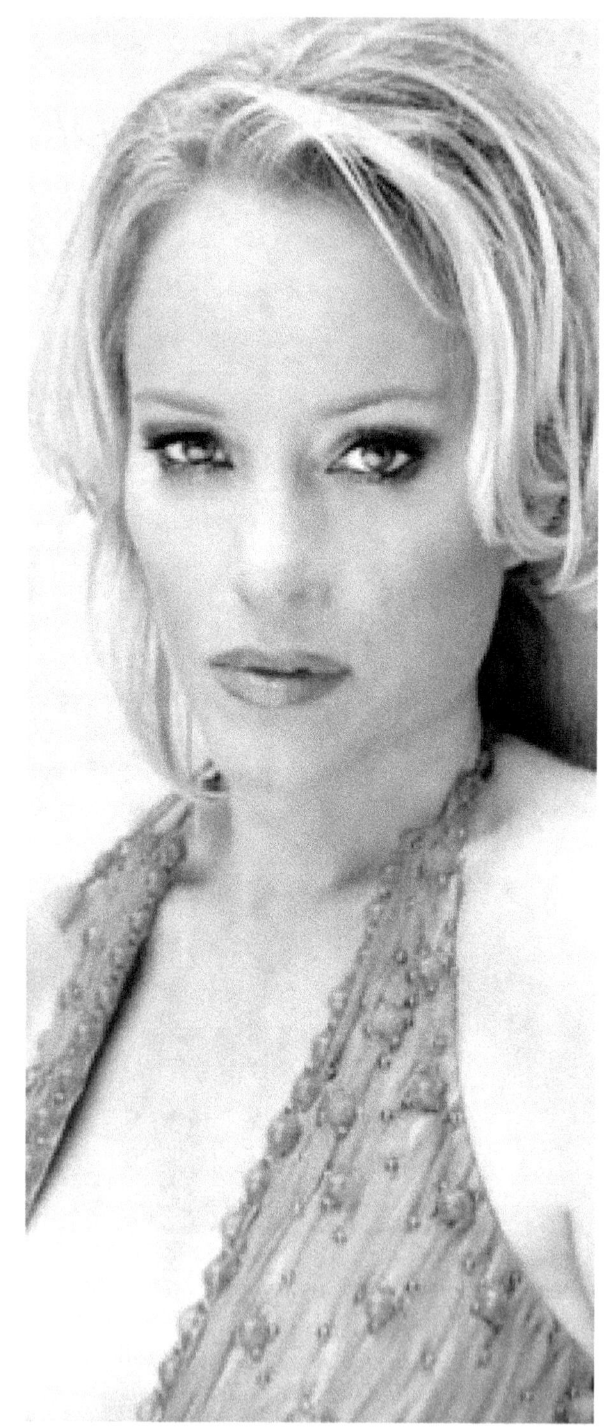

Interview with Jenny McShane

ACTRESS/SINGER IN HOT DEMAND

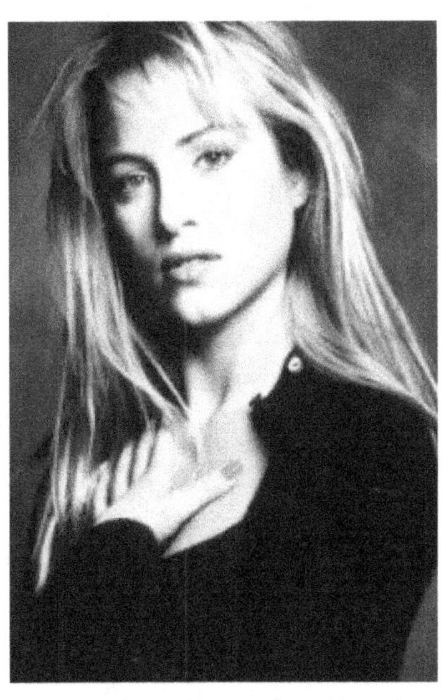

Betty Dravis: Welcome to Dames of Dialogue, Jenny. Christy Tillery French, co-founder of this select band of female authors, appointed me as celebrity interviewer of the group. As you know, the Dames usually interview people in the publishing industry, but since I co-author a series of *Dream Reachers* books, they think it will add fascinating variety to interview people from the other arts. You are one of the most popular artists in *Dream Reachers* and were so helpful to me and Chase Von during its production that I wanted to interview you again for this edition.

Jenny, you have done so much in the entertainment industry, I'm sure our readers will enjoy you as much as your current fans do. I know from your section in *Dream Reachers* about your father's job choice, but can you tell us a little about that and how you went from there to being such a successful actress?

Jenny McShane: I wanted to be an actress since the age of three when I tortured neighborhood kids by performing on a ledge in my basement with an empty paper-towel holder as my microphone. I asked my parents for a piano when I was in second grade. I had a deep desire to get whatever it was inside out, I think! Most people who know me say I like attention, but I think it is more than that—I like to see people happy. I think music and entertaining lets people momentarily escape whatever stress they may have. When I see people's faces respond with a happy gaze, it makes me happy. Entertaining helps me to escape, as well, and gives me a deep inner peace.

Betty Dravis: You chose your career for an admirable reason, Jenny, but it looks like it chose you, too. I have to grin at the image of the "little girl you" in that basement. I bet you get a lot of mileage from being the "daughter of a pig farmer" too…and a lot more laughs, all good-natured and in the right spirit, I'm sure. Nobody can argue with success. I'll get into some of your movies and your leading men later, but can you tell us about when you first started singing and playing guitar?

I understand you formed your own band for a while, but that you recently joined an up-and-coming band with a very unusual name. Do you mind sharing about how you met "Harry the Dog" and where you're currently performing?

Jenny McShane: I do, oddly enough, get a lot of mileage out of the Pig Farmer's Daughter line. My mother gets so upset, especially when they included Pig Farmer's Daughter in an interview *The New York Times* did on me. "Couldn't you say Hog Farmer's Daughter, Jen?" she asked. "It sounds so much nicer."… I think the funniest thing that ever happened with the pig stories was meeting Smokey Hormel. Smokey was the son of the famous Hormel family, which is where I drove with my family to take our pigs when it was time for them to go to market. Smokey became a guitar player in Bruce Willis's band. I started playing guitar and singing when I realized I could get out of some more work.

When we were growing up, my parents made a music room for us in the house. Mom and Dad loved to listen to me play the piano at night after chores. I honestly liked playing but knew it would also make them forget about extra things that might need to be done. My father is one of twenty-two children. His brothers and sisters and mother were all very musical and I was in heaven when I went to my grandma's house and heard them all singing and playing various instruments together. It was so beautiful. My grandmother played the violin and was an expert tap dancer, so she was always the highlight of the show.

It was such a sense of achievement when I learned to play guitar and piano and could sit in with Dad's family and keep up. I took piano lessons at the convent next to the Catholic school, from Marguerite McPartland, another Irish lass. The piano was great, as you can read music and it helps you learn other instruments easily. I can play accordion and guitar based on the basics of the piano lessons.

I did have my own band, called Little Rubie, for a little bit seven years ago. I put it together to keep myself busy when I wasn't working in acting. In April of this year I joined a band called Harry the Dog and the Traveling Soul Circus. My boyfriend is from England and has a whole crew of English

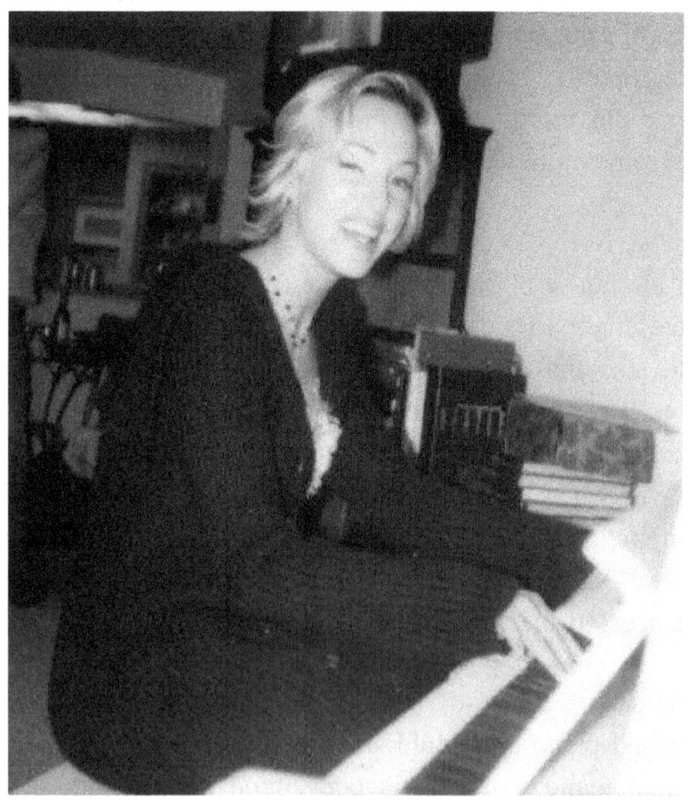

people in LA who really stick together like a posse. He is friends and a big fan of Harry Bridgen's band. I accidentally ran into Harry at an English pub called Cat N Fiddle on Sunset. I overheard one of Harry's friends saying they were looking for a female guitar player because a girl in the band was going on tour with Pink. When I heard Pink, that grabbed my attention! I am a big fan of Pink, so I asked if I could audition to be in the band and Harry agreed. I took Bruno Frasca, the expert guitar player in the band, to Chateau Marmont and proceeded to play the piano and the guitar for the guests that were there that night. The last song I played on the guitar was "The Gambler" by Kenny Rogers. All the other hotel guests joined in; even the actor Josh Hartnett enjoyed it and was singing along. Needless to say, I was invited to join the band. I am on guitar and back-up vocals for the group. I also helped the band write and record a very cool song titled "American Man."

Betty Dravis: That's a fun, interesting story, Jenny. Best of luck with the group! I haven't had the good fortune to be in the LA area to see you perform, but I've seen YouTube videos and photos on various Hollywood websites. You certainly are a good singer, pick a mean guitar and your energy is endless. How do you keep in such fine shape? And please give us some links to your various websites.

Jenny McShane: I do have a lot of natural energy. I think it was growing up with all the manual labor. Now I have to work out at least five times a week just to feel like I am doing something. It makes my spirit positive to run, lift weights, ride a bike, etc.

I think if you are an entertainer it is your responsibility to respect your fans and show them you have morals and drive. I love to watch Rocky as many times a year as I can; it inspires me. Drive and being in great shape is something I admire in any performer. Who likes to drive a dirty car? is how I look at it! I love that Clint Eastwood is in top shape to this day. Any of the performers I admire are always in great shape in person!

I have my own website which is www.jennymcshane.com, but I need to get some updates on there! I also post my current gigs on my Facebook page.

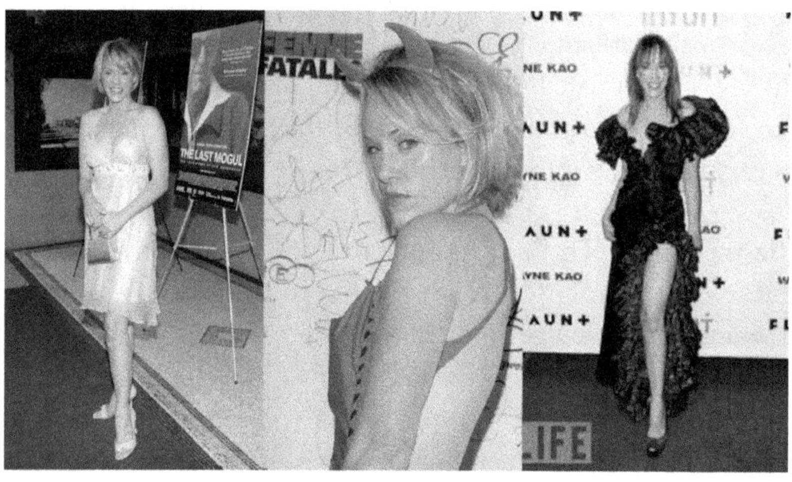

Betty Dravis: I hear you loud and clear about updating your website, Jenny. That seems like an endless task, especially for someone who does as much as you. I've seen five of your movies: *Furnace*, which is your latest (with the very handsome Michael Pare); *Shark Attack*, in which you starred with Casper Van Dien; *The Watcher*, starring Keanu Reeves, where you played the lead female detective; *Shark Attack 3*, where you co-starred opposite John Barrowman; and *Stag*. I expected *Stag* to be an actual stag party, which is not to my taste, so was pleasantly surprised to see that it was about something tragic that happened at the beginning of a stag party, rather than going in-depth with a so-called "sex" movie. It has some nudity, but is more of a thriller, IMO. How many movies have you been in, Jenny? *Dream Reachers* went in-depth on this subject, so keep it brief. Then tell us about some of your modeling jobs. I'd love to hear your take on that, as I'm sure our readers will.

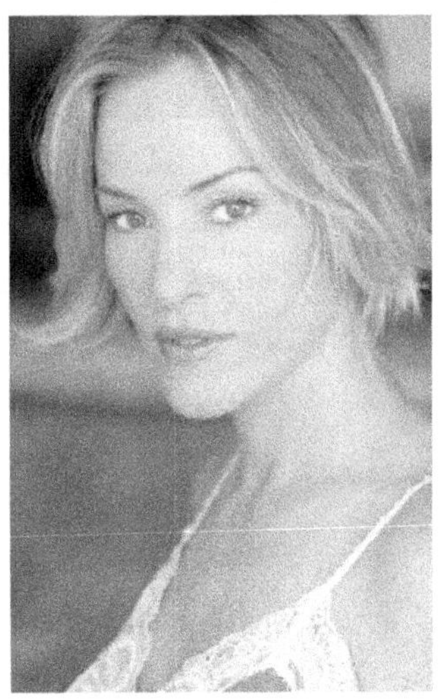

Jenny McShane: I have been in about twenty movies, but only on four television shows. I never keep an exact tab, though. The movie *Stag* has a real message. The film is quite scary as it shows kids and adults that some of our decisions can end up affecting our entire lives. After filming *Stag*, I met a director in

London who told me his eighteen-year-old son had been drunk driving and hit and killed two people and would be serving the rest of his life in prison. The character I played in *Stag* was difficult to play. The original script had the back-story that was not included in the movie. The mother of the two sisters in the movie was dying of cancer and since they didn't have insurance, they stripped to get the money quickly to help the family.

Modeling is the way I started in the business. There is some misinformation about modeling. Modeling is a job description and every model isn't perfect. The majority of modeling I did was commercial as opposed to editorial. Editorial models were stunning, in my eyes. We commercial models were basically girl-next-door types. I did a lot of Budweiser/Anheuser Busch ads and catalog shoots, as well as Target and Dayton Hudson ads when I started. I also did a lot of industrial shoots for various companies, including Fingerhut, 3M, etc. I don't consider photos that I do now to be modeling, but rather publicity for my likeness.

Betty Dravis: That's a modest appraisal, Jenny. I can see the girl-next-door in you, but I also see the "stunning" that you see in others. In fact, you look so different in so many photos and movies that you're like a chameleon… which is a wonderful attribute for an actress, so keep on doing what you're doing. But back to the acting, who was the first big actor you met and what were your feelings at the time? Cowboy actor Jim Davis was the first one I met. He was quite popular in the 50s, if I have my dates straight, but I remember him more as J.R.

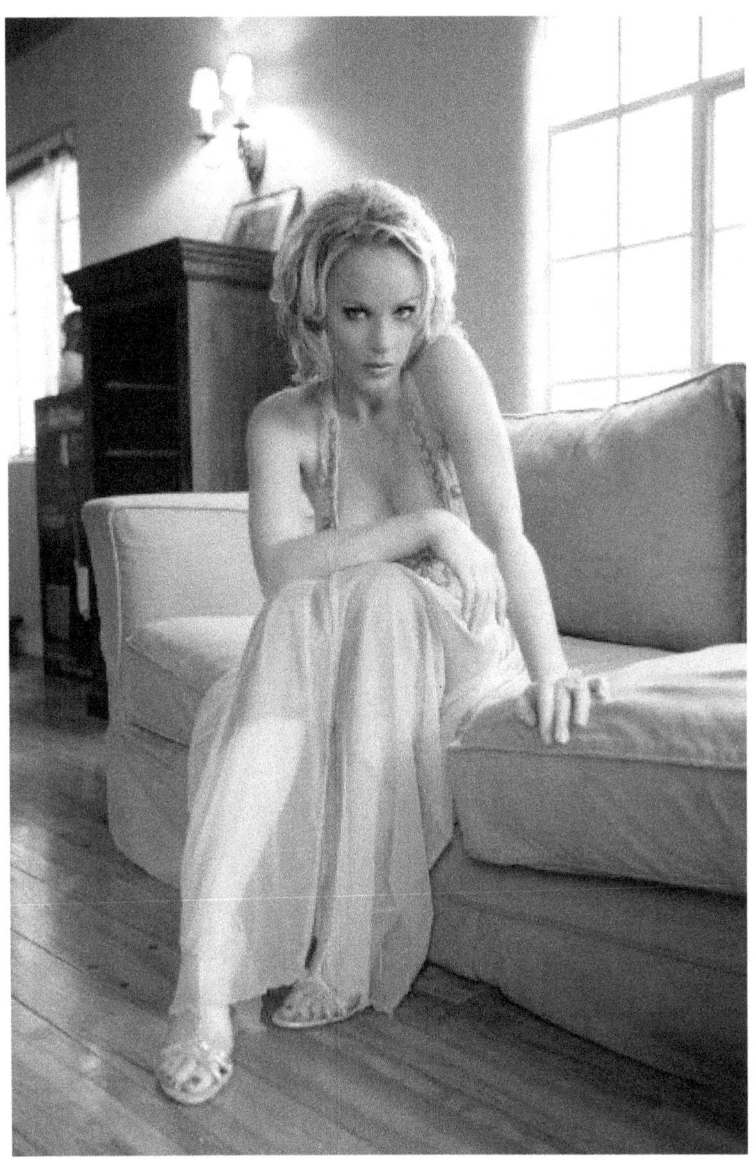

Ewing's father in the later *Dallas* TV series. Meeting him was impressionable, but it didn't move me nearly as much as meeting Clint Eastwood later, a story I relate in *Dream Reachers*.

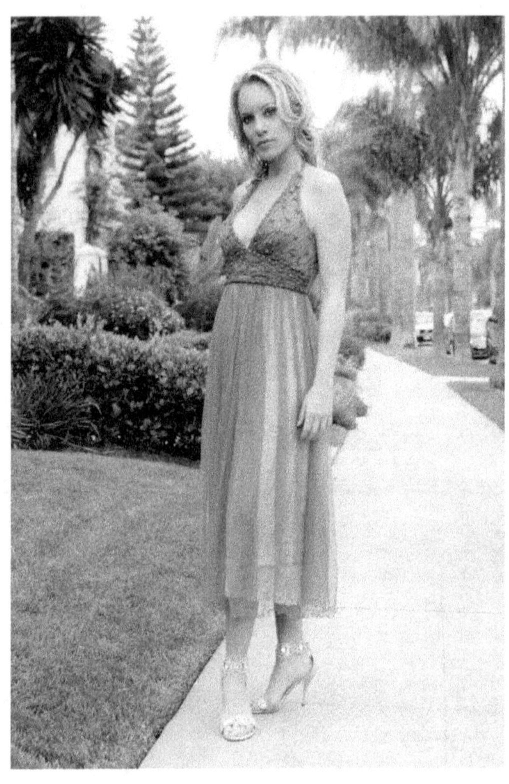

Jenny McShane: Oh, Betty, I love the story of how you met the iconic Clint Eastwood. He's one of my favorite actors. The first actor I met was Kyle T. Heffner. I met Kyle in a café in Chicago, during one of my mother's visits. He was the third lead in a film I loved— *Flashdance*! He also starred on *Golden Girls* and *Seinfeld.* He was working in Chicago in a play with Brian Donehy, another actor I loved. My thought when meeting him was: I have just met somebody who can tell me how to become an actor because he is one! Since then, Kyle has coached me on any role I really wanted. I think it was meant to be, as he knows everything about me and keeps me the person I first was… And I guess I do that in return, now that I have had some success. I keep him in check and he does the same for me! Being in the business for a long while now. I have seen people get big breaks and totally screw them up with bad decisions. I think the acting profession can be compared to gambling: There are no guarantees and it feels like you are walking a tight rope at all times. I don't think there is any performer who has had smooth sailing. My profession isn't an easy life.

Betty Dravis: I've heard that you're well respected in Hollywood for your dependability and professionalism, Jenny. That says a lot for what you've learned. What is your routine when working on a movie…your schedule? Which role was your biggest challenge? And are you between roles now? If so, what do you do to fill the time while waiting?

Jenny McShane: My routine when I am working on a movie is to get my environment situated and feel at home first. Next I try to get into the community and find some down-home people to hang out with after work. As a performer you can't take a drive with a stranger, so it takes a little bit of detective work. But I usually find some good people and end up keeping in touch years later. I like to find out about the places I am working in, if I can, and what the people are like and what makes them tick. One of my first movies was shot in Moscow, Russia. Wow, did I go through some scary moments there. The

Russian people are very scared of "The Americans" and don't trust us, so that was a very uneasy time. I guess it was like being a skunk and thinking you could go hang out with the cats after work.

I have had the amazing opportunities to work on films in Bulgaria, Russia, India, London, South Africa and Canada. I am between jobs right now and I know a lot of fellow actors are, as well.

Work is very lean out there right now, but it is for everyone, so I am keeping busy with my band until I land the next gig.

The people at Gibson Guitars have been amazing by giving me different guitars every time I play with my band. That inspires me to play as much as I can because I love Gibson Guitars. Currently the band that I am playing in, Harry The Dog and the Circus of Lost Souls, is doing a series of four concerts at The Unknown Theater in Hollywood.

The Unknown Theater is four years old and is a nonprofit theater similar to Steppenwolf in Chicago. If you haven't seen the theater, you have to go just to admire the beauty of the place.

I have a few bites on the line, in fishing terms, as far as jobs go, so as soon as I land a job, my vacation is over. I pray that our economy and world come to peace, the troops come home from Iraq and we can all have a great Christmas and end 2010 with a bang!

Betty Dravis: That's my prayer, too, Jenny… I suppose most actors do similar things to fill the time, but now tell us what you love about acting? What do you hate?

I'd enjoy seeing you in a hit TV series…one that would make you a household name. What are your thoughts about that? This curious mind wants to know…as I'm sure our readers do.

Jenny McShane: What I love about acting is getting paid to do something I love which I know a lot of people would love to do. I meet people every day that are doing manual labor just to support their families and give their children education and opportunities they never had. I also love the actors I admired when I was growing up and have now had the opportunity to work beside.

There is nothing I hate about acting! I love it all! I would love to be in a hit TV series. I had a blast in an episode of Don Johnson's TV hit *Chase Nash*; I played guitar and sang my rendition of "Desperado."… I have a great casting director fan that is a fan of April Webster. I came close to getting two TV series with April Webster. I think I will when the timing is right. It has to be the right fit. I wish I could play a gunslinger in an old Western. The character has to be totally ME, so hopefully it comes my way soon. I am a big fan of *The Mentalist* and *Mad Men*.

Those television series fit the actors in the cast like gloves! Hopefully, one of those talented writers reads this and thinks of me…

Betty Dravis: You have certainly met a lot of big names… people you led us to while creating *Dream Reachers*.

Chase and I are grateful to you for introducing us to the famous photographer Jim Marshall, who photographed huge talents, like The Beatles, Janis Joplin, Rolling Stones, Jimi Hendrix…too many to list. In fact, he was the only photographer used by The Beatles near the end of their career.

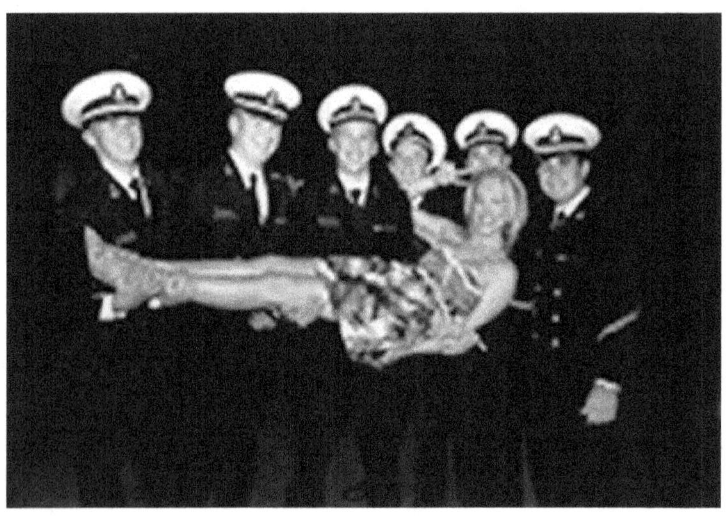

You graciously gave me his phone number and he was so helpful, putting me in touch with the right people at *Rolling Stone* magazine when we needed to use a picture of Tanya Tucker on one of their old covers. What a charming man! And you put me in touch with Mike Regan, VP of Marketing and Acquisitions for Melee Entertainment, when we needed permission to use movie stills from Avi Lerner, the BIG producer of *Slumdog Millionaire* and other huge box-office hits. But for your next question, what advice do you have for aspiring actors?

Jenny McShane: Be prepared for the opportunity. Know your craft and then make the steps to go for it. If you want something bad enough, you can get it!

Betty Dravis: That's great advice, Jenny… thought provoking… Do you have a current mentor? If so, tell us about him or her and about others who have influenced your life…your career.

Jenny McShane: My current mentor is Jonathan Brayley (my boyfriend of six years) who came from England to be an actor. He is a great film editor and now is directing a documentary.

He never studied to be an editor. He met people from England who wanted to see him succeed. I believe that if you are a nice person and passionate about what you want, it happens triple fold. My boyfriend never had the opportunity to become an actor, so he gives the actors his best performance as an editor.

I have also learned to never give up! Another one of my mentors I had the good fortune to meet is the great attorney Robert Shapiro. He and his family have a large number of people they have helped through the years. The Shapiros lost their son to an accidental overdose a few years ago and have created a foundation to inform and help other families who are dealing with similar circumstances. Robert Shapiro is a strong man who has seen it all and keeps fighting to make the world a better place and set a good example for the human race.

Betty Dravis: I've read about the Shapiros and they are true humanitarians.

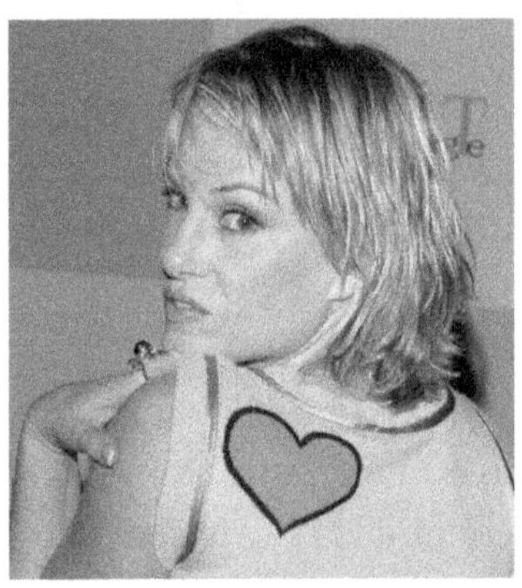

Thanks for sharing their story. But LOL, Jenny, this question was going to be about Jonathan. Since you beat me to it, I would like to know more about his current project.

Jenny McShane: You knew I wouldn't go long without talking about him, didn't you, Betty? Thanks for your interest... Jonathan is currently directing and editing a documentary about the state of the United States economy. He traveled to most of the states to interview people who have survived tornadoes, bombings, Hurricane Katrina, etc. before the economic crash happened. It is a great piece that shows us that we can get through this economic crisis if people who had everything taken in all those other disasters are still standing and surviving.

Betty Dravis: That sounds like an inspiring, uplifting project. Tell Jonathan I wish him great success and to let us know when it's released… But now for the fun question! I waited till near the end to put you on the spot, but do you mind sharing the most embarrassing thing that ever happened to you in connection with your acting or your music?

Jenny McShane: The most embarrassing thing that ever happened to me while acting was when I fumbled a line and actor Don Johnson screamed at me, "Where did you go to acting school—in the barn?" LOL… If he only knew… But he pushed me to give the best performance, so I'm not complaining.

That brings to mind another embarrassing thing, but this is a hard one… It's something John Barrowman said on film, but before I tell about that, let me say that John is an amazing actor and singer. He has won Tonys for his Broadway and West End performances. The award I most admire and envy is the Tony for the opening of Sunset Boulevard (on the West End with Patti LuPone). John is one of those actors who likes to keep the crew on their toes at all times and, to my understanding, never encountered any farm atmosphere, if that makes sense; like mosquitoes in your hotel room (which you find out later were recently emptied Bulgarian Army Barracks) or other situations like that. Well, I am used to this as I grew up in that atmosphere, so when actors were freezing in Russia, I was taking my peanut butter jar out of my pack with my long underwear and having a nice sleep. So with that said, the crew on *Shark Attack 3* was a little upset by the fuss John was creating and he sensed it, so he wanted to bring them back by jolting them with a line I have never heard in any movie! The crew and the director laughed for more than a half hour at that line. It was so weird and out of the blue that I didn't know how to respond. I never thought the line would be left in the movie––but it was! I heard that Lions Gate purchased the movie without watching the whole thing, so it was a blooper that the editor kept in the movie. The line was so often repeated that it actually made the movie and made Lions Gate a lot of money because no one who sees it can believe it. They repeat it and then everyone has to see the movie themselves to hear it with their own ears.

I can't repeat it in polite company, and I don't know the links where your readers might hear it themselves, but there are takes all over YouTube. Look under *Shark Attack 3*. Incidentally, the director Eli Roth sent me an email recently informing me that *Shark Attack 3* (AKA *Megalodon*) has a cult following because of that line. I had heard that and I still think it's very weird. I do have to say that there were clips of John and me on England's popular Jonathan Ross Show; it was in front of one of my favorite actresses Emma Thompson and they didn't show the line… Thank God… That showing helped my name and likeness in England.

Betty Dravis: I heard that infamous line in the movie, Jenny, and I think it was too crude of Barrowman, joke or no joke! But if it helped the movie sales in the long run and no harm was done to you, then…all's well that ends well. Speaking of endings, Jenny, your last question may take a bit of thought, but it's a simple question. I polled my friends and they agreed on what most women would like to know: Of all your co-stars, which one is the best kisser! This would also be a good place to share a few impressions of your other sexy co-stars, if you don't mind.

Jenny McShane: That question doesn't take much thought at all, Betty! Hands down, Don Johnson is the best kisser ever! Don Johnson has that Elvis thing going on! I think he will make the ladies melt until he's a hundred!

As for my other co-stars, Casper Van Dien and Keanu Reeves were hilarious. Keanu invited me to a premier of another movie he had done after *The Watcher*: *The Gift*, at Paramount Studios. I didn't know that Casper Van Dien, my co-star from *Shark Attack,* was there, so when Keanu quipped, "I guess all your boys are here tonight, McShane," I burst out laughing.

I was also surprised when Keanu asked me how it was...working with Casper Van Dien. I hope this comes out right... I mean, Keanu Reeves was about to make sixty million dollars for Matrix 2 and 3 and he still has a deep caring and curiosity about others. What...? That blew my mind. Keanu has to be the nicest actor I have ever worked with, hands down. I heard that he split his back profit on *Matrix* with the crew! Isn't that awesome?

Michael Madsen is another giving and amazing actor. Michael is so nice to the crew and actors and is just fun to be around. John Barrowman and I had a blast in Bulgaria, chasing each other on go-carts. Ja Rule, Danny Trejo, and Michael Pare on *The Furnace* were all amazing.... And I can't forget Tom Sizemore! What a character! Who needs to watch movies when you have that character on your set—living and breathing...?

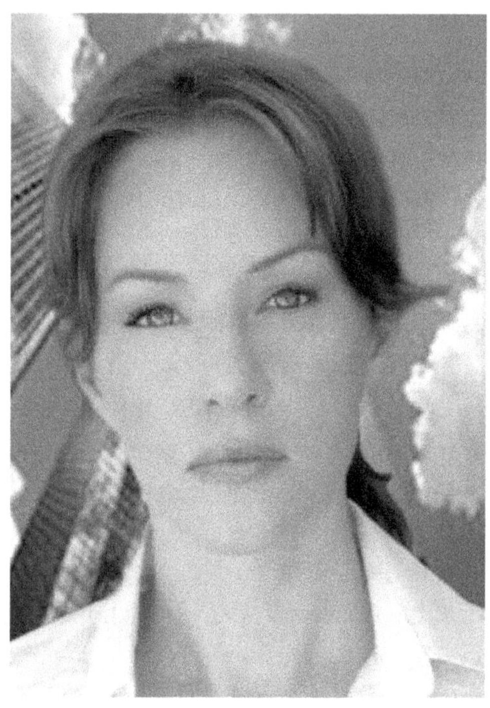

I am also honored to know and learn from Danny Trejo. He has been in the business a long time and is finally shooting the hugest movie of his career, with Robert Rodriquez directing. Cheech Marin and Don Johnson are in it. It's called *Machete!* How weird is that? It's interesting to think that the same Danny Trejo who helped Ja Rule and me learn better angles and fighting stances in *The Furnace* is now going to be a megastar! Which reminds me—Cheech Marin is amazing too. He is a big guitar player and so are Don Johnson and Keanu Reeves. I have found with most actors I have worked with that music and acting run hand in hand.

As long as I have my guitar, I can always play at the beach for lunch, if all else fails!

Betty Dravis: Wow, Jenny, all those stories are fascinating. You certainly have an exciting life and I doubt if you'll end up singing for your supper…but come to think of it, that's what you do with Harry and the Dog. Hmmm… I've enjoyed our time together, Jenny. Thanks for sharing your life with the Dames of Dialogue and our readers. As you so often tell others, you rock!

Jenny McShane: This was a fun interview, Betty, and thanks, Dames, for having me. Keep writing those awesome books. You all do, indeed, rock!

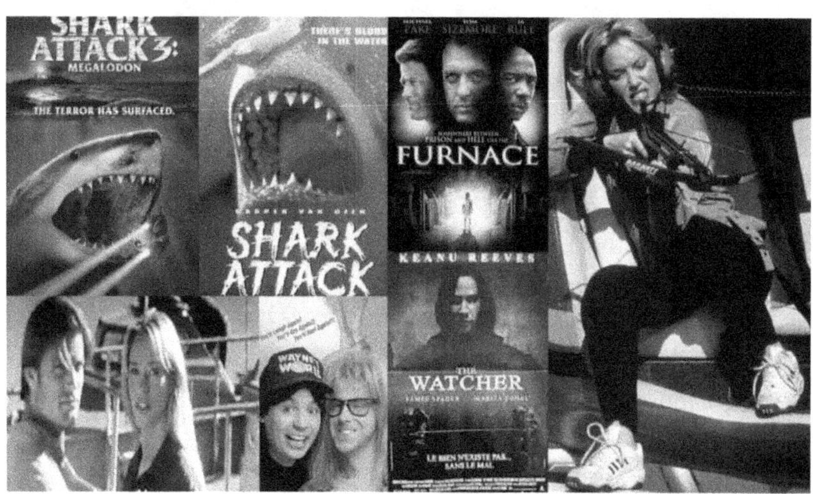

Interview with Bryant McGill

PEACE TREATY FOUNDER IS MAKING A DIFFERENCE

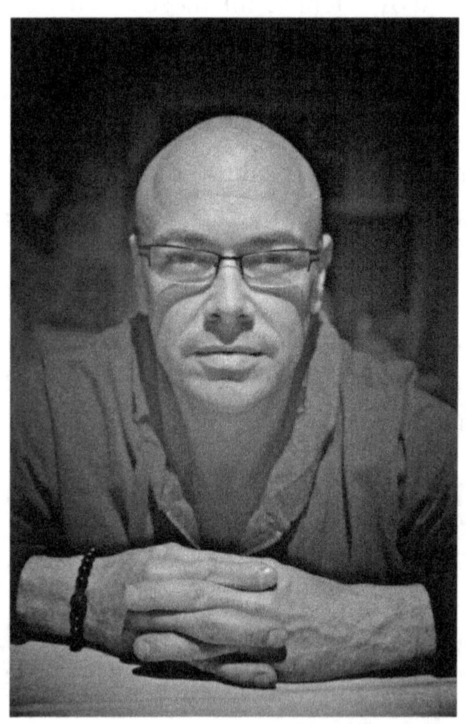

Betty Dravis: Welcome to Dames of Dialogue, Bryant. I'm honored that you found time in your busy schedule to be with us and share your life journey. I met you indirectly through my *Dream Reachers* co-author Chase Von, but we have many friends in common.

As I understand it, your main mission in life is to create peace and harmony, not only throughout the world, but in individual lives. Since you reach and touch the lives of tens-of-millions of people, you have achieved beyond anyone's wildest dreams. Where were you born, and what were you like as a child? I'd also like to know how and when you got started on your current path. Were you always a soulful person "with a mission?"

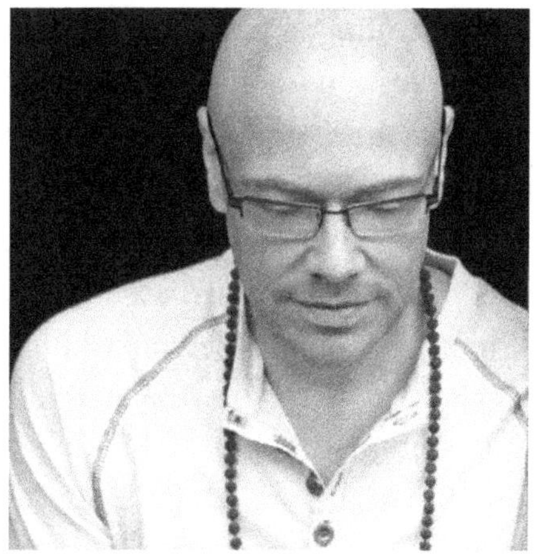

Bryant McGill: First, let me thank you, Betty, for the opportunity to participate in this interview. I have always been fond of your *Dream Reachers* books, mainly because they reveal to others the power every person has to live amazing and purposeful lives; purposeful in the deepest sense. I am also thankful to Chase Von through whom we met.

You asked where I was born and what I was like as a child. I was born in the deep south, in Mobile, Alabama, which is also known as the Azalea City. I was raised on a little dirt road in the country, in a town called Semmes. I spent much of my childhood outdoors. We had animals and horses and acres of open fields. I would hike deep into the woods, drink from running streams and sit in pear trees, eating pears, cut with a child's pocketknife.

I was a sensitive, creative and funny child, who liked to make people laugh. But there was also a part of me which was defiant, willful and curious. I was born asking the question we are disingenuously encouraged to ask and always punished for when we do… That question is, *Why?* That question, more than anything, will get you into trouble if you are a child, or an adult. And so it *was* that I was a trouble-maker, and a natural system buster. I think secretly, many people hope someone will ask the questions they themselves are afraid to ask, even though they will likely punish the person asking.

I guess that is my optimistic way of looking at "Tall Poppy Syndrome." Deep down I wanted to know *why* and if the answer did not agree with my own instincts, there was a hardened steel of defiance in me; a rock that the hammer of so-called authority broke upon, when trying to forge me into its likeness. I realized many years later, that my methods of exerting and protecting my independence and originality had been deeply flawed, immature and ungraceful, in a brute-force way. You see, my understanding of power and strength, were modeled after the society in which I was raised; a spiritually sick society. To me, strength was a show of force; strength was hardness; strength was toughness. This is what most people learn about strength from observing the alleged seats of power, in the form of police, government, military…and from school, TV and society in general.

Fortunately, as a seeker and lifetime student of the world, the seeds of softness and sensitivity had been sown in my soul by wiser, gentler hands, and I found my way to a more graceful understanding of the true nature of true power. As the Sufi's once knew, I now know: that just like water, softness overcomes that which is hard. I know this sounds counter-intuitive, but water, though it is infinitely yielding, will cut through a canyon of the hardest granite. It reshapes the hard and strong, in the contour of its flow of energy. No power can overcome water, though it can easily be conquered.

There are gentle ways of sculpting one's life, and the world, with time, invitation, gentleness, cooperation and surrender. There is a subtle beauty and power in surrender; a cooperation with the divine. When one learns to focus energy through surrender and sensitivity, they become what I call, "reality benders." I have had a wonderful journey from childhood to this time called, the NOW. And because it was my wish, I have become the best parts of my childhood. All I ever wanted was to be that pure child. A child's world is a magical place. My life is still magical and always will be. So if you want to know what I was like as a child, the essence of that child still lives within me and his gentle innocence is my truest strength.

Now, to answer your question about how I got started and if I have always been a soulful person with a mission… Well, from a young age, something kept whispering to me that things were not right with the world; that something was not right with *me,* as a product of an unnatural and dis-eased society. There was a call in my heart to journey beyond the confines of the path placed before me and one day I answered that call. As a troubled teen, with deep turmoil and fear in my heart--and with two apples and twelve dollars as my only possessions--I opened my door, walked to the highway at the end of my country dirt road, stuck out my thumb and like a leaf in the wind, blew away into the great, wide-open world. I hitch-hiked thousands of miles away… I left my friends, family and hometown, and did not return or communicate much for twenty years. I went on a journey…a journey within.

At a certain point on this journey, I began disconnecting myself from the construct of lies and illusions people feed on in the consumer-driven, consensus-reality called, "the modern civilized world." I turned off the television for twenty years. I unplugged myself. I worked to erase the programs that had been written into the fabric of my consciousness by our hidden masters. I began dismantling the artificial edifices that had been erected in my heart, mind and soul from birth, by unknown builders. Brick by brick, word by word--advertisements, slogans, clichés, judgments-- layer by layer, I took down the false idols and symbols of identity, belief, self, pride, ego, ambition, and so-called knowledge. I questioned every belief and fact a person can "know." I doubted everything, especially that which I "knew" with no doubt.

Something in me told me not to believe! "Unknowing" became my comfortable friend.

Decades later when I would learn of the Zen mantra "great doubt, great awakening; little doubt, little awakening; no doubt, no awakening," I could only smile knowing this simple truth had transformed my life in so many ways. Buddha's admonition that one "Believe nothing, no matter where you read it, or who said it, no matter if I have said it, unless it agrees with your own reason and your common sense" had been a golden path I had instinctively followed, that led me to a grand reunion with my original self, my authentic-self, my higher-self, my true soul, and my innermost beauty.

I turned off the lights and lit a candle. I opened the window and listened to the wind, and in that quietness I could hear the whispers from within, "Freedom… Truth… Beauty… Peace… Love…" I stood outside and looked up into the vault of the heavens. I invited truth and God into my life. I let the animals, the sun, the stars, the moon, the insects, the fire, water, elements and the quietness become my teachers. And as the saying goes, "When the student is ready, the teacher will appear," so it *was* that when I was ready, the teachers did appear. One after the other, some of the greatest minds in history would open their lives and hearts to me with their friendship, mentoring and tutelage. Eminent naturalists, great poets, renowned thinkers, prolific authors, great spiritualists; these elders, all appeared one-by-one, each offering me a gift, which was given in love and selflessly, for they knew then what I know now.

Then one day, I looked around and saw that the ugly world was a different and more beautiful place, because I was different and more beautiful. I had somehow emerged on the other side of the looking glass. I was on what I call "The Beautiful Path," a positive life path, walking hand-in-hand with the dreamers, believers, lovers and keepers of the faithful vision of a kinder and more beautiful world.

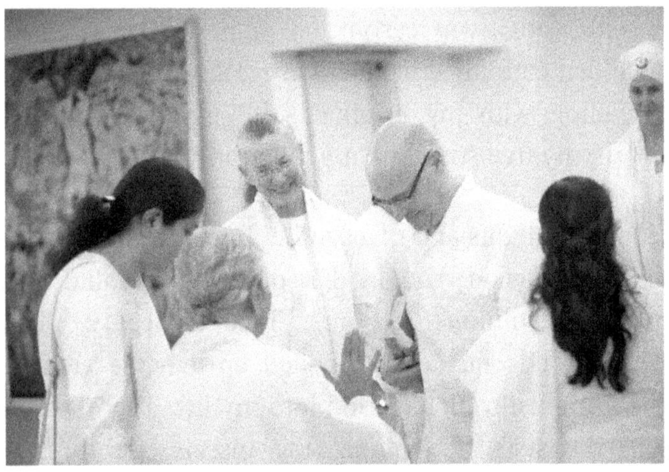

Betty Dravis: Oh, Bryant, my heart goes out to that young boy who had to run from home to find himself… But it worked for you, and you have accomplished so much that it's difficult to choose the highlights for this interview. Having observed you for years, I know you try to remain modest, so I hope you don't mind if I mention some of your most phenomenal accomplishments. To me it seems that founding the Goodwill Treaty for World Peace--along with being acknowledged and upheld by so many individuals and government bodies as a *de facto* Ambassador of Goodwill around the world--are some of the brightest stars in your crown. Further, being formally recognized with a Congressional Commendation by the United

States Congress, honoring your "highly commendable life's work as a Goodwill Ambassador at Large, for World Peace" must feel like an enormous validation of your work, ideas and principles. How does all this make you feel?

Bryant McGill: You know, Betty, some of these recognitions you are speaking of were given to both myself and my beautiful friend in all things positive, Lesley "Chase" Barton. It is really because of Lesley that some of these astounding honors were awarded. Lesley has done so much for others…and for me. For me personally, when these grand things happen, I feel like it is not really happening to me. Later I forget, and then when I remember I am amazed at what has happened. There are times I can hardly even believe it myself. But always after the elation, soberness is usually not far behind because I know that with these honors come deep responsibilities.

The acknowledgments I have received are not only exciting, they are useful, and given with a purpose of encouragement. Each recognition represents a small transference of power, energy and permission to operate in a jurisdiction of worldly affairs; they are tools that make moving forward and opening doors easier, allowing me to inevitably do more good work in the world. I view each of these honors as a trust granted to me by society; a trust that must not be broken.

Betty Dravis: Spoken like a man of integrity, Bryant. Your statements are deeply profound… Now, many people learned through the news--and even more widely, through your national, public service announcements on TV with Lenny Kravitz and Lou Gossett, Jr.--that you had been nominated for a Nobel Peace Prize. How did you feel to know that a group of deans, college chancellors, professors and politicians would respect your work enough to make such a nomination possible?

Bryant McGill: I was really shocked and surprised. I am, of course, grateful to those people, and I feel that it was a sign that we are on the right path, but truly, the journey has just begun. The state of the world is sad, and when I say the world, I mean the real world--the source of the current world's state--I mean the world makers, the creators: *us*.

There is no "world" outside of what *we* create.

We can do so much better. *We must. We will.*

I can do so much better. *I must. I will.*

I have literally just scratched the surface; I have just begun. I know that many sense a new age of simplicity and peace on the horizon, and many are ready to begin the wonderful service of making that world real. I know you also mentioned the World Charity Day PSA, and I would like to thank them for my inclusion in their project. It was a lot of fun filming in Hollywood and participating with them. And I must also say that I love Lenny's music and style, and I hope to collaborate with him one day…to write songs about peace. *I would just love that!* I can't help it. I love all the musicians, artists, dreamers and believers. Let's just all believe together and we will be amazed at what will happen next. As a humanity of people, we always create what is in our hearts; we always bring that which is within us *out* and make it real in the world. Creating peace and beauty is easy. It is just a matter of what vision and desire we carry in our hearts.

Betty Dravis: Bryant, I knew you were a popular man—what today they call a "hot commodity"--but until I started researching for this interview, I didn't realize how famous you really are. Even though your life goals are very altruistic, in many ways you remind me almost of a socialite monk, or a humanitarian rock star… If there is such a thing, you are *it!* I get that impression because you are everywhere. The *Wall Street Journal* even ran a front-page article about you and your celebrity friends, and you are constantly seen in all the glam places around the world, with living legends like the late Michael Jackson, to popular film stars, billionaire business moguls, and even royalty.

You have "hung-out" with hundreds of the most prominently successful individuals in the world.

You must have an incredible time with some of these very creative and talented people.

What are some of the things you have learned through your experiences?

Bryant McGill: I love to be around cutting-edge, creative people, Betty. I find that many of these people are also on the cutting edge of humanitarian and social issues. However, I actually spend most of my time alone and meditating, writing or creating. My time alone is very important. Believe it or not, even though I am a very public person, I am also a very private person. I spend much more time alone--on creative endeavors, or working with my clients, or involved in humanitarian projects--but, when I do get out, I like to shake things up, have a good time and meet stellar new friends.

I have learned so many things from these experiences you mention. I have worked with many of these people as a life coach--or what I sometimes call a "soul coach" or motivator. I have worked with celebrity entertainers, top CEOs, doctors, professional and Olympic athletes, politicians, and top performers during career turn-arounds and personal breakthroughs.

Through these experiences I have learned some very important things. First and foremost: money prestige and power have absolutely nothing to do with happiness. The more money you have, the more zeros your problems have on the end. If you were to talk with the richest people on earth, they would probably tell you that they need another billion dollars…and fast. When you get rid of any problem in life, like money, you get a whole new set of problems. The trappings of materialism and material pursuits are ubiquitous and permeated through all layers of the social economic strata, from the very bottom to the very top. I have learned that there is no such thing as a human experience without pain, turmoil and strife. It is very easy to look around at the illusion of life placed before you—

other people driving nicer cars, wearing nicer clothes, making more money, having more toys--and to think that these people "have it made," and to wonder to oneself, *How did these people do this, and why can't I have this type of success and happiness.*

But the truth is: that behind the scenes of any great or idyllic life there exists the same exact personal crises--emotional turmoil, family problems, financial dilemmas and painful human experiences, losses, trials and tribulations--that exist for every other human being who has ever lived.

I have found this knowledge to be an important part of my own development as a person of compassion. Because I now know that every person I encounter, no matter who they may appear to be, is likely to be dealing with powerful problems and having a very difficult time in some sphere of their life. They may be a billionaire, but perhaps they don't get the love they feel they need from their significant other. They may walk in the nicest clothing, with a strong and confident gait, but around the corner and in their quiet places alone, they wilt into tears over losses, guilt or regrets.

Life can be hard for everyone and this is why it is so important for us to all treat others gently, with courteousness, patience, and with an open mind and heart. You never know what that other person is going through at that moment, or how your smile may make it possible for them to make it through another day, or how your impatience or unkind words, may devastate them, sending them into deeper despair. *This is why I am so careful, so conscientious, and so very mindful about the way in which I deal with others.* I am very mindful, not only about my words, but also about my energy and how it affects others. I made the conscious decision that I wanted to be a blessing in the lives of others and to raise every person I encounter to a higher level with my energy, efforts, words, actions…or just a gentle and authentic smile.

I do this because when I see another person, I see myself.

One of the great benefits I have also enjoyed by being around "successful" people is the unique opportunity to observe and identify success patterns--which through study, I have reduced to behavioral models of extreme simplicity--that can be used by anyone desiring to remove the obstacles to their unique path of purpose. I have learned much about the unlimited capability of each soul to have abundance and fulfillment through kindness, compassion and love.

I used these secrets I learned to turn my own health around, transform my energy and body, lose weight and achieve many of my dreams.

As a coach, I now teach others what I have learned from some of the most amazing people in the world, from top celebrities, world spiritual leaders, gurus, and champions of all fields. I discovered that the best-of-the-best are often deeply spiritual and evolved beings.

Through invitation, reverence and communion with the divine in one's own self, all things are possible. Above all activities,

I love helping others, and so that is what I do, and I am so blessed that I can be a simple joy.

Betty Dravis: The world needs more sincere, caring people like you, Bryant, and it's encouraging to know you are teaching and helping so many.

I know one of your close friends is Susaye Greene, the legendary singer from "The Supremes," who wrote hit songs for Michael Jackson and co-wrote songs, performed and traveled with friends Diana Ross, Ray Charles and Stevie Wonder. I bet she has some fascinating stories to share. How is she to work with?

Bryant McGill: Susaye is such a ray of sunshine, Betty. I just can't say enough fine things about this exceptional lady. Susaye and I share a special friendship and a true soul connection. I see in her such a beautiful and radiant woman who deeply loves life, and who through her immense heart, loves nothing more than creating beauty.

One of the things I enjoy the most about Susaye is that she has a rare dignity to her manner and a comportment about her person that lets you know you are in the presence of a kind and wise master.

We have been involved in projects together for many years and are always energetically connected. She has a strong online presence and is heavily involved in the arts community, so I encourage everyone reading this interview to look her up on Facebook and on her websites.

Betty Dravis: Wow, Bryant, there is much more to successful people than most of us realize. Thanks for sharing such fascinating information about Susaye. She is someone I'd love to know.

In addition to what we discussed above, you also are a speaker at many universities, corporations and government functions and your books and software are even used as part of the curriculum at the university level. I recently saw in the Los Angeles media that--in your role of Goodwill Ambassador -- you delivered a speech at a televised event with many dignitaries: the Los Angeles Mayor's Office, Sheriff Leroy Baca (LASD), Charles L. Beck, the Chief of Police of the Los Angeles Police Department (LAPD), Gerald Levin, the former CEO of Time Warner, Sergio Duarte, the High Representative for Disarmament Affairs for the United Nations, and the world famous artist and activist Lin Evola, the Founder of The Art of Peace Charitable Trust. What was your latest speech about?

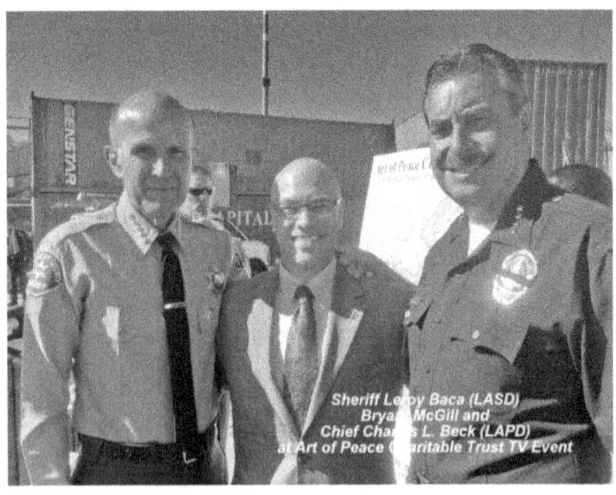

Sheriff Le oy Baca (LASD)
Brya McGill and
Chief Cha s L. Beck (LAPD)
at Art of Peace aritable Trust TV Event

Bryant McGill: I was there speaking at an important and truly historic occasion--the commencement of the transformation of illicit weapons to create The California Peace Angel project.

My message that day was on the impact of illicit weapons, and I was there speaking in support of my friend Lin Evola, a fellow master creator and artist. The first time I met Lin I was profoundly affected by her and her vision, her purity, devotion, commitment and sense of *duty*. My commitment and faith in her and her vision is absolute, because her visionary project is about transformation, peace, and love. It is a project she would say belongs to the world.

There are so many ways in which we hurt one another and sometimes it is with illicit weapons that we hurt others. But, it is *always* the intention to hurt another that does the harm, and likewise, it is also intention that is the antidote to such terrible sufferings. Like the intention to lay a gentle and caring hand upon a broken spirit or limb, and heal and make whole, through the transformational powers-- of art, peace and *love*. Lin's Peace Angel project is a beautifully powerful metaphor of the transformation within; a transformation we must all continually make. I was honored to speak at that event and to make my intentions known. My intentions are for a more peaceful and beautiful world, and we are *now creating* that world together.

I was grateful to be there to enjoin my energy, mission and purpose with other creators to say, "I *believe* in the power of peace and love to heal." It was also so encouraging to stand with some of the nation's greatest *peace* officers, to look them in the eye, and to witness that these visionary leaders, truly do believe in and see a greater world; a more beautiful world where all people are free, safe, and at peace.

I am meeting with the sheriff and chief of police again soon, to sign the Goodwill Treaty for World Peace and to have further constructive dialogues about the ways in which all people can make the world a safer and more beautiful place.

Betty Dravis: It's odd, Bryant, but I received the final answers to this interview from you on the very day I faxed my signed Peace Treaty to the people involved in gathering signatures. Please tell us more about the Treaty and how and why you founded it? Who are some of the people who have signed it? In what countries has the Treaty been represented, and how were you received by the populace? I saw photographs of you with many politicians and celebrities signing the Treaty. What is it like to personally meet with, and get to know, such amazing individuals who all care so deeply about the state of the world?

Bryant McGill: Much of my life and work is concerning what I call "simple reminders," and teaching people about their power of intention. I feel that we are so off-course as a human species that what we often need is to be reminded about the simpler things, which so many have forgotten or erased. We have lost touch with much of our humanity and our real creator-power. We need less information and less complexity.

We need to create a quiet and calm place to allow the healing of that beautiful expansion of love within each of us, *which is the seat of possibility for all great and good things.* We need simple reminders of who we are, what we are and what is possible. *All things are possible, through invitation and love.*

The Treaty was born from the philosophy that a simple reminder and oath of intention could re-awaken in a consciousness what it already knows deep inside: that the world should be, could be, and will be a more beautiful, safe and peaceful home for all creatures and people…*if we choose.* I have always believed that one person really can make a difference. *I AM that person, and so are YOU.* There is nothing special or magical about what I do, or have done. All I have done, and will continue to do, is simply carry a torch of faith, optimism and enthusiasm for a safer and more harmonious world. A passionate fire for a more beautiful world burns within me, and it is that same warmth within you that will tame the coldness of indifference and cruel apathy.

I love all people, all creeds, and all nations. I am deeply in love with life. I am grateful for life and have a profound and abiding reverence for life. At a deep level, all people understand this basic respect for life, even those who do great harm… We *all* understand that life is a beautiful gift. I want to appeal to that simple understanding inside of each person, whether they are a president of a country, a celebrity, or a local neighbor or new friend. My intellect is nearly useless and words are limited, but the humble heart whispers its quiet truth to each soul we encounter, and beauty always inspires greater beauty. In a world that wants me to be something else, I hope to simply have the courage to be beautiful, and let my heart's unbridled truth flow and move upon each person I encounter. I hope to merely be a simple instrument of encouragement; a reminder of what every person innately knows, but may have forgotten. *Is that so much to ask?* Let us all encourage others to let their love flow freely. There is a great endless river of love and creative power in each soul, and when the artificial dams that restrain us are breached, the resulting flow can turn a desert of suffering into a paradise, containing all of the colors and blooms of each unique, vibrant soul.

I see that beautiful, peaceful place in my heart. It is real. At every moment "The Beautiful Path" is but a single choice away, and I will choose that path again, and again, and again. I deeply pray that each person will choose to walk upon the beautiful path with me. It is upon this path that we will encounter the famished and forgotten souls, who we will lift gently in our arms and nourish, with the nectar of our hearts-- *LOVE.*

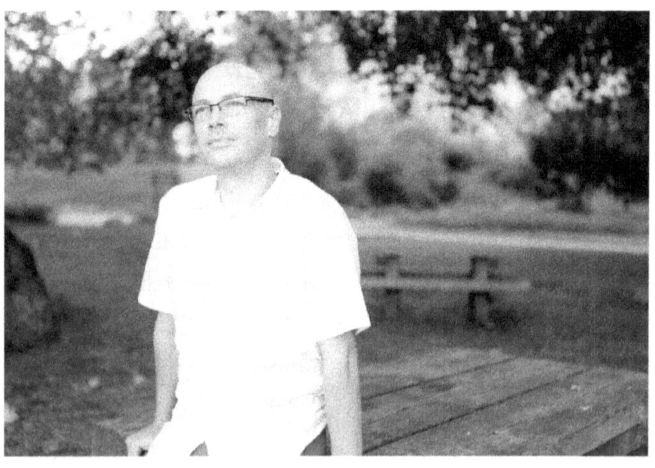

The Treaty has been represented in Italy, Australia, New Zealand, France, Sweden, Jordan, England, America, The Vatican, Japan and many other countries, both privately and in cooperation with governments, NGO's and international bodies. As you mentioned, many celebrities, politicians and social leaders have signed the Treaty, and you asked what it was like to meet with these people in person. In every instance of our travel we have been received with open arms, love and goodwill--which is nothing short of an inspiration.

I have met personally with entertainers and serious activists, such as Matt Damon, Ben Affleck, Don Cheadle, Jason Alexander, Montel Williams, Gary Busey and Raymond "Ray" Romano, who all enthusiastically put their signatures and hearts into the project and its simple message. I have met with, and shared the message, with sports stars like Charles Barkley, Ray Lewis, Hines Ward, Wade Boggs, Michael Strahan, and Evander Holyfield, just to name a few from a very long list.

I have held private meetings with musicians such as the late Michael Jackson, Celtic Women, members of Earth, Wind and Fire, and most recently, Dave Mason who signed the Treaty, though he and I have not yet had a chance to sit down together.

The last Treaty signer I met with privately was Her Divine Grace Dadi Janki, the beautiful, ninety-four-year-old spiritual leader from India. Some of these people became my friends and I have traveled with them and stayed in their private homes; they have expanded my vision of the world through their unique perspectives.

Betty, to me, it is so refreshing to see people with such public responsibility who are still able to think and act without publicists, managers and overseers. These are people who can think for themselves, and who take the responsibility to say: *This is my oath, this is my signature, and even if we don't know how to create it, even if it seems impossible, no matter what, this is what I stand for and this is what I believe.* That courage, optimism and leadership is beautiful to see in this world today.

So each time I meet with one of these people what I think and feel is gratitude. I think to myself, *I am proud of you, and I am blessed that I can witness another soul exercising their unique power to declare before all people that they believe, like little children, in the power of LOVE, to transform the world.* I believe in that power more and more every passing day.

Betty Dravis: You're right, Bryant. Love is powerful and it's people like you and others you mention who will make a difference. And as you are quick to point out, people like me and my readers too…

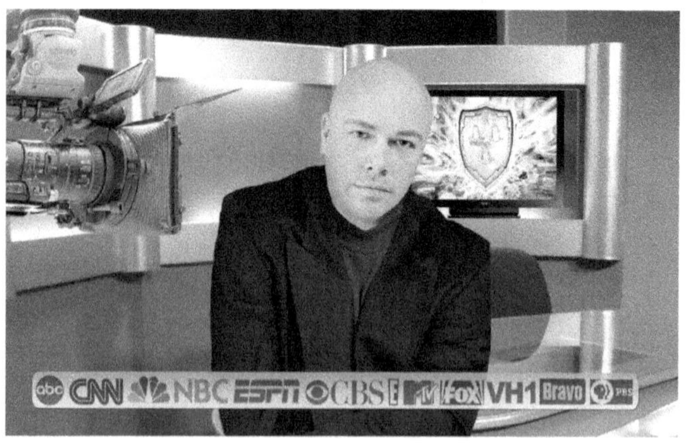

But now I'm curious about something: When you met Dadi Janki, India's revered spiritual leader, you gave her a very special gift, a large precious gemstone that you dug from the earth with your own hands, and later cut yourself. It's been said that for ten years you looked for a pure heart to whom you would give that stone, and that you had even considered kings, princesses and holy men. It warmed my heart to learn you had presented it to Dadi Janki when she signed the Peace Treaty. I was touched when you told her, "We are all precious…we are all gems, and you are a precious gem, Dadi." That was very insightful of you and you made a wise choice.

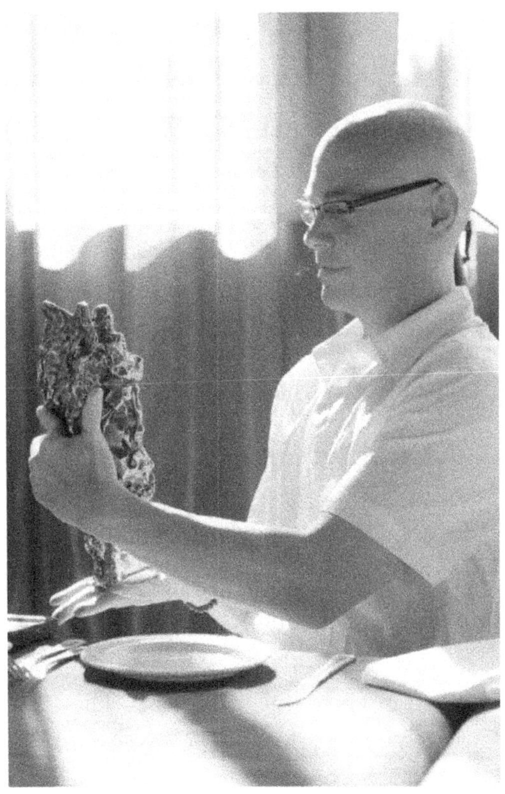

Bryant McGill: Do you want to hear something amazing, Betty? Something that will stir your soul? I can hardly believe this myself, and it is what I call a miracle. Two nights before meeting Dadi, while lying in my hotel bed almost asleep, in a half dreaming state, a voice in my dream told me I needed to have a very special, large gemstone I had cut many years ago, sent to me and that I was to give it to Dadi Janki. So I phoned home and asked that it be shipped overnight to the resort.

The next day, the stone arrived and I took it with me to the event. As I walked in, I was astonished at the sight of large, colored-glass gems everywhere! As it turned out, the whole program was about how we are all "Gems." Dadi Janki was handing a glass gem, blessed with her love, to each person in the crowd. After the program, a table had been prepared for our private meeting where Dadi was to sign the Goodwill Treaty. I sat across from Dadi and we silently looked into one another's eyes and souls for a very long time. I took her hand and placed my gemstone in her palm. I told her about my dream and how I sent for this real gemstone, which I had mined and cut by hand.

I told her, "Dadi, we are *all* precious… We are all gems, and you are a precious gem, too, Dadi."

And then Dadi handed me a glass gemstone in return. The space between us was charged with high energy as we exchanged *drishti.* Our souls smiled at one another as we basked in the warm spirit of the synchronicity and beauty of that sacred moment moving upon us. There was a great knowing and transmission of information in that moment.

It was divine and it was perfect.

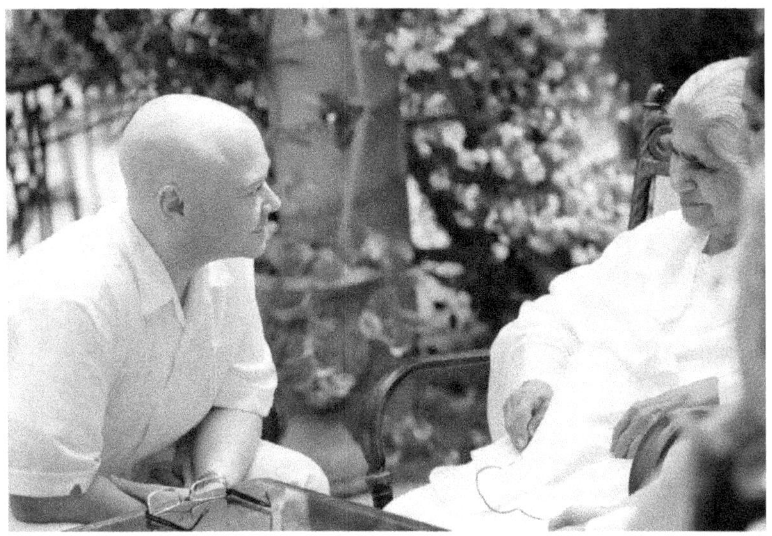

Bryant meeting with 94-year-old Indian world spiritual leader Dadi Janki

The following day, I met with a woman who had contacted me on the Internet and who was in deep distress. Her distress came from not knowing where home is, or what it means to truly have support and love from a family. She had suffered through profound abuses and neglect.

When I travel to different cities, I make an effort to meet with one or two people that my inner-voice tells me to meet. So, in following that inner-voice, it was decided that I was to meet with this woman who had reached out to me. I had a small window of time, so I called her and let her know I was available.

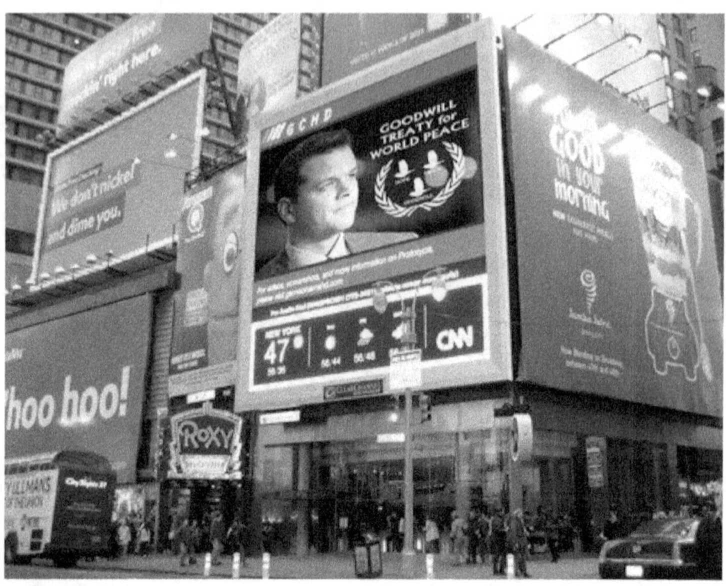

A few hours later she arrived at the resort where I was staying and we met in the lobby where there was a comfortable and private area for us to sit. We sat facing each other and holding hands as we listened with care and with ease, while surrounded in quiet and divine grace.

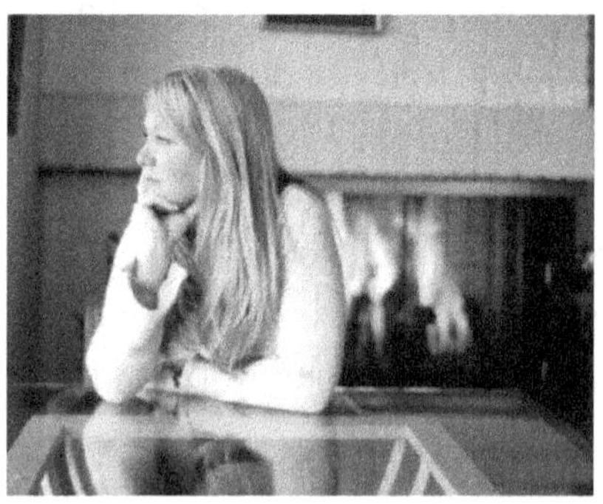

Lesley Chase Barton

After a while of heart-felt conversation, I paused for a moment and pulled out the gem Dadi had given me and said, "This was a gift from Dadi Janki. It was blessed by her and will bring blessings and protection to whoever possesses it. I want you to have it."

She immediately broke into sobs of gratitude and healing. She then told me, out of all the people in the world, she had just been watching videos of this extraordinary, yet humble soul the world has come to know as Dadi Janki. The purest and highest spirit moved upon us and tears streamed from both our eyes.

The *circle of giving* was now complete, and in that moment the world was perfected and all we could feel was pure unconditional love. *The highest place in me met the highest place in her.* We were both there because we had listened to our hearts, and we were both being taught beautiful lessons about listening to the quiet promptings that led us to a moment we each will remember forever. The special gift I gave her was simply my open heart, and there is no gift greater. *The act of true giving is indistinguishable from receiving.*

Betty Dravis: You're right, Bryant; your story does stir my soul. That's a wonderful, moving example of the power of giving *and* receiving.

When you described the exchanges between you and Dadi Janki and between you and your Internet friend, I could feel the love flowing freely…feel the bliss in those breath-taking moments…

I also heard you recently met with the "hugging saint" Amma *(Sri Mata Amritanandamayi Devi)* and received her blessings for your mission. I'm a "huggy" kind of person, so please share those moments with us.

Bryant McGill: Meeting Amma and receiving her blessings and *Darshan* was such a beautiful experience. I met with Amma close to San Francisco where I presented her with the Goodwill Treaty for World Peace. It was a very powerful moment. Amma took the Treaty in her hand, laid it upon her bosom, and pulled me into an embrace…with the Treaty between us. During *Darshan,* Amma blessed the Treaty and my path in life, that I would be protected as a humble instrument in my mission to bring more goodwill and love into the world. It was absolutely wonderful, and her heart and smile are with me forever.

Betty Dravis: You paint a vivid scene, Bryant; I can just picture that spell-binding moment. Now with those fascinating experiences in mind, this seems like a good place to ask a lighter question. If you could spend an entire day with anyone else in the world (living or dead) who would you choose?

Bryant McGill: I would wish to meet any human being on Earth who is low and lift them up. *What we do to another, we do to ourselves.*

Betty Dravis: That's a perfect answer, Bryant; one worthy of your purpose and the true purpose of all life. And what would you say to a person who is low, depressed and desperate?

Bryant McGill: To the low and downtrodden I would say: *Rise-up and allow me the privilege to be your humble servant. I am just a simple student of the world; what lesson do you have for me? Let me be your brother and friend. Let me be a hospitable and comforting voice. I am no more than you. I am only a simple reflection of divine light--the eternal image of creation. What good you see in me is God's good. We are all illuminated with the same universal light. I do not want to squander my divine gifts through weakness, so please help me to be complete by allowing me to serve you. I am not higher, better, wiser or greater, just because you seem low at the moment. No! In fact, I look to you as my teacher. I am just a student who learns by looking at the divine architect's creations and art-- YOU. His art is incomprehensible! Will you be my teacher? Will you lift me when I am low? Will you take my hand when I have fallen? Will you love me when I have failed? No matter, I will do these things for you, for you are the creator's beauty that I will protect. What, or who the creator is, I leave entirely to you... Whether you believe in random destiny of chances, child of Darwin, intelligent design, cosmic consciousness, or a monotheistic God, it does not matter; you are still a beautiful creation, and all respect and honor to the true author and architect of your beauty.*

It is never too late, and love will heal you—your love. Many of my readers, and especially those in the prisons where I sometimes speak, have had very troubled lives and have been neglected and abused. If you have been hurt, do not wait for love to come find you and heal you. Remember the important truth that love works as an agent of healing both ways; by not only receiving, but also by giving. We are made whole only when we make others whole.

If you have not been invested in as a person, or have been neglected or abused, do not be bitter. Instead, ask yourself, "In whom can I invest my heart, love and service?" As the great Mahatma Gandhi advised, we should all be the change we wish to see in the world. Growing up, every person may not have had the best of families or experiences, but in this time called now, each person can experience that love and beauty they wanted...through the lives of others they touch. What a beautiful chance to experience what you may have missed from another perspective, by giving another soul what you know all people deserve.

Betty Dravis: I didn't anticipate the complexity of your answer, Bryant, but it's very thought-provoking and sincere. Really, quite simple when one ponders your truth…

How do you stay so humble when you are surrounded by worldly glamour and materialism, and when you are adored by so many? How do you not get lost in it all? What is your idea of humility?

Bryant McGill: Humility and full consciousness are inseparable, Betty. Once you become fully conscious and self-aware, or awake, you are immediately humble. Only unconscious people and "sleep-walkers" who do not know themselves and what they really are, can lack humility. True humility is greatness. Humility and greatness are not mutually exclusive, but are fully compatible. God is great, and God is good, and we are to be as God-like as possible. I seek to be both great and good. Humility is not weak. *Not being great is a form of extreme arrogance, while being great is an act of true humility.* You see, it is arrogant to not be the great and marvelous being you were intended to become. It is supremely neglectful and insulting to the heart of creation to squander your divine birthright. It takes an act of absolute humility to accept the mantle of greatness which was written into each of our destinies. All strength comes from humility. So I ask, are you humble enough to be great?

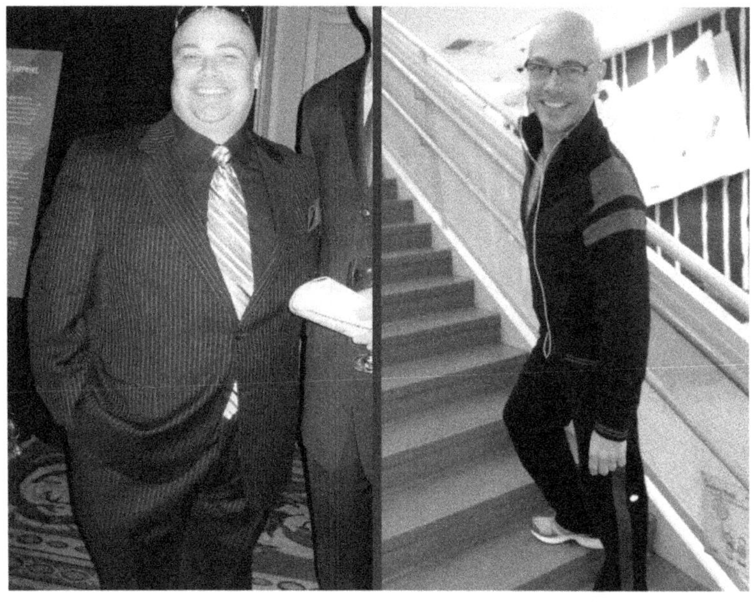

Betty Dravis: I'd like to say you are a stellar example of what Chase Von and I call "Dream Reachers" in our books of the same name. You might not know it, but our creed is: *Only*

Those Who Stretch to Reach Their Dreams Find Themselves Living Them. Bryant, you are the ultimate Dream Reacher, having your dreams fulfilled in a grand way.

And speaking of great accomplishments, I see you have lost over a hundred pounds of weight and have transformed your body and health. How did you accomplish this amazing goal?

Bryant McGill: Thank you for the compliment, Betty. I AM…living my dreams, and I am so happy for that fact. As far as my health is concerned, I was really worried and afraid I was going to die because I was so unhealthy. I could not even walk up a flight of stairs without being out of breath. I was truly, and frighteningly, unwell. The first step to achieving wellness for me was learning humility. To abuse the gift of life and one's own precious body is a form of extreme arrogance and self-hatred. So one of the keys for me was reacquainting myself with the beautiful gifts that can exist for a being who has respect, gratitude and humility for all that is available for us, to sustain our bodies in health and longevity.

There was also a decision that I made wherein I concluded that I wanted to live life with health and vigor. I decided I wanted the energy and vitality to do and experience all of the wondrous things in life that are available to all people. I wanted the strength and stamina to lead a life of activity, exploration and true excellence. Ultimately, it came down to me deciding whether I wanted to advance toward the grave in a state of decrepit stupor or rise and advance in life as a fresh, vital being, full of youthful energy and joy.

In my quest for understanding, I realized something very important one day: that the human body is an unfathomable and miraculous microcosm of divine order. The intelligence, complexity and order of even a single cell rivals that of a large modern city. *Our bodies love us!* Just think about it. The universe within-- your trillions of cells all cooperate in a grand orchestration to serve and heal you. Your cells work around the clock in total unison and harmony, cleaning, repairing, restoring and nourishing your entire physical being. Every person's body wants nothing more than to cooperate with them in achieving optimal health. But I realized that I was *at war with my own body.* I was waging a terrible war of violence against my body by bombarding it with stress, toxic environments, lack of sleep and the most terrible and dreadful toxic foods known to man--otherwise known as the modern American diet and lifestyle. Obesity is not only a life choice, it is a disease.

When you are obese you are chronically diseased and you are moving toward the grave at a rapid pace. My body had become addicted to heavy greases, oils, animal fats, highly refined carbohydrates, sugars, salts and an endless array of toxic chemicals.

I discovered that simply by getting out of my own body's way, letting it do its job and cooperating with my body, *it* would heal itself from the dreadfully debilitating sickness of obesity. To lose weight I did very little outside of gentle and peaceful cooperation with the inherent wisdom and intelligence of my own body. Through meditation and gentle and peaceful cooperation, the body will heal itself with little or no effort. When we are at peace with ourselves the total expression of that true peace includes our outer being…our body. Losing weight and being healthy is so simple and easy. I'm now writing a book called "The Peaceful Body" that explains all of the details of my program. I am on the first year of a two-and-a-half-year transformation process, where my goal is not weight loss, but rather true health and respect for the gift of life.

Betty Dravis: Wow, Bryant, I've seen photos of you "before and after" and the visible change is simply astonishing. This might sound like a cliché, but you truly do look many years younger now. You really are, as they say, a living example of transformation—of mind *and* body.

During your radio show, through the Internet, your books, and as a soul coach, you give many helpful success tips to your followers. What simple advice do you have for our readers to start them on the right path?

Bryant McGill: First and foremost, turn off your television and seek quiet meditative places as often as possible. To all of your *Dream Reachers'* readers out there, I say, *Go for your dreams!* Go for your dreams and never allow the opinions of others to discourage you. *To dis-courage means to take away courage.* Be courageous in the face of criticism and "nay-saying," personal attacks and passive aggressive "supporters" who secretly wish for you to fail. Do not listen to cynics, critics, skeptics or negative people. Do not let negative entities have any power over you. Negativity is a disease of the mind. If they try to block you with a wall of negativity, just walk through it like a ghost.

I realize a lot of starting authors, actors, artists and creators in all fields receive negative feedback about their so-called, lofty goals, their "dream world," their "unrealistic" plans and their delusions. They are often told they need to be more "realistic" and "down-to-earth." Never listen to small minds and small imaginations. These people suffer from delusions of no-grandeur. They suffer from *extreme* delusions of no-grandeur when all evidence points to the contrary, showing that there is great grandeur to be had, and creations of opulence await only your unique spark of imagination. That is how every marvelous thing in the world was created-- by someone who did not listen to that sad nonsense.

Learn to market and share yourself and your creations, whether it be books, poetry, paintings, music, pottery, inventions or ideas. Be proud of who you are--your output in the world, in the form of your creations--and share your unique-self and your beauty, unapologetically. Ignore any person who frames your efforts at sharing as "shameless self-promotion" and narcissism. There is nothing more shameless and narcissistic than tearing down others--their plans, efforts and dreams--just to make themselves feel higher and better. This happens less when you are more established and "successful," but when you begin a journey, these broken people can be vicious and devastating to your plans. People who presently live in fear and darkness will always be shocked, unsettled and even afraid of authentic creator power. Their dark and low vibrational energy will sometimes attack what it cannot understand.

I get about a thousand emails a day, and only around one nasty email a month, so that tells you just how rare and sad these afflicted individuals are. I could never imagine myself actually putting life-force and energy into writing a person a letter just to say something critical or cruel. What a waste of my creator energy, and how very mean-spirited. I would rather use that same energy to send a stranger a letter pointing out something nice or supportive, and I do that all the time.

Remember, what we do to another, we do to ourselves.

I love these words by Theodore Roosevelt, and I think you will too:

"It is not the critic who counts; not the man who points out how the strong man stumbles, or where the doer of deeds could have done them better. The credit belongs to the man who is actually in the arena, whose face is marred by dust and sweat and blood; who strives valiantly; who errs, and comes short again and again, because there is no effort without error and shortcoming; but who does actually strive to do the deeds; who knows the great enthusiasms, the great devotions; who spends himself in a worthy cause; who at the best knows in the end the triumph of high achievement, and who at the worst, if he fails, at least fails while daring greatly, so that his place shall never be with those cold and timid souls who know neither victory nor defeat."

Like I said to a very nice woman on Twitter who asked for my advice when she was being attacked: "Be as light as a feather and as they reach for you, blow by them without them ever touching you."

Many years ago I had a realization that, at that time, was very helpful for me, and I hope it is possibly helpful for your readers. I realized that one day I will face death, and I will die and depart this realm.

No other person can die for me; this I must do on my own. So, while I am alive--and since no single critic is going to lay down and die for me--I will absolutely not allow any person to tell me how to live. This is my life and I will live it how I choose, without worry or distress over outside opinions. I do not need any person's approval, except my own. I would be devastated if I were on my death bed filled with regrets of things I wish I had done, but did not do, because of criticisms and lack of approval from others.

My advice is also to get on and stay on, what I call, "The Beautiful Path." A person on The Beautiful Path always seeks beauty without and within, in all they do and experience. In every person they see beauty, and in every experience they find beauty because beauty has been cultivated within.

Even with harsh and mean people, they find themselves appreciating that person in some way, and even during hardship and tribulation, they receive their lessons for growth with gratitude.

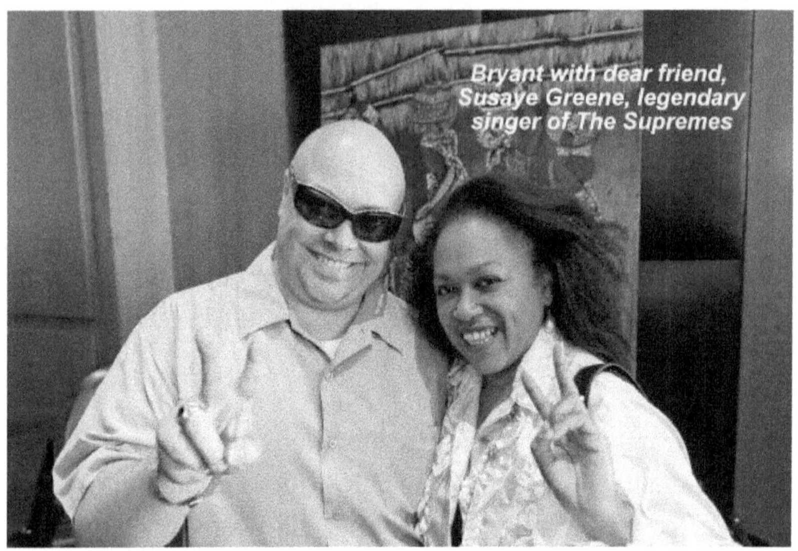

Bryant with dear friend, Susaye Greene, legendary singer of The Supremes

The Beautiful Path is not a place outside of yourself, but is a place you carry with you everywhere you go. The Beautiful Path is the place you want to be, to re-center; it is the garden of peace you seek, but is not a place that exists in the world--it is within. Go there, within, and if you nurture a beautiful garden in your heart, the singing bird will come and fill your world with beautiful music.

A person on The Beautiful Path is also on their path of purpose. Find your unique path of purpose. When you are not on your path of purpose you are sure to be miserable. Any time a person denies their heart's calling in life, because of so-called duty and responsibility, they are cheating themselves…and the world. Always ask yourself: "Responsibility to what, or to whom?" Is it responsibility to mediocrity, subjugation, materialism or economic enslavement? What sick institutions are you bound to upholding through your "responsibility" and to what master do you suborn yourself day-in and day-out? You have a greater duty to be true to your heart and your purpose in life. You have a great responsibility to become the full expression of your true-self and to rise to the full measure of your unique potential.

Every soul has a gift and greater purpose. When we suppress our desire to be true to our greater purpose in life, we can become depressed, and over time, we may even become physically ill. To deny the course of our own nature is a crime against our own humanity. Imagine a world where all the great artists, musicians, inventors, Olympians, healers and dreamers had surrendered their dreams and yielded to the mundane responsibilities of common existence and common expectations. *What a sad, deprived and cheated world that would be!* Live your life with worthy pursuits that are to the benefit of all people. There is only *one you.* Live your true purpose and share your unique gifts with the world.

Also as a good piece of advice, I suggest that everyone meditate, and do the introspection required to find yourself. It is so important that you understand what you really are--and *trust yourself!* There is nothing external of yourself that you need. Everything you need is within. Learn to quieten your mind and be present, mindful and in the now--*even with your own self.* Do not dwell in the past, or in the future. The past is inaccessible and the future is ever advancing, and therefore, also inaccessible. There is only this blessed moment called *now,* and beyond that, there are no guarantees. As Prince

Gautama Siddhartha, the founder of Buddhism wrote: "*Do not dwell in the past, do not dream of the future, concentrate the mind on the present moment.*" So, simply be the glorious creation you are and let your radiant heart smile for all to see…and become love. Finally, and most importantly, do not allow people or creatures to suffer.

Betty Dravis: There is great wisdom in what you say, Bryant, and I've experienced more than my share of nay-sayers during my writing career. It takes much thought, time and patience to arrive where you are, but it appears you are helping many people get there.

It is truly mind-boggling to even think about how you manage it all. You have come a long, long way from that dirt road in Alabama. How do you manage to run so many successful operations? You must be terrific at organizing and delegating authority. How do you accomplish so much?

Bryant McGill: I do accomplish a great deal, Betty, but I accomplish so much by doing as little as possible. I call it "do nothing and accomplish everything." The main action I take to move forward is a form of inaction: being still and quiet. Too much aggression and work will move what you desire further away. Creation is an act of cooperation, not force. You do not rape the universe, you make love with the universe. For me, all things are accomplished by the meditative act of releasing illusions and simply becoming. My main tools are invitation, patience, time, gentleness, cooperation and surrender. I have let go of everything and that is how you get everything; you let go of everything. When we try to control, we become controlled; when we release, we become free. Creativity is the greatest expression of liberty. Creation is an act of *freedom,* by a creator consciousness. I do *very* little outside of being free.

Betty Dravis: It took you many years to get where you are, Bryant, and it almost sounds magical in its simplicity. I admire your diligence and will power in achieving your heart's desire by becoming your own person, not to mention what you are doing for others.

Regretfully, we're nearing the end of our interview, but I can't leave without asking about your beautiful daughters. How important is family to you, and in general?

Bryant McGill: There are many types of families. We love most those who we serve most, and with families there are endless ways in which we serve. Our children and other members of our families are independent entities. We do not own them and they do not belong to us; we can only know them. They belong to the world and to themselves, and for a brief period in this ephemeral existence we have the privilege to share time with them and serve them and their needs.

I remember in vivid detail the moment each of my darling girls was born into life's keeping. I am a contemplative person by nature and there has seldom been a period of time that has gone by wherein I did not reflect back to the moments my children were born. What I remember most--having had a true lasting impact on me--are two things. Of the two, what I consider most awe-inspiring was their first breath. I have thought intently about it over the years; about its profound implications on my understanding of the mysterious world around us and, ultimately, about its beauties.

There I stood in each case as they came into the world, and I witnessed their very first, amazing and miraculous breath. With that breath came the animations of life and their helpless, compelling cries.

The second thing that has continued to impact me is that as this happened--in that instant of their springing to being--I helplessly wept tears of utter and absolute humility and joy, as a witness to the sacred gift of life and creation. Each time I think about the moment of their births, it poignantly reminds me that I have, continue, and will forever cherish each and every breath and beat of their precious hearts. It also continues to remind me that each soul I encounter once took that first breath, and was, and is, also a beautiful child.

As Kahlil Gibran (1883-1931), the famous Lebanese poet, philosopher and artist, once wrote of children:

"Your children are not your children. They are the sons and daughters of Life's longing for itself. They come through you but not from you, and though they are with you, yet they belong not to you. You may give them your love but not your thoughts, for they have their own thoughts. You may house their bodies but not their souls, for their souls dwell in the house of tomorrow, which you cannot visit, not even in your dreams.

You may strive to be like them, but seek not to make them like you, for life goes not backward nor tarries with yesterday. You are the bows from which your children as living arrows are sent forth. The archer sees the mark upon the path of the infinite, and He bends you with His might that His arrows may go swift and far. Let your bending in the archer's hand be for gladness; For even as he loves the arrow that flies, so He loves also the bow that is stable."

My children belong to the future, which is a place I cannot visit, but for now, in this moment, I am blessed to call them my friends, and to witness their beauty and growth, and to be a mirror to them, that shows them their uniqueness and true beauty. No matter what I create or accomplish in life, my children will always be my greatest co-creation.

The most important thing I can say about family is we are all family. I hope one day we can all evolve from the clannish institutions of isolation of the people outside of exclusive family boundaries. We are all children of creation. We are all one, we are all brothers and sisters, we are all one beautiful human family.

Betty Dravis: Confidentially, Bryant, I read that Gibran quote about the "bows and arrows" when my children were small and it let me know in no uncertain terms that I did not "own" them. I didn't like it at the time (laughs), but it gave me pause to reflect and impressed me deeply. Thanks for reminding me. I'm reluctant to leave you because there is so much more to you; more than time and space allow. But I'll console our readers by giving your web addresses where they can find you.

For a last tidbit, I hear you have an upcoming speech you will be delivering with a former United States President, as well as the possibility of meeting the president of India and Gandhi's family. Please mention any additional plans or events coming up in the near future.

Bryant McGill: Well, Betty, currently I am working on a weight-loss and wellness book called, "The Peaceful Body." I am doing a lot of Soul Coaching, as well as wellness and weight-loss coaching in Los Angeles. I have also just opened new business offices in Beverly Hills. I have a reality show in the works and a documentary under production.

I have a lot of web addresses on the Internet. The simplest way to find them is by Googling my name.

Betty Dravis: I knew there was more, Bryant. (laughs) And since you were also interviewed by a best-selling author from the UK, Lisa Tenzin-Dolma, I look forward to getting a copy of *Mind and Motivation: The Spirit of Success,* not only to compare notes about you, but to learn from other experts she interviewed in their chosen fields in the arts, sciences and psychology. These sound like inspirational, motivational and revealing personal stories of how they attained their goals. This book sounds a little like our *Dream Reachers* with a focus centered more on "the mind."

You are definitely a Renaissance thinker who leads from the heart toward a world of unlimited possibilities. It's been a pleasure meeting you and enlightening to learn more about you. I hope you continue your quest "to prove that life is still beautiful and that all people have the power to have a better life and world–*now.*" You have certainly inspired me to take a different approach to make my dreams come true. Thanks for everything, and please keep in touch.

Bryant McGill: Thank you for the honor and privilege to be included in your series of interviews, Betty, and I wish you and all people a life of great purpose and joy.

"The act of true giving
is indistinguishable from receiving."

--- Bryant McGill

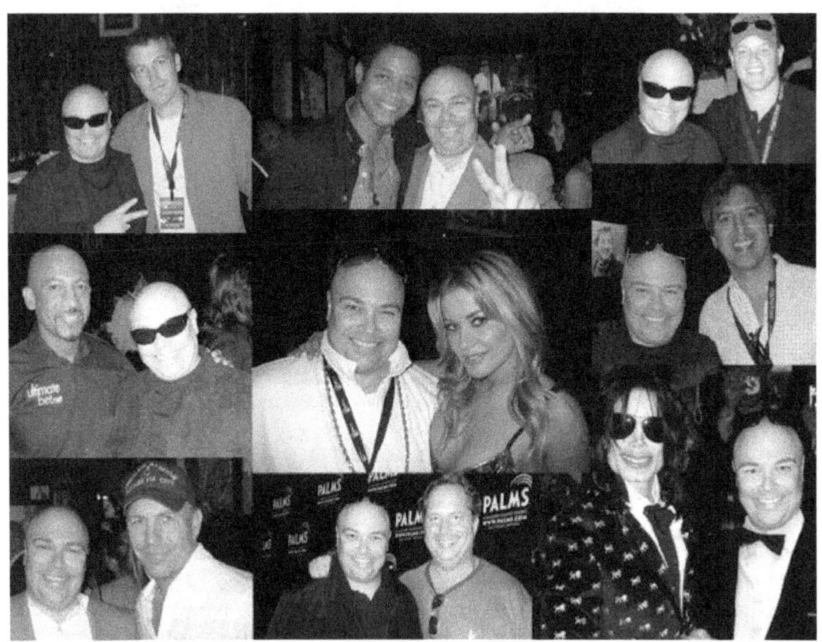

Interview with Katherin Kovin Pacino

"ATOMIC BLONDE" IS STEP-MOM OF AL PACINO

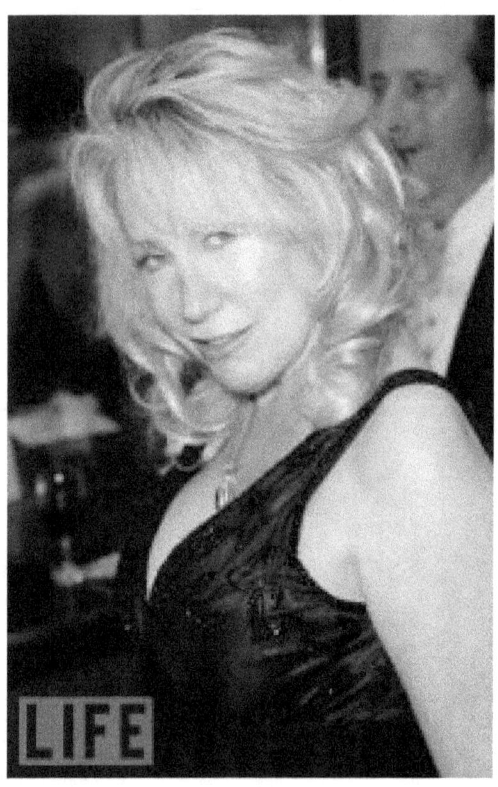

Betty Dravis: Welcome to Dames of Dialogue, Kat. It's a pleasure to have such a fine actress and Hollywood "insider" with us today. I met you on Facebook, of all places–which isn't as odd as it seems in today's high-tech world. I related to what you said beneath your profile picture: "I believe in actors helping actors. When I find a good thing to share, I like letting people know! It's all about the *art*...and giving from the *heart!"*

Since I feel the same way about authors helping authors, you hooked me up front. You sounded so interesting, I just had to look up your film credits and read your biography. Needless to say, your fascinating background intrigued me and I knew our readers would love to meet you. I hoped you would be open for an interview...*and here you are!*

As you know, my interviews are all about high achievers who aren't afraid to dream big and to act upon those dreams to see them to fulfillment. Since you are so successful in all you do, you are the personification of the ultimate Dream Reacher.

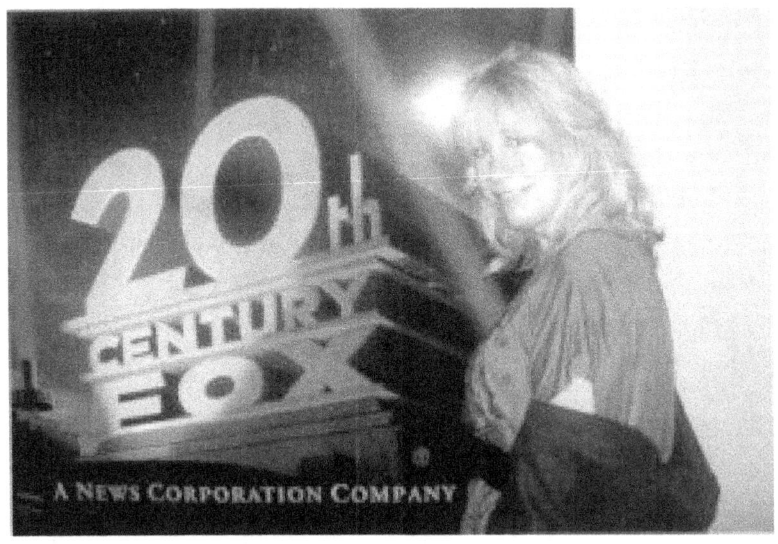

I read that you were born in Chicago, grew up in St. Louis and moved to Escondido, California with your parents when you were a teen. I'm wondering how you went from being the "pampered daughter of a jewelry tycoon/businessman" to Hollywood where you eventually made your film debut in *Holy Hollywood.* You played a principal role as "Tyler's mom" when that film was released in 1999. I bet that first role was thrilling. How did you feel at that time? Have you acted all your life, or just when did you get the acting bug?

Katherin Kovin Pacino: Thanks for inviting me to be part of your project, Betty.

I read *Dream Reachers* and really enjoyed learning new things about various artists, some I know, some I don't, but it's a fun, informative, inspiring book.

About my parents, Arnold and Rozalind Kovin, they owned the Arnie Kovin Jewelry store chain, also Arnex Watches. And they did spoil me to some extent because I had all the luxuries, but they also taught me family values, respect for others and all I needed to know to succeed in life. I'm adopted and they loved me so much… I'm lucky. But *no,* my dad was not exactly a tycoon… He was a multi-millionaire… A very good, hard-working successful man…and Mom was all I could ask for in a mother.

Yes, those first years in acting were thrilling, but every time I go on stage or before a camera, I still get that magical feeling, that surge of energy. I love everything about acting and ever since I was a young girl I wanted to be an actress. I started out by playing extras and began getting better roles, so the *Holy Hollywood* role was not my first, just my first larger role.

Betty Dravis: Your second film followed three years later. In *I Soldati—The Soldier* in the U.S.–you did an impressive job in a supporting role, which happened to be the love interest of your own husband, Sal Pacino. Kat, I don't mind telling you that my ears perked up when I learned you were married to the late father of the living legend Al Pacino. Since Sal was an actor first, is it safe to say that he encouraged Al to follow in his footsteps?

Katherin Kovin Pacino: Truthfully, Betty, he didn't have to encourage him; Al always wanted to be an actor. When he was a little kid, he saw an old Ray Milland movie and ran around reciting some of the lines over and over. In fact, when he accepted the AFI's Lifetime Achievement Award in 2008, Al said, "By age three, I was doing Al Jolson. I found, in the theater, this place I could go to. I found this peace." Sal said that even at three Al was a charmer and Sal supported his son in everything he did… They had a close relationship.

Betty Dravis: Although Sal passed away in 2005 and you've managed to get on with your life, I wish to express belated condolences. That was a sad time for you, but our readers would appreciate hearing about the fun times when you met Sal. I'm a sucker for love stories and am curious about how you met, where you met, and if there were any humorous little anecdotes from that time. I admit that I'm dying to know if you had much interaction with Al…as are our readers! Would you care to share, Kat? (How did you two get along? Was there any conflict because you are younger than he is? … Just little things like that…lol…)

Katherin Kovin Pacino: (laughs) Everyone asks me about Sal and Al, Betty, and I love talking about them too. It brings back some of the happiest times of my life. I was devastated when my husband passed away… I'm glad you asked me about the happy times because I'd rather think about the good times. Playing his love interest in *I Soldati* was interesting and fun. It seemed like an extension of our off-camera life because he was always so loving and supportive of me and such a joy to be around.

I met Sal through a mutual friend who had known him over twenty years. The friend was after me but I thought he was too young for me, so set him up with one of my girlfriends. That lasted about three days, but Sal and I lasted over twelve-and-a-half years.

We clicked right from the first and were married in Las Vegas in the Little Chapel of the Flowers…a candlelight ceremony for close friends and family. Sal always joked that it was "love at first fright."

Sal was in the insurance business for over thirty years and in addition to acting, he was a Union negotiator, which was fortunate for me due to the good benefits packages that give me more security, even now.

As for Al Pacino, yes, Betty, he's a living legend—an enormous talent–and we are extremely proud of him. Since he became so famous, he is always so busy that we don't see him as often as before. When his father was alive, we all got together for private family events: dinners, birthdays, anniversaries…things like that. But after Al's phenomenal success in the *Godfather* trilogy, the studios had him hopping from one box-office hit to another. I respect his privacy, but he won't mind my sharing that he still keeps in touch as much as he can. Whenever he's in a show or wins an award or something, he always sends tickets…and we bump into each other at social events, at the Sheraton-Hilton and other places. He's just too busy to keep close touch with anyone, really.

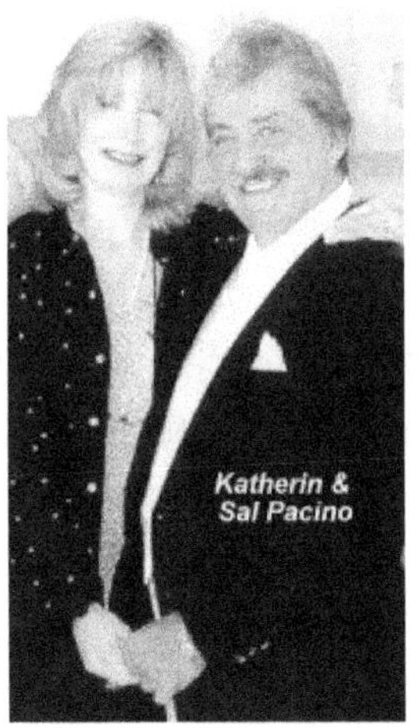
Katherin & Sal Pacino

Al and I always got along fine and there was no jealousy… Sure, Al is older than I am–this month marks his 70th birthday–but that was never a problem between us or anyone in the family. I was his father's fifth wife, so Al was always understanding and accepting of that. He and his father were close, as I said before, and accepted each other's life choices.

Betty Dravis: Now that the big, important subject of Al is out of the way, I admit I'm more curious about you, the independent Katherin. Let's talk about your movie and TV career a little more, and then I'll get into your other interests in and outside the entertainment industry. Tell us about the role of Lady Catherine in your last movie in 2005. And what is the favorite role you've played and why you liked it so much?

Katherin Kovin Pacino: It's an odd coincidence that you should ask about my role as Lady Catherine, Betty. That was the part I played in the documentary *Bolivar: Path to Glory* and it's my favorite role. It was made in 2005 by Bob DeBrino Entertainment and was set in Venezuela. The reason I favor that role is because I got to act with Sal again and traveling to Venezuela to shoot was like having a family vacation while doing what we both liked best—acting! Venezuela is a scenic wonder and seeing the country and meeting Venezuelan stars was the frosting on the cake. With that film we had the best of both worlds. He was excellent in the role of General De Miranda, but sadly, it was our last movie together. We worked well together…

Betty Dravis: That does sound like a dream role and a dream vacation, Kat. I enjoy seeing husband-and-wife teams in movies. Two couples that come to mind are Richard Burton and Elizabeth Taylor and Paul Newman and Joanne Woodward, not to mention Brad Pitt and Angelina Jolie. I'm glad you had the pleasure of acting with Sal and have those beautiful memories.

Now, switching subjects… If I recall the facts, Mickey Rooney played a cameo role in one of your films. Since he's also a living legend and beloved throughout the world, can you share any behind-the-scenes stories of him and his interaction with the cast? I and our readers would appreciate your sharing more of your former connections and adventures along the way, but we'll get to those later.

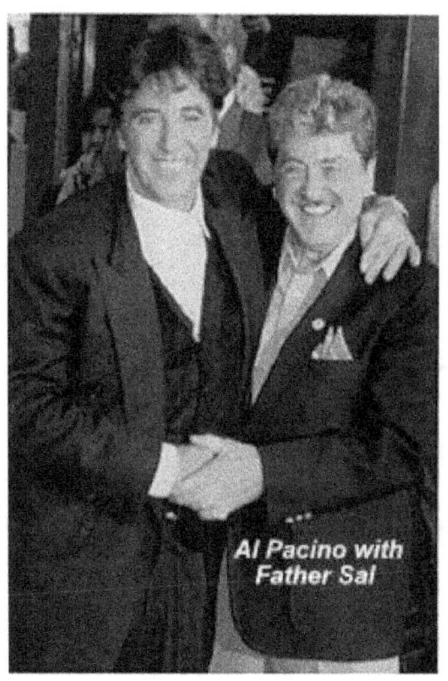
Al Pacino with Father Sal

Katherin Kovin Pacino: Well, Betty, Mickey was easy to work with, very nice and supportive and a lot of fun to be around. I admire him so much. It's hard to believe that he'll be ninety this year and he's in another movie, *Johnny Blue,* which is in preproduction. He's led a fascinating life, and according to Hollywood lore, as of 2007, he's the only surviving screen actor to appear in silent films and still continues to act in movies into the new millennium. His debut was in the movie *Not to Be Trusted* at the age of four. That astonishes me.

Betty Dravis: Wow, I didn't know that, Kat. That is amazing! No wonder he received the Lifetime Achievement Oscar!

You must have met a lot of important industry people in your life, but do you have one that stands out above all others? And who are some of the people who had the greatest influence on your life?

Katherin Kovin Pacino: Sal, of course, my current husband Bill Lashbrook and my parents were great, positive role models for me. They stand out above the crowd, but as for classic stars, I've been most impressed by Barbra Streisand and Bette Midler. Both have outstanding talent and have tackled other ends of the industry too. It's awesome what they've accomplished.

Betty Dravis: Kat, I know that you've done a variety of important things in your life. You have worked as a makeup/fashion/image consultant to companies such as Merle Norman, Revlon, Clientele, and have done makeup promos for Estee Lauder, Borghese, and other famous lines, as well. In addition to that, you've worked for public relation people such as the late Irving Zussman in New York, also as an entertainment business manager with Martin Licker, CPA (who handled names such as James Caan, Gary Sinise and several other celebs).

I enjoy working with famous, accomplished people because they're so stimulating, so that must have been exciting. I admire James Caan's acting ability and was captivated by his role of Sonny in *The Godfather*. What a blockbuster trilogy of movies that was! Did you have any personal dealings with Caan or any of Licker's celebrated clients?

Katherin Kovin Pacino: Believe it or not, Jimmy Caan never came up there. However, I did meet his ex-wife, his son Scott (now an actor himself), his brother, and his fun-loving aunts, whom he helped support. They came to the office about every two weeks for their "upkeep" check. It felt like *Godfather* all over again! (laughs)

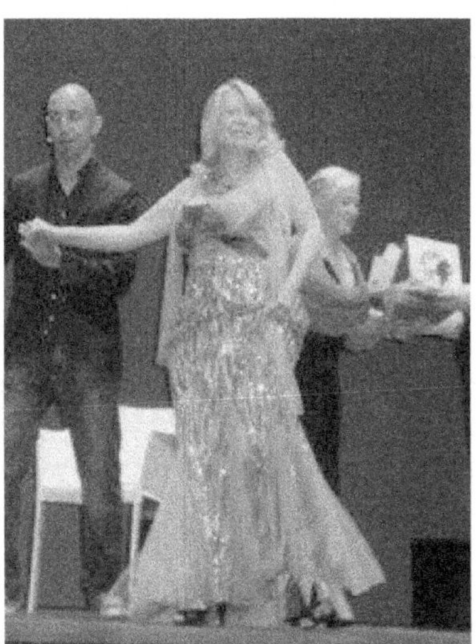

I also met Gary Sinise, who since then has made a mark for himself. He was such an earthy, nice guy… It's no surprise that today he ships supplies to the men fighting abroad for our country! And I met Jeff Wald who was totally very rude, to say the least. I remember that I answered the phone one morning, and he greeted me with: "F*** YOU!"… Since he represented some of the biggest names in show business, I expected more class from him. This was the same guy who was married to Aussie singer Helen Reddy of the "I am Woman" fame. That song was number one around the world, so I guess that went to his head…or was it the coke? That marriage ended in divorce and he married Candy Clark of *The Blob*.

That ended in a divorce just a couple of years later, too! Gee… No wonder… Are we surprised? (laughs)

Betty Dravis: What goes around, comes around, Kat…but we don't always see it. It's always rewarding to see the nice guys like Gary Sinise go on to achieve their dreams. I always admired him and was happy when he won an Oscar for Best Supporting Role in *Forrest Gump* (1995). In fact, he has won an Emmy and so many other awards, it's hard to keep track of. Wow! Go, Gary!

And then there are the jerks like Wald who was so rude to you. I understand that he has a son by Reddy and that marriage lasted fifteen years, but he only lasted a year with Clark. I guess we can speak of his addiction since it's reported in his biography on IMDb (Internet Movie Database). His former addiction to cocaine is public knowledge. I also read that he has cleaned up his act and is once again producing. I have no idea if he still manages any big names, but among his former clients were Sylvester Stallone, George Foreman, James

Brolin, Tom Skerritt, George Carlin, Elliott Gould, Donna Summer, Flip Wilson and Marvin Gaye, and musical groups such as Deep Purple, Chicago and Crosby Stills & Nash, to name only a few. I suppose success like that could go to anyone's head. Since everyone deserves a second chance, I'm glad that he ultimately overcame his addiction and has made a come-back. Hopefully, he has learned respect for others during the rehab process.

You know, Kat, that Clint Eastwood was my first big celebrity interview when I was a young, starry-eyed journalist, and he was a class act; treated me like an equal, like a lady. He influenced me to dream big and act on my dreams, as he did. He's awesome. Have you ever run into him around Hollywood?

Katherin Kovin Pacino: I never met Clint, but came close to it once. I was invited to meet him at a luncheon, but I was married then and was always careful to consider my husband's feelings, so I had to decline.

Betty Dravis: Kat, the people with whom I've discussed this interview speak very highly of you; the first words that come out of their mouths are: elegant…gracious…lovely. In my short time with you, I have to agree with them. You are all that and more! I've also come to see a lighter, more playful side to your nature. I know you don't wish to be thought of as perfect, so to add to your mystique and send our readers away with smiles on their faces, can you share your most embarrassing moment, onstage or off, with us?

Katherin Kovin Pacino: That's a hard question to answer, Betty. I honestly can't think of an embarrassing time in the context you mean, but there is one big embarrassment that still bothers me. And it is not the "laughing matter" kind of story. I can't give too many details without embarrassing others, but I can say that the head people were having trouble booking a hotel for an important industry event and I offered to help. I booked the place for them only to find out later the hotel didn't have the proper speakers and camera equipment. It was a big mess, but once again I stepped up to the challenge and it all worked out.

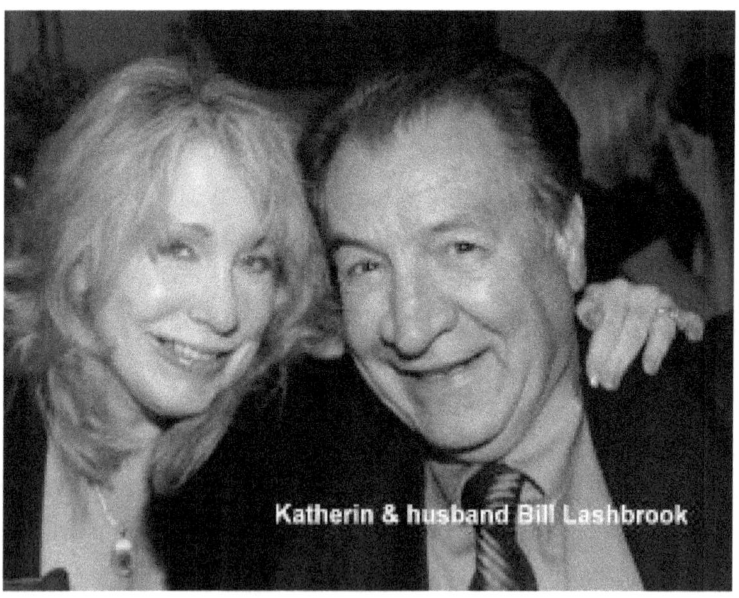
Katherin & husband Bill Lashbrook

Betty Dravis: OMG, I thought you would come up with something like you spilled a drink on a lead star when you were an extra or you tripped onstage…something in retrospect that would be laughable... But you came up with a real whopper! That *would* be embarrassing, Kat, but at least you found a solution.

I don't mind admitting, Kat, I'm intrigued by your acting career, but am also impressed that you played a big role in starting the West Hollywood International Film Festival (WHIFF) with Martin DeLuca, an Argentinean filmmaker and photographer. I have a photo or two to share with our readers from the recent awards ceremony, but I'd like to hear more about WHIFF. When was it founded? How you got involved? The latest buzz, please...

Katherin Kovin Pacino: The Festival is only two years old, but the idea for the Festival was a collaborative effort and I worked hard to help put it together. It was exhilarating work and I was happy to serve on the board of directors for a time. I stepped down when my other commitments got too heavy, but I took part in this year's awards ceremony. It went great this year, so I hope they make it and it becomes bigger and better.

Betty Dravis: We'd all like to hear more about your new projects, Kat, but now I'd like to ask you a lighter question. If you could spend the day with one person besides your husband–someone in history, a favorite author, a public figure, a character in a book, etc.–who would you choose and why?

Katherin Kovin Pacino: I have always admired Shirley MacLaine. I'll never forget her role in *Some Like it Hot*...and all the huge roles that followed. Her breakout role was the one following–*The Apartment*, a melancholy comedy with Jack Lemmon–but I have always liked her later roles too. She was hilarious in *Steel Magnolias*. She has a lot of talent but I like her zest for life and would like to spend a day with her. I could learn so much… The closest I ever came to her was when I was an extra on a set.

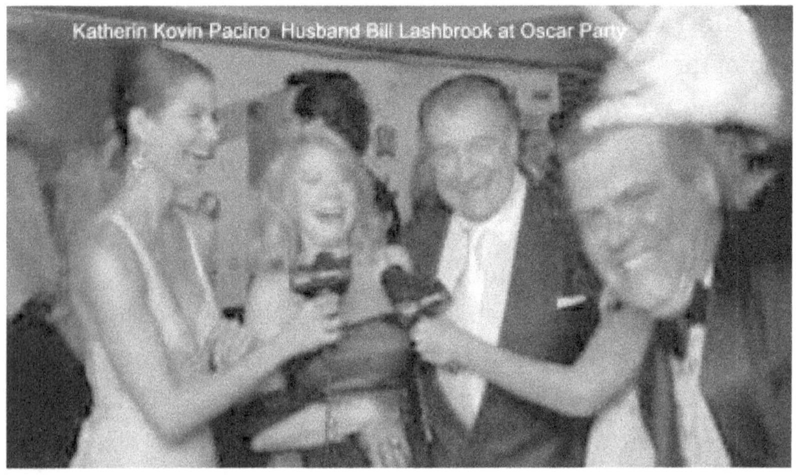
Katherin Kovin Pacino Husband Bill Lashbrook at Oscar Party

Betty Dravis: I like her, too, Kat. Her role in *Steel Magnolias* was also one of my favorites…and she was superb with Jack Nicholson in *Terms of Endearment.*

But moving on, you now split your time between Hollywood where your career interests lie and Marin County, near San Francisco, where your husband Bill Lashbrook grew up. Both places are breath-taking areas, vibrant and alive with talent and natural wonders. You've shared with me in our chats that Bill is a successful businessman and interested in Shakespearean acting. What line of work is he in and how is he involved with the Shakespearean community? He's such a devoted, supportive partner, working with you in many capacities, but I'm also curious about how you met. Guess I'm just a romantic at heart, so I hope you don't feel this is too intimate to share. If so, we understand.

Katherin Kovin Pacino: Exactly, Betty… Bill is a successful businessman but is now venturing into public speaking and is interested in consulting. He's very charismatic and alive with energy, so he'll succeed in whatever he sets his mind to. We work well as a team, so I'll help him as he helps me. We both enjoy Shakespeare and attend some plays and lectures whenever we have time. Bill was never in film, but enjoys stage acting…classical acting. He's a Shakespearean actor of the old school and will be the first to tell you it was more of a hobby than a career, but it brought him many years of pleasure.

But now to satisfy your "romantic nature," Betty, I'll share how Bill and I met. (laughs) As with Sal, we met through a mutual friend. It was shortly after Sal passed away and I lucked out in love again. Bill is wonderful and we've built a happy life together. We both have a great love of theatre; whether on camera or onstage, it's our great passion, so we work on most of our projects together. Currently, we're both interested in voiceover and would like to find a good teacher.

Betty Dravis: Voiceover is cutting-edge at present, I believe, Kat. It's a coincidence, but Chase Von, my co-author on *Dream Reachers*, recently interviewed Joan Baker, a fascinating woman who is one of the most sought-after voiceover teachers in the industry; she's also an author and has some awesome credits. Have you ever heard of her? She's based in New York, but may have a branch in LA. Anyway, she's on Facebook, too, so you might want to send her a message to ask her. At any rate, she could recommend someone in the LA area. But first check her astounding website on MySpace. She has photographs with actor Will Smith and others you may know.

Now that brings us to more of your current projects, Kat. I hear that you have a lot of things in the works…from writing books to producing your own movies. It's rumored that you're helping develop a WWII movie too. I'd love to hear about those exciting endeavors. The versatility of actors blows my mind. It's inspiring to me that you have such multi-tasking abilities and dare to venture into the writing and production end of the industry. I can see why Bill calls you the "Atomic Blonde."

Katherin Kovin Pacino: (laughs) Well, I do keep busy, but that World War II movie is off the table at present. As far as my current and future workings, I'm attached to several IPs (Intellectual Properties), one written by American playwright David Mamet with William H. Macy, as an associate producer; also associate producer of a comedy *Tall Order of Love* by J. Porrazzo; and am acting in J. Porrazzo's *The Queen of Hollywood.* Also, since I'm a spokesperson with Prince Ali of Afghanistan on his record *Party All Night* and am also a background recording artist on that record, you can see why Bill calls me "Atomic Blonde."

I also have other future attachments that are hush-hush at this time, and I have plans to write several children's books and a "How To" book about romance… the do's and don'ts, you know. *Katherin* (laughs as she refers to herself in first person) is still showing the ladies-*and* men—the proper application of makeup, the skills to put together a wardrobe, and the correct use of color/Image. Since I was brought up in that background, those skills come natural to me. I enjoy "paying it forward," as they say.

Betty Dravis: Yep, *Katherin* is showing us all how to be more glam, that's for sure! Actually, I'm beginning to think I have a Wonder Woman on my hands. That's an intimidating array of projects in the works, Kat. You also have a second Facebook page called Kat's Meow that gives people tips on where to get the most bang for their buck; from quality clothing to inexpensive bling to fine dining, you point them in the right direction. I enjoy reading the comments on that page and the opportunity for your fans to share their tips too. That's a fun, interactive site.

Since I love writing, I'm very interested in the books that you plan to write. Be sure to keep us informed when they're released and when any of your movies premiere too. Writing must run in the family; I understand your brother has also written a few books recently. Since our readers are not only interested in the entertainment industry but also in books, I'm sure they would like to hear more about him. The buzz around LA is that he also owns a popular restaurant. The scoop, please, Kat…

Katherin Kovin Pacino: Of course, Betty… I love spreading my brother's good news. His name is John Adam Kovin and he's written two books: *How to Play the Game of Life and Win* and *Taking God to Bed With You: The truth they don't want you to know about God, sex and the way the world really is.*

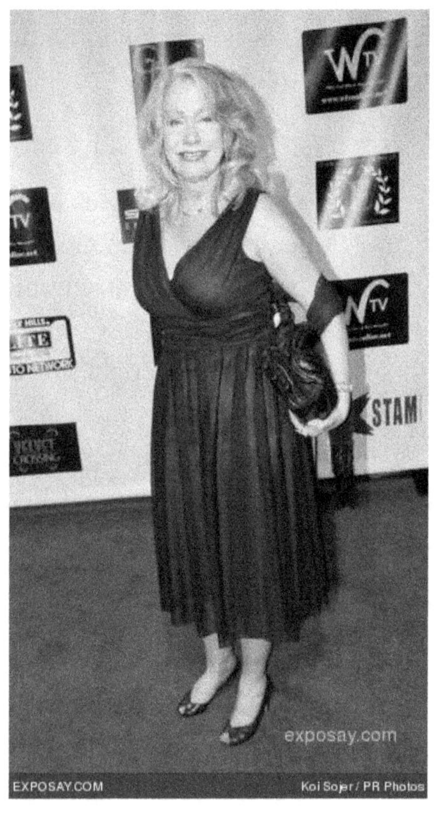

John also owns a restaurant, Chili Addiction, on Restaurant Row. It's located at 408 N. La Cienega Boulevard in Beverly Hills. His chili is to die for and he also serves a concoction I bet you haven't heard of—french-fried sweet potatoes. (laughs)

I tried them and they're delicious. If you ever get down here, Bill and I will take you to dinner. You'd love my brother; he's a real go-getter.

Betty Dravis: OMG, we all love chili! *But french-fried sweet potatoes?* I can honestly say, Kat, my friend in Maine told me about them, but I've never tried them. They do sound yummy, though, and I'll take you up on that dinner offer when and if I get to Southern California again. That's very kind of you and Bill. By the way, does Bill call your brother "Atomic John?" (laughs)

Kat, I appreciate your sharing so openly with us about your life. I enjoyed learning more about your brother and Bill's family too. Bill shared that his daughter, Jessica Lashbrook, owns Marin Feed and Tack in the quaint, colorful township of Fairfax, near San Rafael where my son lives. When I tell Bob and his Patty how gracious you and Bill are to me, I just know they'll be dropping by Jessica's business to say hello.

It's been a delight getting to know more about you, especially your new endeavors. I'm sure our readers will want to know even more about you, so in closing, is there anything you'd like to add? I think you're seeking a new agent, so I hope any who read this will get in touch with you.

You have so much to offer with everything you do. You're an exceptional woman; not only are you a talented actress, you have the necessary business acumen. How can interested parties get in touch with you? I know you're easy to find on

Facebook, but do you have any websites or links you would like to share with us?

Katherin Kovin Pacino: I'm glad for this last chance to add a few things, Betty. Since we first talked, I do have a new agent. I'm excited about that; his name is David Brown and he's one of the best in the business, in my opinion.

I also forgot to mention two projects that are dear to my heart: I have a part in a documentary *Sudan Hope.* Les LeMotte is executive director on that project. As you might know, he's also an award-winning songwriter.

I also have an acting role in *The Tim Brooks Story,* a movie about the first African-American cowboy. Musician Ben Rombouts and Rodney Allen Rippy, the child actor who is so famous for his Jack in the Box commercials, are affiliated with this film. I look forward to working with them.

I don't have a website yet, but I can be found on Facebook on the Internet, as you said, Betty. As for my biography, photos and film credits, they're listed on the Internet Movie Data Base. I also have a fashion page on Facebook – The Kat's Meow.

Betty Dravis: Thanks again, Kat, and best of luck with your novels, producing those movies and with your acting. Please keep in touch and let us know when any of your projects go live, when your next red carpet event takes place, etc. *Inquiring minds want to know!* (laughs) It's been a pure delight working with you on this interview. You are, indeed as elegant, gracious and lovely as your fans told me.

Katherin Kovin Pacino: The pleasure is mine, Betty. Thanks for inviting me. It's been fun and I look forward to meeting you in the near future. I'll keep in touch, via email and Facebook, of course. Xo

ENDNOTE: I had the pleasure of having dinner with Kat and her husband Bill Lashbrook on April 10th in San Rafael. My son Robert, his girl-friend Patty Carrillo and her mother Roma Vargas joined us. We had a delightful time: chatting, eating laughing. Pictures are posted in my Facebook albums. (My website: http://www.bettydravis.com)

"It's all about the ART... and GIVING from the Heart."

--- Katherin Kovin Pacino

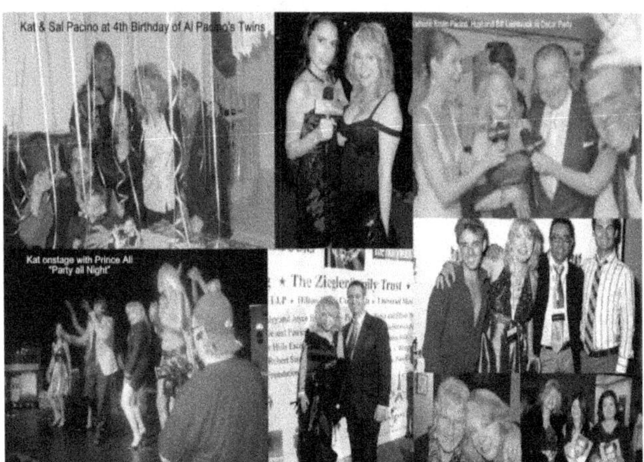

Interview with Tony Tarantino

ON THE MOVE IN HOLLYWOOD, VEGAS, ITALY

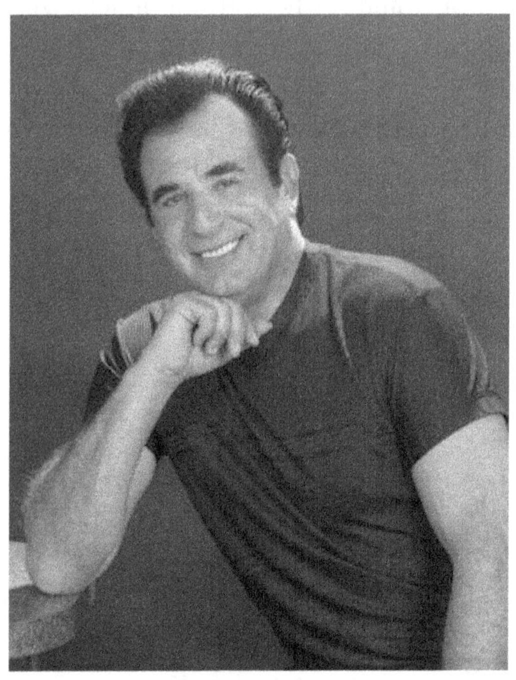

Betty Dravis: Welcome to Dames of Dialogue, Tony. It's a pleasure to have such a talented man from the film industry with us today. Actress Katherin Kovin Pacino recommended you to me for this interview. Of course, everyone has heard of you—you're a household name–but I visited your websites to learn more about you. Among many other things, you're an actor, a screenwriter, director and also have your own production company. Very impressive, indeed…

As you know, my interviews (and those of my co-author Chase Von) are all about high achievers who aren't afraid to dream big and to act upon those dreams to see them to fulfillment. Since you're so successful in all you do, you are a perfect fit for our book, and that's why I'm delighted you agreed to be in *Dream Reachers: Vol. II* when it goes to press. Thanks so much.

Tony, I have so many questions for you… I had no idea where to begin, but then I read something on your MySpace website that made it easy. You wrote: "The film industry has been our way of life for generations." You also spoke about your father Dominic being successful in silent films, speaking of him as "an original cowboy actor." That certainly takes us back in time and I'd like to hear more about him. How and when did he get started and did that lead to your acting and, subsequently, to your son Quentin's interest in the movie industry?

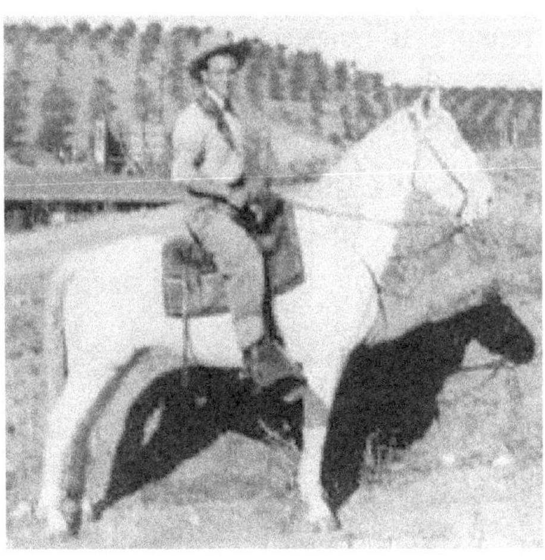

Tony's father Dominic on Tom Mix's Horse

Tony Tarantino: You're right, Betty, acting has been in our family since my father Dominic appeared in several Westerns with stars such as Buck Jones, Tim McCoy, Tom Mix, Hoot Gibson and Fred Thompson. That was in the thirties…

I grew up listening to my dad tell his stories about Hollywood, the people he worked with and many of the ones he met. This started as far back as I can remember. Just from listening to his stories I knew I wanted to be an actor. I can't speak for Quentin, but I caught the acting bug from my father. It must be in the genes. (laughs)

Betty Dravis: It sounds like you had an interesting, adventurous childhood, Tony, and your fans are happy you followed in your father's footsteps. I hope you write a book one day, recounting some of those stories about old-time actor friends of your father. Thanks for sharing the photo of him riding the horse of famous cowboy actor Tom Mix. That must be a family treasure. I bet you laughed out loud when you learned the name of the horse was "Tony." (laughs)

Your father sounds like quite a guy! I remember watching cowboy movies when I was a kid; it was mostly Gene Autry and Roy Rogers in my day, but I recall seeing Tom Mix, Tex Ritter and some of the others too.

But moving on, if I recall correctly, your first acting role was in *Where the Boys Are* when you were eighteen. You've been in many movies since then—including *Blood Money, Holy Hollywood, All the Rage,* and *Family Tree.* Do you know the exact count…or roughly? I know you have much experience and have honed your craft to perfection. Can you describe your emotions when you landed that first role? We'll get into the details of your production company later.

Tony Tarantino: I believe the count to date is about sixty films. I was happy to land that first role, but I may have been even happier when I auditioned for and was accepted into the Pasadena Playhouse after graduating from LA's Washington High School. That's a long way from my hometown; I was born in Queens, New York and raised in Brooklyn. If my parents had not moved me and my sister Diane to Los Angeles in 1952, my life might have taken a different course.

Betty Dravis: Tony, I can't believe all the skills you learned at Pasadena Playhouse: acting, modern dance, guitar, singing, etc. You even played guitar and sang folk songs in local coffeehouses…for the joy of it and for tips. I bet those tips came in handy for a young student.

But all that wasn't enough for a fun-loving, ambitious young man like you!

You wanted to be as well-rounded as possible to land as many roles as you could, so you also earned a pilot's license; became proficient in Western quick-draw; won awards for marksmanship with handguns and rifles; earned a black belt in Karate and Kung-Fu; became skilled with bow and arrow, even touring with the Malibu Roving Archers. Do I dare mention: boxing, tennis, swimming and playing accordion?

I confess it blew my mind when I learned about all your early achievements. That's awesome and I bet that list isn't complete, is it? (laughs)

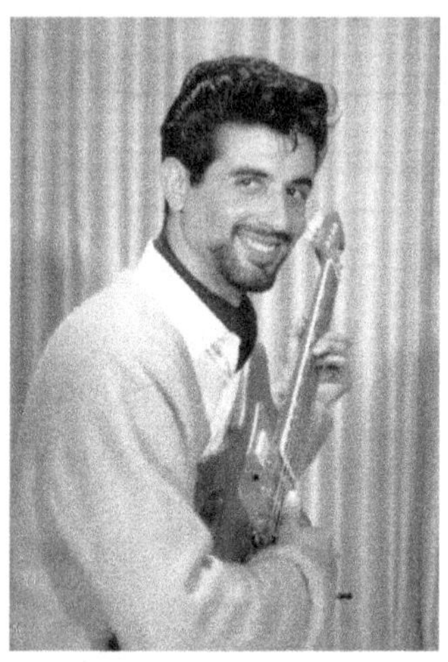

Tony Tarantino: Well, Betty, I did do a few more things… (laughs) I love music and that led me to form several bands where I played lead, rhythm and bass guitar in supper clubs and night-clubs in Los Angeles and the South Bay area. Those were heady years. We had a lot of fun back in the day.

More recently, I produced a television interview show, co-hosted a radio talk show and in 1998 worked on four films, starring in one. There is more, but I don't want to bore you…

Betty Dravis: The path to success isn't easy, is it, Tony, and you are anything but boring. (laughs) I enjoy all your show biz stories. In fact, you're being modest not to mention some colossal awards you have earned: in 2001 you took home the coveted Los Angeles Music Awards "50 Years Tribute to the Sunset Strip" for your contribution to music spanning your career. The award was given out at the Whiskey A Go-Go.

It must have been fun to go back to where you also played on many occasions. Also winning awards that evening were Gary Busey (for his *Buddy Holly* portrayal), Peter Tork of *The Monkees,* Jackie Shannon and Ollie Woodson of *The Temptations,* David Gates of *Bread*, Chuck Negron and Lenny Williams of *Tower of Power,* Devo, and Larry Flynt for the Freedom of Speech Award.

You certainly were in good company, to say the least… What a night that must have been! And to go down in musical history that way is incredible!

Tony, you have proved that the road to success can be fun and rewarding. I'm glad you enjoyed the journey to where you are today. All of those skills blend together to form the accomplished actor, director, screenwriter, songwriter and producer that you are today…so that's a *good* thing…

You also won Best Comedy Drama at The San Fernando Valley International Film Festival (VIFFI) Awards in 2004. And in January, 2010 you hosted *Elvis – Happy 75th* at the Grove Theatre in Upland. On the bill was Elvis tribute artist Sage Matthew Vincent and actor/belly dancer Tanya Lemani who performed the role of Little Egypt in Presley's 1968 NBC comeback special. (For you Elvis fans, a clip of that dance can be found on YouTube.)

Another well-received project you did in 2000 was an exercise video, *Silver Foxes,* with the lovely actress Stefanie Powers. I hear that the real Silver Foxes is actually a group of celebrity parents: you, father of Quentin; the late Sal Pacino, father of Al; Patsy Swayze, mother of the late Patrick; Jenny Crawford, Cindy's mom; Christine Johnson, Magic's mom; and Nikki Robbins, Tony Robbins' mother.

I understand that *Silver Foxes* is the brainchild of producer David Krieff. That video must have been a change of pace for you. Do any of you ever get together now?

Tony Tarantino: Thanks for mentioning some of my awards, Betty. And as for seeing my co-actors in *Silver Foxes, no,* I haven't… We are so far apart in distance, it's not easy to do, but we have spoken on the phone on many occasions. I think I have spoken to Patsy the most because she is here in Southern California. Sal Pacino and I were real close, almost like father and son, until his passing in 2005. I enjoyed many good times with him and his wife Katherin.

Betty Dravis: Katherin Kovin Pacino also told me that you and Sal were very close. I was saddened to learn of his death; belated condolences on his passing.

And it's understandable that you don't see the others so much, Tony. It's a crazy world nowadays with everyone carrying such heavy loads… That video sounds like a clever idea. We all admire strong, caring parents and their successful offspring. And the entire world fell in love with Stefanie Powers when she starred in *The Girl from U.N.C.L.E.* and the TV show *Hart to Hart* with the esteemed actor Robert Wagner. I read that her latest is a Hallmark TV movie *Meet My Mom.* It's heartening to know she is still active.

Do you still exercise using the Power Pilates techniques of stretch and relaxation as featured in the video, or how do you stay in such fine shape?

Tony Tarantino: Stefanie Powers is a great actress and a wonderful woman. I've had the pleasure to interface with her on several occasions.

But as for an exercise regimen, *no,* unfortunately, I haven't had the time to work out as I should. To keep in shape, I used to exercise with personal trainer P.J. Bowen, and I trained for boxing with Hervi Estrada. I keep telling myself I have to get back to it. Once you stop, it's real hard to start back.

Betty Dravis: Well, you certainly appear to be in great shape. At six feet, one, with your natural lankiness, many men must envy you…

But on with the interview, I know you wish to keep much about your family private and I honor that. I saw a video of a reporter questioning you about Quentin, and you said, "I have great respect for my son. He's probably the finest filmmaker of our time… Definitely the most copied artist of all time."

Is there anything else you'd like to share about your family?

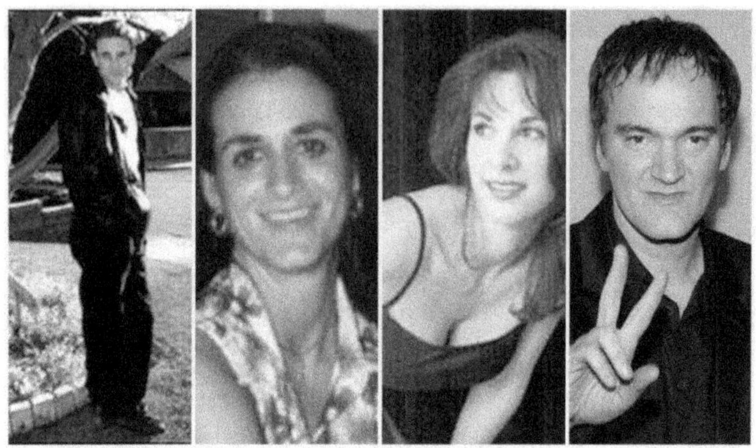

Tony Tarantino: I have four children: Edward James, Tanya Marie, Ronnajean and Quentin. I'm very proud of them all. You have my permission to use photos of them, Betty, and any photos from my various websites, but I would rather not comment about my family at present.

Betty Dravis: I understand, Tony, and it's generous of you to offer use of your photos. Many people in the public eye are very protective of their families, and I think that's admirable. One can't be too careful in today's crazy world. But speaking of pictures, I saw one of your mother Elizabeth. Was she an actress too? She was certainly beautiful enough for leading roles.

Tony Tarantino: Thank you for the kind words, Betty. *No*...my mom was a full-time, stay-at-home mom. She never was an actress. She devoted all her time, her love and her energy to my sister Diane and me.

Betty Dravis: Thanks for sharing about your mom, Tony. From the way you and Diane developed into good, caring adults, your mother was undoubtedly a fine role model.

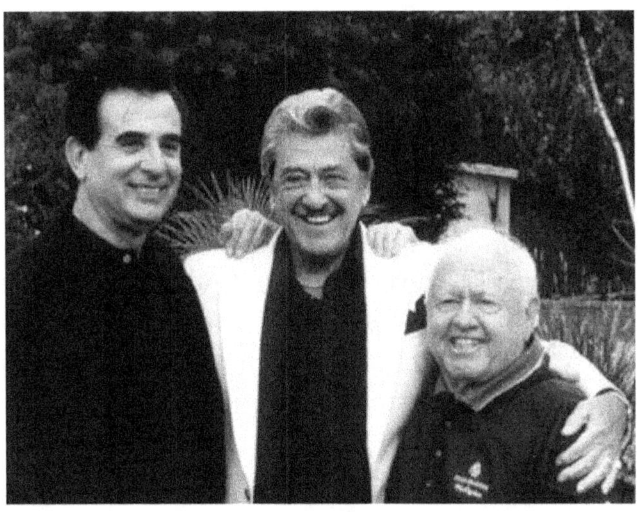

Tony with Sal Pacino and Living Legend Mickey Rooney

And I bet your father had a great deal to do with that, also, being a "cowboy" of the Golden West and all. (laughs)

But speaking of beautiful women, I saw a YouTube video in which a TV personality is questioning you and that gorgeous actress Susan Kennington at a Charity Masquerade Party (supporting the leukemia, cancer cause). In the video you two spoke about the projects you were working on at the time. You mentioned that you were producing *Prism*, based on the book *Color of the Prism* by Thomas J. Nichols. I know it often takes years to finish a film, but can you tell us a little about the progression of the filming? (For our readers, the video link is: http://www.youtube.com/watch?v=Yx6wI6WBoNs).

I also read in a Las Vegas newspaper about you having three films in pre-production, including *Prism.* We'll get into the other two below, but for now tell us about *Prism* and when we can expect to see the premiere. Also, for an outsider like me, explain the difference between "in production" and "in pre-production."

Tony Tarantino: Like everyone in the industry, I enjoy talking about my films, Betty. *Prism* is a large budget film and that makes it a bit harder to finance. On this film I'm the screenwriter, director and also play a supporting role. *Prism* is a blending of fact and fiction into a journey of intrigue, love, betrayal, greed and tragedy; a present-day police thriller set on the Arizona-Mexican border. *Prism* is in pre-production.

The difference between in production and pre-production is: Pre-production is where you put all the pieces together–the cast, the crew and all that's involved in the actual production. Production is when you have started principal photography.

Betty Dravis: Wow—three movies! That's a real coup, but an awful lot of juggling. (laughs) We all love movies, not to mention how some people idolize entertainers!

Thanks for explaining about production and pre-production… Now I *get* it! And your description of *Prism* stirs my writer's imagination; I can't help anticipating in what direction the plot will go. I look forward to seeing all your movies, but that one really intrigues me.

Since Susan Kennington acts and writes for some of your movies, is it too fresh of me to ask if you and she are an "item," as they say in Hollywood? She certainly is a gorgeous woman and I hear she's a fine actress too. I haven't had the good fortune to see her on film yet, but I hope to remedy that in the near future. I've chatted with her on Facebook and she seems to be such a fascinating, down-to-earth, caring woman. Since she's so gorgeous and glamorous, I have to chuckle at her calling herself a "girly tomboy sporting stiletto boots."

What a woman! In fact, I relate to her so much I actually landed her interview for this book. (laughs)

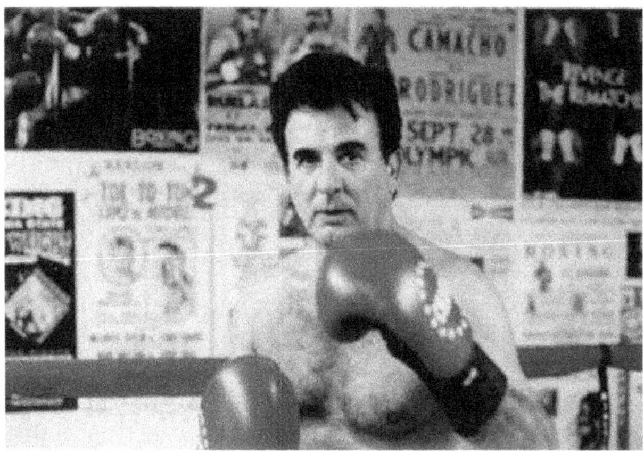

Tony Tarantino: I'm glad you chose Susan for this book, too, Betty. She deserves all the accolades she can get! I enjoy sharing about her… Susan and I are very close friends. She's a very talented actress, a wonderful person and we work well together. We attend many networking functions and red-carpet events together to promote the work we are doing as a team and the work we do as individuals.

Betty Dravis: Thanks for clearing that up. We can't have too many good friends… Next, I'm dying to know about your other projects, but before you enlighten us I'd like to know what motivated you to switch from acting to directing and producing.

When did you start your own production company?

Tony Tarantino: My dad and I started Tarantino Productions in 1958 as a general partnership. I didn't incorporate it till after his passing. I consider myself a storyteller, and acting and directing are big parts of telling a story. As a younger man I concentrated on acting. As I got older, strong parts became harder to come by. If you are a major star, an A-list actor, then it's not a problem. I haven't made it to that point, but have always been happy just to be part of the process in any way I could.

I have come to love the directing and producing end of the business, but must admit that directing and producing is no gravy train. You've got to be quick witted in this business and never underestimate anything.

Betty Dravis: I love the way you express your "feel" for your industry, Tony. I feel the same way about writing… When you dream, you dream BIG! You know what you want and you go for it! Our motto with our *Dream Reachers* books is: *Only those who stretch to reach their dreams find themselves living them.* That describes you: you set your goals and certainly stretch to reach them. No wonder you are such an outstanding Dream Reacher.

Would you please give us the inside scoop about your movies?

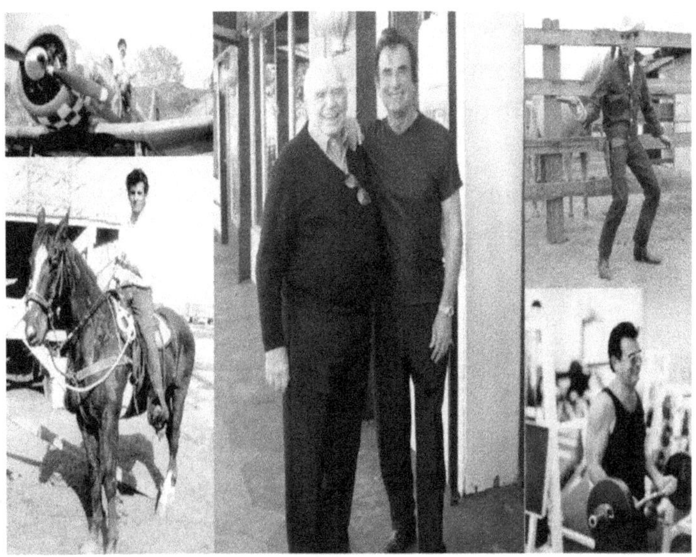

Tony Tarantino: It will be easier to answer this by copying from a news article written about me. I'll leave the portion about *Prism* out because we discussed that above.

Tarantino Signs On For Three Films

...The second film, The Keeper, is also in pre-production and is scheduled to start shooting as soon as Prism is completed filming. In this production, Tony has been contracted to direct

this true story of Richard Etheridge, born into slavery in 1842, who rises to national heroism during a time of racial prejudice and discrimination in America.

Third is Death Keeps Coming, with Tony as producer. This 1880s Western with a supernatural twist stars Martin Kove. (Best known for his role in all four Karate Kid films.)

Betty Dravis: Those movies all sound like winners to me. I can't wait to see them. It will be years of hard work, but I wish you all success with each of them.

Now to take a short break from the film industry, I have a lighter question this time: If it were possible to spend the day with anyone throughout history, who would you choose…and why?

Tony Tarantino: Well, this is an easy one for me, Betty. I'd like to spend time with Christopher Columbus because I enjoy adventure and travel. I love America and would have enjoyed being part of the discovery of this great country. My ancestry is Italian, but I'm a second generation American. I'm very proud of my father Dominic who was a WWII Marine and served on Guadalcanal and Iwo Jima.

Betty Dravis: That's a great answer, Tony. It was men like your father who gave so much to assure our freedom. Thanks for sharing that.

Your choice of whom to spend the day with is fitting. You and Christopher Columbus would have had a lot to talk about; with your entrepreneurial spirit and inquisitive natures, you have much in common.

And now, Tony, for a little "fun" question. Most people have had embarrassing moments at some time in their lives. Have you? If so, please share one of them with us. As we all like movies, we also like a good laugh from time to time.

Tony Tarantino: I was at a party and a well-known actor whom I have since come to know came up to me and said: "Hi, Tony," and I called him by the wrong name. Not only was it the wrong name, but it was the name of another well-known actor. I can laugh about it now, but it wasn't funny then.

Betty Dravis: OMG, that's what they call a grand *faux pas.* That *would* be embarrassing, but since you became friends later, that actor must have had a good sense of humor and a bit of humility. (laughs)

But moving on, I hear that you have a beautiful home in the hills of Southern California. I bet you hated to leave all that when you recently traveled to Italy on business and to visit friends. Do you travel abroad extensively?

I know in younger days you raised and trained horses and enjoyed a bit of roping and cutting, but how do you relax at home now? Also tell us a little about your work with Screen Actors Guild.

Tony Tarantino: I wouldn't say I travel extensively, but I do manage to get away occasionally. Yes, I do miss my home when traveling, but Italy is beautiful and I enjoy my times there.

I also write screenplays, so I do a lot of writing and business from my home. That's relaxing, in its own way. You, as a writer, must know that… As for the Screen Actors Guild (SAG), at one time I volunteered three hours a week reading to K-3 classes as part of their BookPALS program. I haven't read to them for a while because I can only do it between films, but it's fun to help the children learn to read and to appreciate books.

I miss it when I can't do it; kids have a way of keeping us grounded.

Betty Dravis: I'm sincerely impressed by the caliber of the talented professionals you work with. Incredible!

And I admire you for helping the future generations, Tony. Paying it forward is a wonderful thing to do…a great way to show your appreciation for your blessings. But now we're nearing the end of this interview, so before I tell our readers where they can contact you, is there anything I missed that you'd like to share today?

And what advice do you have for young people just getting started in acting and/or filmmaking?

Tony Tarantino: I don't think you missed much, Betty. (laughs) And the advice I give to all young people is: "You don't lose until you quit."

Betty Dravis: Well, that may be short, but it's good, solid advice, Tony. It's been a real treat to chat with you. You're inspiring! I certainly learned more about you and the movie business; I'm sure our readers will enjoy you as much as I do. We will be watching for your new movies. (Might I add that you have a charming Italian accent with a hint of French for good measure?)

I like this line from your website: *TonyTarantino.com is your online source for everything Tarantino. Watch his latest trailers, see his production calendar, order merchandise, get the inside Hollywood dish and famous celebrity news articles right here.*

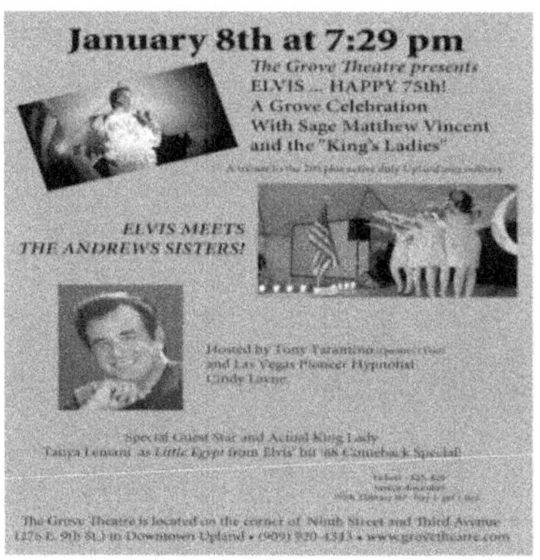

That said, instead of publishing Internet links, as we did on Dames of Dialogue, I'd like to let my readers know that they can find you on Facebook, Tarantino Productions and by simply Googling your name on the Net.

One of the best places to find all your movie credits is the Internet Movie Data Base.

Thanks again, Tony, for this open, honest interview. I find you to be an intelligent, well-spoken man of the world and I'm sure our readers will agree.

Ciao, as you always say, and God bless you and your impressive volume of works. We have thousands of words in this interview and I never even touched on your screenplay *New Horizons* that you wrote with Tom Cruise and Catherine Zeta Jones in mind for the lead roles. Perhaps we can do this again sometime.

Now, as they say in your industry, "That's a wrap" or in mine, "Let's put this baby to bed!" (laughs) Stay in touch…

Tony Tarantino: That's a deal…and thanks, Betty. It's been real fun and I'd love to do it again, perhaps when one of my movies is a wrap. I'm juggling a lot of plates at the moment, but this was an enjoyable interlude. *Ciao*…

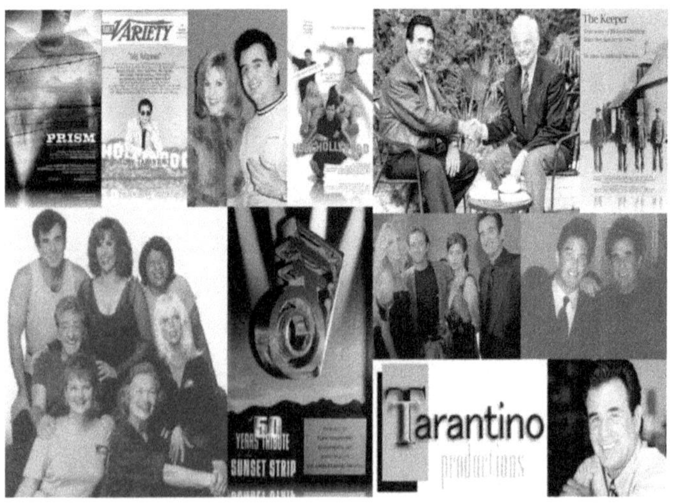

Interview with Antonia Tosini

ACCLAIMED SCREENWRITER, ITALY'S AMBASSADOR OF GOOD WILL

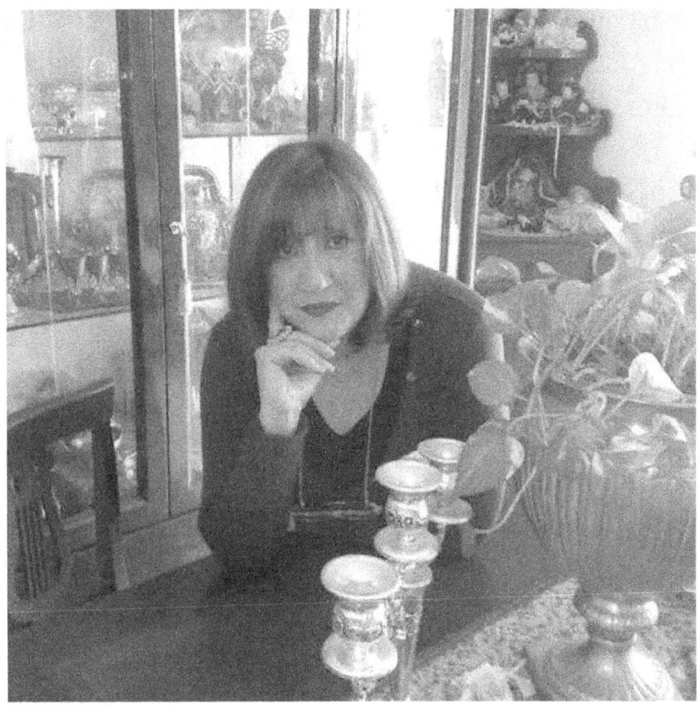

Betty Dravis: Welcome to my world, Antonia Tosini. I'm honored to have such an icon of Italian literature and cinema as my guest today. Not only are you the Ambassador of Peace for your home country of Italy, but I hear that you also write cutting-edge screenplays and have a best-selling book in France…among many other things.

You come highly recommended by many of my friends with connections to Italy: Tony Tarantino, Susan Kennington, Katherin Kovin Pacino and Romina Arena, to name a few. I've had the good fortune to interview all four of those outstanding Dream Reachers recently and am delighted that they're featured in *Dream Reachers: Vol. II* along with you.

Since having our works become movies is every writer's dream, your huge writing success fascinates me. Not only that, you enthrall my readers, too–since many are authors with high hopes of seeing their books and screenplays filmed. Many more of our readers are in the entertainment industry and they're always seeking their next great role. I can think of a dozen or two who would love to be cast in your next movie. (laughs)

We'll talk about your many successes later, but now I'd like to know when you first began writing? Do you remember your very first work? And what was it like growing up in Italy. Since you currently live in Napoli, is that where you were born?

Antonia Tosini: My dear, allow me to thank you for this interview. I started my career not so very young because I wanted to give priority to family and my two children. (laughs)

At any rate, in my film there are already some American actors, and I can tell you that I understand fully also the dream of the writers that is to create a film, but I can assure you that it is not easy. After I write a script, I have to work hard to find a production that wants to accomplish it–and do not always succeed. What I can recommend to people who do this job is to believe in what you write and move on, very, very determined.

I was born in a mountain town in the Abruzzo region (Avezzano, L'Aquila), but I grew up in a town of sea: Pescara (always in the same region). Mine was a very quiet childhood and adolescence. My father was cinematographer, so I breathed an air of film cinema.

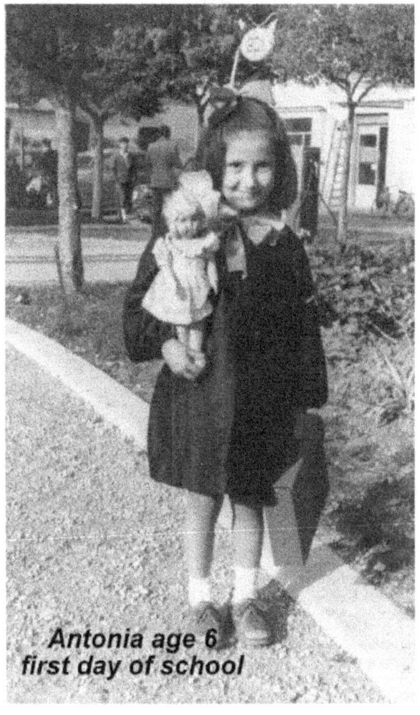
Antonia age 6
first day of school

As a child I started my career by writing diaries, poems and short stories, the legendary "Newspaper of the Small." (laughs) Thanks to my teacher of primary school where I told the wonderful world of emotion that I tried to convey to friends (about the natural world and the universe). Now I am reminded of a memory of my childhood and I want to tell you. Usually, when you have three or four years, children spend their time playing with toys. The way I passed the time was different. I remember that I put on my Latvian parents, surrounded by about fifteen books scattered on the bed. Next to me was my favorite doll. I opened a book and I began to "read". Of course it was all fantasy, because at that age I could not read. My love for cinema and a passion for books are my two souls. With passing time, I grew more and more passionate about the cinema and so I attended a directing course at the Film Academy in Rome. My first job was a documentary dedicated to the Shrine of Our Lady of the Arch, by title: *Life and Miracles of Ex Votive.*

Betty Dravis: Well, Antonia, you are an original now and from your childhood I can see you were always unique. Like you, I wrote poetry as a child and started my real writing career late (age forty to be precise) because I devoted myself to my six children during their formative years. And your answer to my question about "writers desiring movies from their books" is perfect. We all can relate to how hard it is to find a good publisher and/or producer. (laughs) You are also right in that it takes determination…

Your childhood in Italy, growing up in a house where your father "lived and breathed" cinema is different from our experiences, but I think we all relate to your sweet anecdote about reading to your doll. What a precocious child you were! (laughs) Thanks for sharing about your first documentary, also.

That must have been exciting and was a great start for you. I wish they had it on DVD for posterity, but I'm sure they don't.

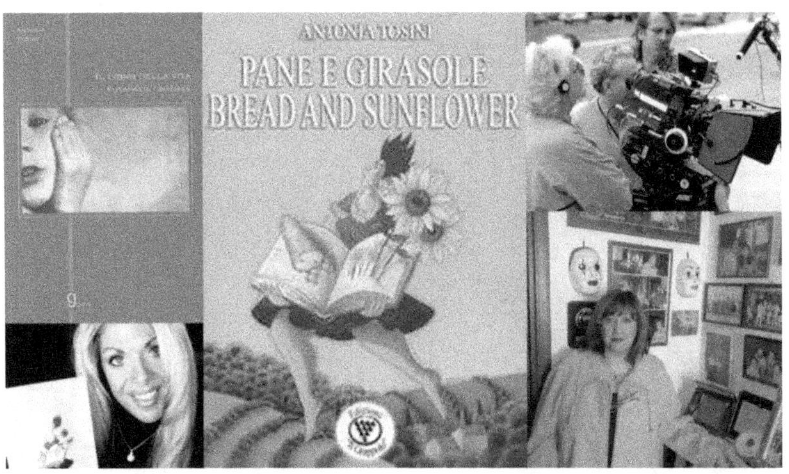

But moving on, what was the title of your first novel? I understand you also have a novel that's a best-seller in France. That's phenomenal and I'm dying to hear about the books you've written. And when did you write your first screenplay? How many screenplays have you written? And please talk about some of the directors and producers you've worked with.

Antonia Tosini: Those are good questions, Betty, and I'll try to answer them all. (laughs) I cannot say that I have written many books; I have written more screenplays. The first book is entitled *The Book of Life/Euthanasia Social* and is a very dramatic story, written in a surreal way, with the tone of a fable, a kind of philosophy that is reminiscent of the Greek theater. The story it tells is of a young couple who suppress their newborn son because he is deformed. The second *Bread* *and Sunflower* is a book of poems on human rights; the third, *The Pink Wound,* is on the rights of women (abuse, rape and violence against women); and *Hourglass* is a collection of short stories (to be published next year).

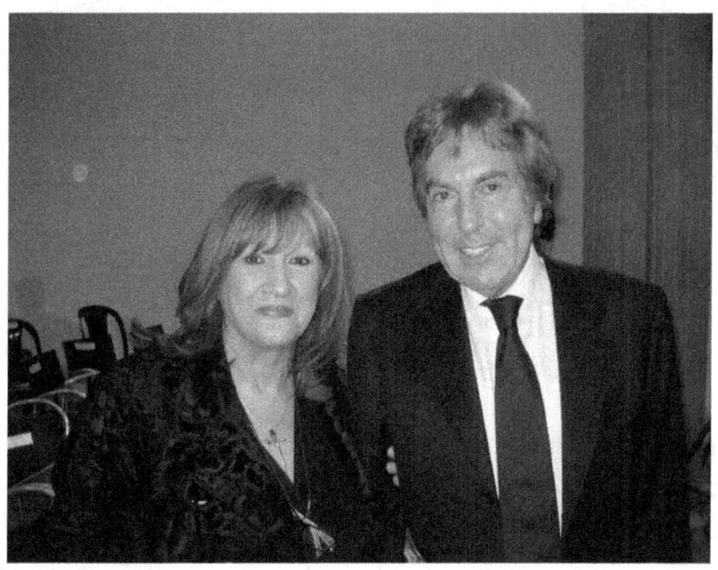

Antonia with Director Fabrizio Del Noce

I started about fifteen years ago (not so young), with the title of "Director in the Drawer" in a not-very-special time in my life. As I said, until then my time had been prioritized by the family and not to my dreams. To recover the lost time, I did an unbelievable race against time. I worked in theater as an assistant and assistant director; I did some small theater directing (I've made a documentary), but nothing blatant. So after a while I shelved the idea of the direction and I am dedicated exclusively to writing.

The shift to cinema was laborious: On this new path, I have worked with various writers and directors more or less known. Among these I will mention one: Algerian Rachid Benhadj, a great director who is famous for the film *Pane Nudo.* He is a director of an almost maniacal precision–one that puts all the passion into his works. He taught me much and is a true master.

If I remember correctly, I wrote my first screenplay in 1978 and I have written about twenty-five screenplays. I wrote scripts for plays and made the dialogue for television drama … I wrote on commission… In the end, I gained a good appreciation and consideration by some colleagues and producers with whom I worked for a while and I gained very wide experience.

Among the producers, I worked with many of Italy's biggest: Ennio Pontis on *Tetraktys* (and am working with him again now). I like to recall the experience of writing in the production of *Cinema International Communications* (CIC) of Giuseppe Colombo ("Beppe" for friends). He is a man very famous in the world of Italian cinema. He has produced international major motion pictures with major international directors. Some of his credits: *The Bee Keeper*, directed by Theo Angelopoulos, screenplay by Tonino Guerra; *The Stendhal Syndrome* that starred Marcello Mastroianni, directed by Dario Argento (with Asia Argento, Thomas Kretschmann, Marco Leopardi, Paolo Bonacelli). Beppe also produced the *Wax Mask,* directed by Sergio Stivaletti, supervised by Dario Argento (with Robert Hossein, Romina Mondello, Valery Valmond, Gabriella

Giorgelli); *The Phantom Of The Opera*, directed by Dario Argento, script by Gerard Brach (with Julian Sands, Asia Argento and many others…) Beppe is a person of great experience, a man of class. To work with him, for me it was a great learning experience. With him I have still a beautiful friendship…

Betty Dravis: Wow, Antonia, you have an incredible background working with the best Italy has to offer. As for your books, we'll talk about *Bread and Sunflower* later, but at the moment, I'm overwhelmed with all of your cinematic accomplishments. I've heard that working with Giuseppe Colombo and Ennio Pontis is the American equivalent of working with Steven Spielberg and George Lucas. *Now that blows my mind!* I would be in seventh heaven if I could work with them!

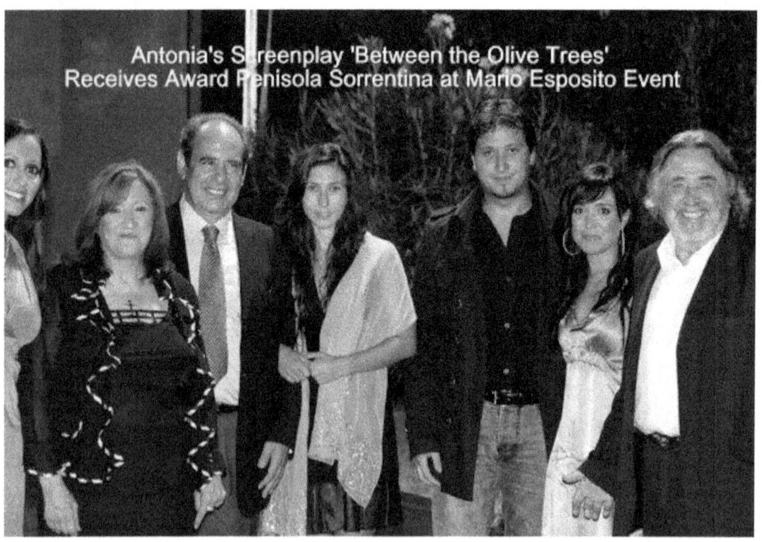

Antonia's Screenplay 'Between the Olive Trees'
Receives Award Penisola Sorrentina at Mario Esposito Event

Everyone has heard of *The Bee Keeper* and *The Phantom of the Opera,* but other than that, my knowledge of Italian cinema is very limited. I apologize for that, but please continue. I hope you don't mind talking about the most recent movie for which you have written the screenplay.

Antonia Tosini: I wish I could share all about this one, my dear Betty, but we're still in negotiations, so I can't talk too much about it or the French producer. But he's a great director/producer and I'm completing a screenplay for him. I can say the story is set in the suburbs of Paris…in an underground where the discomfort is palpable and where there is a constant danger of promiscuity and violence.

Betty Dravis: I'm cool with that, dear Antonia… I understand contract restraints… So let's move on to the next question: Are any of your screenplays in production now? If so, tell us about it. If not, please update us on what you are working on now.

Antonia Tosini: I am currently working on various projects, but my own screenplay *Between the Olive Trees* is more imminent. It's in pre-production and will be directed by David Worth. I state that the director was originally to be Tony Tarantino. He's a skilled professional and I respect and am very fond of him. Our work together links us in a long and sincere friendship.

Unfortunately, there was a scheduling conflict, in the sense that we were unable to reconcile our time with him, but I hope to work with him on another project in the future.

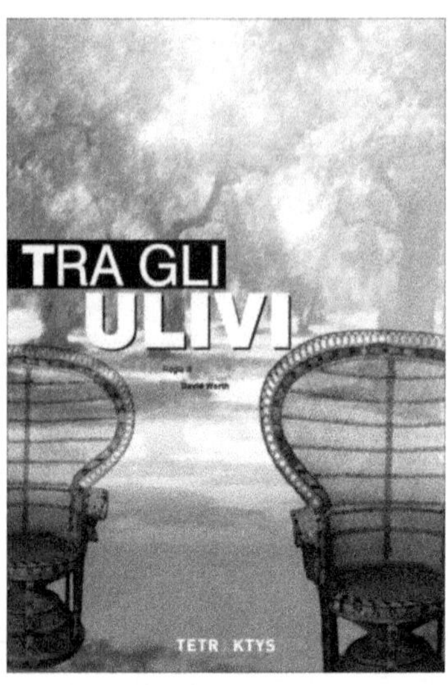

I'm humbled and grateful because in September *Between the Olive Trees,* the project and the script, was awarded the "Award Penisola Sorrentina" at an event organized by the journalist Mario Esposito. The motivation of award is: *For the project Between the Olive Trees, an example of a significant insight of Mediterranean creativity, imagination and intelligence combined with the psychological excavation. The mystery and the plot twist are in the best tradition of the thriller genre.*

Antonia's screenplay & the project "Between the Olive Trees," was awarded the "Award Penisola Sorrentina" at an event organized by the journalist Mario Esposito.

Now back to the production: After the split with Tarantino Productions, Ennio Pontis, the producer, contacted David Worth, who knew of the fame and brought the script. After he had read it, Worth wrote a very nice message, adding that he found the story very compelling and, of course, was happy to do the directing. Worth is a man of great culture, is a director and cinematographer with a great experience. He has worked with big names in international cinema, such as Clint Eastwood, and directed films such as *The Game's Prophet* with the great actor Dennis Hopper and the series of *Shark Attack,* just to name a few. Between us has now established a good relationship of respect. We write often and we exchange views on international cinema.

While with Robert Reed Altman on *Psicopompo,* a paranormal genre film, I have to say that he, after reading the script, wrote a message that was very rewarding to me. I think he's a great professional, a person with a great delicacy in relationships, in that he has a lot of respect and consideration for people. Robert ("Bobby" to his friends) is an extraordinary person who has much respect for the name he bears. I state that I have always been a big fan of his father, Robert (Bernard) Altman, who was defined by many–the "adorable hateful" of America–as a "renegade," but who was later recognized as one of the greats.

MASH (the film), *Gosford Park* and *A Prairie Home Companion* are three of his better-known works. Working with his son, for me, is almost like working with him. Bobby is exceptional in his work, is loved and respected by all. He has worked on more than sixty successful films, as director of photography. I am convinced that in addition to the physical resemblance to his father, he has inherited the same energy and brilliant directorial skills, typical of the best Masters.

The other project deals with a social issue relevant today and problems with racial issues. It's set in Italy, tentatively titled *The Face Of The Moon* and with the *Bravo* director/producer Ziad H. Hamzeh, an artist of Los Angeles, who has won over forty awards for directing, producing and writing, including the coveted Kennedy Center Achievement Award.

Betty Dravis: Ohmigosh, Antonia, you are beginning to sound like Superwoman! How do you manage to do all that and remain so gracious and always look so elegant? That's a mind-boggling list of screen credits and you are working with the "big boys," as we say in America: David Worth, Ennio Pontis, Robert Reed Altman…and your own "Beppe."… (laughs) Those are names even I have heard of…and I am by no means a "film buff." As for the Altmans, Robert Reed Altman last worked with his father on *A Prairie Home Companion.* Our American readers will relate more to the TV shows your "Bobby" has recently worked on: *Boston Legal, The O.C. and Lost in Hawaii.*

Antonia, I'm sorry it didn't work out with Tony Tarantino because I would love to have seen him direct your film *Between the Olive Trees.* Nevertheless, I'm pleased you'll be working with Worth because I have a personal liking for the *Shark Attack* movies. My dear friend, the beautiful actress Jenny McShane, played the female lead in *SA1* and *SA3*. She was interviewed for our first *Dream Reachers* book by my co-author Chase Von and we three became good friends after that. Unfortunately, she had to turn *SA2* down because she was working in *The Watcher* with Keanu Reeves at the time. In fact, I enjoyed her life story so much I decided to interview her (from a woman's viewpoint) for this second *DR* book, making her the first person to be featured in both books.

I, personally, am intrigued by the title and plot of your film *Between the Olive Trees* and can't wait to see it on the big screen. Which brings to mind, what do you enjoy more…screenwriting or writing novels?

Antonia Tosini: *Mi* dear Betty, I look forward to reading about Jenny and all the beautiful people in this book and am honored to be a part of it.

I like to write about everything and I love to find the key language in every theme and every kind of writing, but I do not deny my love for the script because this allows me to experience the emotions of my characters more than any writing.

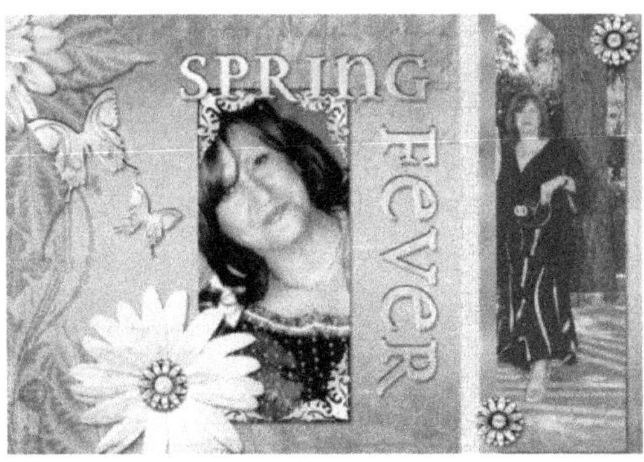

Betty Dravis: I sort of anticipated that response, Antonia. Filmmaking is a fascinating business and working with the actors and actresses would be a thrill for me. You know, you are a lot like the man you admire so much, the late, great Robert Altman. This quote by him reminds me of something you would say: *"Filmmaking is a chance to live many lifetimes."*

When I Googled your name for research purposes, I got 77,500 results and that was only their 24-second finding. If I had done an advanced search, no telling how many would have come up. That's a lot of info about one little lady, my dear. (laughs) I can see why, though, since you do so very much. I see photos on the Internet of you with a lot of influential people, including your current producer Ennio Pontis, our own Tony Tarantino and a man named Bruno Garofalo. The first two are pretty much "household names," but since I'm not familiar with Italian cinema, who is Garofalo?

And at what event were those photos taken?

Antonia Tosini: My dear Betty, the pictures of which you speak were taken during the visits for location of the film *Between The Olive Trees.* Bruno Garofalo is the art director, which is his role in many films, including *Scusate il Ritardo* and *Scugnizzi* by director Nanni Loy. He is also a famous director of theater…very, very good.

Betty Dravis: Thanks for telling us about Garofalo, Antonia. Now tell us something about your husband Tony Sorrentino. I understand that he's an accomplished star in his own right; *huge* among Italian musicians. Exactly what does Tony do?

And since I'm such a romantic, I would love to hear how you met him and to learn something about your children.

Antonia Tosini: Well. Tony is a good musician, graduated from the Conservatory of Music. He's a pianist, composer and conductor. He has participated in various transmissions and shows

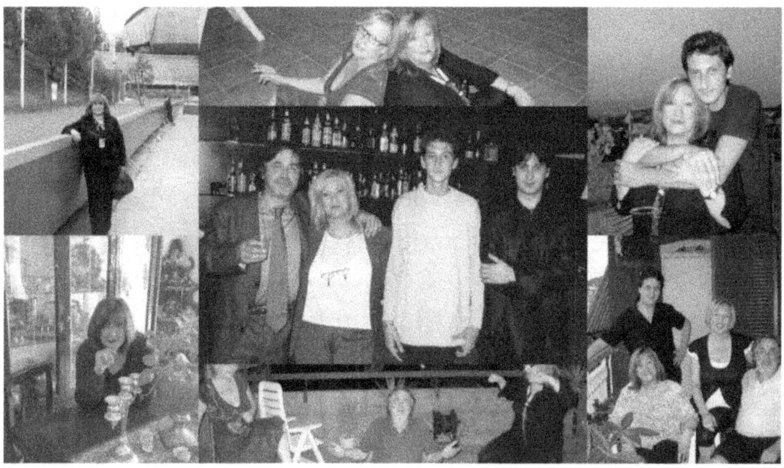

for Italian television RAI and radio. He has worked with the great orchestras, including also with the great master Roberto De Simone, with whom he toured the world with his works, and with two myths of Italian songs: Sergio Bruni and Claudio Villa, famous in all world…and other singers. In the '80s Tony began his parallel career as a theatrical composer, alternating with being a conductor. For ten years he wrote numerous music for plays and important musicals for the Sannazaro Theatre in Naples for actress Luisa Conte. Among his most popular musicals are: *Women in Parliament* and *Lysistrata* by

Aristophanes, just to name a few. And for twenty-five years he composed for the *compagnie* by great actor Giacomo Rizzo, but also for theatrical companies Nazional.

Tony is a very famous composer and conductor.

I met Tony thirty-seven years ago in Pescara in Abruzzo. We were very young… At the time, I studied singing and one day he came to replace my teacher who was due to travel to Milan for other commitments. We fell in love and married eight months later. From our union were born two sons, Massimo and Daniele, who followed their father's footsteps. In fact, both are musicians. In addition to doing concerts, they also compose music for theater, documentaries and film.

Their latest work is a short film entitled *House Hunting* by the American, Angela Kennedy, and now they are in talks with a Los Angeles director for another soundtrack. I'm also pleased and humbled that our sons, Massimo and Daniele, have been selected to compose the music for *Between the Olive Trees.*

Betty Dravis: That's incredible, Antonia, that your entire family is so gifted, but to know you can sing along to their beat…well, that's a "toe-tapping" thought… (laughs) Musicians are special people and we all need music in our lives. I know you're proud of your husband and sons. I bet Tony has influenced and enhanced your career and is one of your prime supporters. Since you've met and worked with so many important people, who are your other mentors and how have they affected your life?

Antonia Tosini: Surely, my husband is my great supporter, but as I already told you, since childhood– thanks to the occupation of my father–I love the film. I can tell you my point of reference: Although I never worked with him, my mentor was the late, great Robert (Bernard) Altman, a creative genius, an unconventional man, critical… Most people failed to agree with him and few supported his thoughts, but he defended to the last, winning against all the odds. I *think* like him and fully endorse his work. I consider myself a very creative person and I believe in what I write, and I do not ever adapt to castrating market logic. That's another reason I was so grateful to work with his son, Bobby Altman.

Betty Dravis: What you are saying is that you admire your mentor, Robert Altman, for his independence and not "caving in" to public opinion that would change what he created… He had his own vision and stayed true to it, despite those who called him a "renegade." You know, I suppose that's one of the many reasons I always admired my mentor, Clint Eastwood, who is quoted as saying, *"I have to keep challenging myself and try something I haven't done before. The studios aren't always happy with that... But playing it safe is what's risky because nothing new comes out of it."*

Antonia Tosini: *Mi scuso,* Betty, but I wish to state that I have admired and loved Robert Altman for everything he was and stood for. He never bartered his art and his thinking. *He WAS the Art!* And no one ever has surpassed him (this is my point of view, of course). He left to young people a great deal of material to study and learn. Blessed are those who knew him and worked with him. They surely have learned many great lessons of life and cinema. The only thing you cannot learn is the genius. The genius is not taught; it is a gift that is not given to all…but Robert Altman had it. A characteristic of Altman's was to never take anything for granted and to seek new opportunities to direct.

In my opinion, the directors of today tend more to the technical special effects, which certainly are very important for film, but only if combined with the heart, the history and inventiveness. First of all, it would be necessary to form a good basis for critical-theoretical approach to film with philological method–view and review films. The legendary French director Claude *Chabrol* said that the technique is learned in four hours.

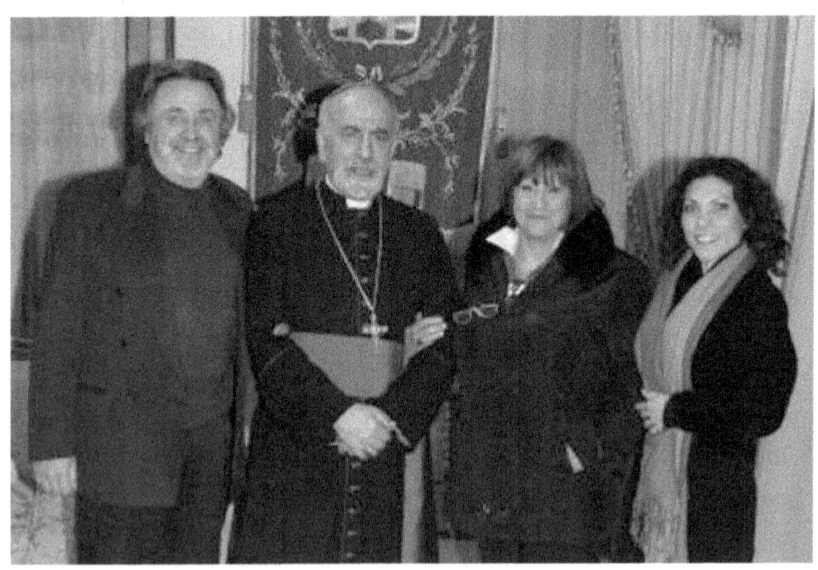

Antonia and Tony with Archibishop and Mayor of WP

Betty Dravis: I think you are a lot like your mentor and certainly learned much from him. In my opinion, you are a genius among filmmakers too. You, Antonia, are not only an extremely talented writer who understands human nature, but you are also an intelligent, outspoken, independent woman. That's as it should be when your original creations are on the line; no one knows better than you what you mean by your writing and nobody understands your characters as well. Truthfully, I love and respect that part of your nature, and Altman would be proud of you following his example.

Along those lines, I have another question: If you could spend an entire day with one person from any period in history, who would you choose and why?

Antonia Tosini: Without a doubt, I would choose Cleopatra. She was a great woman–smart, intelligent, spoke several languages, was a writer, and a skillful strategist. She was the last Queen of Egypt; after her, nothing, total vacuum… Her history fascinates me.

Betty Dravis: *Great choice, Antonia!* I was hoping you'd choose a strong woman like yourself, and you didn't let me down. (laughs)

At this point in the interview, I was going to ask the question about one thing you would do to change the world, but since I learned that you are Italy's Goodwill Ambassador, I already know the answer to that: *You would seek peace at all costs.* Right? (laughs)

This brings to mind a quote I once read by the late Mother Teresa: "I was once asked why I don't participate in anti-war demonstrations. I said that I will never do that, but as soon as you have a pro-peace rally, I'll be there." Those are words of wisdom that I can imagine you saying.

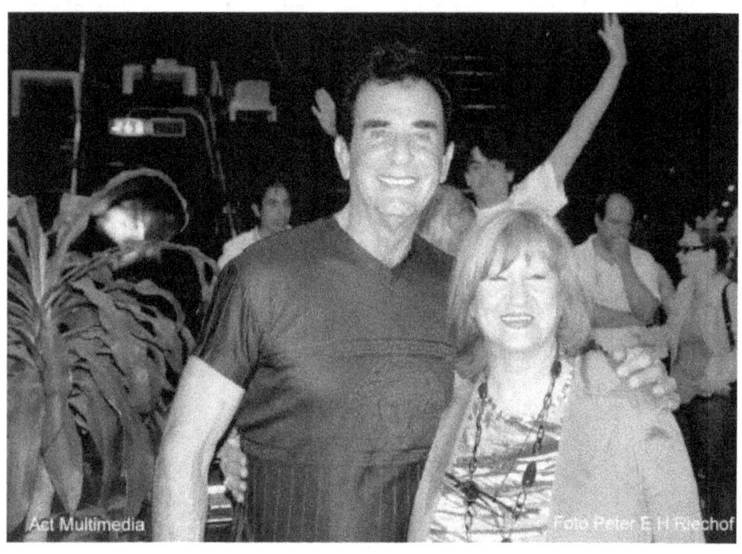

Antonia with American Actor/Director Tony Tarantino

But moving on, Antonia, I'd like to say that as much as I admire your phenomenal writing accomplishments, I'm super-impressed with your status in Bryant McGill's growing movement.

Bryant, as you know, is the founder of The Goodwill Treaty for World Peace and a great humanitarian that I had the pleasure of interviewing for this book. Is he the one who chose you to represent Italy…or was it done by a committee?

Antonia Tosini: My sweet friend, I think the right way to go if we want to change the world is to learn how to unify the *heart,* reason and faith. We should all start making small changes and have the force of the weight of our ideas and great responsibility to carry them out. It is not an easy thing, but humanity must learn to love and to respect what God has given us.

In this regard I would like to dedicate to your readers, this poem from my book *Bread and Sunflower.*

PRAYER

Oh God I pray you!
let our world be everyone's homeland
let nobody ever use your name
to make war…on our earth
metallic glares explode like drums
and incessantly turn around agonizing
peoples subject to the world and to the sound
of the absurd…souls overflowing with smoke, hunger
and solitude, the livid oligarchy dribbles magma
plunderer, which dominates and accumulates lands
and capitals in a scenery of living dead
lying on a cradle adorned with crosses hammered
by the yelling thirsty power…let there be
no longer hate for the colors codified in the
chromatic scale of your skin, let the world belong
to everyone and nobody outrage his brother anymore
let there be no more homelands to save and
let the world be living without conflicts.
That's the only way, oh God, we could be people living in
peace!

As for Bryant McGill, he is very beautiful person. I remember that he had a call from Chase Lesley Barton, Goodwill Ambassador, to propose me to become an ambassador of peace in Italy. I felt very honored by this endowment which made me change my way of acting. At first, my words on peace were few, but from that moment on I tried to do something for those people who not have vision and speech. As I always say, I'm not a rich person (*matrialmente,* talking about), so I had to invent something concrete to give to help the persons who are weak. So I started writing books for solidarity.

My dear friend, in knowing about *Bread and Sunflower,* you seem to be informed about everything. (laughs) I admire the research you did to conduct this interview. But I want to add that my book *Bread and Sunflower* has gained the appreciation of the Italian President Giorgio Napolitano and the French President Carla Bruni Sarkozy and that honors me greatly.

Betty Dravis: Congratulations, Antonia, to be recognized by the President of one's own country and of France, too, is the very highest honor, indeed. I'm proud to call you my friend.

I want to devote some time to your book *Bread and Sunflower*, so we will discuss that more below, if you don't mind. But first I'd like to talk a bit about the Peace Treaty. Since it is McGill's goal to have almost everyone in the world sign the Peace Treaty, one of your duties as Goodwill Ambassador is getting signatures for the Peace Treaty. Is that right?

What are some of your other duties?

Antonia Tosini: That's right, Betty, and if you and any of your readers would like to sign it, here's the link: http://www.goodwilltreaty.org/. Other things I'm doing are spreading the word and getting contributions for the cause. Contributions that will help people in need...

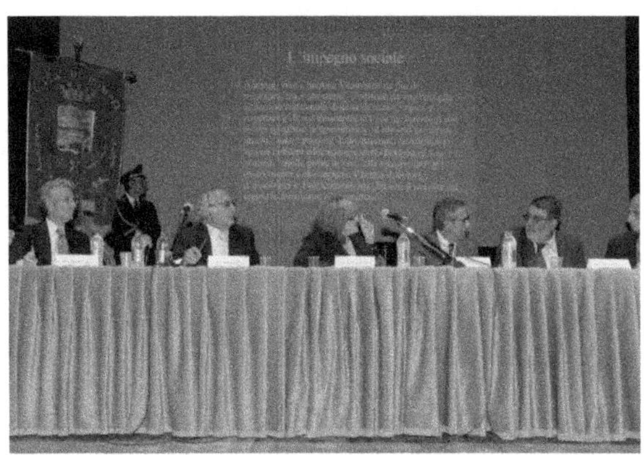

Antonia Addresses Peace & Human Rights Conference

Betty Dravis: I notice that in addition to your "Antonia Tosini" Facebook page, you also have a second page under "Antonia Tosini – Author & Screenwriter." I understand that page is something you're doing for World Peace. What's that all about, Antonia?

Antonia Tosini: My dear Betty, this page is devoted to my book *Bread and Sunflower*. I hope to sell more books through this page because I'm donating all the proceeds to African children. Proceeds will be donated to the Onlus "Tram African" to help build a hospital in Kenya. For more information, please email: info@trameeafricane.org.

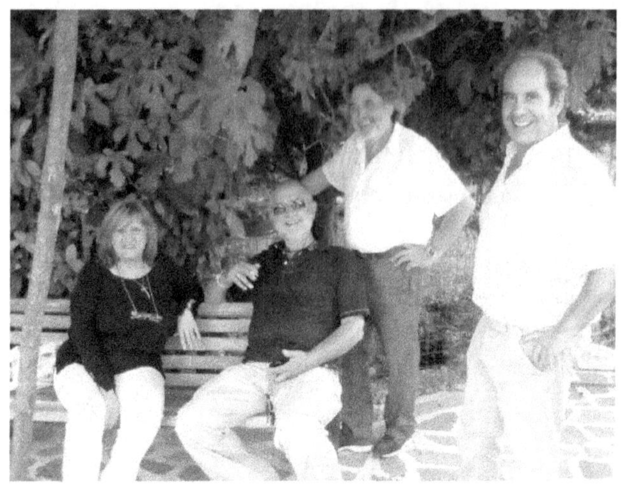

Antonia taking a break during a work session with Bruno Garofalo, her husband Tony Sorrentino and producer Ennio Pontis

Betty Dravis: Wow, Antonia, you really are amazing! That's generous and so caring of you. I can see why you are so dear to the hearts of your countrymen and all who know you.

Since you're a humble person, I hope you don't mind my talking more about your special book. I was pleased to learn that Bryant McGill was chosen to write the preface and be a contributing author for *Bread and Sunflower,* which is a book of bilingual poems and meditations on peace and human rights.

It's also beneficial to know that it's written in Italian and English and features cover art by the Florentine painter Maurizio Vinante and notes by film director Rachid Benhadj. It must make you and your family proud (in a good way) that your book has received official sponsorship from the United Nations Educational, Scientific and Cultural Organization (UNESCO) and support and sponsorship from European Parliament, Parliament of the Council of Ministers and Social RIA Television.

Here is a portion of what the great Bryant McGill had to say about you: *"Antonia Tosini's masterful tribute to human rights and peace, Bread and Sunflower, is a collection of ideals worthy of every reader's time and meditation. Ambassador Tosini's commitment to peace and human rights is commendable. Her visionary work in this book and her humanitarian efforts around the world are a gift to us all."*

That boggles my mind! I'd be dancing a tango with Al Pacino if any of my books reached that stature. (laughs) But seriously, Antonia, you're a remarkable woman. I'm proud to count you among my friends. Congratulations again…

Antonia Tosini: Thanks, Betty, I'm a lucky woman to be doing what I love for a living. And I would enjoy to see you tango with that great actor Al Pacino. (laughs)

Betty Dravis: Hahaha, Antonia, I guarantee it wouldn't be a very graceful sight, so I don't know if Al would be too pleased with me. (laughs)

But now, before leaving you, I'd like to mention some of your other interests which are rather self-explanatory: Friends of the Dalai Lama, The United States of America, *Il Libro della Vita*

(Eutanasia Sociale), "Butterfly Kisses" Parent Bereavement Group (Loss of a Child), Super 8 International Filmmakers Association, Wild Hanlon Cartoon, etc. And you enjoy horror books, which is something else we have in common. I enjoy reading them as well as writing them. I have one coming up in the future and hope you do, also…or at least a gory screenplay. (laughs)

I regret that we must part, my dear Antonia, but it's time to thank you for spending so much time with us. After chatting with you, I predict a long, prosperous future for you in writing and the cinema. I'm looking forward to reading your latest book of short stories, *Hourglass,* and to seeing your works on the big screen in the USA. And may God bless your humanitarian work too.

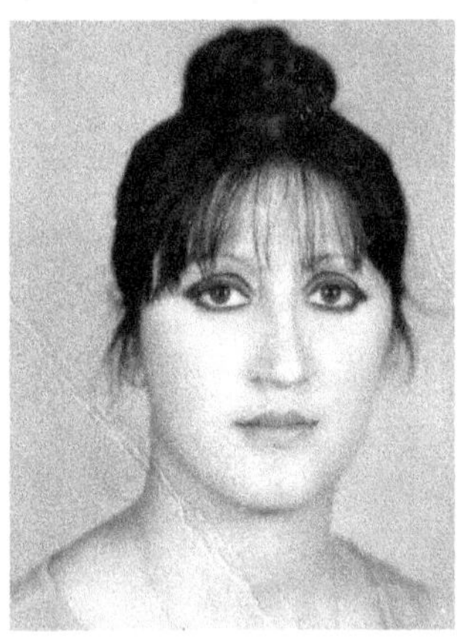

Antonia Tosini

I know it's your dream to win an Oscar one day, and I think you will. Your cinematic works are *magnifico.* I'd like to remind people to Google your name to find all about you on the Internet.

As you know, I don't speak or read Italian, but through your magic, this interview was made possible. I hope you keep in touch to update us from time to time about your career and your personal life. Please let us know when your book *Hourglass* is released and when your movie *Between the Olive Trees* premieres… And now, to use words that you and Tony taught me, I'll bid you a fond farewell: *Ciao, bella donna... Molto bello...*

Antonia Tosini: Thank you, very sweet and professional lady. It's my pleasure to be with you, your readers and the Dames of Dialogue. Cheers, as you say in America. See you soon and BIG hugs.

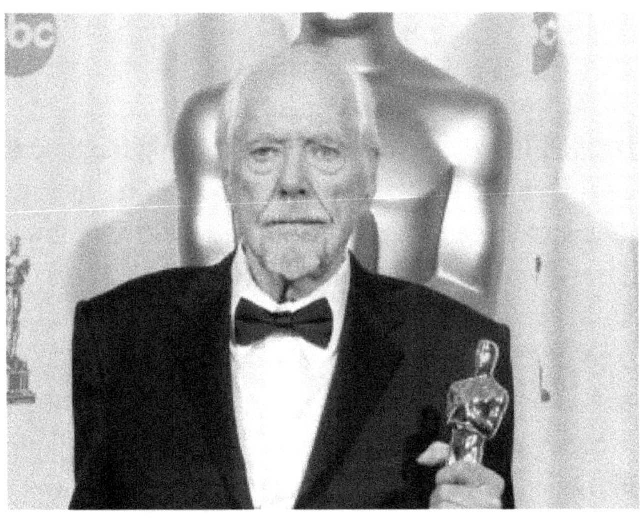

Antonia's Mentor the late, great Director Robert Altman

Interview with Frank Nappi

NAPPI IS EVERY AUTHOR'S DREAM

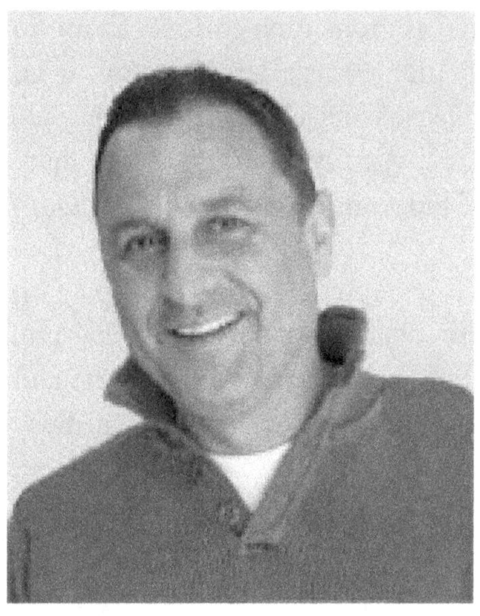

Betty Dravis: I'm delighted that you're taking the time for this interview, Frank, especially now that you're in such hot demand as an author. We formed an Internet friendship after I read and reviewed your first novel, *Echoes from the Infantry* (St. Martin's Press). That heart-warming book was released in October of 2005 and I discovered it in January of 2006. I was so impressed by your plot and writing skills that I named it my favorite debut novel of that year. You might recall that my Amazon review title read: *Nappi Is a Rising Star in the Literary World.* Sometimes I scare myself… (laughs)

Well, it's always exhilarating to catch a rising star and I'm proud to say that you proved me right. Your star burns brightly! *Echoes* received national attention, not becoming the movie I had hoped for, but it won the Silver Medal for Outstanding Fiction for the year 2006 from the Military Writers Society of America. And it paved the way for what happened next! Since then you have written two more books and both are being produced on film.

Wow–and even though I felt this would happen when I read your debut novel, I'm still stunned!

But even as I extend my hearty congratulations, Frank, I must confess to a modicum of envy… Every author I know would love to be in your shoes! As we have discussed many times during our four-year friendship, it's my dream for one of my books to become a movie… preferably all of them. (laughs)

Please share with us what inspired you to write *Echoes* and your best-selling second book that followed a few years later, *The Legend of Mickey Tussler,* (also with St. Martin's). I'm sure our readers would like to know when and where they can see the movie of *Legend.*

Since I want to go into detail about the awesome deal with your third novel, let's keep that information for later…as a surprise for our readers. Okay?

Frank Nappi: First of all, thank you, Betty, for the opportunity to share my story with you. As you know, there is no greater honor for an author than to be acknowledged by another successful author.

As far as the inspiration for *Echoes* is concerned, I had the good fortune of meeting two very special WWII veterans–to whom the book is dedicated–during a Veteran's Day speaker assembly I arranged for my interdisciplinary classes more than ten years ago. My students were captivated. I was too. The stories they told me haunted me in a way I could never really describe. I became very close with both of them. I got a glimpse into what it was like to walk around, post war, with a whole other life in your head; how difficult it is to manage both. God, if that is not fascinating, I don't know what is… I began writing short stories, ultimately weaving them together with some creativity. Prior to that, I had always entertained the thought of writing a novel, but I lacked that "Muse," as the expression goes—the right inspiration. Eddie Hynes and Bill McGinn took care of that.

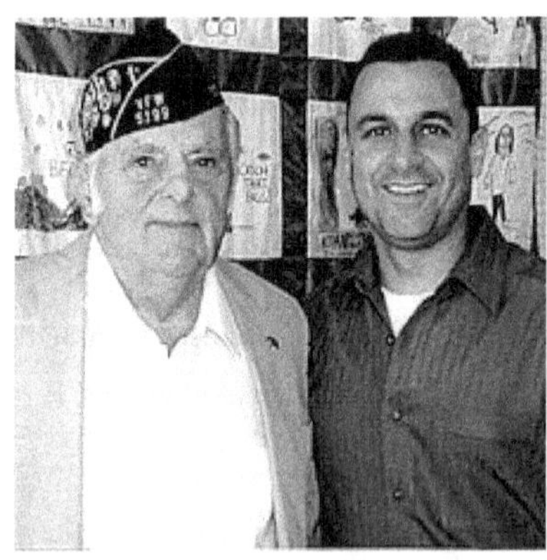

Frank with his friend Eddie Hynes, WWII veteran

Betty Dravis: Frank, your respect for veterans and their families is evident and that's what enraptured me as I read *Echoes*. It's the first book I read wherein an author depicted how war affects not only the serviceman but his entire family. In that heart-warming, yet bittersweet novel, you showed that trying to recapture what they left behind is almost impossible.

Since you are a high school instructor on Long Island and met and interviewed many veterans in the course of writing *Echoes,* it was natural that the setting for the book be your home turf. Please share with us the setting for *The Legend of Mickey Tussler* and why you chose that location.

Frank Nappi: Well, I needed an era and a geographic location where Mickey's story could be plausible. Milwaukee, post World War II, was the perfect time and place for such an improbable tale. The city is small and intimate, dotted here and there with local shops and breweries. The people are also simpler– and I do not mean that in any pejorative way at all.

What I believe is that these "Milwaukeeans" love and appreciate what they have, and that includes their beloved Brewers. They are God folks. I don't know that Mickey Tussler would have had a shot in the concrete jungles of New York City.

Betty Dravis: Milwaukee—perfect! As I read *Legend,* I recall thinking you had made a wise choice: that's baseball country… And with what you say about the people there, your choice was perfect. I know *Legend* is a best-seller all over, but I bet it has a huge fan base in the baseball and the autism communities since the main character, Mickey Tussler, is autistic.

In order for our readers to relate to *Legend* and our interview, this seems like a good place to share the synopsis:

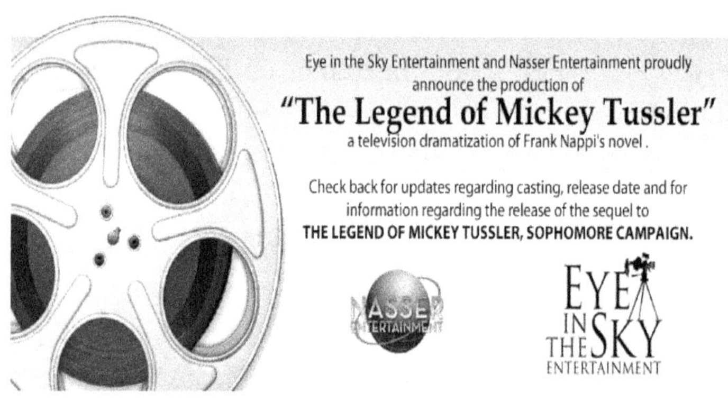

Seventeen-year-old Mickey Tussler is recruited to play for a minor league affiliate of the Boston Braves. Arthur Murphy swears Mickey has the greatest arm he has ever seen, that anybody has ever seen. And it might be true. But Mickey's autism is prohibitive. It keeps him sealed off from a world he scarcely understands. Lost both in the memory of his former life with an abusive father and the challenges of a new world filled with heckling teammates, opponents and fans, there's no way Mickey can succeed. But his inimitable talent–one of the most gifted arms in the history of baseball–gives him a chance. Can he survive a real-life dream? Or are the harsh realities of life too much for him? This is the powerful underdog story of how a young man with an extraordinary gift comes of age in a harsh and competitive world.

I lifted the book description from your Amazon page and am curious: Did you write the synopsis, Frank, or did Amazon? I know with my own books, I have to supply the synopsis to Amazon, so I think I already know the answer to that one. (laughs) I'm also curious about where the bulk of your reviews and fan letters (email) comes from. Do you receive more input from baseball fans or people who champion the cause of autism? Since both are popular with mainstream America, this book has widespread appeal. Do you think that's the secret behind its great success and why filmmakers chose to preserve it on film?

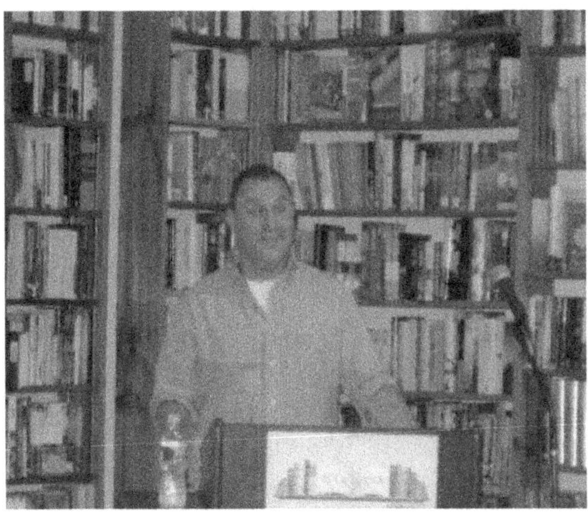

Frank talks "books" at Barnes & Noble

Frank Nappi: The description was written by one of the editors at St. Martin's Press. I believe it captures the essence of the story. Actually, so many of the emails I receive also focus on the unusual dichotomy presented in the book. I was most pleased that the baseball community, including Alex Rodriguez of the NY Yankees, Hall of Fame pitcher Fergie Jenkins and *New York Daily News* award-winning sports journalist Bill Madden embraced the book the way they did. The baseball scenes have been celebrated by many as some of the best ever written. I don't know about that, but it sure is nice to hear.

The other segment of the population that has really become enamored with the tale of Mickey Tussler includes the many groups that advocate for special needs children. I believe they were touched by the concept of a "special" young person who possesses an extraordinary talent, rather than the "woe is me tale" that has regrettably come to define these extraordinary individuals. Many parents have written about how inspirational Mickey is to them and how they hope he becomes the face for special needs kids everywhere. I imagine the hope is that exposure leads to understanding and ultimately tolerance. I am pleased to be able to contribute to this movement in some small way.

Betty Dravis: It's encouraging to hear you say that, Frank, because I know the desire to help others is a big part of who you are. I also hope that exposure leads to understanding and more tolerance of those less fortunate, also.

Now before going on to the phenomenal news about your third book, Frank, I'd like to share the review that *Publishers Weekly* wrote about *The Legend of Mickey Tussler.* I forgot to mention that there is a bit of romance in the book, too, making it well-rounded and even more realistic, but this review touches on that:

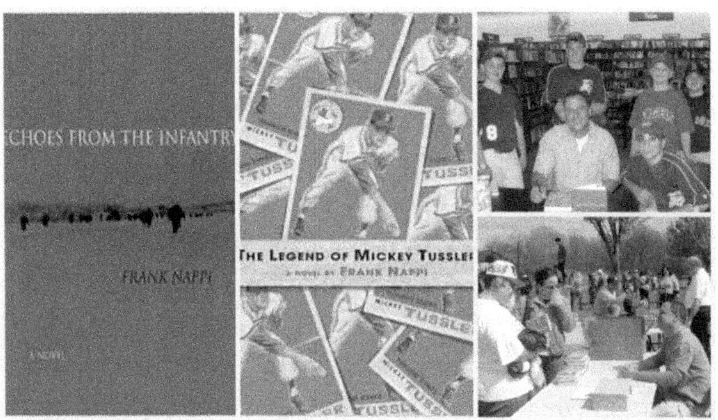

"Nappi (Echoes from the Infantry) has produced a knowledgeable yet unsentimental book starring an autistic teenager with a fearsome fastball. Milwaukee Brewers' manager Arthur Murphy recruits 17-year-old farm boy Mickey Tussler as a pitcher for his team. And though Mickey's slowness enrages his impossibly cruel father (who abuses his wife and derides Mickey as a "retard"), the boy's dad is happy to collect his son's pro baseball salary. In short order, Mickey achieves local stardom despite his mental disability and his teammates' clubhouse pranks. Lefty Rogers, the Brewers' southpaw ace, resents Mickey's triumphs on the mound and plots to sabotage his rival's budding career. At the same time, Murphy romances Mickey's much-abused mother and leads his resurging team in a hot pennant race. The writing is clear and direct, and there's no confusing who's a good guy and who's a

bad guy. The baseball elements really sing; baseball fans will find much to appreciate, while the sports treatment of triumphing over adversity adds crossover appeal to the YA market." – Publishers Weekly

Is that a fair summation of your *Legend,* Frank, and how did you feel when you read it…since *Publishers Weekly* is among the most sought-after reviewers? In your answer, also touch on why you chose to write this as a YA (young adult) book and how it, indeed, crossed over to appeal to readers of all ages.

Frank Nappi: I guess I see the story as multi-faceted, with the characters of Mickey Tussler and Arthur Murphy driving most of the action. Clearly, this story is as much about the frustrated baseball-lifer Murph as it is about his amazing discovery, the fire-balling phenom Mickey Tussler. The chance meeting between the two proves most fortuitous for both, as each of their lives changes dramatically because of the other. Each also undergoes some sort of self actualization, although Mickey's is limited due to his condition.

I am also pleased with the way the character of Molly, Mickey's mother, rounded out the story.

Her story is one that I believe many readers, especially women, will find poignant and thought provoking. I love her as a character. She is warm, genuine, and remarkably resilient in the face of much adversity.

It is easy to see why Mickey loves her so much and how Murph cannot help but begin to fall for her.

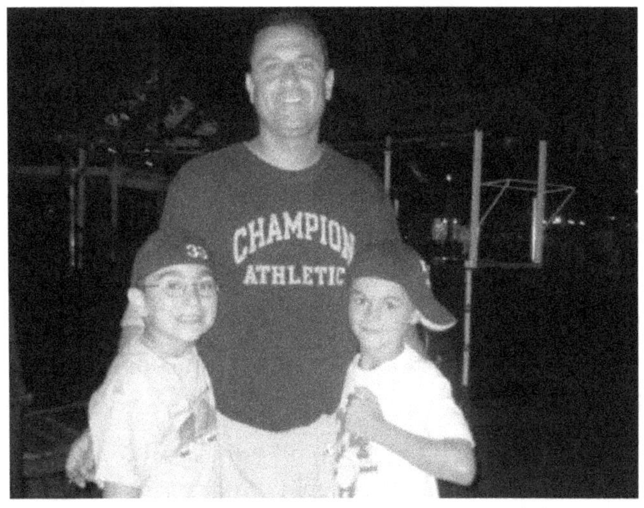

Frank's own baseball players, sons Nicholas & Anthony, at Hershey Park

The YA angle was really a natural outgrowth of having a story with a teenage protagonist. I feel as though young readers can relate to what Mickey is feeling at various points in the story, even though many of his emotions and reactions are colored by his Aspergers. The fact that the action includes concepts like hatred, bigotry, intolerance, sacrifice, love, and of course baseball makes the book a good read for everyone.

Betty Dravis: Absolutely, Frank, and the way you wrote about the characters brought them to life…another plus of a good book. Since you are a high school instructor, it doesn't surprise me that your books are first rate. When did you realize you wanted to be an author? Please share a little about that and about the college you attended. Were you born on Long Island and have you always lived there?

Frank Nappi: Well Betty, I have always written. Even as a teenager myself, I would spend time playing around with short stories and essays. Some were good, some awful. And like many other writers, I had no luck publishing any of them, except for a couple of pieces that appeared in *New York Newsday*'s "500 Words Or Less" column. That was sort of pivotal for me, I suppose, because I loved the way my name looked in print. But then I sort of floundered a bit, you know, looking for the perfect outlet that would satisfy this certain something inside of me – this creative drive, something untapped that was gnawing at me. In retrospect, what was missing was the trigger or impetus. And, as I said earlier, that was provided by my two special friends, Eddie and Bill.

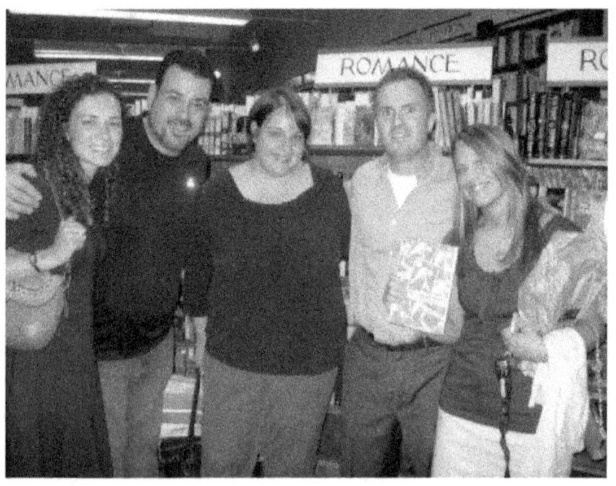

I attended Hofstra University, right here on Long Island. I have lived here my entire life and did plan on expanding my horizons, albeit an hour away, in New Rochelle at Iona College, but a baseball injury derailed what I had hoped would be a stellar career there. I transferred to Hofstra as a business major. What a horror! Do people really talk and behave that way? I quickly changed my concentration of study to English, particularly American Literature, and fell madly in love with the likes of Faulkner, Fitzgerald and Hemingway.

Betty Dravis: All *male* authors, Frank… (laughs) But I agree, they are fine examples of stellar writing. For your next question, who has been your biggest inspiration in life and who are your favorite authors? Your favorite book? I notice that in your own reviews you often quote from wise sources. What is your favorite all-time quote that applies to your own life?

Frank Nappi: Biggest inspiration? That's a rough one. This is going to sound like a cop out, but I don't feel that one person, at least in my case, is responsible for who I am. I believe that all of us are a composite of several influential people we meet along our journey. Naturally, my parents played a major role, providing me with love and nurturing, and of course now my wife Julia and two sons, Nicholas and Anthony, are very instrumental in the things I do. I had fabulous teachers as well, both in high school and in college, and my friendships with people like Eddie, Bill and even you, Betty, also contributed to who I am. The exciting thing is that there are people I have yet to meet, individuals who will also continue to shape who I am.

I have certainly read many insightful quotes from brilliant minds. If I had to choose, however, I would have to say Shakespeare's line "There is nothing good or bad, but thinking makes it so" is the one that resonates most. At some point, we all face heartache and disappointment, and it's essential for our well-being to be able to place these moments in perspective–to find the good in what appears to be misfortune. I'm not a huge fan of Shakespeare, like some are, but I do like *Hamlet* and some of the philosophical exchanges in the play. I guess I am more of an F.Scott Fitzgerald disciple. He was a true master of the language, and wrote the way the birds sing. His work is effortless and beautiful. *The Great Gatsby* has to be the finest work of American Literature. There is so much there. I read it every year with my classes, and always find something else to admire.

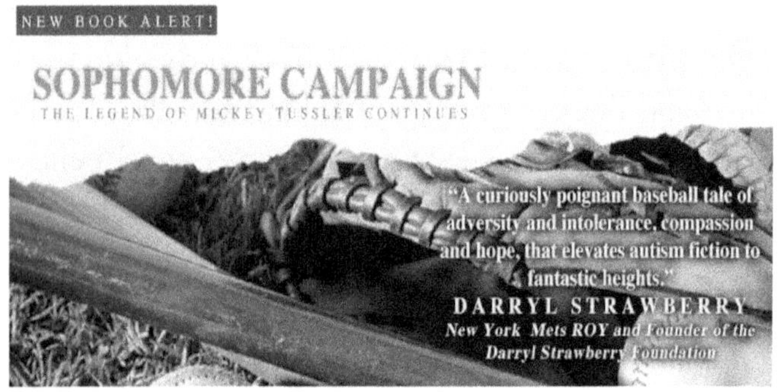

Betty Dravis: I agree with your philosophy that we draw bits and pieces from everyone we meet along life's path and I'm looking forward to absorbing new people, places and ideas into the fabric of my life, as you are. Awesome answer, Frank…

I am in awe of the powerful message in that short line of Shakespeare's quote. I'm flattered that you used that line in a review of my book *1106 Grand Boulevard.* I always favored your review because you seemed to understand my main character so well, but now I treasure it.

And thanks for sharing your depth of feeling about *The Great Gatsby.* I saw the movie, but have never read the book; now I must go back and read it.

Gee, Frank, just as you admire Fitzgerald and other excellent wordsmiths, you are rapidly gaining your own admirers. I hope you don't mind my sharing that Alex Rodriguez of the New York Yankees wrote a rave review of *The Legend of Mickey Tussler*. He said, "In my work with the Boys & Girls Clubs of America I see all kinds of challenges facing kids today, and this book does a very good job of treating gifted kids and teenagers with sensitivity and understanding in coping with and meeting these challenges."

That's very impressive and it must warm your heart to know your book will inspire children. You touched on that briefly above, but how does that make you feel? Have you met any other famous people since becoming such a hot property yourself? And has casting been done on Legend yet? If so, who are playing the parts of Mickey Tussler and Arthur Murphy?

Frank Nappi: I think that any time you are told that what you have done has helped kids, it's the ultimate reward. If the book touches even just one life and makes the difference for just one kid, then the endeavor can be deemed a success. I guess I'm not as hot as you think, Betty, for I have yet to meet anyone famous. Well, aside from you, that is! However, casting for the film version of Mickey Tussler has begun, with a verbal commitment from actor John Schneider to play the role of Arthur Murphy. We are still searching for Mickey.

Betty Dravis: John Schneider from the *Dukes of Hazard…* Cool… He seems like a great fit for your Murph and would be about the right age now. The last I saw him was in a Nip/Tuck episode. He just gets better with age.

And I'm not as hot as you think, Frank—I'm not famous. I just happened to rub elbows with a lot of famous people during my newspaper days. (laughs)

One of the things I enjoyed most "back in the day" was meeting celebrities like Jane Russell, Clint Eastwood, Senator Ted Kennedy and Tanya Tucker. And now that I've commenced interviewing again, I'm meeting more high-achievers: you, actors Kitty Kavey, Jenny McShane, Shawn Richardz, Darcy Donavan, Jason Seitz, and award-winning singers and musicians like Alina, Nhojj, Kashy Keegan, MT Robison… I recently interviewed Katherin Kovin Pacino, an actress/producer and soon-to-be author, who just happens to be Al Pacino's step-mother. My co-author Chase Von and I call all those who are featured in our *Dream Reachers* books "Dream Reachers" because you stretch to reach your dreams.

You all inspire people in your own ways, so I can relate to what you're saying.

Now, this might sound frivolous and off the subject, but it helps us to know you better, so I'm going to put you on the spot:

What is the most embarrassing thing that ever happened to you and how did you handle it?

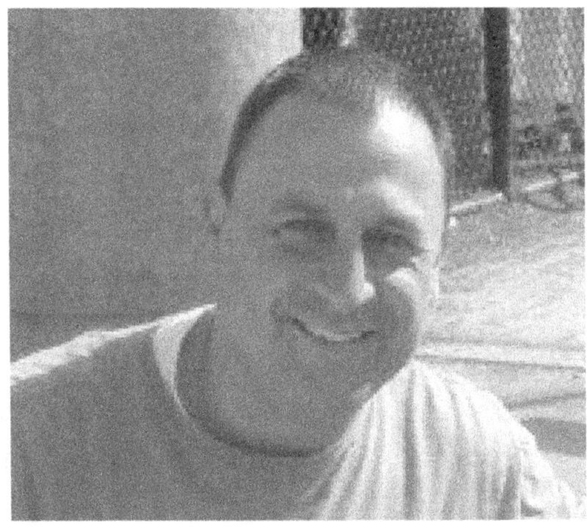

Frank Nappi: So now I'm a Dream Reacher, am I? Well, I sure am in good company, so that's way cool… I'll be pleased to be featured in *Dream Reachers: Volume 2* when it comes out.

As for embarrassing moments, I am no stranger to those; I have had my fair share. However, the one that always comes to mind is the morning I was sitting in my 20th Century American Fiction class at Hofstra. I had been out late the night before, at a concert, and had gotten little or no sleep. In addition, I hadn't eaten anything and it was real warm in the room. I started feeling a little woozy, so I put my head down on the desk. The next thing I saw was a patchwork of faces, including my professor's, looking down at me. I remember thinking, "Wow, Professor Zimmerman and a bunch of people from my class are in my dream. How strange…"

Then, as the gap between dream state and consciousness began to wane, I realized, much to my utter humiliation, that I had fainted in class and everyone was looking at me. I could not get out of there fast enough! The only thing worse than leaving was coming back two days later for the next class. I think I said something funny when I came in, like: "I'll try to make it through the whole class today, but if I can't, who's going to catch me?" The professor was cool about it. It helped a little.

Betty Dravis: Wow, that's a whopper, Frank. As they say on the Internet, I'm LOLing…*with* you, not *at* you, of course. And I must add that your response to the class upon returning was cool.

Now I'm curious about something else. If you could spend the day with one person besides your wife–someone in history, a favorite author, a public figure, a character in a book, etc.–who would you choose and why?

Frank Nappi: Great question**…** There are so many names that come to mind**.** I already spoke about my admiration for Fitzgerald, so you know I wouldn't mind hanging out with him, drinking and talking about writing, etc. But, if I had to choose another, I suppose it would be Babe Ruth. I love baseball, and nothing fascinates me more than the history of our nation's pastime. Naturally, Babe Ruth was and still is the most iconic figure in the game. I think I would really enjoy gaining some first-hand insight into the man's psyche…and watching him in action.

If the Babe was unavailable, I would consider giving Marilyn Monroe a call. (laughs)

Betty Dravis: Ah-hhh, the divine MM… You and a million other guys, Frank! Can't say that I blame you there, and what I wouldn't give to have met and interviewed her. I came close by interviewing Jane Russell, her co-star in *Gentlemen Prefer Blondes.* She was quite the "bombshell" herself …and is still around, helping children with her WAIF program.

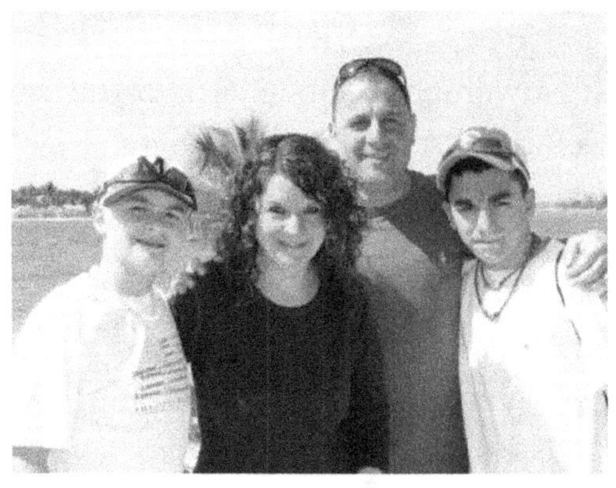

Frank, Julia, Nicholas & Anthony at Key West

Your answer is the perfect lead-in to my next question: Since most people are romantics at heart, I'd also like to know a little about your wife and children and what role they play in your writing. Their reaction when they learned that two of your books are soon hitting the big screen? How you met your wife? … I hope you don't mind sharing on a more personal level.

Frank Nappi: My wife Julia and sons Nicholas and Anthony mean everything to me. I spend as much time with them as possible. They are truly the wind in my sails. Julia and I met at Oceanside High School where both of us still teach. She is my best friend and will proofread for me or read scenes that I have yet to finalize. She is an avid reader, so she has a good eye. My boys are not really involved in my writing, except for the time they surrender so that I can get some of it done. They are thrilled and so proud that I have had the success I have had. They are campaigning as we speak to be cast as "extras" in the film version of Mickey Tussler. It means the world to me.

Betty Dravis: Now, Frank, getting back to your books, I know the thrill of seeing a first book in print, but outside of that what has been the highlight of your literary career…the thing that made you jump up and down with joy?

Frank Nappi: As you know Betty, this is a tough business, replete with exhilarating highs and devastating lows. With the exception of the chosen few, we all experience this wicked cycle. I have been fortunate enough to have several of these highs, but the most memorable to date is the sale of my first thriller/mystery *Nobody Has to Know* to Eric Parkinson of Hannover House/Target Development Group. The deal is somewhat unique, for Mr. Parkinson also purchased the film rights simultaneously. His publishing company is actively seeking literary properties with big screen potential. So, when the book is released in January, 2011, plans for a film version will already be underway. Pretty cool, huh?

Betty Dravis: OMG, Frank—*cool?* That's the *hottest* news I've yet to hear from any publisher! I must say the press release they sent out about you and your book, Nobody Has to Know, is one of the most impressive I've ever read. Parkinson has to be the most innovative, cutting-edge publisher in the world. To actively seek books not only to publish but to film is mind-boggling to me, but since they have their own film subsidiary that makes perfect sense. What a coup for an author to get "in" with them. That is one company that thinks "out of the box."

WOW!

The usual way a book sells is after publication, so to sign a deal for a book and film in one fell swoop… OMG, that blows my mind! Now I understand why you're constantly wearing that big-toothed grin. (laughs) But, as you said, you had your "waiting" period, just like the rest of us, and have earned your day in the sun, to use on old cliché.

Congratulations, Frank. After what you went through, I'm absolutely thrilled for you. It couldn't have happened to a more deserving person… I'm glad you found Hannover House and wish you the best of luck with the book and the movie. Since I had the honor of writing a blurb for the cover of *Nobody,* I have read the manuscript and can't wait until its release in January of 2011, and later to see your characters come alive on the big screen. Needless to say, I'll be first in line at the movie.

But now our readers and your fans are eager to know a little about this phenomenal book, so let's share a brief synopsis: *Nobody Has to Know* tells the story of Daniel Baldridge, a college instructor who finds himself as the central figure in the mysterious murder of one of his students. Stalked through text messages he receives from the dead girl's phone, Baldridge fights for his life against an extortion plot and a deadly revelation.

In my personal opinion, this book screams for a sequel. Do you plan to write one? I would love to know what happens next in the lives of your characters, especially Baldridge. It will be fun to see what actors are chosen for those parts, too, but it's much too early for that. Please share the scoop about a sequel to *Nobody Has to Know,* Frank, and any other works in progress (WIPs).

Our readers are an inquisitive group of artists and want to know all… (laughs)

Frank Nappi: They do say great minds think alike, Betty… Yes, I am currently playing with a sequel to *Nobody Has to Know*. The story will resume a couple of days after the final scene (can't say anything else) and follow the same sort of twisted mystery as the first. I have not worked out all the details yet, but it's underway. I am also working on a third Mickey Tussler story–*Season Three: Welcome to The Show.* As you know, my plan is to re-release Mickty Tussler in paperback, along with the sequel, *Sophomore Campaign,* just in time for the film. Then my boy Mickey is off to the major leagues, where he and Murph encounter a whole new set of challenges. Fingers crossed!

Betty Dravis: Fingers definitely crossed, Frank. I am so impressed with the string of books you're tackling. I have another one in the works, two to get back in print and two finished manuscripts I haven't even submitted yet, so I know all about multi-tasking. But that's a dedicated writer for you; always juggling WIPs.

I hate to let you go, Frank; there are a million questions I could ask, but the news about Hannover House sort of leaves me speechless.

It's been a delight getting to know more about you, especially the exciting news about your books going into film. I'm sure our readers will want to know even more about you, so in closing, is there anything you'd like to add?

How can those interested in you get in touch with you? I know you're easy to find on Facebook, but do you have any websites or links you would like to share with us?

Frank Nappi: Yes, Betty, just go to Facebook and type my name and it will take you to my page. I have some photos posted there of my book-signings, some military and baseball friends and a few of my wife Julia and our two sons.

I need to update my website with the news about *Nobody Has to Know*. I've been so busy writing that I just haven't gotten around to that. (laughs) I have only a few pictures posted there, but it does contain contact information in case anyone would like to write me. The link is: http://www.franknappi.com/. I try to answer all my correspondence. Thanks for taking the time for this great press about me and my books and best of luck with your endeavors!

Betty Dravis: You are very welcome. It's our pleasure… We appreciate your talking so frankly with us, Frank, (pun intended…) and for writing intriguing books that hold our interest and entertain us for hours. We all look forward to seeing them on the big screen. Again, I am so pleased for you… Keep in touch and let us know when *Nobody Has to Know* is released…in print and on film. See you at the movies…

"A curiously poignant baseball tale... elevates autism fiction to fantastic heights."

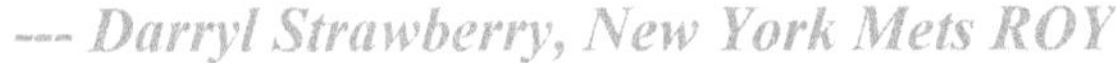

--- Darryl Strawberry, New York Mets ROY

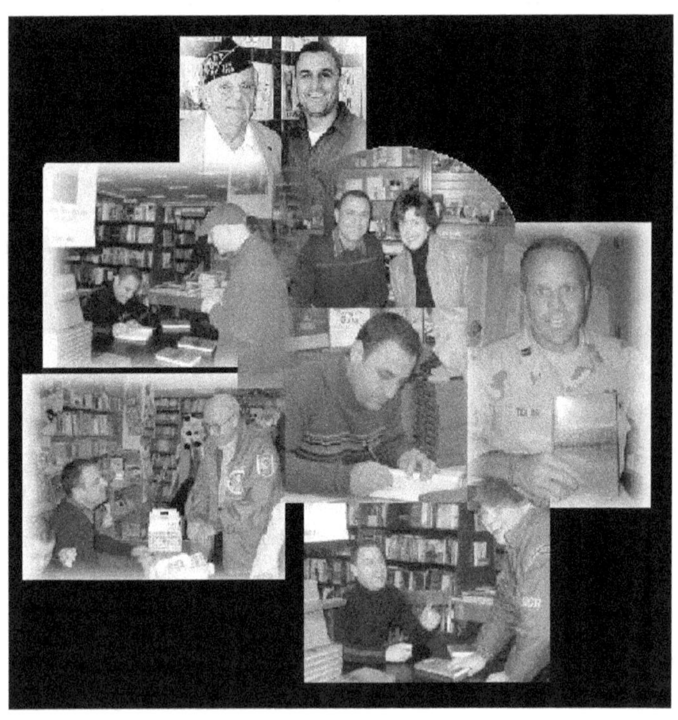

Interview with Susan Kennington

GORGEOUS ACTRESS & SCREENWRITER

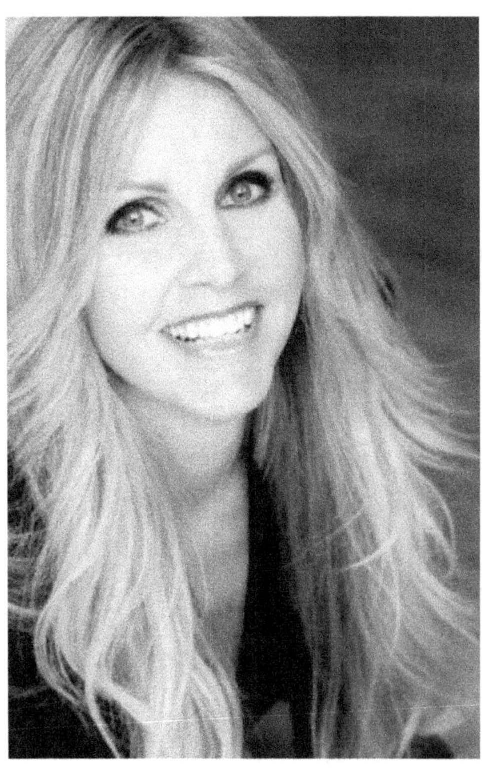

Betty Dravis: Hey, Susan. I'm honored that you found time in your busy schedule to be with us and share your life journey. I met you through Tony Tarantino for whom you are writing and who is directing some of your next acting performances. I can't wait to know what's happening on the big screen and your other creative interests, but first I want to know about your childhood.

It intrigues me that you were born in Germany because your father was a military man and the family traveled extensively.

Chase Von, my co-author, also spent some time in Germany and is the first to call himself a "military brat." I bet you got a lot of that while growing up. (laughs) Please share some highlights of your childhood, such as when your family returned to the U.S. from Germany and what you dreamed of being when you grew up.

Susan Kennington: Thank you, Betty. It's my pleasure to be interviewed by such an accomplished writer as you.

Before my family returned to the U.S. we moved to the Philippines when I was about three years old. I have vivid memories of living in a home that was raised above ground with a screened-in lanai underneath. At night, lizards would cover the screens and I would talk to them before I went to sleep. My parents bought the most beautiful bamboo living room set with hand-carved teak accessories. I can still remember the fragrance. At that age, I recall several trips to the emergency room. Everything from high fevers to split lips from trying to roller-skate down the hall. I also climbed the counters and cupboards and reached the baby aspirin… *My poor mom and dad!* I seemed to have put them in a state of panic on a regular basis. (laughs)

From that location, we returned to the states…to North Carolina. At the age of four, I began to understand the importance of southern hospitality by observing my mom and her friends. And there were more trips to the emergency room: neck injuries and other minor abrasions. Once I split my eye open and I still have the scar from that one. I suppose it's safe to say I was quite active.

Boston was next, where I received an excellent first- and second-grade education, becoming quite a proficient little reader. I'm glad I had the chance to experience what it was like to live in the snow and all the fun that went with it, as well as tour all of the historical landmarks.

My father was in Vietnam much of the time, so it must have been very difficult for my mom, but she never complained. We drew very close to our friends whose loved ones were also overseas. My mother was in a state of constant service and we always seemed to have enough of whatever was necessary to help whoever was in need. I will never forget how she so completely gave of herself. She was the strength of all who knew her–a true steel magnolia.

From Boston, we moved to southern California, then further north to Alameda where my little sister was born. Finally I wasn't the baby of the family, so my parents loosened the reins. I was thrilled to have a little sister to help take care of.

After the sudden passing of my father, we moved back to southern California where we had previously purchased a home. It was a sad time for all of us, but my little sister–who was barely a year old at the time–kept us smiling. My imagination was, and is, very vivid, so I dreamed of life from

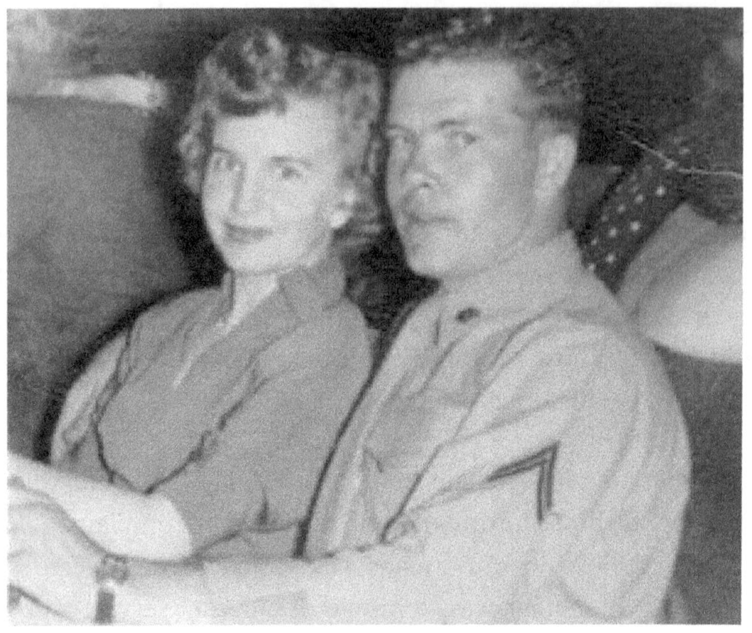

Susan's parents Virginia and Norman Engstrom

one end of the spectrum to the other. I had a magic carpet in the living room that I would "ride" when I was four. I would change my name each day, so it made it difficult for my mom to know what to call me. One dream that was always constant was that of being a mother. More than anything, I'm grateful to say that wish came true, and I am living my dream.

Betty Dravis: Traveling sounds like an adventurous beginning to an active, fulfilling life, Susan–*but talking to lizards! Yikes,* I would have been hopping around, screaming. (laughs) And I can just see the "little tomboy you" taking all those trips to the E.R., riding your magic carpet and then changing your name on a daily basis. You sound so cute and precocious, Susan. *Your* *poor mother*–but I bet she enjoyed every second with her precious daughter!

As for being a mother, I think that's what most women dream of first and foremost, and I'm glad we both have our beloved children in our lives. That's what life is all about.

Before getting into the heavy stuff, I have a confession to make. You've commented on some of my photos that you think I'm an attractive, elegant lady. When you say that, it astonishes me since you're one of the most beautiful women in Hollywood. That's so satisfying to my ego that I go around with my head in the clouds for days. (laughs)

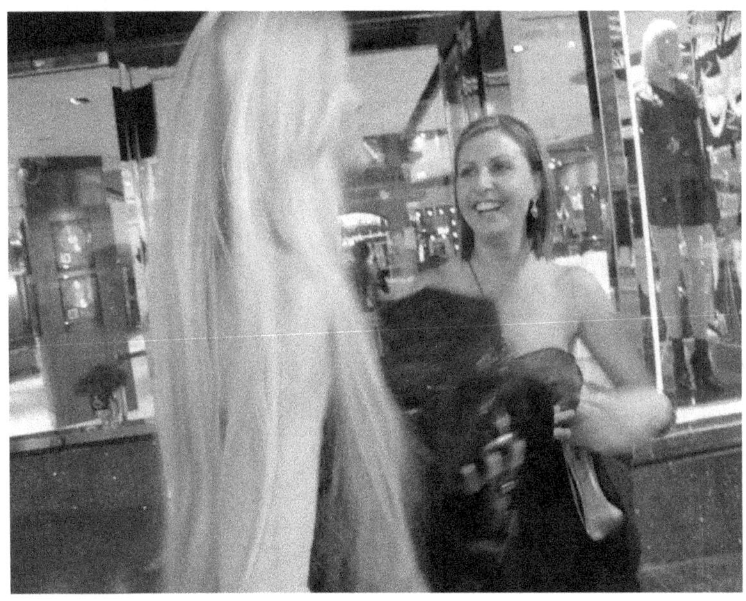

Susan & daughter Tressah en route home from Kodak Theater

But seriously, Susan, you are gorgeous and have the most magnificent head of hair I've seen since the famous actress Jane Seymour (when young) and popular songbird Crystal Gayle. Crystal's hair is her trademark and I wonder if you're known for your tresses, also–in addition to your acting ability and great beauty, of course. I imagine those long, golden locks have gotten you many acting roles, but has your hair ever kept you from getting any role you've coveted?

I imagine not, since you can always pin it up into a bun or draw it back. There are many choices…

Susan Kennington: Thank you, Betty. I must give credit to my mom for my hair. She passed on the gene to me and to my children. I've thought about cutting it many times, for the exact reason you mentioned. Long hair can sometimes be a distraction. Yes, it can go up or back, so that helps. I don't pay much attention to it and rarely visit a salon, so it has gotten very long lately. By the way, I love the pictures I've seen of you throughout the years. *My goodness,* I am sincere with my compliments regarding your beauty!

Betty Dravis: There you go again, Susan… But needless to say, I'm flattered. Thank you so much. I also give my parents credit for whatever genes I inherited from them. They were lovely, down-to-earth people.

Everyone wants to know all about your acting career, but before discussing that, I'd like to know when the acting bug bit you.

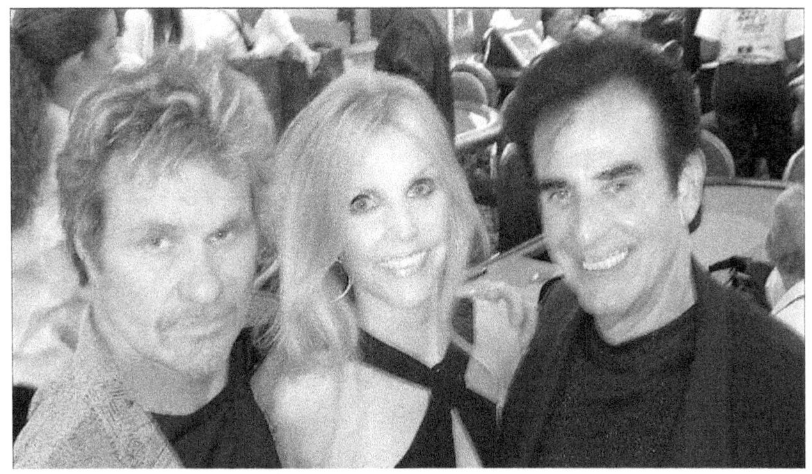

Susan at a charity event with Actors Marty Kove & Tony Tarantino

Susan Kennington: From my earliest memory, I enjoyed entertaining my family, especially my dad. In the living room, at the dinner table, during long drives in the car… It didn't matter *where,* we were always "on stage." (laughs)

My dad had an incredible voice and was very funny, so we had a lot of fun together, especially when doing impersonations of celebrities.

When I was twelve, I was part of a young women's organization within our church that I had recently started to attend. Our leader was Susan Laughton. She had extensive professional experience with stage, music, writing and composing and was an exceptionally talented woman. She spent hours with us after school and during vacation time, teaching and training us. I still remember the songs from her musicals. Susan Laughton took a publicly shy young girl under her wing and before I knew it, I was out of the living room and on the stage singing and acting. I can't stress the importance of how valuable her volunteer service was to me.

I also took drama, choir, voice and dance classes here and there throughout school and college and performed in various community productions. At the age of eighteen I became engaged and a new chapter of my life started, with my acting and singing re-locating from the stage to the kitchen. That chapter was put on hold for many years while I did other things, and then a few years ago–through a series of interesting events–it became apparent that I would be moving in that direction again.

Betty Dravis: Wow, your memories bring flashbacks of when I entertained my parents by singing *Wabash Cannon Ball* for Dad and *The Ballad of Barbara Allen* for Mom.

I couldn't sing worth a darn, but Dad and Mom got pleasure from it and didn't seem to mind at all. I guess Dad's keen sense of humor and Mom's unconditional love for her children overcame our deficiencies. (laughs) And what a huge break it was for you when that incredible teacher took such an interest in you.

Susan, I hear that you're an awesome mother, so please share what your family means to you. Have they been supportive as you strive to reach your other dreams?

Susan Kennington: As I said, Betty, while in college I became engaged and then married a few weeks after turning nineteen. During that period of my life, I was given my dream of having four incredible children that have enhanced my life with indescribable joy. I built several custom homes with my (former) husband. I enjoyed the entire process of shopping and investigating land, working with architects, procuring permits and seeing the project through to fruition, including the interior designs, marketing and selling the homes…and then moving on to the next. It was an amazing experience that provided a creative outlet, as well as valuable knowledge. Among other things, I also did volunteer work, taught and led youth groups and took college classes when my schedule would allow, and of course, raised my children.

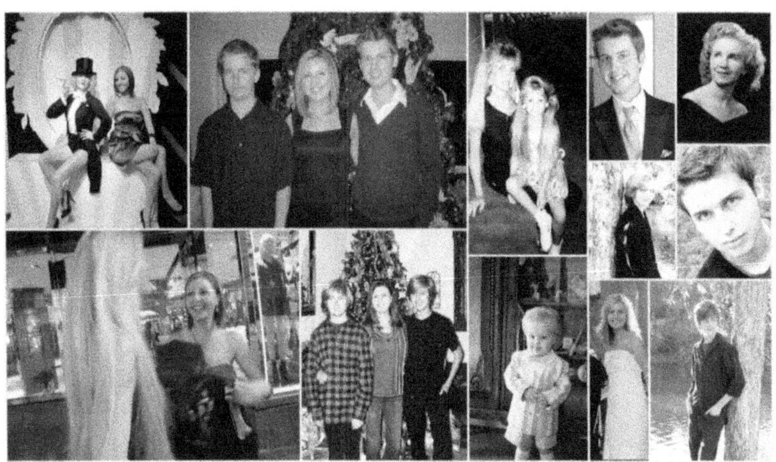

I'm glad you asked about my family because my family is absolutely everything to me. I have always been a hands-on mom and have structured work around raising my children, not the other way around. There is nothing more important than them. They have been my priority from day one. Shane, my youngest, is now sixteen, and I enjoy every minute I can get with my kids. They are supportive, but the entertainment industry isn't something we talk about often. There are too many other things that occupy our combined thoughts and activities. I guess you could say we live a somewhat un-Hollywood, down-to-earth life.

Betty Dravis: Having had six children of my own, Susan, I certainly relate to that. I also share a love of construction with you. Not that I ever actually built any structures, but I owned *Construction Labor News* for over fifteen years and fought many editorial battles for working people's rights. There are no people on earth who work harder than men and women in construction.

Wow, Susan, I knew you were a dynamite actress, business woman and mother, but to learn of your actually building houses is awesome. Another reason to admire you…

But getting back to show biz, a little bird told me that your very first acting assignment showed you being "transfixed" on George Clooney as he delivered a speech. I read that *that* scene required a Coen Brothers' style of humor. Was that scene in the Coen Brothers' movie *Intolerable Cruelty* where you played an attorney? Just what *is* that style of humor, Susan? And how did it feel to be ogling one of the top stars in the world?

Not a bad way to start… (laughs)

Susan Kennington: Yes, Betty, that scene was in *Intolerable Cruelty.* I find the Coen Brothers' work interesting and in a realm of its own. As for their comedic style, most people either find it quite funny or they just don't get it at all. I'm one who "gets" it. I've had experience with many of the characters they create, so their films just crack me up. Oftentimes you don't realize the full impact of their humor until a beat or two later. *Quirky brilliance at its best!*

Yes, my first day on a set and my assignment was to stare at George Clooney… It does *not* get any better than that. (laughs) He's even more handsome in person, very professional and a fantastic actor. He performed the same speech countless times and worked for hours so they could shoot different angles, expressions, etc. I had not been to bed the night before because I was at a bonfire with my boys' scout troop…in the middle of an orange grove until late in the evening. Then I had to go home, get ready, pack and drive to L.A. in order to be in Beverly Hills by about five a.m. After working all day, I think it was about nine or ten p.m. when someone came over to me and said Mr. Coen wanted me in the front to shoot some close-ups for the next scene. That's when I was given my special instructions. I was thrilled, but also smiled at the irony of looking so haggard from no sleep.

It was a great opportunity that I'll fondly remember with giggles and gratitude.

Betty Dravis: I can't imagine you looking haggard, Susan, but you're a trouper and came through for the film, regardless. I (and the majority of women) envy you meeting George Clooney, but that's just one of the perks of your profession. (laughs)

After that, I understand that you joined the Screen Actors Guild (SAG) and met many big stars.

Do you mind telling us about some of the ones who impressed you the most and with whom you would like to act in the future?

Susan Kennington: I have been impressed with every one that I've had the chance to be on set with. Kevin Costner was very nice. I would love to work with him. Billy Ray Cyrus, David Zayas and Eric Allan Kramer stand out as being exceptionally warm and friendly too. There are several more, but honestly, I can't think of anyone that was not very kind. I don't go up and pester stars, so maybe that's why I've had good experiences with the ones I've been around. I'm in awe of directors and crew who manage to keep it all together and run a smooth and productive set. I would love to have the chance to act–not only with those I've already mentioned–but with Javier Bardem, Harrison Ford, Al Pacino, Michael Douglas… I could go on forever.

They are all incredible and I think just about anyone would love to work with all of them.

Betty Dravis: I'm probably behind the times, but I don't know Zayas, Kramer and Bardem, but all the others are "household names" by now. Great choices and you named two of my all-time favorites: Harrison Ford and Al Pacino.

With those hunks in mind, Susan, I must ask you a question that's proven popular with our readers. I hope it doesn't embarrass you. I have asked a few actresses the same question and it's a big hit with our female readers. The question: What star that you've worked with is the best kisser...onscreen, of course? (laughs)

Susan Kennington: I have yet to experience a kiss with a major star, but I will say I watched a movie recently, *Frankie and Johnny,* with Michelle Pfeiffer and Al Pacino. The way his character kissed her character was extraordinary. Don't tell anyone, but acting is also very technical, so without the mutual passion, it may look the same, but nothing beats the real thing. (laughs)

Betty Dravis: Oh, yeah, Susan... A kiss without passion is like a taco without the hot sauce... (laughs) You know, I hate to admit it, but *Frankie and Johnny* is one of the few Pacino films I've missed. Now it's at the top of my list. As soon as I finish your interview, I'm going to go online to Amazon and order it. I might learn something important. I saw them together in *Scarface* and they do seem to have that certain onscreen chemistry.

But moving on, I've heard you refer to yourself as "a tomboy in stilettos," and after hearing some of your childhood misadventures, I understand why you said that. Nevertheless, that statement endeared you to me and made me chuckle, but now it brings to mind another question. Susan, since your many public appearances call for a rather extensive wardrobe, if you could buy only two garments for this coming fall season what would they be? Who are your best women friends and do you enjoy doing the girly things together, like shopping at out-of-the-way boutiques and dining at little sidewalk cafes?

Susan Kennington: For fall, I would buy tall, slender boots and a tailored jacket. My best women friends are my daughter and my sisters. I always enjoy my time with them. My sisters are like comediennes, so we cause a ruckus wherever we go. And my daughter is always up for anything fun. We share so much in common, yet have different interests, too, so there's always something new to talk about and explore.

Betty Dravis: Since you're tall and statuesque, Susan, those boots sound like the perfect choice, and a tailored jacket is versatile and a real wardrobe stretcher. Good choices… I also like that you enjoy your sisters and your daughter so much.

I bet you all have fun, outrageous times together. *Girl power!*

Now that you're an accomplished actress with much experience, I would like to share some of your past credits before going on to your current projects. I'm pleased to report that, in addition to *Intolerable Cruelty*, you've had roles in the following films: *Memphis Rising: Elvis Returns* (G.T.M. LLC/M.Z. Silverz, Director) wherein you played reporter Lyn Martin; *Flying By* (Eric Abrahamson/Jim Amatulli) where you played a Runion guest named Summer. And then there was *Carnivale* where you played the mother in a featured family film for HBO.

That's quite a start, Susan, and now you're acting in four upcoming movies that we'll discuss below. I'm excited for you, not only for getting so many good roles, but also for other skills you've developed. But first, for the benefit of aspiring actors among our readers, please tell us where you studied.

You spoke above about getting started in college, so this question pertains to what happened after.

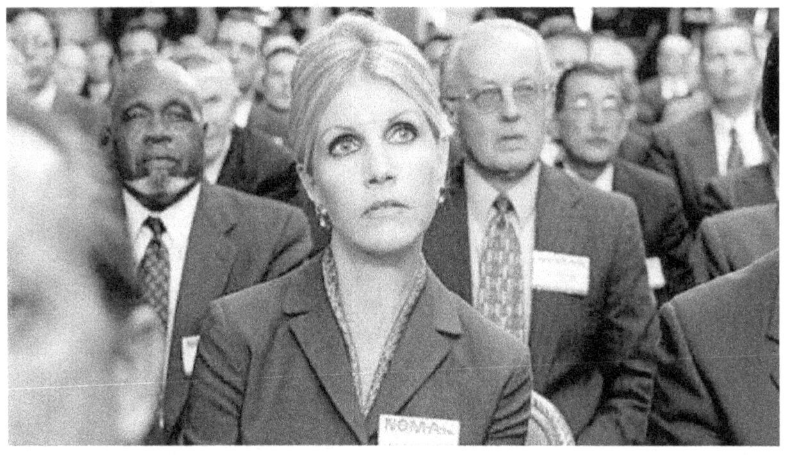

A scene from *Intolerable Cruelty* where Susan plays an attorney

Susan Kennington: Well, Betty, I won't bore your readers by describing each movie and scene I've been in and all the classes I attended, but I studied with various acting instructors throughout the Los Angeles area and participated and graduated from a specialized on-camera training course for actors at Actors Certified Training in North Hollywood, now located in Burbank. I've also taken a screenwriting workshop by Linda Seger, taken firearms training by Jim Bowan and attended classes by Joel Coleman, Susan Laughton and Steve Nave, to name a few. I like to give the instructors credit because they are so important to the entire entertainment industry.

Betty Dravis: I can't imagine you ever being boring, Susan, but I dislike long lists of things when reading, also. And I agree with you about the importance of teachers…no matter what career one is in. But now I'd like to hear about your writing. I'm impressed that you started writing somewhere along the way and have recently turned to producing. I know that you've contributed to A-list scripts, are also writing your own original screenplay and producing and developing a film based on historical events, set in the South Seas. What's the latest buzz with those demanding projects?

Susan Kennington: It's true, Betty, I am a screenwriter, but I haven't sought to have my own work published yet. Everything I've done has someone else's name on it. One dream at a time, and that's one of my next goals I need to reach before I can live my dreams to their fullest.

The film *The Shark Hunter,* which is in early development, was written by J. Robert Shaffer and is taken from his historical fiction novel, *Samoa,* to be released in early 2011. It is set in the islands of Samoa during the late 1800s and is a cross between *Braveheart, A Perfect Storm,* and *The Patriot.* Inspired by true events, it is one of the greatest tales of courage, integrity, love and forgiveness–with a starring role played by Mother Nature. The project was placed in my hands by my dear family friend, George Molifua, shortly before he passed away. He and J. Robert Shaffer were extremely close. As you might surmise, this film is of particular importance. There has been some studio and A-list interest, and our website–built by Kodi Zene who was introduced to me by marketing expert Edward Earle–will be up shortly.

Betty Dravis: Both those films sound like high concept to me, Susan. I'm so excited for you, and I look forward to celebrating with you on the red carpet when your very own film premieres. Woo-hoo…

In addition to all of that, you're also an associate producer for a fitness DVD that's in development and for a business strategy show, now in production. Considering the many projects you're involved with, I'm curious about how you keep on track and remain organized. What's a typical day in your life like?

Susan Kennington: The fitness DVD was more than a year ago, Betty, as well as the business strategy show, although that's about to take off again under a new format, from what I understand. It is tied to the consulting work that I do.

Some things overlap and others have taken place during different time periods. In the film business, there is often a lot of waiting for final funding to occur. I don't wait on anything, however. I always have something else to work on during those times. I stay organized by remaining dedicated, taking one thing at a time and focusing on top priorities.

Betty Dravis: Your fitness video brings to mind another question, Susan. Since you're five feet, nine inches tall and quite slender, I would describe you as a "willowy beauty." How do you stay in such fine shape and what are your favorite foods?

Susan Kennington: "Willowy beauty…" Hmmm, that's a nice way of putting it, Betty. (laughs) I do some form of exercise nearly every day, even if I can only fit in a ten-minute workout. I've found that keeping the discipline going is very important. My favorite form of exercise is running, particularly by the ocean. I find tremendous energy by moving water. It's quite a physical, spiritual and creative experience for me. I also have a small portable stair-stepper that I use at home for quick intense workouts. My diet consists of mostly raw foods: fruits, nuts, vegetables, seeds, herbal plant foods and lots of salads. When it comes to food, I basically eat what I like, but in small portions, especially if it's something that isn't quite so healthy.

Betty Dravis: Your exercise and food choices sound sensible, Susan, and like you say, it does take discipline and the regimen of doing it on a daily basis. I admire anyone who can stick to it.

Since I recently interviewed your good friend and business associate, Tony Tarantino, who is also an important industry figure, IMO, and one of my favorite Hollywood people, I'm really jazzed about your work with him. In addition to good roles in three of his movies that are in pre-production, you're also a staff writer and associate producer for Tarantino Productions. That must keep you hopping, so tell us something about your work.

I would like to know if the writing evolved out of your acting and exposure to the entertainment industry. And please tell us about your favorite role in a Tarantino production: Is it the role of Margo in *Prism,* or of Belinda Rhodes in *Death Keeps Coming,* which Tony produces in association with Karl Adam Entertainment/Derek K Milton?

Susan Kennington: My experience with producing, in general, is very similar to building a custom home, Betty. It takes patience, self-initiative, tremendous drive, vision, hard work, paying attention to details and being organized, as well as being very good at working with various personality types. I'm an endless well of ideas and I have a huge amount of contacts. These are some of the things I've been told that make me stand out as an asset on projects.

I used to write down my thoughts, often in the form of poetry and song lyrics, and then throw them away. Throughout my life–through natural correspondence and expression of opinion, emotion, communication and language–I was often asked if I was a writer, and if not, why wasn't I. When Tony and I became friends, he was very encouraging of my writing skills, and also my acting skills–which he wasn't even aware of until long after we became acquainted. He happened to be with me one evening during a class I was enrolled in… That's when he started asking me to be in some of the films he was working on, and it's just grown from there. Assisting with, and contributing to the screenplay *Prism* was a wonderful opportunity for me. I soon realized I had the knack and wanted to keep moving forward with it. The same thing happened musically. His sincere feedback and encouragement has fortified my confidence and desire to cultivate that part of my creative nature. I'll always be grateful to him for that.

As for my favorite role, there are aspects of each character that I will be playing that are of particular interest. I helped to create and develop Margo and had an enjoyable time expressing her wit, intellect and feminine nature, so she is close to my heart. I've always wanted to act in a western, so the role of Belinda Rhodes, the wife of a rancher who is confronted by a paranormal presence, will be an amazing experience.

Betty Dravis: I find *that* with my friends who encourage my writing, too, Susan. The ones who keep their faith in me and inspire me to move forward will always be remembered with undying gratitude. In the end, it always seems to boil down to people helping people. That's what makes the world go round.

Well, Susan, we've spoken about so many aspects of your life and I think it's been definitely established that you're a human dynamo…a real Dream Reacher. After reaching the stars and *living your dreams,* what inspires you to reach for more stars and do something even more extraordinary? And what advice do you have for those who are disillusioned and thinking of quitting?

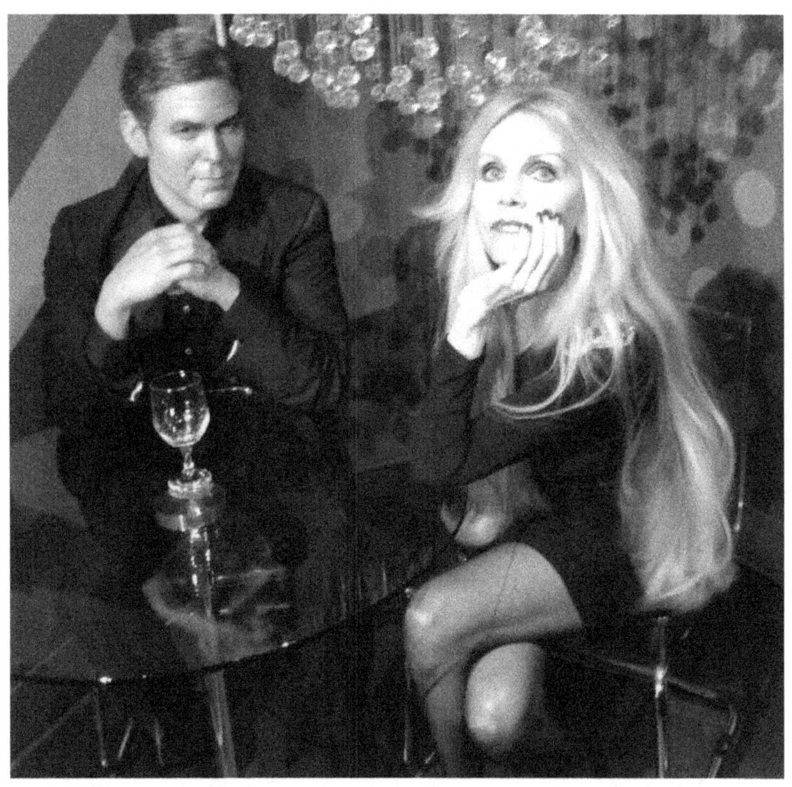

Susan at an Industry Event with wax image of George Clooney

Susan Kennington: I learned at an early age that life on earth, as we know it, can end very quickly.

I have said goodbye to many loved ones as they have passed on, including my parents and my first child.

What inspires me is pure love: love of God, love of family and friends–both here and in the spirit world–love of our existence on Earth, and love for all that is possible.

For anyone who is feeling discouraged, know that with all of life's experiences there is knowledge to be learned. This alone is a valuable gift, no matter what we are blessed with or what we must endure. Find ways to elevate yourself when feeling low. This might come in the form of music, exercise, an inspiring film or laughter. Develop a talent, release your tears… Whatever works for *you.* Most of all, I can't stress enough how vital it is for me to be spiritually in tune and connected.

Betty Dravis: That's excellent advice, Susan… And please accept my condolences on the loss of your loved ones. I, too, know the pain of losing a child… But now we need a break from heavy to light, so what is the most embarrassing thing that ever happened to you—onstage or off?

Susan Kennington: Oh, I have a great story… (laughs) It took place about twelve years ago. I was with my family at Disneyland, including my sisters, nieces, nephews…the whole gang.

The day was winding down and we stopped in front of Sleeping Beauty's Castle while waiting for the parade.

Actually, it was the parade that never came…because it didn't, but that's a whole different tale.

Well, the kids were little and getting restless, so I bought an armful of *churros* and was feeding them like tiny seals. I had this bright idea to stand on a bench that surrounds the castle, but sat instead on the ledge above it while I fed the kids their treats. Seemed like a good idea, but the ledge was polished stone, so in an instant I slid off and disappeared–except for my feet that were sticking up. I landed in a tree below the bench/wall and couldn't move. My boys were ecstatic because it was just like Buzz Lightyear when he fell out of Woody's window into a tree, and they proudly told me this when they stuck their little laughing heads over the wall to get a better look. All my sister could say was *Susan!*…amid paralyzing laughter. Finally, their dad popped his face over and said, "*Susan!* What did you do that for?"

It was an "I can't believe he just asked me that" moment…

What was I supposed to say: "Well, apparently, I thought it would be entertaining to lie jack-knifed and incapacitated in this tree waiting for you to decide when might be a good time to yank me out."?

He extended his arm and in a split second I was back on "land." We laughed so hard I thought we might be escorted out of the park. Yes, I still have my Buzz Lightyear scar on my arm and wear it proudly.

Betty Dravis: That's one of the funniest things I ever heard, Susan…but leave it to you! And dare I laugh at your expense? (laughs) But before I double over with laughter, I better ask the next question: If you were given the chance to spend an entire day with one movie director or producer (besides those with whom you currently work) who would you choose and why?

Susan Kennington: Anyone who has their budget in order and is ready to shoot and get to work! Dreaming is nice, but doing is better. (laughs) I recently watched several Al Pacino movies and gained a high degree of respect for his abilities as an actor, which I suspect would translate into him being a fantastic director. He's directed a couple of films that I'm looking forward to seeing. As for Kevin Costner, he "appreciates the lines on a woman's face as she gracefully journeys through life." What an experience that would be, to work under his direction. Pacino and Costner are two that come to mind very quickly, but there are so many.

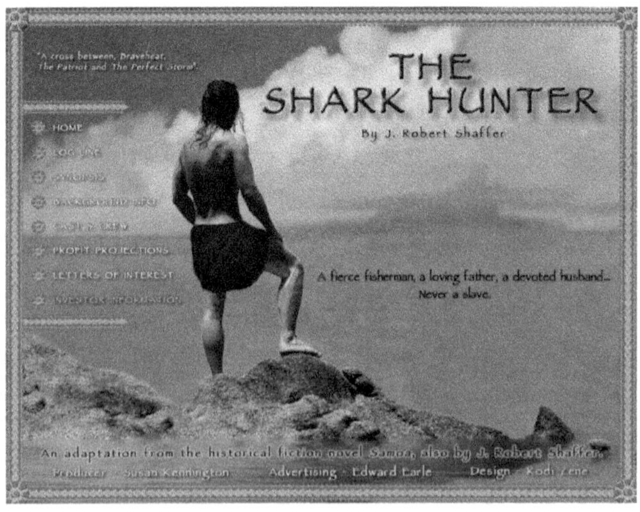

Susan is producing this movie; date to be announced

Betty Dravis: That seems like a sound way of choosing, Susan. I agree that Pacino is so gifted he could branch out into directing and be brilliant. I bet our readers will readily ditto that thought. (laughs)

But now, since the world is in such chaos at present, if you could influence any one thing in the entire history, the present or future of the world, what would you choose to change and why? This can include how something works, also. For example, you might want to allow automobiles to fly. (laughs)

Susan Kennington: Well, since you've mentioned it, Betty, I've often fantasized about being one of the Jetsons while traveling from San Diego to Los Angeles. (laughs) But all kidding aside, if I could change one thing it would be that every child on earth would be born into a loving and tender environment. One that would enrich and support the pure essence and potential of who they are and what they will become. If that were to take place, nearly all other problems of our society would cease to exist and the real beauty of our existence on this planet we share would flourish.

Betty Dravis: That's the most beautiful thought I've heard in a long while, Susan. You are remarkably sensitive and caring of others.

Since you're an actress, you receive a lot of public acclaim, so can you share one story that is especially close to your heart; something someone said or did that moved you and made you glad you were able to help (or inspire) that person?

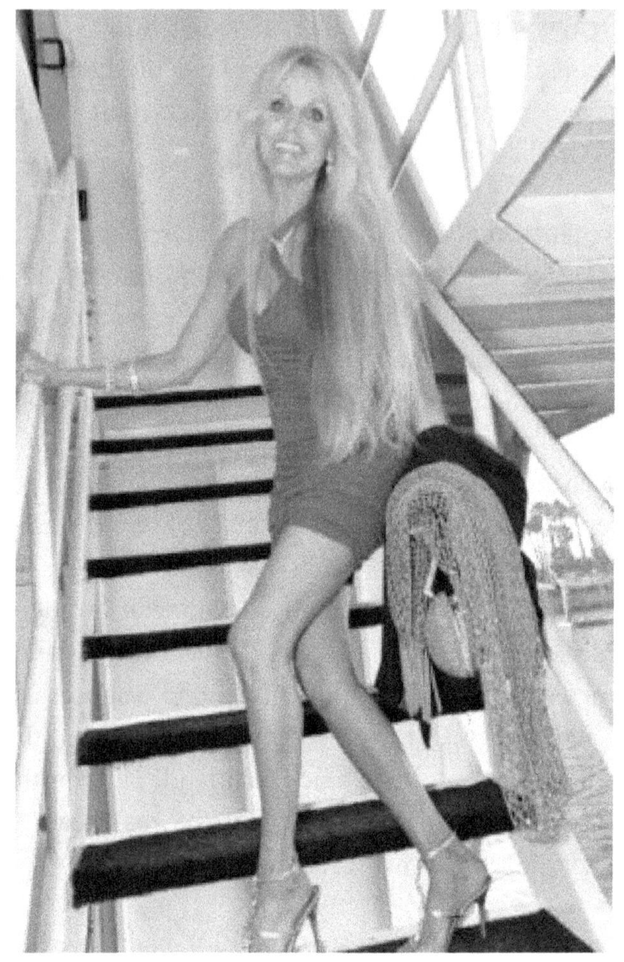

Susan Kennington: Oh gosh, I'm not aware of any public acclaim! (laughs) There isn't one person in particular, but rather a gratitude that I have for a constant and steady stream of notes and personal conversations that come my way, expressing the inspiration and insight I've somehow been able to share with others. I find human interaction one of the greatest things I can do to add depth and meaning to my life.

It's a good feeling to hear that I've provoked thought in someone…caused them to think about things they never thought of before. The greatest is when my children share moments with me that affirm in my heart I've done well as their mom, and they know they are loved and treasured.

Betty Dravis: That's the kind of humble answer those who know you would expect from you, Susan. Your entire being is unbelievably kind and attuned to others.

Thanks for ending our "chat" on a positive note, but before leaving, I'd like to offer you the chance to discuss anything of importance that I may have missed.

Susan Kennington: I don't think you've missed anything, and I want to thank you, Betty, not only for this interview, but for all that you are and all that you mean to me.

You are a treasure, and I'm grateful our lives have crossed paths. I look forward to reading more of your work and to many years of continued friendship.

Betty Dravis: I appreciate that, Susan, and I feel honored and blessed to be your friend.

I'm reluctant to leave you because you're such fun to be around, but I'll do so if you promise to send post-production info about your films and news of your other projects. (laughs) I know our readers will want to be kept in the loop. Meanwhile, they can visit your various websites, which are easily found by simply Googling your name.

Well, Susan, I guess that's it for now. I've had a blast chatting with you. It's refreshing to know there are still such wholesome, wonderful, caring people in the southern part of our glorious state of California. Thanks for being here and for being *you!*

Since you're learning to speak Italian now that you're spending so much time in that lovely country, the next time you're there, please give Antonia Tosini a big hug from me. Since she's the author of the screenplay *Between the Olive Trees,* you should be running into her at one event or another. And in closing, I hope Tony won't mind if I borrow his favorite farewell: *Ciao, baby...*

Susan Kennington: *Grazie, and ciao mia amica bella!*

"I find human interaction one of the greatest things I can do to add depth and meaning to my life."

--- Susan Kennington

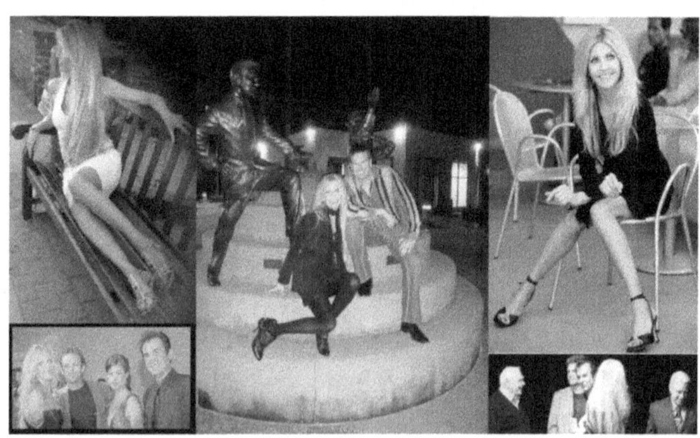

Interview with C. Robert Lee

ESTEEMED PHOTOJOURNALIST OF THE 50s ERA

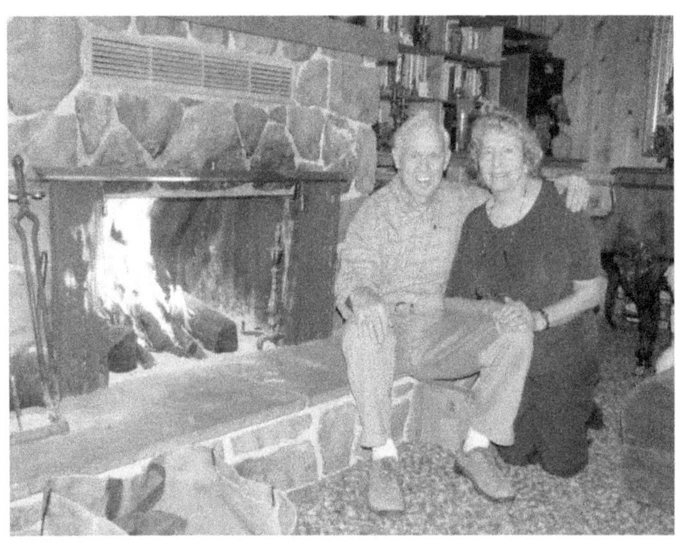

Bob and his gracious wife Ileana at home in Idyllwild

Betty Dravis: Welcome to Dames of Dialogue, Bob. It's a pleasure to have such a distinguished photojournalist with us today. I'd like to make it clear upfront that I know you personally, having been friends back in the day…waaaaay back in Hamilton High School (Ohio) when we were classmates. You just happened to be my first movie date, but that has nothing to do with why I am interviewing you, of course. I selected you because you are a Dream Reacher of the first caliber and have been very successful in your chosen career.

That said, I'm curious about how you got started; did the photography come before the writing or vice-versa? And which do you enjoy doing the most?

Bob Lee: Well, Betty, I think I could be described as an "in the moment kind of guy." Whatever I'm doing gets my full attention. When I was in junior high school, after seeing me hunt-and-pecking on her old, black Underwood typewriter, my mother predicted that when I grew up I would be a writer. (Incidentally, she was timed in a typing competition at one hundred ten words a minute. She was so fast the keys often stuck together…)

In my first year of high school I built a small darkroom in the basement and taught myself how to process film and print photographs. The best of my prints of classmates ended up taped to the inside of my school locker door—especially the shots of two pretty classmates wrapped in white towels over their swim suits. At graduation ceremonies I was chosen as the student most likely to become a Hollywood photographer. Both predictions were to come true before I was twenty-nine. Whatever I'm doing, I like best. To discover a truth from a chain of words that tumbles from your mind that you didn't know was there that literally sings to your heart and brings tears is the most satisfying gift of all.

A few years after graduating from Hamilton High School, I decided to move to California, but detoured in Denver, Colorado—planning to work my way to California. (More details of that below…)

My first break in photography actually came through the US Air Force. In Denver in November of 1951, I enlisted in the Air Force and was assigned to the 307th Bomber Wing stationed on the island of Okinawa where I ended up in a photographic unit processing aerial photos of bombing raids by B-29s on North Korea's ammunition factories and dumps. Magnesium flares were dropped to light up the ground and the photos were used to evaluate the success of the mission.

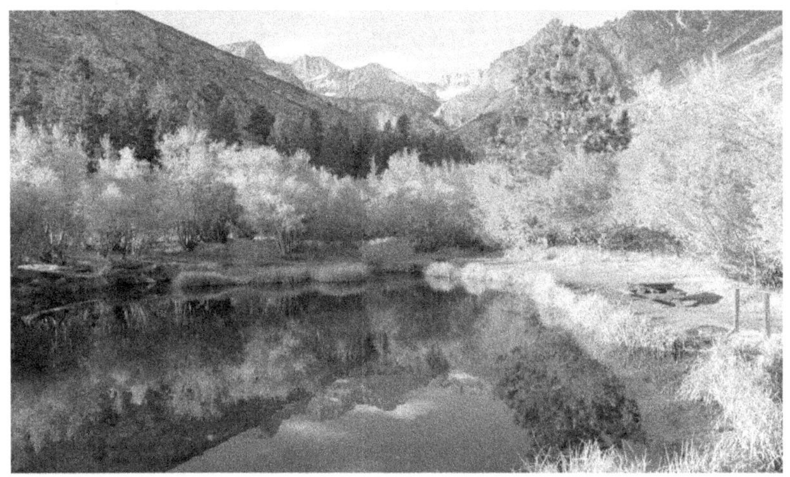

C. Robert Lee's all-time favorite landscape

The airfield had great photo processing facilities that we photographers were encouraged to use to expand our photographic skills in our free time. I bought an expensive German Rollaflex camera. On weekends and holidays I toured around the island going into many of the small, out-of-the-way villages and beaches on a bicycle I bought for ten dollars.

I took hundreds of pictures of local scenes and people. Then I used the base labs to process film and make prints when the labs were not in use. Later, I took 8×10 prints to some of the people I had photographed. My commanding officer really liked my work and suggested that I had a natural talent for composition and "timing the moment with people." He encouraged me to consider becoming a photojournalist when my tour of duty was over. The CO gave me a third stripe and placed me in charge of the copy lab which was a smaller darkroom with a workroom set up for making copies.

"As long as you can keep up with your work flow for me, you can do your own work anytime you feel like it," he said. That was the luckiest break in the world for someone who wanted to be a first-class photographer and had two more years to serve in the Air Force. The CO saw something in me that was planted and shaped by my hard-working, Christian parents.

When you're given a job to do, do it beyond what is expected and it will be noticed and rewarded. It turned out that I had this darkroom all to myself for the rest of my tour on the island and I didn't have to pay for any supplies but my film. I was the only one of the photographers who worked in the labs who wanted to be a photojournalist.

Betty Dravis: I can tell you're proud of your parents, Bob. They set a good example and now you're setting one for your children. I relate to our high school class predicting you would be a photographer. Coincidentally, the Class Prophecy, as we called it back then, also predicted I would be a writer.

And it's also a coincidence that we both ended up in California–at opposite ends–after taking different paths to get where we are.

As I noted above, I have known you since my youth, but failed to state that we were not in contact during the majority of that time.

I hope you don't mind if I share the unusual story of how we renewed our friendship after many years. When my first novel, *Millennium Babe: The Prophecy,* was published in December 2000, as part of a public relations campaign I bought a copy of a Hamilton High School Directory that listed my classmates with last-known addresses. You were one of the ones who received the letter I composed and you immediately wrote to me (snail-mail). Later we started emailing, exchanging "war stories" about our careers and families. Since then I have met your lovely wife, Ileana, and you two have been up North to visit me several times. Crossing paths again more than fifty years after graduation is mind-boggling, but I am grateful it happened. We have shared a lot of laughs since then and learned new writing skills from each other...not to mention life lessons.

Bob Lee: You're right, Betty. Whenever I relate that story, my friends are astonished. But to tell more of what happened after graduating from high school in 1947, I worked for a wholesale automotive parts store for two years. It became boring and repetitive and I yearned for something new and exciting and one day at the local library I found it: *skiing!*

I decided to put dreams of California on hold, move to Denver, Colorado and learn how to ski.

The store I worked for was the Savage Auto Supply Company, owned and operated by three brothers and their aging father. One day I asked Bob Savage, the oldest brother and general manager, if he knew anybody in Denver in the auto parts business. He had met some men at a national convention several years earlier who owned ten stores throughout Colorado and he volunteered to write a letter of recommendation and introduction. Bob also phoned his friend and he offered me a job over the phone. I accepted and within a week I was on my way in my 1942 Buick Roadmaster convertible, with everything I owned in the trunk and back seat.

By 1951 we were in a war with North Korea, so I enlisted in the Air Force for four years. When I returned from Okinawa I was stationed at Travis Air Force Base, a few hours' drive north of San Francisco. I was assigned to the base photo lab along with forty other photographers and only enough work for two.

Most of us were free to wander about the base at our leisure. It was obvious after a few weeks that we were not going to get an early discharge, except three months early was granted to those who enrolled in college. I enrolled, but that still left me with a year of service. When I started gaining weight I began going to the base gym to workout with pick-up games of basketball. Then one day in the Special Services Lounge my ace-in-the-hole jumped up and hit me right in the eyes. Goosebumps ran down my back and arms. There it was again: *skiing,* my salvation from boredom. The Air Force owned a recreational ski lodge on top of Donner Summit. The notice of its existence was on a small sheet of paper on a bulletin board. The details of using it were pitiful.

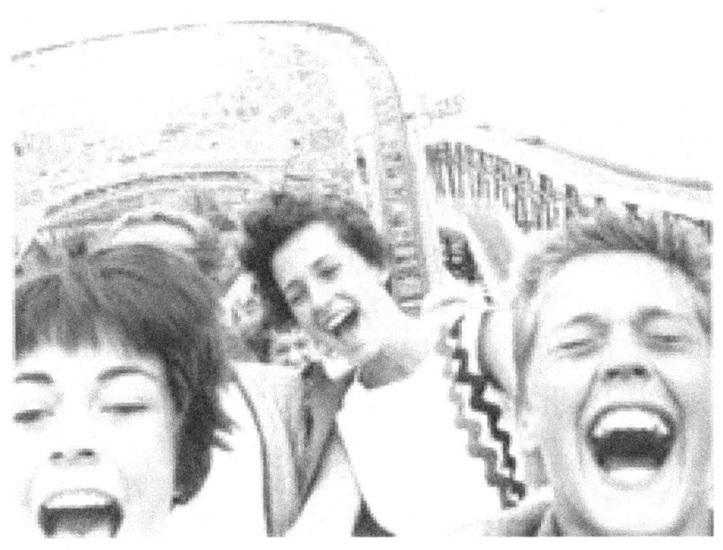

Award-winning photo: *Roller Coaster Joy*

I asked around and finally got in touch with the CO of Special Services, Colonel Rhodes.

To make a long story much shorter, I got my CO to transfer me with Colonel Rhodes's approval to Special Services and assignment as the ski instructor to replace the one being discharged in three weeks. The photographs of my ski trips to the Japanese Alps from Okinawa are what convinced the Colonel to request my transfer. I put together photojournalistic posters that were displayed around the base with the visual and written details that made the lodge desirable. This chapter of my life is a novel in the making. I spent that winter on the mountains of the Sierra Nevada making friends with all the ski resort owners, photographing ski races, dating female Olympic racers and photographing them. All these contacts were going to serve me well after I graduated from college and began my career as a freelance photojournalist. There is more, but I need to follow a chronological line of thought.

Betty Dravis: That sounds good to me, Bob…whatever works for you, works for me. But before you continue, I'm glad you mentioned playing basketball in the service; that reminds me that you were captain of our school basketball team back in the day too.

It's interesting that your career got started in Colorado and really took off when you hit California. The photos and stories you wrote are intriguing and published in prestigious magazines, and I'm impressed by some of your interview subjects, especially the late, great, iconic producer Aaron Spelling.

I really enjoyed all of his famous TV productions; the list is too long to place here but it includes *Charlie's Angels, Dynasty, Burke's Law, Beverly Hills 90210* and *Melrose Place*, all phenomenal hits.

Bob Lee: I didn't publish or write anything until after I was discharged from the AF in September of 1955 and had graduated from The Art Center School in Los Angeles with a degree in Photojournalism. Students in their last year at the Art Center are required to create the equivalent of a Thesis for a Doctorate, except there is no tolerance for sky gazing with wooly-muffle prose that has no chance of being published. I decided to shoot for the stars by writing and photographing a couple who had unsuccessful first marriages and in their second marriage they were living on Donner Summit year round, raising Husky sled dogs and small children and experiencing some of the largest snow storms of the twentieth century. My project was patterned after *The Saturday Evening Post's* "How America Lives" series.

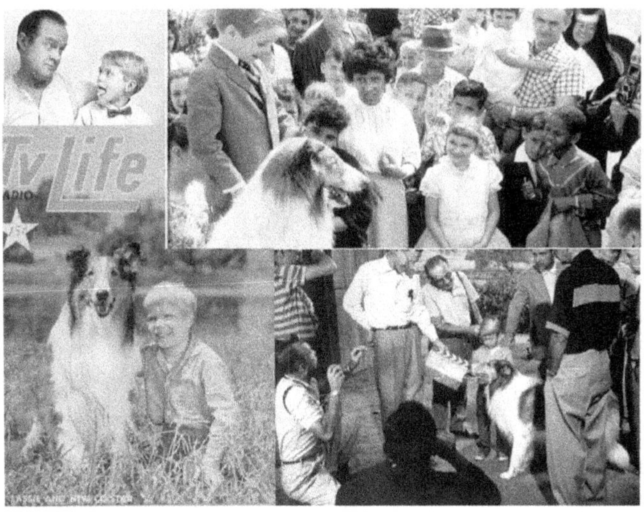

After Will Connell, my PJ professor gave me an A+, I sent *New Love—New Life in the High Sierras* to the photo editor at

The SEP. She rejected it, but her letter was very encouraging.

She wrote, "This story is the finest, most complete free-lance submission I have ever received. We plan our stories a year ahead of time and we already have our winter stories set for this winter. It would be wrong of me to ask to hold it for a year; it's too good. Please send it to another magazine."

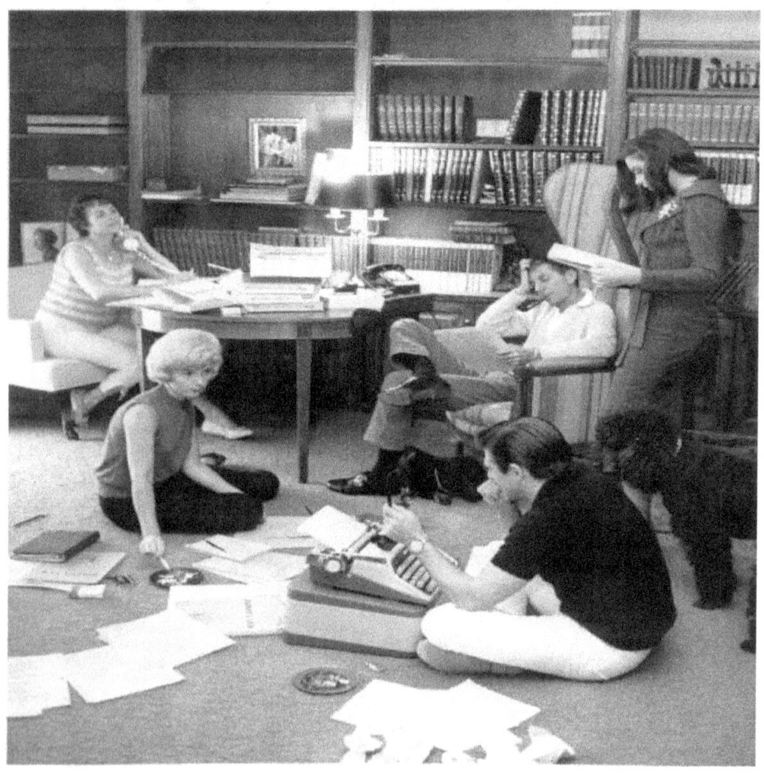

Bob captured the late, great Aaron Spelling in a brainstorming session for Burke's Law

This rejection was a disappointment, but I have always believed that I have a powerful guardian angel. I would be graduating two months later and I had other work to do for other classes. Within a week, I was called into the Dean's office to meet a widely published PJ from New York and Florida named Carroll Seghers, lll. Carroll was looking to hire an assistant photographer with knowledge of the city, a good car and a good eye for "people" photography. He had three assignments for New York magazines.

The Dean had recommended me, if I was interested. *Fifty dollars a day and all expenses! Would I turn that down? Not on your life!* Carroll was to become my most influential mentor. He was living the life I wanted to copy. The next four months of my life changed so fast that only a grace-bestowing God could bring all these elements to fruition in such a short period of time.

Betty Dravis: Wow, that's exciting, Bob. I'll never forget my first big break in journalism when I was a free-lancer and invited to interview the popular actor Clint Eastwood and shortly after that, the sexy movie star of the 50s, Jane Russell! Those were heady days for both of us, it seems.

Your list of credits and the big names that you photographed and wrote of are very impressive: producer Aaron Spelling, actors Zsa Zsa Gabor, Gloria Swanson, Vivian Leigh, June Allyson and Gene Barry (during Aaron's TV production of *Burke's Law)*...not to mention the 1960 Winter Olympics. And it must have been fun to photograph Bob Hope with Jon

Provost, the new (at the time) boy in the popular *Lassie* TV series. And the list of magazines who published you reads like a Who's Who of magazines: *Time, West, Cosmopolitan, TV Life, Saturday Evening Post.* You even had assignments for the *Encyclopedia Britannica*; the list of credits goes on and on…

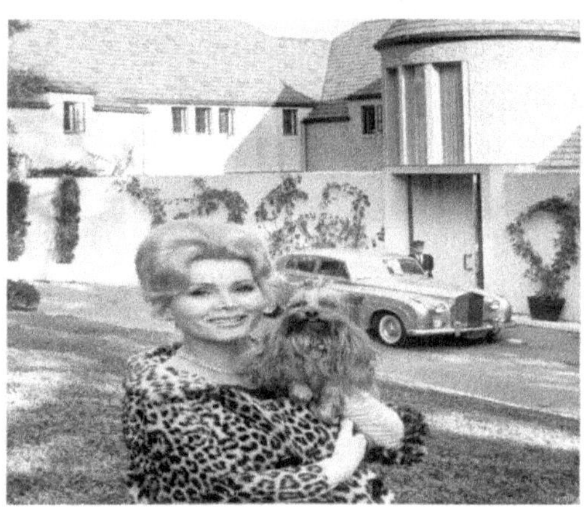

The Fabulous Zsa Zsa Gabor from an episode of *Burke's Law*

Bob Lee: Thanks, Betty, it was the most exciting and rewarding period of my life at that point and I'd like to share more: In the last four months of 1958 I graduated from the Art Center School with "distinction." Carroll Seghers read *New Love—New Life in the High Sierras* and loved it. He phoned Robert Atherton, the executive editor of *Cosmopolitan* magazine and praised my story. Robert said, "Send it overnight express." Within three days the story was sold for $750. Carroll's first assignment was to photograph Frank Sinatra while acting in a new movie. That went well. Next, was a story about a complete cast change in one episode of *Lassie* for *Life Magazine.* The PR rep for the show asked Carroll to take some pictures of the new boy, Jon Provost, that would make a nice cover for *TV Life* magazine. Carroll suggested that I do it. I think it paid three hundred dollars and Carroll told me to keep it all.

The next story was a photo study of the life of teen-agers in California for *Cosmopolitan.* The editor chose to use two of my shots. By the time Carroll was ready to return home, we were bonded friends and I had learned so much from him that I integrated over the next several years. His parting advice was, "Get some ideas together for stories you want to do and take them to New York and contact as many editors as you can. Bob Atherton told me that he thinks you have a bright future and wants to meet you. Your story is going to run ten pages and he's not changing one word. I don't suppose you're aware that he has edited Hemingway, Faulkner and Fitzgerald."

I was delighted, to say the least, so I followed Carroll's advice and went to New York where I bunked down at the Manhattan YMCA near Grand Central Station for three dollars a night. On the flight I considered that maybe I should try to get an agent. In the yellow pages I found the literary agency listings. I didn't recognize any names until I reached the s's and saw Ad Schulberg. I remembered reading a book called *What Makes Sammy Run* by Budd Schulberg and decided to give this Schulberg a call. After I told her that I had sold a story to *Cosmo* that was going to run ten pages in the December issue, she invited me to her home that was a beautiful apartment on

Fifth Avenue in the heart of Manhattan. She was a small, elegant-looking lady with a friendly, engaging smile and demeanor. After a few minutes of conversation, I learned she was Budd's mother and for years had been a talent agent for some of the most famous movie stars in Hollywood. Her husband was the president of RKO and later, Paramount. In one book I read later she was referred to as "The Queen of Hollywood." She preferred the less stressful agenting of writers. She agreed to represent me and asked me to have dinner with her that night. She had two tickets to a classy supper club where a new singer named Barbara Streisand was performing. It was a grand evening.

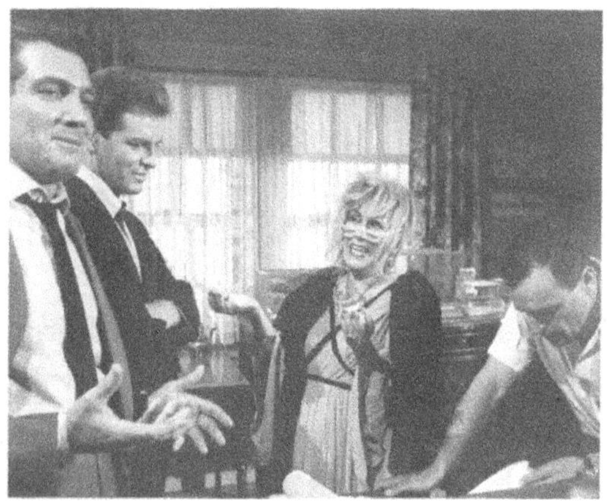

Gene Barry & Gloria Swason on set of *Burke's Law*

The following day, Bob Atherton took me to lunch. I told him about my experience as a ski instructor during my last year in the Air Force and that I wanted to do a story about the

Alexander Cushings of Squaw Valley and the coming 1960 Winter Olympics. He said he would think about it and let me know.

After a week in Manhattan, I had four pre-sold assignments and had met ten editors that I could approach by phone later with ideas. I was on my way…

Back in California I decided to make the rounds of the LA advertising agencies with my portfolio of children's photographs. I sold two to a young account executive named Angela Fox Dunn. She asked me where I had taken the pictures. The answer necessitated telling her about *New Love-New Life.* She wanted to read it; she was a frustrated writer and after reading it, she invited me to a picnic on the beach where we discussed writing. I learned that she was in love with an Italian man whose sister had recently returned from Spain after two years of working in Madrid for an American contractor as an interpreter. "Her name is Ileana and she speaks four languages, lived in Milan, Italy through WWII. You two would really like each other. She's from a good family and she graduated from Scripps College in 1956. She will make someone a fantastic wife. You're both the same age."

Angela's uncle is William Fox of Twentieth Century Fox Studios. Her mother is the story editor at Fox Studios. Angela has published several hundred movie star profiles in *the LA Times*, but most important to me, as it turned out, Angela was a born matchmaker!

She hosted a Christmas Eve dinner party for Ileana and I to meet and invited another couple that she had brought together. The Fox family in LA is sizable and some of them take turns hosting holiday parties between Christmas and New Year's Eve every year and Angela took us to every one of them. After the fifth night-party at a beach house north of Malibu Beach and under a full moon I proposed to Ileana and she accepted.

We stopped at Coffee Dan's in Santa Monica to drink a toast to each other and plan how to break the news to our families.

As timing would have it, the following morning I had a call from Bob Atherton in New York. "Good news, Robert. We've decided to go ahead with the Cushing Squaw Valley Olympics piece, but you'll have to be in Squaw Valley early morning New Year's Day to get the pictures we need. Okay?"

"Why the rush, Bob, I'm planning to get married in a few days."

"I apologize for the short notice, but the three Cushing daughters are attending a private school in Virginia and are home for the holidays, but they are returning to Virginia by train at 3 pm on January 1st. We need pictures of the entire family on the mountain showing the valley below."

I hesitated for long moments before Bob interrupted my thoughts by saying, "I appreciate your dilemma. Let me sweeten the pot to present to your fiancée. We will pay all your honeymoon expenses by giving you a second assignment of

"How and Where Californians Have Fun" and you can take all the time you need—within reason, of course."

"Okay, Bob, it's a daunting task, but I'll try. I've got to schedule a preacher, get a blood test, a license, buy a ring, put my ski gear together, organize my camera gear, then notify all the family on both sides. I'll ask Ileana and get back to you shortly."

I phoned Ileana and she said, "Let's do it." And we did! That turned out to be the most important and luckiest day of my life.

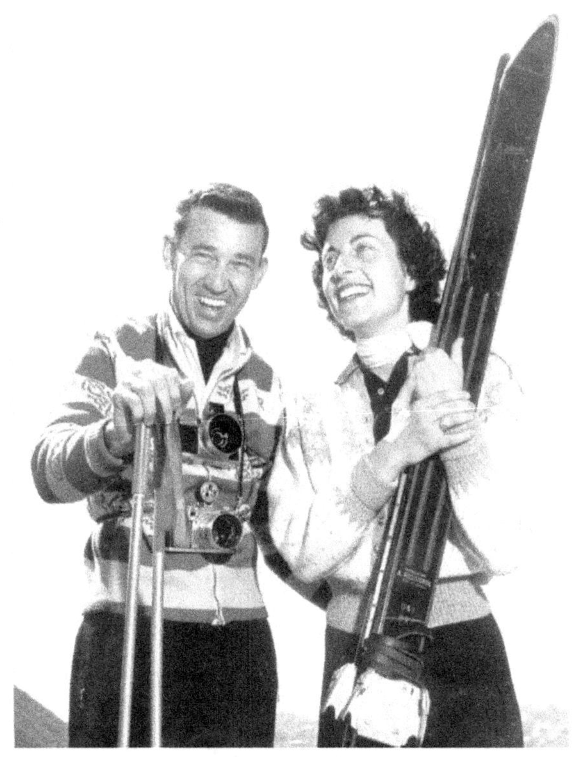

Betty Dravis: Sounds like your guardian angel was working overtime that day, Bob–fantastic photography deals and a lovely wife in one fell swoop! Your life was taking off to stratospheric heights… But time flies, and you and Ileana now have a grown daughter and son and reside in Idyllwild, California, with a second home near Palm Springs. Both locations are among the most beautiful places on earth. I'd like to ask a simpler question about photography and then move on to your novel. I love talking "books," but since I know you also photograph breathtaking landscapes and seascapes, I would like you to share your favorite one with us.

Bob Lee: That may be a simpler question, Betty, but since I love nature in all its manifestations, I can't choose a favorite. Is it okay if I e-mail you a selection of my best nature shots and you choose your favorite?

Betty Dravis: That's a deal, Bob! I'm the winner in this situation because I get to see a number of your lovely works. I won't name the one I select now because the story is finished before I select the photos; instead I'll post my favorite here. It will be hard to choose between a mountain mirrored in a lake and a glorious sunset or sunrise, for example, but I'll do my best. Thanks for the opportunity.

And now on to your adventures in Peru and a bit of book talk: I know that you have some connection with Peru and a trilogy you are creating is set in that country. Bob, I have read your unpublished manuscript and it's a powerful, dynamic accomplishment with unforgettable characters. I hope it gets published soon because you've worked on it for over twenty years and it's a remarkable story. I think the world is ready for something so well-written and original. I think it would make a blockbuster of an action movie with a strong love story.

Please tell us about your adventures in Peru and whether that inspired *Circles of Destiny.* Feel free to name the books that form the trilogy, capturing the essence of each in one line…which is the hard task that publishers ask us authors to do.

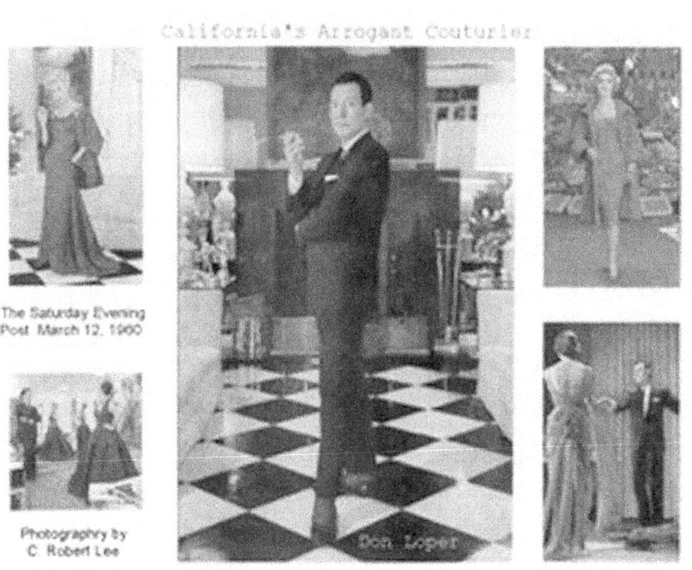

Bob Lee: My daughter's Godmother, LiLita Fraser Mellon was born and raised in Peru. A close friend of hers was in the San Pedro area looking to buy five used tuna boats to take back to Perù because the local boat builders had lost too many unseaworthy new boats and there were millions of tons of anchovies running just a few miles off the Peruvian coast.

We entertained this wealthy young man at our Lake Sherwood home. I traveled to Peru with his fleet of five tuna boats and was welcomed into the Fraser household as a family member by LiLita's physician father and her mother, brother and sister-in-law. All of them had been guests at our Lake Sherwood home. I was also welcomed into the homes of all of LiLita's friends that she had written letters to. Her brother was a very well-connected businessman. The eldest daughter of the vice-president of Peru taught me much about Peruvian society. I had many adventures in Peru and they did inspire the writing of the novels, but at the time I wasn't conscious of gathering research.

As you know, Betty, it's almost impossible to put a story concept in one line, so I hope it's okay if I give a portion of an overview that I use with my submission letters:

In 1968, the year of the assassins, an angst-driven priest, Father Doug Ryan, is sent to Peru from Los Angeles to investigate an Andean padre accused of using mission funds to buy guns for Communist guerrillas. He is mistakenly identified by a dictator-in-the-making as the source of the Andean padre's gun money and is marked for torture and death. Choosing to take a dying street urchin to a hospital, rather than meeting with the Cardinal-Archbishop of Lima, saves the priests' life. The death of the street urchin creates an unbreakable bond between the priest and the doctor who tries to save the boy. Several hours later, the doctor chooses to risk his own life to help save the wounded priest who is being chased through downtown Lima by two squads of counter–revolutionary soldiers. The doctor hides the priest in his nieces' bookstore with her help. The realization that the dying boy as well as the doctor and his niece, Chabuca Barcea, has saved his life compels the priest to follow a treacherous path to fulfill his spiritual mission.

By helping to save Father Ryan's life, Chabuca is forced onto an unknown path to preserve her life and her father's manuscript.

She volunteers to be Ryan's guide and Quechua interpreter by going into the Andean wilderness with him to find the renegade priest. Their journey turns into a quest for spiritual peace, an epic blend of fiction , history and personal experience.

The narrative continues in the second book of the Circles of Destiny trilogy, *Heart of a Warrior – Soul of a Saint, and comes full circle with a satisfying, dramatic ending in the third book. It's titled Spirit of the H.A.R.P; it's a work in progress and is almost finished.*

Chabuca and Doug continue the search for her father's assassins until she is kidnapped by a communist guerilla leader, Pactimbo the Russian. The ransom is that her uncle, a senator, write and persuade the legislature to pass a land reform. After the dictator's attempt to assassinate the president fails, a coup d'état succeeds, and the secret policy of genocide continues against the landless Indian population.

Betty Dravis: I know you are not a man of few words, Bob, so am not surprised that you didn't wish to condense your ambitious, exciting trilogy into one sentence per book.

Whenever an agent or a publisher asks me to do that, I often think how unrealistic it is, but I try to go with the flow. I'm happy you gave this more lengthy description. It's very well presented here and will surely intrigue all who read it. Since you're retired now and have always believed in following your dreams to fulfillment, I assume that getting your trilogy published is your next big dream. Is it out to submission currently and what do you hope for your writing career in the next few years?

Bob Lee: Yes, Betty, I'm very excited by the prospect of getting these books in print. The first book of the trilogy is with one of Hollywood's leading literary agents, Joel Gotler in Beverly Hills. I'm awaiting some news, but have learned to be patient when dealing with agents and publishers.

Betty Dravis: You already mentioned the influence of Carroll Seghers, lll on your life, but who are others you look up to? I, myself, have had a lot of mentors and mine are as different as the sun and the moon: Clint Eastwood influenced me when he went on after I interviewed him to reach astronomical heights.

He taught me to dream big and not let anything stop me; Eleanor Roosevelt was a font of wisdom; and my parents taught me all about honesty, kindness, the importance of dreaming and to follow Biblical teachings. And like many writers, my favorite authors inspire me: from famous ones like Pat Conroy, Joseph Finder and Maya Angelou to soon-to-be-famous writers like my friends Christy Tillery French, Chris Platt, Chase Von, Laurel Rain Snow, Caitlyn Hunter and Maggie Bishop. I'm wondering who your favorite authors are and which one inspired you most.

Bob Lee: Pearl Buck, *The Good Earth;* John Steinbeck, *The Grapes of Wrath;* Graham Green, *The Power and The Glory: Les Miserables* by Victor Hugo; all the books of Thomas Merton; all the books of Carl Jung; *Soul Mates* by Thomas Moore; *The Life of Saint Francis* by Nikolas Kazantkazakis; *The Agony and the Ecstasy* by Irving Stone*; Lust for Life* by Irving Stone; *Scene and Summary* by Leon Surmallion. I also spent twelve weeks with Lajos Egri , a Hollywood script doctor and renowned Hungarian playwright who wrote the quintessential *The ART of Dramatic Writing* and several others.

I've learned much from each one of these men and women, but the most inspiration comes from my Lord and Savior, Jesus Christ.

Betty Dravis: I can see His influence on you, Bob, and find that admirable. If you had the capacity to change anything in the history of the world, or the present or the future, what would you choose to change and why?

Bob Lee: The Bible tells us that "God hates a Liar." President Abraham Lincoln said, "No man (or woman) has a good enough memory to be a successful liar." I would vote for a law that says, "Every politician that lies to those who have put their trust in them shall be subject to jail time at hard labor based on the severity of their lies and the damage their lies have done to innocent lives." Just being voted out of office into a cushy retirement income for the rest of their lives is cultural suicide and unjust to those who have to work harder to pay the increased taxes to keep these lying thieves in the luxurious lifestyles they've become accustomed to.

Betty Dravis: That might sound harsh to some readers, Bob, but most Americans have political savvy and would agree with you; politicians have gone too far and have caused catastrophic damage to too many people, to the detriment of our great nation.

Now for another question: If you could spend the day with one person (someone in history, a favorite author, a public figure, a character in a book, etc.), who would you choose and why?

Bob Lee: Jesus Christ, because He gave me mercy, grace and love, cleaned up my life and offered me the gift of eternal life. I've accepted that gift with gratitude.

Betty Dravis: Bob, I too am a believer and I admire your faith. Now this question is really two in one, and I think I know how you will respond: Next to your faith, writing and photography, what is your passion and what is your pet peeve?

Bob Lee: You probably guessed right, Betty. My passion is to honor each day and thank God for one more day of life on this beautiful earth and to revel in the miracles of life all around me. My pet peeve is a liar who lies about his lies.

Betty Dravis: Thanks for sharing so openly with us about your life, Bob. It has been a delight learning more about you. I'm sure our readers will want to know even more about C. Robert Lee, so do you have any websites or links you would like to share with us?

Bob Lee: Not at this time, but people can reach me on FaceBook.com.

Betty Dravis: I'm on FaceBook, too, Bob, as are all the authors I know, many Amazon reviewer friends and many members of my extended family, including grand nieces and nephews. It's a great place for quick, easy communication.

In closing, I would like to add: I know *Circles of Destiny* has received pre-reviews from a cross-section of people with well-developed critical faculties and impressive credentials. I don't have room to share them all, but I would like to leave this one for our readers to digest because it's the opinion of Norman Corwin, a writer-producer-director who holds visiting lectureship chairs at five major universities; chairs two Motion Picture Academy Award committees; has won twenty-two major awards in media and the humanities and has published seventeen books. A documentary film, *The Golden Age of Norman Corwin* was awarded an Oscar in March of 2006.

After reading parts of *Circles of Destiny* to his advanced

writing class at USC, he told the students: "The scenes of the dying street urchin, the feeling of impotence, compassion and loneliness on the part of Father Ryan, and how he and the good Doctor Tomas tasted the boy's death in their souls haunted me to the point of tears. It was only my long professional training that got me through." After lengthy discussion, Norman ended the session by saying, "As you have seen and felt, this writing achieves great power."

Corwin's evaluation is a perfect way to end this interview, Bob. Thanks again for sharing with us, and best of luck with *Circles of Destiny.* Check back with us and let us know when it's published.

Bob Lee: Thanks for the opportunity to put my story out there, Betty. I'll certainly keep you updated on *Circles of Destiny.* It's been great fun chatting with you again. Ileana sends her love too.

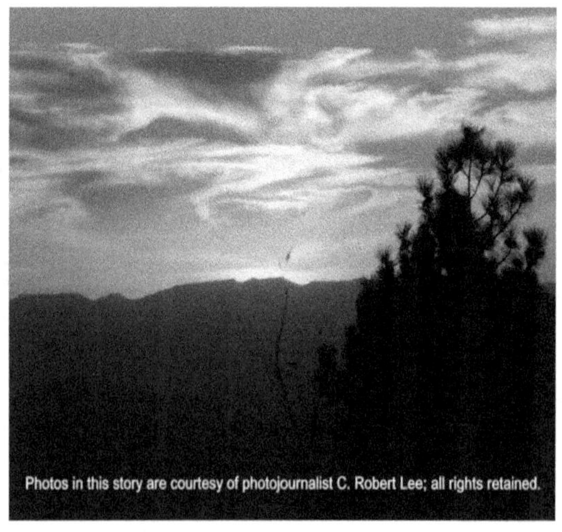
Photos in this story are courtesy of photojournalist C. Robert Lee; all rights retained.

Interview with Cheryl Kaye Tardif

BEST-SELLING CANADIAN SUSPENSE AUTHOR

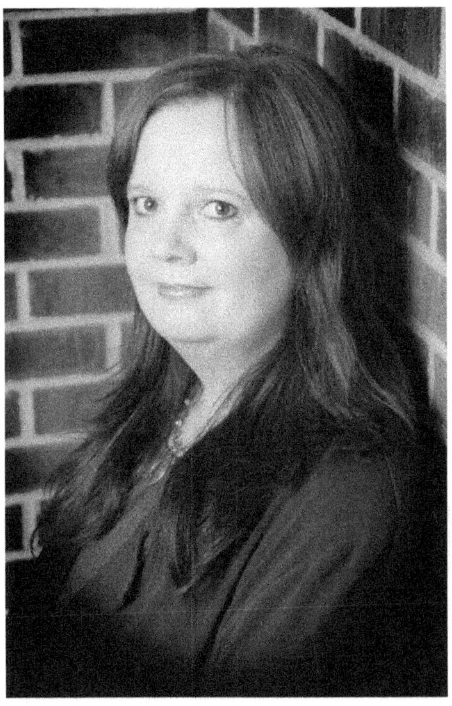

Betty Dravis: Welcome to Dames of Dialogue, Cheryl. It's our pleasure to have an award-winning author from north of the border with us. I know you have more going for you than your passion for writing, but it's all related, so I hope you enlighten us about the many plates you juggle. Thanks for taking time from your multi-tasking to visit us.

I heard about you a few years ago from your fellow-Canadian who is an Amazon reviewer. Since then I've read all of your books and enjoyed each one. We're always interested in how an author gets started, so please clue us in: When did you first know you wanted to be a writer?

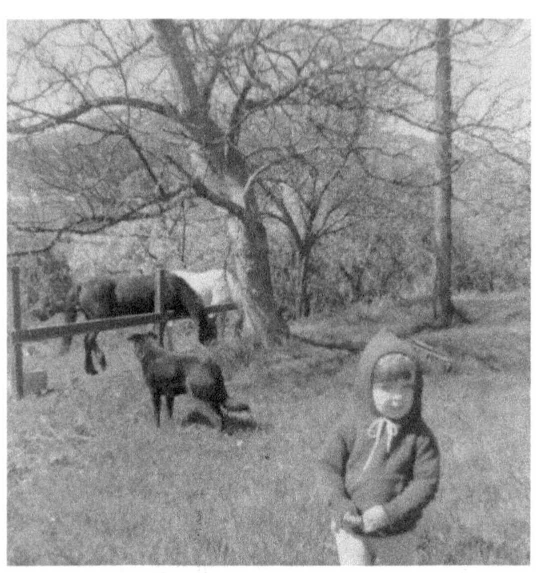

Little Cheryl helped Dr. Seuss

Cheryl Kaye Tardif: Multi-tasking is right, Betty. Whewwww... It never ends! But I always make time for an interview; it's the best public relations authors can get, and everyone knows authors love good press. (laughs)

But to answer your question, I recall the first stirrings of interest in writing when I was in elementary school. Every time I was assigned a story to write, I was ecstatic. And I always got high marks and praise from my teachers. My mother says this passion started even earlier. Apparently, when I was very young, she discovered me scribbling lines underneath each line of a Dr. Seuss book. She thought I was defacing the book. Horrified, she asked me what I was doing. I replied, "I'm writing the story." I guess I felt Dr. Seuss could use a little help. (laughs)

As a teen, I started writing creepy short stories. At sixteen I began my first novel titled *Beckoning Wrath*, inspired by my author idol Stephen King. After completing my horror novel in just under a year, I brought it to school, anxious to get my Language Arts teacher's opinion. But someone broke into my locker and stole my manuscript. Sadly, this was way before Microsoft Word and the "save" button. I'd typed that manuscript on my mother's typewriter; it was the only copy and I think it was about 60,000 words. I never saw *Beckoning Wrath* again and I don't remember the plot. Even so, my desire to become a published author was strong and it never wavered, even though I was distracted by life.

Betty Dravis: I love Stephen King, too…and Dean Koontz, John Saul and James Patterson; great horror and thriller writers.

But what a precocious little kid you were, Cheryl. I can just picture you "helping" the famous Dr. Seuss. (laughs) And it's too bad your first novel got lost that way. I can't imagine losing 60,000 words, but we've all experienced similar losses…not from theft, but from computer crashes when we failed to back-up our works in time.

Even though you must have felt crushed back then, your readers are lucky that you were persistent enough to keep on writing. Otherwise we wouldn't have such great books as *The River, Divine Intervention* and *Whale Song.* I read somewhere that you call your first published novel, *Whale Song,* your "heart book." I'm dying to hear why it's so dear to you.

Cheryl Kaye Tardif: Betty, *Whale Song* is–and always will be–my "heart book." I say that because I am connected to it on so many levels. The story was in my head and heart for two years before I wrote one single word. I knew the title instantly… And I knew it would affect people who read it; I just didn't know how much.

It's also my "heart book" because of a sadder connection. My younger brother Jason was murdered in January 2006. Police were having problems finding his next of kin. I was his only family in Edmonton, but our last names were different. When detectives questioned Jason's friends, all they knew was that my brother had a sister who wrote a book about whales. Police then searched online. And they found *Whale Song*…and me.

When I went to empty my brother's apartment, I found the battered, stained copy of *Whale Song* I'd given him three years earlier. To understand how that impacted me, I must explain that my brother was living on the street for a while and had lost most of his belongings along the way. He also suffered from alcoholism and mental illness. For him to have held onto my book meant the world to me. I later heard he'd told his friends he was proud of me.

Shortly before my brother was murdered, he called me. We talked about forgiveness, something that is very key to the theme of *Whale Song*. During that call, I forgave my brother, he forgave me, and more importantly, he forgave himself. *Whale Song* is my "heart book." *How could it not be?*

Betty Dravis: Oh, Cheryl, I'm so sorry about your brother. *What a tragic loss!* Please accept my belated condolences.

Cheryl Kaye Tardif: Thank you, Betty. It *was* tragic. My brother's murder was very hard on everyone in my family, especially my parents. Jason was so young (only twenty-eight) and hadn't even begun to live. Our only consolation is that he is at peace now.

Betty Dravis: I read on your website that since *Whale Song* was first published in 2003, it has gone on to great success, winning book-cover awards and achieving bestseller status on Amazon. Some of your fans have said *Whale Song* changed their lives. Do you mind sharing a few of those stories and how they make you feel?

Cheryl Kaye Tardif: It is one thing to write a novel that is so close to your heart, like *Whale Song* is for me; it's another thing to have your writing impact people's lives in ways you never expected. I've received emails from people who have said *Whale Song* literally changed their lives.

From my words they found some message, some form of redemption or help. *How powerful is that?*

I am awed by the response my novel has received. Aynsley Nisbet, a struggling artist, had found herself in a rut–with her art and her life. I believe she was going through depression. She saw the cover of *Whale Song* in the window of a bookstore and was drawn to it. She finally bought it and read it. Ever since then, she has blossomed into an amazing artist. I've bought many of her works, including the first one she painted after reading my novel. She aptly titled her painting "Whale Song" and she allowed me to share her story on my blog and site. I was so honored and so proud to see all that she has accomplished since I first met her.

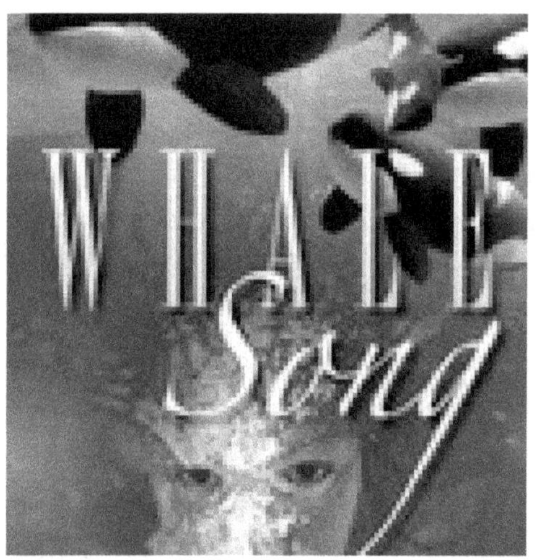

Other testimonials to my "heart" book: One adult daughter read *Whale Song* after her mother died and she said it helped her deal with the loss of her best friend–her mom. A man in his sixties read it and tearfully shared it with his lady friend. A mother and daughter who hadn't spoken to each other about anything important because of resentment and old grudges read

Whale Song and told me it changed their relationship–for the better.

There is power in my novel and I'm not sure I'm completely responsible for the words. Maybe I was led to write them. All I know is that *Whale Song* has become more than my "heart book"; it has become a message of forgiveness, redemption and love that has crossed borders and countries.

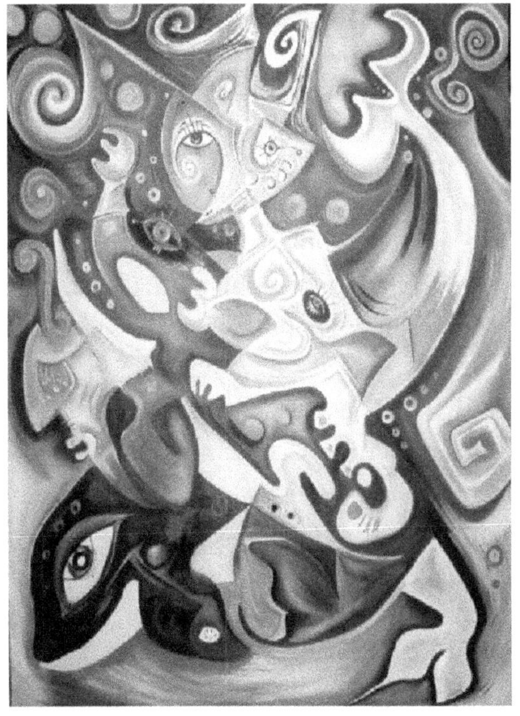

Whale Song painting by artist Aynsley Nesbit

Betty Dravis: Those testimonials are awesome, Cheryl, and Nesbit's painting is lovely…so cheerful and bright. What a rush that must give you to know your book helped her and so many people. I'm sure there are more who never contacted you to tell you. I've read it and it's a very moving story. I know how great that makes you feel because I've had reviews of my book *Millennium Babe: The Prophecy* wherein people share how the story moved them. My favorite is from a woman in the wine country of California who bought *Babe* to read during a long-anticipated trip to Russia. Unfortunately, her husband had a heart attack en route. To relieve the stress of waiting, she read *Babe* and said she completely lost track of time and was grateful to me for "writing a really exciting book that filled up every moment" she sat in that waiting room.

Thanks for sharing those touching stories, Cheryl. It appears your books are just as popular with school administrators and teachers. I hear they're using them in classrooms for novel studies. How do you feel about this?

Cheryl Kaye Tardif: I feel completely honored, Betty. I've had schools from across Canada and the U.S. inform me they're using *Whale Song, The River* and even *Divine Intervention* in their English classes. I've even done some Skype visits with some of the schools. I recall the first student to email me, telling me she'd written a book report on *Whale Song.* I ended up surprising her at her school and she rewarded me with her book report. She'd received an A. I surprised another student with a school visit. These are two great memories for me. And recently, I was told that a NATO school in Germany was using *Whale Song* and *The River* for book studies of Canadian authors.

Since then I've sent more books to the students.

Betty Dravis: That's very impressive, Cheryl, and kind of you to drop in to surprise them. It just gets better and better as word spreads, doesn't it? Now tell us about other projects on your plate. I hear that you and your daughter Jessica appeared on a *Celebrity Chefs* TV show a few Christmases ago. Share the buzz on that little adventure.

Cheryl Kaye Tardif: Yes, that was one of the crazier things I've done as an author, and this time I dragged my daughter Jessica along for the ride. *Celebrity Chefs* is a CityTV program and when I was asked to appear on it, I knew it would be a blast.

The TV crew came to my house and while I was being interviewed about my novels, Jessica and I prepared strawberry dumplings, a dessert that my mother used to make quite often; it was my brother Jason's favorite. It's safe to say that no fire extinguishers were harmed while making this short clip, which aired on television and was posted on CityTV's website for a while. (laughs)

The strawberry dumplings turned out divinely and the cameraman and host settled into a bowl once we were done filming.

Betty Dravis: I don't consider that crazy at all, Cheryl; it's part of the fun of being an author and another great way to get noticed. Besides, TV seems a natural for someone with your outgoing personality; you're definitely not known to be shy. (laughs)

I hear you have other claims to fame–besides being a respected author and a "Celebrity Chef." You've also done a little acting along the way; no stranger to cameras and directors calling---Action!

Cheryl Kaye Tardif: You caught me, Betty. (laughs) While I'd love to say that I'm really an A-list actress hiding behind a pen name, I can't. However, I did work as a background actor in Vancouver for a year. My agent was Ralph Streich with *Local Color* and he got me work on two hit TV shows (in the '90s). During filming of *The Commish,* a popular crime series that starred Michael Chiklis, I was fortunate to meet the lead actor, though I'm sure he doesn't remember. I think when I was introduced to him, they thought I was one of the other major actors. At the same time, I also met one of my producer/author idols, Stephen J. Cannell.

The other TV series I worked on was *The Heights*, produced by Aaron Spelling. That show came out around the same time as the original and very popular *Melrose Place*. In one episode I played a female escort to an older man. At least that's what I told my background actor partner. We were having dinner and champagne in a lounge, while a terrible singer performed. I think that was my first "role." I recall another episode where two of the stars sat on a bench. One was eating a hot dog and every time we did a new take, they gave studies of Canadian authors.

He didn't look too good after the tenth or so take. (laughs)

I guess I should confess that I was also a contestant in a wacky TV game show called *A Total Write-Off!* In my segment I was paired with another writer and a ventriloquist. (Yeah, a real dummy! lol)

We had to write a short story based on cues from the host, actress and comedian Barbara North, and from the live audience. *A Total Write-Off* was produced by Panacea Entertainment and aired across Canada, including *Book Television.* Sadly, my team lost, but it was a crazy, exciting moment I'll never forget.

Betty Dravis: Way to go, Cheryl! I admire your versatility and acting sounds like great fun. In fact, the more life experiences authors have, the more "rounded" we are, in my opinion. Who knows when some of what you learned from acting will work its way into one of your novels?

As a writer who writes mainly suspense–*The River, Divine Intervention* and your YA novel *Whale Song*–you've explored death, murder, conspiracies, stem cell research, psychics, serial arsonists, native lore, assisted suicide, racism, bullying and more. Cheryl, I also know you've crossed over to the dark and steamy side of romance, and that you have a new pen name. Tell us about Cherish D'Angelo.

Cheryl Kaye Tardif: You're right, Betty. Cheryl Kaye Tardif writes suspense thrillers, horror, and YA. Cherish D'Angelo is my alter-ego and she gets to delve into the world of romance, love, lust and danger. I just can't seem to write a novel without killing someone off, so when I decided to venture into writing romance, I felt it had to be romantic suspense. Cherish writes books *with* passion and *about* passion. *These ain't your Gramma's romance novels.* (laughs) While I don't write erotica, some scenes Cherish writes may be more explicit. This is one of the main reasons why I wanted to separate her writing from Cheryl's. I don't want my young *Whale Song* fans reading my romance novels–not until they're mature enough to handle the language.

Betty Dravis: Well, Cherish, (laughs) I may be your old-fashioned grandmotherly type because I don't enjoy erotica at all…but to each his own. I have read portions of one of Cherish's books, however, and after I skipped through the in-depth romantic description, I truly enjoyed your story. It kept me turning pages as fast as I could. But for many reasons, I think it's wise of you to use a pseudonym. But *that* aside, how did you pick your pseudonym?

Cheryl Kaye Tardif: I wanted a name that meant something. Cheryl, my real name, means beloved, dear one. So does Cherish… D'Angelo came to me when I was trying to find a last name that also meant something to me. I collect angels so that was an easy choice. Put them together and Cherish D'Angelo means "cherished one of the angels." Mostly, I think it looks awesome in a flowery, romantic-looking font.

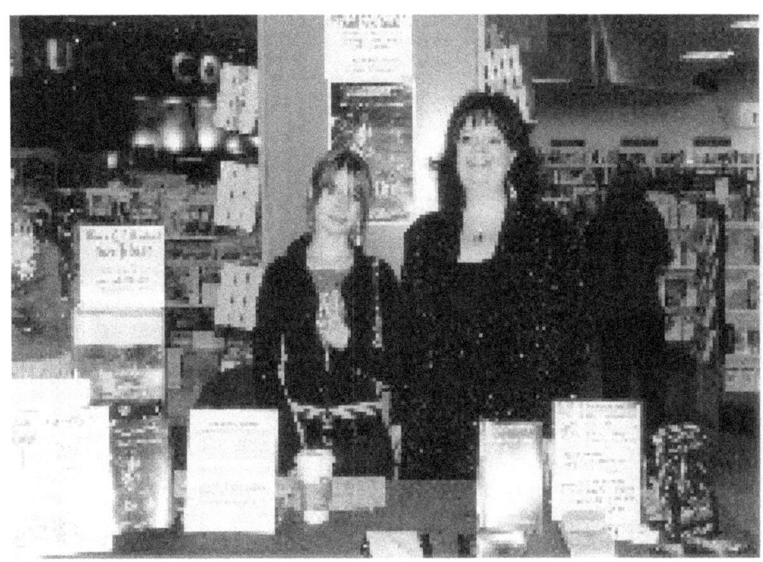

Cheryl at *Divine Intervention* book launch with daughter Jessica

Betty Dravis: I think that name is perfect for your pseudonym, Cheryl. In addition to having special meaning to you, it's a lovely name that conjures up an image of a beautiful, sexy woman.

You might get a laugh from this: I once did a skit with a friend who speaks French. We chose names and I chose Chou Chou LaRue off the top of my head. I thought it was "cute" and it sounded like a can-can dancer to me. Later I looked it up and learned that *chou* had two meanings: cabbage and darling (or pet). I prefer the "darling," of course. And *LaRue* in French is "the street" or "the red-haired one." Go figure...but guess which one I preferred. (laughs)

But getting back to Cherish D'Angelo, what works has she written?

Cheryl Kaye Tardif: I'm happy to talk about Cherish, Chou Chou, you darling red cabbage. (laughs) Cherish D'Angelo is the proud author of her first novel, a romantic suspense titled *Lancelot's Lady.* This novel first started as a contest entry in the Dorchester Next Best Celler contest that was hosted on Textnovel.com back in 2009. *Lancelot's Lady* made it to the semi-finals.

Not only was it a semi-finalist, it was voted by readers as the #1 Most Popular entry for the first three months of the contest and the #3 Most Popular for the remaining three months. Though it didn't make the finals, *Lancelot's Lady* went on to win a 2010 Editor's Choice award from literary agent and CEO of Textnovel, Stan Soper, before its publication and release as an eBook in late September 2010. Cherish is working on another romance novel.

Cherish's catch-phrase is *Cherish the romance.*

Betty Dravis: Great catch-phrase, Cheryl, but you're very creative with those. You use another one I like in describing the promotional side of this book business. You call yourself "shameless book promoter." I love it! Aren't we all…in this day and age? (laughs)

But since I've read parts of *Lancelot's Lady* and like the storyline so well, I hope you'll give a brief description of that romantic suspense.

Cheryl Kaye Tardif: I'd love to, Betty. *Lancelot's Lady* is a contemporary romantic suspense set in Florida and the Bahamas. Here's my tagline:

A Bahamas holiday from dying billionaire JT Lance, a man with a dark secret, leads palliative nurse Rhianna McLellan to Jonathan, a man with his own troubled past, and Rhianna finds herself drawn to the handsome recluse, while unbeknownst to her, someone with a horrific plan is hunting her down.

Lancelot's Lady is available in the Kindle Store, KoboBooks.com and Smashwords.com. It should also be available through various apps on the iPhone and iPad.

Betty Dravis: Simply hearing you describe *Lancelot's Lady* brings back the story to me and I'm happy to tell our readers that Cherish may write in a different genre, but her work is just as intriguing as Cheryl Kaye Tardif's.

Cheryl, I mentioned how great you are with taglines and promotion above, so this is a good place to tell about your career in advertising and promotion. How did you learn how to successfully promote yourself?

Cheryl Kaye Tardif: Betty, though I'd love to say I've always been a writer and found success easily, I can't. From the time I left home and studied hairstyling to just before I published my first novel, I worked in fields that required me to learn how to market and advertise myself and my other business endeavors. It wasn't always easy. In fact, my desire to become a published author was put on hold for many years after facing rejection after rejection, and this led me to try other things.

Years later, I analyzed my careers and realized that in every one of them I had to sell or promote something. I went from hairstyling apprenticeship and owning my own salon (I was the youngest salon owner in BC at the time) to leading hundreds of people weekly as a motivational speaker for an international company; from there to managing a telemarketing division for a home security company. Then I ran a private home daycare, developed and published a childcare directory, sold Pampered Chef tools…and other jobs in between. In each career I found ways to write something and my creative and entrepreneurial spirit helped me with advertising and marketing in these fields. It was this experience that I brought to the table when I was finally ready to delve into my dream to become a published novelist.

Betty Dravis: All of your experiences not only have made you a better writer, Cheryl, they have also made you more proficient at "selling yourself." You now help other authors with your "book marketing coach" business. I would appreciate your sharing a bit of that and your marketing website link.

Cheryl Kaye Tardif: While marketing my own books, I discovered that some methods work better than others. Some are less expensive. Some are more fun, while other marketing approaches are grueling. As with everything I ever tackle, I instinctively analyze what works and what doesn't, what is time efficient and what's a time suck, and cost versus value. Most published authors will tell you it's the marketing that is the hard part. Not everyone has the knowledge or talent, but marketing techniques can be learned.

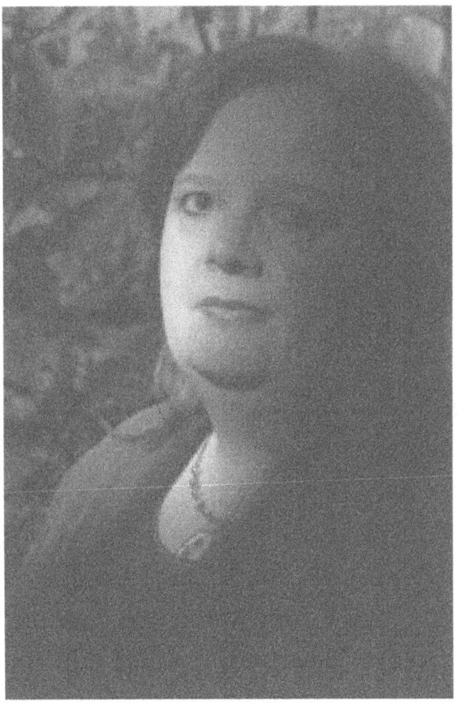

Shadow portrait of Cheryl; appropriate for a mystery writer

Over the past seven years, I've been helping my fellow authors by writing articles that teach them select promotional strategies. My nickname in the book industry is "Shameless Promoter," though I've also been called a "marketing whiz" and "guru." I don't really consider myself a "whiz" or a "guru," though. I just love sharing what I've learned in my journey–and what I'm still learning. I've had emails from writers who have used my techniques and become successful as a result. This led me to branch out last year as a book marketing coach. While I gave away my methods years ago and still do at times, I've realized that many authors need a more personal approach and want a marketing plan that will work specifically for them. The only way I could justify spending the time and effort in helping them to this degree was to charge for it.

With me as your book marketing coach, you get a business partner of sorts, a cheerleader and, hopefully, a friend who is very interested in your success. I am so pleased when a client reports they followed my strategies and something wonderful happened as a result–whether they get more sales, more traffic to their sites, more hits on their blogs, or more interested agents or publishers. Clients can run their own ideas past me, too, and many times I can help them iron out the details or get organized. Four of my most popular coaching topics are creating an Internet identity, agent/publisher queries, virtual book or blog tours, and sponsorships. Clients also ask me how to handle pitching to agents/publishers at writers' conferences, physical book tours, promotional items and web design or creation.

You can learn more about what I do as a book marketing coach by checking my Shameless Book Promoter site in the Internet. Be sure to check out my prices as I often have specials on. While there, take time to read endorsements by satisfied authors who have benefitted from my experiences.

Betty Dravis: Cheryl, I hope I haven't kept you too long, but I assure you, I'm almost finished. Just a few more questions, if you don't mind… I always ask celebrities I interview who their mentors are and if they could spend an entire day with any person in the world (living or dead) who would they choose. It will be fun hearing your response to those questions.

Cheryl Kaye Tardif: First, I have to thank you for even considering me a celebrity. (laughs) It's not something I'm really used to. I have a few mentors. Stephen King is my author idol and I guess you could call him a mentor, even if he doesn't know it. Through reading about "The King" and his career, I have learned so much about writing and marketing. His book *On Writing* is in the drawer beside my bed, and at one point I owned every Stephen King novel, including his Bachman books.

As a teen, I knew I wanted to be just like him, which was why my first two novels were suspense/horror. I would give anything to spend a week with him, follow him around, see what he does during the day, watch how he writes–basically be his stalker for the week. I'd need a week because I'd have to decompress after each day so as not to wake up screaming in the middle of the night. I am positive he would scare me…

Ironically, I almost had lunch with him a couple of years ago. I was invited to be a guest speaker and panelist for a writers' conference in Valley Forge and they were hoping to have Stephen King as the keynote speaker. They'd arranged a special lunch and I was one of the honored few invited to it. To my dismay, he couldn't make the conference.

My other author idol is Gail Bowen. She's a Canadian crime novelist with a series of books featuring Joanne Kilbourn. Gail is one of the most gracious authors I know and she's helped me in many ways, including critiquing some of my work and providing a wonderful review blurb for *Lancelot's Lady* (it's on the front cover). I am inspired by her journey as a writer, by her commitment to a series and set of characters and because her books were made into TV movies starring Wendy Crewson and Victor Garber.

I would love to spend an entire weekend with her…by a lake, sipping tea and chatting about who dies next in our books.

One of my other mentors is Jerry D. Simmons. Jerry worked for Warner books for about twenty-five years. When he left, he was the VP, Director Field Sales and he has seen both the publishing and self-publishing sides of our industry.

Because of his unique experiences, he shares his knowledge with writers of all genres at his site WritersReaders.com. I admire him so much and had the great fortune to meet him (at that same Valley Forge conference).

Since then, he has become my greatest mentor in all things

publishing and marketing. He has given me fantastic advice on many areas of my career and has been extremely supportive. I've written articles for his newsletter many times. Jerry now offers another option to writers–the option to self-publish as an independent author yet still have distribution similar to what traditional publishers offer. His company, Indi Publishing Group, offers many services to writers.

Betty Dravis: As to what constitutes a celebrity, I and Chase Von, my co-author on the *Dream Reachers* series, think that anyone who achieves a dream–whether large or small–is a celebrity.

You, Cheryl, have dreamed big, worked hard and definitely are a celebrity, in our book (pun intended). (laughs) In fact, every life is a celebration…or it should be.

As for your mentors, I think King is every author's idol, but Gail Bowen and Jerry Simmons are great role models too. I've been in contact with Jerry Simmons and he is, indeed, all you say; that man has it all together.

Before finishing, I'd like to mention one more honor you've received: you were nominated for the Lieutenant Governor of Alberta Arts Award in 2004. That's quite an honor; belated congratulations on that and all your successes.

Cheryl Kaye Tardif: Thank you, Betty. Though I didn't win, being nominated for the 2004 Lieutenant Governor of Alberta Arts Award was such a huge honor. I was nominated by a fan who had read *Whale Song* (2003) and *Divine Intervention*

(2004). Before the nomination I hadn't even heard of the award and I was so surprised when I got the notification of nomination.

I have never forgotten that fan. She made me believe that I had talent and a gift, and it kept me strong in my motto: "Dare to Dream…and Dream BIG!"

It's reviews like this that give me confidence, also: "Tardif, already a big hit in Canada…a name to reckon with south of the border." – BOOKLIST

As a child I had a big dream. I wanted to be a published author and to write stories that people would remember. As a teen and in my early twenties, I attempted to start on that path, but hit so many roadblocks that I thought my dream would never happen. Instead, *life* happened. And that's exactly what I needed. With life came experiences that only served to deepen my writing and marketing abilities. Throughout this, I kept my eye on my main dream. Then in 2003, I made that dream happen and *Whale Song* was born.

I'm very fortunate to be able to do what I most love, what my heart has always yearned to do.

Dr. Seuss, move over! Cheryl Kaye Tardif and Cherish D'Angelo are in town, and they don't plan on leaving… lol

Betty Dravis: What feisty ladies you are, Cheryl and Cherish! (laughs) So to help you along, I'd like to let everyone know they can find all your fascinating websites by Googling your name on the Internet.

This is your last chance to share anything else you'd like to mention that we might have missed. I would also enjoy hearing about your current WIPs (works in progress).

Cheryl Kaye Tardif: I have so many WIPs that I sometimes wish I could clone myself, though I'm sure my husband would say something like: "One of you is quite enough." (laughs) I never run out of ideas and he's so used to me telling him about my newest plot idea. Currently, I am working on *Submerged,* a thriller that explores drug addiction and redemption. I am especially excited about *Submerged* because it has a cool tie-in to a thriller my agent is pitching right now to publishers. In *Children of the Fog* there is a secondary character and a main setting that overlaps in *Submerged*, though the two novels are complete stand-alones and unrelated other than this. I am so intrigued by the main character in *Submerged;* he's based on a high school friend who went through a similar battle with drug addiction. My friend Mike has been an awesome source for research purposes. In many ways, *Submerged* is *his* story.

I'm also working on a YA novel titled *Finding Bliss*. It will definitely resonate with *Whale Song* fans, and I believe schools will be especially interested in it for novel studies. I have no idea when either of these works will be published.

Betty Dravis: They all sound intriguing and we wish you as much success with them as you've had with your other novels.

Well that's a wrap, Cheryl… Once again, thanks for sharing your interesting life and all about your books with us today. In closing, I'd like to also share with our readers something I wrote long ago in my review of your novel *Whale Song:* "One doesn't simply read a Tardif story, one experiences it!" I mean that, Cheryl, and I wish for our readers to have the same delightful experience. You are a master wordsmith.

Cheryl Kaye Tardif: Thank you so much, Betty. *You are a doll!* Your quote above expresses my deepest desire for my readers, that they "experience" my stories, hopefully in ways that move them emotionally. I've enjoyed your questions and as always, I'm in awe of your own exciting life story. Thank you for allowing me to share mine. I wish you huge success with *Dream Reachers: Vol. II.* I am so honored to be featured in it, and I wish you the very best in all your endeavors. *Dare to Dream…and Dream Big!*

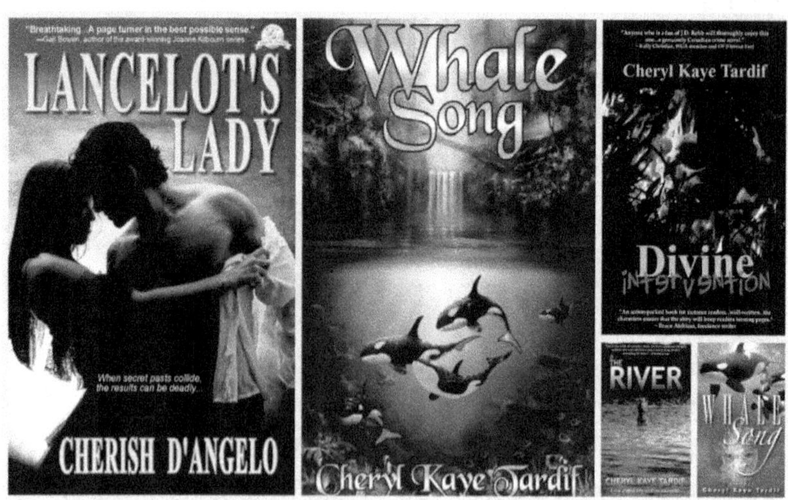

Interview with Marissa Autumn

GORGEOUS, MULTI-TALENTED ACTRESS/SINGER/DANCER

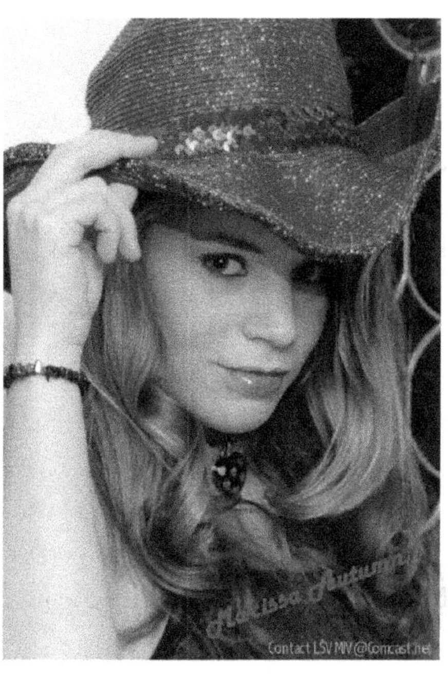

Betty Dravis: Welcome to Dames of Dialogue, Marissa. Chase Von, my co-author of the *Dream Reachers* series, saw you on NextCat and sent you my way. After viewing your videos, reading your resume and seeing your outstanding pictorial portfolio, I'm astonished at all you have done. You not only sing, dance, model and play several instruments, but you've also been in movies and on TV. It blows my mind to know you do all that while attending college on a scholarship.

Since you're only nineteen years old, I'm curious to know what age you were when you started performing? Can you tell us a little about your childhood and why your mom named you Autumn?

Marissa Autumn: I started at age three doing a dance commercial for the preschool I attended. I also sang in church at that age; I was an angel. At the age of nine, I did a commercial for the clean waters of Canada and was given free camping tickets for their parks…and clothes saying Canada on them. The principal of my middle school told me I was a great performer and had me perform in every event that took place at the school. That sparked my interest and it was so much fun, I just kept on. By the age of thirteen, I was singing at fairs and performing in plays throughout the state of Michigan. At the age of fourteen, I won a ten-thousand-dollar scholarship for performing a concert at the local fair. It was not a contest; someone in the crowd took an interest and chose me. I was sent to Pittsburgh to train with a famous choreographer from California so I could be in an MTV video with J. Lo (Jennifer Lopez).

It was a hurry-up affair: They called my mother and said they had a scholarship for me, but I had to take it by Wednesday. It was in March and my school was having soccer tryouts. I love soccer, but I chose the scholarship and went to Pittsburgh. It was so exciting. One performance led to another and at sixteen, I did the Super Bowl XL in Detroit and was starting to perform Country/Rock/ Pop concerts in Michigan, Ohio, West Virginia and Iowa.

My modeling career also took off at age fifteen. I started modeling for Nordstrom's with the girls from the movie *Mean Girls* and went on to be the "Gap Girl." I made arrangements to do a concert for Hurricane Katrina victims, raising $ 20,000 the first hour. I don't know what the final total was, but was told a lot of money was donated. It was an awesome feeling to know I was helping others.

All the time I was doing this, I also played on a traveling soccer team; performed in the high school band (I play the flute, piano and saxophone); served as varsity cheerleader; and was on the school dance team. I was in the school band for nine years, starting in fourth grade. I was also an honor student, but truthfully, I could not have done any of it without my family's encouragement and my mom driving me all over the place.

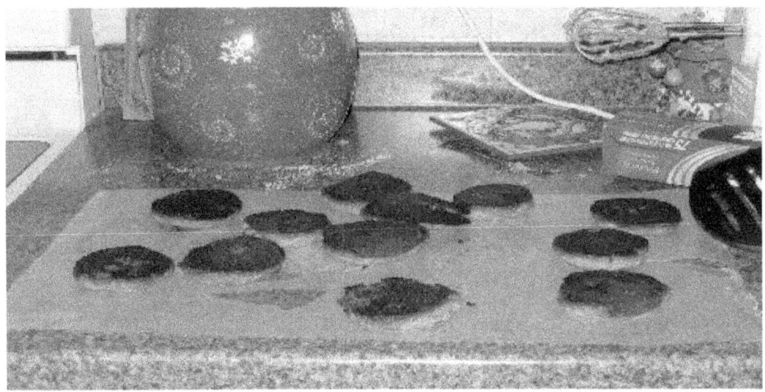

On the domestic front, I also was trained by my mother to make floral arrangements. That is something she does, so she was pleased when I won all kinds of blue ribbons at the local and state fairs and from Women's National Farm and Garden shows for on-the-spot floral arrangements. But I can NOT make brownies to save me…or cookies. LOL…

My mom said she kept me very busy so I would not have a lot of time to think about the fact that I was adopted. It worked! I was adopted at the age of five weeks and when my adopted mother saw me all she could see was my hair. It had so many different colors of gold, yellow, brown and red that she said she had to put Autumn in my name because my hair looked like autumn leaves piled on top of my tiny head.

Betty Dravis: I see what she meant, Marissa. Your hair is gorgeous. But my mouth is hanging open… I read about some of your accomplishments, but never knew the full extent. Thanks for telling us more. You are amazing! Would you share a little about your college life and how you manage to do so much. What is a typical day like for you?

Marissa Autumn: Well, Betty, today is one of the days I am working in *Red Dawn.* Filming starts at seven-thirty p.m. I got up early, ate breakfast and hurried to get to college by eight; came home for lunch at one; went to work at one-thirty (internship with veterinarian starts at two). Then I went home at five, ate a very quick dinner, dashed to change clothes, put curlers in my hair. By five-fifteen, I was putting makeup on in the car, while mom raced me to the film location. I also studied in the car. I'll spend all night there making the movie, studying between takes. Then Mom will pick me up at seven in the morning and drive through Wendy's for breakfast, then race to get me to college which is about an hour away from where the movie is being filmed. Then another day will start all over again.

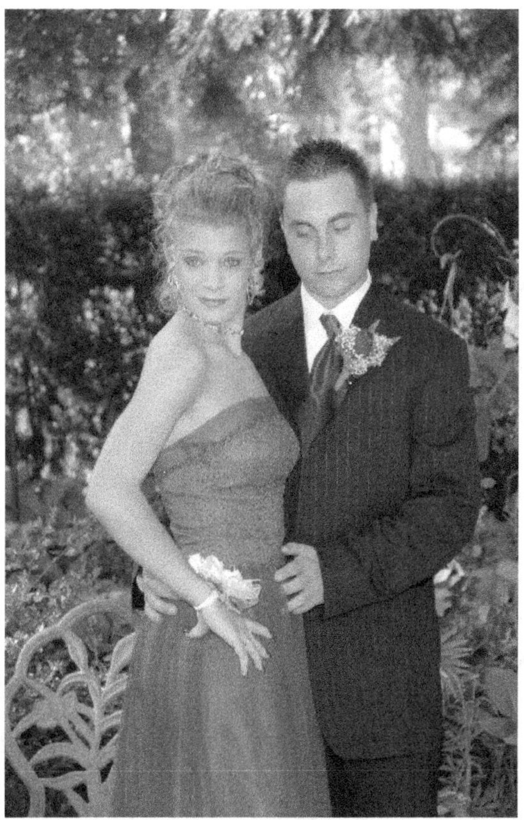

Marissa and Kyle

Betty Dravis: Yikes, Marissa, it makes me tired just hearing about it. It's a good thing they don't film every day or you would never get any rest. With your busy schedule, this may seem like a silly question, but you're a vibrant, active young woman and at your age you must date some. Do you have a steady boyfriend, if they still call it that in the new millennium? If so, how does he feel about you keeping so busy?

Marissa Autumn: I did date a young man for five years, but decided I wanted to date other guys to make sure what I really want, so I broke up with Kyle. Plus, I wanted to do my own thing. I am too young to settle for one person at this time of my life. Kyle still comes to all my performances and some of my rehearsals. We are good friends, but I am now dating a few different guys.

Betty Dravis: That seems sensible at this time, Marissa, and I'm glad you and Kyle are still friends. Now since you do so much, can you narrow it down to three things in your life that you couldn't live without? And since you sing, what song do you find yourself singing most often in the shower?

Marissa Autumn: The three things I want most in life are: To meet my real parents someday, a very good education (seven to eight years of college) and to have the lead role in a big-screen movie that would feature all my talents: acting, singing, dancing, etc. When I am doing anything—acting, singing or playing a sport–I am performing and I want to be the best at it! If that means more training, then I am ready to do it. There is one other thing I love doing and that is helping others. From the time that I can remember, I have been helping other children in need by doing concerts to help raise money for them. One of my favorites is the Festival of Trees for Children's Hospital. I started very young in helping them…and the USA soldiers is another group I perform for.

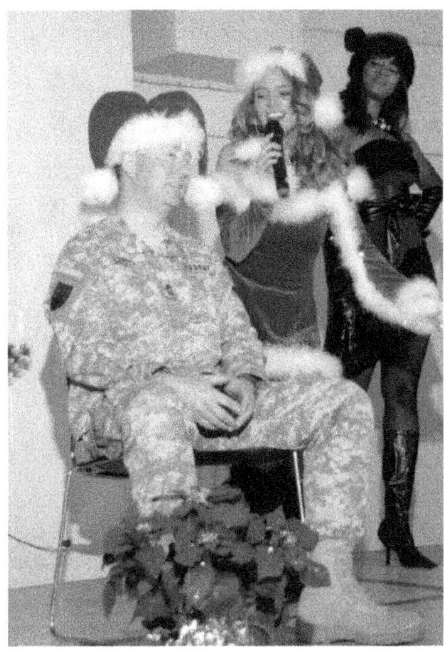

I don't sing a lot in the shower… LOL. But on-stage I love doing pop music, but the crowds enjoy it a lot when I do country too. Gerald Dodson, who is a USA security officer in Washington D.C. from the White House, and Rick Young, a music teacher who owns Talent Live Studio in Michigan, are the ones who wrote my original songs: *The Girl, Take Me,* (pop) and *Whirlwind* (country). *The Girl* is my favorite and I'm hoping someday they may want to use it in a movie. Gerry and Rick have another song, *Making Love in the Rain,* for me to record in the future.

Betty Dravis: You certainly have a lot of people encouraging you in your career, Marissa. You are very lucky! From your website, I see that modeling is also a big part of your life. You are a stunning beauty, so I can see why. You have done runway and print modeling for so many big names that I couldn't possibly list them all here. Among them are: Katerina Bocci's Bridal Show and her private showings, Dior Cosmetics, St. Pucci, Macys, Saks, Nordstrom's, Gap, MGM, *Hour Magazine* and you were chosen to model at *Renu Magazine*'s launch party. It must have been fun to combine your talent for singing in some of the larger shows. Since everyone thinks of models as being perfect, can you bring that "down to earth" for us by relating a runway mishap or a funny incident that happened during any of your modeling assignments?

Marissa Autumn: There are two times that come to mind. One was when I modeled the fabulous $40,000 red gown by Katerina Bocci. Just as I was ready to step onto the runway someone hit my shoulder causing me to fall. The other embarrassing time was when I modeled and sang at MGM for the grand opening of *Renu Magazine*. You had to be twenty-one to walk through the casino to get to the event room where I was to perform and model. I had to use my sister's ID to get in the place. Since she is blonde, a little older and larger than me, I told the security guard that I lost weight, had plastic surgery and dyed my hair. I don't know if he believed me, but he let me in. But some mean-spirited person called, saying there was an eighteen-year-old modeling, so before the show started they did another security check. I hid in the bathroom, but they asked everyone to come out and show ID again. Fortunately, the same security guard was there; he looked at me and said, "She's okay! She's over twenty-one. She just had a lot of plastic surgery!" I was so relieved to be able to perform that night! I got a laugh from that because that nice guard had no idea how ironic his remark was: The grand opening was put on by a well-known plastic surgeon, Michael Gray.

Betty Dravis: That's a funny story, Marissa. I notice on your resume it states that you are open to roles from fifteen to thirty. I was taken aback when I first saw the age thirty limit; I can't imagine you looking thirty. But now that I've seen the sophisticated shot of you in that red gown with the extremely chic, more grown-up hairdo, I believe it. Now getting back to your acting, I'm intrigued by the photo of you with the famous singer/actor Billy Ray Cyrus. How did you meet him and where was that picture taken?

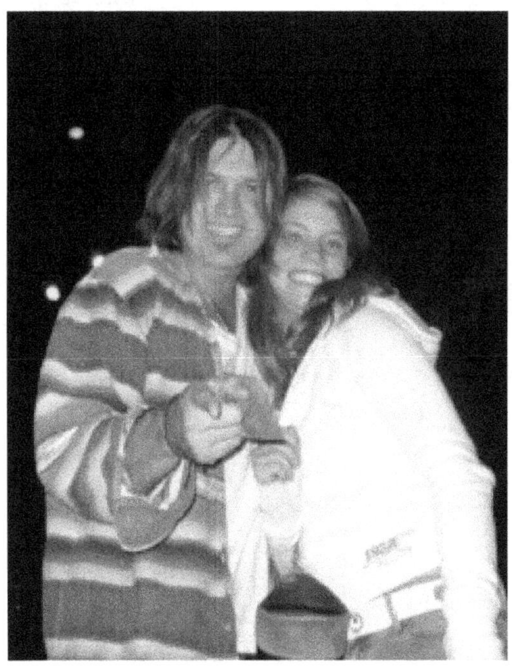

Marissa with singer/actor Billy Ray Cyrus

Marissa Autumn: I met him about two years ago…just before we did a concert in Canton, Michigan. He is a very nice man and compared me to his daughter at the time. I was happy to perform the last song with him; he was a lot of fun to work with.

Betty Dravis: Speaking of actors, there's another photo of you with comic actor Rob Schneider who got his start on *Saturday Night Live*. I've been a fan since his 1999 movie *Deuce Bigalow: Male Gigolo* and its 2005 sequel *Deuce Bigalow: European Gigolo.* He's a riot! It was cool to see him on Jay Leno's show recently. You told me that you played the part of a college student in one of his films, *American Virgin*; I'm wondering if you played a friend of the main female lead Priscilla, played by actress Jenna Dewan? What was it like working with Dewan and Schneider? Is he as funny off-screen as he is on?

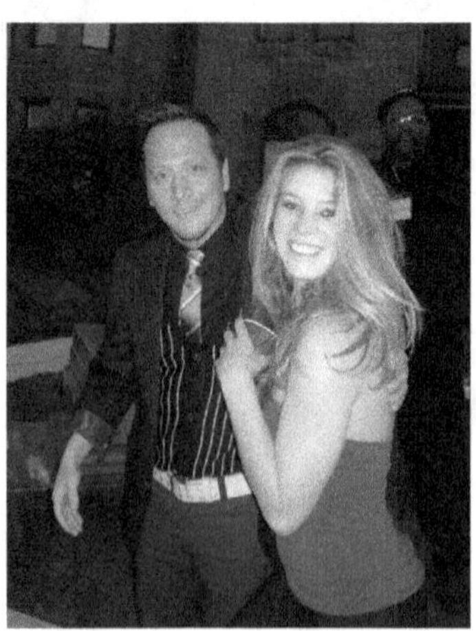

Marissa with comic actor Rob Schneider

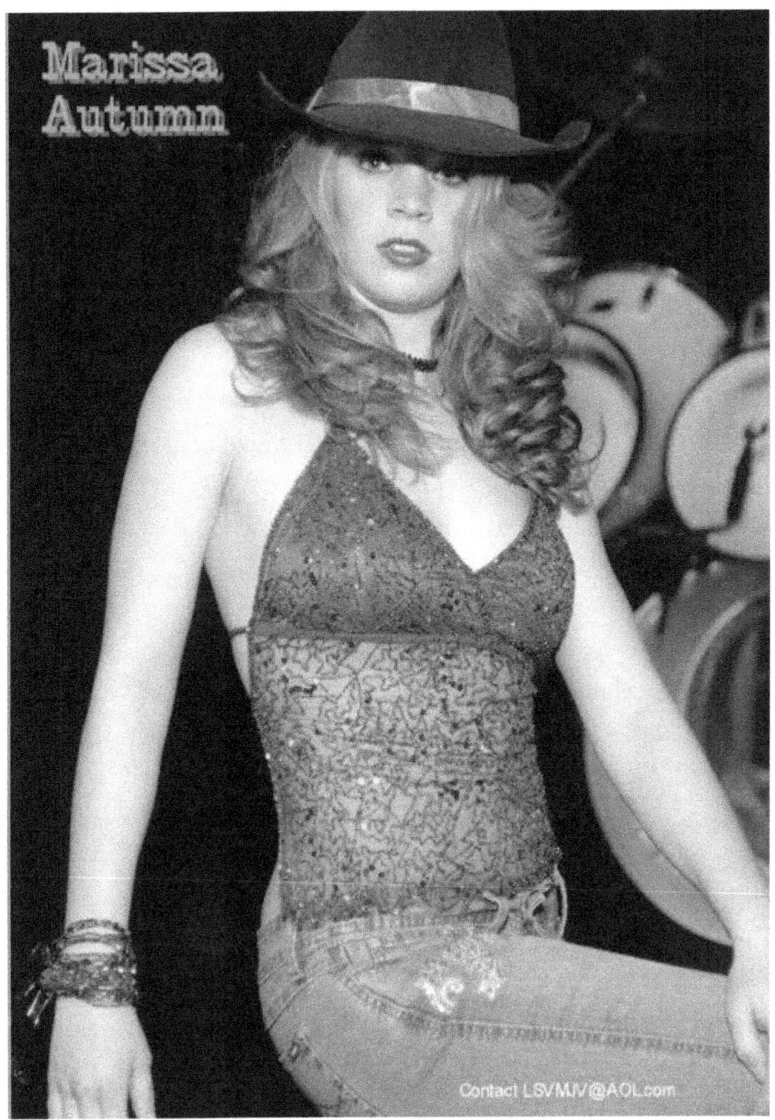

Marissa Autumn: Yes, I played a friend of hers at the pretend college which was filmed in Greek Town, Detroit. We attended a lot of the same parties throughout the movie and we were doing what most college kids do: partying, drinking, dancing…and some were having pretend sex in the movie. *Not me, though!* Dewan was very quiet on and off the set, but Rob is a lot of fun. In one part of the movie he is just about all naked. This movie was a lot of fun to be in.

While waiting for the set to get ready, Rob and I would sometimes sing together.

Betty Dravis: An interesting bit of trivia I learned during research for this interview is that *American Virgin* started shooting in New Orleans with the title of *Virgin on Bourbon Street,* later changing to *American Virgin* when they decided to shoot it in Michigan.

I understand you have been in two big-screen movies, two HBO films, had a part in a Jennifer Lopez MTV video, and performed a concert at Detroit's Super Bowl XL party at Somerset Collection. How do you handle such early success? And since you share some of the attributes of Jennifer Lopez, is she one of your role models? Did you learn anything from her while working on the MTV? If so, I'm sure our readers would enjoy hearing all about it.

Marissa Autumn: I am so busy I don't have time to think about that stuff. I am usually studying or going from place to place. Yes, J. Lo was very interesting…and really pretty. At that age (fifteen), I was very impressed with everything she did. I remember her telling me to get used to learning a whole new dance in one day or even overnight. While in Pittsburgh, I had to practice dancing from seven a.m. until eleven at night. It was a long day… I was taught by a choreographer in Pittsburgh that had been flown in from California just for this video. J. Lo was right; I had to learn some new dance moves--and learn them fast!

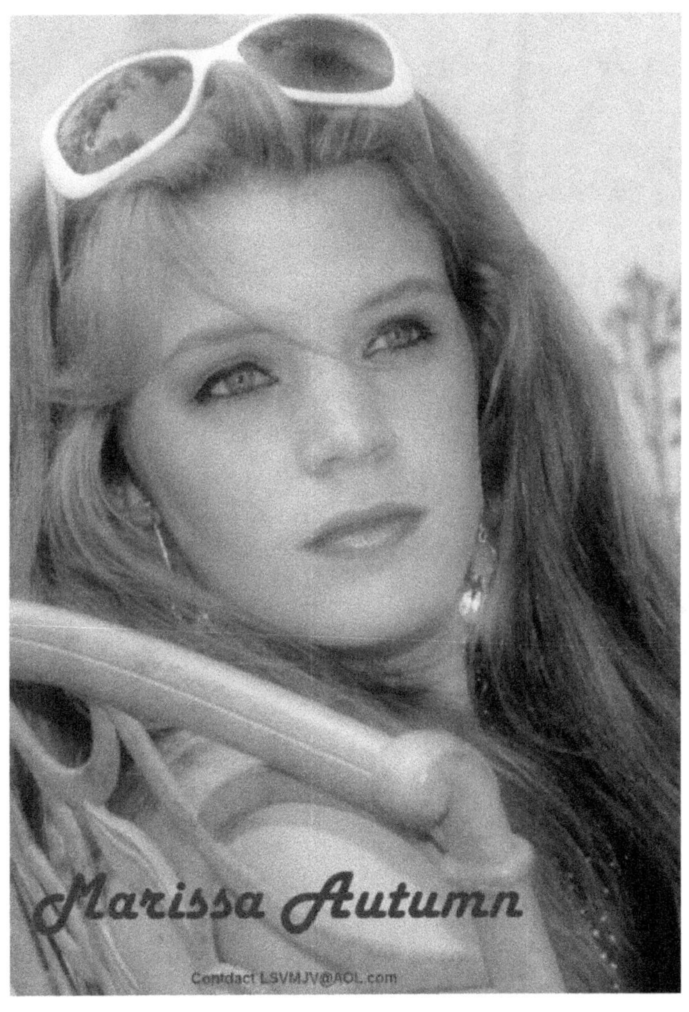

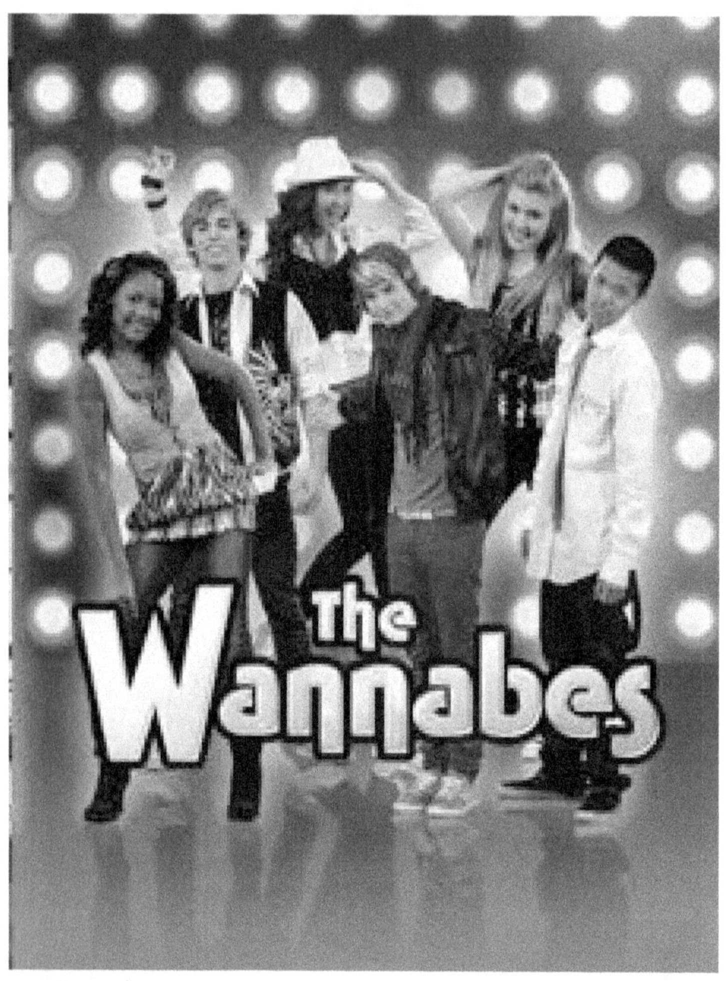

Betty Dravis: Most of your parts have been small parts so far—from college students to aggressive shoppers—but you said above one of your goals is to have a lead role that showcases all your talents. Please share your life's ambition and some advice for those who wish to be in the entertainment industry.

Marissa Autumn: Yes, I want the *lead* role in the movies, but I still want to do my singing and dancing too. I think that an entertainer should be able to do all three and do them well if trained the right way. I have watched many movies where the actor is acting, singing and dancing. I am going to college year around hoping to get my degree in a shorter time so I can spend more time acting. By the age of twenty-one, I will have completed my four years of college with honors. By that time I hope to have been in a number of different movies, also.

Betty Dravis: I admire your determination and ambition, Marissa. That's great advice and smart thinking. It's always good to have a back-up plan. Being a veterinarian, to me, would be an exciting, rewarding career choice too. Perhaps someday you can combine the two. Do you have a current mentor? If so, tell us about him or her and about others who have influenced your life…your career.

Marissa Autumn: I love acting, but want to make sure I have a good backup. Just in case the acting doesn't make it all the way, I could be a veterinarian…but now I'm doing both and having a lot of fun. My mentor in my life was my principal in middle school Mrs. Jo Kwasny.

She saw me perform at the school talent show and told me I have to be an actor. She said that when I performed her eyes were always on me, like the other kids were not on the stage, even though they were. She encouraged me to act, sing and to get good grades. I can't thank her enough.

Betty Dravis: Regarding your music, you have a lovely, natural voice and the best way to describe your vibrant stage presence is to say you have tremendous sex appeal and you "glow."

I've seen some of your videos and you are just as appealing singing pop as you are doing country and rock. I read that you've been compared to LeAnn Rimes, Carrie Underwood and even Shakira. That takes me back to when I interviewed country/western superstar Tanya Tucker when she was only fourteen. At the time she was being compared to Brenda Lee who also got a young start. I hope your being compared to these big names is a good omen for your bright future, also.

Your versatility is awesome and you certainly get your audience revved up and wanting more. During each performance you appear to be having the time of your life. Is it as much fun as it appears? And how does it feel being compared to those famous entertainers?

Marissa Autumn: Yes, it is a lot of fun. And it feels great! At first it was a little scary because some people were chasing me, taking pictures and shouting my name and all I wanted to do was make it to the bathroom before I had to do my concert. It really feels good when the whole crowd shouts my name when I walk on stage to do a concert. I love it! And to be compared to some of the performers who have won so many awards is awesome… To win the same awards as those top entertainers is something I dream of.

Betty Dravis: Since this interview will come out around Christmas, I'm accompanying this story with a photo or two from your Christmas concert last year when you entertained some of our U.S. soldiers. You told me earlier that show "was a story in itself." What did you mean by that? Also, where was this performance and do you have one lined up for this Christmas?

Marissa Autumn: Yes, I am working on doing a holiday concert for the soldiers this year in Michigan. I make the concerts as much fun as possible by having the soldiers put their names on pieces of paper and put the papers in a basket. I have a number of different business donations–CDs, video games, phones, games, gift cards–and other items for them.

After my concert, I pull from the basket and give every soldier a present. At one of the concerts last year, I had them video one of the soldiers and me for YouTube. After the video was out for about two months, I got an email asking me to remove the video from YouTube because I was way too sexy to be with the old man in the video. Here is a picture of the "old man" and me. He's far from being old; a nice-looking young soldier… Aren't people funny? LOL

Betty Dravis: That is odd, Marissa, but they were probably being overly protective of you because you're so young. But you are so fascinating, I'm getting carried away too. We mentioned two of your big screen movies above, but I understand you are also in one that was just released in

November: *What's wrong with Virginia?* It stars Ed Harris,

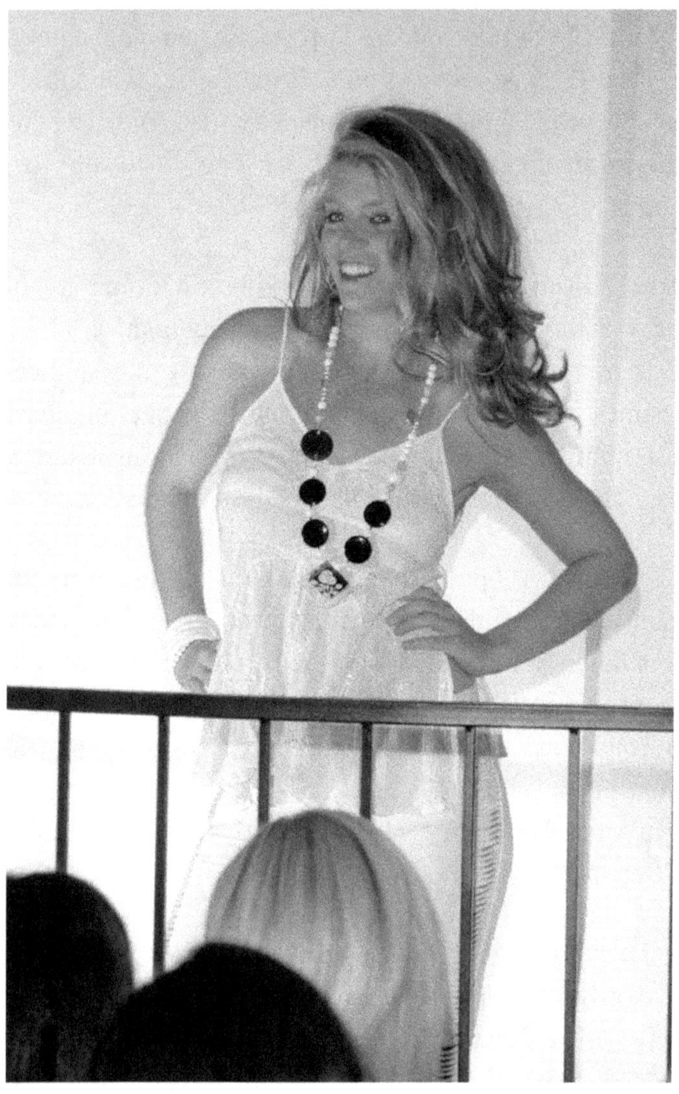

who happens to be one of my favorite actors, and Jennifer Connelly. Please tell us about your role in this movie and whether you had any personal interaction with Harris or Connelly. Can you tell us a little about your on-set interactions with them?

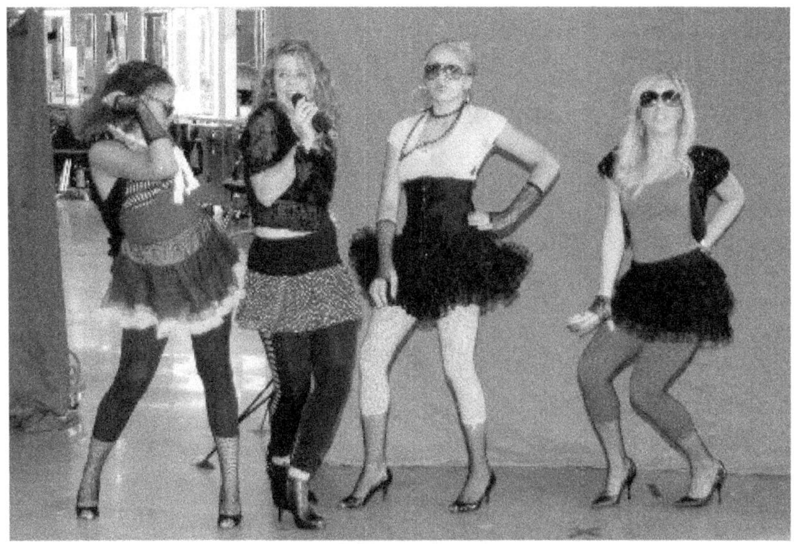

Marissa Autumn: It was a very exciting movie to be in, Betty, because it has a lot of twists and turns. I played a young lady in the town. The place where the film was being shot was two-and-a-half hours from my house so that time I had to stay in the city. Because of that I was there when we were finished for the day of filming and was able to have dinner with them at times.

That was fun. Ed and Jennifer were both very nice to me, and Jennifer said she liked the different colors in my hair. I get that a lot…

Betty Dravis: I bet it was fun, Marissa. I'm not as familiar with Jennifer Connelly, but I agree with her about your hair being absolutely magnificent. And Ed Harris is one of my all-time favorite actors. I wish I could have joined you; that would have been a blast.

Well, that ties up the interview, young lady. You certainly have an exciting life, and I've enjoyed our time together. I doubt if you'll end up as a veterinarian with such a great start in the entertainment industry, but like I said above: both choices are ideal careers and you're smart to have a back-up. Thanks for sharing yourself with the Dames of Dialogue and our readers.

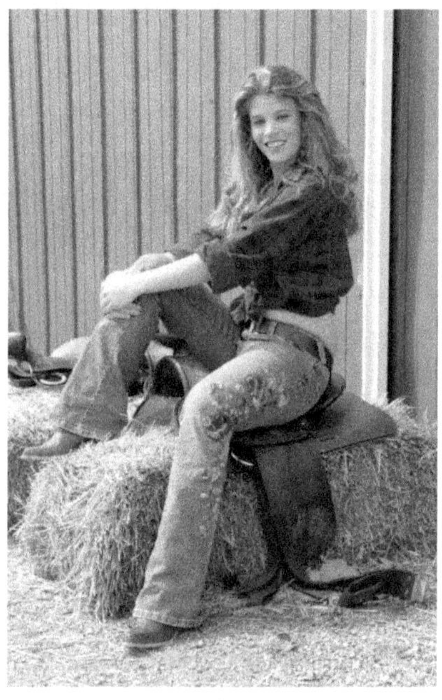

You are just the kind of all-American girl that we love to see succeed. Keep us posted on your career, and before you leave I'd like to tell my readers to Google you and they'll find multiple websites, complete with amazing photo galleries.

In closing, I'd also like to remind our readers to catch you in *What's wrong with Virginia?* I'm also impressed that you were in the Disney presentation of the *Wannabes* in December, 2010. It was great seeing you perform with that fun group of young people… You will also be entertaining the US soldiers again with a Christmas concert. Don't forget to send us some new photos to share on our various websites.

It's been a lovely, inspiring visit, Marissa. We hope to see you on the big screen in that lead role before too long. Keep in touch.

Marissa Autumn: Wow, Betty, I'm honored to be featured by you and can't wait to be in your next *Dream Reachers* book. Thanks much and I'll keep in touch…for sure. Bye for now.

"I love acting, but want to make sure I have a good backup."

--- Marissa Autumn

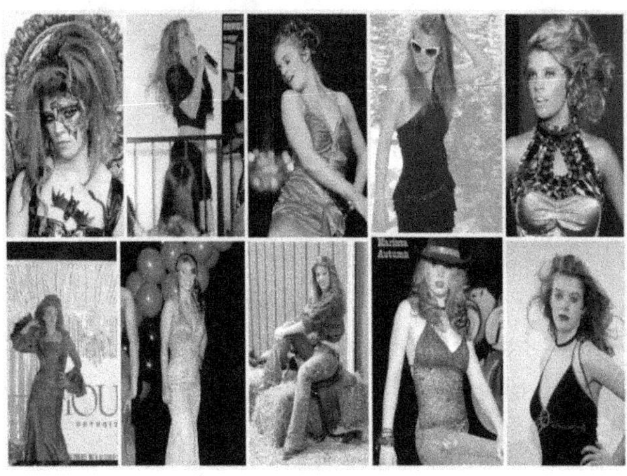

Interview with Stan C. Countz

PUBLISHER, PRODUCER, PROMOTER & POET

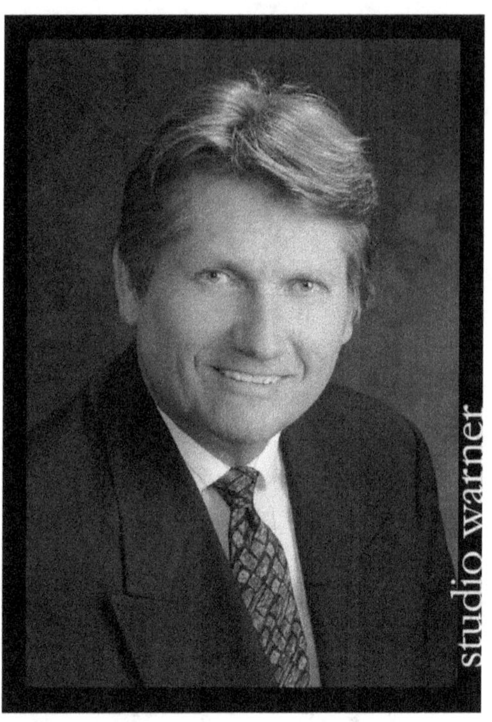

Betty Dravis: Welcome to our growing slate of Dream Reachers, Stan. It's a pleasure to have such a talented man from the California Central Valley with us today. I moved from Silicon Valley to the Central Valley two years ago. While I live in the smaller town of Manteca and you live in the booming metropolis of Modesto (laughs), we're in the same "neck of the woods." I met you on Facebook and you drew my interest because you promote local merchants, have a background in publishing, TV show production and are a prolific poet and wordsmith. When I saw the quality of your full-color *Valley Views Magazine,* I knew you were a man of vision…a man I wanted to interview.

Before we get to know "Stan the adult," I'd like to give our readers a peek at "Stan the child." Where did you grow up? What were you like as a kid? What were your first ambitions?

Stan C. Countz: Thanks, Betty, I'm happy to be here. To start at the beginning, my parents met and married in the Central Valley city of Turlock during the fabulous fifties. My mom, Myrna Louise Wymar, was an avid horse enthusiast and barrel rider and a member of the Turlock Cavaliers. My dad, Charles Alvin Countz, was like the original "Fonzie." He wore his hair in a duck-tail and was a member of a car club, like most guys in those days. They fell for each other and, before you know it, I was on my way. They got married and moved to the Bay Area where my two brothers and I were born and raised. I lived in Martinez, Walnut Creek, Danville and Alamo before moving back to the Turlock area in 1967. From the sixth grade through high school, I lived there; my parents built a countertop manufacturing and installation business (Countz Counter Tops).

In high school, I was a member of the track team and during this time I was confronted with the claims of Christ and decided to accept Him into my life. This decision was to have tremendous impact on the course of my life and the lives of my family and friends. This was at the height of the "Jesus Movement" of the early 70's. After receiving Christ, I was walking on "Cloud Nine" from about the middle of my freshman year through my senior year in high school.

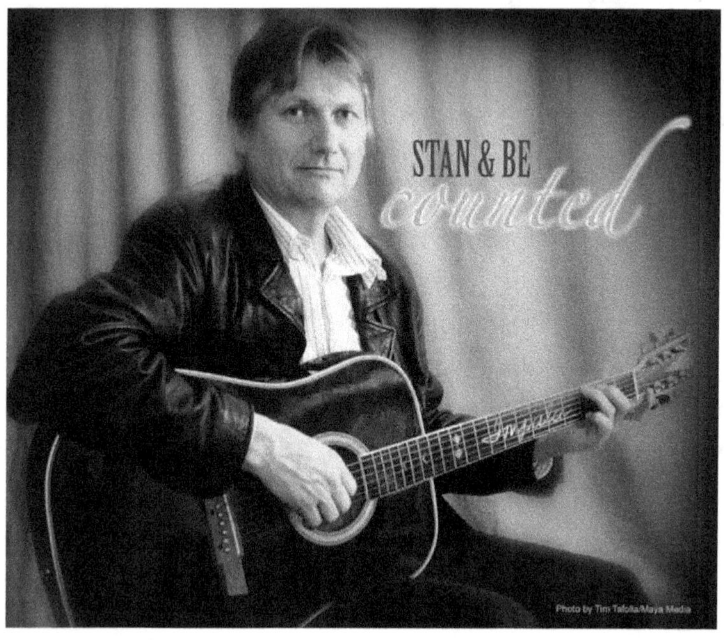

I was one of those guys that brought my Bible to school and actually read it. I was involved with the early days of contemporary Christian music and enjoyed listening to early Christian rock artists such as Barry McGuire, Larry Norman, Randy Stonehill, Chuck Girard and other pioneers of that genre. During this time, I had a voracious appetite for Bible Study, prayer, evangelism and Christian fellowship. I wrote a weekly column in *The Turlock Journal*, entitled "For Real." Several articles were picked up by national publications. I took a class taught by Margaret J. Anderson, author of The Christian Writer's Handbook, who happened to live in Turlock at the time.

Betty Dravis: Your parents sound "Fifties Cool," Stan. Thanks for painting a vivid picture of that era; your description brings back pleasant memories for me. It's also interesting to hear about your accepting Jesus into your life.

Your interest in singing may have been sparked by those Christian singers and your interest in writing must have gotten a big boost when a few of your articles made it national. I find it interesting how everything in our lives tends to blend together to form who we become as adults. Using myself as an example, I started writing poetry at about age eleven, took private elocution lessons, favored English, journalism and creative writing throughout my school years. It didn't surprise anyone when those skills followed me throughout my working life.

Stan C. Countz: You're right, Betty; that's how it was for me too. After graduating from Turlock High School in 1974, I majored in English and minored in Journalism at Modesto Junior College. I wrote for the college newspaper and was inspired to continue writing when I won an award for an investigative journalism piece from the California Community College Association.

Unfortunately, writing jobs were not too plentiful, so after graduating, I took a few minimum wage general laborer jobs before I discovered I could sell. My first sales job was working for Fuller Brush, selling degreasers, germicidal cleaners and brushes door to door. I met my wife Teresa at Modesto Junior College and hired her to deliver and collect on all the products I was selling. I went from selling brushes to selling freezer food plans.

When I made enough money so I didn't need to take just anything that came along, I interviewed with media companies–including TV stations, radio stations and newspapers–and was hired by a new FM radio station in the Modesto area. K102 (today referred to as Sunny 102.3) was the first contemporary station on the FM dial in the Modesto area. I was given ninety days to "sink or swim." Luckily, I excelled at radio-advertising sales and subsequently started a Christian radio show, *The Right On Rock,* which eventually aired on three rock stations in the Modesto area over an eight-year period.

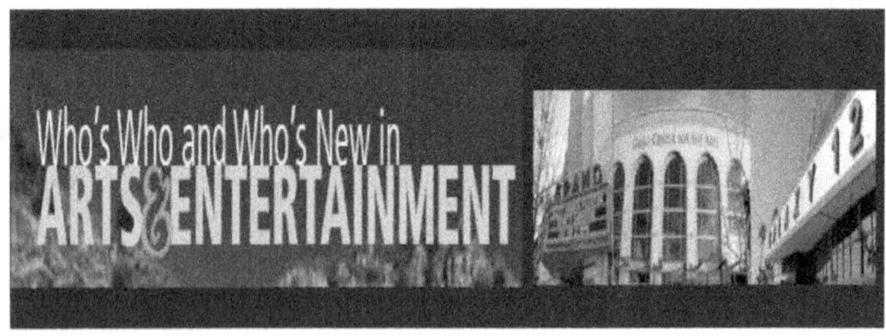

In 1979 I left the radio station as an account executive and was hired by a local advertising agency where I had the opportunity to produce TV shows, direct mail-coupon mailers, bus-bench advertising and other innovative local advertising programs. In 1979 I launched *Advertising Alternatives* and began publishing specialty tabloids and publications. In March of 1980, I founded *Valley Views* magazine.

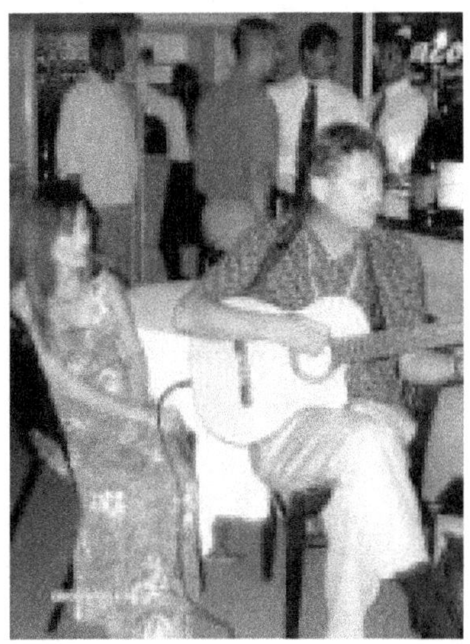

Betty Dravis: Well, you earned your way to the top, Stan, through diligence and hard work, the old-fashioned way. (laughs) It's great that your wife worked with you to help you get started. That's impressive and says a lot for both of you.

My research shows that *Valley Views* magazine was the first city/regional magazine ever published in the Central Valley. Before telling us about your current projects and your ambitious plans, please tell us what happened to the original publication and what you did in the interim…before starting up again.

Stan C. Countz: I put out thirty consecutive issues of the original *Valley Views* between 1980 and 1983. The magazine was a victim of its own success. After approximately twenty-eight issues of the magazine, I convinced myself that I needed investment capital to take it to the next level. I spent hundreds of man-hours with my business consultant Brad Schuber, putting together a complete business plan. The first person I showed it to, a CPA, jumped at it and brought in his printer business associate.

They offered to set up a new corporation and issue me 40% of the stock in the new entity. I had always told myself that I would never give up controlling interest in any of my businesses, but I had convinced myself of the need for this capital. Well, in a nutshell, I was left holding the liabilities of the sole-proprietorship and all the assets were transferred to the new corporation. Once this was done, these investors surprised me by asking me to step down from my role as publisher. Once I did that, there was no one to assume my responsibilities and so they put a couple of issues out without me, but, basically, there was no one who could generate the ad sales so the magazine took one last breath and "gave up the ghost" after I stepped down.

Remember, I did all of this while I was in my early twenties, way before anyone else even thought of producing a magazine for the Central Valley.

Betty Dravis: That's really something for someone so young to build a magazine like that, only to have it "snatched" from beneath you by unscrupulous businessmen. I bet you learned valuable life lessons from that venture. Seems like they "cut off their noses to spite their faces," though, so you must have had the last laugh. So, what happened next, Stan?

Where did you go from there?

Stan C. Countz: I was disheartened by that setback, of course, Betty, but I carried on and stayed in the advertising field for another twelve years. I produced direct mail coupon books and published *Modesto Lifestyles* and *Stanislaus Business*, special-interest newsprint publications. In 1990, I was the top ad-sales rep for the *Valley Yellow Pages* for Stanislaus County and Sacramento County. In 1993, I decided to pursue other business interests… All that time, I missed the publishing business; it gets in your blood, as you must know. So in 2003, I decided to go back into the publishing and advertising business.

In the previous twenty years, publishing technology had changed drastically, so I was in for a steep learning curve. I hooked up with graphic designers, freelance writers and photographers and a heat-set web printer and put out a forty-page magazine. This was followed by a fifty-six-page magazine. Once I changed the name back to *Valley Views*, it jumped up to eighty pages and then a hundred. The success of *Valley Views* magazine spawned and inspired other magazines as well. For example, as soon as I changed the name of the magazine from *Modesto Homes & Lifestyles* to *Valley Views*, almost every paper in the Valley changed their names.

Tony Zoccoli, who published two Valley magazines, confided in me over the phone years later that he had watched for every new issue of *Valley Views* to see if he could match the quality of the content and the design. He changed his distribution strategy and format of his publications to mirror *Valley Views* and today is still publishing a successful magazine covering the San Joaquin County area.

In an attempt to diversify my brand and add depth to my coverage, I also launched a website and a TV show *Valley Views Spotlight* that featured "documercials" promoting life in the Valley, Bay and foothills. We produced four episodes of *Valley Views Spotlight*. A successful developer, who had bought up much of downtown Sutter Creek, saw the potential of doing some "destination marketing" and jumped on board prior to the building of the bypass that everyone knew was coming.

Betty Dravis: That's interesting, Stan. I enjoy hearing about your publishing career because I relate to your struggles and your successes. For fifteen years before my retirement, I owned and published a 20,000-circulation newspaper in Silicon Valley. *Construction Labor News* was the "Official Voice of Labor in Silicon Valley and Beyond." It was a highly political newspaper, as you might guess, because our subscribers were Unions affiliated with the Building and Construction Trades Council.

But, aside from my interest, I'm sure our readers will enjoy learning more about you and your ventures. You have an outstanding video on the Internet wherein you speak of the original *Valley Views Magazine* and your plans for your new "baby." You rekindled fond memories of my own publishing days when you spoke of the old-fashioned way of cutting-and-pasting with an X-Acto knife. I remember those days from when I edited the *Gilroy News Herald.* In fact, we always needed "filler" stories in various lengths to fill gaps in layout when the writers didn't "guesstimate" length correctly. It was funny when the "paste-up man"—which is what we called our graphic artist in those days–stuck his head in the door, saying, "We need a three-inch story." (laughs)

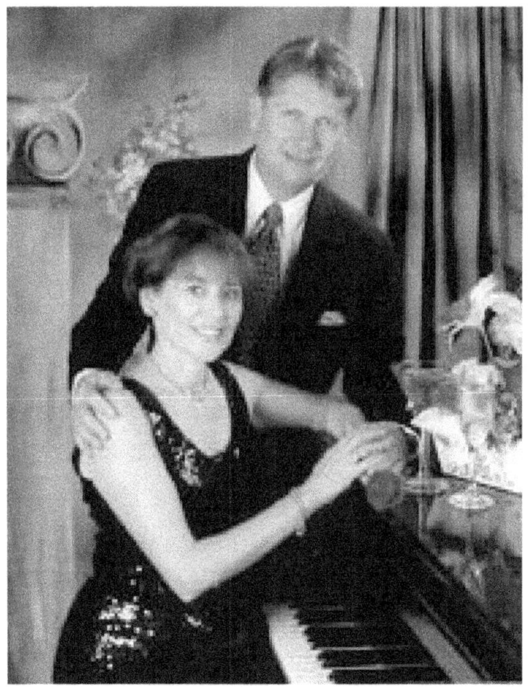

Stan & Teresa (Bustamante) Countz

Since you openly discuss *Valley Views Magazine* in one segment of the video, while other segments feature great places to visit in the Central Valley, I'm sharing the Internet link with our readers: http://www.valleyviews.biz/.. It's a fascinating video and I hope our readers take time to watch all the segments and surf the site. I couldn't drag myself away from it; all that yummy food, breath-taking scenery, the news segments, etc. The Central Valley is, indeed, a lovely area with much to offer residents and visitors. I hear you have launched a big "Local First" campaign. Tell us about it, Stan.

Stan C. Countz: Well, I think many communities throughout the country could benefit from being in better touch with their local resources, local talent and local business and non-profit organizations. Also, I believe a community resource guide can inform and educate people about the importance of supporting locally-owned and locally grown companies, non-profits and talent. For the last three years, I have been working on ways of rewarding consumers who think and shop locally first. To this end, I believe I have found several creative ways to tap into the growing "Local First" movement by launching a local search portal and publishing local community resource guides and/or coupon directories that educate, inform and entertain their respective communities while rewarding local consumers with local shopping rewards, online, print and video coupons.

The community resource guide ought to profile successful local business leaders, non-profit organizations, artists, entertainers, authors, actors, models, etc. and ought to be a source of community pride and solidarity. It should cover the "Who's

Who & Who's New" in the community. Due to the current economic downturn, however, we thought it prudent to format the publication in such a way that the break-even point is reached easier than was the break-even point for *Valley Views*.

To this end, we have come up with a simple, duplicable print and online publishing platform and format that would work in nearly any cohesive community that wants to improve the economic climate of its local economy.

Betty Dravis: So it appears you're no longer publishing *Valley Views* and are back into promoting again. I thought that Tim Tafolla, your ad designer and associate on *VV,* was quite talented. What's he doing now that *VV* is no longer being published?

Stan C. Countz: Well, Betty, *Valley Views* is still a brand we want to keep and promote, but we are holding it for when an economic resurgence occurs. That's why we're doing smaller, less-ambitious community resource guides for ultra-local neighborhood target marketing. We organize a "school of little fish," instead of trying to land a couple of "big fish." Many of the big fish have moved to deeper waters.

Thanks for asking about my friend, Tim Tafolla, Betty. I'm sorry to report that his office building was gutted by a tragic fire about eight months ago. He had to start all over again from scratch, so he moved to North Modesto where he's currently operating his photography and graphic-design business from his home.

He is moving towards fashion photography and videography and is going forward in his business. I designed his website and his company. His new company name is Maya Media Studio. I believe he is also managing another business as well.

Betty Dravis: It's too bad the magazine is out of print, but the print industry has always been a hard, competitive business that's prone to huge shifts in advertising revenue as the economy rises and falls.

I hear that you're contemplating a different kind of TV production for the Central Valley, Stan, and I think this is a good place to give readers an impression of its size: As we Californians know, the Valley stretches approximately 500 miles (800 km) from north to south. It boggled my mind when I learned that it's around 42,000 square miles, making it roughly the same size as the state of Tennessee. Its northern half is referred to as the Sacramento Valley and its southern half as the San Joaquin Valley. With that in mind, is it too soon to talk about your new venture?

Stan C. Countz: As you may have noticed, there's nothing I like better than talking business, Betty. (laughs) When the economy took a dump in the fall of 2006, I curtailed my plans for both the magazine and the TV show. However, through Tim Tafolla, I have recently been connected with a very talented video editor who is looking to co-produce a TV show for the Spanish-speaking Central California market and I am in discussions with him exploring the possibility of producing a show for both the Anglo and Hispanic markets.

The show would air on a couple of English-language and a couple of Spanish-language broadcast channels out of Sacramento and would beam all over the Northern San Joaquin and Sacramento Valley. This program would give us an opportunity to promote local businesses, local artists and local events and destinations to an audience of millions of regional viewers.

Betty Dravis: That sounds fascinating, Stan, and is something I think the public would favor. If anyone can make it work, you can. Best of luck.

Stan, you send tempting Facebook invitations to the most fabulous places in the Valley, but you spoke about that above when telling about the Shop Local and Who's Who and Who's New campaigns. I can tell you're proud of this area we call home. You certainly promote it well and belong to all the civic organizations. I saw some of your videos and am impressed with your on-camera persona and with the logos you created.

The premise makes lots of sense to me and I understand it's sweeping the country, with Chambers of Commerce and local leaders joining the national trend. And as seems to be your way, you're on the cutting edge again.

Stan C. Countz: Yes, I am proud of this area, Betty; my heart, my home and my family are here. I'm sure you have seen, heard or read some of the sensational stories that have been produced or written about our area. If one is to believe all they have heard about our region, no one would want to live here, much less raise a family here. Our media outlets have become very adept at airing our "dirty laundry," but, for some reason, they are reticent to cover any story that shows our region in a positive light. They can never be found when someone "does it right."

I would like to try to rectify that. I think the local media should be there with our video cameras, our microphones and our notepads when someone does something noteworthy or worthy of praise, rather than following the scent of blood, like a bunch of crazed bloodhounds. I believe we can make a difference in our local communities by supporting locally-owned businesses, local talent and causes in which we believe.

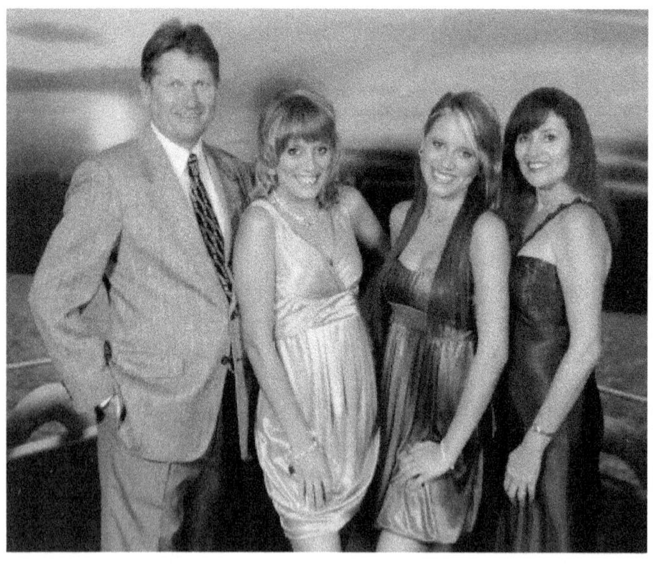

Stan & Teresa with their beautiful twin daughters Vanessa & Jessica

Betty Dravis: You're right about that, Stan, and I think that holds true of all the media: sensationalism is the name of the news game nowadays, it appears. I, personally, enjoy shopping and dining in my little corner of the Valley. I've found some amazing restaurants in Manteca, not to mention some fabulous clothing and shoe shops. (laughs)

Among many other things, Stan, you also sing, play guitar and compose lyrics. I've seen videos of you singing your own compositions and like them very much. I especially enjoy one entitled "Stand for Somethin' or You'll Fall for Anything." That's sound advice, Stan, and confirms that

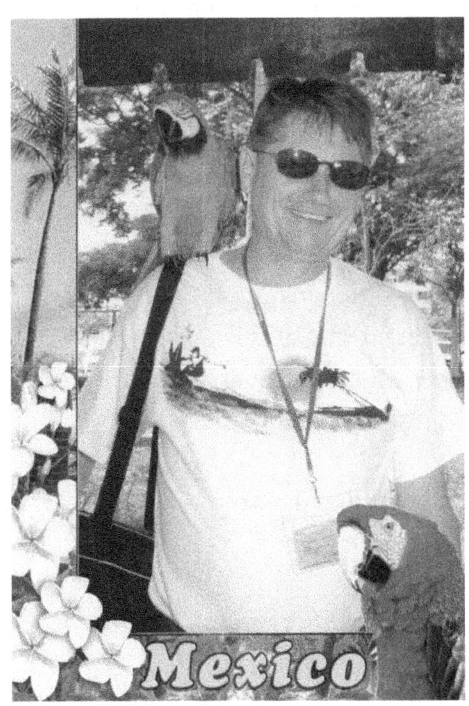

you are a true Dream Reacher, a man who believes in stretching to reach your dreams. But how and when did you start writing verse, Stan?

Stan C. Countz: In the spring of 2005, my mother, Myrna Louise (Wymar) Countz, passed away at the age of sixty-six. About a year after she passed away, out of the blue and unexpectedly, I started writing poetry and verse. Perhaps it was a "coping mechanism," but I prefer to believe that it was a gift of God. All of a sudden, I started writing lyrics and verses and poems like a madman. Since that time–I think it was 2007–I have become quite prolific in my lyric-writing. Two of my poems have been featured in international poetry anthologies.

Several of them have been re-tooled as songs, been recorded by bands and are being played on radio and on the Internet all over the world. One song, *Recipe for a Broken Heart,* was recorded in Chet McCracken's studio; Chet was the original drummer for The Doobie Brothers when they were featured on the cover of *Rolling Stone Magazine* in their heyday. This song was recorded by the band Big Rain, out of Aptos, California, and played on radio stations all over the world. I wrote the lyrics and Bruce Guynn wrote the tune.

Here's a little something I wrote, entitled *I Write a Lot,* that describes my writing habits:

I write quite a bit, usually every night and sit in front of my computer composing megabits of verse and rhyme. How often do I do it? All the time...to my wife's shock and dismay, I write around the clock and every day. I never stop or have writer's block. But I'm still trying to make it pay. I've written hard rock, doo-wop, country and pop. It may seem silly, but I write non-stop for hillbillies, fillies, tikes and tots. Some say I'm crazy, some say I'm not. Some say I'm lazy. Some say I'm hot, but either way, I write a lot.

Betty Dravis: That's sad your mother passed on so relatively young, Stan. My belated condolences…

And I must say, the end of your little ditty above is really funny, but the poem is a little hard to read in places. For better effect, I'd like to hear you sing it…or speak it as poetry.

Do you still sing and play guitar? And do you have any albums or CDs recorded yet?

Stan C. Countz: Yes, I still sing and play—every chance I get. (laughs) I also play drums, Betty. I have recorded enough of my songs to produce an album, but I need to focus on pulling everything together, get everything tweaked and mastered and released. I did my first wedding last month and would love to do more weddings and events. It was great. I especially enjoy performing for "Baby Boomers," since I write for them and they "get" my lyrics better than any other age group. But I will perform for any group or gathering, if given half a chance. I also enjoy discovering local talent and promoting it. I have been producing some local talent showcases lately and would like to expand the effort to a monthly. On the Internet, check out http://localfirst.biz/local-talent.htm.

Betty Dravis: As I said above, I've heard a few of your tapes and you have a definite talent, Stan, but I can understand how and why Local First is your main focus now. Since you also help plan many grand openings and special events, serving as master-of-ceremonies at many, do you ever perform at any of these events?

Stan C. Countz: Right again, Betty… My main focus right now is promoting the Local First message. Along with a huge media campaign, we are looking to organize Local First Local Talent Showcases and networking events to introduce the local business community to the non-profits and the local talent. We had our Local First kick-off in Turlock July 7th at Sweet River Grill and had a standing-room-only launch that pulled three times as many people as the venue expected.

Betty Dravis: Congrats on the Turlock event, Stan; I hear it was a lot of fun. Best of luck with all your projects.

You have an impressive array of photos on Facebook; from cruise ship to playing guitar to weddings to your lovely family to magazine covers. These photos represent many facets of your life. I could comment on each of them, but I'm really curious about those awesome convertibles from back in the day. They are way beyond cool, reminding me of the movie *American Graffiti.* Tell us about that photo, Stan. And while on the subject, were parts of *American Graffiti* filmed in Modesto?

Stan C. Countz: Although *American Graffiti* was loosely based on George Lucas's life growing up in the Modesto area, it is my understanding that the actual filming of *American Graffiti* was done in the Petaluma area. However, Modesto has had a love affair with cruising since I can remember. We used to have Graffiti Night in Modesto when people came from all over to cruise up and down McHenry Avenue. Several years ago it was outlawed, but now they have converted the entire month of June to Graffiti Summer. Check out this video produced by *Valley Views Spotlight* (my former TV show) that chronicles some of the 2006 activities in the Modesto area.

Fans can locate it on the Internet by Googling my various websites.

Betty Dravis: That is, indeed, a famous movie; we're all enamored of that era. But moving on: Stan, how important is family to you? We would enjoy knowing a little about yours.

Stan C. Countz: I have been married to my saint of a wife, Teresa, for nearly thirty-three years. We have twin daughters who are eighteen years old and we are getting close to becoming "empty nesters." My mom, both of my brothers and my dad have all preceded me in death. I'm the last of the Mohicans, so to speak. My daughters are working on getting their driver's licenses and buying their first cars. We are very close with my wife's family. She comes from a family of seven and has three sisters and a brother who all live in the Modesto area. Her mom and dad only live ten houses down from us. Her mom is originally from Chihuahua, Mexico and her father is originally from Mexico City. My wife and all her siblings were born and raised in Modesto. My wife is very close to her family. Her family members are some of her best friends and confidants.

Betty Dravis: Nothing beats a close-knit family, Stan. You are surely blessed.

Okay, now for a lighter question: If it were possible to spend the day with anyone throughout history, who would you choose…and why?

Stan C. Countz: I would like to stay for a day with Jesus, son of Joseph, during his three-year ministry as he went about the Judean countryside. In fact, I wrote a lyric entitled "Carpenter's Son." It paints a scene that might take you back in time to when He was turning water into wine and giving sight to the blind and blowing the Pharisee's minds.

Betty Dravis: Jesus is the perfect choice, Stan; that would be a divine blessing, for sure. I hope to be able to hear you sing that song one day. That would be a real treat… But moving on, I know how important the Central Valley and home are to you, but everyone likes to get away from time to time. What are your favorite vacation spots? And what do you do for recreation?

Stan C. Countz: We like to get away to Pine Crest up in the Sierras or the Santa Cruz/Monterey area on the coast. We also enjoy the Morro Bay and Pismo/Avila Beach area. My wife enjoys scrapbooking and I enjoy writing poetry and songwriting. (laughs)

I also enjoy jamming with other musicians and creating memorable songs that change the way people think.

Betty Dravis: I'm happy you get away with the family, Stan. My children and I take to water too. In fact, as I conduct this interview, it's Labor Day weekend and my adult kids and some of the grandkids are headed to the beach home of friends in Santa Cruz. I'd be with them, but I have to work. (laughs)

There's a lot of talk about "paying it forward" in recent times, so tell us, Stan, how do you show appreciation for your good fortune in life?

Stan C. Countz: I like to encourage talent in all forms where I find it. Talent comes in all shapes and sizes. I like to encourage people to dig in, set their goals and don't let anyone steal their dreams. There is so much that is discouraging out there. I want to be that one bright light in the night that shines its beacon and warns of the rocks and shoals ahead, so the ship can make it safely into harbor. If I find a flower blooming in a desert place, I want to water it, fertilize it and see how big it will grow.

Betty Dravis: Good analogy, Stan… Encouraging talent is an admirable way to pay it forward. In a way you are doing what Chase Von and I do when creating our *Dream Reachers* books: inspiring people to dream big! I admire that about you, Stan.

Keep up the great work. But now we're nearing the end of this interview, so before I tell our readers where they can contact you, is there anything I missed that you'd like to share today?

And what advice do you have for young people just getting started in journalism or writing, in general?

Stan C. Countz: Read good writing and write good writing. The way you spot a counterfeit is to become so familiar with the real thing that when a fake comes along, you can spot it immediately. Become acquainted with good writing, so you can recognize it when you see it. And I encourage writers to keep a journal or online blog. If you do not know how to set up a blog, contact me. I'll get you all set up.

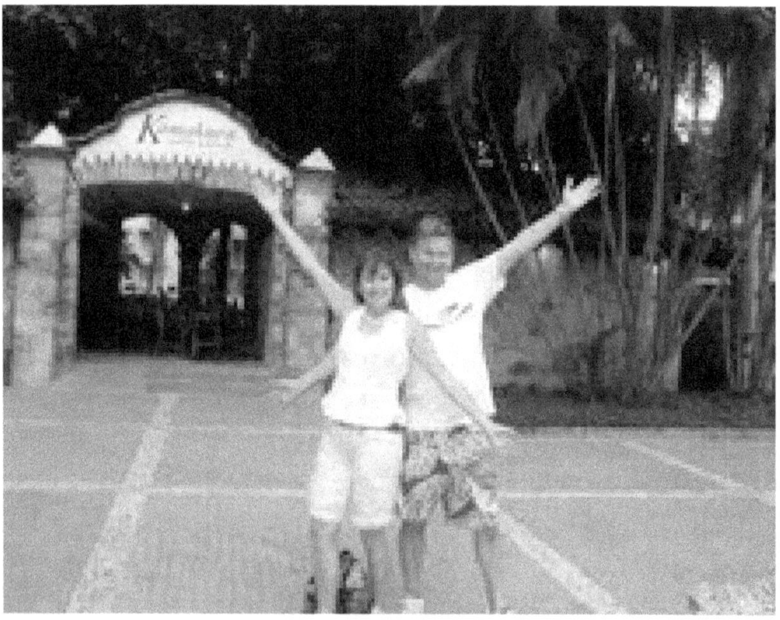

Betty Dravis: I'm sure your advice will be welcome, Stan. It's been a pleasure talking with you today. Thanks for sharing your dreams with us and for standing up for your convictions. *That* said, this is the perfect place to tell people they can learn more about you by Googling your name to reach your various sites on the Internet:

Thanks again, Stan. Blessings on all your projects… I'll be seeing you on Facebook, Twitter and in the pages of *Who's Who & Who's New,* I'm sure. (laughs) Don't forget to check back with us and keep us in the loop.

Stan C. Countz: It's been fun, Betty. Thanks for including me with all these fascinating high-achievers. I'll try to live up to your expectations and stretch to become a top-notch "Dream Reacher." And don't forget: *Shop and search local first.* (laughs)

"I started writing poetry and verse.
Perhaps it was a 'coping mechanism.'"

—-Stan C.Countz

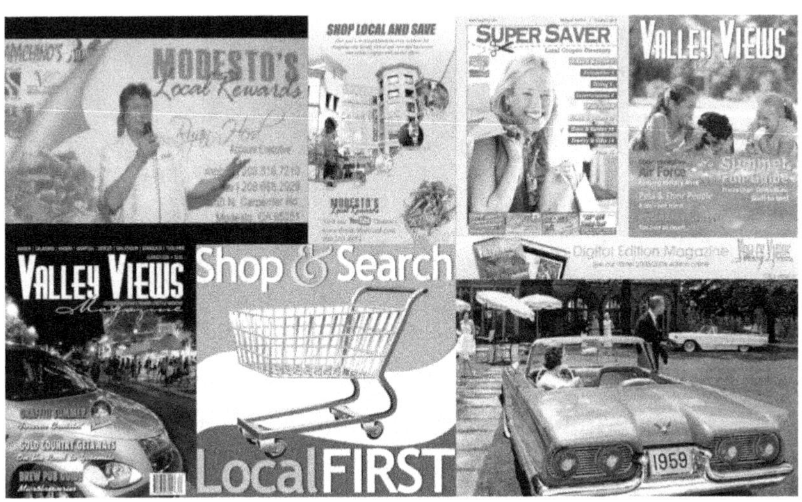

Interview with Jessica Gilbert

FOUNDER OF
TALENT SPOTLIGHT MAGAZINE

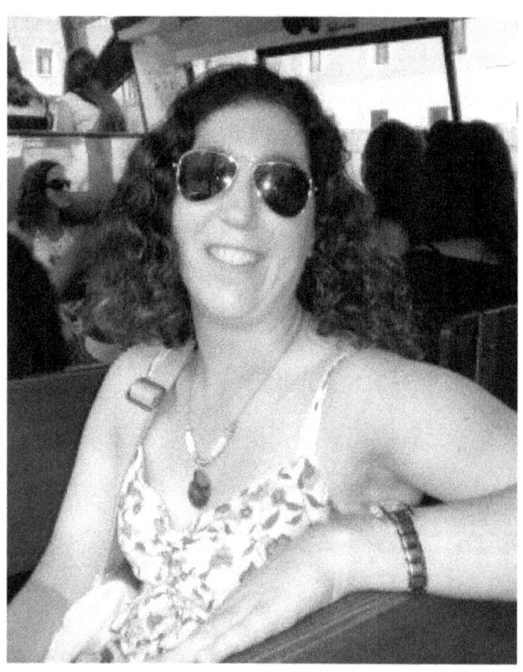

Betty Dravis: Hey, Jessica… It's great to see you. I'm overwhelmed by the number of entertainers and artists who suggested you for this interview. You're a promoter of new talent, building fan bases for them, but it looks like you have a big fan base yourself. (laughs) On your various websites you state that you couldn't live without music in your life. I assume that's why you love entertainers so much and want to help them succeed.

There's so much I want to ask you, but where to begin? Hmmmm... How about at the beginning...with your childhood in Canada? What kind of precocious kid were you, Jessica? When did you first start swaying along to music and realize you enjoyed it so much? Were you pushing your little friends off the merry-go-round, encouraging them to sing and dance instead? I bet you did something like that. (laughs)

Jessica Gilbert: Hi, Betty. Thanks so much for having me here. I feel very honored to be among so many wonderful and talented people.

You're right, music (and the arts) is something I can't live without, but I never went so far as pushing my childhood friends to perform. (laughs)

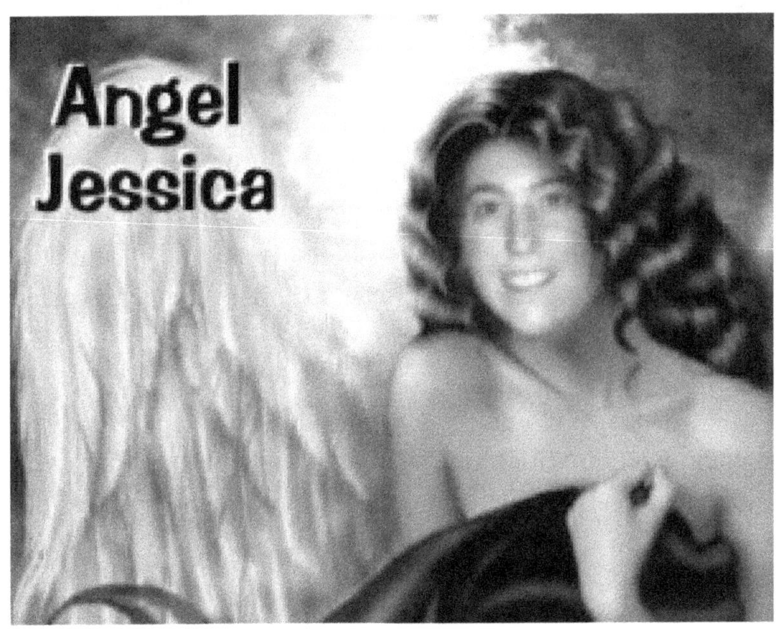

I truly *love* working with artists and being a part of their journey to the top. There is so much great talent out there and being able to assist an artist in even a small way makes me feel good because it's one step closer to helping them reach their dreams.

I was born in Montreal, Canada, but left as a baby for Houston, Texas. I spent my childhood there until the age of ten. I was, generally, a very good and independent child because I was as happy doing things on my own as I was being with other children or adults. As a child I liked creative endeavors too: drawing, painting, coloring, writing and especially puzzles. I had learned the alphabet through the medium of puzzles by the age of two, which apparently was unusual, according to the playgroup *"directrice"*...much to my Mother's surprise. I loved the performing arts: took ballet and tap-dance lessons; enjoyed singing to myself and making up songs and recording them as I came up with the words. At about age eight I organized a school play, *Return to Oz,* in which I was involved in all parts of the production, placing myself in the lead role. (laughs) I was also engaged in fundraising activities for various causes. In fact, at my school I was the first child to initiate a fundraising activity which led to many other student fundraisers.

Betty Dravis: Just as I suspected, Jessica, you were a precocious child. I bet your parents were very proud of you. And then when you grew up, did you start attending concerts? If so, can you recall your first concert... (who you were with, who was performing, etc.)?

Please share the emotions the live music aroused.

Jessica Gilbert: Yes, Betty, I've been fortunate to have had the opportunity to attend many concerts! My first concert was Tina Turner in Målaga, Spain at age ten with my parents and sister in the summer outdoors. I can't say it was the best concert experience because it started really late. It was also hot, buggy and I got tired of standing. However, I still loved seeing her *live!* Back then I played Tina's music a lot as she was one of my top favorite artists (still is today), so getting to see her in concert was an exciting experience for me. I was overwhelmed with joy to be there.

I'm not sure what I'd do without music because not only is it great for entertainment or inspiration, but soothing to the soul. Literally, I go to sleep listening to music, listen to it when I wake up and throughout the day have some music playing. Music gives me an inspiration to think, create, write and relax.

Betty Dravis: Wow, Jessica, that's a lot of music, but if it inspires you, that's what matters. I can understand how that works for some people, but do you choose different music to create different moods? For instance, what do you listen to while writing? While relaxing?

Jessica Gilbert: Yes, Betty, the kind of music I listen to depends on what I'm doing, time of day, how I'm feeling, etc. For instance, while writing or painting I like inspirational music. While relaxing or before bedtime I like soft music. I even have a playlist in my iTunes called "Relaxing Mix."

Betty Dravis: That sounds sensible for a person so attuned to music, as you are. I'm curious about your writing, Jessica. In addition to articles for your new online magazine, what type of writing interests you? We'll talk about the magazine later.

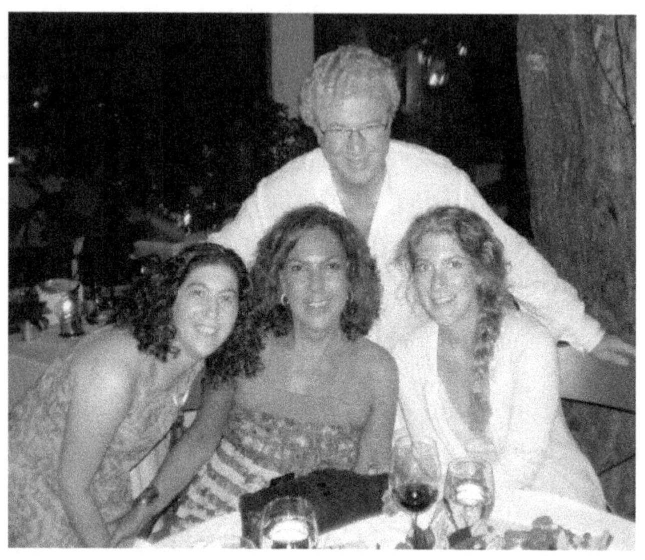

Jessica with parents
Freda & Adrian Gilbert & sister Lauren

Jessica Gilbert: I've written short stories, and screenwriting has always been an interest of mine. In college I took a film-writing class, so learned the technique for this type of writing. For the class assignment, we had to write a seven-minute script, which turned out to be a success. Subsequently, I thought it would be great to turn it into a feature-length script. I also have an idea for another one inspired by actual events in my life. However, any screenwriting I do will be an extra thing when time permits.

Betty Dravis: I wish you luck with all your projects, Jessica. While on the subject of writing, in your Facebook notes you posted a lengthy list of biographies and autobiographies of famous people. It contains a fascinating array of movie stars from Rita Hayworth and Ray Milland to Jane Fonda. What prompted you to post that?

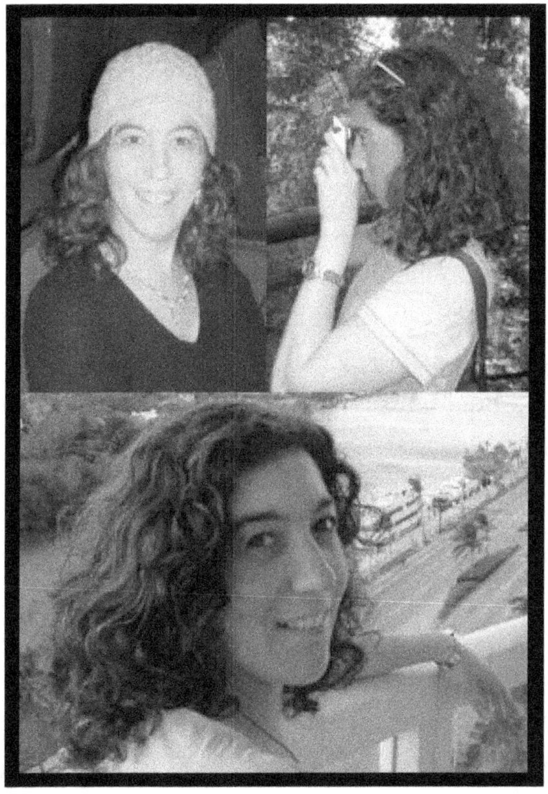

Jessica Gilbert: Betty, the list of biographies and autobiographies that I posted was for a friend of mine who has this book collection for sale. So, I wanted to help spread the word about it.

Betty Dravis: He certainly has an interesting collection. Do you aspire to write a book someday? If so, are you interested in fiction or nonfiction?

Jessica Gilbert: Yes, I'd love to write and illustrate a children's book. Since I like to draw, paint, write…and I love children, I think this kind of book would be a great opportunity to combine all these elements together. Actually, Betty, I have a couple of ideas for children's books. (smile)

Betty Dravis: Oh, you'd be a natural for children's picture books, Jessica. I'm here to tell you that they are a joy to write; takes one back to one's own childhood. I've only published one YA, *The Toonies Invade Silicon Valley,* but I have three unsubmitted picture books that are partially illustrated by my granddaughter, Kristy Soza. I would so enjoy doing my own illustrations, but, unfortunately, I don't have the talent of a kindergartner. (laughs)

But changing the subject, you wrote somewhere: "I'm not your average girl." What do you mean by that, Jessica?

Jessica Gilbert: Well, Betty, I'm not your average girl because I've lived a life that many people don't get to experience. I've lived in three countries (USA, Spain and Canada) and traveled extensively throughout much of Canada, USA, Europe and the Dominican Republic. So I feel very fortunate to have experienced living in different countries and cultures. Also to have been able to do all the traveling I've done up to this point in my life.

Betty Dravis: You're right about that, Jessica: You are fortunate. I'm about twice your age and have only been in two bordering countries and about twenty of our United States. (laughs)

I hear you just returned from Italy, which is one place I would love to visit. I'd enjoy going there now to experience Antonia Tosini's screenplay, *Between the Olive Trees, being produced.* I could kill three birds with one stone: meet Director David Worth, Actress Susan Kennington who has a prime role in that movie, and Antonia Tosini, talented and iconic screenwriter. Now *that* would be a thrill.

Was your trip vacation or business? And did you meet any new artists while there?

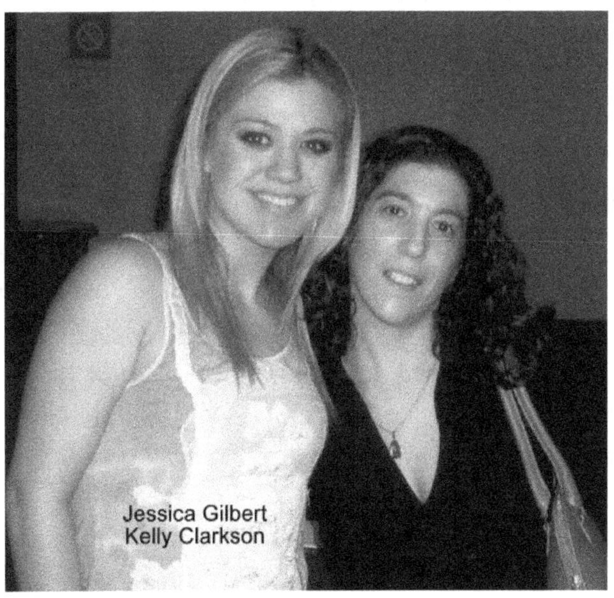

Jessica Gilbert
Kelly Clarkson

Jessica Gilbert: Betty, my trip to Italy was a much-needed vacation. (smile) I had such a blast traveling throughout Italy and got to see so much in twelve days. The highlights of my trip were Venice and Capri. I *love* Italy, so hope to make it back there again soon. I didn't meet any new artists while there, but finally got to meet one of my MySpace friends in person…a gifted photographer.

Betty Dravis: I saw photographs of your trip, Jessica, and Italy's as picturesque as you say. Breath-taking, in fact. I know you love to travel and get around much more than the "average girl," so I'm sure your time there is a treasured memory.

But I'm the most curious about the promotion aspect of your life. I know that you promote a number of talented people: musicians, authors, singers, dancers, artists, etc. But from the sheer number of musicians you help, it's obvious you prefer them. I know you promote singer/guitarist/lyricist MT Robison and The Messengers and are a huge fan. I met you through M.T. after he was featured in our first *Dream Reachers* book. He's awesome and has some clever promotion going on himself. For instance, he calls his fans his "Street Angels" and a white feather is one of his trademarks. Like you, I'm a Street Angel, too, Jessica; I adore MT. He certainly has it all "going on": the look, the voice, and the creativity—not to mention a huge stage presence. He can't miss with a publicist like the talented Linda Shrader in his corner.

How many fan clubs have you founded and who else do you promote besides M.T.?

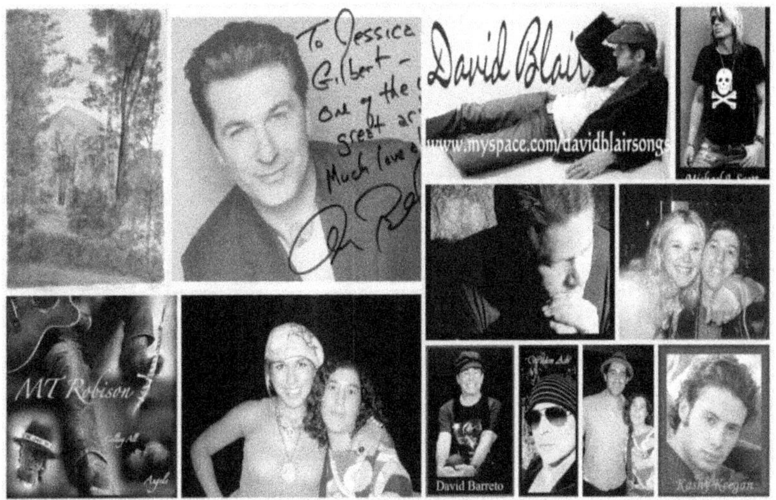

Jessica Gilbert: I do promote many musicians, but it isn't that I prefer them over the others because I love all types of artists. I just end up connecting with more musicians simply because so many more come my way on the various social networking sites. Yes, I do promote MT and The Messengers. I adore MT so much…as both artist and person.

Linda Shrader is amazing and he truly is lucky to have her as his publicist.

I've founded eight fan clubs for various musicians. To tell you about all the wonderful artists I promote would be a whole interview itself because there are so-ooo many of them. However, to name a few: Kashy Keegan, Wildon Ash, Michael J. Scott, Neil Barlow, David Blair, David Barreto, Kadesha, Lizann, Daz, Elena Vogt, Tima Montemayor, Olivia Gray, Tobiah and Orly Vardy. They are all amazing artists that can be found on MySpace and I highly recommend checking out their music.

Betty Dravis: That's quite a roster, Jessica. I expect many of those to be big names in the future; you certainly have an eye and ear that's attuned to the pulse of the world. You were even kind enough to start a *Dream Reachers* Fan Club on MySpace and on Facebook. My co-author Chase Von and I are humbled by that. Just to be included on the same page with all your talented friends is an honor. Thanks so much for your faith in us.

Speaking of MySpace, your MS page is incredible, chock-full of talented people and current bios and links. Each time I visit your page, the photos and art are so appealing that it boggles my mind. I feel like I felt the first time my mom took me to an ice-cream parlor. How could I choose just one flavor? I wanted them all... That must be how you feel when deciding who to promote. What's the first thing that draws your attention to a promising artist, Jessica?

Jessica Gilbert: It was my pleasure to start a *Dream Reachers* Fan Club for you and Chase Von. It's a wonderful and inspirational book that everyone would enjoy reading.

When I visit ice cream parlors I always have a hard time choosing flavors too. (laughs) Yes, I feel exactly the same way when deciding which artists to promote. It's going to be really hard choosing who to interview for each issue of my magazine because I really do love so many artists. What draws my attention the most to a promising artist is how much they give of themselves, which leads to our connection. One of the qualities I value most of all, besides talent, is originality.

Betty Dravis: You probably don't know this, Jessica, but originality is the first thing I notice when choosing a book to read and review, also.

Since you currently do the publicity and promotion as a labor of love, do you plan to make a career of it? If so, is your forthcoming magazine the first step towards making your dream come true? I know you "wear three hats" with the business: publisher/managing editor/freelance writer. As a former print newspaper owner myself, I can testify that there are many more hats than that. (laughs) But tell us more about *Talent Spotlight Magazine,* Jessica. When will you launch your debut edition? And can you give us a sneak peek at a few artists you're interviewing for the first edition?

Jessica Gilbert: Betty, I would like to make a career in artist promotions (and possibly even in other aspects of the music or film industry) because I'm passionate about promoting and working with all types of artists. Perhaps I might work for a record company in the PR department.

Talent Spotlight Magazine came into creation as a result of my desire to participate in the creative process of talent. It is very fulfilling for me to offer artists a creative venue to promote their talent. As well, selfishly speaking, I hope this creative venue will be a good means to get myself out there as a promoter. I've thought about doing something like this for a while now and always wanted to work with a magazine. So, now I can…with my *own.* (smile)

TSM will be an online magazine that will come out bimonthly, starting this October. It will feature in-depth interviews with talent from all genres of the arts: music, photography, art, film, print and more. The magazine's primary focus will be on new and emerging artists. However, it will feature more established ones as well. Each issue will also feature an organization or cause–there are so many wonderful causes and organizations out there that I feel it would be great to promote them too–reviews and more! It will have a whole variety of different artists in each issue, making it a more diverse magazine. Some of the artists that will be in the launch issue are two of your original Dream Reachers: Kashy Keegan and MT Robison. I will also be featuring April Star Davis, a jewelry designer whose designs have been featured in numerous fashion magazines and in various movies. Her jewelry has also been worn by many top celebrities.

Betty Dravis: Great minds think alike, Jessica: I thought about interviewing a famous jewelry designer for *Dream Reachers: Vol. II,* but due to heavy demand for the available slots, I didn't have time. I look forward to reading your story about April Star, and of course, dear Kashy and MT. As you know, they were interviewed by my *Dream Reachers* co-author Chase Von for that book.

Your first edition sounds like a winner.

I understand that the talented writer Michelle Jackson will be working with you on the magazine.

Did you know that she wrote the following about you?:

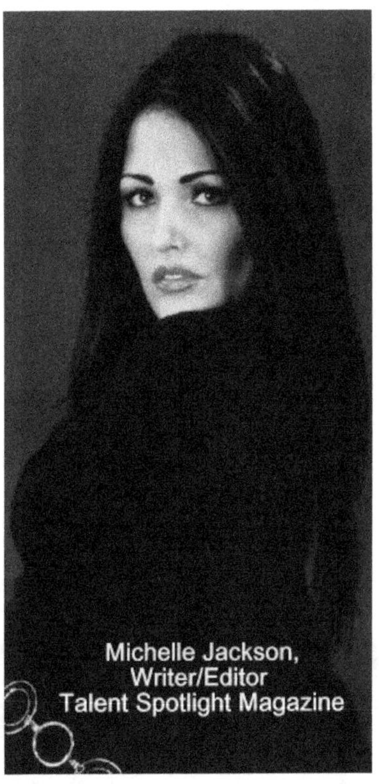

I am wonderfully blessed to call Jessica my friend and to be on this great journey with her. She is extremely talented in the arts and has a heart of gold, reaching out to others who possess the same passion. She is motivated and driven to help artists of all genres to reach their dreams in this great Industry. I have great hope that she will succeed in achieving these goals.

That's high praise, Jessica, and "heart of gold" is how many of the artists describe you. Can you tell us a little more about Michelle and her duties with *TSM?*

Jessica Gilbert: Yes, Betty, I'm blessed to have Michelle Jackson working with me on the magazine. I connected with her instantly awhile back through a friend. We share a love for the arts, plus she's also a wonderful writer. Michelle is a great singer too and I have told her she should put her music out there. Then I can promote her as well. (smile) I didn't know what Michelle wrote about me until it was up on the *TSM* MySpace site. I'm infinitely grateful to her for her kind words and generosity. She will primarily be a contributing writer with interviews for the magazine.

"I'm passionate about promoting and working with all types of artists."

--- Jessica Gilbert

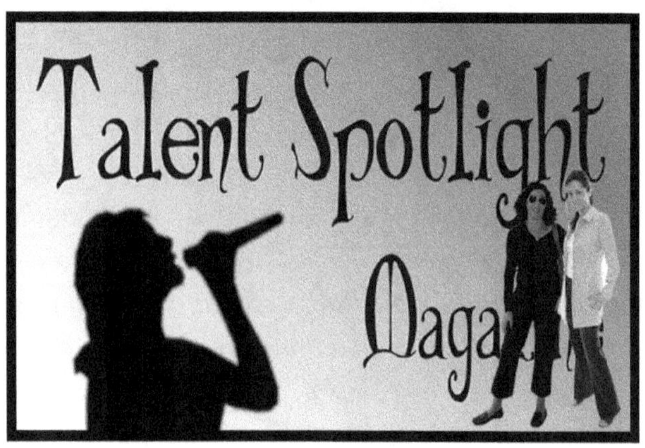

Betty Dravis: Michelle sounds like a real "keeper." You two have a lot of mutual respect and admiration for each other. I look forward to reading her articles too.

Talent Spotlight Magazine–that's a perfect, self-descriptive name, Jessica, and your logo is very attractive. It's all the buzz with many artists that I know. I've been hearing about *TSM* for months and months. We're eager to see your first edition and wish you incredible good fortune.

Jessica Gilbert: Glad you like the magazine name and logo. (smile) I designed the logo myself and received positive feedback on it, so am pleased that people like it. Awhile back in Canada, I took an intensive graphic design course as I enjoy playing with graphics as well. I know that many people have been anxiously waiting for the launch of the magazine and I promise that wait will soon be over. Thank you, Betty, and to everyone else for your tremendous support for *TSM.*

Betty Dravis: The late promoter Bill Graham, who was the best in his day, had some incredible stories to tell about how he got started. After meeting the San Francisco Mime Troupe at a free concert in Golden Gate Park, he gave up a promising business career to manage the troupe in 1965. After Mime Troupe leader Ronny Davis was arrested on obscenity charges during an outdoor performance, Graham organized a benefit concert to cover the troupe's legal fees. The concert was a success and Graham saw a business opportunity. He was an American impresario and rock concert promoter from the 1960s until his death in 1991. We wish you fame and good fortune, too, but hope your success begins with less public scrutiny than Graham's. (laughs)

Jessica, being such a lovely, dynamic and active young woman, when do you find time for dating? Or is that something you're postponing for the time being?

Jessica Gilbert: That's interesting about Bill Graham, Betty. I bet he *did* have great stories about his work as a promoter! Perhaps after I have more experience, I'll write a book about it someday.

But to answer the big "dating" question: While I *am* busy with all the work I do, I always have time for dating. (smile) Finding Mr. Right and settling down is high on my priority list.

Betty Dravis: I thought you'd say that, Jessica, but I'm glad to hear you confirm it. All work and no play makes Jessica…well, you know how that old saying goes. (laughs) Okay, now that your priorities are settled, let's move on…

I hear that the very talented David Barreto, one of the musicians you promote, wrote a lovely song about you. Tell us about him and how that made you feel? I find that incredibly romantic. Do you have a link where our readers can hear the song and do you mind sharing the lyrics with us?

Jessica Gilbert: Yes, David Barreto did write a wonderful song about me titled "Jessica." I was really honored and flattered he did this song for me and will cherish it forever.

Friends who have heard it said he really captured the essence of me. I don't have the lyrics, but people can hear the song on my "Jessica's Artist Network" page. David truly is a talented and amazing musician, one I proudly promote. (smile) BTW, he also did a *Talent Spotlight Magazine* jingle for the website.

Betty Dravis: Oh, Jessica, I love that catchy jingle; the way David drags out the words (Talent...Spotlight...Magazine) is so cool. Makes me want to dance... Since you're multi-tasking now, Jessica, do I dare ask if you have a "day job?" If so, where do you work? If not, let us in on the secret of survival without working.

Are you an heiress or some rich man's daughter? (laughs)

Jessica Gilbert: LOL, Betty... I've been taking Spanish classes in the mornings to brush up on my speaking skills. The rest of the day is a combination of artist promotions, magazine work and painting/drawing. Recently, I got back into my art and would like to build up a body of work to sell (originals and prints). My background is in art, as I majored in studio art with an emphasis on painting/drawing at university. Soon I shall also be offering an official listing of my services and rates for online promotions and management.

Betty Dravis: I'm glad to hear you'll soon be going professional with your promotions, Jessica, and the news about your art is welcome too. I would love to have an "original by Jessica," so keep us posted about that too. Meanwhile, I invite our readers to view your online gallery (under Art in your

Facebook photos) and if they see anything they like, to contact you.

Since we all must prioritize our schedules, here's a food-for-thought question that might be fun to answer: Can you name three things in your life that you couldn't live without?

Jessica Gilbert: That's an easy one, Betty… I can't live without my family/friends, travel and live music.

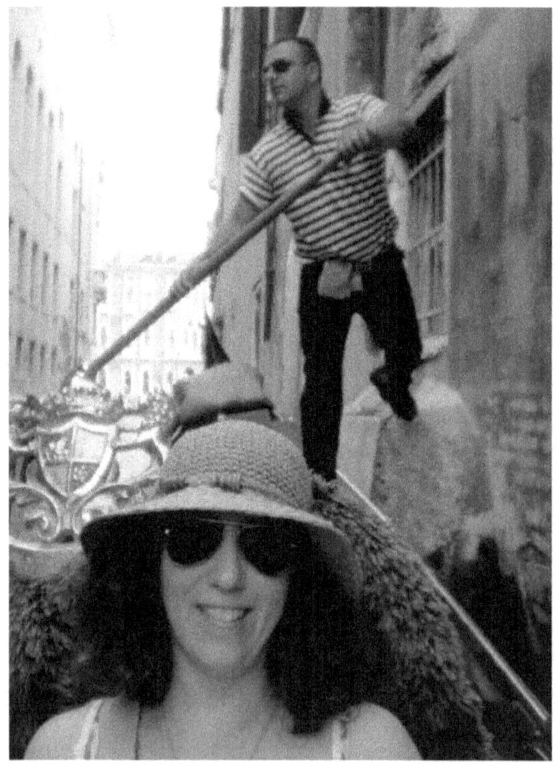

Jessica in gondola in Venice

Betty Dravis: Well, that's short and sweet, Jessica, but it says a lot for your character and values. Thanks.

Another question that usually brings out the humor in people is: What's the most embarrassing thing that ever happened to you?

Jessica Gilbert: You know, Betty, I really can't think of an embarrassing thing that has happened to me. I'll share a funny story with you instead. For my tenth birthday in Texas (it was also my last one there before I moved to Spain the first time around), my dad got a *piñata.* For people who don't know what it is, it's something made from either a clay container or a cardboard shape covered in paper mache. The tradition with a *piñata* is that you fill up the inside with sweets and goodies.

Then everyone is blindfolded and hits it with a stick until it breaks and the sweets fall out. However, that didn't quite work out the way it should have. My friends and I were hitting the *piñata* non-stop, waiting for all the sweets to come out–but no traces of any.

What my dad didn't know was that he was supposed to fill the *piñata* with sweets himself. So, all the hard work hitting that *piñata* to get it open didn't pay off with sweets. This was one of those occasions where you just had to be there. (laughs)

Betty Dravis: Oh, no-ooo, Jessica… That's hilarious! You poor kids, but I feel sorry for your father too. I hope the kids didn't get after him with those sticks… (laughs)

Now for another question: If you could spend an entire day with just one person (living or dead) who would you choose and why?

Jessica Gilbert: This is a tough question, Betty, because I'd like to meet people from all walks of life who work in different fields because everything fascinates me and I can learn something from everyone I meet. But since I have to pick one, I'd choose to spend an entire day with Ellen DeGeneres because she has had all types of people on her show and must have many wonderful stories to share about her experiences meeting them all. An entire day would be needed to hear about much of them, plus I think she would just be so much fun to hang out with in person. (smile)

Some celebs I'd love to have an encounter with include: Julie Andrews, Wentworth Miller, Anthony Hopkins, Barbara Walters, Brad Pitt, Alec Baldwin, Robin Williams, Scott Wolf, Bette Midler, Adam Lambert, David Cook, James Blunt, Bon Jovi, Enrique Iglesias, Five For Fighting, INXS, Daughtry, Red Hot Chili Peppers, Jewel, and lots of others.

There are so-ooo many celebs I'd love to meet. I've been fortunate to have already met some of them, including: Cyndi Lauper, Bryan Adams, Rob Thomas, Rosie O'Donnell, Gary Sinise, Kurt Browning, Joss Stone, Kelly Clarkson, Joshua Radin, David Usher, Suzie McNeil and some others. I received a phone call from Alec Baldwin when he filmed the TV mini-series "Nuremberg" in Montreal and came close to meeting him.

I would still love to meet him.

Betty Dravis: Wow, you've met a lot of celebs, Jessica. My daughter Allie used to adore Cyndi Lauper. In fact she resembled her so much that she dressed like her one Halloween; a dead ringer in that pink dress, black mesh hose and black-and-white, high-top sneakers. A wonderful memory…

As for meeting Alec Baldwin–*you and me both…* The funny thing about Alec is that I like him better today in his maturity than I did when he was younger. I often wonder why that's true with certain actors. But you must share the story about how you came "close" to meeting Alec. I want to hear all the juicy details… (laughs)

Jessica Gilbert: Well, Betty, it was simpler than I thought it would be. I just sent Alec Baldwin a note expressing my appreciation for his work; included my number and also shared some pix of my art. So, one night I got an unexpected call from him. That took me by complete surprise since this doesn't happen often–at least not between a celeb and fan. When we spoke, he expressed interest in meeting and seeing my art work, saying that he would get in touch with me again if it were possible. I never heard back from him, so that's why the meeting never took place.

However, a couple months later I did receive a lovely, personal note from him mentioning how much he admired my work and one day hoped to own one of my pieces. So, I actually sent him a small painting as a gift and got a nice thank you note from him.

Anyway, he's not the only celeb I've received mail from; I used to enjoy sending letters of appreciation to many of my favorite celebs. I have over a hundred autographs. Some I did write to through the film's production office when they filmed movies in Montreal (at one time they were filming tons of movies there).

However, with Gary Sinise and Nicolas Cage, I left letters for them with assistants on the movie set. I was actually one of the thousands of extras in that movie; you can't see me though.

I had an awesome day, watching the filming in action under the direction of Brian de Palma, and also had a free lunch and t-shirts imprinted with the name of the movie and cast.

In response to my letter to Gary Sinise, his personal assistant called, inviting me to the wrap party. I went, of course, and met Gary there. Unfortunately, I didn't get a pic with him. His sweet, pretty assistant told me he was overwhelmed with pictures. But I received two signed pix in the mail later on. It was also unfortunate that Nicolas Cage and de Palma weren't present at the wrap party; they had already left town. Nicolas Cage also responded back to me, signing and writing a short message on the pic I had enclosed.

I want to share this story about Cage and Sinise with you, too, since it's a nice story.

Betty Dravis: You're right, Jessica, those are heart-warming stories, reinforcing my opinion that high-ranking people are not much different than you and me. The majority of them are hard-working, sincere, down-to-earth and friendly. I've seen that same caring quality in many of the celebs I've interviewed. It's good to know that about Alec, Gary and Nicholas; thanks for sharing.

Well, Jessica, we're nearing the end of the interview, so this is a good time to mention anything that I might have missed. I'll post your links in closing, so your fans and friends can find anything else they might wish to know about you.

Jessica Gilbert: You didn't miss much, Betty, but I'd also like to add that I have a children's page dedicated to all causes and organizations related to children. People can check that out on my Artist Network page. It's called "Jessica's Precious Treasures of Hope." At some point in the near future, I'd like to create some kind of fundraiser project to raise money for some of those that I strongly support. If anyone would be interested in working with me on something, please get in touch with me.

Betty Dravis: That's an important point to mention, Jessica. Children are our future and I'm pleased to know you have plans to help them also.

It's been delightful chatting with you, but the time flew and I must bid you a fond farewell. We learned a lot more about you today and definitely look forward to reading and becoming a fan of *Talent Spotlight Magazine*. It will be cool to follow the careers of you and your clients…your awesome artists! I'd like to remind our readers that you can be easily found on the Internet, by simply Googling your name or the name of your magazine.

Thanks for sharing your dreams with us. You're a caring, dynamic woman with a heart of gold, as you have heard many times before. May all your dreams come true, and keep rocking to the beat of your own drummer! I'm so happy to add you to the growing list of Dream Reachers.

Jessica Gilbert: Betty, thank you so much for inviting me to be here, and I will keep you posted on everything! Love and Blessings xo

ENDNOTE: Since this interview was done, Jessica's Talent Spotlight Magazine has launched to huge acclaim and is in about its fourth edition as we go to press with this book.

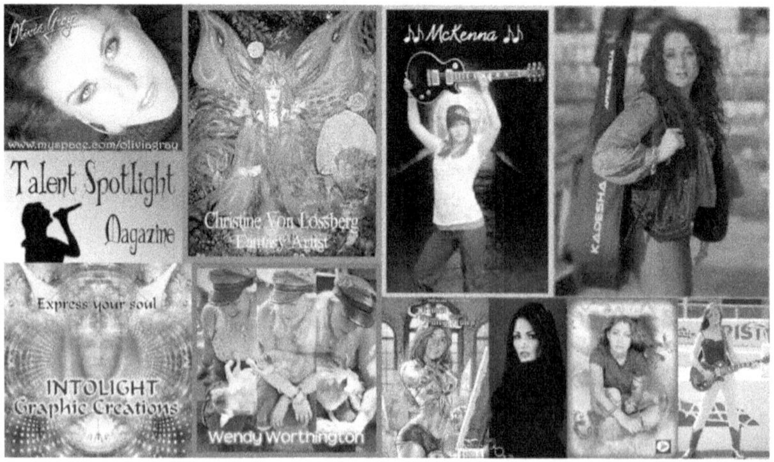

Interview with Sherwin Buydens

TALENTED MAN-OF-MANY-FACES

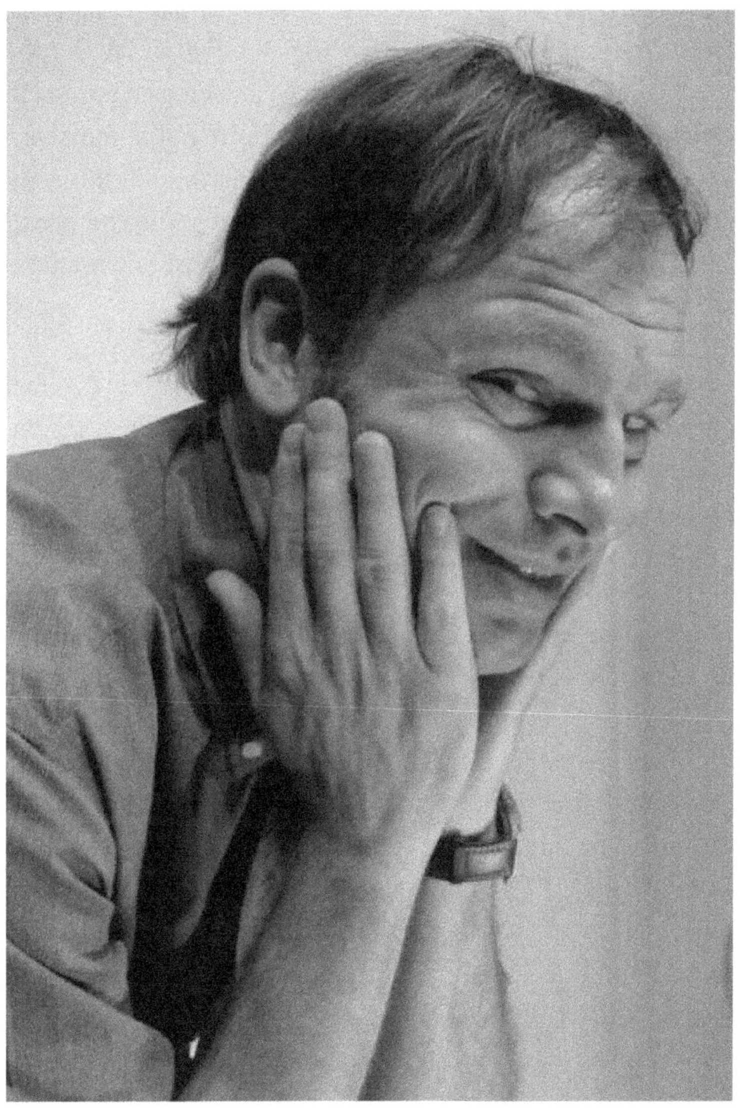

Betty Dravis: Hey, Sherwin! I just read your biography and am intrigued by your unique approach to life and your way of expressing yourself. After I met you on Facebook and viewed some photos of you. My first thoughts were: *Wow, that actor has a wonderfully expressive face; A man of many faces. I've always said that about the amazing actor Robert De Niro, too...* I see that you're quite versatile as an actor and are active in other areas of the industry, as well. You're not at the peak of your dreams yet, but you're working hard and things are beginning to happen for you. But before we get to the present, let's dig into your past. When did you know that you wanted to be an actor? How old were you at the time?

Sherwin Buydens: Well, thank you for comparing my facial expressions to Robert De Niro. He *is* versatile… Such a fabulous actor, and an actor whose career heights I can only dream of reaching.

Ms. Dravis… Betty, my whole acting career really started out with a change of mind, after taking Don S. Williams's course "On Camera Scene Study." Don was the executive producer and director of his own longest- running TV show in Canada, *The Beachcombers* (1971-1991). At one time during the course, an American actress Maria Louisa Figura was substituting for him. When she took me aside after one of the classes and said, "You could be a working actor," I felt like the manna of Heaven had descended down upon me and rays of light had filtered their way through the clouds of Vancouver, Canada. (laughs) *I could be a working actor! I could be a working actor. Wow!*

I was about 26 when Maria saw me acting in Don's class and that was the turning point in my life! My possible destiny was then chosen for me. You see, at that time I was in a rather cushy English-as-a-second-language job that I disliked and would soon receive a settlement for a small motorcycle accident I had been in.

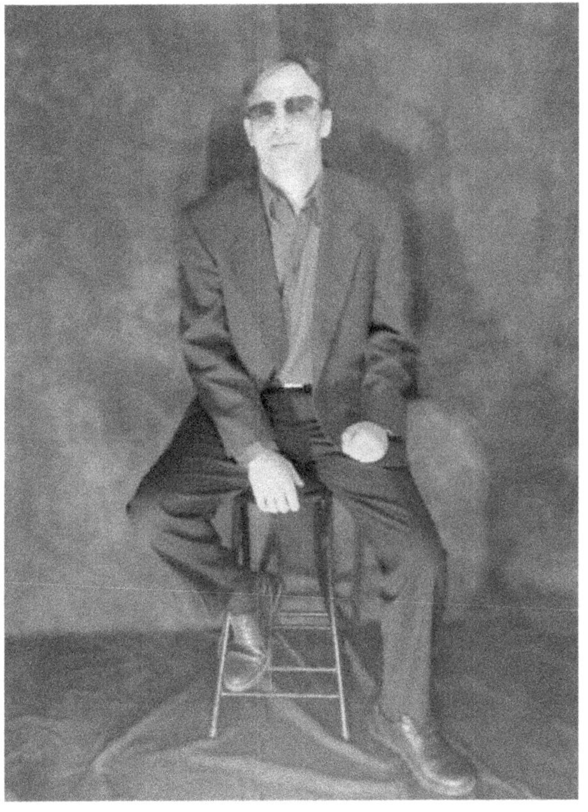

Up until then, Betty, I treated acting largely as a hobby. I did all right in acting class, in my opinion, and I took a Fine Arts Minor in college. My long-term friend Bob Phipps is also an actor, but I hadn't yet connected the dots in my mind. "Don't quit your day job" was always in the back of my head. The other thing that always concerned me was that J-O-B stood for "Just Over Broke."

I knew that if I was ever to transcend being more than middle-class in title–the prices in Vancouver are almost as high as Los Angeles–I had to think of a lasting opportunity to propel me forward in life. I had to quit treating acting as a hobby and get serious. I also knew I needed money to carry me through until acting roles came along, and that I was capable of more.

Betty Dravis: Thank God for putting people like Maria in our lives…people who first recognize that spark in us. Whether one has a talent for ditch-digging, plumbing, acting, writing, or any skill, we all need encouragement to believe in ourselves and pursue our dreams. Sherwin, I'm forever grateful to my parents and to my high school writing teacher for first believing in me.

And I'll never forget the icons that came later: Clint Eastwood, Jane Russell, the late Senator Ted Kennedy and others who spurred me on, not to mention my children, my best friend, you, my co-author Chase Von, actress Katherin Kovin Pacino, actor/director/producer Tony Tarantino, actress/singer Jenny McShane, photo-journalist C. Robert Lee and many other Dream Reachers in these books.

Let's discuss your mentors a little later in this interview, but for now I'm eager to know what happened next. Did you make it to Hollywood? And how did you support yourself?

Sherwin Buydens: It's fun to look back on that, Betty… Fast forward six months, and with settlement money in hand I was off to Los Angeles to check out the scene. Fortunately, I was trading commodities in oil and cattle, both of which were paying handsomely at the time. I was selling short on oil because before the spring of 2005, "Crude Oil" had never traded above $40 a barrel. That meant, whenever the price of oil approached close to $40, I made fistfuls of money when the price went down quickly. If you like nostalgia, that's nostalgic enough for me. (laughs)

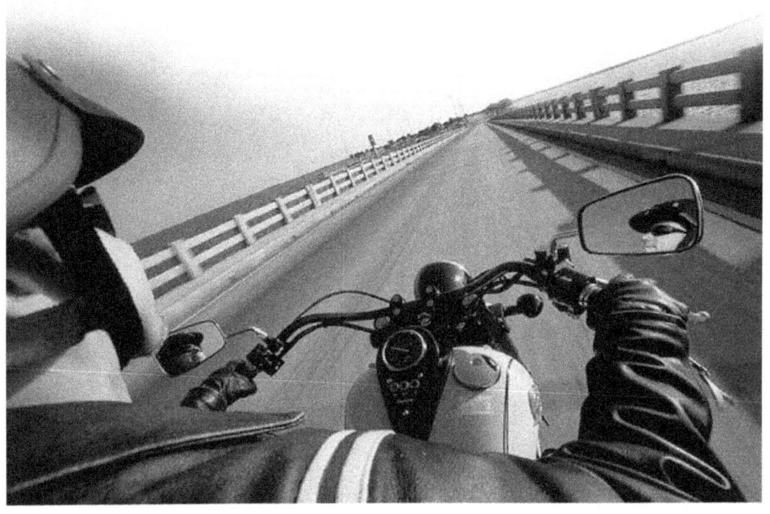

And I only traded "Live Cattle" because of the "Mad Cow Scare" that essentially dropped this commodity to fifty-five percent of its original price. I rode the price back up to ninety percent of the original. Ironically, later that would be the topic of a film I acted in called *Mad Cowgirl.* (laughs)

Fortunately, my world in commodities ended in 2005–and for the better. I discovered real estate, which was the second key to my life. I had come to discover this was the vehicle that many film producers use to finance their own films. It's all beautiful to say, "I've got this project in the works," and "I've got that project," but unless you are really marketable, how is that film going to be produced? The number one challenge to all filmmakers is cash. Ideas abound, but ultimately money in your pocket is how your project gets done. The biggest stars–Tom Cruise with the *Mission Impossible* series, for example–largely self finance their own projects, so why should I do anything differently?

Betty Dravis: I read a story about that recently, Sherwin. With the multi-millions it takes to make a film in today's economy, it's a wonder any films get done, but if they get a blockbuster they recoup their investment many times over. And if they bomb, well that's another story… But it certainly is smart of you to find something to tide you over until you establish a firm foothold in show biz. It sounds like you're laying a good foundation. I don't understand the world of commodities, but I do know a little about real estate. Second-hand knowledge to be sure, since my daughter Mindy James is a Realtor in Los Gatos. I know enough to know that the bubble burst, but that's a subject for later.

But for now, Sherwin, my readers and I are eager to know if you ever hear from Maria anymore? Did she become your mentor and who are other mentors in your life?

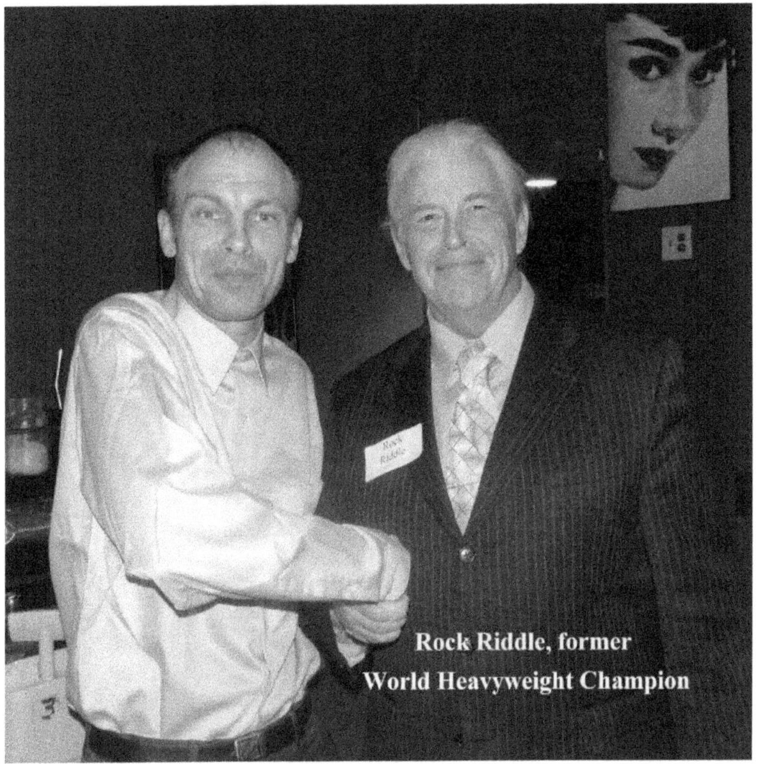

Rock Riddle, former World Heavyweight Champion

Sherwin Buydens: Strangely enough, I have not kept in touch with Maria. She was like an angel that came down to me at the right time and, somehow, many like her have entered my life at just the right time. Maria is still a beautiful woman and a consistently working actor herself. You might want to check her out on the Internet.

I enjoy remembering those days and the many wonderful people I have met along the way. Probably first in the ranks is Andrew Magliolo whom I met in Santa Monica.

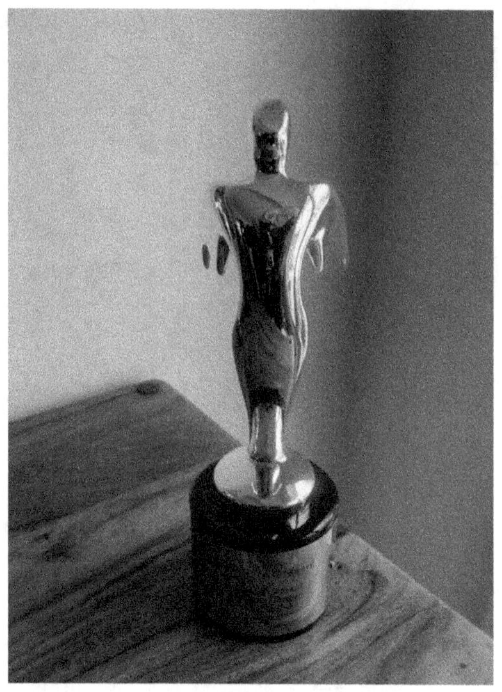

Sherwin and Bruce Schwartz won the Telly Award at The Chicago Film Festival for *I Stand Here Ironing*

He is an accomplished actor /producer, an intelligent, articulate man and successful in real estate. He emphasized to me the meaning of discipline in this business because acting is part of "show business" and how having money to pay the bills should be first on any artist's list of priorities. I remember him saying, "It took me seven years until I landed a co-starring role on *Designing Women.*" He has been a personal mentor to me and others in life, stressing financial responsibility, advocating discipline, not losing focus on the big prize and making it as a working actor.

Betty, another person of huge importance was Rock Riddle who preaches a similar theme, emphasizing the "business" part of the industry. Rock has been in the entertainment business for nearly thirty years, first as a wrestler, but also as a film and television actor, Beverly Hills agent, manager and now a promoter.

Through his ideas I have met a wide variety of people, including Tony Tarantino, whom you interviewed recently. Since I'm a person who wants to reach the highest echelon of achievement–and acting is one of those industries where most people are working a day job to survive—it's instrumental to reach out and meet people of prominence and deliver excellence.

One such example was at the American Film Market where I met Bruce R. Schwartz, back in November of 2004. He is the son of Sherwood Schwartz, probably best known for being one of the head producers of the television shows *Gilligan's Island* and *The Brady Bunch.* Bruce had an upcoming educational short film titled *I Stand Here Ironing* that would be a period piece taking place in both the 1930s and 1950s. Even though I was slated to be only an assistant producer or perhaps an associate producer, I relished the opportunity. So when Bruce's number-two person became ill with Lyme Disease, threatening to kill the project, I was determined to make that project work. I felt it was my calling.

I had remembered–after assisting in production at the theater level–how important details were to making a project work and what might be needed to make this project successful. Young people today may think of Elvis Presley as being an icon of popular culture for the 1950s, but for a 1950s middle-aged couple, there is no way they would be listening to Elvis Presley. Instead, we dressed this set with Mario Lanza, another icon for a different generation that my late grandmother adored.

Even though I did no more than background work for this piece—performing the role of an out-of-work person in a 1930s soup line–I certainly was believable. I simply made the most of the opportunity that came my way, Betty, and in the end, I was given credit for co-producing this film. I was very happy when it received two awards, the best being a Telly Award at the Chicago Film Festival. I have this award posted on my Facebook page.

No matter how large or small, when opportunities come your way, you must take advantage of them whenever possible. I bet you've learned that along the way, too… (laughs)

Perhaps one of the most inspiring anecdotes on that note is a certain character actor by the name of Kelsey Grammer. He, as I understand it, was slated to work on just four episodes of an upcoming television show called *Cheers*. As we all know, through his brilliant portrayal of Dr. Frazier Crane, he became a season regular and then gained his own show.

Of course, Hollywood is known for sexy stars, but we character actors can also do very well when the opportunities arise.

Betty Dravis: Wow, Sherwin, it sounds like you moved to L. A. at an opportune time and met many successful people. That's exciting and those are stimulating people to have in your life. I know that when I interviewed people like Tony Tarantino and others in this book and the first Dream Reachers, it invigorated me anew. And I agree with you about taking advantage of opportunities. That's been the key to whatever writing success I've achieved and I certainly regret the ones I've missed along the way. It's often in the choices we make too. We live and learn… (laughs)

I enjoyed the anecdote about Kelsey Grammer going from character actor to lead role all on the strength of his acting abilities. That's awesome! He's one of my favorites; he can sure deliver… And I'm impressed at your taking such a small part in your first movie and turning it into an award by being a team member and helping wherever you could. I wish you the same good fortune as Grammer and other TV stars that went on to major success–like the stars of the colossal hit "Friends."

But to lighten the subject, what's this I hear about you having an "affair" in America?

Sherwin Buydens: So you've heard about that, have you, Betty? Well, it's not what you think! It's not an affair "in" America! It's an affair "with" America! (laughs) As you know, I'm proud to be Canadian, and it's a wonderful country to live in, but at the moment, Canada is number two on my list. At present I'm having an affair with a lady that stands 150 feet tall, is made of copper and is proudly American. And so I am fiercely proud to be in this country too…pursuing her dream as well as my own.

Betty Dravis: I see, Sherwin! Thanks for making that clear. I love America, too, of course, and may God continue to bless us here.

You've been blessed by being in some movies. I know this is just a start, but you played the role of Ned in the short feature *Ned the Caveman;* Mo Lester in *Mad Cowgirl;* and an orthodox man in *Driving to Zigzigland.* I'd also like to share the links to two powerful videos, *Crow Magnon Man* and *Military Man* that impressed me, especially the depth of your voice and your wide range of expression, which I mentioned above.

I also saw a photo of you behind the wheel of a Vegas cab and the poster for the movie *Vegas Cabbie.* That's certainly a colorful, eye-catching, intriguing poster. I hear that you not only acted in that movie, but you also directed and produced it. How did that come about? Is it out yet? Please share the latest with our readers.

Sherwin Buydens: That film has not come out yet and I may have a hand in being the assistant director in it. The film needed a poster, and the best role I could fit in was the British gangster in an Elvis costume. This certainly is a colorful character role and I'm simply so grateful to have the opportunity. Even if you may not fit the role, you never know what role will make your career. Henry Winkler, who for many people defines the motorcycle-riding Fonz on *Happy Days,* didn't know how to ride a motorcycle. Yet, the most memorable picture of him in my mind is in the opener where he rode a motorcycle–and apparently crashed it afterwards. (laughs)

Betty Dravis: Well, good luck with *Vegas Cabbie,* Sherwin, and thanks for the bit of Hollywood trivia about "The Fonz." That's cool…

Now tell us, besides the acting classes in Canada, have you studied with anyone in the States?

Sherwin Buydens: I had taken an auditioning class with Jeff Rector some time ago, but really acting classes, overall, I would argue, are not that important once you know how the camera operates. Auditioning is important because if you can't land the acting role, you won't get hired. Keanu Reeves is an excellent example of an actor who made it in the industry because of his sensational auditioning skills. In my mind, film and television actors should also be strong theater actors, and if there is anywhere I want to improve, more theater is in the future for me. I have already performed as the doctor and old man in a Scottish play, as a soldier in *Antigone*, and as Telygin in *Uncle Vanya.* I am confident in my acting skills because I have had to perform the same roles over and over again with fresh enthusiasm each night, and because all of the great actors at one time came from the stage. If a person wants to have a career like Spencer Tracy or Jack Nicholson, or even Kelsey Grammar, there is no substitute for stage-acting. The same is absolutely true, too, for the women, such as Katherine Hepburn or Elizabeth Taylor who also added Broadway to their resumes.

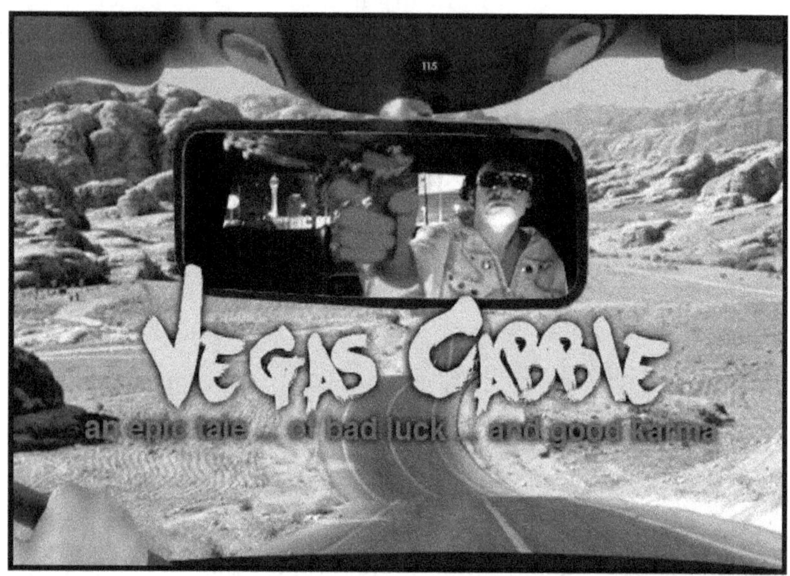

Betty Dravis: I never thought of it like that, Sherwin, but it makes lots of sense. Show biz certainly is fascinating.

I understand that you went from commodities to real estate as a means to finance your film career, but before we get serious again, I'd like to ask you a few lighter questions. If it were possible to spend the day with anyone throughout history, who would you choose…and why?

Sherwin Buydens: Fascinating question… There are two people that come to mind. One is Nostradamus and the other is William Shakespeare. I, like most people, am fascinated by the unknown. I definitely trust my intuition, and I would say my clairvoyant skills are a fair amount above average. Because I have a certain ability to “see” into the immediate future, I find Nostradamus especially interesting for his ability to look hundreds of years ahead.

My knowledge is based on a rough deduction based on current events and their probable statistics. There’s also a certain amount I can derive from people’s personalities. Nostradamus, though, was truly touched by the finger of the Almighty, for his predictions were not even remotely conceived by anyone during his life

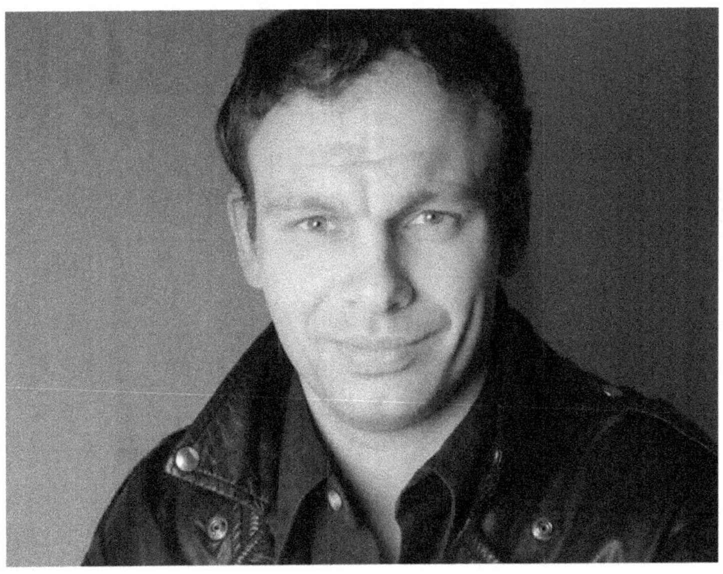

The other person far beyond others is William Shakespeare because he is, perhaps, the most articulate and intelligent writer in the English language of all time. By reading and performing Shakespeare, I find myself not only improving my acting, but

also my vocabulary, history and general intelligence. He not only had an IQ over 200, but his wit and wisdom is truly uncanny. Shakespeare's plays have endured thus far in history and probably will endure as long as there's an English language because the concepts and level of meanings that he conveys speak across classes that even people today–with some practice–can well understand. The politics of art has changed dramatically since his time, yet the brilliance of the depth of the context of his characters is truly astounding.

Betty Dravis: Your choices are incredible, Sherwin, and I think you picked perfect ones for an actor.

And now, I'm going to put you on the spot… (laughs) Since most people have had embarrassing moments at some time in their lives, do you mind sharing one of yours? It can be funny or sad, but I find they are always interesting in retrospect.

Sherwin Buydens: Betty, I don't have any embarrassing moments I wish to mention that will not get me arrested–*and I have more than a few!* I do have one defining moment when I was young that made me who I am today. Many people would find this embarrassing. When I was twelve I was chosen to deliver a sermon in front of the church on the topic of "Faith, Hope and Love." Speaking in front of 400 people at a relatively young age, I believe, helped instill my confidence in speaking publicly…and even today I enjoy it. Public speaking sure can be embarrassing, as George W. Bush learned the hard way. He's given us plenty of fodder for decades to come. Even though I've made an idiot of myself many times, if you don't put yourself into potentially embarrassing situations, how will you grow?

Betty Dravis: Ah-hhh, the famous "Bushisms" of both father and son… (laughs) Their verbal boo-boos have spawned several books, Sherwin, but I think if you scrutinize anyone who speaks a lot in public you'll find many such errors… But moving on, since you haven't mentioned your family, it would help us understand you better if you told us a little bit about them. Do they support your dream of becoming a great character actor? I understand that you live in Las Vegas now, but plan to return to L. A. Will that be soon? And how often do you get back home to Canada?

Sherwin Buydens: Well, Betty, to answer your last questions first, Canada is a bit of a distant memory already. Last time I was up north was in 2008, and I'll probably make it back early next year. As for Los Angeles, it's definitely in my near future. My feeling is, when the time comes, I will be ready and waiting. Los Angeles is already my second–nearing first—home, but when will I move? My best guesstimate is a few months…

In my family, Dad was the entrepreneur, and although he was never thrilled about me becoming "just an actor," he definitely accepted my decision when I got involved with anything financial. As for my mom, that side of the family contains the artists and athletes, so she understood and promoted my dream with enthusiasm. My grandfather was a talented fiddle player; a cousin on that side of the family has danced for the National

Ballet of Canada; another cousin has played for the women's Canadian national soccer team. And my mother's older brother played semi-professional baseball.

Betty Dravis: Hey, you're a pretty diplomatic man, then, Sherwin… You hit on the very things that keep both parents happy with you: real estate and acting. (laughs)

But moving on… This might seem trivial, but what are your favorite foods and restaurants in Vegas? You also appear to be slim and trim by nature. Does that make it easier for you to stay in top condition in order to keep up with your many interests?

Sherwin Buydens: Absolutely, Betty! The foremost purpose of food is to keep your mind and body healthy. Thanks to Mom, I'm slim by nature and I, generally, eat very healthy. Spinach is one of my favorite foods and if I ever grow up, I want to look like Popeye. (laughs) As far as restaurants, anything cheap and relatively healthy is good. I like hotdogs as much as the next person, but I'm more likely to eat at Subway. The Klondike has the $1.59-24-hour breakfast with eggs, bacon or sausage and toast, which can be addictive. Cici's Pizza has an all-you-can-eat lunch buffet for $3.99. The Orleans has some good cheap food too. Vegas is a fun place to eat, no question about it. The area around Vegas is also scenic and wonderful for hiking and walking, which I also enjoy.

Red Rock Canyon makes an excellent day trip and I can often be found there. It is easy to see why *Star Trek,* and other television and films have scenes that were shot there.

Betty Dravis: Having lived in Reno for a few years after retirement, I know that in "gaming" towns, it's easy to find excellent meals at very reasonable prices; they offer lower prices on food to lure the gamblers to their casinos. It's only good business… Thanks for that information, Sherwin, and for telling us about the scenic wonders of the Las Vegas too.

Now, before we get into your real estate interests, what advice would you give to anyone aspiring to break into the entertainment industry?

Sherwin Buydens: Well, Betty, anyone serious about acting–or any business, for that matter–needs to understand the business and learn from the masters of personal achievement. People like Bob Proctor, Wayne Dyer, Deepak Chopra, Burt Goldman, Vishen Lakhiani and Earl Carmichael should be at the forefront in their world. I also believe it's *easy* to make it in the acting world.

In Los Angeles the prime determining factor for people is money. Marketing is huge and your contacts will help you succeed. If you can volunteer in a worthy project you are usually "in" because people of talent with ambition and enough money to cover their bills will rise to the top.

Betty Dravis: Everyone else says it's hard to make it in "Tinsel Town," but what you say makes sense if one is willing to work from the bottom up. Your attitude is spot on!

What's your favorite quote, Sherwin?

Sherwin Buydens: I have many, Betty, but I'd like to share one that will give everyone some food for thought. It's from Napoleon Hill who wrote for Andrew Carnegie, the second richest man ever: "Whatever the mind can conceive and believe, the mind can achieve."

I also recommend that everyone view his YouTube video.

Betty Dravis: That's powerful advice, Sherwin. I've watched several of those inspiring men on TV and they are, indeed, masters at motivating people to reach the heights in whatever they do in life. Thanks for sharing that.

And now, tell us about your real estate ventures. I hear that something big is in the works. Before sharing that, please tell us your thoughts on real estate. How are you doing so well since the bubble burst and so many were hurt by losing their homes?

Sherwin Buydens: The latest opportunity in my life has been commercial real estate. Why buy houses when you can buy apartment buildings? We all know many areas of the country are in a residential-housing mess. So, too, another potential mess is coming up if one wishes to cash in at the commercial front. I am not the first proponent of the saying "Think Big and Kick Ass," as used by Donald Trump, because thinking small will land anyone from any walk of life in the slow lane, as I'm confident you know. These days I'm partnering in buying apartment buildings of at least 100-150 units. My position will be the asset manager. I find the deal and help implement the management which will assist in changing a potential gem of an asset into a moneymaker.

Strangely enough, I didn't have to go out into the world and learn this skill. My grandparents were caretakers of an apartment building before they passed away and I took an active role in cleaning and landscaping it. From them, I've gained a true understanding of the industry from the bottom up, and yet pursuing acting has led me on *this* career path, which is fascinating, lucrative and life changing.

Betty Dravis: You certainly are versatile, Sherwin. Most people would be happy simply to make it in real estate and own all that property, but you burn with ambition to be an actor.

With that attitude, I expect you to go a long way.

How did you gain such confidence?

Sherwin Buydens: I've always used a Raymond Aaron reference about taking a look back on your life. Pretend this day is your last day on the planet and ask yourself what you have contributed. My life has already had some big challenges with playing semi-professional, under-eighteen soccer, playing piano and failing in the first year only to get first class honors four years later. So I'm not starting from a position of a lack of self-confidence.

That's not to say I have any greater or more obvious talents than anyone else. I simply have searched to work with the best

I can, and for that reason there will be some big challenges ahead.

Betty Dravis: Who is the man in the photo of you with a product called Elbow Friend? What's that and why are you posing with it?

Sherwin Buydens: That's my friend Stephen Goetsch who has directed and edited numerous projects in both television and film. Like me, Stephen is an ex-athlete, in the tennis world—and girls, he is still single. (laughs) We're posing with the pink Elbow Friend, which is the latest color in the ergonomic armrest cushion line, because he had many requests for the color pink and finally found the right fabric. You well know the line: "Know your audience," and that line works in many genres of life.

Betty Dravis: I watched the video about that product and wouldn't mind trying it myself, Sherwin. I have no problem with my elbows, but I do get neck tension from typing so much. I see that it could help in that area, also.

What do you hope for in your future, Sherwin?

Sherwin Buydens: I want to reach my highest purpose, Betty. (laughs) I believe what you and Chase state on the cover of *Dream Reachers: Only those who strive to reach their dreams find themselves living them.* And I'll work as hard as I can to make my dreams come true. I want at least one Oscar in my future, a whole list of real estate assets, and I want to meet more people to obtain maximum growth in this life. Currently, I'm very close to signing my first apartment deal–176 units in Dallas, Texas. That's exciting because I'll own a full fifty percent!

Betty Dravis: That's incredible, Sherwin. Congratulations! It appears that you're well on your way to reaching your dreams. You may end up being a Donald Trump and Kelsey Grammer combined in one big bundle of happiness. I certainly wish that for you. That's why I wanted you to join our growing rank of Dream Reachers.

Now, since we're nearing the end of our interview, is there anything I missed that you'd like to share today?

Sherwin Buydens: You went into more detail than I had hoped for, Betty. I cherish the opportunity to work with like-minded people such as you, and I really wish to create a legacy I can be proud of. Then, like Andrew Carnegie, I can give away much of my wealth. My first goal financially is to obtain a thousand units. Every day I re-affirm to myself that I deserve to be great! Here is another quote for you from Muhammad Ali: "I am the greatest… I said that even before I knew I was."

Betty Dravis: Good ol' Ali! *How right he was!* And, Sherwin, don't forget me when you start giving that money away. (laughs) You're certainly an ambitious man… I admire that in you and let me repeat: from watching your videos, I'm truly impressed with your acting skills, your voice and your wide range of facial expression.

By the way, I'm really impressed with the Internet Movie Data Base, a website that shares so much about artists in the entertainment industry. It's a fabulous research site for writers and those in the entertainment industry too. For all your fans, you can be found there also.

Thanks for sharing your busy time with us, Sherwin. This has been a fun, fascinating interview. We wish you all the best and please keep us posted about your life and your dreams. We'll be seeing you on the big screen, and on Facebook, of course. (laughs)

Sherwin Buydens: Well, thank *you,* Betty. I've really enjoyed doing this. There, no doubt, will be plenty of fantastic news on the horizon and I promise to let you know when more develops. We spoke of opportunities above and I'd like to thank you again for taking time with me for this opportunity. I'll be looking for more books written by you and Chase Von. And whatever I can do to make *your* dreams come true, please don't hesitate to ask. Take care…

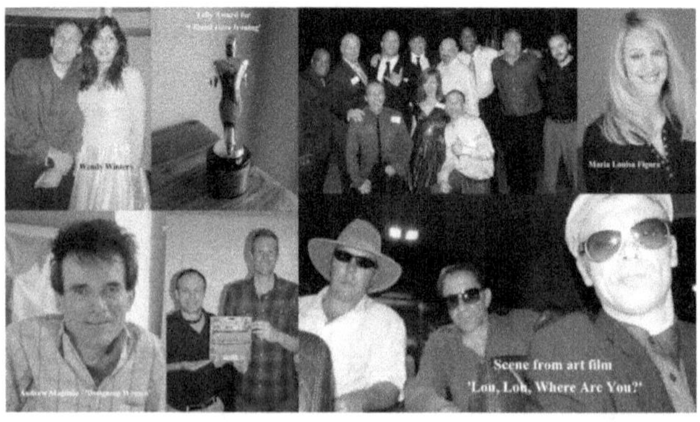

Interview with Dr. Linda Salvin

PSYCHIC RADIO HOST: 'BEACON IN THE DARKNESS'

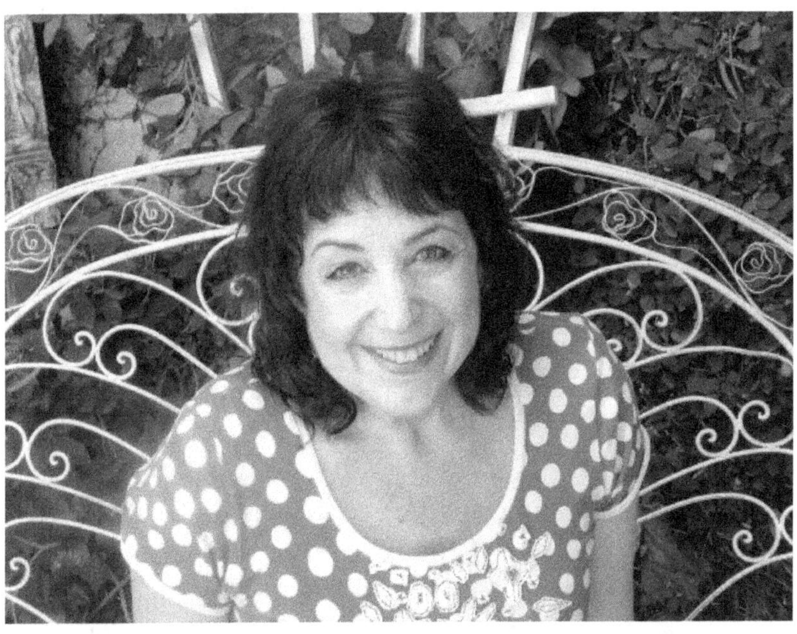

Betty Dravis: Dr. Salvin, you are a *first* for me! I have never interviewed anyone with your special skills before, so I hope that we both learn from this interview. Since I am a devout Christian, I'm somewhat of a skeptic–but a skeptic with an open mind…at least during the course of this interview (laughs).

I know that you believe in God, too, so am eager to see how your psychic skills fit in with His plan for your life.

As you know, my co-author and I write books called *Dream Reachers* and they're all about high-achieving people and the problems they encounter in reaching their dreams. I chose to interview you because you definitely fit that category. As well as being on popular websites like Dames of Dialogue and Student Operated Press, your interview will also be included in *Dream Reachers: Vol. II.*

I met you through Facebook and you come highly recommended by actress Katherin Kovin Pacino who is one of your best friends. Tell us how you met Kat and exactly what it is you do. I read that you had been a successful public health official and that you got started on your new path through a series of traumatic accidents. Can you share about that? I realize your life reads like a book, so please share the highlights.

That said, let me welcome you to Dames of Dialogue with open arms. It's always fun talking about the unknown, so I suspect we will have fun. I know our readers enjoy reading about interesting people and *you,* Dr. Salvin, are *that* and more.

Dr. Linda Salvin: Hi, Betty…and please call me Linda. We have chatted enough on Facebook to be on a first-name basis. I prefer the informality of places like Facebook, as I know you do.

First off, let me thank you for inviting me to participate with your *Dream Reachers, Vol. II* publication as well as the Dames of Dialogue and Student Operated Press. I am honored to be considered a high-achiever among your other featured people. You have such an impressive catalogue of celebrities you have interviewed throughout the decades, I cannot see how I got so lucky to be included in your collection. Again, my heart-felt appreciation…

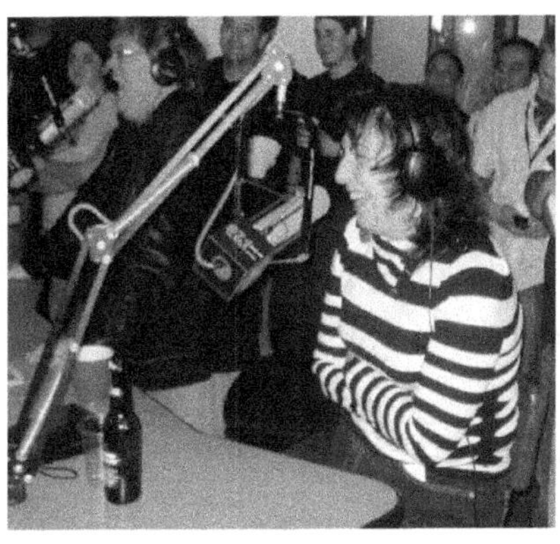

To answer your first question, my background is Health Education and Epidemiology, the study of epidemics. Many people thought it was skin, which is dermatology. (laughs)

Although I will discuss my educational background in depth below, once out of school, many strange events began to take place in my life. The first occurred in the fall of 1977 after I returned from Europe. I had just been offered a position at General Dynamics in Pomona for an Industrial Hygienist. The job entailed creating a program to ensure the health and well-being of the manufacturing plant from chemical and toxic exposures. The weekend following the interview, I had a bizarre fall in the bathroom where I passed out, was rushed to the hospital and found I had sustained a concussion when my head hit the toilet and broke a chunk of porcelain. I was laid up for about ten days, called the company and asked if they could hold the job for me.

All the while, something inside me told me not to take it. I ignored that little voice and worked there for two-and-a-half years. I established the Industrial Hygiene program just as OSHA was coming of age in the late '70s. I was one of four professional women in a very male-dominated industry of many ex-military personnel; certainly not the place for someone like me who once walked moratoriums for the Vietnam War in high school!

During my years in the health field, among other things, at USC I did brain tumor research as well as research on Vietnam veterans exposed to Agent Orange, developed the drug abuse program for Cal State Northridge, taught AIDS education to kids on parole in the California Youth Authority. But the funny thing was, I just could not figure out how I ended up working at a gray metal desk with my window looking out at barbed wire fences. I quit my job without having another to go to. My spiritual journey was about to begin…

Betty Dravis: Sorry you had the accident, Linda, but perhaps that ended up for the better since it probably had a great deal to do with your rethinking your job situation…even if you did go on to work over two years in that program. (laughs)

And NO, I can't picture you behind a "gray metal desk," but it's heartening to know that you were helping people in both phases of your career. But please continue. I'm eager to learn all about your spiritual journey and everything you do now. I know you're a popular radio host with a big following, but other than that… Hmmmm…

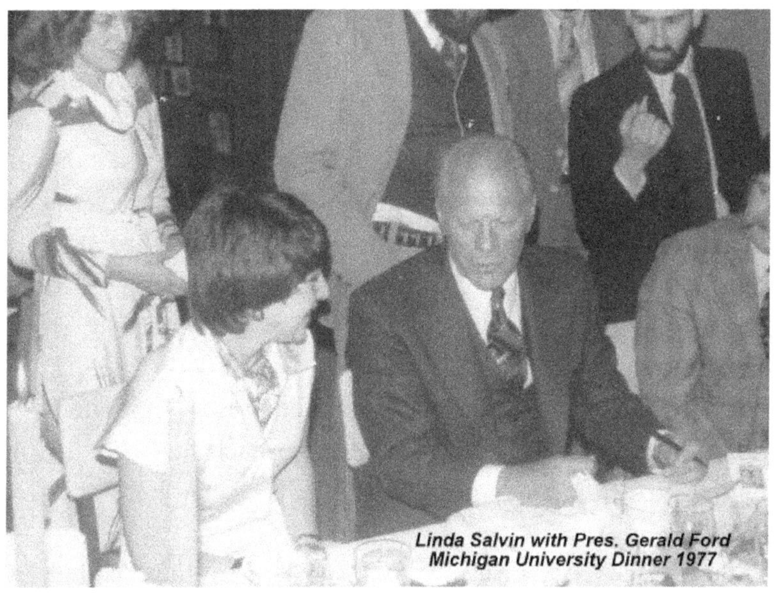
Linda Salvin with Pres. Gerald Ford
Michigan University Dinner 1977

Dr. Linda Salvin: Well, Betty, I'm just as eager to tell my story. Talking it out is cathartic, in a way. OK, after leaving General Dynamics in early 1980, a friend from San Francisco asked if I wanted to house-sit their home while she and her husband traveled through Europe. (I had actually known my friend in high school and ran into her in a college class in San Francisco.) Her offer came at an opportune time for me, so I took advantage of the offer to partly decide if I would want to relocate to the Bay Area again and partly to escape many of the conflicts I was facing.

Not sure what I was going to pursue at the time, I decided to return to what I have termed, "the scene of my crime" to figure out what happened to me along the way. I moved back to San Francisco for two months, but loved it so much that I stayed five–until deciding to return home to Los Angeles where I planned to enter the music industry once and for all.

I had begun my spiritual trek a year or two before, seeking out what God and the universe really meant to me, had in store for me and what spirituality might mean to me. I went on unemployment, taking time off after six straight years of college followed by a few years of work. It was time to think things through.

While there, I interviewed at UC Berkeley for an Epidemiology appointment, was flown down to Long Beach for an Industrial Hygiene position. I was offered both and rejected both.

While in San Francisco, I took what was then called est training, a popular self-awareness workshop. After that experience, staying with friends and finally getting ready to make a commitment again, I packed up my car, drove down the coast and landed in my parents' home in Beverly Hills. It was also their 30th wedding anniversary party and I wanted to be there to celebrate with them.

In December, 1980, I interviewed with an insurance company for an Environmental Health Specialist position which I was offered. I was in training just two months when I received my first out-of-town assignment; it was in San Jose, California. I drove to Newport Beach to meet my partner and then to John Wayne Airport to catch a plane to San Jose. We were to test ethylene oxide exposure in an autoclave to determine chemical exposure levels in a hospital. We needed to determine the safety and toxicity levels to insure health standards were in effect. An autoclave is where surgical instruments are sterilized. We instructed the staff not to open the autoclave door during the next four hours. At the two-hour-check mark, we discovered someone had tampered with our sampling and invalidated our entire day's work.

We decided to pack up and head back to the airport. While sitting in the coffee shop, I turned to look at the parked plane and said, "Doesn't it look like it could crack there?" When my partner turned, he did not see the exhaust or settlement line that I did, which seemed to appear beyond the wing of the plane.

An hour-and-a-half later, our plane crash-landed to avoid collision with another plane taking off on the same runway. Statistically, the probability of all of us surviving was about two billion to one. *But we did!* I guess you could say that was my first premonition.

My life changed forever that day, February 17, 1981.

I spent many years confused, frightened, spiritually challenged, alone and trying to figure out what had happened to me. When I say alone, I mean few people could identify with my challenges, feelings or sensations. I didn't know I had become so God-conscious and psychic at the same time. I did not know where to turn, who to talk to. Even therapists could not identify with me. I was in conflict for at least six years, to say the least.

However, during that time, I had a number of “wake-up calls”: my car was hit by a fire-truck; in 1984, I totaled a car; and had the white-light experience and was given a choice to live or die. Had I not experienced all of this, I would not believe it either…

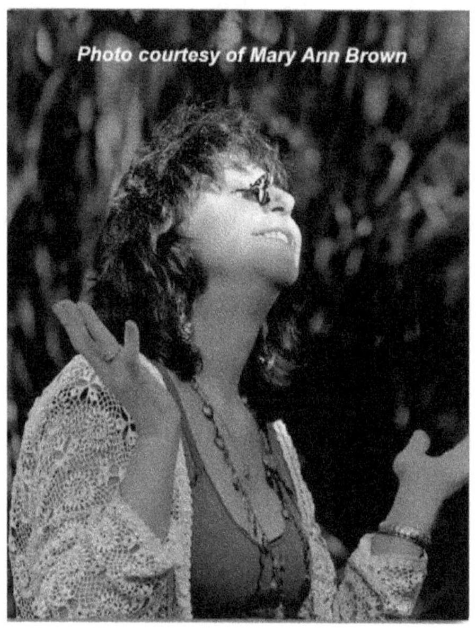
Photo courtesy of Mary Ann Brown

Yes, there is a God in my life! Although raised Jewish, my awareness of God broadened. Yes, I believe there is something out there directing us all on our journey–especially when we veer from our truth–or to encourage us to move more toward our higher and ultimate purpose if the soul’s yearning to grow is such. I know I had a thirst for knowledge I did not understand in high school but was philosophical in my own right. Yet, as an adult, I entered the world of science and was less creative than I had been.

We all change through our decisions. What I have learned is that if we get off the path, by opening spiritually, we can return to our God-given self and become who we were intended to be.

The plane crash opened my eyes, as did all the other accidents. I was going toward music but then psychic abilities took over and although I ran for eleven years–while attempting to work in public health, health education at a local university, working as an epidemiologist in cancer research, etc.–things still did not sit right within me. I became restless and uncomfortable within my own skin and did not know why. It was as if a surge of energy was pushing me. Intelligence, attractiveness, education, a nice salary and *gee*, something still wasn't right.

Betty Dravis: Frightening accidents and experiences like that would make anyone sit up and take notice, Linda. Yours was a hard path to get where God wanted you to be. Thanks for sharing your San Francisco college years. What other colleges did you attend? Since your parents lived in Beverly Hills, is that where you were born? A so-called Valley Girl at that time? (laughs)

Dr. Linda Salvin: I grew up in Sherman Oaks, Betty; my parents moved to Beverly Hills when I was in grad school. My college education extends beyond San Francisco State University. I began undergraduate work at Los Angeles Valley

College in Van Nuys, California and left in my sophomore year, February, 1973. This is where I made a very big mistake in my life that now is just a chunk of time for learning a big lesson–a painful one at that! I followed a boyfriend up to college even though we had just broken up. I did not have the courage to say I no longer wanted to attend that school, so I left home and went anyway. Not a good experience for me but I did earn my BA in Health Science in May, 1975. I can still hear my mother asking if I wanted to come home and my reply of "No!" How many times do I wish I had said, "Yes?"

That summer after I graduated, I was working as a camp counselor at a Girl Scout camp when I received a phone call from my mother, saying I had been accepted to the University of Michigan in Ann Arbor for my Master's in Public Health Epidemiology. I really liked studying disease and thought it would be exciting to do and I considered becoming a doctor. I quit camp, went to visit friends in the Bay Area, returned to LA and prepared for grad school.

Four years after grad school was the life-altering plane crash. *Gee, did my life change!*

In 1989, I was working for a private organization where we taught AIDS education to kids on parole in the California Youth Authority. On a weekend night, I was hit in my car by another car that jumped the lane, spun out on the Hollywood freeway. I was so frightened, I just said, "Oh, God, help me!" as I scrambled for the brake pedal. Like the Red Sea parting, all eight lanes heading north into the San Fernando Valley that night came to a halt and somehow, by the grace of God, I was able to turn my car around and drive over to the right shoulder where there were a few other cars who had been involved in the accident. I was not at fault. I had to get all the information from the other people. I knew I had a headache but did not know the extent of it at that time.

Each accident I had been in damaged my back, neck and arms, but they also took me out of my body and closer to God. After the last accident, I had such agonizing headaches that the neurologist told me it would take at least two years of treatment before I felt better. But after what I had been through since 1981, there was no way I'd spend two more years healing.

I was determined to get well fast, so I found a wonderful chiropractor who was able to unlock the pinched nerve and assist me. Thank God for chiropractors.

Betty Dravis: Those headaches must have been awful to endure, Linda, and I'm so glad you found help from a chiropractor. That's a wonderful testimony to their skills. My son-in-law Nick Rodriguez is a chiropractor. He and my daughter Allison own O'Hara Chiropractic in San Jose. He sure was a blessing to me when I suffered a pinched sciatic nerve. But please go on, your story is gripping.

Dr. Linda Salvin: Your son-in-law and daughter are healing people, too, Betty. I'm pleased to hear that. God's blessings on them…

The odd thing is that after that accident, I became more psychic, but due to the headaches, I quit my job, took on odd jobs and played music around town. But fate stepped in again: In 1991, I fell ill and needed emergency surgery.

My gynecologist explained that as a result of tumors, if I didn't have surgery, I would end up dying. I remember him asking how important having children was to me. Having already bypassed a few of the relationships I had ever considered having children with, I knew the decision to surrender my child-bearing abilities for my life was my next challenge. So there I was, facing another very difficult and upsetting time…again.

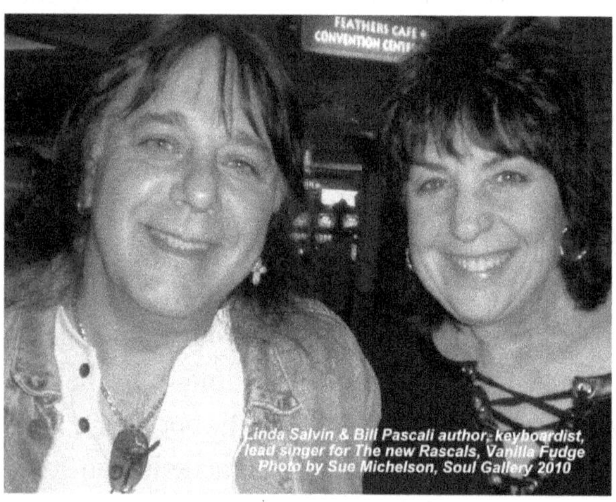
Linda Salvin & Bill Pascali author, keyboardist, lead singer for The new Rascals, Vanilla Fudge Photo by Sue Michelson, Soul Gallery 2010

The upside was that shortly after I began to heal, the energy from my hands began to flow from me and the healing gift I have today emerged. I did stand-up comedy for awhile and the joke was that they took out my uterus and I became a healer. Go figure… (laughs)

Betty Dravis: You've certainly had a lot of pain in your life, Linda, but you are such a giving, caring woman, I know you would suffer it all over again in exchange for the gift of healing and helping others. You're an amazing woman; a less strong woman wouldn't be able to endure what you did and then joke about it in your comedy routine. Wow! Tell us more… I'm eager to hear how you got started in radio, and I bet our readers are, also.

Dr. Linda Salvin: Well, Betty, I do have more to say, but I'm not used to talking in-depth about myself, so stop me if I go too far. (laughs) On the other hand, I could talk all night about my career. I love explaining the spiritual and metaphysical sides of life.

But first, I'll respond to your radio question: I got started in radio in1994. I worked for Psychic Friends Network, was in their Infomercial with Dionne Warwick for two seasons (1992-93), worked awhile as a psychic and then went out on my own. Shortly after the 1994 earthquake here in Los Angeles, I was selected out of 365 people to be the night-time psychic on Los Angeles's KBIG 104 FM radio. The station was one of the largest rock stations in town.

By that summer, I had built a following and was known as *the* radio psychic. The creative director there, who is still a great friend today, suggested I start my own show. I took his advice and after sixteen years, I have been nationally syndicated on AM/FM, cable and now I have my own Internet station. I hope to grow over time… as word gets out.

Betty Dravis: Congratulations on going national, Linda. That's a huge leap in the right direction. By stretching to reach your dreams, as we urge in our *Dream Reachers* books, you have fulfilled dream after dream. I'm sure your following will reach the stratosphere. I'm familiar with your show from your website and on Facebook and I got a taste of just how popular you are: When you and I started conversing there, I suddenly started receiving friendship requests from quite a few people who are huge fans of yours…and from your competitors, as well. (laughs) It was obvious, because they mentioned you in requesting my friendship. You can't keep any secrets on Facebook, can you?

Dr. Linda Salvin: I didn't know that, Betty, but you're right… (laughs)

I love Facebook. It's a wonderful way to network, to meet people and, hopefully, help them with their everyday and health problems. Thanks for sharing that about my "fans" who contacted you. However, fans is such a presumptuous word. I like to think of them as clients, even friends.

But you asked about "all" I do, so I will start with metaphysics which is a combination of religion, psychology and esoteric beliefs. After all I had experienced and how I had grown, changed and evolved, I felt it best to validate my educational and professional side with the top degree to complement my previous academic degrees. I returned to school and received my PhD in 2008 from the American Institute of Holistic Theology.

In the late '90s, I developed a candle line called Wicks of Wisdom® which are "…like a prescription for your soul."®

These candles include three per set with essential oils, herbs and powders to assist spiritually to increase finances, love, health, luck, win legal cases, balance dysfunctional relationships and much more. For years, I have received testimonial after testimonial from my clients and that–along with the readings, healings and channelings–gives me great satisfaction. Knowing I have been able to help others achieve something on their journey through life makes it all worthwhile. People can see the candles on TV and our website pages that can be found by Googling my name.

I mentioned channeling, Betty, and most people are interested in that. Here is the odd, painful way I came to learn I could channel: After the hysterectomy and the healing work, I discovered my body was developing more and more benign tumors. At one point I had about forty tumors removed from hips and thighs. They needed to come out as they each had their own independent blood supply, called angiolipomas.

I eventually discovered I was placing the energy from healing people back into my body. One day after surgery, I was wearing shorts, slapped my hands down on my lap and saw it: many of the scars of the various tumors that had been removed were in the perfect shape of my eight fingers and two thumbs.

That's when I realized I had to change the way I dealt with energy.

I had three more surgeries for tumors by 1999 and each surgery seemed to elevate my gift. I have learned that since anesthesia is the closest thing to death, it may also have had something to do with the spiritual changes I went through while removing the negative masses of energy I had accumulated in my body (which are considered tumors).

After the first surgery to remove the tumors, I had a client come to see me. He asked about his wife who was deceased. I began to speak as if she were coming through me. He said I was just like her. I was pleasantly surprised to learn that I was given the gift of transmediumship after that surgery. All in all, the accidents led to opening up, finding God, knowing there is a force out there guiding me, you and the rest of the planet.

It appears that the first surgery took me to a new level and the following surgeries opened me up to yet a different world to help people, read, explore and comprehend the different dimensions of life. I do not have enough time (or space here) to write a complete dissertation of my ideas of what this all means, Betty. I do know there is spirit; I do know there is something outside of ourselves and not just within ourselves that directs us. I feel that aligning and integrating is the key for the true life's happiness and purpose. Love, work, fulfillment, happiness, contentment come when doing God's will. There are challenges, decisions, choices and free will. I have learned how my will caused me upset and by becoming aware of spiritual laws, life's flow and synchronicity timing of people, places and things, life took on an entirely new meaning and path for my purpose and fulfillment.

Even while in therapy for treatment of the post anxiety stress disorder I suffered following the plane crash, I could not heal or recover properly. I had difficulty sleeping and awakening.

The only way I began to feel comfortable was when I found God in my life. I began to trust the universe, the energy, and the messages of the universe. I began to see that everything happens in time for a reason; that God's rejection is God's protection; and a coincidence is God acting anonymously. I began to understand the synchronicity of life.

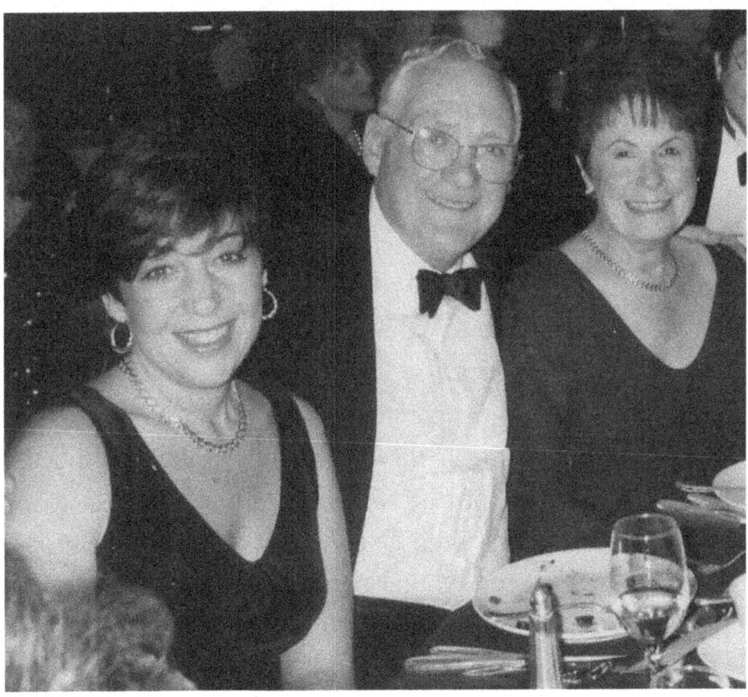

As I said above, a year after the plane crash, I was hit by a fire-truck and in 1984 had totaled a car and experienced the white light, where I was given the choice to live or die. Regarding the white light experience, I was driving home on a rainy night.

The street lights were out. I was heading north as a car entered the intersection going west. I broadsided the car. I said to myself, "They're going so fast! I want to go home." Next thing I knew, my car spun out and as I was spinning and came to a halt, and–as God is my witness–a white light went from the top of my head, through the ceiling of my Camaro and into the heavens. I heard a loud voice say, "You can come with us now or stay and do…" And I was given a message I choose not to share at this time.

Freaking out, I chose to stay. Paramedics pried me out of my car. When I stood on the street, I cried, "They want me off the planet! They want me off the planet!" I was rushed to UCLA for observation. After all the accidents from 1981 to this one in 1984, I felt like something was out to get me, change me and finally, redirect me. I know, many people say they would never drive with me. The truth is, I have been through so many different events that most people never go through…or perhaps only once. But I've been through many which continued to alter my life and perspectives. After a while, I began to feel like I had a connection to the "other side," like a bumper car is connected by a metal rod to the electrical system above to drive around and bump other cars.

My first clients were through the Psychic Friends Network, even though after the plane crash my friends kept saying that everything I told them kept coming true. I knew I had become psychic but ran for eleven years before I embraced it and surrendered to using the gift for a career. The calls on the network helped me gain the confidence to read for people accurately.

Within months of my readings, I had several repeat callers telling me I was one of the few who knew what they were talking about, whose predictions actually came true and that I could help them. Six months into this, I received a call from the Psychic Friends Network office asking if I would be interested in being in their upcoming infomercial. I agreed and from there my psychic career took off. I worked the line a couple of years, was invited to do a few TV interviews like CNN-FN, Hard Copy, John & Leeza, etc. and one thing led to another. I had no idea what I was doing other than I created a business for myself using faith…with one foot in front of the other. Word got out on and off the radio, my client base grew to include celebrities and now, sixteen years later, I have read, healed and/or channeled for close to 18,000 – 20,000 people.

At the beginning of this interview you asked how I had met actress Katherin Kovin Pacino. Well, Betty, Kat and I met via my radio show. She was a listener, then a client. I read her a few times; she had already lost her husband Sal Pacino and I remember she had just met her current husband, Bill Lashbrook…or had just married him. We eventually became friends.

She is a very down to earth, lovely person who I trust completely.

That is difficult in the Hollywood scene. She is one of my friends who does not abuse my gifts and we understand each other. I do offer to assist her, to guide her.

One of the sad things about my career is that there are people who want me only for my gift, but Bill and Kat see me as the person I am, as I see them for who they are, not what they do.

Betty Dravis: *Twenty thousand people!* Oh, my, that's impressive to think you've touched so many lives… Thanks for sharing how you met the gracious, charming Kat. I met her on Facebook and I'm grateful she led me to you. I agree, she's a lovely woman…inside and out.

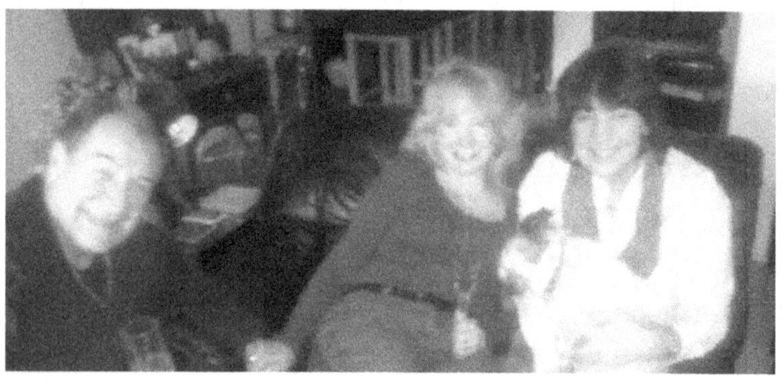

Bill Lashbrook, Katherin Kovin Pacino Lashbrook & Dr. Linda Salvin

I was fortunate to meet her and Bill during the course of an interview for this book. My son Robert, his girlfriend Patty Carrillo and her mother Roma Vargas accompanied us to a fine Mexican restaurant in San Rafael. We had a wonderful time and it delights me that you both will be featured in our new book.

Dr. Linda Salvin: I heard about that from Kat, Betty, but I'd better get back to the question of how I got started in radio…before you get impatient with me. (laughs) I know you have a deadline: In 1994, after experiencing all I had in the '80s during that lost decade of mine–when all my friends were becoming yuppies and I was becoming psychic and spiritual with three near-death experiences–I had toyed with my music career again, but it never went anywhere. (Some news on that front is happening now, but I'll share that below.)

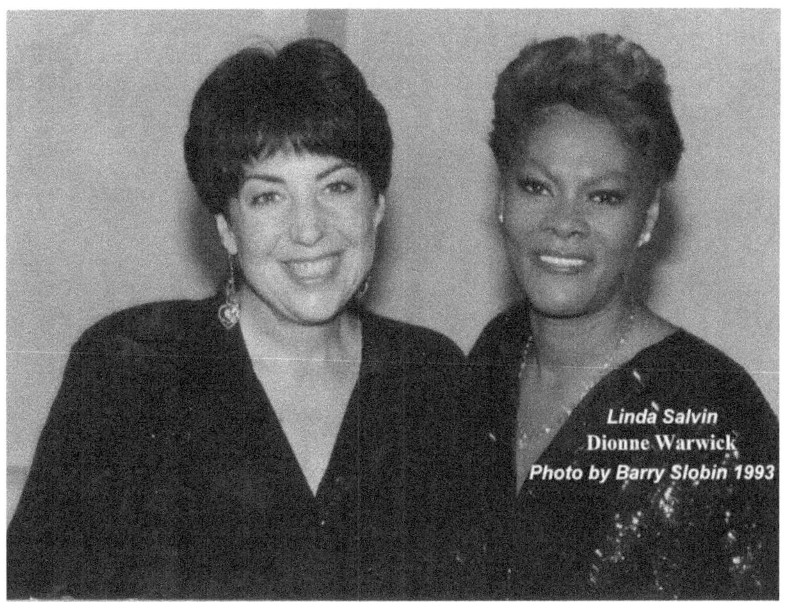
Linda Salvin
Dionne Warwick
Photo by Barry Slobin 1993

When I was accepted into the radio gig, I saw immediate financial results and opted to concentrate on radio and psychic work to help people (instead of my music). I gave up music for radio.

But my big news for today is that in February (2010), I just signed a new contract where I am being branded by a company for the new Dr. Linda Salvin Psychic & Astrology Network which is going to be a terrific new psychic and astrology line with great readers. I will be heard on *national* radio doing daily commercials for astrology and returning to terrestrial radio (AM/FM) with my two-hour broadcast, in addition to what I do currently online. The link is on my Facebook page. We will be on hundreds of radio and TV stations advertising the line. The line will also upsell Wicks of Wisdom and the company will be airing my Infomercial. Therefore, everything I have done on my own until now (these past sixteen years) is being integrated and elevated to a new and grander level. Hopefully, we will go *global.*

Betty Dravis: OMG, Linda, your life story is mesmerizing. That white light experience would send the average person around the bend, but by that time you were deep into understanding your gifts, so were able to infiltrate them into your growing awareness of yourself and what you hope to achieve with your life. More power to you! *And going national!* All I can say is that you served a severe apprenticeship and are ready for it… Now, we have reached the point where you must share your other good news with us—your *music* news! I bet you are happy to finally be able to use your lifelong love of music as well as your psychic gifts. The future must look very rosy at the moment.

Dr. Linda Salvin: Gee, Betty, I thought music would simply be a form of pleasure and relaxation for me in my downtime at home. But as God and the universe would see it, after you asked me to write this, my dear friend George Brown (of Kool & the Gang) has offered to produce my music. We are meeting to discuss my songs which are quite spiritual and folksy. I began playing guitar at age nine and have never been able to evolve my style. I always sound like me, a folk singer, no matter what style I try to cover. I am most comfortable as a folkie, but was embarrassed by my style for many years. But now in the digital age, with online opportunities, it seems all genres are acceptable and music, which is the language of soul, is as unique as each of us. I have recorded demos of songs I've written and play rhythm acoustic guitar and am happy to finally be returning to the studio.

The future does, indeed, look rosy. *Very rosy!* I am excited about the national syndication and the possibility of having my songs produced. I can't wait to see what develops.

Betty Dravis: That's encouraging, Linda. Music is a big part of who you are, also, and this opportunity will give you a healthy balance between the serious Linda and the fun-loving Linda. Go for it! But now, since we all love chocolate, I want to hear about this "heavenly healing, body-fortifying" chocolate you have on your website. I want some…and I want it *now!* (laughs)

Dr. Linda Salvin: Oh, I couldn't forget *that,* Betty! (laughs) Well, as I began working for myself, incorporating the spiritual trek I had been on–the numerous accidents, setbacks, career choices, the search for God and healing and what to do with myself–I reflected upon my education and realized what we need out there. As an undergrad in health education, I remember one professor pounding the definition of health into our heads: "Health is the state of physical, mental, emotional and spiritual well-being and not merely the absence of disease." Ok… Well, after the accidents, I found that physical therapy, acupuncture, massage, psychotherapy, and other treatments I sought to calm my fears and suffering were not as helpful as seeking spiritual guidance with God and energy. So it dawned on me to incorporate my experiences and help others understand spirituality, spiritual health and integrate with my new gifts of sight and healing. So, I'm a spiritual psychic, metaphysical healer and medium.

Now here's where the chocolate comes in: I find products that work to help others, much like the healthy chocolate on my website. I have a very severe sugar sensitivity which I have battled most of my life but only in recent years have begun to understand and cope with. The smallest drop of sugar offsets my insulin levels so severely that my moods change drastically.

I can become depressed, angry or weepy for a few days. *Not a pretty sight...* Remove the sugar and I'm fine. The same occurs with white flour products. Most of us do not understand that we really are what we eat.

While in New York in February, 2009, some friends introduced me to the product. I was nervous about trying it as I had not had sugar for nearly eighteen months. This was different, made for diabetics–which I am not. I am the opposite; my pancreas overproduces sugar. I guess I'm just so-ooo sweet! (laughs)

Anyway, the product is full of antioxidants which destroy the free radicals in our body–which of course can cause our disease–so I decided to see what would happen. I had spoken to others and read miraculous health benefits from cardiovascular to diabetic.

The product is Xocai. The link is on my website. If any of your readers are interested, I would suggest they watch the video then contact me directly before purchasing so I can fully explain the product, health benefit and marketing abilities to make an income, too. If it works for me, it will work for you.

Here is the link to the site. The video is amazing. Again, please contact me directly before ordering:

http://mxi.myvoffice.com/lindacsalvin/index.cfm.

In nine months on the chocolate, my cholesterol dropped forty-seven points; I visited the chiropractor twice in a year and not weekly as a result of the decrease in pain, an increase in flexibility and movement with synovial fluid; my arthritic pain and inflammation disappeared and I now have full range of motion in my neck where before I had about sixty percent from all the trauma in my past. The product works! The company says three or more a day is equivalent to eating a pound of broccoli. Which way would you prefer to ingest your antioxidants?

Betty Dravis: You don't have to be psychic to know the answer to that, Linda, so bring on the chocolate. I have nothing against broccoli, but much prefer the yummy taste of chocolate. (laughs)

But now tell us, was your family behind you in your new calling? I know that most people don't deal well with change, so are there any humorous incidents from the time you switched careers that you'd like to share with us?

Dr. Linda Salvin: It pains me to say, Betty, but NO, my family has been very unsupportive about my chosen field as it is not something they understand, approve or respect. They were happy when I had my scientific title, and would have been more supportive if I had remained in the public health field. It has further isolated me from them with the additional challenges I have faced in building my business. No one could understand why I would be a psychic, let alone believe I *am* a psychic. I suffered quite a bit of ridicule from my family and even some friends, but when the infomercial ran and my parents' friends commented about seeing me on air, I got a little respect.

Unfortunately, there are the gypsies and fortune tellers who give us bad names and there are skeptics for whom I love to prove my psychic abilities.

No one could understand! I couldn't understand! All I knew was that I had developed a gift and after running from it for eleven years, I had to embrace it. I began my psychic career at age thirty-eight, radio at forty, received my PhD and launched the infomercial at fifty-four and here at fifty-six, I have an entirely new opportunity again.

Many people misunderstand the work, so there is no humor involved until I begin to ramble-off *all* the things that had happened to me. Before I reach the end, people do tend to grin a little…at the preposterousness of it all. And believe it or not, there are some things I haven't even mentioned. For one, I failed to mention that the City of Los Angeles denied the fire-truck accident… Well, enough is enough, I'm sure… (laughs)

OK, how many lives have I had? I'm still here and wondering what all of this means and *why me?* I have scars inside and out, but I am how I am. If I can't find the humor past my own pain, how can I help others? I read, heal and channel with laughter even though many people do not understand my personality.

Laughter is natural medicine for the soul. I cry, I laugh. I heal, I love. I teach, help, heal...

Betty Dravis: Linda, I must say I don't know anyone else who has had that many bad things happen to them, but even I can see the humor in the way you describe them…all lumped together that way. Sort of a *Divine Comedy* up close and personal…or is it just the *Inferno* part of that classic? (laughs)

But I admire your positive attitude and I, too, believe laughter is a natural medicine. Is that an additional reason for how you survived it all?

Dr. Linda Salvin: Well, most of the time it did feel like an inferno, Betty. (laughs) And I do believe that laughter, perseverance and God helped me survive…and it does to this day! I have fallen down, scraped my knees, cried my eyes out and yet, look outside on a beautiful day to see the trees, dogs, cats, flowers, birds and know that in the end, there is a reason for all of this and I do not give up. Now, as I mentioned, I have a company behind me when a year ago I thought it was dead for good. It was simply a trying transition.

The infomercial call center was not converting our sales, the radio station I had been on for three years went off the air and my mother passed away unexpectedly. All the plates I had been twirling–from radio, infomercial production, PhD, private clients, and whatever else I was doing–crashed….hit bottom.

We can only do so much.

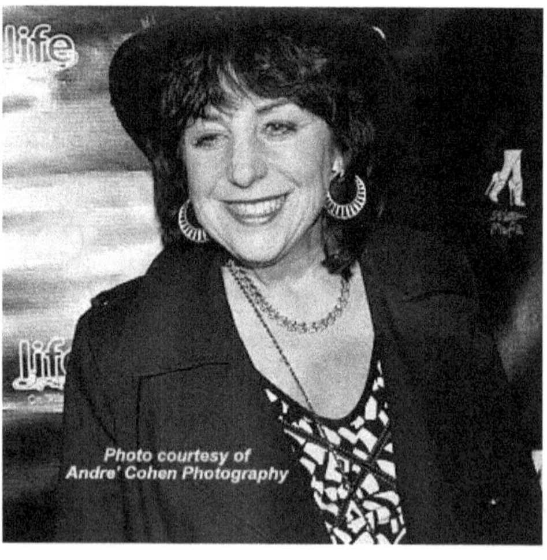

The universe will only give us as much as we can handle and allow us to see, heal and then start up again *if you do not give up.* Meeting the face of adversity is scary, painful and discouraging. I am not married (YET!) and have no one to fall back on except myself. And when I fail, I have nowhere to go but to God. Of course, I have friends, mentors, associates, family, etc. but when confronting some of the deepest and most spiritual transitions and experiences of my psychic gifts, accidents, surgeries and ascensions, I really had nowhere to turn, Betty. I just learned to go day-by-day and trust, believe and develop faith at such a level that people, places and things were put in my life for a reason. Most of the time I was right.

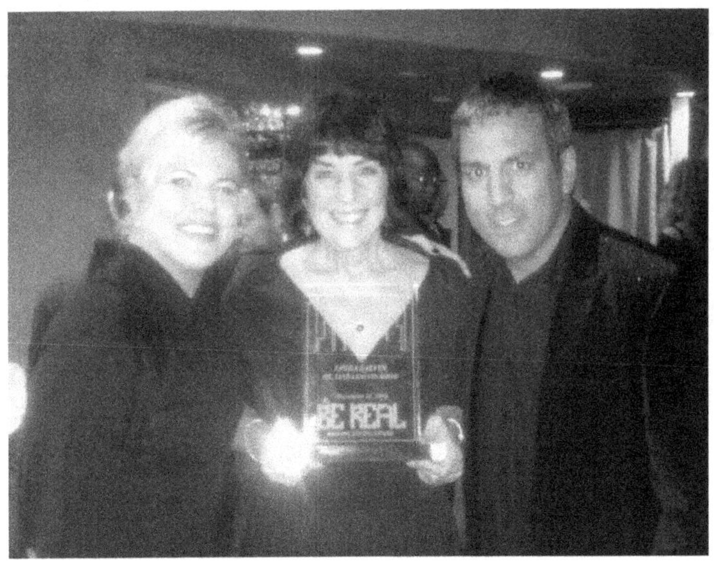

Tracee Theisen of CBS and Talk Host Leo Quinones congratulate Linda on receiving the Real Broadcasting award

Sometimes we are forced to reinvent, redesign, rediscover and recreate ourselves. Not everyone is handed life on a silver platter with opportunities without hard work. Some people seem to have an easier time than others, true. I feel a lot is timing, chance and preparedness as well as the ability to create what you want and be willing to seek the opportunities as they present themselves. I know I have by-passed opportunities I regret in hindsight and I wonder what I will tackle next for the future. Each decision leads to another on the journey.

Betty Dravis: I have not had an easy journey, either, Linda, and I admire your ways of coping. I, too, trust in my faith in God and his son Jesus to see me through. But now I'm curious about something else: Most people in your line of work notice—or someone in their family notices—that the person has some psychic ability at an early age. Did you have any special abilities or did it all evolve after your accidents? And have your skills heightened as you inter-relate with more clients with special needs

Dr. Linda Salvin: As a child, I remember certain *déjà vu* experiences and a few past life experiences. I did not understand them at the time, but once I opened up, I began to remember. I recall something that occurred when I was about four years old: My father was showing me the sky in our backyard and I remember thinking to myself, *Here I am again…* meaning, I recognized that I had been here before.

I know I am not of the earth plane. I did not understand it at the time.

I thought I had a pretty average childhood except I saw two planes collide in midair at age four. I began working for my parents at age ten, was a girl scout and sold cookies too. (laughs)

Even then I knew that I was sensitive and intuitive, but I would not say I was psychic until after the plane crash awakened it and brought it *all* to light, so to speak. When I slid down the ramp from the plane, I noticed I was standing five feet, eight inches on the right side of my body and about fifty feet outside of my body on the left. That feeling (of being split in half) lasted about three or four months. I later learned I became what is known as a "walk-in," where someone is close to death and a new soul enters. Ruth Montgomery wrote a book called *Strangers Among Us* around 1979. She describes the theory of walk-ins and referred me to the book.

I had no idea what it meant until a psychic explained the concept to me a month after the plane crash when she herself said, "You're a walk-in" and I asked what that meant.

Working with clients over time certainly helped me to hone in on skills, accuracy levels and my ability to immediately diagnose a situation with a client. I work quickly when I hear a person's problem.

As for clients with special needs, I have healed people from schizophrenia to heart pain and hives… I have lists of what I have done for people that traditional doctors or therapists have not been able to do. It is part of my spiritual gift. I just need to get it out to the universe on a grander level to reach more people. Your interview will also help me do that, Betty. Thanks again for this opportunity. Unfortunately, I cannot perform any techniques on myself, just as a psychic cannot read themselves! (laughs)

Betty Dravis: Your website lists many things that you do for your clients–readings, channelings, healings—and it also tells of your Wicks of Wisdom Candles and special healing chocolate. I admit that the idea of channeling and reincarnation is not in my belief system, but at the same time I believe you have some type of genuine gift that the average person doesn't have.

I suppose that time and seeing how your predictions come true are the real tests.

Thanks for explaining all that to us; people can visit your website to find out more and to read testimonials of how you helped so many others. But now will you please touch on a few downsides of your gifts?

Dr. Linda Salvin: One of the downsides, Betty, is that I am so sensitive that being in a mall can drive me nuts due to the various lights, sounds, voices. I tune in quickly in restaurants, can often read people at a distant table and feel their discomfort, lies and joys. I have learned over the years to turn it down and monitor my wave-lengths, so to speak.

Another upsetting factor is that many people abuse the fact I am psychic; they phone me as my friend when, in reality, they want help and are far from my “friend.” When I shut down or put my boundaries up and state they need to pay, their attitude changes; they feel I owe it to them. I make a living professionally at this work, which is draining, tiring and often disturbing. But, people feel they deserve answers whenever they want, forgetting I am human, have a life, outside interests and try to work a schedule. The abuse that takes place is unbelievable and I really tire of it. My true friends do not cross that line. They pay me if they need me. Otherwise, we are friends and can enjoy life, love and fun outings together…without my reading for them. The biggest downside can be loneliness and being misunderstood.

Betty Dravis: You must have anticipated this question because you touched on it briefly above: I read somewhere that a lot of what a psychic does is a drain on his or her own system. Since you have experienced it, how do you prepare for a client session or for a radio show? And how do you unwind afterwards…with a glass of wine, as many people do when returning home from a hard day’s work? (laughs)

Dr. Linda Salvin: Psychic, healing and channeling work is extremely draining. Many people do not understand the type of energy it takes to truly read. I pull energy from people. I am clairsentient, so I pick up emotions and practically get inside the other person or become them. I often hear people say, “He said that…” or “That’s what I told my boyfriend…” or “How did you know I felt that…” and I simply say, “I’m psychic.” Some people are more difficult to read than others as they are not as spiritual or psychically aware.

Others test or play "stump the psychic" to see how I do and then I have to work twice as hard.

Many times I became angry as I pull their anger and give it back to them. My spirit mirrors them and the answers are revealed. In healing I absorb their negative and have to release it properly so I do not get ill.

Channeling is a very different process. There are times I have been nauseous all night and when a client called for her appointment I explained I may not be able to read due to feeling so ill. Her response was, "Oh, you have Sally, she died of stomach cancer."

On another occasion, I did not sleep for two nights prior to a session; turned out the channeling was for a woman's deceased husband who died of sleep apnea. Another time I had an excruciating headache, only to find the client's friend passed of a brain tumor.

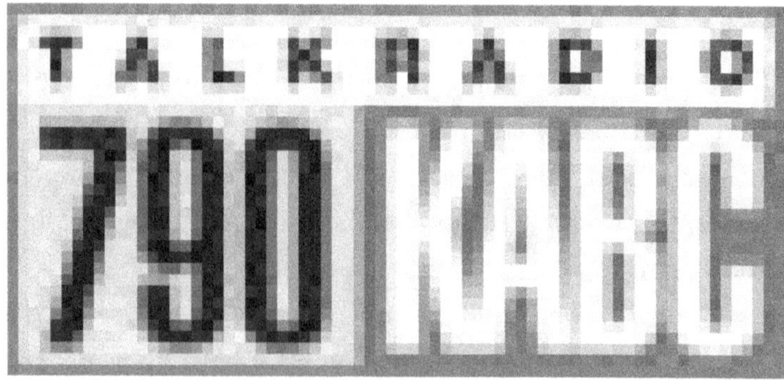

Channeling is draining, the energy comes in on the right side of my brain; I bring in one voice or spirit only; I am not good with party lines, as I call them, with more than one spirit. I translate what I hear and convey the messages.

People are stunned at messages that come in about their childhood, clothing, food, events, cars, places they went, etc. Those are confirmations that their loved ones are around. There is a fine line between the physical and spiritual world. I communicate to give comfort and closure with love.

Despite the drain on my emotions, the letters of gratitude, emails, and testimonials on the radio over the years have made the work more than worthwhile. To know I have somehow touched the lives of others during grieving periods, painful periods, healed where doctors failed and eliminated frustrations…or a prediction about a sale of a home, getting a new job, meeting a new mate came true is gratifying. The excitement in a person's voice is overwhelming and pleasant.

As to how I prepare… Well, Betty, I prepare with a bit of meditation and protective shielding and sometimes with prayer to protect against negativity. I know I have protection, but when some negative spirit enters me it will throw me off balance even for a few days before I realize I am not myself; that an entity is attached to me or is in me.

Many times, standing under a hot shower for awhile is the most healing and cleansing I can do for myself.

There are essential oils and salts I bathe with at times to prevent the spirits from harming me, as well. This work can be damaging, which I do not even understand.

I do not drink alcohol. Lots of water, tea, and coffee are my liquids of choice. I try to drink a lot of water more than anything and flush my system of toxicity. I relax by looking at the sky at sundown as the colors of the day change. God paints a different sky each night, you know? The night sky is fascinating to me. I love the constellations, the Milky Way, watching the moon rise and shift in the sky. I observe certain planets and stars. Sometimes I look up and wonder why I'm here and whisper, "I want to go home," but I know I'm not done yet. I usually go out to dinner with friends in the evening, catch a movie or listen to live music. That is how I relax.

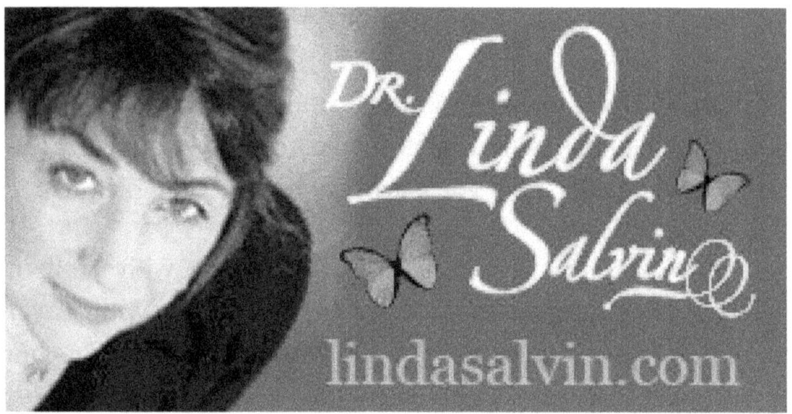

Betty, I could write a book on the channelings I have conducted and that would take up too much space for your interview, LOL. If I had not experienced psychic abilities, metaphysical healings or channeling the spirits with such great effectiveness, I would be skeptical. I have lived it, so I know it is real. I do not know *why me* or how I was chosen, but I was. *It is not what I thought of as a good time when I was growing up.* I did not seek this, it came to me as a result of surrendering my path to God's will and allowing the universe to use me as I was to become…a vessel of information to help others on a spiritual level.

Betty Dravis: I am amazed at how much you love people, Linda. To be willing to open yourself like that is extremely loving and caring. You are a very strong person and I admire you so much. In fact, your life story is mesmerizing.

I especially enjoyed hearing a few of your success stories and if our readers want to know more, they are welcome to visit your website.

Now for a lighter question: Since you reside and work in the LA area, do you have any famous clients besides actress Katherin Kovin Pacino (who is also the stepmother of the living legend, actor Al Pacino)?

Dr. Linda Salvin: Some of the famous people I have worked with include movie producer Christine Peters; actresses such as soap stars Elaine Princi and Jasmine Blythe; singers Dionne Warwick, George Brown (Kool & the Gang), Chuck Negron (Three Dog Night), Vince Neil (Motley Crue) and Chris Poulson (Superficial Saints); actors Courtney Cox, Shadow Stevens, Rick Dees, Caroline Rhea, Cheech Marin (first known for Cheech & Chong, but who became a respected performer in his own right); *Reality TV* star Chad Rogers; author & infomercial king Kevin Trudeau; and an ESPN reporter when I predicted a world series in 2000…and many, many others.

The list is on my website.

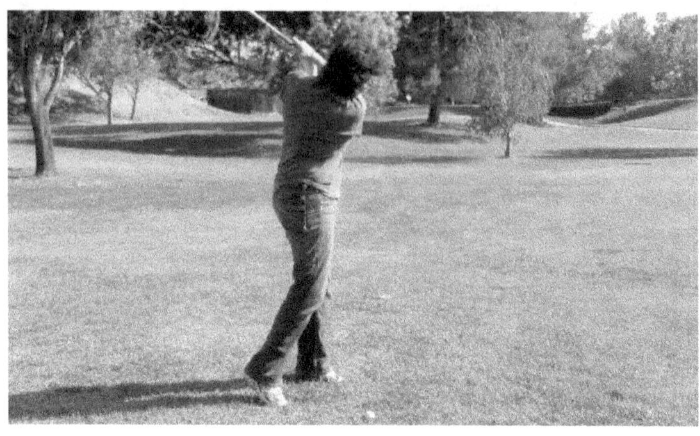

Betty Dravis: Wow—that's an impressive list, Linda. Now I'm curious to know if you've ever met a real, live ghost…er, make that a real, *dead* ghost? (laughs) Or been in a haunted house?

Dr. Linda Salvin: Betty, paranormal is not my thing. I prefer light to dark. It is fascinating to record sounds, voices and observe sightings, but it is not my specialty. But since you asked, *yes,* I have seen ghosts and I'll relate a few experiences for you: I had been on TV for a local show in Los Angeles called *9 on the Town* which is not on anymore. I was asked to visit the Queen Mary in Long Beach to identify all the haunted areas on the ship. In the show, you see me on tour with a staff member of the ship and I accurately identify the spirits, ghosts and locations of deaths on the docked Queen Mary.

Another incident: In 1992, a rock star passed away. He attended my high school, although I had never met him. He began channeling through me three days after his death. I have had messages from him for several years and effectively bring him through on the Ouija board. Yes, Betty, there are ways to effectively communicate with spirits *safely* with the Ouija board…and it can also be very dangerous. Anyway, on two occasions, he made himself present in my homes. The first time I saw him, he was standing in the doorway of my bedroom and hallway of an apartment in 1993. I was not scared; I was comforted, actually. The second apparition occurred when I rented a small home in the canyons.

I had a fire going in the fireplace and he was sitting on the ledge of the fireplace. I just stared at him and he stared right back.

I've also seen shadows of my deceased animals walk by. I have not seen my mom who passed last March, 2009, but my father saw her in his new condo recently… *Spirits and ghosts are real.*

I felt spirits in a haunted hotel once and in a cemetery, I literally could hear voices of the deceased speaking to me in a certain row, yelling, screaming and requesting that I take them with me, get them out of there, release them from the grave, etc. I thought I was nuts but then I remembered what I do, who I am, why I was there, and I'd be ok. Two rows over, it was quiet. Go figure… Yes, spirits are alive in the graveyard too.

Betty Dravis: I might be a big sissy, Linda, but that gives me the creeps, but then I love horror movies, so go figure that oxymoron. Now what do you think of Sylvia Brown, the psychic that TV personality Montel Williams presents on his show so frequently? And John Edward (McGee), famous for his TV show *Crossing Over*... Do you believe his claims of communicating with the spirits of the audience members' deceased relatives?

Dr. Linda Salvin: In 1994, prior to the earthquake, I was given Sylvia Brown's book *My Guide, My Self.* It is the only one of her books I have ever read. She has "ghost' writers," of course, speaking of ghosts. (laughs) Her book was fascinating and I related to it. I will not condone or condemn her work. I know that no psychic is one-hundred percent accurate and I do not believe any psychic should charge $750.00 for thirty minutes.

There was a time when I received many of her clients, as well as James von Praagh's. As for John, I really do not know his work. I know people who have been to his seminars and simply adore him. I am sure he is extremely talented as a medium.

Betty Dravis: On the lighter side–and I do have a lighter side, Linda (laughs)—what is the best advice you ever received from your mother?

Your father?

Dr. Linda Salvin: My mom used to say, "Always finish what you start." God knows, there are projects left undone, paths yet to be traveled. She would warn me not to get involved with certain guys, so of course I did. And, I paid the price later. My dad would say, "Don't worry what others think, worry about yourself," but I was too insecure to understand for a long time.

He would always want me to "give it the ol' college try" when I was down. When I complained that the good guys are either married or gay, he'd say two things: "They broke the mold when I was born," and "Linda, there's an ass for every chair that's built." My parents' advice served me well, but the one thing my dad said that is most helpful in my business is: "Get it in writing."

That's my dad! Just so you know, my parents built a company when I was young that was number fifty-eight on the NASDAQ. It went international and they travelled more than any rock band ever did. They were married fifty-eight and a-fourth years when my mother died. It was a soul-mate love affair. They were very happy and great parents. I still have my dad, thankfully.

Betty Dravis: I'm sorry to learn of your mother passing; belated condolences. But I'm glad you still have your father and it's wonderful to hear of successful marriages. I never tire of soul-mate stories. You were blessed to have such warm, loving parents. Even though they didn't understand your gifts, at least they raised you properly and gave you a great start in life; truths to fall back on.

But you can breathe a sigh of relief soon, Linda… I'm nearing the end of your grilling, but first I want to put you on the spot. Since you do telephone readings and answer on-air questions from your many followers–even on an international level–have you been able to "read" me through our Facebook and email correspondence. Please share what you have "picked up" about me…but be gentle. (laughs) I don't want to be a fair-weather friend, always seeking free answers and taking advantage of you, so I promise this will be a one-time thing…for the sake of the story.

Dr. Linda Salvin: OK, here goes, Betty… I feel you are jovial, fun, light-hearted and have a zest for life. You take each day as it comes, but with the strife we all do. You were brave in your day and are even braver and more carefree today. You are in excellent health, love your family, are down to earth and have three to five more publications still unwritten and yet to be published. Another contract is offered this summer/early fall for you. You also have a trip coming up this summer. October appears to be significant with publishing and family, so we will see what that brings. People love you and you love people, but you are selective as to who really gets to know you. You do have your boundaries… The person who crosses you will be sorry.

You have a legend to leave the planet down the road.

Country and nature are very important to you.

How's that for starters?

Betty Dravis: That's a fine start, *Linda*, and it intrigues me. It's odd to hear anyone tell me about my future. Since it is all positive, of course I love it, especially the part about my publishing and a new contract offer. There is, actually, something in the works; I'll let you know when it works out.

And you are *spot on:* I do love people and am selective about who *really* gets to know me. I certainly hope no one crosses me because I truly don't want to make anyone sorry. (laughs)

But speaking of love, your love of people comes across in your on-air delivery and on your various internet sites. It has been said of you: "Her love of people is a beacon in the darkness."

That description reminds me of a lighthouse, a fitting metaphor for you, IMO. You are warm, cozy and light the path… I haven't seen you on TV, but your dear friend and client, actress Katherin Kovin Pacino, tells me that you positively shine on camera—and I believe it! Even your Internet personality is endearing. You glow…

Before ending this interview, is there anything else in your immediate future… in addition to the fantastic news about your show being syndicated and going national and that your music may soon be produced?

Dr. Linda Salvin: I'm most excited about the new Dr. Linda Salvin Psychic & Astrology Network, of course. We discussed that above, but going national is a dream come true! As for other projects, in addition to the TV shows I mentioned above, I have a resume of shows on my website, but another exciting thing is that I recently did a pilot for a new psychic show. If it is picked up, I will be featured in thirteen episodes.

I also have a few treatments and a script for a sitcom, talk show and movie, but so far have had no luck in selling them; all are based on my experiences as a psychic. And I'm also working on my autobiography.

Also, I would like to mention that I'm published in a book called *Chopped Liver for the Family Spirit* that consists of stories of overcoming adversity with people like Peter Marshall, Shelley Berman and the late Lloyd Thaxson.

Betty Dravis: That is certainly a full plate, Linda. I wish you the best of luck with all your projects. Now, if you will, please share three things that you couldn't live without.

Dr. Linda Salvin: Betty, I have to mention *four* things I couldn't live without: First are my father and friends. And it's obvious that I couldn't live without being able to help people, so my abilities are extremely important to me. I also love to travel and have been through most of the US, Europe, Japan, Thailand, parts of Mexico and Canada. And last but not least, I need my music in my life. I am beginning to return to music again. I'm playing guitar and re-writing songs. I have met new collaborators. Where I had once given up, doors seem to be opening.

Betty Dravis: I'm so happy for you, Linda. You are already a star in the LA area, but with your show going national, I hope you will soon be a household name…recognized by everyone. I wish you much success with your new show. That's awesome!

I think we've established that *you*, Dr. Linda Salvin, are a dynamo…a regular whirlwind of energy who finds great satisfaction in helping others reach their goals and dreams…to live happier, healthier, more productive lives. And that's why we selected you to be in our *Dream Reachers* book. Before departing, Linda, please share with us how interested parties can reach you. Radio call letters, phone numbers, etc. will be very helpful. Of course, you don't have to repeat the ones mentioned above.

Dr. Linda Salvin: People interested in a private, paid consultation for a reading, healing, channeling session or to purchase Wicks of Wisdom can call my office at 818-788-6077 direct or leave a message at 888-509-1077. The website is www.lindasalvin.com which also has my internet radio station.

I play several pre-recorded radio shows 24/7 as well as do a live show on Saturdays at eleven am PDT, which you have called in and spoken with me. I will be returning to KABC and that show will be syndicated. There will be astrology spots on sixty-five stations nationally soon. People will soon hear about the Dr Linda Salvin Psychic & Astrology Network where they can call fabulous readers for spiritual and psychic advice.

Betty Dravis: Thanks so much for sharing your goals and dreams with us today, Linda. I truly enjoyed visiting with you. Keep us posted on your future achievements and I'll let you know when your predictions for me come true.

Dr. Linda Salvin: I would love to continue keeping you posted with future events, phone numbers and releases as I evolve into the next phase of my life. The activities are multi-faceted because I love so many things. Ultimately, though, I hope to find the love of my life and partner with my twin. I feel I recently met him. Let's see if I'm right…if things turn out the way I hope.

Before I leave, Betty, I forgot to add something about how my faith and trust in the universe helped me overcome all the adversity and somehow it is leading me back to some of my original goals and passions, as well. Therefore, God has a plan and we never know what it is. *Everything happens for a reason! There are no accidents.* We just have to become willing to surrender and follow His will, which may not be ours.

OK, that's it! I promise…no more! (laughs) Thanks to you, your co-author Chase Von and the other Dames of Dialogue for letting me express myself so openly. Keep up the great Press and please keep in touch.

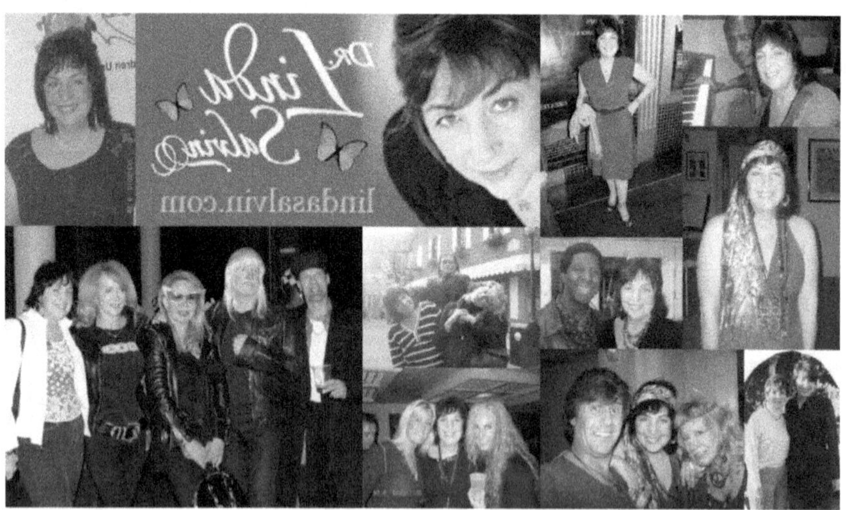

Interview with John Manha

VIETNAM VET LIVED HIS "ISLAND DREAM"

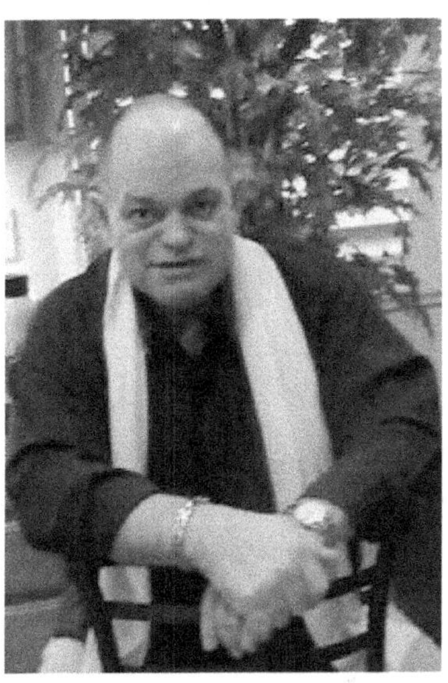

Betty Dravis: Welcome to the wonderful world of Dream Reachers, Johnny. You're a first for me because it's the first time I've interviewed someone so close to the family. But you're more than worthy to bear the title because you overcame huge obstacles to fulfill your dream of having a home on an island and all that goes with it: blue skies and sunshine...gentle sea breezes...the splendor of tropical storms...endless stretches of aqua-marine water...hammocks lulling you to sleep on hot summer days...lovely *chicas* dancing around you... (laughs)

All that was yours for a time…

You know, Johnny, just about everyone dreams of living on an island or at least by the ocean, but before we get into how you achieved that, I hear you had a double-whammy—*two* traumatic experiences–that changed your life drastically. What happened?

John Manha: Thanks for interviewing me, Betty. I've always wanted to share my story. But where do I start? I suppose the best place is when life-changing things began to happen. I'm a veteran and had already served in Vietnam. When I was about thirty-three years old, something started happening with my left foot: it felt heavier and didn't lift on its own like before. It would "catch" on things. That confused me because I didn't know what to make of it, but it went on for seven years; all the while I was growing weaker and weaker. I couldn't understand what was happening in my body or even try to explain to my wife. Even when the doctor diagnosed my problem as multiple sclerosis, it was too complicated to understand, let alone explain. MS is an inside job; you can look real fine on the outside…at least for several years.

I was fortunate with my job, though. I had a union job and I pushed on through as long as I was able to function. I'll never forget the day I quit. It was a sad day, indeed. I was forty years old and forced by health to take a disability.

About a year later I was divorced. Heather, my daughter by my first wife, was just sixteen and I had custody of her since she was nine. She had seen me go through two divorces and I didn't want her to see it again. That and chances of my health deteriorating made me decide it would be better for her to live with her mother who, fortunately at that time, was stable and in a very good marriage.

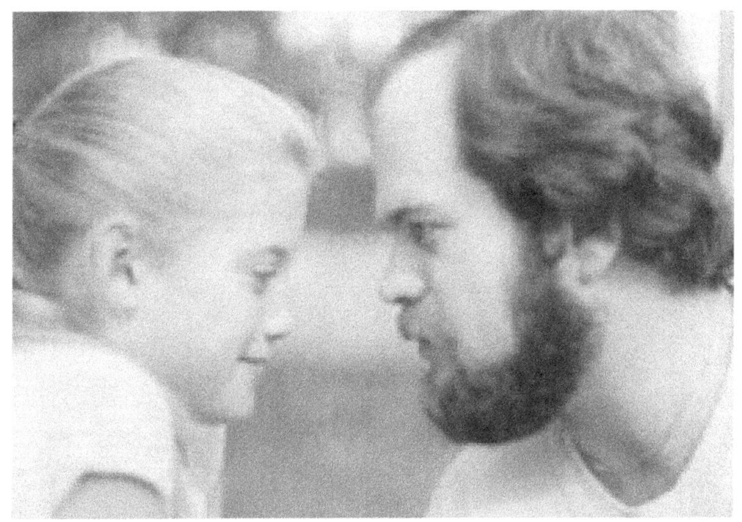

Johnny & Daughter Heather back in the day

She even had a pink Mustang for Heather to drive! Obviously, my daughter was not too happy with me, but since the divorce was messy, I felt then—and still feel–that I made the best choice for her.

Betty Dravis: Heather is now a lovely young woman, a fantastic wife and mother, so it worked out in the long run and that's what matters. Johnny, it's good that you have no regrets because those can eat away at your soul.

I'm so sorry you developed MS and were forced to retire early, but what's the second major trauma. It doesn't seem fair you should get hit with anything else.

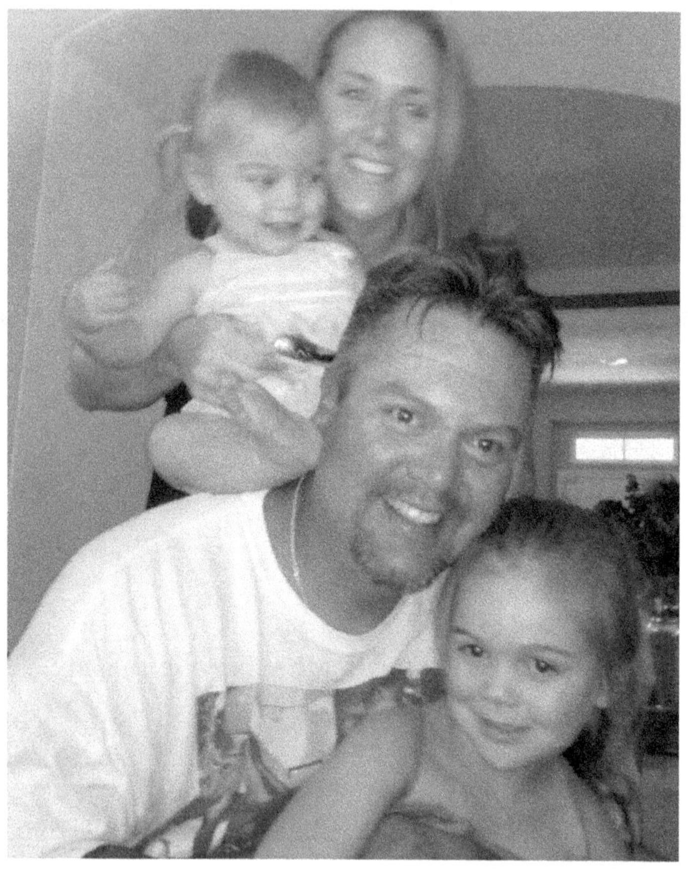

Heather & Jesse with daughters Mia & Andi Rose

John Manha: Life isn't always fair, Betty, but I've learned to take it one day at a time. No use complaining.

My second major trauma came the night after my thirtieth high-school reunion. I was wheelchair-bound and had to have help getting there, but I ended up having a great time.

However, the following morning, I took a shower and was sweating like crazy. It was November 1998 and pretty cold outside. When my roommate came home and saw my condition, he immediately called an ambulance.

I was having a heart attack and when I arrived in the ER, they called in the best cardiac team available that day. While I was giving the nurse my closest relatives' phone numbers, I began to feel euphoric. I asked her if she had everything she needed and if she was ready to go to work. When she answered, "Yes," I slumped over and immediately was surrounded by the most beautiful lights I had ever seen.

It sounds funny, but I was looking for my baggage and I had none. And then I looked straight ahead and saw a Biblical scene on the wall; people were standing before it and more beautiful lights were behind them. I thought that I would like to be closer and *just like that–I was halfway there!* The people I saw did not look right at me and I got very sad because I knew I was not going to be able to stay. I turned around and saw an undulating tunnel that resembled the inside of an intestine. It was very long, but I saw the ER room at the end. Strangely, it looked very, very close. I could see the medics working on my body and immediately got impatient with them. "Leave him alone," I said. "Just let him go. It's all right."

I turned to go back to the lights when something warm and fuzzy came over me and I was whirling through that tunnel, back to the world. Grasping, screaming, contorted people were embedded in the walls of the tunnel. They seemed like monsters to me and they were trying to grab me, wanting to go back with me. I was frightened witless… I whizzed through that tunnel and flew right through the physician and into my torso with a loud thump. I remember punching at the nurse. "Johnny, it's all right," she said.

I remember answering, "It's *not* all right… You people are rude."

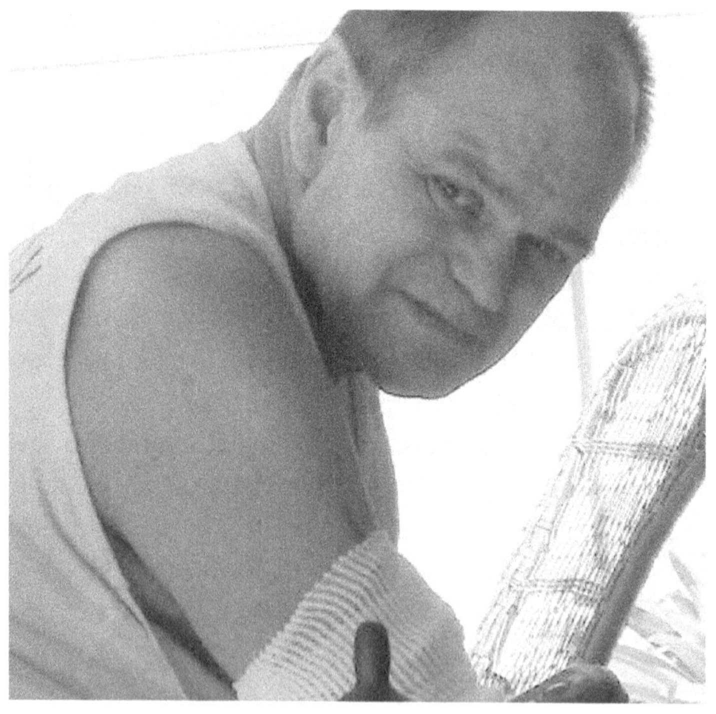

Later in the recovery room, I was crying and the nurse asked me if I had had an out-of-body experience. I told her I had and she asked if I had wanted to stay there. I told her I did. It was such a feeling of euphoria on the other end of that tunnel…where the bright lights were. She told me they could tell because I fought real hard and that I was dead for seven minutes.

In retrospect, since I was raised Catholic, I thought that tunnel was Purgatory and the bright lights were Heaven. You know, Betty, I'm really a blessed man. I recovered from that in six days… What's more, it was the best I had felt in years. On top of that, it was such a rejuvenating experience that it changed me forever, making me grateful to be alive. The experience left me knowing that there is life after death. I'm now taking time to smell the roses and sharing my belief with anyone who will listen.

Betty Dravis: I'm sorry you had to suffer through a heart attack, Johnny–*but what a story*! Your out-of-body experience is dramatic-- frightening and inspiring at the same time. A number of people have reported supernatural experiences like that and lived to tell about them. Those stories always fascinate me.

I empathize with you, but I'm certainly glad you came back. I suppose God isn't finished with you yet. Perhaps He enlightened you for a reason and you're meant to inspire others by sharing it. All who know you certainly admire your positive attitude and determination to proceed with your life, even though you're now confined to a wheelchair. You're an inspiration to us all.

But now tell us when you first thought of living on an island?

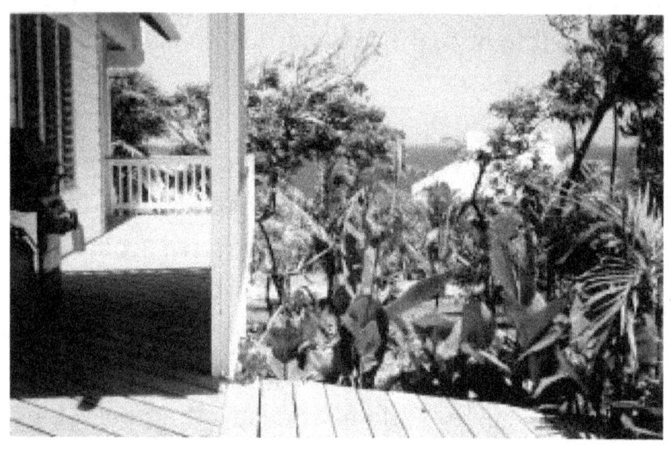

Ocean View from Johnny's Front Door

John Manha: I don't know exactly, Betty. The idea could have come when my sister started talking about moving to Hawaii. Then I really became interested when my friends, Ron and Karina Smith, moved to Roatan Island to open Bananarama, a dive shop with bungalows. I read about Roatan and learned this: *Roatan off the North Coast of Honduras in the Caribbean, is part of the Bay Islands and is a vacation paradise and home to pristine, white, sandy beaches, amazing tropical jungle-covered hills with a diverse and unique reef system and heartwarming people. It has a unique culture and authentic Caribbean charm. Roatan and the Bay Islands are often called the Caribbean's best-kept secret.*

When I read that, I visited my friends and fell in love with the place. That's when I started fantasizing about living on an island–*and Roatan was it!*

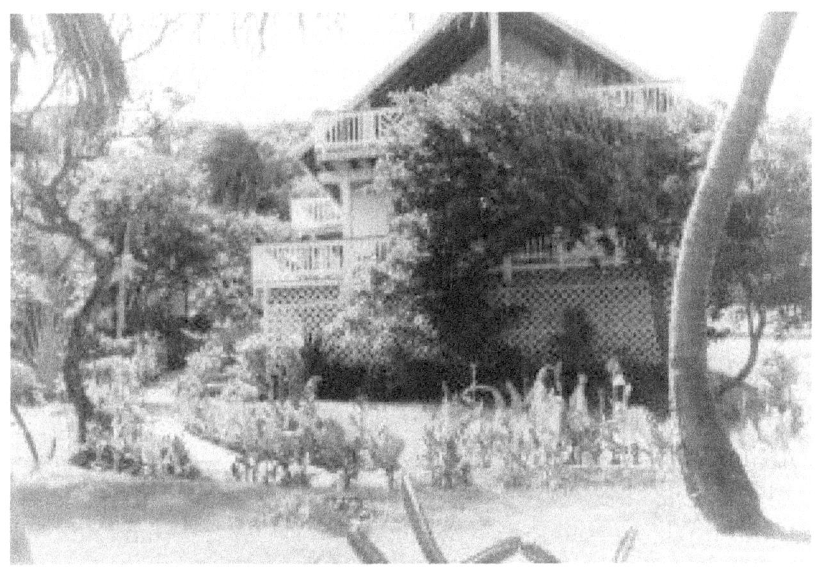

Johnny's Island Home

Betty Dravis: That's interesting, Johnny, and it's so important for everyone to have a dream. So tell us how you finally fulfilled your dream. Did you immediately formulate a plan of action, or did it come gradually over a number of years and circumstances?

John Manha: The idea evolved gradually. I often talked to my daughter and her mother about it. I kept on doing things around my Livermore, California home—like repairing the roof and such–but I began picturing myself on an island. It seemed like paradise to me… It took some time to settle my affairs in the States, sell my home and contract with a Roatan Realtor to find a site to build my dream home. From the time Ron and Karina moved there, it took about three years before I finally made it.

Betty Dravis: I understand that your Realtor found you a good site that you approved, sight unseen. Since you were in a wheelchair, how did you get around when you first arrived on Roatan to look at your property and arrange for the construction? Who greeted you at the airport?

John Manha: It's so funny that you ask that question… (laughs) I rolled out the doors of the airport and there was a woman sitting on the bench who immediately got up, grabbed my wheelchair and took off with me across the parking lot. I was telling her to stop, while trying to stop at the same time…and I couldn't. She was very strong and didn't understand a word of English. I didn't speak any Spanish either, so was at her mercy.

She took me to my Realtor, T. J. Lynch of RE/MAX, who had been handling my affairs since January of 2001. When I asked about the woman pushing my wheelchair, he replied, "That's just Candida."

When I said, "Oh, that's just Candida," he burst out laughing, explaining that he had hired her to take care of me at the airport. All I could say was, "Wow, TJ! You are *the man!*" I never suspected at the time, but years later Candida would become my fiancée.

Betty Dravis: Oh, that's a funny beginning for a romance, Johnny. I can picture you fuming and fidgeting as an unknown woman pushes you across the airport. (laughs) That seems like poor communication from the Realtor for not informing you ahead of time, but it worked out.

I'm dying to know more about how your relationship with Candida evolved, but let's take things chronologically. Even before your home was completed, Candida introduced you to a young woman named Rosa who became your housekeeper and personal assistant. You also met more helpful friends. Tell us a little bit about Rosa and your friends, including Candida.

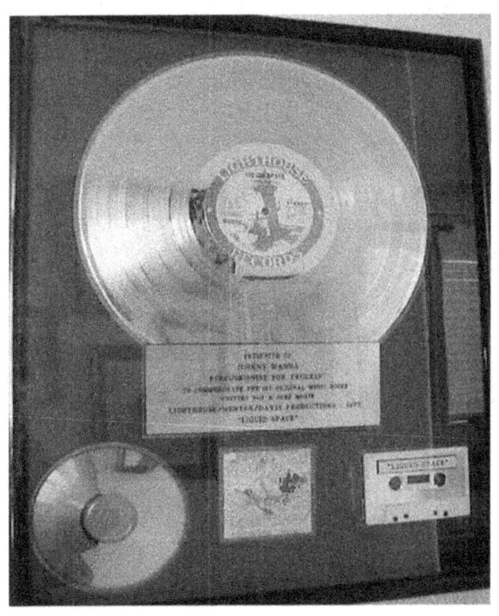

Album from Johnny's band "*Truckin'*" back in the day

John Manha: Well, Betty, Rosa was an interesting girl. When she first came to work for me, she was only eighteen years old and already had a two-year-old child…a baby girl. I immediately took a real big liking to Rosa and treated her as a second daughter.

I rented a house across the road from my building site, so I could easily supervise construction. I also hired Rosa to come in and help me five days a week. Meanwhile, Candida started dropping by several times a week to visit. We three became friends and I learned that Candida had three children that were already out of the "nest." She was forty-two at the time and was running a hotel in the West End. She was an intelligent, strong, caring woman and I grew to admire both women. We learned to communicate and I picked up some Spanish from them and they learned some English from me.

I also became friends with the contractor, many of the workers, restaurant owners and supermarket owners where I would cash my checks. There was a nearby bank, but it had very slow service. It was easier to cash my checks at the supermarket; all I had to do was call and they'd have the cash for me the following day. Sad to say, but I would've had to wait three days for the bank to handle my transactions.

Betty Dravis: So you and Candida learned to speak each other's language a little. Well, Johnny, that's a far cry from your first meeting at the airport. (laughs) But thank God for putting people like Candida and Rosa in your life…people who recognized that you are unique and did everything they could to keep you moving in the right direction. But when your home was completed, what was a typical day in "Paradise" like?

Did it resemble your long-awaited fantasy?

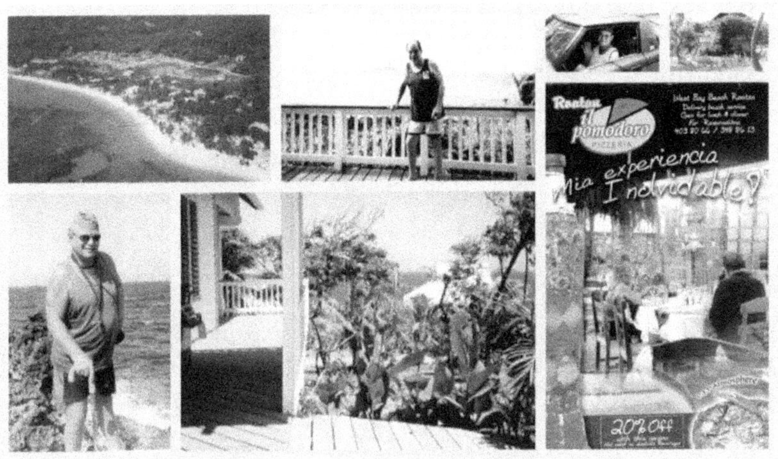

John Manha: Betty, when my home was completed and I could really relax, my day went something like this: Rosa arrived about eight-thirty in the morning, made coffee and cooked my breakfast. I would wake up when I smelled the coffee. Go ahead and laugh, but it's true. (laughs)

I greeted Rosa and went upstairs to the outside deck. Around nine, she served breakfast and ate with me; we talked about what I wanted to have done that day and structured a period of time for her schooling. I was very big on insisting that she finish school.

By the way, by the time I had to leave the island, she blessed me by graduating from high school with honors. She also had two more children by then…sort of the "island way" for young girls there.

Anyway, back to my day… After breakfast, while Rosa worked, I walked over to the hammock… excuse me, I *rolled* over to the hammock. I had 190° view of the ocean from my deck, with seven- to -ten-mile-an-hour breezes blowing almost every day. With the temperature always somewhere between 80° and 95°, it was heavenly… It was so relaxing, I often fell asleep there.

I had a lot of CDs which Rosa loved hearing, and the music was soothing as I swayed in my hammock. That was the time of day when I would count my blessings as I thought about all the fantastic people that had helped me get to that point.

And of course, never forgetting God's part…

If I woke up before lunch, I fooled around on my computer or made a few telephone calls. On some days I went to the swimming pool and floated around on my raft. No matter what I was doing, Rosa always found me at noon when we would have lunch outside on the lower deck.

After lunch, I sometimes went to the West End beach in my electric wheelchair. I would visit my friends at the dive shop and maybe go diving or snorkeling or just fool around on the beach and meet people. I not only met locals but people from all around the world. They all had great stories to tell.

Since Rosa left at 3:30 every day, if I returned home later, she had something made for my dinner, leaving a note telling me what happened while I was gone…if anything at all. After dinner, friends often dropped by. If not, I watched a couple of movies or perhaps messed around more on the computer and then went to bed.

Since I could still get around a little with a cane in those days, I often went for drives in my little 1983 Mazda RX Seven, which was the only sports car on the island.

That's how a typical day on the island went. It was a little paradise…

Betty, I also had a cycle of alternating my time between the States and Roatan; staying in both places three months at a time. I tried to rotate with the best seasons in both places. That way I got to see my daughter, and the bonus was that I kept a year-round tan. (laughs) Another advantage of going back and forth was that each time I returned, all my female friends welcomed me home in grand style…in exchange for the trinkets I brought them. (laughs) I really was a jet setter and an expat. I lived like that for seven years. I was living my dream and loving every minute of it.

Betty Dravis: That does, indeed, sound like an idyllic life, Johnny. So why did you eventually sell your island paradise and move back to the states?

John Manha: Unfortunately, I developed a severe infection, Betty. It started in both feet and my right leg. When I first got to the island, Candida had given me a dog. I used to take that strong little puppy out for walks, holding the leash from my wheelchair. I guess my foot got tangled in the leash or something, but it ended up caught in the caster of my wheelchair. That started the infection, but it never seemed serious until later in the summer of my fifth year there when a red line crawled up my right leg. I passed out following a shower and was rushed to the hospital.

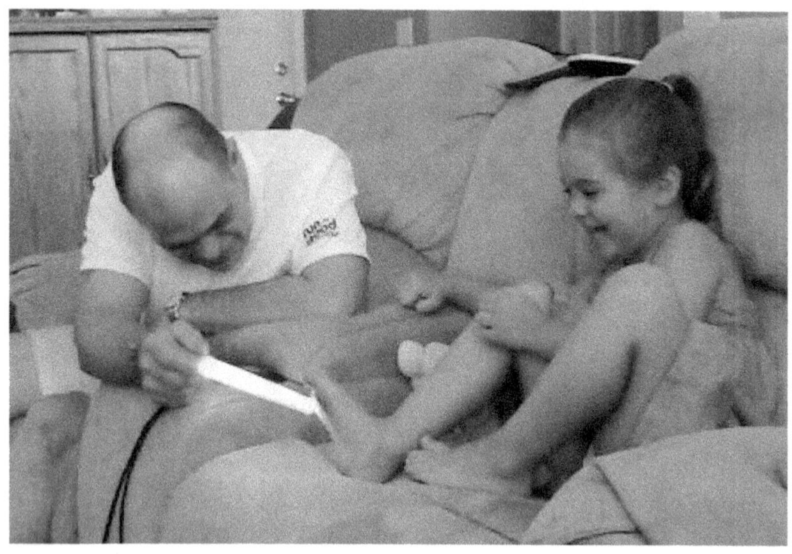

John Teases Granddaughter Mia at his 60th Birthday Party

Due to better medical care in the States, my daughter Medevaced me from Roatan to San Jose, California. They sent a little Learjet with a pilot, copilot, nurse and doctor. It was pretty exciting to me. It really was a class act, for which I am grateful because the infection was very serious. I spent four days in the hospital where I received intravenous antibiotics and then spent several more months in a rest home. I was determined to go back to my island paradise, so after a few months in my cousin's home, I want back…only to get infected again.

Three months later, I was back in the States, in a little home in Manteca. I could get better medical care here and I wanted to be near my granddaughter Mia, too, so I reluctantly sold my island home, bought a custom van, complete with ramp and all comforts, and later purchased my new Del Webb home. Since then, Heather and her husband Jesse Rodriguez have had another girl, Andrea Rose and are now expecting a son.

Betty Dravis: I'm very sorry you developed the infection, Johnny, and that you were forced to return to the States in an emergency situation. Since you now have two granddaughters, Mia and little Andi, and have purchased a lovely home in a luxurious Del Webb community, it all seems to have worked for the best. How do you like your new home?

John Manha: *You can say that again, Betty! I love my house! I love this community!* Of course, I miss the ocean and my island life on Roatan, but this place is another kind of paradise. It is luxuriously landscaped, has a lakeside clubhouse complete with an exercise room, several swimming pools and hot tubs, library, billiards room, all kinds of planned activities and much more. *My, oh my!* I really didn't think I was going to like living in Manteca or anywhere in the United States for that matter. And I believe Candida is going to love it too.

Betty Dravis: Johnny, now that you mention Candida… That isn't the end of your Island Dream because something else happened while you were there that promises to change your life in the future. Since I and my readers are suckers for a good love story, please tell us what happened after you left Roatan?

John Manha: You know, Betty, "love" was never mentioned between me and Candida during the seven years I was there.

We got along well and were good friends, but as I started settling into Manteca, I started feeling like something was really missing. It drove me crazy. Then one day I realized I was missing Candida. I called her and told her how I felt and asked her if she felt the same way. She told me I was "stupid" not to realize that she had loved me from the first day.

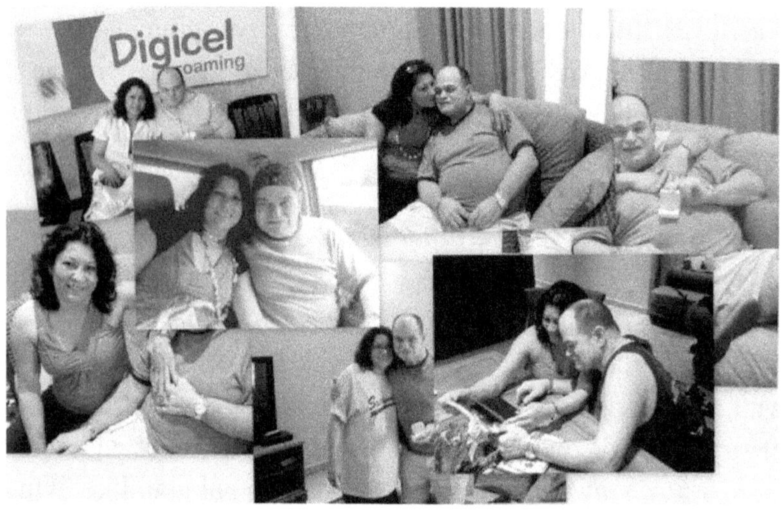

We immediately started filing papers for her visa. The government needed a letter stating why I wanted to marry this woman. I told them the story–starting from the airport–and how we remained friends for a very long time until we realized we loved each other. I laced it with all kinds of cute anecdotes. The process has taken almost two years so far because we've had communication problems with the attorney handling our case.

Candida and I still feel the same about each other, even though we're far apart, so in February of 2010 I flew back and officially proposed to her. I spent three days there and it was wonderful. I had heard about relationships like this working really well, but had always thought that wasn't for me. *But here I am—and loving it!* What I mean is that we're handling the delays well, even though it's hard. I can't wait till she gets here and we can marry in that lovely gazebo at the clubhouse.

Betty Dravis: That's a beautiful love story, Johnny, and I hope all goes well for you and Candida. I've seen photos of her and she's a lovely woman, as well as being a nice person. But you're not the type of man to stop at one dream. I hear you have another one you're working on—an entrepreneurial dream this time. Tell us about the new business venture that you're embarking on.

John Manha: I believe you should always have a new dream, and what I'm doing now is something I never ever dreamed of trying. I am an investor now, flipping houses. Before this, I learned how to sell notes. Between both, it involved almost a year of training and learning…not to mention *money*. Anyway, I am really excited about this. I'm working on my first deal now, and I know it's going to explode. I hope I explode right along with it! I'm pretty sure I will. Succeeding with my island dream gives me confidence that I can tackle this project and succeed, as well.

Betty Dravis: I've seen you do many things others thought were beyond your capabilities, Johnny, so I have no doubt you'll succeed in whatever you set your mind to. There's a lot of competition in the housing market, but if anyone can do it, you can.

You are *that* determined: a never-give-up guy with a positive attitude.

Now, Johnny, who has been your biggest inspiration in life? Do you have a mentor or someone you'd like to pattern your life after?

John Manha: Putting aside my personal feelings that Donald Trump has done some asinine things in his private life, I admire his business dealings.

Others are Preston Ely, Than Merrill, Kenny Rushing, Pete "The Ninja" Skouras, Al Aiello, the income tax genius, Ron Le Grand and Anthony Morrison. If I could grasp their knowledge, I'd be a millionaire in a month, perhaps less. I guess I'm one of these people who just want everything *now*. Yeah… (laughs)

And of course you, Betty! You have been an inspiration to me like no other. Your schedules and work habits just blow me away; the hours you keep are simply incredible. And you're prettier than those others too. (laughs)

Betty Dravis: I hope so, Johnny… (laughs) I do admit to having a good work ethic, but I've never come close to the big bucks, so you better stick to those successful men…while mimicking my perseverance. (laughs)

And now, I'm going to put you on the spot. Since most people have had embarrassing moments at some time in their lives, do you mind sharing one of yours? It can be funny or sad, but I find they're always interesting in retrospect.

John Manha: I never have gotten embarrassed too easily in any situation, Betty, but thinking about this, I would have to say it was when I got married the first time. I had already been playing in a band and was used to people looking at me, but this was really personal stuff! It felt like an intrusion into my soul. It didn't last very long because I had nothing to hide in there. (laughs)

Betty Dravis: That's too funny, Johnny… People watching you exchange vows embarrassed you, while being pushed through an airport by a stranger didn't! (laughs)

This might seem trivial, but what are your favorite foods and restaurants? I know you have a sweet tooth, so I won't divulge your consumption of ice cream and cookies, if you share your favorite "good" foods with us. (laughs)

John Manha: Well, I like shrimp, lobster, steak, chicken and all fruits and vegetables, including asparagus. Then there's the "goodie" department… Many members of our family like to dine at Applebee's; their "Triple Chocolate Meltdown" (cake and ice-cream) is out of this world. I remember someone taking a photo of you with that dessert. It *was* decadent, wasn't it?

Betty Dravis: You're right, Johnny, our families have had many fun dining adventures at Applebee's. As for that huge slice of chocolate cake with ice-cream and chocolate dribbles, it was yummy. I paid for overindulging later, though. (laughs)

Now let's leap from eating to exercising, since you like your sweets a little too much… I know how important keeping upper-body strength is for you, so how do you keep fit enough to perform all that heavy lifting you do? You know, by leveraging with your wheelchair… (laughs)

John Manha; All of my life, Betty, I have done many jobs that required lifting. I've been a hod carrier, a plank setter, a scaffold setter and bucket-loader operator. I've also used a pick and shovel, and like any other guy, I've split wood for the fire.

While I was living on the island, I did exercises in the swimming pool or in the ocean, using water as resistance.

Since moving into this Del Webb Community of Woodbridge, I've been working-out with a weight trainer. My family and everyone who sees me move furniture and other heavy purchases are amazed at how I use the principle of leveraging, applying it to my wheelchair. I love a challenge, so for me it's kind of fun.

Betty Dravis: That weight trainer must be a big help, Johnny, and I am one who has seen you maneuvering heavy items with your wheelchair. *Quite a feat!*

If you could reach more people in wheelchairs, what advice would you give them about making the most of their individual situations?

John Manha: I'd like to tell them to accept their situation as it is and work with it, always keeping a positive attitude that tomorrow could be better. You never know what new medical discovery might be just around the corner. Meanwhile, don't become a recluse. Get out and mix with other people as much as you can. As for heavy lifting, the first thing I want to say is to read a book on leveraging weight. Then try lifting things, always keeping your limitations in mind. You might start with shopping. At the grocery store, see how much you can get in one of those little baskets and then hang them on your wheelchair. This works well with an electric wheelchair, but a regular wheelchair would probably be impossible. And remember, necessity is the mother of invention.

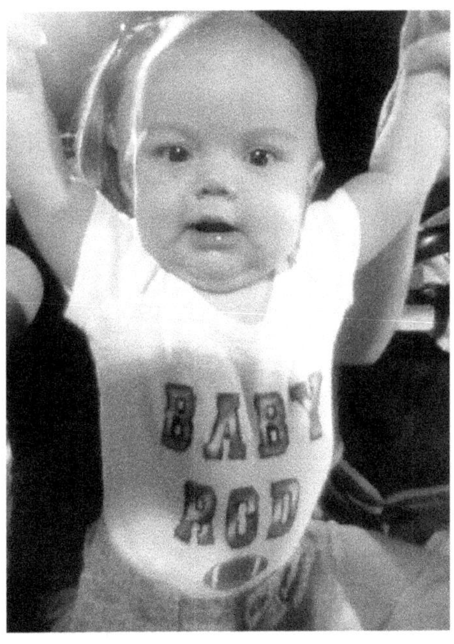

Granddaughter Andi Rose

Betty Dravis: That's a positive way of looking at it, Johnny, and I hope you inspire others to make the most of their own lives.

What's your favorite quote?

John Manha: I have a couple: "It's easy to get to the top once you get through the crowd at the bottom." That's by Zig Ziglar. And the other is, "Success is not so much what we have, as it is what we are." – Jim Rohn.

Betty Dravis: That Zig Ziglar is funny, but does he tell you how to get past that crowd? (laughs)

And Jim Rohn is absolutely right about success having little to do with material things. Thanks for sharing those.

Because you're such a versatile man, Johnny, it would be easy to overlook something in this interview that you'd really like to share. Before closing, if I missed anything, please share it now.

John Manha: Well, Betty, you didn't ask about my pet peeve.

My pet peeve is too much swearing, exaggerated street life and scantily-dressed young women in too many movies. Would it be too much to ask the producers to lighten up. It's a bad influence on our children.

Betty Dravis: I agree with you there, Johnny, and we, as individuals, can do our part to stop it by not purchasing or attending those kinds of movies.

Thanks for sharing your busy time with us, Johnny. I wish you the same luck fulfilling your entrepreneurial dreams as with your island dream. With that same positive attitude, determination and drive, you will make it to Millionaire's Row.

You certainly have a lot of powerful men partnering with you.

And for those who want to converse with you or learn more about you, they can find you by Googling your name or one of your company names, Lazy J Enterprises.

Be sure to come back and tell us how it all works out. Cheers, my friend!

John Manha: Thanks for the interview; I enjoyed it very much and am honored to be included in such talented company. As for keeping you informed, with our families so close and your nose for news, you'll probably be the first to know. (laughs)

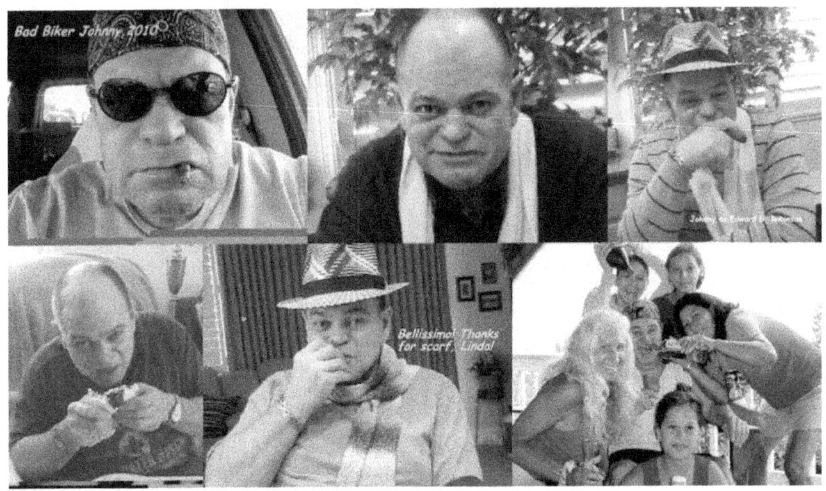

Interview with K. Michael Crawford

AWARD-WINNING CHILDREN'S BOOK AUTHOR/ILLUSTRATOR

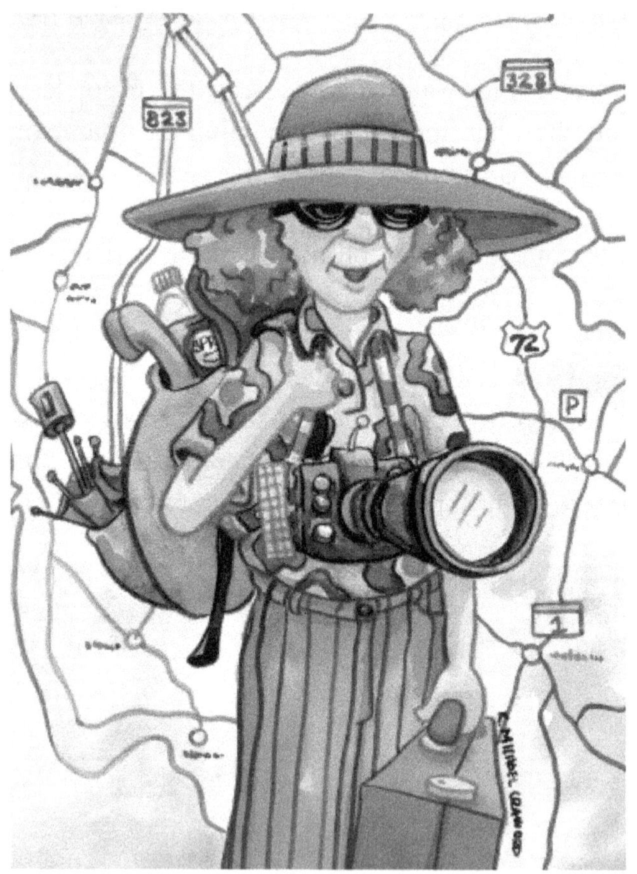

Betty Dravis: Good day, K. Michael Crawford, thanks for visiting Dames of Dialogue. It's great having a visit from the famous, award-winning children's book author and illustrator of a certain classic that is beloved around the world. We can't divulge all our secrets up front, so we'll talk about that famous book later.

You come highly recommended by a publisher friend because you are tops in your field. I know you're in hot demand and have many projects in the works, so it's kind of you to squeeze us in.

I've seen many of your illustrations and you're the most creative illustrator I've seen to date, and I've been around a long, long time. (laughs) Just browsing through your website is like a trip to some wondrous fantasyland filled with the most colorful, charming characters… Creating such original characters must be a labor of love. I bet you have more fun than a child at Disneyland. I recommend that all our readers visit your website for a real treat. They will be awed, I'm sure. The link is: www.happilyeverart.com/.

K.M., it's a good thing God gave me a talent for writing, since I can't draw as well as a kindergartener. I'm wondering if you have always had this amazing talent. Can you tell us a little about your childhood? Did you start then…or were you a late bloomer?

K. Michael Crawford: Well, Betty, my childhood, as well as my life, has been very quirky to say the least. You might even say enchanted. I have had the most magical things happen to me over the years and been surrounded by the most waggish people all my life. I discovered at a young age that I could put some of those quirky adventures and people down on paper and call it art. With my imagination, this job is perfect for me, full of enchantment and magic. Plus, I can sometimes go to work in my pajamas… Some of my ideas come from my imagination and some, if you can believe, come from my own life.

It also helps that I never grew up. I am just a big kid at heart and love to be silly. I find the humor in everything. At a young age, I was taught to see the magic in life. A magical life is the only way I live my life, otherwise, there is that whole messy thing called "reality," which I avoid at all costs. Edward Gorey once wrote, "We all create our own reality." I just prefer mine to be make-believe.

Betty Dravis: Ah-hh, K.M., I may have met my artistic soul-mate; I never grew up, either, and I love being silly… Just as quirky seems to be one of your favorite words, it's one of mine too. *That* and funky… I have no idea why. I suppose because they conjure up fun images in *my* active imagination.

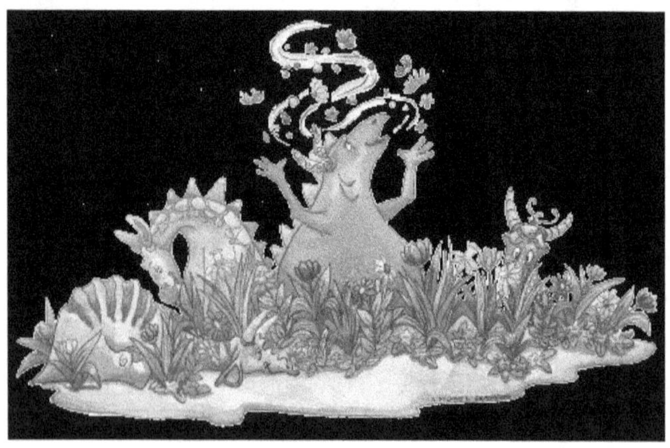

By the way, as a writer, I relate to going to work in pajamas. I often get carried away by my book characters and forget to get dressed. (laughs)

K. Michael Crawford: I love strange words, Betty, and always have. I love words such as inkling, waggish, quirky and tingling. I try to use them as much as I can in my writing and on my answering machine: “Please leave a message and when I have an inkling I will get back to you. *Beep!”* (childish giggle)

Betty Dravis: Oh, K.M., all the unusual words you use are casting a spell on me; I have to smile when reading your answers to my questions. You *are* a silly one, but that’s why children everywhere adore you and your work. I also think writers and artists must have fertile imaginations to be good at their craft. Would you believe that my Muse rides a shocking pink Harley, dresses in biker gear–complete with silver studs? She races through my mind, her long, blonde hair trailing two feet behind her as she tosses the most outrageous story ideas my way? (laughs)

But back to you…I read that your first work was with a crayon, K.M… That tells us something about your age at the time, since parents don’t usually give pencils to young children for fear of accidents. Do you remember the subject of your very first drawing and do you still have it? Did your mother post it on your refrigerator with a magnet, as parents do nowadays?

K. Michael Crawford: Ho-ho-ho, Betty. I love your Muse! She sounds quite waggish herself. What silliness is this?

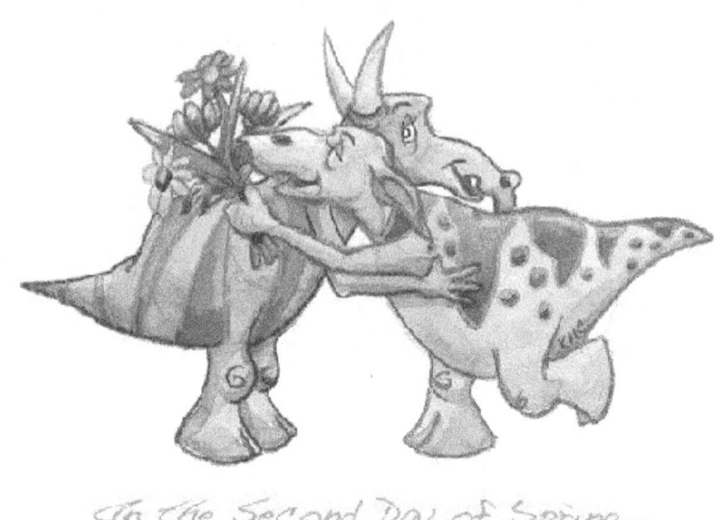

On the Second Day of Spring...

But to answer your question, I don't ever remember not drawing or using my imagination. Even at a young age, I figured out that every day I could go on a fantastic voyage or a strange adventure just by using my imagination. No batteries, buses or airline tickets required… My parents always gave me creative toys where I had to use my imagination to play with them. To this day, one of my favorite toys is "Incredible Edibles"; they are sort of like Gummy Bears you make yourself. You cook them in this contraption–which will explain my fascination with contraptions –love them–and then you peel them out to eat. They taste horrible, but you have to eat them after you make them. So I would imagine that I was creating some magical potion that could turn you into a toad or a fairy. There goes my mind again off onto something silly. (childish giggle)

I think my mom kept a few of my childhood drawings, but when I was growing up we hung our drawings in our rooms or put them away. Refrigerators were only for keeping stuff to eat and you never left the door open, even if you were just looking for something tasty to snack. You had to figure out what you wanted to eat before you opened the fridge, go in fast, grab it, and then shut the door. Now, if you left the front door open in my house, you were reminded that you didn't live in a barn; which is funny, because if you left a barn door open, all the animals would get out. Now you know I didn't grow up in a barn, either. *Shucks!* That would have been a fun adventure. (childish giggle)

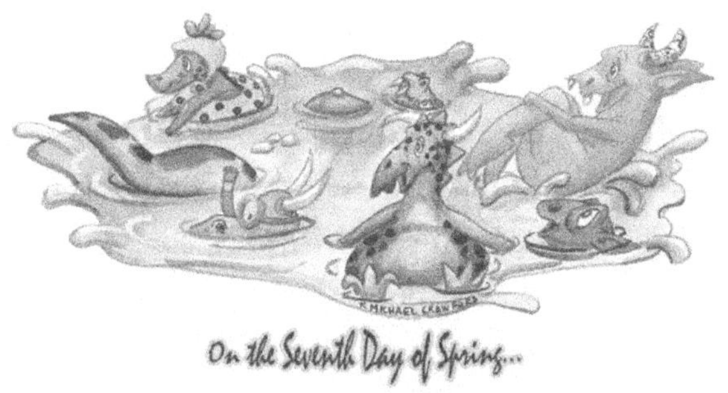

On the Seventh Day of Spring...

I don't remember what I liked to draw back then. I have always loved to draw animals, so it was probably animals. Imagine my delight when I realized that you could take parts of different animals to create a mystical creature. We had two family farms where I hung out a lot as a child. By the way, you should never try to ride a dairy cow and if you plan to swing by a rope from the loft and land in a pile of hay, make sure there's no bees' nest in the hay. *That's some of the great wisdoms I got as a kid!*

My mom kept some of my art from high school and a very funny sketchbook from college, which I have now. When I need a good laugh, I pull them out. No one gets to see them until after I am gone.

Betty Dravis: Oh, making us wait to see the "good" stuff, are you, K.M.? But just where are you planning on going? (laughs) You are cracking me up here… I'll certainly remember what farm animals *not* to ride and to look for bees' nests in any haystack I run across…for sure… (laughs)

By the popularity of your books and illustrations, your fans must be very happy that you *did* discover using different parts of animals to create those clever characters in your work. It must be very rewarding to see so many of your characters in book form. You create everything from pirates to dragons and I, for one, am enamored with your dragons, especially the purple and pink ones on your website. I can't help but smile when I see them and all of your charming critters.

Where do you get the inspiration for such magical characters?

K. Michael Crawford: Someone once asked me, while looking at some of my artwork, if all the stuff in the painting was in my head. I said, "Yes, that's the stuff that can come out." (childish giggle)

Before I explain how I go about creating characters, I need to thank Mr. Foley, my ninth-grade English Teacher, and writer Ray Bradbury for helping me to increase my visual creativity.

Mr. Foley used to read us Ray Bradbury's books, all of them, throughout the year. So while he was reading, I was picturing the whole scene in my head. I tried to thank Mr. Foley, but couldn't find him. I did get the chance to thank Mr. Bradbury in person. To this day, I still picture the illustrated man and how his skin changed pictures when he told a new story.

So here are the basic steps when I create, but not totally guaranteed. Sometimes, I will see someone that needs to be made into a character.

1. I see something or someone I like.
2. I put an idea to what I like.
3. The idea goes in my brain.
4. Then I start asking the question, "What if?"
5. After I mix it up in my brain blender,
6. I let the idea ride my brain roller coaster. Let the idea get thrown around a bit.
7. Then I brew it like a wizard's concoction.
8. Finally, after the idea has gone through all of the above and if the idea is still good, it comes spitting out on the page as a bright and multicolor image. If it's a character, I bring it to life.

Sometimes an idea or character goes in and comes out totally backwards. A funny thing is, you can tell when I am about to go into a very creative spell. I start talking backwards. I say whole sentences backwards. It's pretty funny to hear. It's also a good way to find out if someone is listening to what I have to say.

Betty Dravis: Your creative process is quite fascinating, K.M. I can just picture your "waggish" face as you work your magic. You are a laugh a minute. (laughs) And I suppose that "What if?" gets the juices flowing for artists *and* writers. I often use that when working on my own book plots.

I read something about your work that amused me. Someone asked the question: "What do you get when you cross a purple hippo with a bear?" What's the answer, K. Michael?

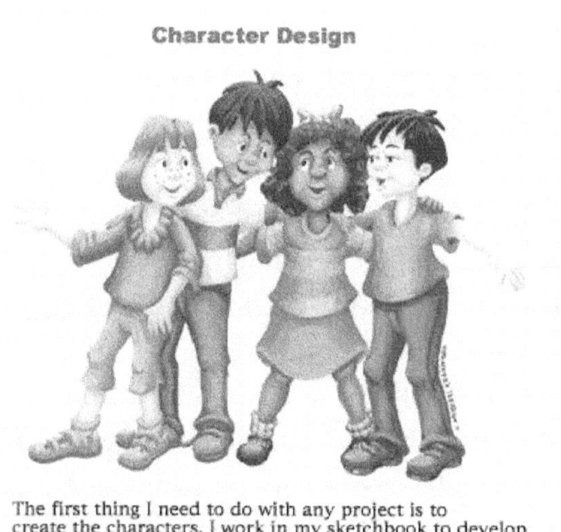

K. Michael Crawford: The answer is: *K. Michael Crawford's work!* (childish giggle) By the way, I have dressed up as a blue M&M and a cow for Halloween, but I have never been a purple hippo/bear. Oh, maybe this year I will be… But I have seen one, and thank goodness for that. Otherwise, I wouldn't know how to draw one. I have also seen a bucksnort, but that's a whole other story.

Betty Dravis: That's a great riddle, K.M.—and the answer is so-ooo *you!* You have such a variety of wonderfully outrageous characters on your website that I may have seen a purple hippo/bear, but have no idea what a bucksnort is. (My younger brother's name is Buck and he gives a pretty *mean* snort, but I don't suppose you're referring to him…) Na-aaa, you haven't even met him… But seriously, you'll have to share that bucksnort story with us one day; perhaps in a new book.

You certainly have a sharp sense of humor and a joy for life that comes through in your drawings. Each character is so unique; they look happy, boisterous and filled with life. How do you manage that?

K. Michael Crawford: When I create a character, I sort of feel like Dr. Frankenstein because in order to create a good character that everyone will like I have to bring that character to life. I need to give them personality and attitude –what they like and dislike. Everyone has to want to fall in love with that character and if it's a villain, they really have to hate him.

Dramatic music and a spooky laugh as the good doctor throws the switch... Presto, a new character has come to life! I have a wonderful lab in my basement just for that purpose. No visitors allowed, unless you are willing to donate a brain or something. (childish giggle)

Betty Dravis: K.M., I was going to visit you, but now I've changed my mind; no spare brains to donate–even if it is for a good cause: *children's laughter!* (laughs)

Seriously, it's refreshing to meet such a highly regarded artist who can call yourself "silly" and attribute your creativity to that side of your nature. In that way you remind me of Steve "The Woz" Wozniak who good-naturedly calls himself a "geek." Being a long-time resident of Silicon Valley, I was there when he and Steve Jobs created their first Macintosh. As you might know, The Woz is the brilliant techie who actually invented the first user-friendly computer and Jobs is the charismatic super salesman behind their business success. I've always admired "The Woz" because none of the fame-and-fortune went to his head. That tells a lot about him, and your attitude is just as humble as his. What else can you tell us about your attitude towards your work?

K. Michael Crawford: That's an interesting comparison, Betty. I may have met The Woz in my Frankenstein lab once… (childish giggle) But seriously, when my head gets too big and about to float away, a character will sit on me to keep me in line and grounded, somewhat. Family is also good for keeping you grounded. They remind you of all the embarrassing things you did when you were growing up. If that doesn't keep you grounded, nothing will. My dad had a big influence on my attitude towards my work. He always told me puns and showed me that life is so much better when you are laughing. Never take yourself too serious and always be the first to remind yourself that you are still human.

My art is my art and how I create it seems normal to me. How I look at things also seems normal…until I see the funny look on someone's face after they have looked at my art. That's when I realize that the way I see things and the way I think is *not* normal.

I can look at any garden and see all kinds of magical creatures running through it. Under my bed lives a whole host of characters that will wake me up at night if I haven't fed them. In my studio, the whimsical beasts tell me when they need to go out. So I don't think of what I do as work; it's just who I am. There is a fine line between my art and myself as a normal person–which has become blurred–and I believe that's the way it should be with any artist.

Betty Dravis: Well, K.M., too much is made of being "normal," and I agree with you.

In addition to your fabulous art, you also write children's books. Did you discover your writing ability at about the same time you began to draw? And which do you enjoy most?

K. Michael Crawford: I have always liked to write, Betty, but I first worked on the art side of creating and then started to focus on the writing side. Here is the funny part: I have had four English teachers throw their hands up at me, saying that I would never learn grammar. Okay, I am the first to admit that grammar doesn't click with me. I don't think it ever will… I write like I talk; never mind that when I write I switch tense in mid-sentence. *But if there is a will, there is a way!* So I hired an editor, Andrew, to proof all my work before it goes anywhere. I have also read that Mark Twain had trouble with grammar and his editor worked his/her magic so his stories could be told. So at least I know I am in good company.

Betty Dravis: I would say that Mark Twain is the *best* company, K.M., and you're fortunate to have found a good editor.

Where did you receive your formal art training and what age were you when you sold your first book *Timbo and the Butterfly?*

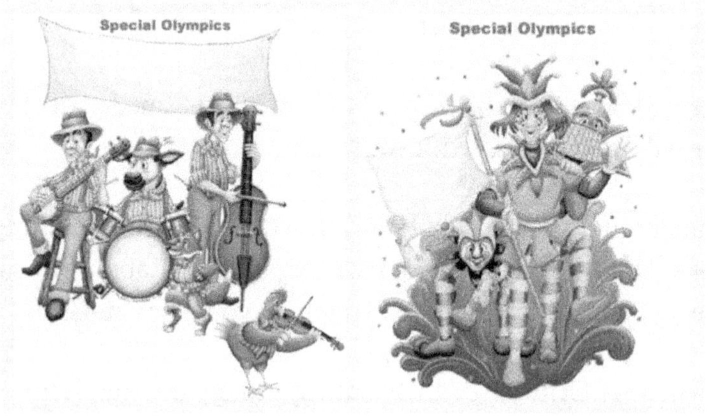

K. Michael Crawford: I went to the University of Maryland, College Park and got my degree in Advertising Design. As you can see, that degree worked out well. Actually, it has helped me a lot in children's books. I only worked in the field for eight years and then went into children's books. But while I was in college a friend of mine, Steve, suggested that we do a book together. I created Timbo as a character first and then Steve wrote the story to go with the character. Timbo will always be special to me because he was one of my first characters I created for a children's book.

Actually, we did three books together. They were the first three books I ever illustrated in this career. We published them to give to family and friends and sold some of them in a local bookstore. *The Baltimore Sun* even did an article about our books. Right then and there I knew I was hooked and wanted to write and illustrate children's books for the rest of my life.

Another friend keeps telling me that she is going to make millions from selling one of those first books on eBay. I hope she does! (childish giggle)

I also took illustration classes at Otis-Parsons School of Design, Art Center of Design, American Animation Institute and Associates in Art to learn as much as I could about art and how it worked. I am still learning about art and plan to keep learning until I am done with what I don't know.

Betty Dravis: That's interesting how Timbo came to fruition; sounds like a good collaboration with Steve. And you took a lot of courses to enhance your natural talent. I admire your drive for more and more knowledge, K. M.

I recently interviewed you for a Dames of Dialogue internet blog wherein I asked the question: How do you celebrate when either finishing or selling a manuscript? Your answer was clever and humorous, capturing some of the essence of who you are. Please share it with us again, if you don't mind.

K. Michael Crawford: This is how I answered, Betty, and I enjoyed reading other authors answers too: *Once upon a time...there was a magical place with lots of magical characters and some strange folks, but not to worry, I just finished my latest book... First, there will be dancing around the drawing table and a big WAAHOO! heard from coast to coast. Maybe some chomping on some M&Ms and then a little more dancing. Then I realize in my silliness I have a new idea for another book. Well, hi-ho, back to work I go, dreaming up a whole new magical place to put between the pages of a book. So the story goes...and all the magical creatures and strange folks lived happily ever after, once their creator got back to work.*

Betty Dravis: What an original and fun way to celebrate, K. M. That's the attitude I've come to admire! I can picture you whistling (or perhaps even yodeling) as you dance a jig and chomp on M&Ms while drawing to your heart's content. (laughs)

Now tell us, K. M., have you written any adult books? But the big question is: How did you get your first big career boost? I'm eager for you to tell our readers what that "career boost" was. It's very inspiring to me.

K. Michael Crawford: Well, Betty, one night I was sitting in my lab, lost in my own imagination, when a ringing appeared in the dream. Where was it coming from? Who or what was making that ringing sound? *Poof!* It was the phone beckoning to be answered. It was Ideal Publishing on the line, asking me to illustrate *Chicken Little.*

You see, I had been sending out postcards to publishers in order to get work as an illustrator. I sent out one postcard, once a month, to two hundred and some publishers for six months before I got that phone call. Ideal Publishing got one of my postcards and gave me a call. *It was so exciting!* Up to that point, I had only illustrated for Educational Companies, such as World Almanac and Highsmith. *Chicken Little was my first big break!*

As for writing for adults, it's a little hard for me to write for adults when I'm so young at heart. But I have been told that adults love my books. So I guess, in a way, I *do* write for adults, but I still think my talents and imagination are better suited for children's books.

Betty Dravis: Well, this is one adult who adores your books, K. M., but back to *Chicken Little,* I know there have been many versions of it through the years. I read that the author is unknown, so what can you tell us about its history?

K. Michael Crawford: I don't know who created the original story of *Chicken Little,* but I had such a great time illustrating that book. The publisher let me go "hog wild" on the illustrations and pretty much gave me free rein to do what I wanted. So when I started to draw, I decided to add my sense of humor. I made Ducky Lucky sitting in a duck blind. (You have to live on the East coast to know what a duck blind is.)

Henny Penny decided to grow her own corn. *Hey, a girl has got to eat!* So does Goosey Loosey, who is fishing beside the lake.

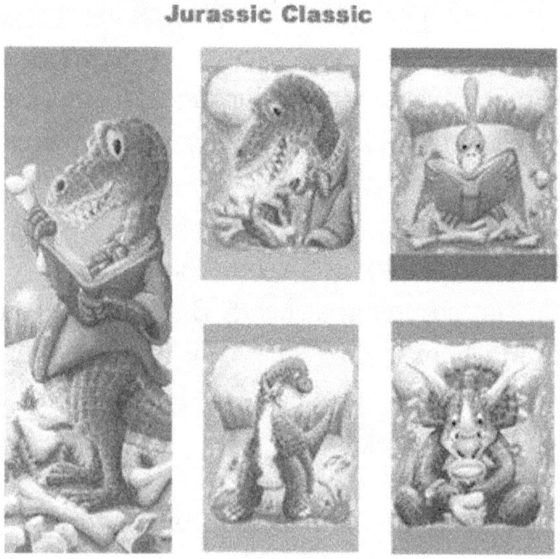

Jurassic Classic

Another creative campaign for Upstart/Highsmith.
The campaign was a seven piece project.

Betty Dravis: You certainly have a heart for your characters, K.M. and your illustrations work for me. I chuckled at the "girls" fishing and growing corn. But we do have duck hunting in California, too… (laughs)

After that incredible, unexpected offer from Ideal Publishing, I heard that you became a hot commodity and have been illustrating "happily ever after." I understand your works have been distributed throughout the United States and you've worked for many big names in the business: Special Olympics, Disney, Warner Brothers Studio, Scholastic and Hanna Barbera, to name a few. Your list of prestigious awards in the field of children's literature is also impressive. Parents Choice is one I recall and I'm delighted to know one of your latest books–*The Mystery of Journeys Crowne*–has won a Biblio Best of 2009 Award. That's another tremendous achievement.

Can you give a brief synopsis of the next book in your Bazel Lark series, *The Island of Zadu?* I understand it just went to press. Will it also be published by Virtualbookworm.com Publishing?

And when is the release date?

K. Michael Crawford: Argh, Matey! *The Island of Zadu* is a high-sailing sea adventure based on the same idea as *The Mystery of Journeys Crowne.* The reader has to answer clues to know what to draw on the page. So get your sea legs ready to set sail soon!

Happily Ever Art Publishing is a publishing company I started to publish all of my first-of-their-kind drawing books. Virtualbookworm is handling the printing and distribution of these books. Between creating the books, promoting them and all the other things I have to do these days, I was glad to have someone else distribute and print the books.

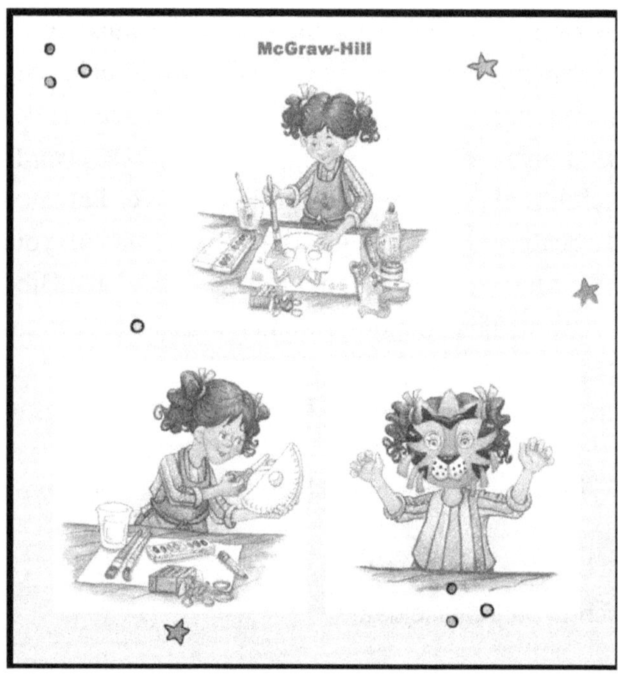

Betty, when I lived in Los Angeles, I was very lucky, because I had a friend who did a lot of work for the studios. She hired me to help her with the illustration jobs, so I worked on *Magic School Bus* video covers, *Winnie the Pooh* ornaments and *Looney Tunes* books. That helped me out until I got more of my own illustration work. It also helped me define my style. When you are drawing other people's characters, you have a chance to see what you want to put in your own work. One of the things you have to do to be a good artist is to determine your own style of art. That comes from how you want to show the world how you see stuff and is very important to defining your style. Painting tons of paintings also helps to create a style.

Just as writers need to learn their voice in writing, so do artists in drawing.

Betty Dravis: Wow, K. M.! You're a human dynamo, like so many of our Dream Reachers. I can't believe you started your own publishing company too.

As for your Bazel Lark series, there's a story behind why you wrote them. Please clue us in.

K. Michael Crawford: At the time I came up with the idea, I was teaching kids Comic Book Art. When I first started teaching kids, in a class of fifteen students I would only have to help jump-start the imagination of about three kids. As the years went on, it got to be more and more kids who needed help. I decided to create special books to help kids learn to use their imagination all their lives. Kids who use their imagination have an easier time making the right choices for themselves and can see all the possibilities that life has to offer. If anything, using your imagination teaches you to believe in yourself, because it teaches you to believe.

Once I had a student who didn't believe in all those make-believe things: dragons, tooth fairies, aliens and such. I made a deal with him; I told him that by the end of the classes I would get him to believe. I didn't say what I was going to get him to believe, but if he didn't believe by the last class I would owe him a treat. So the last day of class, he came up to me and said,

"Well, you owe me a treat because I still don't believe." I looked at him and said, "Oh yes, I did get you to believe." He gave me a quizzical look. "What did you get me to believe?" With a smile on my face, I replied, "In yourself…" His mouth dropped open and he then said, "Yes, you did!"

Betty Dravis: Well, K.M., if there's anyone who can make kids believe, it's you with your magical pen and writings. That must be a wonderful feeling.

Now that we've talked about your series, tell us about another recent work, *Batty Malgoony's Mystic Carnivale*. That's a clever name, by the way… Since my name is Betty, I've been called Batty a few times, as you might imagine. (laughs)

So I can relate to Batty. Please tell us a little bit about this appealing character.

K. Michael Crawford: Ray Bradbury's book, *Something Wicked This Way Comes*, has always stuck with me from the first time I read it as a child. Besides, I love carnivals, fairs and circuses. So what better way to use the quirky side of my character than to create a book; like instead of a cow catcher on the train, I put a cow.

Batty lives in Wicked Springs, Wyoming when he is not traveling with his Carnivale. I would tell you to stop by for a visit, but he might make you into one of his acts. He's very good at recruiting new people. He is still trying to get me to walk the high-wire, while being an all-person band. He is just your basic quirky and waggish character that I hope kids will like.

Betty Dravis: A cow on a train instead of a cowcatcher! You're too much, K.M.! (laughs) And thanks for the information about *Batty.*

Speaking of children, you must receive a lot of input from them about your works. K.M., can you think of any funny things kids or their parents have asked you? And what advice do you give people who want to be artists?

K. Michael Crawford: Yes, Betty, when I do presentations, the kids do say the funniest things to me. I ask them to help me create the character we are drawing and they start telling me that their mother was sick all night and slept on the bathroom floor. I think they are supposed to tell me those things so that I can use pieces of their tales in my art. There's always been something about my personality where kids feel it's okay to tell me all kinds of things about their lives and families. I have yet to meet a normal family or person, so that shows that the quirky art I create is not so *out there*.

As for advice, Betty, when I'm talking to a future artist or writer, I always tell them one thing: *Eat your vegetables!* No, really, I tell them to always follow your heart, because it will never steer you wrong. Do what you love, love what you do and never give up on reaching for your dream. You can be anything you want. Sometimes it takes a little hard work and elbow grease, but you will get there. Funny thing is, sometimes we get there and don't realize it.

Betty Dravis: Great advice, K.M., and I, too, know many people who have "arrived" and don't realize it. Life is strange…

I know you've created dozens of awesome characters, but do you have a very favorite? Do children seem to favor one over all others?

K. Michael Crawford: I love them all or I would not have created them. The ones I don't like end up in the round file next to my drawing table. Once I learned that I not only need to create the characters, but I also need to bring them to life, I learned to create the kinds of characters that fit with my art and style. I gave them personalities, likes and dislikes… Most of the time, I already have them created in my head before I even put pencil to paper. Kids are the first to tell me whether they like a character or not. They don't hold back on me.

Betty Dravis: From your vast menagerie of fanciful critters, K.M., I would have a hard time selecting a favorite, also.

When, in an earlier communication, I asked what the initial K stands for in your name, you said you liked keeping your private life separate from your art. I respect your privacy, but can you tell us a little about your home state and what you like to do in your spare time. I understand that Maurice Noble, a Disney animator, once told you that if you want your work to be 3-D then you need to have a 3-D life. What did he mean by that and what have you done to follow his advice?

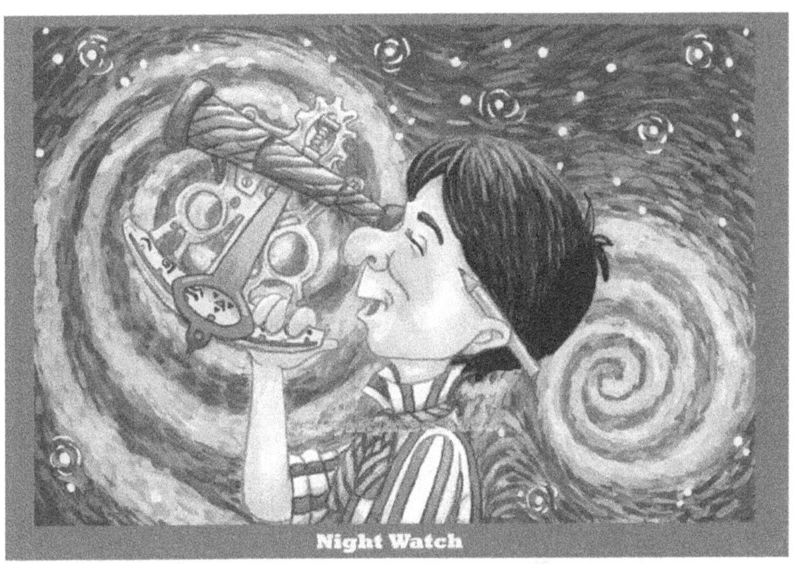
Night Watch

K. Michael Crawford: The "K" stands for Kalamazoo or Kentucky. It could be Kakapo or Kangaroo. I prefer Karakul. It just depends on what mood I am in on that day. That's the nice thing about an Initial; it can be anything you want.

I live in Maryland at the present time, but that can change at any time. I have been known to pack up and move somewhere else at a moment's notice. There are too many wonderful places to live in the world. *Why just live in one?* I am hoping that the Queen asks me to come and visit with her for a bit. I drink tea, so I would fit right in. I would be more than willing to bring the crumpets. (childish giggle)

Maryland is known as "Little USA" because it has a little bit of everything; there are mountains, oceans and a bay. There are cows, deer and creatures of the forests. There are tall people and some of them are short. We had Edgar Allan Poe for a short bit, so should I say more?

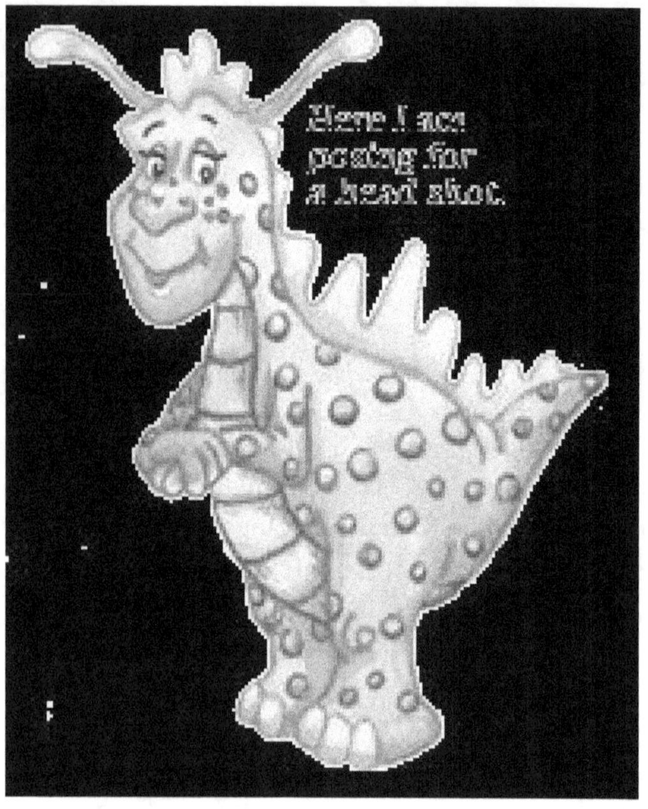

When I am not doing my art, I am usually off on an adventure to get more stuff to use in my art. I have the most unusual adventures–par for my life–and I see the most wonderful things just by taking the road less traveled. (Sidebar: If I see a road I have never been on, I will turn and go down that road just to see what is there. It drives the people riding in my car crazy, but they wind up having the most fun). I try to see all kinds of things and have all kinds of experiences, so that I have a broad perspective. I visit museums, parks, gardens, and the strangest attractions. Yes, if I drove by the largest ball of yarn I would stop in and see it. That was what Maurice Noble was talking about. The more experiences you have, the more you can put in your art.

I have been known to spread a little wackiness in kids' lives by teaching them how to draw. I think that they mostly teach me… Do you know that every time a fly lands it throws up?

That puts a whole new meaning on a picnic. I don't know if I have been on one since I learned that tidbit.

I also enjoy sailing and have had a few adventures on the high seas as well. I would like to recommend that it's best not to sail during thunderstorms or snowstorms. *Been there! F*rosted eyelashes are not fun. Wait–I think I hear a new adventure calling me now. Off I go!

Betty Dravis: *Karakul Michael!* That's not too catchy, so I think I'll stick with K.M. (laughs)

Hang with me a little longer before you go dashing off… I'm almost finished and am curious to know if you have had any mentors and what children's writers and illustrators you admire most.

Another illustrator who awes me, though, is Sarah Davis of Australia. Sarah began illustrating for children in 2007 and was awarded the Children's Book Council of Australia's 2009 Crichton Award for her first picture book, *Mending Lucille,* by J.R. Poulter (Lothian/Hachette Livre) which was released in 2008. In 2009 she illustrated several other books (Harper Collins/Random House/Scholastic). And another book that Sarah illustrated, *Fearless* by well-known English/Australian children's book author Colin Thompson, has been shortlisted for the Children's Book Council of Australia's Book of the Year award. I must say that's very impressive for such a short time in your business. She's the daughter-in-law of my closest friend, Linda Bulger of New York, and I'm wondering if you've heard of Sarah yet.

K. Michael Crawford: I am sorry to say that I haven't heard of Sarah Davis, but lately I have been really bad about keeping up with all the wonderful authors and illustrators out there. It's amazing to me all the talent I'm part of as a children's book author and illustrator. It's just incredible.

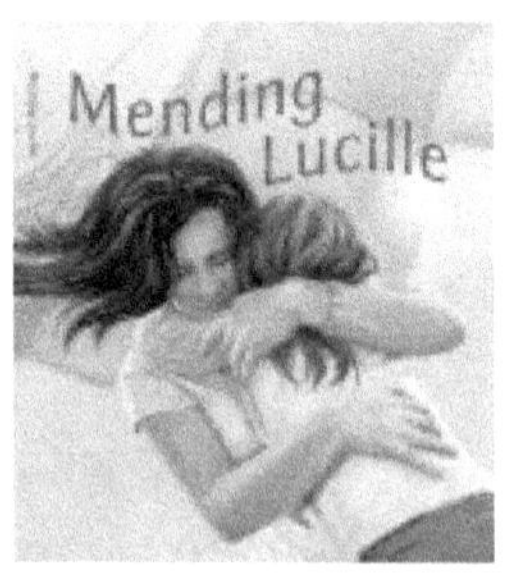

Illustrations by Sarah Davis

And did you know that only five percent of the world's population is in the arts? That's a lot of entertaining, dancing, acting, singing, designing, writing and creating we have to do for the rest of the world. I guess I better get back to work, so that I contribute my share.

As for mentors, there are so many people that have left their mark on me and what I create that it would take days to list them all. Two of the major ones are L. Frank Baum and Ray Bradbury. For artists, I would say a lot of the masters and illustrators whose work I have enjoyed. The illustrators I like the most have found a way to create energy in the lines they put on paper. That's not an easy thing to do.

My inspiration comes from lots of different things. It can come from people I see out and about, or it can come from something someone does. You do have to be careful around me; I don't miss a trick and lots of things I see out in the world go into my work.

I was once asked if you could mirror the career of any other author, who would it be and why? I answered that I was having too much fun writing my own life story to want to mirror someone else's life. But there are a few authors I would want to have their royalties sent to me.

Betty Dravis: Oh, yeah, K.M., I wouldn't mind having just one percent of Stephen King's royalties. (laughs) As for being careful around you, I'm not a very cautious person, but thanks for the warning. On second thought, though, I'd enjoy being the subject of one of your projects.

This seems like a good place to toss this question into the mix: If you could spend the day with anyone (living or dead) who would you choose and why?

K. Michael Crawford: There are *three* people I would like to spend a few days with and I would like to create one book with them. Those three would be Leonardo de Vinci, Walt Disney (although I heard that he could be a little cranky sometimes) and Dr. Seuss. *I could see it now!* The Lorax would learn to fly up in the sky and the Butter Battle Bunch would ride a wooden bike or maybe take a hike with Bazel and Batty in the happiest place on earth. Dr. Seuss taught me to read, Walt Disney got me to see the magic and Leonardo de Vinci taught me to dream.

Betty Dravis: K.M., it blows my mind to think what you four brainiacs could concoct together! *What a mind-boggling thought!* (laughs) But what are you currently working on and what do you hope for your writing career in the next few years?

Any goals that you have yet to reach?

K. Michael Crawford: I just finished my latest book called *The Island of Zadu*. It just went to the printer. It's the next book in the Bazel Lark series. *The Mystery of Journeys Crowne* is the first one. Thanks for mentioning those above.

I am also planning to get back on a funny book I started last fall: *Professor Horton Hogwash's Museum of Ridiculous.* Believe me when I say it will be ridiculous. I called it that so I could learn how to spell the word ridiculous. I am still learning that one; thank goodness for spell check. One of the rules in the book is, "Never, ever pick your nose's friends" just to give you an idea. The reader/artist is asked to fill in all of the museum's collection and treasures in the book and each room has a theme the reader must follow. The sillier things they draw on each page, the better.

I have ideas for at least six more books after Horton's book, but my big dream is to build a magical place/park where kids can come to use their imagination in real life. I haven't worked out the details yet, but I have a whole notebook of ideas.

I think if I stop dreaming, you might as well put me in the ground, feet pointing up. I hear the strangest things sometimes: *If a person is buried with their feet pointing down it means they weren't a good person in life.* I was in the middle of a cemetery when I heard that one, so it was okay if I heard it. Somehow, someday, that bit of information will show itself in one of my paintings. It always does…

Betty Dravis: From viewing what you've already created, K.M., I'm certainly happy to know that we can expect much more from you. That theme park is a grand idea. Please let us know when it happens.

And congratulations on the start of production on your Island book… I hope the series becomes a best-seller like most of your books. I bet you had another celebratory dance, didn't you, K.M.? But before leaving, let's remind our readers that they can Google you to view your fantastic art and to find your latest projects.

Get Caught Up in a Good Book

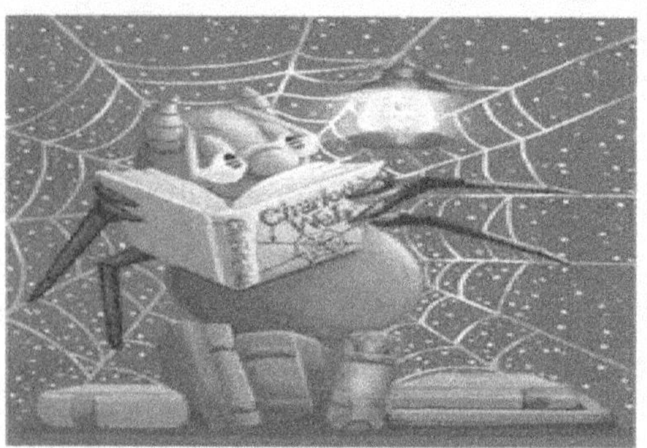

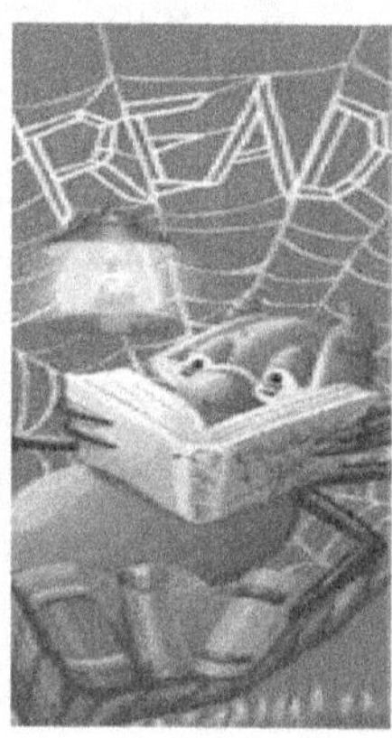

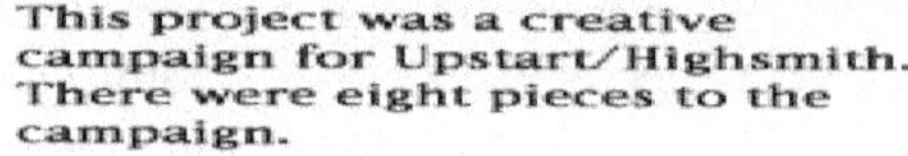
This project was a creative campaign for Upstart/Highsmith. There were eight pieces to the campaign.

K. Michael Crawford: Thank you, Betty. This has been fun and I hope silly to read… But while we are at it, let's everyone get up and do that good celebratory dance together. It's always good to dance your way through life. I wouldn't have it any other way.

Betty Dravis: It's our pleasure, K. M. You're a lot of fun…

Your website is pretty comprehensive, but if you have other links, feel free to add them. This is also the place to mention anything you would like to add to this interview; anything important to you. Oops, I forgot to mention that you also sell some of your art on your website. I would love to have one of your drawings on my office wall, so I'll be in touch on that. Details are found under PRINTS on your website. I'm wondering if you also sell any of your colored drawings, like the pink dragon.

K. Michael Crawford: *Hold the presses, Betty!* Batty just sent a Carnivale clown over with another bit of great, waggish news: Nancy Allen's book that I illustrated, *Trouble in Troublesome Creek,* was selected to represent the state of Kentucky at the National Book Festival in Washington, D.C. this fall 2010.

Betty Dravis: Another honor, K. M.—that's awesome! Congratulations, but I'm too tired for another dance. I fear you would keep me dancing till the cows come home. (laughs)

That makes us all want your art work even more, so tell us whether that's possible?

K. Michael Crawford: I'm still floating in nether space about that honor, Betty, so I'll dance later…in private. (childish giggle)

It's funny that you wondered about buying my art, because recently I decided to send more of my children (paintings and artwork) out into the world because I'm running out of room to keep them. I am always interested in finding good homes for my art and there is no application to fill out or waiting period to get some. I even do commission work… If anyone is interested in buying from the gallery section of my website, they can contact me there. I don't even charge an arm or a leg.

I am a little less willing to sell the original art from a book that I have illustrated because someday the publisher or printer might need the art again. It would be funny to me if someone hung an illustration from Bazel's or Batty's book. It would look like an incomplete painting, but who knows? I have seen incomplete paintings in museums.

I also have videos on youtube.com for my books. They are silly videos I created to promote my work. One person told me they were going to have trouble sleeping after they watched Batty's video. (childish giggle) I have a new video that I will be adding soon to promote only my art.

I think I might do what James Patterson does when he advertises one of his new books. He clearly states that he is going to kill off one of his characters if you don't buy his book.

Well, I am going to start saying that I am going to send one of my monsters to live with you if you don't buy one of my books. They will eat you out of house and home, while making a mess in every room. They don't smell too good, either. Just imagine trying to sleep while one of my monsters is under your bed, belching the alphabet song. You are also going to pay for postage when I send you the monster. Imagine the cost of postage for a two hundred pound monster?

It would be so much easier just to buy my books.

Betty Dravis: You are baaaaad, K. M. That is too funny. (laughs)

I hate to leave the fun and games, but thanks for becoming a part of our growing list of Dream Reachers. You are in good company and my co-author Chase Von and I are happy to have you in our rather exclusive "club." Like the subjects of our other interviews, you dream big and have stretched to reach your dreams. I really enjoyed getting to know more about you and wish you best of luck with all your future projects. Your journey through life is an inspiring adventure.

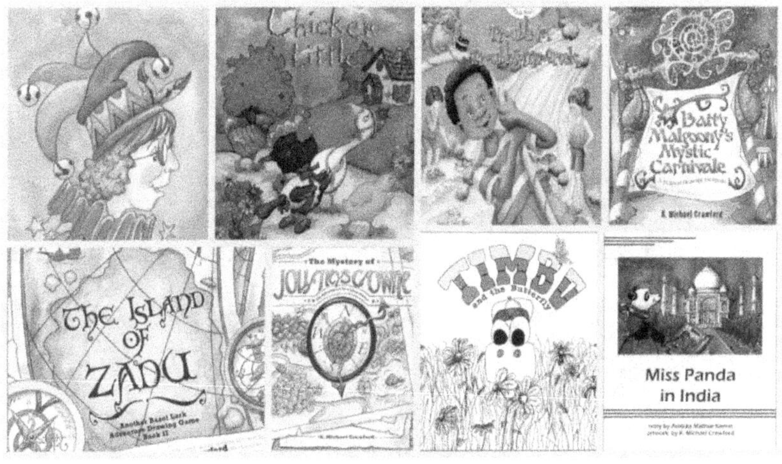

K. Michael Crawford: Thank you for all your wonderful comments about my work. It's always nice to hear that someone else is enjoying my silly art and quirky books. I don't even want to think about not being able to pick my nose's friends or sail to mysterious islands. Those who like my art and books allow me to keep creating those adventures.

I want to also thank you for letting me be a part of *Dream Reachers II* and perhaps, you'll invite me to visit again when you are ready for some more silliness. I will put out the tea and crumpets and we can sit a spell chewing the art. My art comes in flavors… (childish giggle)

"The more experiences you have,
the more you can put in your art."

— K. Michael Crawford

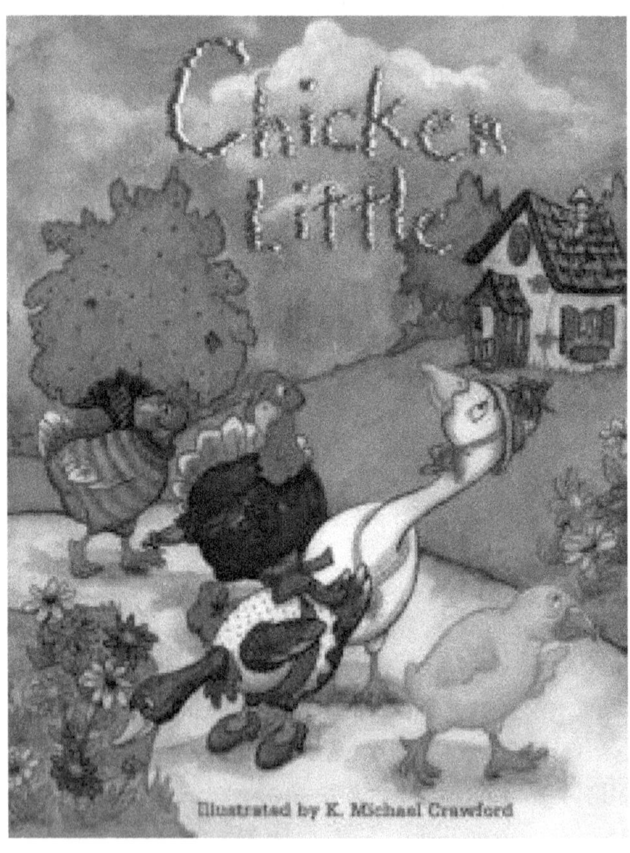

Interview with Rob Waterlander

"PEOPLE WHISPERER" IS A NATURAL

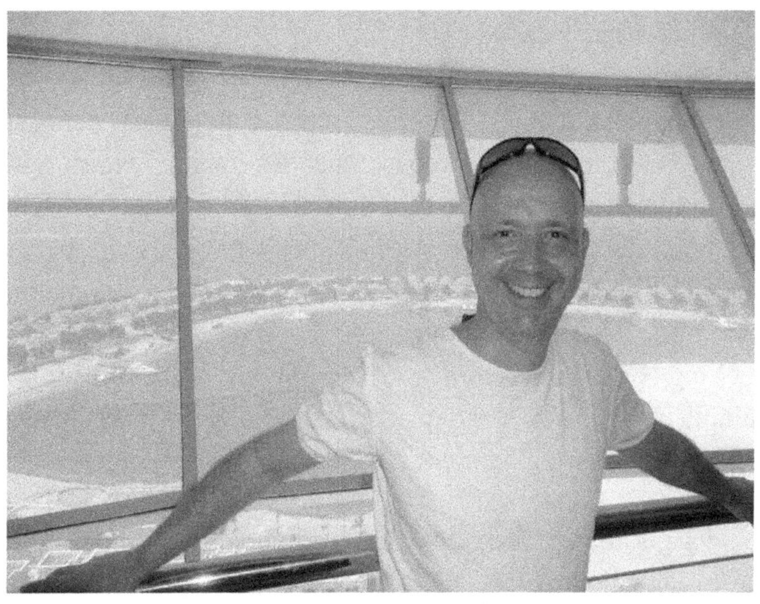

Betty Dravis: Good morning, Rob, It's my pleasure to have you visiting with us all the way from Holland. I'm glad you could make it, and thanks for taking time from your busy schedule.

I'd like our readers to know that I met you through model/award-winning screenwriter Kitania "Kitty" Kavey who starred in our first *Dream Reachers* book. She recommended you highly, but I must confess, when I started researching you it was your logo that intrigued me. Odd to say, but that orange lizard is rather attractive, in a funky kind of way. (laughs)

But first things first, Rob… To relate to people as you do, a person must have inborn intuition and certain powers of persuasion. Did you recognize any special skills as a child? When did the urge to help people start? Please share some of your early childhood with us. I'm especially curious about what it was like growing up in Holland.

Rob Waterlander: Well, Betty, I am not the typical personal, mental or motivational coach people might expect. My intuitive and empathetic nature is something I was born with and have developed over my lifetime. I have always been a beacon–shining and attracting people who were wondering what direction to go–although initially, I wasn't aware in full. Looking back, I think things started moving in the direction of guiding people when classmates started asking for guidance, mainly girls sharing their emotions.

I feel I got my extensive class, or University of Life, the first three months of my life. Long story… (laughs)

Being adopted by two of the most loving parents after I was given away has been the key to unlocking my potential for intuitively seeing and feeling people. It helped me to enter the world of helping those in search of more of what they want.

And by the way, Kitty is an amazing person, gifted and so sweet.

In 1996 I started organizing youth sports events for charity: CliniClowns sports events. CC is a foundation that originated in NYC when Patch Adams started to perform as a clown in hospitals, entertaining children with long-term illnesses, sometimes terminal. These sports events put me in contact with professional soccer players and the rest is history; one soccer player referred me to another, etc. *And I love it!*

By the way, Hunter Doherty "Patch" Adams is one of those special ones on earth. Would love to meet him in real life and have a chat.

As for Holland, my country is probably one of the best countries overall. I grew up in a suburb of Amsterdam, what used to be a little fishermen's village where I felt safe, being able to play, hang out and develop the "real" me.

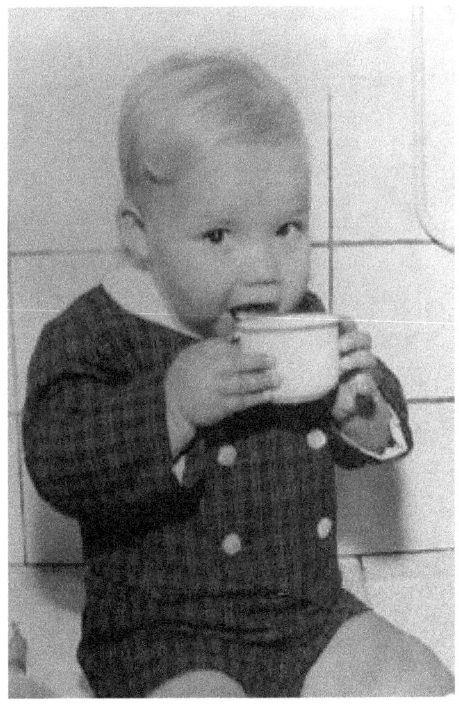

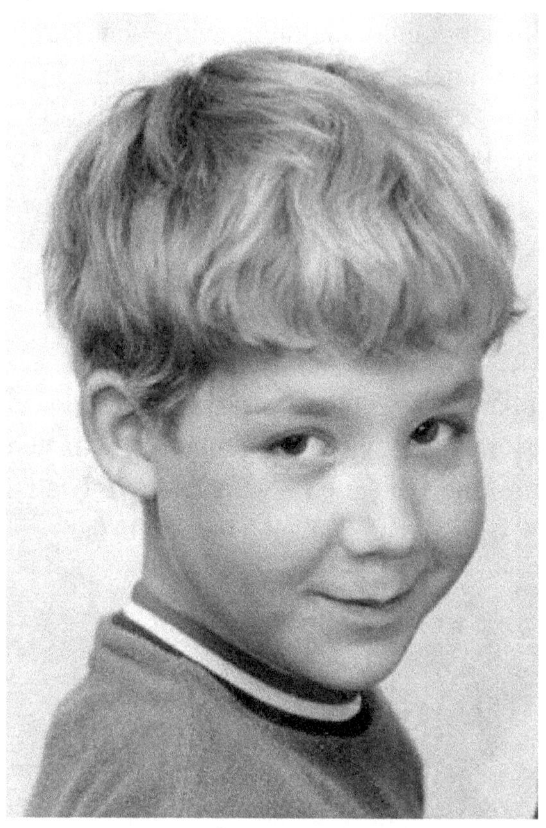

Betty Dravis: That's interesting how CliniClowns started; I recall reading some stories about Patch Adams. I agree with you about him; he had to have been a caring, sensitive man to devote his life to children like that. I sensed when I met you that you were born with this "sensitive" ability, Rob. Thanks for explaining the fascinating details.

This might seem like an odd juxtaposition, but getting back to your logo before I forget: Why did you choose a lizard? And why an orange one…?

Rob Waterlander: I chose the lizard, Betty, because it's associated with intuition and psyche, balance and sensitivity, helping us to detach from our past what no longer serves us. Detachment from ego, power to regenerate that which is lost, facing fear, controlling dreams, conservation, agility… The lizard is an archetype of adaptation, variation, flexibility and shrewdness. The lizard typifies characteristics that I work on every day within my own life, and it helps teach my clients to realize these same skills in theirs.

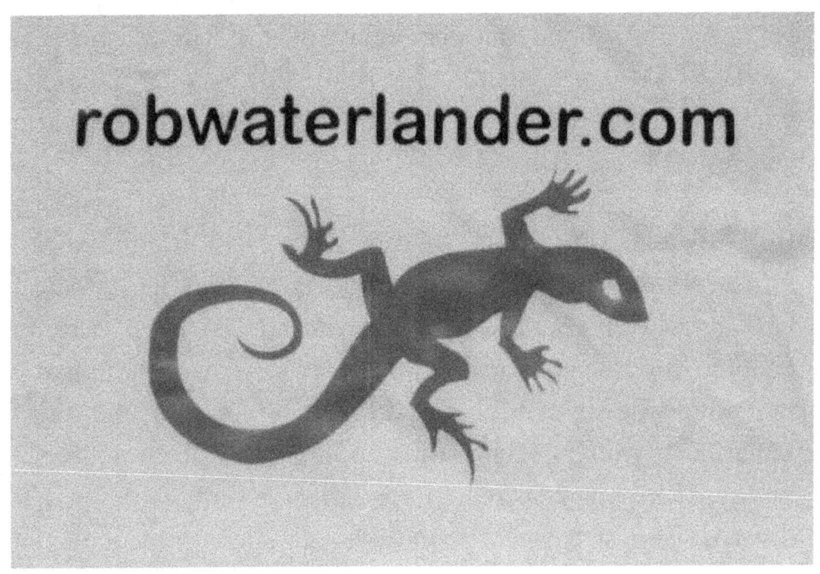

Also, the lizard's stillness and its silence–having the peace and ability to hang-out for hours and hours in the heat of the sun–is something that I can relate to myself. So, as you see, there are various aspects of what the lizard is to me and, therefore, what made me choose it. I listen, absorb in silence, and then intuitively see and feel where the person's next steps are.

Betty Dravis: Well, I can't argue with your wise choice, Rob. I once chose the turtle as the logo for a newspaper I owned…because of its patience. But that didn't last long because my subscribers thought I meant that they were "slow" like the turtle. (laughs)

But back to you, after the lizard, the second thing I noticed on your page was your brilliant smile. It was a pleasure when you visited my home in February to find that the smile is genuine and almost a constant… I found you to be a truly happy, up-beat guy. In my opinion, only a man who has found his true calling in life can be that happy. But before you get into what you're doing now, please share a little about the path it took to get from "there to here."

Rob Waterlander: I am following the path leading to the sanctuary where I want to be, and being on track feels good. I have two lovely souls in my life who are blood related: my children, a son and a daughter. Those two are my link to many things in life that I cherish, given by one of the most remarkable women in my life, the high school sweetheart I married and was married to for almost twenty-one years. I divorced almost ten years ago, although she is someone I am eternally linked to.

There is another woman in my life with whom I have found the connection I so want, leading closer to the sanctuary where I love and long to be. I am feeling good… From here, I have everything to offer to people looking for guidance, joy and releasing resistance in life, allowing them to be who they are and enjoying life in full.

Having been in sales for a long time, I learned a lot about myself and people. I enjoyed doing something that brought me success and acknowledgment of me as a professional: advising and selling roofing constructions for new and re-roofing projects with a contract value of up to more than two million dollars per project. One of the projects I did brought me to Richard Meier, the well-known and famous NYC architect.

My intuitive qualities were a valuable asset to work with project teams and buyers within the construction industry and during those years I developed my qualities extensively.

Betty Dravis: I agree, Rob, that being in sales teaches valuable lessons about others. I bet you felt proud and fulfilled when you actually viewed the architectural beauty of the completed construction projects, also.

I saw some recent photos of you with a lovely, dark-haired woman with a smile that matches your own. Is she the new woman that you spoke of above?

Rob Waterlander: Yes, Betty, she is felt as my mate in the sanctuary. (smiles) Her name is Carly Couweleers and we were brought together by one of her daughters and two of my best friends. She is a guide, too—although a bit different from what I do. She is able to see through people at levels going beyond what most of us see, and I can see us working together with people in the future. It is amazing to experience someone to work with who is guided by spiritual guides and is a woman of God, also. *That* I asked for too…

Betty Dravis: I'm so happy for you both, Rob. Carly does, indeed, sound like a God-send and I can tell by your glowing description that she's "the one" for you. (laughs) You should make a great, inspiring team. Like-minded, compatible people working together can perform miracles,

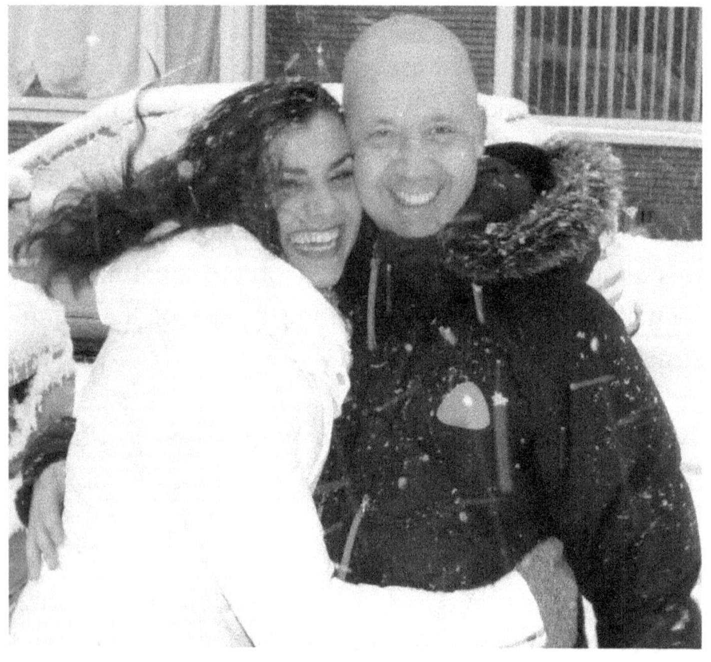

When you decided to take a road trip to visit me in Manteca, you were in the States for client meetings in San Francisco, and after you left you had more meetings in the L.A. area. Were those meetings successful and did you manage to help your clients progress in their search for a more meaningful life?

Rob Waterlander: I was in California for a few meetings with people and some workshops in San Francisco and L.A. I am glad I took the time to also drive down to Manteca from the Bay Area before heading to L.A. Being able to meet up with you, as well as with your friend Johnny, was such a good thing.

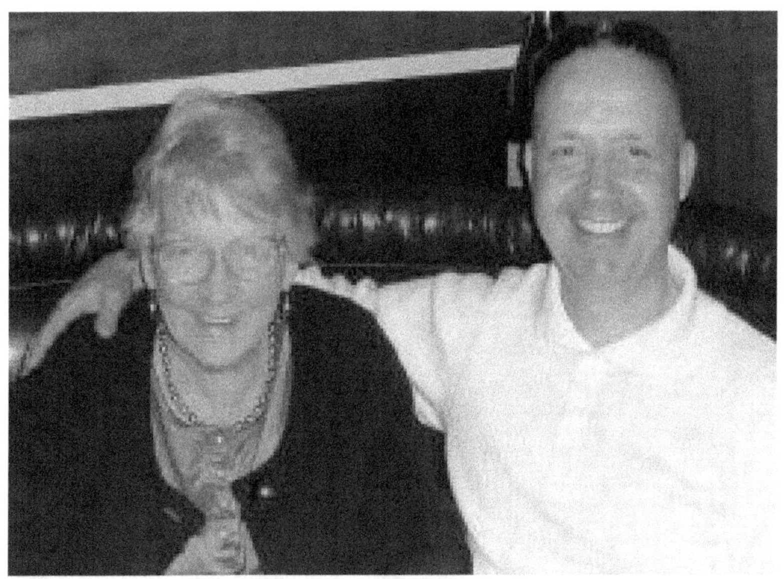

Rob took a road trip from San Francisco meetings to visit author Betty Dravis

You, being a mother, do have the natural drive and joy of wanting to make a difference, but it was Kitty Kavey who told me and still does: "Rob, go to L.A. They need you there." Truthfully, Betty, after having lived in San Diego in 2003, going back there has been a good stepping stone. I am glad I decided to say *yes* to the meetings. Whether the people I met are making the progress they want in their life or not, it is an option I offered to them. As you know, we all have freedom of choice. I love working with those creative guys and gals…and Malibu is *so* my area. (smiles) I am certain to go back soon.

Betty Dravis: It's a great start, Rob, and I'm happy you enjoy working in the States. Speaking of road trips reminds me that you love to travel and have clients in many countries.

What countries have you visited and where did you go on your most recent trip?

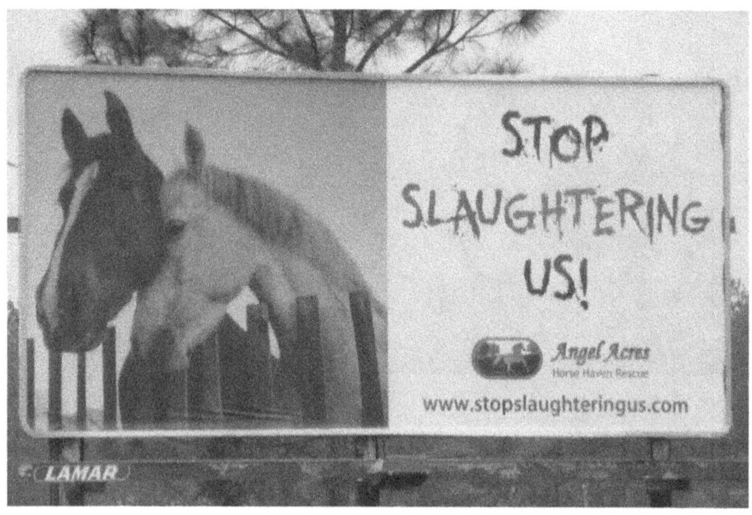

Rob Waterlander: I love the globe–the playground offered to all of us here in the world. The world is huge, although I think it is nothing compared to what is out there and waiting for us, Betty.

My last travels took me to the Middle East and I will be there soon again. It's an amazing area… Also I had the chance to spend some time in Venice this summer.

I have been to many places in the world; except for the Far East I have been to almost all continents, although not all over those continents.

I would love to see more of Africa and the Middle East. Sydney and San Francisco are my favorite cities. Another part in the world that intrigues me is South America; Venezuela and Bolivia showed me extremes in atmosphere.

My next travel will be to Saudi Arabia and Northern Africa, both for business. Then in 2011, I am also traveling to the USA, both for pleasure and business. Recently, I started to look more into the Dutch Islands, close to Amsterdam, and other than the climate, it is so wonderful.

Betty Dravis: *Wow–all that travel boggles my mind!* That's a mighty ambitious agenda, Rob. You certainly do love to travel, and fortunately, you're in the right career to be able to do it. (laughs)

I know cruises are a lot of fun, so what's the funniest or most embarrassing thing that ever happened to you on a cruise?

Rob Waterlander: Wow, Betty… hahahahaha… I had the chance to go on a cruise with my best friend–thanking him for all the years he gave me so much fun while he was playing in one of the leading soccer leagues in the world, the Premier League in England. We went to Norway and met some wonderful entertainers while on the cruise. He had a not-so-nice experience, which to me was very funny… (laughs) We kayaked in a beautiful fjord and he turned upside down while looking backwards; not so nice for him–losing his camera and phone. But I will always remember that cruise as precious because I spent quality time with a dear friend who gave me a lot, both he and his wife. Enjoying food and travel with a dear friend is one of the best experiences life has to offer.

Well, kind of funny, too, my son's luggage not being there when traveling for a cruise departing from Panama and having to shop for new clothes almost every day because each day new promises came our way. Eventually, he had to take part in a formal night and seeing my son actually enjoying being dressed in a tuxedo was worth it. My son said, "The next time, I will probably travel with a plastic bag and an empty suitcase." Six weeks later, the suitcase re-emerged having been to Miami and all over the Caribbean. (laughs)

And very sweet was being with my daughter during a formal night seeing how grown-up and lovely she looked in her in her evening gown.

Betty Dravis: It's odd how those embarrassing moments give us laughs years later, isn't it, Rob? As for your kids in formal attire, I'm featuring a photo of you with your daughter in her formal gown and one of you and your son, also. Your daughter is, indeed, a beautiful young lady and your son is very handsome, but with such good-looking parents, how can they miss? It comes natural, don't you think? (laughs)

Now, getting back to your career, to sum it up, you are an intuitive motivator, "people whisperer," inspirer and guide and you work one-on-one with people to help create the life they want. This means working to ensure their independence and helping them discover or rediscover their personal light in order to continue through life's challenges.

That sounds like a colossal job to me. Do you mind telling us how you begin with an individual? And please share a few success stories.

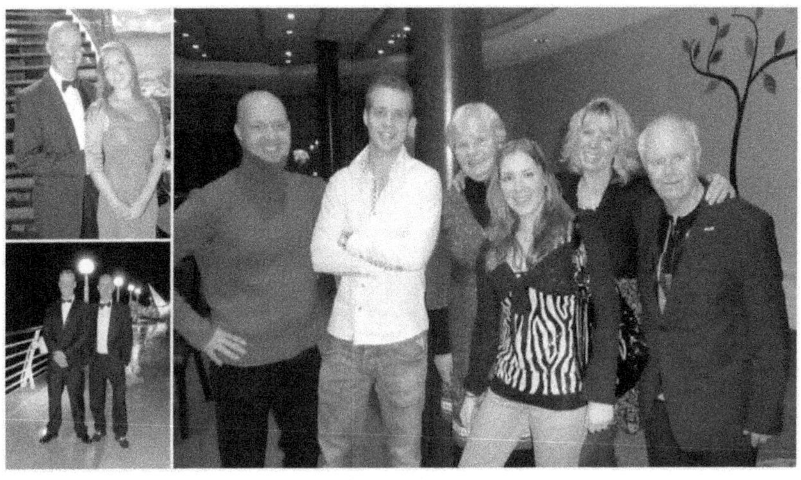

Rob Waterlander: Before I answer that, Betty, let me assure you and your readers that my work is not meant to substitute for those who have addictions or conditions that should be treated, but I can work as part of their team to success. All the possibilities are within each individual and I can help them discover the endless joy and happiness that is there.

Light is essential. Many times we try to see the light in our lives, and we can't.

It may seem there is no light… Circumstances and events can overwhelm us.

Even well-meaning friends and family can discourage us from living our true purpose. Entertainers and sports stars, in particular, are under tremendous pressure to fulfill the expectations of others around them, often losing themselves and their personal focus in the process.

What I always start with is tuning in on people, feeling and seeing behind the masks we all wear in daily life. I am just silent… I listen and, occasionally ask a question. Listening to what they say and don't say, figuring out where they are and where they want to go…

Talking about individual people, I would have to give disclosures that most prefer me not to give. In general, I can say this: Entertainers and sportspeople with level-headed spouses who use common sense should stay in close connection with their partners, enabling them to thrive. When they lack support of a good husband/wife or similar, they might, sooner or later, need a person who is able to give support, guiding them through life's challenges and helping them to focus on what they do so well.

Betty Dravis: I understand and respect the privacy of your clients, Rob, so thanks for generalizing for us. I totally agree that a helpful mate is a powerful force and it's very important to support one another…whether it's a spouse or a dear friend.

I hear that you specialize in working with people in the entertainment and sports community; professional athletes, musicians, singers, movie actors, artists and other creative talent. Why and how did you manage to narrow the field?

Rob Waterlander: As I said earlier, the sports events helped me connect with sports people and those guys kept referring me to other athletes.

Basically, I have chosen these entertainers and sports people, as well as other creative guys and gals, because I enjoy working with people with that specific state of mind. Driven and at the same time fragile somehow. I think all the attention and "The show must go on" stress levels make people prone to stuff that would stress out anyone. There is just no escape when everybody is expecting a brilliant performance and appearance.

Betty Dravis: You're absolutely right about that, Rob. We've all seen some of our favorite stars, whether entertainers or athletes, fall apart due to that kind of stress.

I've heard through the grapevine that you're good at what you do and I hope you don't mind if I share what a few people wrote about you. I'll start with Kitty Kavey since I know her and she's mentioned above.

"Intuitive, kind and empathetic to others, Rob Waterlander is

an absolute joy and privilege to work with. If you're in the entertainment or sports industries, he really "gets" the pressures that we have to live up to–not only our own expectations, but the needs and expectations of those around us and the public. He doesn't preach, or tell you what to do or which plan to follow. Instead he leads each individual to the place within where the answers lie. He gently guides one to what they know, and what they need to know, to not only be successful in career, but also to be able to reconnect with the happiness and peace within. Not only that, but Rob is also an expert in combining the realities of business and marketing (and public relations), with the spiritual/emotional needs of an individual." – Kitania Kavey, Screenwriter, Actress, Model, The Netherlands/Europe

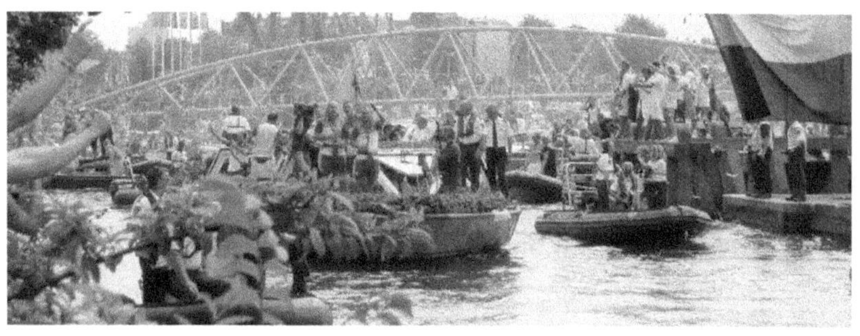

And the following is from a sports professional in the UK:

"Rob is someone who is empowering and directing. He has the ability of communicating at the right moments, pointing out exactly that part I couldn't see beyond at that moment. I call it diving in, opening and showing the pregnant space of possibilities... opening doors to what was waiting so close. In a

way, I wasn't initially aware that I was applying aspects of what he said and shared when we interacted. When distracted by people in my daily professional or personal life, it's easier to feel the patience of knowing whether now, tonight or tomorrow I would exactly see what I needed to see. As an athlete with a focus on performance, once or twice a week having a balanced day-to-day life is essential. Rob is a valued part of keeping focused, knowing that all is well." – Fabian Wilnis, Professional Footballer, UK

Those are powerful words of praise, Rob. Knowing that you've helped those people must be encouraging to you, keeping you inspired and focused on your own dreams and goals. I've heard you say, "An interesting question for many coaches supporting people could be 'who is going to motivate you when the motivator has gone home?'" Please answer that intuitive question for us.

Rob Waterlander: Well, Betty, I feel what works best is when a client is independent, only dependent on their own gained knowledge.

When they absolutely know themselves–their hearts, and can listen again to their authentic selves–only then will they be secure and happy.

I have made it my life's work to guide people towards what always has been waiting for them, and once there, I just stay around to fine-tune, watching from a distance as they live thriving and wondrous lives.

Once I have established a level of clearness with my clients, I try to see them twice a year…up to a max of twelve times.

Betty Dravis: That makes perfect sense to me, Rob, and I see that truth working in the *Dream Reachers* that my co-author Chase Von and I have interviewed. That's good, solid advice and I can see where we could all use someone like you in our lives—someone who really cares.

I saw your gentle guidance when you met my friend John Manha who has multiple sclerosis. You talked with him at length and I saw your compassion and nurturing abilities first-hand. As a strong, determined Vietnam veteran, he's a good judge of character and he was truly impressed with you and admires your calling. He felt your life flow.

Thanks for that and for encouraging him in his personal and business goals.

But we're nearing the end of this interview, so I'd like to invite you to share your Mission Statement. We've discussed everything in the statement, but I think our readers would like it condensed as a refresher.

Rob Waterlander: My Mission Statement as stated on my website is: *My goal is to guide each person to create for themselves the opportunity to have each of their talents and thoughts tuned in to the direction of that which one has a passion for. I know that if the passion and creative direction of each individual is found and followed, then the physical, mental and financial rewards will flow naturally.*

Thank you, Betty, for this chance to get my message across to more people. I sure hope to meet up soon again and have the chance to do another lunch together. Meeting Johnny was felt within… Please say hi to him from me and deliver this message: “I enjoyed talking to you a lot, Johnny. Man, you have an awesome smile.” (laughs)

Betty Dravis: I, too, hope we do lunch again next time you’re in the States, Rob. I certainly enjoy your company. This time I will listen for your “silences” too. (laughs) And I’ll certainly pass on your message to Johnny. He’ll be pleased to know you’re thinking of him.

It’s awesome what you offer your clients, Rob, but I almost forgot to mention that you work with companies too. By now our readers must be eager to learn how to contact you, but before that, tell us a little about your corporate services.

“It saves a company loads of money when the new person is the right one.”

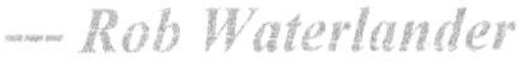
— Rob Waterlander

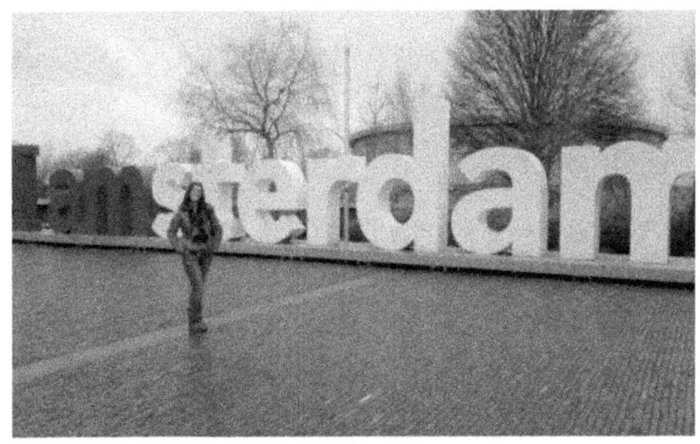

Rob Waterlander: I'm glad you remembered, Betty, because that's a big part of my business. I am available to work with corporate Human Resources Departments and with recruiters and headhunters to help find the right executives for their companies…or the right companies for their clients. In today's market it is imperative to match the job opening with the right candidate before time and money is invested in a position that doesn't work out.

I assess the needs of both the company and the job seeker to ensure a good fit for both. I walk with them on the beach or we cycle… Any activity is great while figuring out whether the company and the candidate are a match. It is so fun to be with a person who has a dream…and spending a while with a candidate for a job enables me to see whether he really wants it or whether he just wants to survive.

I understand it is so much better when a person actually feels excited because the job fits a part of his dream. And it saves a company loads of money when the new person is the right one.

Betty Dravis: You're right, Rob! That's very important in today's business climate. I have several corporate friends who use services such as you offer. Thanks for expounding on that area of your profession. And if anyone wants to know more, they can Google your name on the Internet.

Before closing, Rob, this might seem silly, but I think it will shed more light on the real *you*: If you were stranded on a desert island what three things would you take with you?

Rob Waterlander: *It's the island life! Wooo-hoooo...* I'm so much an island person, it feels like a present to me. Hahahahaha...

This is a good question for me, Betty. Thank you for asking.

Now let me think... What/who I would like to take with me and what I would like to have with me there? I can choose whatever I wish, though only three? Well, that is easy: My children and Carly. And hopefully, there will be available a few jackfruit trees and coconut trees.

I might be pushing a bit now, but if possible, I would like to take my two best friends. I will miss you all, but having my children and Carly will help me to get through. (smiles)

Betty Dravis: Oh-haha, Rob, I guess you would be living on love, coconuts and jackfruit then.

I've never seen jackfruit, but I read somewhere that it's the largest fruit in the world and can grow as large as eighty pounds.

Well, that's a lot of food, so you certainly wouldn't go hungry. (laughs)

I really appreciate your sharing your time and your life with us today. It's fascinating how you found your true purpose in life. I see the principle of "What goes around comes around" working in your life: Helping others achieve their full potential to live their dream enables you to live your dream.

The cost of your services wasn't mentioned, but you do work on a sliding scale and are available worldwide, so that's a big plus in your favor. *That* said, it's been fun getting to know you better, and do come back to keep us posted from time to time.

As for me, I'll see you on Facebook, I'm sure. And I know you're open to answer comments from everyone on Facebook.

Farewell and good luck, Rob…or in your language, *Vaarwel* and *geluk!* Please keep us posted on your activities. Oops—I almost forgot to thank you for the bright yellow "wooden shoe" house-slippers you brought me last time.

Rob Waterlander: Hehehehe, I see some Dutch here… (smiles)

Well, what I do always makes me feel good and that is the most important thing. Feeling good… What I charge depends on circumstances, indeed. Roughly it varies between 1,000 to 4,000 Euro/US Dollars for working with someone a maximum of two days, and people pay/arrange my travelling and lodging.

Thank you so much, Betty. It was fun to answer your questions. I am grateful because it helped me to go back to joyful moments, especially those in the six years of organizing sports events. It was fun and educational to work with pro-athletes, pro-referees and nine- to ten-year-old soccer players of the major soccer teams in Holland, as well as working with TV and radio teams and those who sponsored the events. I learned a lot… One thing I remember so well is what a general manager of Nike said: "Rob, focus on two things at the same time, *max*. That allows you to be successful with what you do.

Just do it!"

And, I am amazed at you every day, Betty. You are the age of my mom, though you run your blogs, write books and do your interviews…

I hope I have the chance to see you again and then I would like you to have some fun in real wooden shoes, instead of the fluffy ones. (laughs)

Thanks again, Betty. Hugs and loving vibes sent your way. Xx

"I listen, absorb in silence, and then intuitively see and feel where the person's next steps are."

— Rob Waterlander

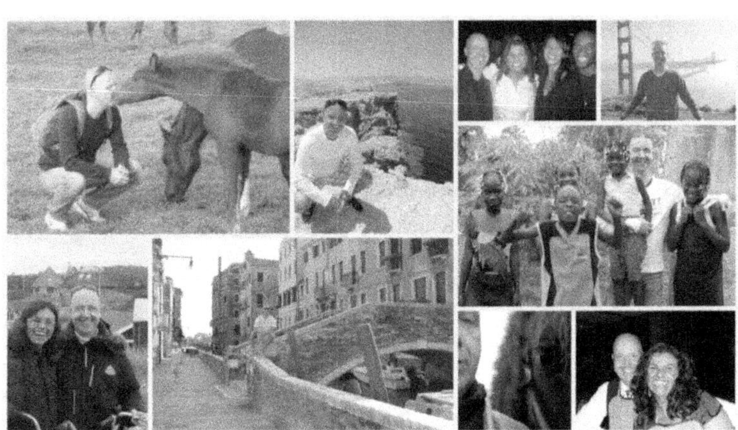

Interview with Jackie Krudop

CO-FOUNDER OF PACINO WORLDWIDE

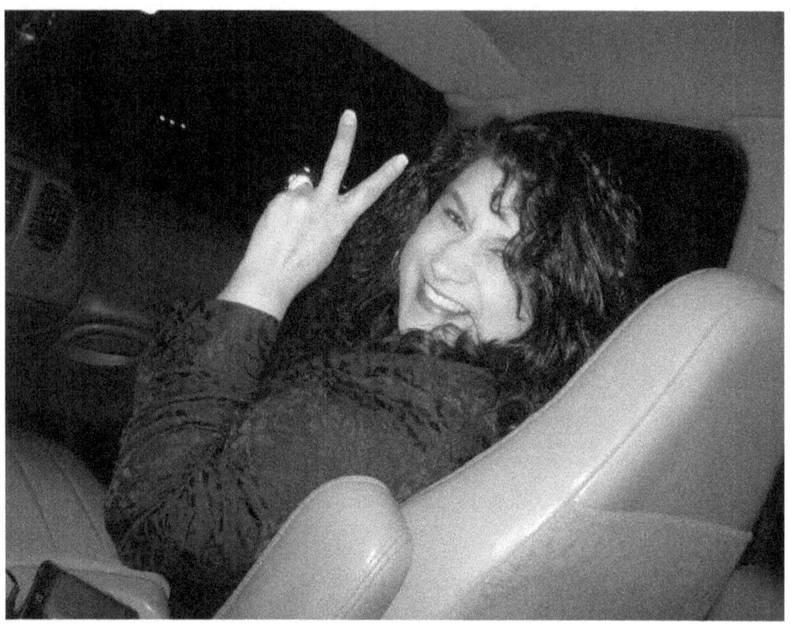

Betty Dravis: Welcome to Dames of Dialogue, Jackie. It's not every day I interview a woman with your special mission in life. In fact, I never met anyone who does what you do… With millions of blogs and websites on the internet, I never even thought of interviewing a site owner–until I stumbled across *Pacino Worldwide* and wondered who was behind the fascinating site.

I did a little research and the more I learned about you and your dedication to the fabulous actor, Al Pacino, the more intrigued

I became. You have a dream and are working hard to make it happen. You are a Dream Reacher and qualify as a celebrity to me and my co-author Chase Von.

Jackie Krudop: Thanks for inviting me here, Betty. I'm pleased with the kindness you've shown towards my dream. Some people may consider it silly, but to me it's a labor of love. I know your *Dream Reachers* books are all about celebrities achieving their dreams, so I get a laugh from that… *I am far from a celebrity!* But when I learned that you and Chase consider everyone's life worthy of celebration and all it takes to be a celebrity is to have a dream and fulfill it, that's when I began to celebrate my own "celebrity" status. (laughs)

In a lot of ways I feel like a celebrity to Al's fans because I get emails and tons of compliments on things I have posted on Facebook, such as photos from events, appearances and such. Maybe I post something that they may not have had the chance to see in their part of the world because of press or what not… That word "celebrity" is still a little new to me, but secretly, it makes the old ego feel realllyy good! (laughs) In fact, Betty, this interview makes me feel very confident right now. I thank you.

Betty Dravis: It's our pleasure, Jackie, and you got it right! Life is as fun as you make it… But now please tell us what your website is all about. I know you adore Al Pacino an d your website states: *Maintaining the integrity of an artist at a level deserving of the man it honors.* Just what does that mean to you?

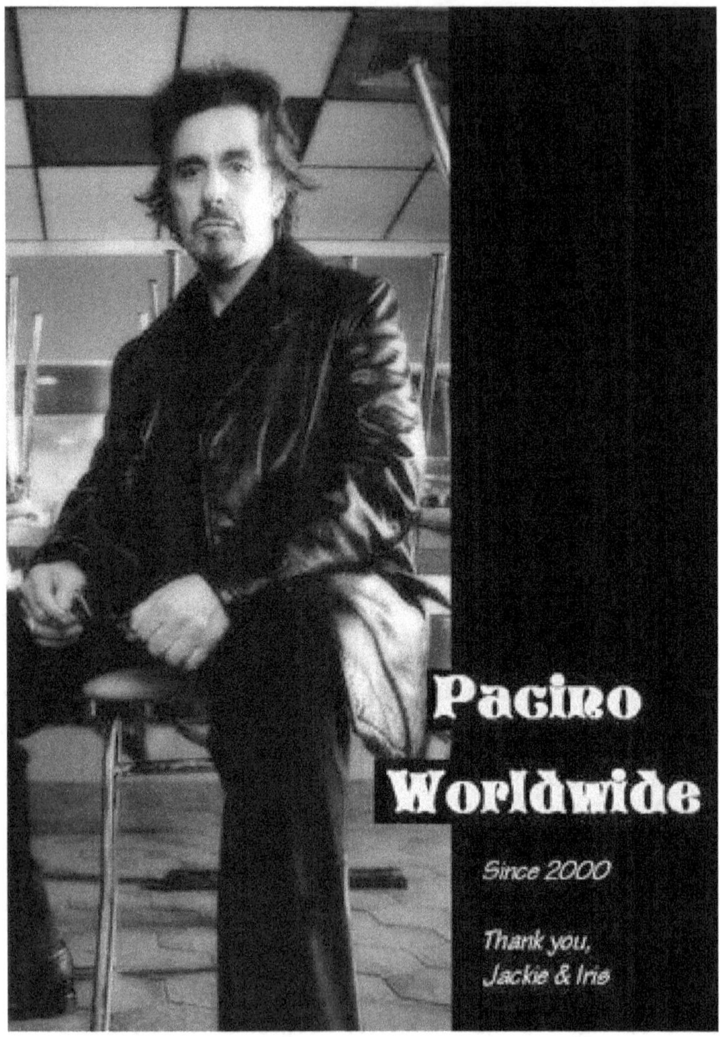

Jackie Krudop: Wow, just seeing our mission statement in print takes me back to the very beginning. I guess that it means that *at all costs,* we will bring to Al's fans the facts–not the rumor mill "b.s." and nothing that will exploit him, his family, his children or anything in his personal life.

I mean, when we first started this, you wouldn't believe how many questions we got about who he's dating, what church he goes to, who he votes for president …just silly stuff like that. It sort of angers me that people claim to admire someone, but then they invade their personal life as if there is truly no respect at all. I don't know…

Sometimes I get a little overly protective of Al, but it's not in a possessive or obsessive way; it's in a humane way. But I wouldn't want all those questions answered by anyone but me, and if Al hasn't answered them, then perhaps no one needs to know. Make sense? (shrugs shoulders)

In short, what that means to me is that when you come to *Pacino Worldwide,* you get facts about Al's art and his works–past, present and future–nothing else. And you will make a friend or two along the way…guaranteed!

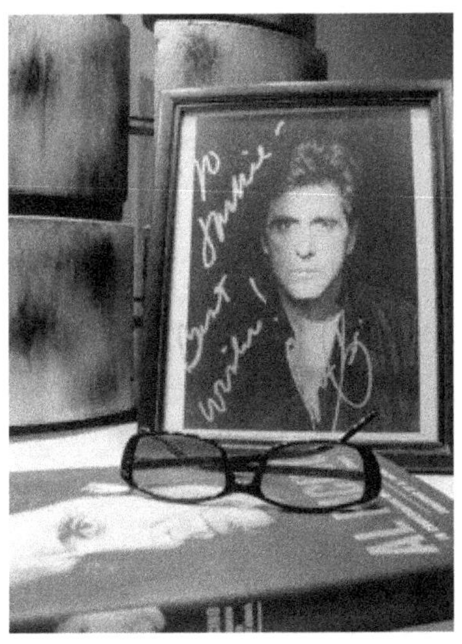

Betty Dravis: It's an admirable mission statement, Jackie. No one could expect more from you than honesty and good information; I'm sure Al Pacino would respect that in you, also. In the eyes of the world, that must make you Al's number one fan! How do you feel about that?

Jackie Krudop: I think about half the fan base of *Pacino Worldwide* would call me more than just a "fan." I used to hate that word because it sounded so "stalker-ish," so I'd rather be thought of as a respectful admirer. Either way, I hope my tribute is known by at least Al himself. I hope that he knows of my dedication to keeping his other admirers in the loop. That's a nice thought…

In fact, my website vice-president and co-owner, Iris Frank, recently said, "In more ways than one, it's Al's name that gets the fans to *Pacino Worldwide,* but it's you, Jackie, that keeps them there!"

I appreciate Iris pointing that out because it is a lot of work… If there is one thing I have learned by being a "fan" and someone who looks "in" from the "outside," there is a constant need to know as much as I can without seeming like some psycho stalker. I started this site as a way to keep fans informed of everything I can with the resources that are available to me that may not be available to them. And along the way, friendships are made. *That's the cream.*

Betty Dravis: Jackie, as a former career journalist, I can understand that in gathering information for the site yourself, you might appear to be stalking. That's the way journalists are often perceived, even the most ethical ones. But everyone who knows you knows you are respectful of Al and always put his interests first.

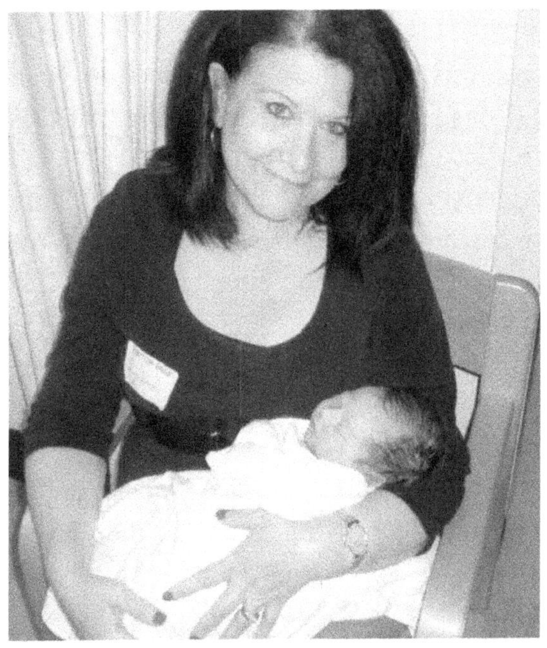

Jackie's PW partner Iris Frank with her first grandchild Jacob Ryan

I like that term "respectful admirer," Jackie. It has class, like you. But hasn't Al or anyone from his entourage ever contacted you to acknowledge the website? If not, perhaps they might read this and get in touch. I hope that someday you get to meet him. That would be another dream-come-true. How do you feel about that?

Jackie Krudop: Well, I certainly wouldn't know the first words to say to the man…really. Honestly, we have had no one from Al's "people" ever acknowledge the site at any time. However, we have written to comment on a few newspaper articles…just to let them know our side of a situation.

If would read this, perchance, and happen to want to get in touch, well, I'm sure they'd know how to find me. (laughs)

As far as my next dream, it would be to not only meet Al, but to see him perform in a live play. I'm a bit of a nut for Shakespeare since high school; but thanks to Al, it seems more educated and more passionate… So to see him perform onstage would be a nice dream too. If that happened to be a current Shakespeare play in New York, then all the better.

Betty Dravis: I know how you feel, Jackie, and I hope that dream comes true. Don't forget to grab the opportunity with both hands when it comes your way. That's the message we hope to inspire with our *Dream Reachers* books.

Even though it's been forty years since I interviewed Clint Eastwood, I would dearly love to see him again. In fact, I would like to have a photo taken with him in the identical pose of the one taken then.

We were both young and "pretty" in those days, but we've fared well and a photo like that would be a blast. Oddly, I think he'd get a kick out of it, too, if I could get past his "people" to request it. I guess I will have to try harder. (laughs)

But moving on, Jackie, when did you first see Al Pacino? In what movie?

Jackie Krudop: My first movie was *Scarface,* but I barely remember seeing it because I had to sneak in the drive-in theater to see it. I hadn't reached the age of eighteen yet (1983), but I saw it, anyway. I just remember feeling so bad when hearing all those "f" bombs being dropped in one movie.

(A bit of trivia Betty: Did you know that Al has said in an interview a long time ago that there were 182 "f***s" in that movie? That's more than some people get in a lifetime!)

Betty Dravis: I never liked too much profanity in movies, either; I suppose they did it to make their characters seem tougher...but whatever, it was never in good taste and was unnecessary, in my opinion. Bruce Willis is one of my favorite actors and I cringed during many of his movies when that word came up too often. I notice they don't use that word as much as they once did. That is a *good* thing...

But back to your first encounter seeing Al, at that point, did you succumb to his dark, swarthy looks or to his acting ability?

Jackie Krudop: The movie that actually "did it" for me was *Scent of a Woman.* It still remains my favorite of his movies. I must have seen it too many times to count. You know, there is just something about his "charm" that just escapes me now (sigh), but the thing about that movie was that I found myself wanting to take care of him or to tell the character to "snap out of it!" Then, of course, the famous tango scene.... Aaahhh...my favorite... Now *there's* the dream!

You just have to see it to know what I'm talking about.

I "succumbed," as you say, more so after reading his first bio *Life On the Wire*. This book was something of a project I gave myself when I was pregnant with my twin boys. I had nothing better to do with my time off work than to take my other two kids to school and read, so I read a bio from the library every week. I went by alpha order and, needless to say, I stopped at the "Ps." That got me to the internet and the rest is history!

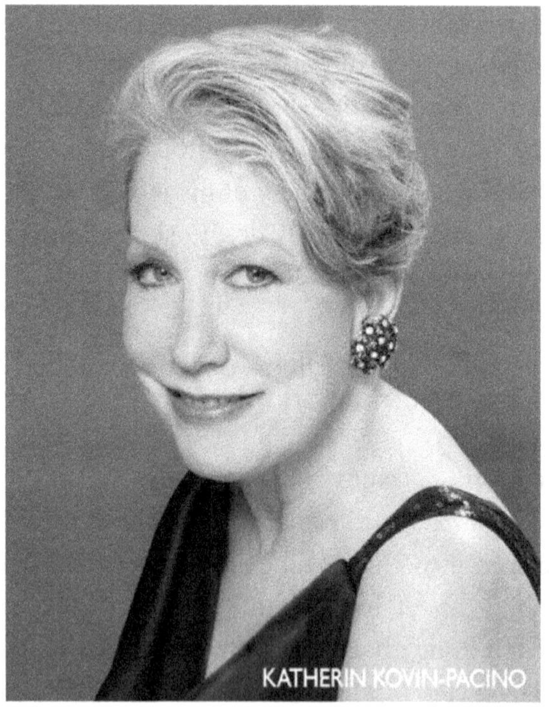
KATHERIN KOVIN-PACINO

Betty Dravis: I, personally, got hooked on Al when I saw him in the first *Godfather;* he was absolute dynamite in that movie, and so good-looking. I'm surprised you never mentioned any of the star-making *Godfather* movies, but you were probably too young when the first two were filmed. It sounds like you were really "hooked" after reading his bio. Did you go on to see all his movies after that? Or have you seen them *all?*

Jackie Krudop: You know, I'm not sure if it was before I created the website or during the process of it all that I decided I better see some of these films. (laughs) I mean, here I am trying to entice people to see the Al that I see and to come to this website, but if I don't know his films, how can I offer opinion or shed light, right? So *yes,* at this point in my "Pacino life" I have seen all but one…and that is *Me, Natalie*. It was from the 70s and it's not out on DVD, so I'm not sure *when* I'll see it, but I *will* see it!

Betty Dravis: You're right, Jackie, you have to have seen his films in order to talk and write about them. His stepmother, Katherin Kovin Pacino, told me he said that "Scent of a Woman" was his personal favorite movie. Have you heard that? And what's your favorite movie starring Pacino?

Jackie Krudop: Isn't Kat just wonderful? Kat has been very good to me. Yes, I have heard that about Al and I know that he is also fond of the work in Scarface too. But *Scent of a Woman* was his Oscar winner, so I can see how that would be his favorite. It just so happens that it's my favorite movie of his too. As I said earlier, it was this film that really got to me. His charm and his tenacity as the blind retired Colonel Frank Slade just brought so much to the film. The film was about strengths and weaknesses, family and self… I just loved it! I watch it about once a month to just hear a big WHHOOHAH!! (Yes, I can actually recite the end speech too.)

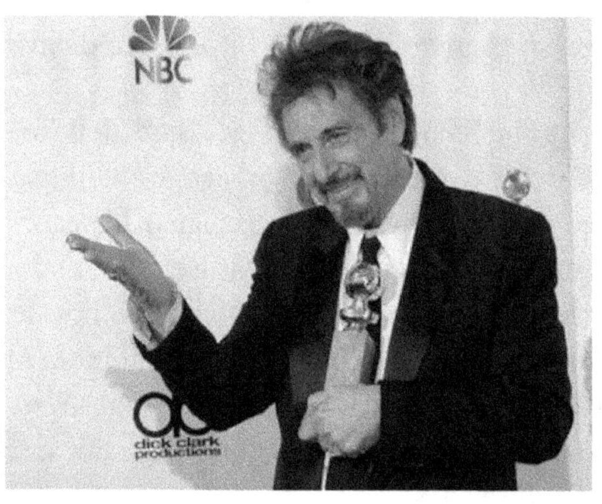

Al Pacino won a Golden Globe for his portrayal of Jack Kevorkian in *You Don't Know Jack* in January 2011

Betty Dravis: I liked that movie myself, Jackie. That tango scene and his amazing speech were awesome, but that "Whhoohah" cracked me up. But did the great Al ever make a film you didn't like? If so, why didn't you enjoy it?

Jackie Krudop: Honestly? At first I wasn't crazy about *Donnie Brasco,* but after watching it for the third time, it took on a different meaning… I think the reason I strayed from it at first viewing was because of the stereotypical "gangster" side of things and the over-acting and over-used accents of some of the actors (not from Al). But the story and the meat of the movie holds plenty to see… I mean, look--it's Johnny Depp *and* Al Pacino! What's not to love? (laughs)

Betty Dravis: Which of his leading ladies do you like best? I, personally, love Diane Keaton who played his wife in the first *Godfather,* but I also like Michelle Pfeiffer who starred opposite him in *Scarface.* She's a gorgeous woman.

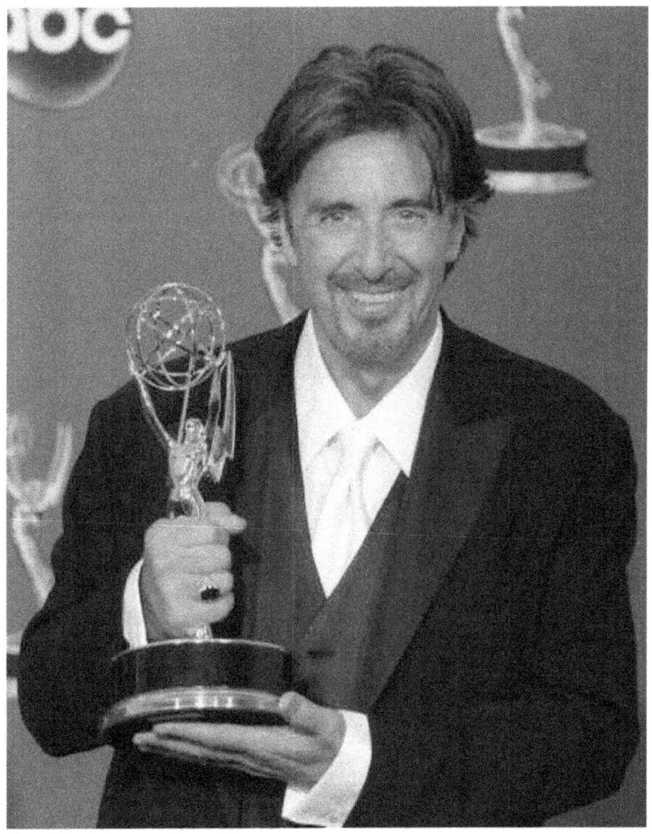

Al Pacino won an Emmy for his role in *Angels in America*

Jackie Krudop: While I do agree with you about Diane Keaton, playing Kay in *The Godfather,* I'd have to say that my favorite is the great Meryl Streep in her role with Al in the Emmy-winning HBO movie, *Angels In America.* She (as Ethel Rosenberg) and Al (as Roy Cohn) just have that "something" that is needed on screen to make it work. They feed off each other's lines as if it were a match in acting Heaven.

Betty, I believe the rapport comes from the paths they have taken in their personal lives. (Meryl was in a relationship with Al's dear friend John Cazale who played Fredo in *Godfather* and Sal in *Dog Day Afternoon.* Cazale had passed away.)

He speaks of his *own* admiration of Meryl in a movie recently released called *I Knew It Was You: The John Cazale Story.* It's currently showing on Cable channels. Their on-screen chemistry worked wonders. It was real from-the-gut acting.

Betty Dravis: I haven't met one person who doesn't admire Meryl Streep. Sorry to say, I never saw *Angels in America.*

Well, Jackie, Al Pacino is a major talent and has won numerous acting awards, so I can understand the attraction. I'm very devoted to actor Clint Eastwood, but never once thought of honoring him in this way.

I met and interviewed him years ago, as everyone in ear-shot must know by now. I'm not shy in bragging about it, but I simply honor him by trying to follow my dreams with as much diligence and creativity as he's always shown.

Since you have a devoted husband and four children, how do you find the time to maintain the site in such a professional way? Does your family support you in this endeavor and if they help you, tell us what they do.

Jackie Krudop: Well, Betty, while they *do* support me and my endeavors (no matter what I want to do) they pretty much leave Mom to her "computer time," and then she'll come back and be "mom" again soon. As far as my husband, he is *very* devoted to his family. He sometimes works more than ten hours a day in a hot stinkin' factory. He has been there for over twenty-five years this July and I have to tell you, there is not one time that he comes home to a dirty home or a meal not cooked or at least planned. My children *all* do their daily chores and make sure that they are *all* contributing members. So thanks for pointing that out and I'm sorry if I strayed from the actual question. I guess that's how this "well-oiled machine" works. (laughs)

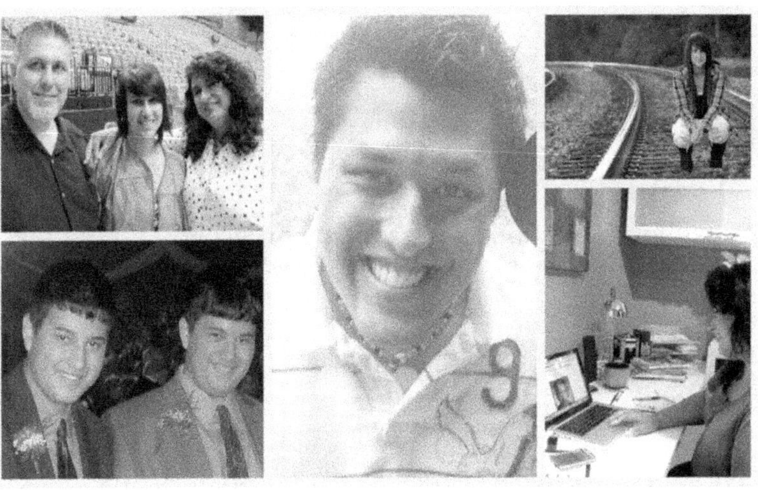

Betty Dravis: I'm glad your family is so supportive of you and of each other, Jackie. Family is what it's all about. So tell me about your daily work routine. Do you have a regular "day job?" And how many hours do you devote to *Pacino Worldwide?*

Jackie Krudop: Hmmm, Betty…my daily routine? I guess I do have one; I do have a day job. I am the office-everything girl for a small, family-owned construction company that shall remain nameless as I promised myself not to talk about bosses or work on the internet.

I'm not sure how many hours you could calculate that I work on the site and on the Facebook page. I am "online" daily because my day job is not that busy, so I take the time to answer questions and connect to fans via Facebook. I guess it's a good thing Al doesn't have me on the payroll then, huh? (laughs) There are some days I work on the site for at least four hours and then there are days I don't hardly touch the computer.

Working on the site, updating it and connecting with the fans on Facebook is a "get-away" for me…therapy of sorts. While others turn to vices such as gambling or alcohol, I turn to web design and "Facebooking."

Betty Dravis: Good for you, Jackie. It's easy to see you're enjoying it.

You are the president of *Pacino Worldwide* and Iris Frank is the co-founder and vice-president. This might come as a surprise to you, but following is a note she wrote telling about how you met. I hope you don't mind my sharing it.

I can't tell you the exact date I met Jackie. I can tell you I was in my forties. I am no longer in my forties. In fact, I am deep into my fifties. I can, however, tell you how I met her. I was hungrily seeking a ticket to see the screening of "Chinese Coffee" at the first Tribeca Film Festival in New York after 9/11. I put out a web-wide email to various Pacino fan groups (never have I taken such a risk!) asking if anyone had an extra ticket. I did, in fact, find a ticket. I also found Jackie, or should I say, she found me. Although ticketless, she responded to the search of a Pacino fan.

Al Pacino's talent and love of his craft are the reasons Pacino Worldwide exist, but also the reasons Jackie and Iris exist. That is a blessed irony... But what you also have when you sign onto Facebook is the wit, drive and dedication of Jackie Krudop. She reminds us that as payback for her effort and her talent we are required to enjoy her handiwork. Her website is here to relax with. She insists you do just that.

Many years, many tears, many arguments and many, many phone calls have passed between us, but our love and admiration for each other remain constant. Take your bow Jackie.

Wow, Jackie, Iris thinks the world of you.

It's interesting how you met and it's heartening to know you became such good friends. Have you ever met Iris in person?

Jackie Krudop: *Have I ever!* Iris comes to visit me here in my humble abode (in the Midwest) every Labor Day weekend for what we call our "board of directors meeting," but really it's nothing else but good old girl time. We have become the best of friends, knowing one another better than we do our own selves. Knowing Iris is a true treasure; we not only share a "Pacino-thing" but so much more. We share so much…tears, laughter… My kids have even grown to call her "Auntie Iris," so what does that say? *I just simply love her!* I call her "sister" all the time, but right now you can call her "Grandma." She's busy enjoying her first grandchild, Jacob Ryan Frank, who was born June 30, 2010.

Betty Dravis: I'm happy for Iris and her family, Jackie. Please congratulate "Grandma" for me and express my best wishes. (laughs)

What legalities were involved in starting *Pacino Worldwide?* How many members do you have? How many countries are represented in your fan base? And who supplies the fabulous photos and movie stills of Al?

Jackie Krudop: As far as legalities are concerned, the only promise I made to Al's lawyers years ago (as the president of *Pacino Worldwide*) was to *never* make money from his name. So therefore, we are a non-profit, tribute-for-entertainment-purposes website. Yes, his lawyer contacted me as to a response to a very "ballsy" proposal we sent regarding the start up of perhaps a "fan club." Not knowing what was in store, he just wanted to make sure of our intentions.

That is when I decided it should be something that *all* can enjoy and get use from; a resource, if you will. That way when fans who have never seen a particular film research that film, they will go to us, hopefully.

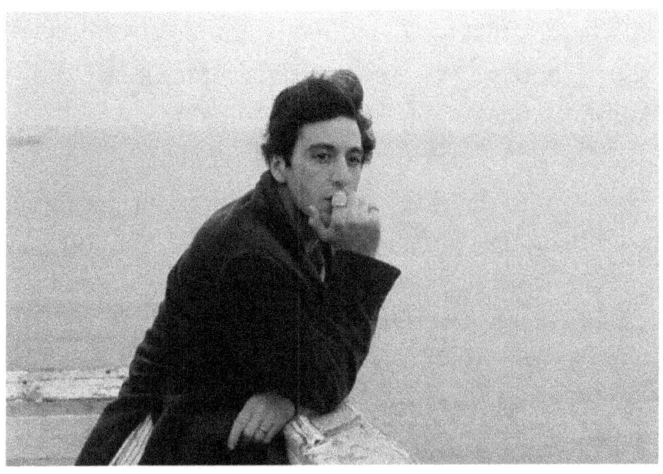

Members consist of fans from all around the world. We are up to 496 fans on Facebook and it continues to grow daily. Only Iris and I "run" the website. It may be "my baby," as Iris called it once, but we both manage it. The photos on the site are mostly photos that we have access to from various sources upon release: Reuters, Corbis, Zimbio… They're available to most–but not to everyone–so as soon as we get them, we pass them on. And *trust me,* there are fans out there who count on us to send these photos. We are constantly researching the web for new pictures and get press releases from Google and Yahoo daily anytime Al's name shows up in the news. *Right now–that's a lot!*

Betty Dravis: That's interesting, Jackie, and you're right about Al: He's a hot commodity now and has been for a long while. He has become a living legend…

Iris mentioned your page on Facebook, so I think she met the *Pacino Worldwide* Facebook page. Your personal Facebook page is where I met you (indirectly through Katherin Kovin Pacino). I notice you post trivia questions and other information about Pacino and your page seems to be where many people first learn of *Pacino Worldwide.* You also talk about your day-to-day life and your children on Facebook. Did you set up that page for social networking or as another means of getting the word out about your favorite star?

Jackie Krudop: Well, to be honest Betty, the personal Facebook page is my own little way of connecting to old friends and family I don't see all the time. The *Pacino Worldwide* Facebook page is a bit of a "coming of age" thing for the little boost I thought that the website needed. It has, indeed, worked! Iris does the marketing and watches our site's numbers/visitors constantly. She says that since the onset of the Facebook page, our "hits" (numbers) increased instantly!

We've gone from 20,000 to 30,000 "hits" a month to over 60,000 just this past June. Now, the numbers get larger once Al is busier, so keep working Al… (laughs)

Betty Dravis: Wow, those are fabulous numbers, Jackie. I'll post the link on my sites around the internet and, hopefully, send more "hits" your way. (laughs)

I mentioned Al's stepmother, Katherin Kovin Pacino, several times above. I also interviewed her for *Dream Reachers: Vol. II.* She's a fabulous, good-hearted, lovely woman and a noted actress. I notice she's your friend on Facebook and approves your website. How did you meet her and is she a help with *Pacino Worldwide*? Also, you call her Katherin the Great… Why is that?

Jackie Krudop: I call her Katherin the Great because I picked it up out of a Facebook post when *you* called her that in a joking manner. I thought it really fit her–*she truly is great!* We met over ten years ago as I was searching for ideas and found myself joining blogs and various other Pacino groups in my quest to know all I could about the man and the actor. Well, I had casually mentioned to Kat that I'd love to start my own website, but that it was probably impossible and that no one would even like it, etc…all the negative stuff you could say.

It was Kat who encouraged me. Because of my age and my "experiences" in life, she knew I'd have a more mature side to Al's fan-based sites. I had pretty much given up when one day she and I exchanged emails about Tribeca tickets and such, and she said something about all the fans from other countries… That's when I realized that I *could* and I *would* do the site and

I'd call it "worldwide" because of how many countries his fans are from. I think, personally, that the name worldwide makes people pause to think…like, *hmmm, maybe…*

Betty Dravis: I noticed that side of Kat, too; she's forever encouraging people…a fascinating, caring woman.

Since Al Pacino has won many awards in his outstanding career, I can't go into all of them, but I'd like to run a quote he made in 2003. His words make me smile, affirming that he has a good sense of humor and has remained down-to-earth and humble.

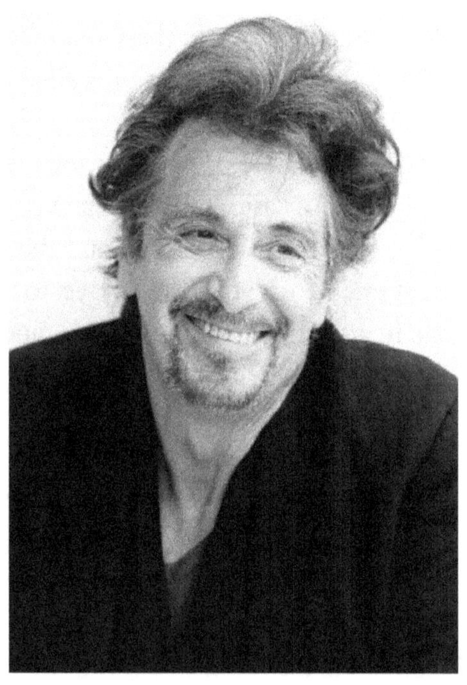

"I'd like to be remembered as the only man who lived to be 250 years old! (laughs) And someone who had a chance to do what he always wanted to do. I like to think I'm a guy who wasn't going to make it, and I did. So it's good to buck the odds. If that means anything to anyone, I will be grateful from

the beyond!" – Al Pacino (from Interview by Ken Burns for *USA Weekend*, Issue Date: January 26, 2003)

Jackie, do you have a favorite quote of Al's…or an anecdote you'd like to share?

Jackie Krudop: My favorite quote of Al's comes from his Oscar-winning movie *Scent of a Woman:* "There isn't nothin' like the sight of an amputated spirit, there is *no* prosthetic for that."

This quote came at the climatic ending to that wonderful film. It had everything to do with the character, Charlie, and the demise he was facing. I think I have chosen this quote because of the depth of it. It says that there is no way to "fake" a spirit. Once someone's spirit is broken, it's hard to build back up and no one has that right to take your dreams and break the spirit that you were born with.

Betty Dravis: I agree that those are powerful words, Jackie; a lot of truth in so few words too. Thanks for sharing that. That was a fantastic movie and Al certainly won that Oscar, fair and square.

On a less serious note, have you had any embarrassing moments in your life that stem from having this website?

Jackie Krudop: Well…I'm not sure if it's embarrassing, but it sure made me aware of what I was in store for by building this website. When Iris and I first got the idea to have a website, I dubbed it *Pacino Worldwide.* So, naturally, at family functions and times with friends we liked to pass on our "good news" by giving them the full domain name and the web address: pacinoworldwide.com. Simple…right? Or so you'd think...

Well, when some friends of Iris looked up the address, a slip or misunderstanding of the words and all of sudden, up on the screen comes "Pacino's *****" which is not our site. In fact, it has nothing to do with Al. *It's Porn!* You can imagine the looks on her friends' faces as they stand there in awe or shock or whatever… Iris corrected her friends and they had a great laugh, but this is how a simple switcheroo can really make for an awkward moment.

Betty Dravis: Oh, that's really funny, Jackie, and that would sure embarrass me. (laughs) But at this point in the interview, I usually ask my guests this question: If you could spend an entire day with anyone in the world (living or dead) who would you choose and why? Since we already know the answer to that, who would be your second choice? (laughs)

Jackie Krudop: (Giggles)… Honestly Betty, I'd love to spend an entire day with Al with all the knowledge and life experiences he has, but truthfully, I'd give anything to spend a day (again) with my departed grandmother. This woman raised me when my own mom worked full time at a factory and when we were in hard times as a child. She raised me from birth to about high-school age. I'm happy that she was able to live long enough to see me married and witness all four of my children. She passed away the summer my twin boys turned a year old.

They're now sixteen, so while it has been a long time ago, I long for dinners and prayers at her table and her good old southern hospitality.

Betty Dravis: I don't blame you, Jackie. I know it would be a thrill to spend a day with your beloved Al, but family comes first. Your grandmother was undoubtedly a strong, wonderful woman and must have been an inspiration to you. Thanks for sharing that touching story.

What other famous actors do you admire?

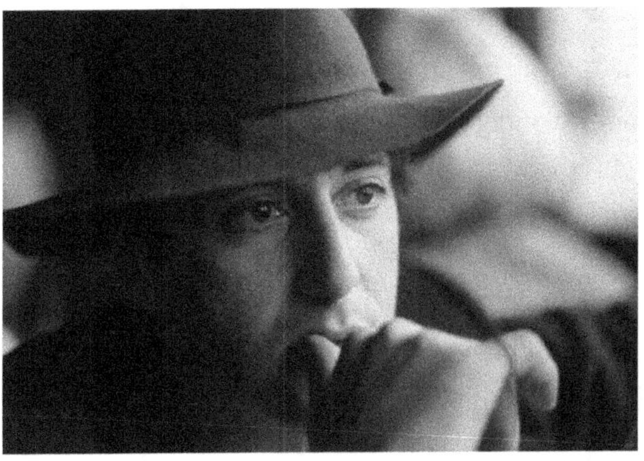

Jackie Krudop: Yes…there are other actors out there, huh, Betty? (winks) Well, let's see…I admire Meryl Streep for her "real" acting methods and being able to also transform perspectives (such as Al). I also adore the singer/artist Billy Joel. I have only seen him once in concert and love the way he brings such soul to his songs… You know, "It's All About Soul" and all his songs, actually. I don't really get a chance to know the names of many of the current celebs. I stick to movies with the people that I've been watching awhile, like Tom Hanks, Robert De Niro, Jack Nicholson, Jennifer Lopez (for her acting ability, not singing) and Bonnie Hunt.

Betty Dravis: You wrote the following on your Facebook page: "Love my husband, my kids and my God…what else is there?" Dare I answer the question by quipping: "There is Al Pacino?" (laughs)

What ages are your children and what do you like to do on family outings?

Jackie Krudop: Thanks for asking about my kids, Betty. I have four wonderful kids, but what Mom doesn't say that…right? They really are, though; they start with my son Matt, age twenty-three, who is taking college courses for interior design, and then my daughter Katrina who is eighteen, just graduated from high school and is bound for cosmetology school in the fall, and last, but not least, are my twin boys, Jerod and Jordan, who turned sixteen on July 19, 2010. Look out, world… (laughs)

My husband John and I have been married for a little over twenty-three years and mostly spend our "family outings" doing whatever the kids want. We like to take our two dogs for walks or play volleyball in the backyard or just go catch a movie! It's all about *them,* and we've found that just doing that and having our own "date night" once in a while, works for us.

Betty Dravis: That sounds like a winning combination to me,

Jackie. Your family seems to be tight-knit and close, which is how it should be…

Before ending this interview, I'd like to know if you have any plans to expand *Pacino Worldwide.* And what's in the near future for Jackie Krudop?

Jackie Krudop: The only plans I have for *Pacino Worldwide,* I'm already doing. I opened up the Facebook Page to fans that had already been with our little forty-member Yahoo Group and now we have 415 fans! *I love it!* The reason I love it is because I get to see how many folks from all ages, all walks of life, and all parts of the globe have the same great sense of awe and admiration for Al. And as they said about Elvis: *forty million fans can't be wrong!* And as I say: *415 fans—and growing– can't be wrong!* **(laughs)**

As for Jackie Krudop, I'm not sure what's next for me… My kid is going to college, so I think I'll stick around home for a while and keep running the website and Facebook page! How's that?

Betty Dravis: Sounds good to me, Jackie. Well, we could talk all day about Al Pacino and his fabulous body of works, but instead I'll ask our readers to Google *Pacino Worldwide.*

Now before closing, Jackie, this is the perfect place to share the good news about Al's HBO movie *You Don't Know Jack!*

And this is your last chance to mention anything we may have missed, so feel free to do so.

Jackie Krudop: As you know, Betty, in *You Don't Know Jack,* Al plays the role of Dr. Jack Kevorkian (1928 –) who in the 1990s defied Michigan law by assisting the suicide of terminally-ill persons. It's an HBO presentation, directed by Barry Levinson. Critics and fans are raving over Al's accurate portrayal of the controversial, single-minded and often antic Kevorkian.

I'm pleased to announce that Al won the Emmy in 2011! We predicted it and are thrilled that he won.

He already received an Emmy for the HBO movie, *Angels in America. We happen to think that Al and HBO make a pretty good team!*

Currently, Al is performing as Shylock in William Shakespeare's *The Merchant of Venice* in New York's beautiful Delacorte Theater for the summer months' Shakespeare in the Park. This is a very big deal at *Pacino Worldwide* and we are even more excited to have gotten news recently that says that there are "talks" of this very show going to Broadway. *We hope!* Any other Pacino news and happenings can be found on our site's "Future Features" page.

Betty Dravis: I saw *You Don't Know Jack* and was mesmerized by Al's performance; he was fabulous. He not only played the part, he *was* Dr. Kevorkian in that film. That's how great he is! He certainly deserves an Emmy. He's one of the best actors in the world.

Thanks for the good news!

In parting, I wish to thank you for sharing your life and your dreams with our readers, Jackie. It's been great fun talking with you. Please keep us in the loop about Al, and I want to be first to know when you finally meet this living legend who has millions of fans all around the world. Dare I call him the "Man of Your Dreams?" (laughs)

Sweet dreams, Jackie.

Jackie Krudop: Thanks, Betty. I'm happy to have this chance to share my thoughts about Al Pacino and to talk about *Pacino Worldwide*. My husband comes first, but in a way, Al *is* "The Man of My Dreams" because I admire him and his legendary acting. Sweet dreams to you all. It's been fun… *Pacino lungo Vivo!* (Long live Pacino!)

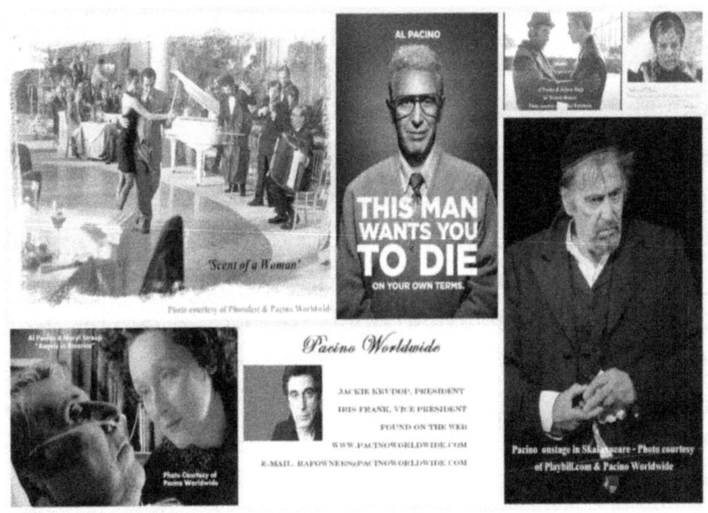

Photos in this story courtesy of
Jackie Krudop & Iris Frank of Pacino Worldwide

Interview with Joshua "Deous" Gennari

PRODUCER WITH A DIFFERENCE

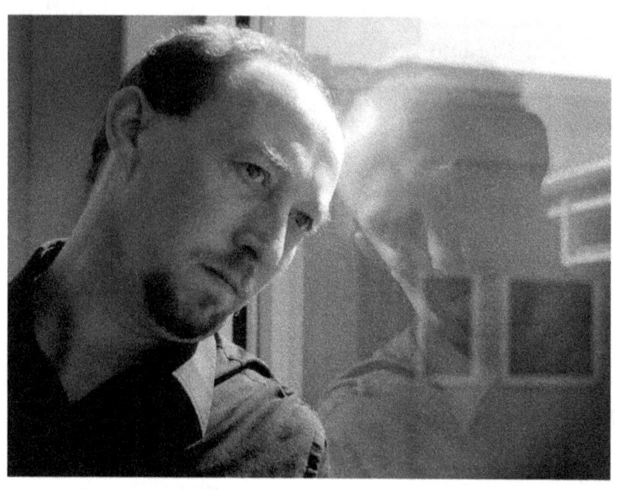

Betty Dravis: Hi, Deous. It's great to see you today. I'm delighted that you took time from your busy job with Area 51 Productions to be with us. Chrissy K. McVay, author of *Soul of the North Wind,* recommended you highly. When she told me about your concept for Area 51 Productions, it blew my mind. No one that I know has endeavored to create movies in the same way that you envision. But before we get into that worthy project–since you are not only a film-maker, but also an actor, singer and dancer–tell us a little about your childhood.

I read that you started acting in 1983 at age nine with the Riverside Children's Theatre in California. My readers are always interested in how artists get started, so how did you first become interested in entertaining? Did your parents push you or was it your own desire?

Joshua "Déous" Gennari: Thank you, Betty. It's great to finally be here with you. How did I get started? My parents were both hugely artistic; I grew up around the arts. My mother did plays in New York, just off Broadway, and my father was a musician and a songwriter.

In fourth grade I did a play called *How The Grinch Stole Christmas*. My teacher, Miss E., thought I should try out, and so I was cast as The Grinch. I absolutely loved the experience. After that, my parents enrolled me in the Riverside Children's Theatre. The very first play I auditioned for was *Alice in Wonderland*. I was cast as the White Rabbit. The Children's Theatre was very much like a weekend school. We had classes on acting, music, and even dance and movement. My love for the arts was set in stone and my parents were, of course, elated.

After we moved to Alaska, I attended school in Nikiski and found they had a dance company led by Phil Morin. It was there I really solidified my appreciation for dance and choreography. Mr. Morin was an incredible teacher and choreographer; my true inspiration for pursuing the dance path.

Betty Dravis: Wow, Deous, with such talented parents, it's natural that you have a grand passion for the entertainment industry. I'm very impressed that you choreographed five musicals and even more ballets by the time you were twenty-one. That's an astonishing start for one so young. Do you mind sharing the progression of your career and why your family moved to Alaska and other places where you built up an astonishing portfolio?

Joshua "Déous" Gennari: Sure Betty… After my freshman year in high school my parents, who were now teachers, decided to move to Alaska. My mother believed it was the Last Great Frontier; we had some family friends who moved there and raved about it. I wasn't excited to leave my whole life (or what I thought was my life) behind. However, as mentioned above, when we landed in Nikiski I was ecstatic to find that artistic outlet to plug into: the Nikiski High School Dance Company.

My parents had developed a new teaching method where they implemented theatre into their curriculum. My father asked me to choreograph the musicals and teach their students. I agreed, on the stipulation that they allot a time solely for dance and allow me to teach dance performance technique.

I don't think my parents initially realized I planned on teaching anything more complicated than step left, step right. My father and mother kept saying, "I think you're getting too complicated." (laughs) But kids are amazing.

Unlike adults, if you don't tell them what they can and can't do, they will just do it.

The first year and first show was when I learned the most. I would set the bar and the students would constantly hit or even surpass my expectations. The hardest part was figuring out what their capabilities were, then setting the bar just out of reach, so they had to stretch themselves.

When they hit the goal, I praised them and once again moved the bar just out of reach.

By the third year, it became a game; the kids wanted to see how high Mr. G. (what they called me) could set the bar. Many times I worried they might not be able to hit the goal, *but every single time, they succeeded!* The very last show I choreographed was a stage adaptation of Walt Disney's musical *Newsies*, with extremely complicated dance numbers. The kids tossed newspapers and dove into a roll to catch them. The timing had to be perfect. They did a beautiful job.

When I started attending Kenai Peninsula College (KPC), I discovered Chris Morin (Phil Morin's wife) was both a professor and the director of the KPC Dance Company, so I got a double-dose of her. Chris was awesome! She picked up where her husband left off as I continued to train and work on my technique.

Later, I moved to Anchorage and made it into the University of Alaska Anchorage (UAA) Dance Repertory and the Alaska Dance Theatre Company. There I focused on Ballet, Modern Haitian and Jazz, as well as method acting. After that I moved to London for a year and started auditioning for shows. *I loved London!*

Betty Dravis: You continue to amaze me, Deous. Your choreography credits are awesome. Here are a few shows you've choreographed: *Annie, Pirates Of Penzance, West Side Story, Wizard of Oz, Oliver,* three modern ballets: *Legend, Both Sides Of The Story, Redemption*, and even a stage production of Walt Disney's *Newsies,* as you mentioned above.

That's a broad array of popular shows, Deous, and if any of our readers would like the entire list, they can visit your Internet Movie Database link (at end of this interview). Do you have a favorite production or one that made an immense impression on you and possibly changed your life?

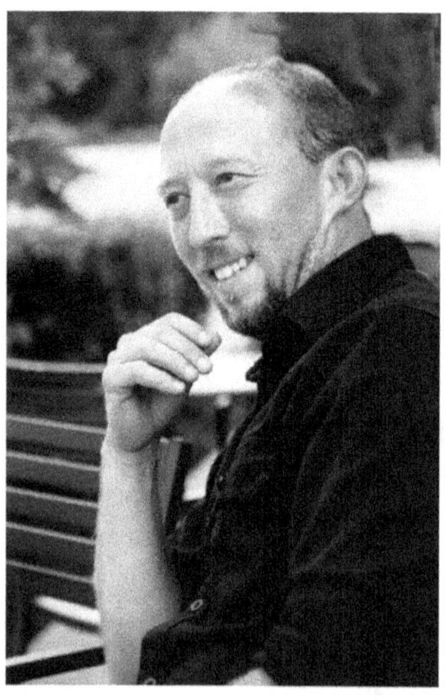

Joshua "Déous" Gennari: Yes, Betty, I do, actually. While I was studying at Duke, I fell in love with the Pilobolus Dance style. The idea of weight-sharing and partnership that Pilobolus employs was intriguing not only as choreography, but life in general. Life is about a give and take and creating those momentary pictures. We come together, we share and then move on to our next picture, where we repeat the process.

It's exactly what we are doing in this interview. You and I share ideas, which will be shared in various media, and when your readers read our ideas, it will, in some way, affect them. Hopefully, in a positive way... This is what Pilobolus is all about: the sharing between two bodies as they move though space. I wish everyone would employ this in their daily lives.

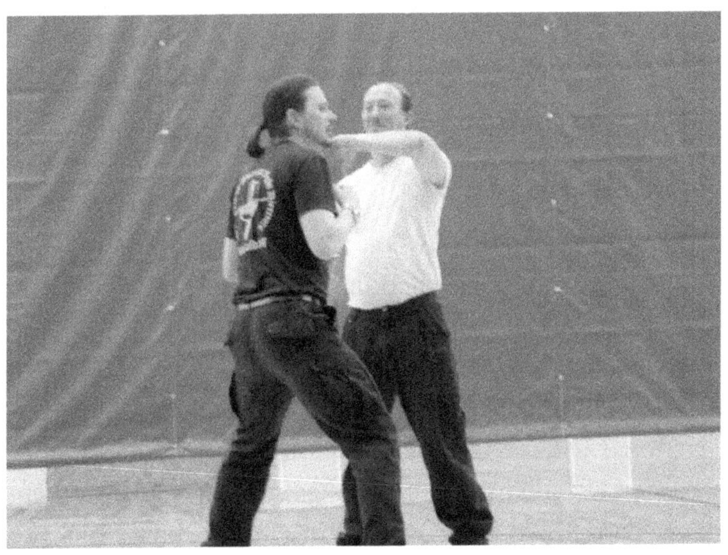

Deous teaching stage combat at Pierce College

Betty Dravis: That's spot on, Deous, and sounds rather spiritual. But in addition to dance, you're also an actor and singer. I understand you've performed the roles of Tony from *West Side Story* and The Lizard Man in *Side Show.* Were those live stage productions? Where did you perform?

Joshua "Déous" Gennari: I performed those roles in community theatres in Kenai and Anchorage. I love musicals and because we love the Art so much, my wonderful wife Jackie and some friends privately recorded multiple songs. These include "The Confrontation" and "This is the Moment" from *Jekyll and Hyde*, "Where's the Girl" and "Into the Fire" from *Scarlet Pimpernel,* "Sunset Boulevard" from *Sunset Boulevard.* My wife and I also recorded the duet "You are my Home."

Betty Dravis: You're what I call an all-around performer, Deous. I know you're not a vain man, but I think I would become vain if I could do half of what you do. (laughs)

But something I'm curious about: How did a man with your talents end up spending twelve years in the military? That's quite a detour from your entertainment career.

Joshua "Déous" Gennari: Well, Betty… What do I say? (laughs) *Life happened.* Up to that point I had been active with the National Guard for seven years. After my first Honorable Discharge I decided to return to theatre; that's when I went to London (partially to escape the memories from the military and part to try to pick up the pieces of my theatre career).

After a year in London, I returned to the States and brought a young lady back with me. Soon after that, we got married and shortly thereafter, she became pregnant, so I had to evaluate the importance of stability for my family. As a result, I joined the Active Duty Army and returned to the medical field. Two years after my son was born, my wife and I divorced. After I was granted custody of my son, he and I started to rebuild our lives again.

I remarried and was deployed to Operation Enduring Freedom. As fate would have it, about six months after getting back I found myself going through another divorce. This time I was completely in the dark and never learned why. She just decided she was leaving, I guess. My son was totally devastated.

After seeing how the divorce affected my son, I decided I wasn't ever going to remarry or engage in a serious relationship again. I never wanted to be divorced once, let alone twice. There is nothing more crushing than the feeling of losing your family, especially after trying everything you can think of to try and save it. It was then I realized sometimes there is absolutely nothing you can do; sometimes it doesn't have anything to do with *you* at all. I realize for many people out there this may not make a lot of sense. Relationships are two-way streets and when one person decides to quit there is nothing the other can do to change that.

I was honorably discharged in November 2005. It took some time, but I finally did remarry. This time I believe I finally found my soul-mate. Jackie is incredible and my best friend. She and I support each other, our endeavors, our children and our dreams. She is my inspiration and my voice of reason.

Betty Dravis: I agree that divorce is devastating, especially when children are involved. I'm glad it worked out for you and you finally found your Jackie. I wish you and your family much happiness and good fortune.

The fates must have conspired with you to keep you in the entertainment industry, Deous. I don't think it's a coincidence that you met Ken Dietiker while stationed at Fort Lewis. Since you both enjoy film creation and the arts, did you guys work together after your discharge? And when did you decide to concentrate on the directing/producing end of the business?

Joshua "Déous" Gennari: Ken and I lived right next to each other. We wound up spending a lot of time discussing film and movie projects we wanted to see completed. After getting out of the military, I returned to school and decided I wanted to start a film production company. Ken is one of the creative directors (and trouble-shooters) for Area 51 Productions.

Betty Dravis: I'm glad to hear that you and Ken are still working together. Good, loyal, like-minded friends are hard to find.

For a man who made his mark in choreography and the military, Deous, you somehow managed to accumulate six years of college at Kenai Peninsula College, University of Alaska Anchorage, Duke University and Pierce College in Washington State where you now reside. You must be brilliant because in 2009 you made the President's List holding a GPA of 3.9-4.0, became an Alumni of Phi Theta Kappa and have been published in the Cambridge *Who's Who of Business.* Is Pierce College where your deep interest in the academic life began to blend with your love of film?

Joshua "Déous" Gennari: I don't know if I'd call myself "brilliant," but like my father once said, "There is only one difference between genius and insanity–perspective." (laughs) Then again, if I had to give a starting point to where the two began to blend, it would definitely be Pierce College. That's where the inspiration to start Area 51 Productions was born. I was working on a project and realized to complete it properly I would need some money, so I decided to write a business grant and start Area 51 Productions.

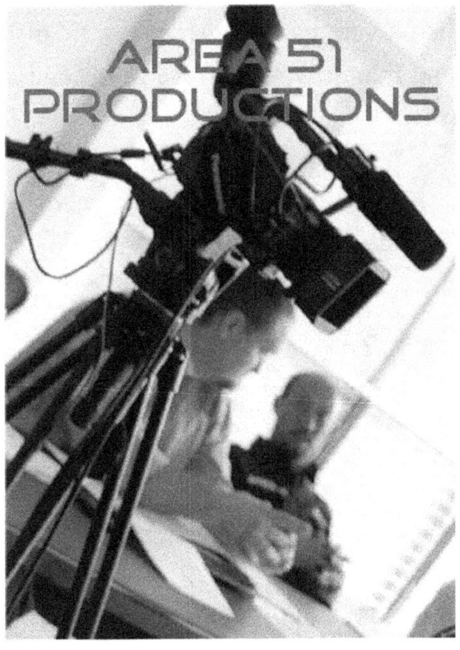

Betty Dravis: Before we discuss more about Area 51, let me back-up for a minute. You mentioned your family above, but

I'm curious about how you and Jackie met. As everyone knows by now, my readers and I are a bit romantically inclined. (laughs)

Joshua "Déous" Gennari: When Jackie and I met we had both been in bad relationships and definitely didn't want to go down that road again. I'll tell you how we met, but you can't laugh. Well, maybe you can chuckle a little. (laughs) I had a friend who talked about this website called E-Harmony. Of course I laughed hysterically and even mocked him because I thought all dating sites were just a waste of time. He swore it was different and explained they had some kind of profiling exam. I laughed even harder. Anyway, finally I decided it couldn't hurt and I could always tease my friend later.

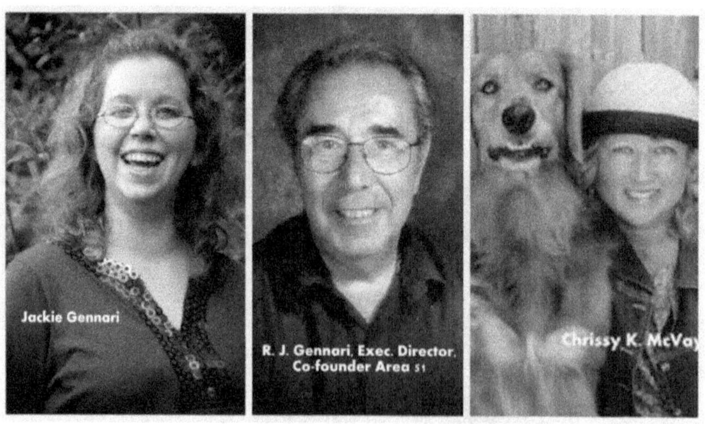

Jackie and I almost instantly popped up on each other's profile. We had all the same interests and even similar backgrounds since I had been a medic and she a phlebotomist (a legal Vampire, someone who draws blood). We both also had a background in music and loved the arts. Most importantly we both seriously wanted a family and someone to grow old with. Jackie had a son named James from a previous relationship and I had my son Josh.

We dated for a while before introducing our children into the mix. Jackie and I fell in love and we have been together ever since. We now have another son, Jaron, and our cross-over to the dark side was complete. (laughs) Just kidding… They're wonderful kids. Jackie and I dubbed our family Sector J-5, since everyone's name starts with a J. All our kids love Transformers and so we stole the idea from Sector 7.

As far as the business is concerned, Jackie is one of my associate producers and the creative mind behind many of our projects. She is also one of the first to read and edit the scripts. As for the boys, Josh is in a Zombie film I'm working on and James just debuted in a horror concept film called *Clown,* directed & written by Bill Read.

Family is always a challenge to juggle with our lives and careers, but we are committed to *family first.* I have incorporated this into my company philosophy: when I schedule shoots I also leave room for my staff to spend time with their family. I decided long ago I never want to cause another family to fall apart. My studio is set up to be a family-friendly environment.

Betty Dravis: Well, Deous, I have the same reaction when I see those E-Harmony ads on TV today. But now I know it can work, so I'll try not to laugh in future. As for you, a man who puts family first can't be all bad. (laughs) I got a chuckle out of Jackie being a "vamp." My daughter Mary Lee was a phlebotomist for a while too. Jackie might get a kick from this, but when a woman asked her what that was, she jokingly said, "A brain surgeon." We couldn't believe the woman believed her.

Another of your outstanding humanitarian traits, Deous, is that you have an incredible passion for uplifting and encouraging people. I read in your bio that this passion was sparked by studying great leaders such as John C. Maxwell, George Lucas, Steven Spielberg and Patrick Daugherty. Tell us how they inspired you. I would also like to know if you have personal mentors that inspired you to great things.

Joshua "Déous" Gennari: Well Betty, John C. Maxwell is a motivational speaker and teaches thousands of executives how to change their thought process from negative to positive. I met him once and his personality was infectious. Patrick Daugherty was a professor from Pierce College who encouraged and pushed me on the road I'm on now. I'll discuss George Lucas and Steven Spielberg later.

I have always believed it is important to have mentors in our lives. My father is at the top of the list. He inspired all the research for our current project and helped found Area 51 Productions. Whenever I have a question about a problem or situation, he is the first person I call. Others would be Elizabeth Sierra-Arruffatt and Jeff Silverman.

Elizabeth is the Area 51 senior photographer and has been with me from the inception. She's also one of the first people I call to discuss an idea for feedback. She is always a positive inspiration to me and everything we are trying to accomplish. Jeff is our I.T. manager. The great thing about him is he is a very technical and logical guy. Whenever I am in a dilemma, I know I can always call Jeff and never worry about getting bashed. He always gives me a straight-up answer about why he thinks I should or shouldn't handle something a certain way. His answers are always logical and basically unarguable. This is great for me because I am very much a person to try to look at things from every possible angle.

Another would have to be Diane Matson. I cast her as one of my leading actresses, but I soon found I wanted her production input and guidance. She is also one of my lead script editors for the *We Were Vampire* franchise (as well as this interview). I respected her input and friendship so much I offered her a co-ownership in one of our current franchise projects *AWL.*

Last, but surely not least, is your friend and mine, Chrissy K. McVay. When I first started writing my novel, I knew I needed someone who had done what I was trying to do in order to accomplish it. I knew nothing except how to tell a story. I sought out Chrissy with the sole intention of earning her trust and respect, hoping she'd be willing to guide me. *It worked!* (laughs) Chrissy also become a highly-respected friend. When she speaks, I listen in complete silence, just absorbing. She not only inspired me, but also provided encouragement every step of the way. I cannot say "Thank you!" enough.

So hugs to you, Chrissy! You're awesome!

Betty Dravis: Oh, I agree with you about Chrissy. She's not only a fine writer, she's very knowledgeable and a great person to have in one's corner. In fact, she's the one who recommended that Chase Von interview me for Student Operated Press. We put our heads together and decided to jointly publish our celebrity interviews in the first *Dream Reachers* book. And now we're working on a second in the series (which is where this interview will be published in print form). I owe Chrissy big hugs too. *(laughs)*

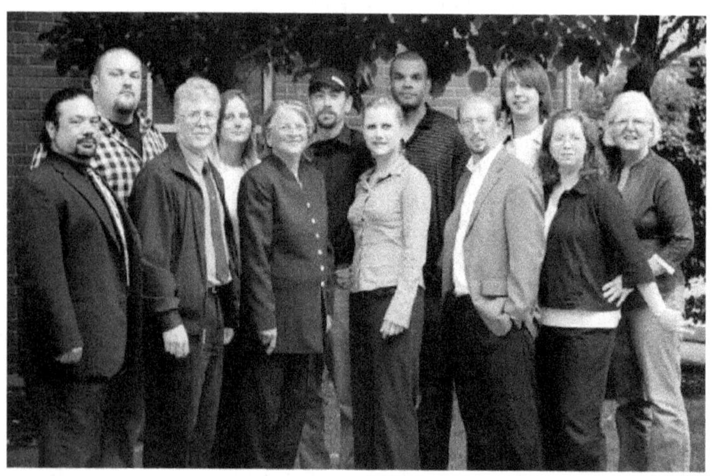

Now for the big news—AREA 51 Productions! I've heard such positive things about your special program that I'm dying to know all about it.

Deous, this seems like a natural progression and a perfect way for you to celebrate all your accumulated achievements in one huge project to benefit many people.

I sense that this is the biggest dream of your life, so please tell us all about it: Exactly what is it?

Where did you get the idea?

And how does your plan differ from what others in film are doing?

Joshua "Déous" Gennari: First, you are absolutely right! It is the biggest dream of my life and, of course, a huge undertaking. I founded Area 51 Productions back in the beginning of 2009. I wanted to establish the largest studio in Washington which could also give a wide array of jobs to unemployed artists and production people. The goal was to establish a company where writers and story creators have active voices alongside the director of the films. So often, stories are ruined because the "Powers That Be" don't consider the story the writer initially envisioned. So I wanted to make the writers and creators an active part of the film-making process.

We also plan to have positions available for students, perhaps with scholarships or as interns. It's so hard for students to go from graduation to landing a job without any real experience. Area 51 will provide that by assigning them to a department in their area of expertise so they can actually work on a real film project.

So my creative team and I sat down and drew plans for a self-contained, green-friendly studio. The building houses many different departments, including an art studio, sound studio,

CGI, special effects, and even a small movie theatre to view the final mix before the project is wrapped and packaged for distribution.

Our goal is to create a creative environment where directors, producers and crew can have all the major elements right at their fingertips. Then I sat down, wrote up a business plan and decided to apply for a Federal Business Grant to pay for start-up costs.

Betty Dravis: With so many people obsessed with breaking into the movie business, this program sounds ideal for helping larger numbers of them. Just where are you currently with Area 51, Deous?

Joshua "Déous" Gennari: Well, Betty, when the economy crashed, all the grant money disappeared (to bail out all the car and bank companies), so the startup companies (trying to help stabilize the economy) were left hanging. While working to acquire funding for the studio, we pooled our resources and started production on a few film projects. My staff has been very patient with the process. I can't thank them enough for all their support. Now we are looking for investors or financial backing for the company. This dream is so big it will take many more people to accomplish it.

Betty Dravis: The economy has devastated and derailed millions of people, Deous, but with so many loyal people determined to work with you to make it happen, it can't fail.

I've heard a lot about one of your productions, *We Were Vampire.* Tell us about that and other films you might have made. I also saw a poster for *Art of the Sacred.* Is that another project of Area 51?

Joshua "Déous" Gennari: *We Were Vampire* started in 2009 with a novel I conceptualized and wrote called *The Sacred.* After I wrote the initial 274-page manuscript, I handed it off to Jenn and Jesse Jefferis, who helped shape the text and also contributed to the story. *We Were Vampire* was originally a short film to advertise the book by using it as a prop. As I wrote the script, I quickly realized this was actually a modern-day continuation of the story. At that point, my co-writers encouraged me to continue and turn it into a feature.

It is a very unique take on the whole vampire concept. It took Rick Gennari (Co-owner, Area 51 Productions) and me about ten years to research the ancient history linked to *The Sacred* and *We Were Vampire*. *We Were Vampire* is now a film trilogy and a continuation of *The Sacred* novel trilogy, which combined, is called *The Sacred Vampire Saga*. This franchise has become at least as large as *Lord of the Rings*. We are now starting the pre-production process by filming webisodes to help advertise this project online.

I have also been working on publishing the first novel in *The Sacred* trilogy, *Genesis of the Forsaken*. The book is nearly ready for a final edit and should get published this year. I am so excited about the books and can't wait to see what the public thinks. All the reviews so far have been excellent–and that was in its rough format.

In addition to everything else, I have also been collecting illustrations for the trilogy. Eventually, these will be published in a separate book, *The Art of The Sacred,* with all profits going to the illustrators.

Betty Dravis: *Books!* Now you're talking something I understand, Deous. (laughs) I'm excited for you—the films and the books. Since you're such a dynamo—acting, singing, dancing, directing, producing, writing—that probably keeps you in shape without the need for much exercise, but I'm curious… You appear very agile in all your photos, so what is your secret for good health and vigor?

Joshua "Déous" Gennari: Well, as you can tell, I keep myself *extremely* busy between business, writing, directing and family. Eating healthy is always a challenge. The important thing is not necessarily to eat three times a day but throughout the day instead. The biggest meal of the day should be breakfast and lunch, *not* dinner. Keep each snack-meal small enough to curb your hunger, rather than until you're full, and you will maintain a much faster metabolism.

Betty Dravis: That's sensible, Deous; many doctors confirm the wisdom of "smaller meals, more often." But what's a typical day like for you?

Joshua "Déous" Gennari: From now until we get the studio built, I work from home, which is great because I also get to look after my three-year-old. So a normal day for me… Well, what is normal? (laughs) Jackie and I get up between six-thirty and seven a.m. and I make us both a latté. Usually, that is a fancy name for an overpriced coffee, but we have an espresso machine so we can make them inexpensively.

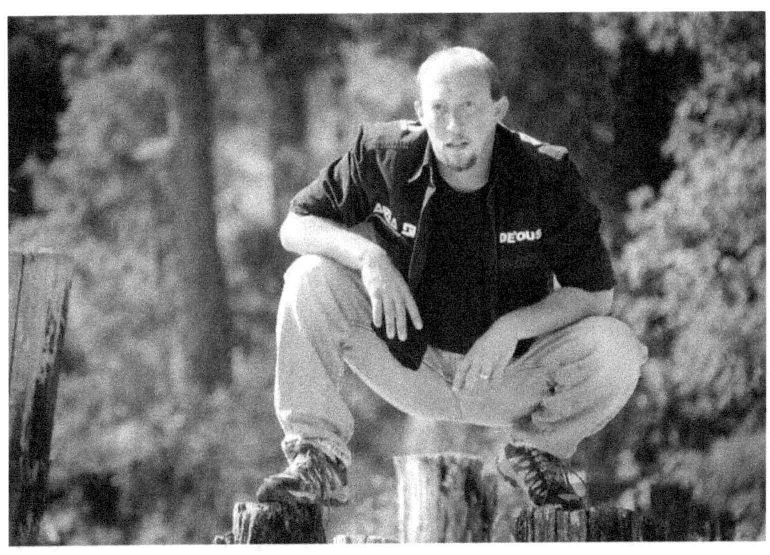

After Jackie is on her way to work, I sit down, check my company emails and respond. If I am in the middle of a writing project, I'll work on that for an hour or two before making business calls or working on preproduction notes. Somewhere in all of that I'm feeding my son breakfast, or occasionally taking him out for a Danish for some father-son bonding time. Then it's lunch and making sure my two older boys get their homework done before making dinner. After the kids are in bed, I settle in for another couple hours of either writing or video editing. That's probably as close to an exact schedule as I can get. Things change sometimes, so I just adapt to situations and go with it. It's the number one lesson I learned from the military–*adapt!*

Betty Dravis: That seems like a comfortable, productive schedule, Deous. One more question about your great state of Washington: Does Washington have a film festival? I, for one, would love to see an Area 51 Film Festival that features only movies produced by you, your staff and the school students. Is that a practical dream for the near or distant future?

Joshua "Déous" Gennari: I'm glad you mentioned that because an Area 51 Film Festival is completely practical. We are working on a program called the NW (North West) Local Film Production Support Program. The program creators are Ken Dietiker, Rick Gennari and me. This program offers filmmakers up to $50,000 from in-house grant money to produce projects which will be shown at the Festival. Both the festival audience and the Area 51 Production staff will vote on their favorite films. The winners will be submitted to other festivals around the world at our expense. Right now, the program is set to house twenty films. Of course, as we grow, the festival will then have the ability to expand as well.

Betty Dravis: I'm pleased to hear that; sounds like your plans are all-inclusive. There are so many talented newcomers just waiting for a chance like this. Film festivals are awesome.

Since you're actually living your dream by doing what you enjoy doing most, what advice can you offer to others who aspire to be in any part of the movie industry?

Joshua "Déous" Gennari: Well, first, establish a good, reliable work habit. Second, for anyone who aspires to do anything great, the greatest advice I could give is *never* give up; it's the difference between failure and success.

Case in point: Thomas Edison was once asked why he didn't give up and why he was willing to *fail* over 10,000 times while trying to create the light bulb. Many people called him crazy and laughed at him. His response was, "I didn't fail 10,000 times. I simply found 10,000 ways it wouldn't work." So remember, failure is never final or certain until you quit.

Betty Dravis: Good advice, Deous! I haven't heard that story about Edison, but have heard some inspiring ones about Henry Ford. (laughs)

Now since show business, like real life, is made up of both drama and humor, I'm sure you've had some embarrassing moments during your long career. Please share one of those funny things with us.

Joshua "Déous" Gennari: Well, Jackie's friend Lynn, her son Michael and I were all joking around one day. Just for fun, Michael and I were trying to one-up each other. He said something about the English language and, of course, going for the instant kill I said something like, "Well, it's a good thing the English language has twenty-seven letters in the alphabet then, huh?" Instantly, everyone in the car got quiet and stared at me.

"What?" I asked.

Everyone broke out laughing and Michael said, “You mean twenty-six.”

Trying to cover my mistake, I responded “That’s what I said.” Of course we all knew that was absolutely not the case. Anyway, to this day Michael calls me “Mr. 27.”

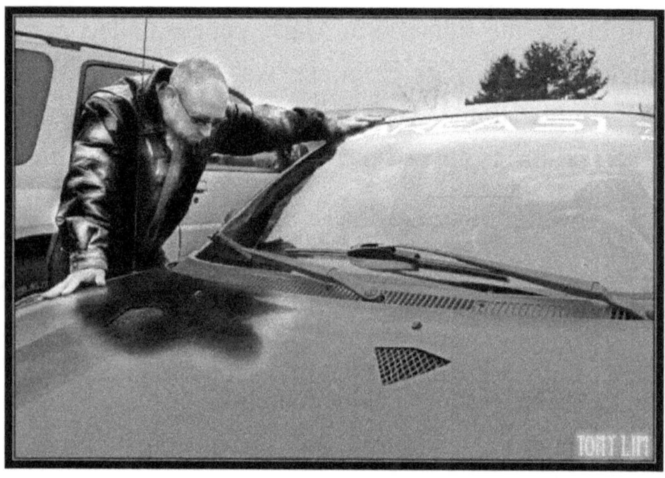

Betty Dravis: That sounds like something I would do, Deous, so I empathize with you. *Yeah... right!* (laughs)

If you were given the chance to spend an entire day with one famous movie director or producer who would you choose and why?

Joshua “Déous” Gennari: *Great question!* That would have to be Mr. George Lucas. I’m so glad I can finally tell you why he is so important, as a mentor to me. I’ve studied his career as a director and producer all my life. His is the perfect rags-toriches story for anyone who wants to be a filmmaker. He wrote a huge Galactic Opus and went through so many struggles just to see the first film completed. When making his next film, his struggles only intensified because he dropped out of several guilds due to their unfair politics. Still he endured. By his third *Star Wars* film, *Return of the Jedi,* he'd lost his wife through a divorce. Yet he didn't quit. Now he is one of the most respected directors of all indie film directors.

While I was setting the foundation for Area 51, I looked at Lucasfilm Ltd. as a model. Although we have never met, I have the utmost respect for him. I would definitely hang out with him for a day, just so I could learn more from him.

Betty Dravis: I wouldn't mind that myself, Deous. He's quite the man! But now, since the world is in such chaos at present, if you could influence any one thing in the world, what would you choose to change and why?

Joshua "Déous" Gennari: I wish people would listen to each other more. We have two eyes, two ears and one mouth. That's twice as many types of input as output. If we would take that to heart and really listen to one another there would be far less anger in this world.

This answer is simple and short, but please think about it…

Betty Dravis: I have often had the same idealistic thought and feel that the difference in backgrounds and experiences is what keeps that from happening, but that's food for much thought.

Most artists receive a vast array of kudos throughout their careers. One of my personal favorites is from a book review written by a woman whose long-awaited trip to Russia was interrupted because her husband had a heart attack. She wrote that while he was in surgery she read one of my books, *Millennium Babe: The Prophecy,* and it took her mind off what was going on inside the operating room, thus sparing her a great deal of stress. Needless to say, learning that my book had helped her in such a special way made me happy. Can you think of one example of a compliment that really made your day? Whatever you wish to share…

Joshua "Déous" Gennari: The best compliments I ever received were from the Area 51 Production core staff members who came alongside me throughout this process and didn't quit. They helped encourage and guide me while remaining steadfast. This is incredible to me because the journey hasn't always been easy. Like any company, we get our share of knocks, bumps and bruises, but nothing fazes them. My staff helps keep everything on course and don't get hung up on the insignificant stuff, so I would like to thank them publicly: Thanks so much to Jenn and Jesse Jefferis, Ken Dietiker, Christopher Hoard, Jackie Gennari, Jeff Silverman, Raemenn Jewall, Elizabeth Sierra-Arruffatt, Richard James Gennari, Dannie Baldwin, Mark Rosenwald and Diane Matson.

Betty Dravis: That's incredible, Deous, and says a lot about them, about you and about the entire concept of Area 51… Loyalty is a divine thing, in my opinion. Now before we finish,

I'd like to offer you the chance to discuss anything of importance that I may have missed.

Joshua "Déous" Gennari: Well, I just wanted to let everyone know that there are several ways to get involved or become familiar with this exciting project. As I mentioned earlier, we have been working on putting the funding together for the first film, *We Were Vampire*, and are looking for investors. For anyone who is interested, you can go to the *We Were Vampire – Web Series & Feature Film Project* on www.kickstarter.com.

You can also go to Amazonstudios.com and leave a review for the script and story. *We Were Vampire* is ranked sixth out of 497 projects in the Action Adventure category. We would love to hear your input, so please feel free to do that as well. For more info about this project you can also visit www.wewerevampire.com. We are very proud of this project and the entire *The Sacred Vampire Saga*. It is going to be like nothing anyone has ever seen before.

Betty Dravis: I wish you and your staff "God Speed" in raising funding for this very necessary, exciting project, Deous. Any saga cut from the same cloth as the legendary LOTR is sure to be magnificent. I read a portion of one of the scripts and I'm overwhelmed by the entire concept. This is one I'm on pins and needles to view.

I'm reluctant to leave you because your projects are all so exciting, but all good things must come to an end. Please keep us in the loop because we're eager to see this promising saga on the big screen. I hope it's soon.

Meanwhile, your fans can visit your websites for more information. As everyone knows, it's simple to Google anyone on the Internet. Your name and videos are all over the place. (laughs)

Well, that's it for now, Deous. I've enjoyed visiting with you. It's been enlightening to learn about Area 51 and your plans for the future. We all wish you best of luck, and once again I'd like to congratulate you for your innovative idea that will help more people fulfill their dreams. Thanks for visiting with us and sharing your life…your dreams.

Joshua "Déous" Gennari: Thank *you,* Betty I have enjoyed being here. Of course I will send you updates, photos, and will keep you posted on Area 51 Productions. Thanks so much for interviewing me. Feel free to contact me anytime.

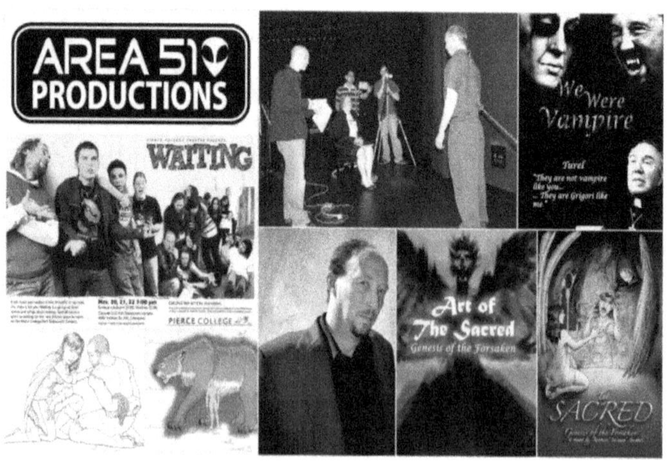

PART TWO

INTERVIEWS BY CHASE VON

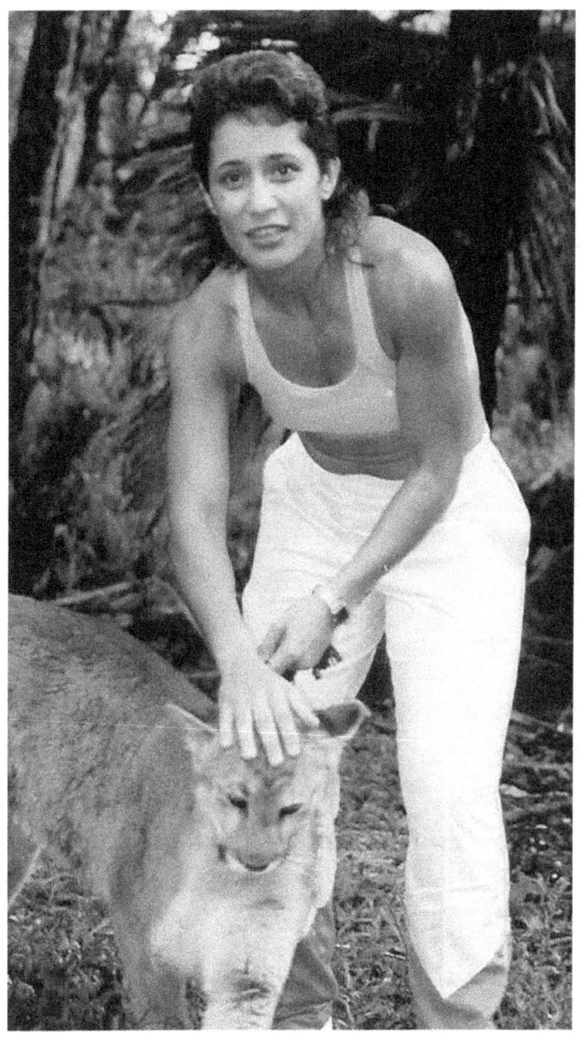

Ada "Ace" Velez sharing a moment with her feline "Friend."

Interview with Hollie "Hot Stuff" Dunaway

FOUR TIME WOMEN'S BOXING CHAMPION

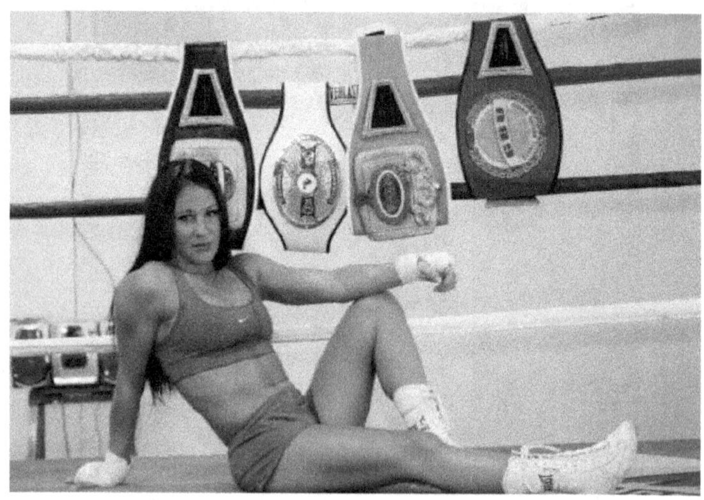

Chase Von: Hey there, Hollie, belated Happy New Year`s to you, and on behalf of the Student Operated Press and myself, we really appreciate you taking the time to share with our readers. We`re starting a new year so I truly consider it an honor to start by interviewing a true champion. So thanks so much again…

Hollie Dunaway: The pleasure is all mine, Chase. It`s an honor speaking with such a talented writer that really thinks outside the box.

Chase Von: In all the fights I`ve seen of you, Hollie, I`m not surprised to learn you've been champion four times and I really expect to see you adding more belts to that in the future. People that haven`t watched some of your fights will have to check them out to see why I say that but you`re a natural. What most impressed me was your ring generalship. No matter what someone is trying to bring at you, you don`t ever seem to lose your composure. I was also shocked viewing two of the fights when they awarded the victory to someone else! Personally, I thought it was robbery but will get to that later.

First, even though it seems like you were born with gloves on, can you tell our readers what your younger years were like? (Smile.)

Were you always athletic? And unlike some people who dream of being champion, you sort of stumbled into boxing. Can you share the story on how that happened?

Hollie Dunaway: Thank you. I was always athletic and have an older brother in the U.S. Army that I had the pleasure of fighting with throughout my childhood. I was raised on a farm in Arkansas and didn`t discover boxing until I was eighteen.

With no amateur boxing career, I guess you could say my first year fighting was on-the-job-training.

Chase Von: Someone else in women`s boxing I`ve come to know is Sarah Goodson. I know I shared with you that she and I were going to do an interview, but she was just too busy training and preparing to fight Krisztina “Baby Girl” Belinszky. She gave it a good attempt but Krisztina won that bout that took place in Hungary. But Belinszky is someone you`ve also fought and beat.

Is there a possibility you and Krisztina will square off again?

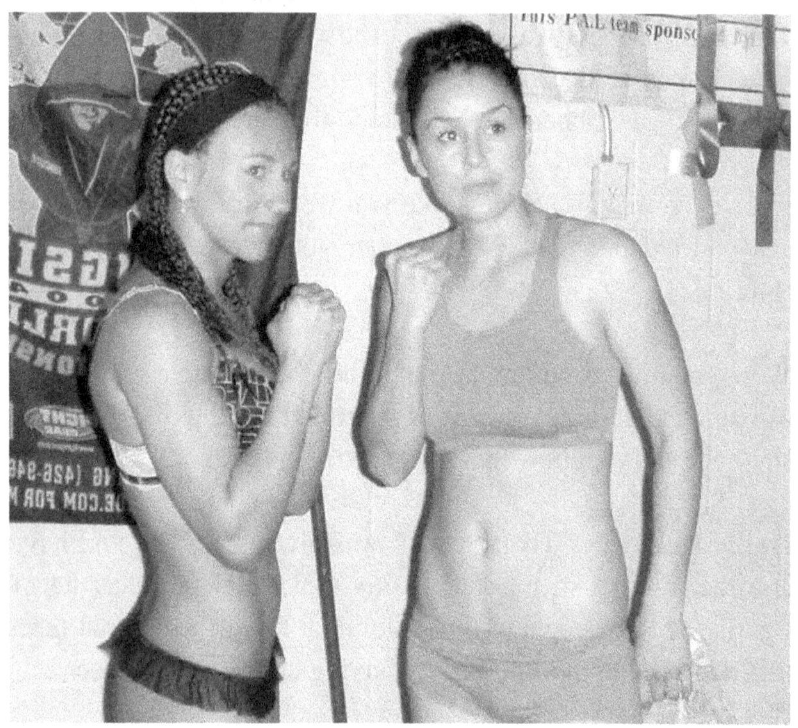

Hollie Dunaway and Chantel Cordova at weigh in

Hollie Dunaway: I would love to fight Belinszky again. Beating her in Hungary to capture her two world titles was one of the greatest highlights of my career.

Chase Von: Two of your fights that I watched, as I`ve told you, I was totally shocked when they gave the win to the other person. I know we`ve also discussed that and you told me how much it hurt when you train so hard, and give up so much to do your best and then get robbed. You also told me that it was far more than those two that were given to people that didn`t really

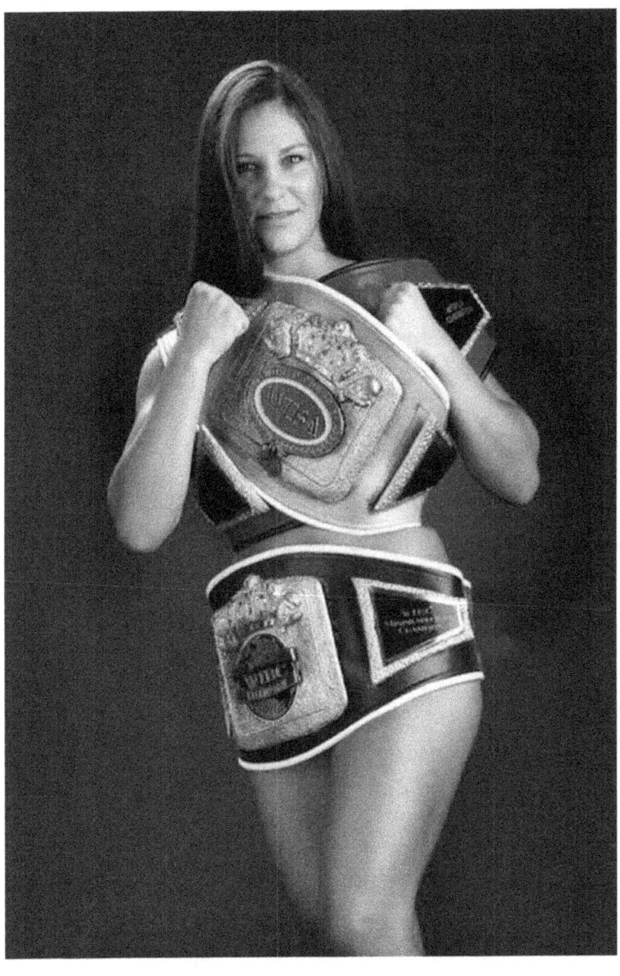

win. I know it happens in men`s boxing as well, but I think it is rarer. Is that a problem you see with women`s boxing in general?

Because when I look at your record, 22 wins, 8 losses, 1 draw and 10 by KO, impressive as it is, I still think just from those two fights alone, you should have two more in the win column!

I`m not saying names because I certainly don`t think the boxers themselves are responsible for bad decisions that are on the judges, but what do you think your record would really be if things were judged fairly? And after experiencing that not once, not twice, but so many times, how and where do you find the strength to train again and give it your all, not knowing if it is going to happen another time? Has that ever made you want to just give up on boxing altogether?

Hollie Dunaway: I see as many robberies in men`s boxing as I do in women`s boxing. There are more televised men`s fights so that may make it a little harder to rob a fighter of a win when such a large audience can see what really happened. My professional record is 22-8-1 (10 ko`s) and I`ve won 4 world titles. However, if boxing were judged fairly every time and there were no bad decisions, then I would be a 9 time world champion with a record of 28-3 (10 ko`s). It just made me sad, sick and angry at the same time writing that.

I just have to focus on the positive and let all the negative go. It will turn me into a negative person incapable of accomplishing anymore in boxing if I don`t keep that attitude.

Chase Von: It`s too deep to get into now I think, but do you agree with what I said; regarding something should be done about bad decisions in boxing? I.e. they do have instant replay in football. How about when it is really a noticeable to even the crowd decision, that they make something like that, reviewed by actual boxers, either retired or still in the game who are respected, so that those things don`t stay as they are?

Meaning, and (we can copyright this now), January, 2, 2010, Hollie Dunaway and Chase Von suggest that questionable decisions are reviewed by three respected people in the field of boxing and if they concur an injustice has taken place, they either A petition it is over turned or B, consider it as if the fight didn`t take place and reschedule it with different judges?

Because seeing someone robbed when they`ve done all that people in sports have to do to even enter the arena to me is not only harmful to the individual, but to those watching it.

Because they too, are left wondering if people saw the same thing they did and eventually time buries it so it can`t be looked at again in the same light.

After all, life moves on, so don`t you think perhaps, in the age we live in, that something really questionable should be given a second look before that happens? And most importantly, no matter who someone might be rooting for, do they really want to see someone that didn`t win get awarded for winning?

If so, why not watch rigged pro wrestling right?

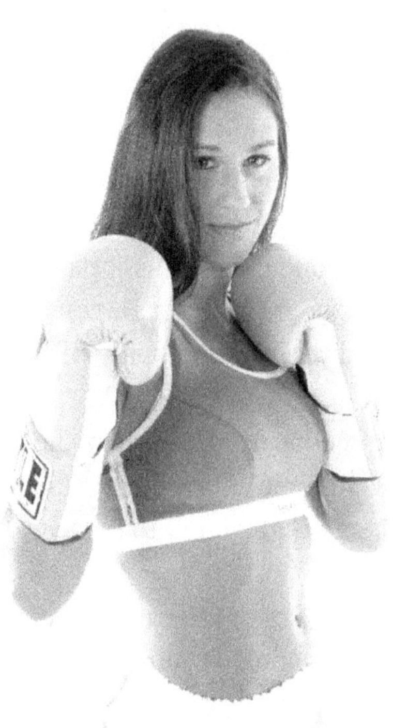

Hollie Dunaway: I agree with you 100 percent! In late 2009 instant replay became an option, but only to review if a foul was committed, not for any other purpose and especially, not to overturn a bad decision. Every state and every country`s commission have a different set of rules. The fact is most judges have never boxed a day in their lives. Boxing, the sport I so deeply love, remains the most corrupt sport in the world.

Chase Von: One of my more recent interviews was with the lovely Joan Baker, a recognized queen in voice over work. I mentioned you in that interview because on one of her web pages, she had *Hot Stuff* and I thought that was a strange coincidence after learning you were down for this interview.

But let`s face it, you are HOT! (Smile.)

You are also going to be appearing in a men`s magazine because you`re also a sought after model. Can you share a bit more about that with our readers? And what your thoughts are in regards to that perhaps helping interest in women`s boxing?

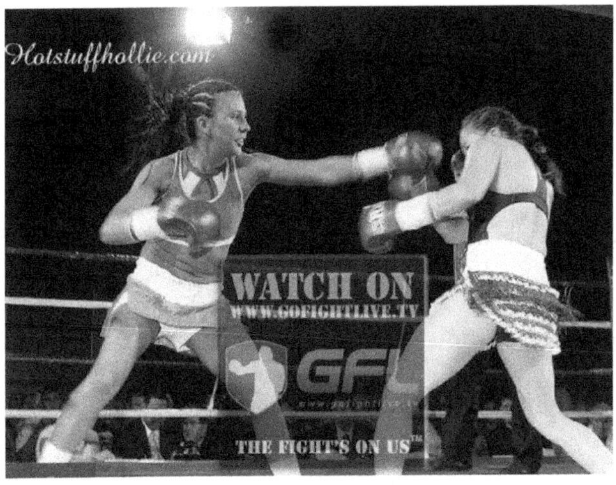

Hollie Dunaway: I posed for *Penthouse Magazine* in Las Vegas several months ago which will be released soon. I suppose I`ve followed in the footsteps of other successful female boxers such as Mia St. John and Regina Halmich who both posed for *Playboy*. After I saw that it helped more than harmed their careers, I believe it will help bring more attention and fans to the sport from people who aren`t usually women boxing fans. Posing nude is not for everyone. I am very proud of the body that I work hard for and am a naturally confident woman. My photos are nude but tasteful.

I wouldn`t do anything to embarrass myself or the sport of boxing.

Chase Von: I can`t imagine what you do to prepare for championship bouts. And that`s something your trainers or yourself might not want the competition to know any way.

But what are some of the things you do to stay fit when you aren`t training for a fight? And what are some of your favorite meals?

Hollie Dunaway: I stay in the gym year around. I just pick up the intensity about 6 weeks out from a bout. I fight in 4 different weight divisions so my diet varies from fight to fight.

When I fight at lower weights, I eat plenty of whole grains and cut out sweets and fried foods but when I`m fighting at a heavier weight, I eat everything in sight to get up to 112 pounds. My favorite foods are chicken, chicken, chocolate, and chicken. (Smile.)

My trick to not put on weight is to cook and eat at home instead of going out to eat at a restaurant. And my favorite pre-fight meal (after I make weight) is chicken fettuccini.

Chase Von: I`m Black, Blackfoot and Cherokee Indian and rumored by family lore, to perhaps have some French in me as well. You list yourself as Native American. Can I ask which tribe or tribes?

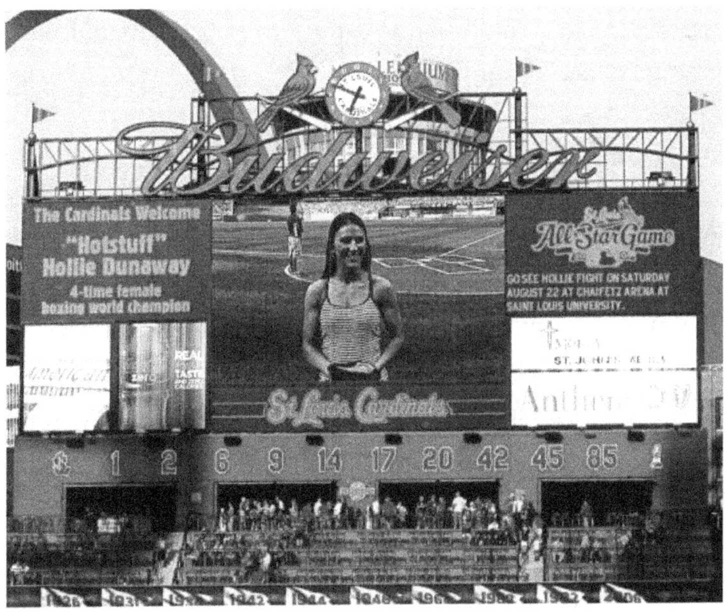

Hollie Dunaway: I am Cherokee Indian. I registered and got my Indian row number five years ago.

Chase Von: What would you say if you were standing before a microphone that could be heard by every child on the planet, and regardless of what language they spoke, they would understand you?

What positive advice would you give the children, if that were possible?

Hollie Dunaway: If you have a dream, always feel as though you can achieve that dream. Some dreams and goals are hard to achieve, but never impossible. You just have to be creative and find ways around the obstacles life throws in your way.

Chase Von: How important is family to you, and what is your take on the state of our current world?

Hollie Dunaway: My family is very important to me. I`ve lived away from my family for the past 3 years but just left Vegas and moved home to Arkansas. I plan to open my own boxing gym here soon. I wouldn`t have felt comfortable tying myself down permanently by starting a business thousands of miles from my family. I believe people are mostly good but living in big cities alone I`ve discovered there are many people in the world that are really just looking out for themselves and will take advantage of you if given the opportunity.

Chase Von: Now a tough one because I always try and ask at least one of those during my interviews Hollie. Mixed Martial Arts is becoming incredibly popular!

And in truth, I enjoy both boxing and MMA but what I`m wondering, is right now it`s like they are treated like baseball and football or basketball to some degree.

If you want to watch boxing, you go to a boxing match or tune into them, and if you want to watch MMA you tune into that when it`s available or attend an event. Various people from boxing and other sports are trying their wares in MMA as well.

But one, do you think you will ever get into Mixed Martial Arts?

And two, do you for see a day when perhaps in the same venue, they will have boxing and MMA combined in one event? You know, first perhaps a few boxing matches, and then MMA or vice versa?

Hollie Dunaway: I will not ever cross over into MMA. I have respect for the sport but it`s simply not for me for many reasons. I`d rather not be elbowed or kneed in the head and MMA gloves are so small, they offer hardly any hand protection or protection to the bones in the face you are punching. I love to see a good fight but when I see someone`s ear cauliflower up in a MMA fight, I realize that is permanent.

I have seen blood pour from the ears in nearly every brutal MMA fight I`ve watched. Most of my fights are ten rounds and at the end, I rarely have a mark on me even fighting world champions. I contribute that to my impeccable defense.

Boxing is an art and I can take a punch if need be but if I were getting physically damaged every fight, I wouldn`t have much longevity in the sport. I`ve fought 7 years as a professional and don`t plan to retire anytime soon. I have seen many shows where boxing and MMA are combined and think it`s a great idea to bring together the 2 audiences.

Chase Von: As anyone can tell you`re very attractive, but you are also very articulate. What`s the likelihood we will see you not only fighting in the future but also being a commentator as well because you certainly know far more than most, when it comes to the sweet science? (Smile.)

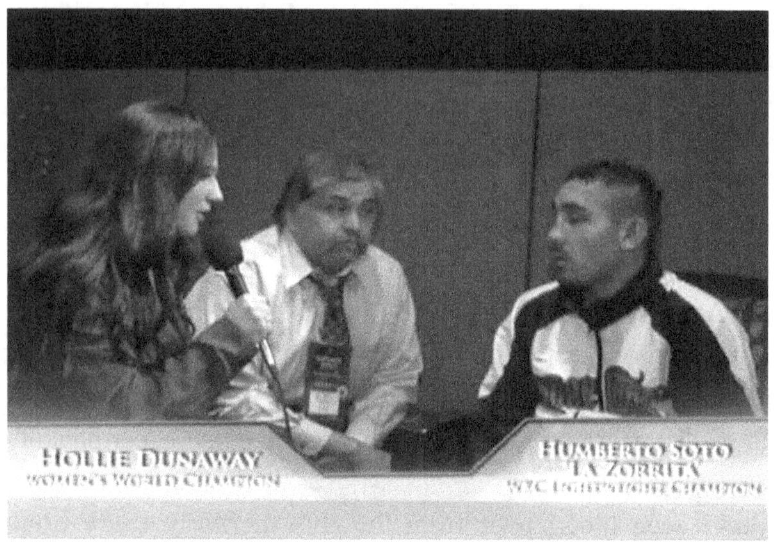

Hollie pursues her other dreams behind the "mic"...

Hollie Dunaway: Thank you Chase. I`m a boxing commentator in my home living room when I`m watching fights on television. (Smiles.)

Seriously though, I would love to do it professionally.

My dear friend, Al Bernstein who is a well-known Showtime boxing commentator even suggested I would make a great commentator after we did a radio show together in New Mexico.

Chase Von: I know I told you, after watching you fight and reading up on you---Particularly your web page where you have what looks like a diary--- The movie by living legend Clint Eastwood, starring not only himself and another acting legend, Morgan Freeman, but also the beautiful Hilary Swank came to mind.

Million Dollar Baby! The ending was really sad but it was a great movie. But will you ever write down your life story in book form?

Because I think it would make an excellent movie and not only inspire but it would be a real true life story!

Hollie Dunaway: You read my mind! I`ve already begun writing my life story. And its way more interesting than the hit movie Million Dollar Baby, which is a great movie that I truly appreciate.

I plan to write for a couple more years and will reveal the great, the bad, and the ugly.

Chase Von: Can you share your various web pages or places where people can find you to learn more about you?

Hollie Dunaway: My primary website is HotstuffHollie.Com. I am also on nearly every networking site such as myspace, face book and my grown-up viewers can visit my at HotstuffHollie.TV

I set aside a few hours every day to respond to fan mail. I receive way too much fan mail to respond to everyone but I at least read every message sent to me.

Chase Von: One thing I`ve learned from Willard Barth, a friend of mine is that we all have to stretch our comfort zones at times or we stay where we are at pretty much.

Just from getting to know you, I know that one of the best things about you, is you have a truly wonderful personality and even numerous commentators have said your manner in which you carry yourself, is a huge plus for women`s boxing.

But do you ever see yourself acting? Because you`ve not only been blessed with great hand speed and power but great looks as well! And though you might not see that in your future, you have spent a lot of time in front of huge crowds of people and because of your natural athletic ability; you would probably be able to do all your own stunts! (Smile.)

Hollie Dunaway: I have considered acting, even studied it a bit but boxing and modeling has kept me so busy I never pursued it. It is something that I would be comfortable doing and will keep an open mind to in the future.

And I would definitely do my own stunts!

Chase Von: Hollie again, true pleasure getting to know you and doing this interview with you, so I can share what a unique individual you are with our readers. I`m wishing you all the good life has to offer and again, because we`ve communicated personally a few times, I hope more learn about how genuinely sweet you are, even though I don`t think they want to step in the ring with you. (Smile).

So continued success to you always and on behalf of myself and the SOP, truly appreciate your taking the time out your hectic life to do this and I do hope you`ll drop me a line every now and then and tell me what other mountains you`re conquering, ***Champ***! (Smile).

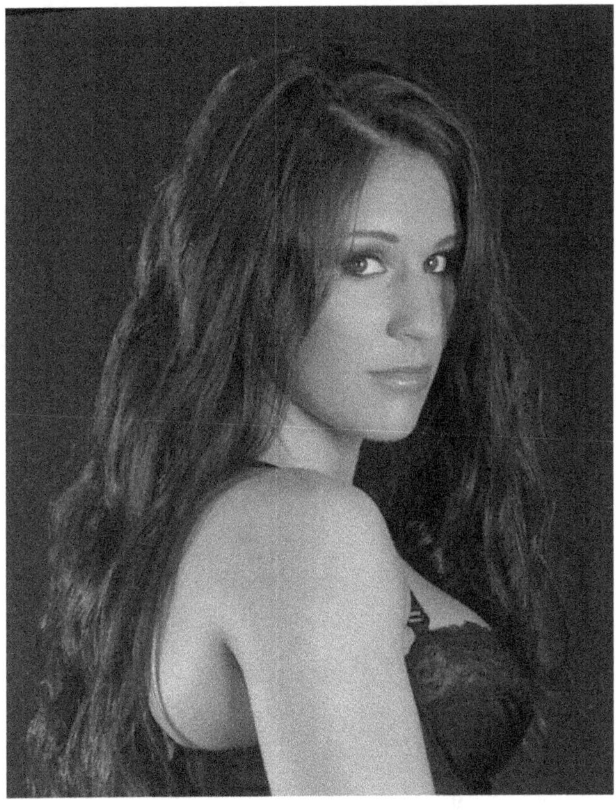

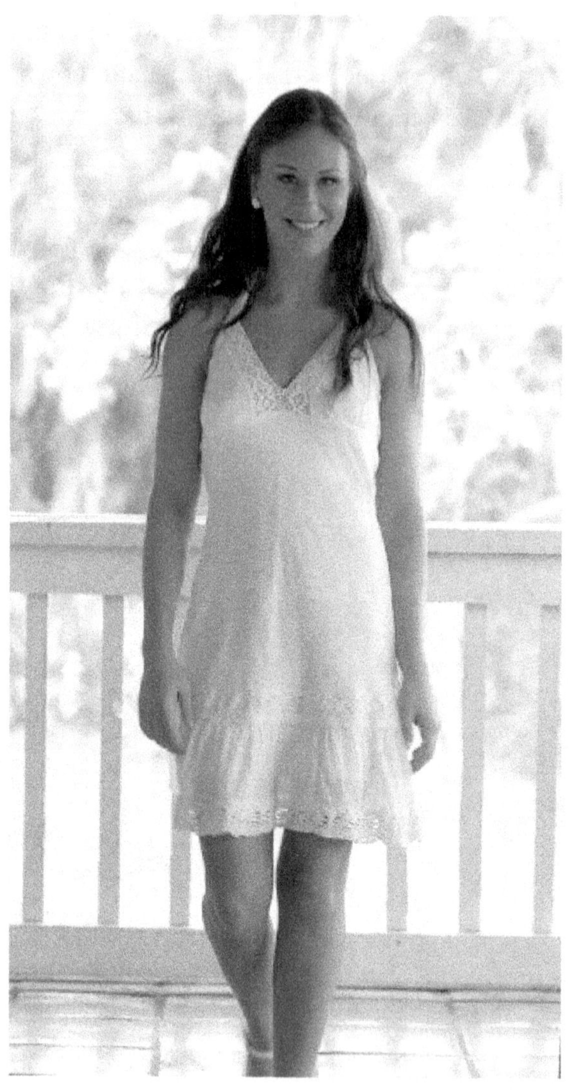

Hollie Dunaway: Thank you so much, too, Chase, and the Student Operated Press for taking the time out to interview me. I`m very fortunate to have crossed paths with you and will definitely keep in touch.

Interview with Ed Roberts

LIFE-SAVING POET

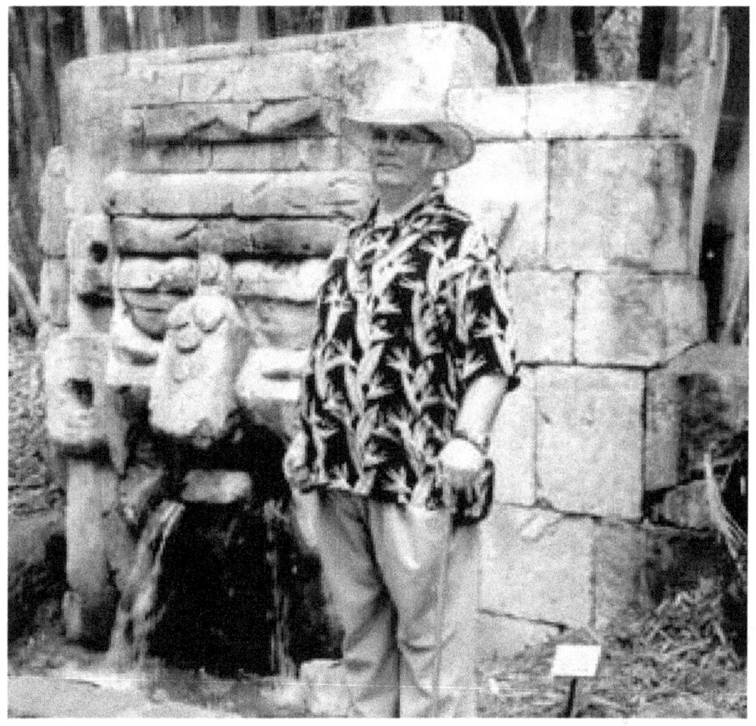

Chase Von: Ed, or Brother Ed, (Smile.) On behalf of the Student Operated Press and myself, this is an honor. You`re also a contributor here and I`ve known you for many years now, so I`m pleased you want to do an interview and even after knowing you all this time, I`m sure there are going to be a few things I learn during this. But again, thanks for finding the time in your hectic schedule to squeeze this in.

Ed Roberts: Thank you brother; not a word I use lightly. Just to let those out there know that though we have never met in person Chase is one of those people I would not hesitate to hand my wallet or car keys over to if he said he needed them. We have been friends and much more for over 6 years now. Trust is something that has to be earned but believe me; he has done this a dozen fold.

Chase Von: We met on line many years ago now, when I was in Kuwait. They had a computer Café of sorts there and you could pay a little on a card and as it ran out, pay a little more and get more credits for computer time. Often there were long lines there just to get on a computer but it was contact with the outside world again, so we willingly waited.

But in addition to being able to email family and loved one`s I also stumbled on your web site, and it was there I read a poem called, *The Man Who Left The Bar* and I was stunned at how powerful it was! I emailed you or left a comment saying pretty much that and was really surprised when you responded back! Since then we`ve pretty much been in constant contact! I didn`t think then we would practically become brothers but that`s pretty much what has happened. (Smile.)

Did you have any idea when first we met, we would still be in contact today?

Ed Roberts: You probably won`t be surprised by my answer Chase, but yes. As you know I hear from many people; some from far away, some from here in the US. There are times I read their words, others I feel them instead. Yours are those I felt. I`m not sure how many will be able to understand but as a poet I spend a lot of time looking past the façade others try to create around themselves and look instead into their heart and soul. It might be a gift or a curse but it is something one is born with. Trying to deny it or drown it simply would drive one mad.

After several years, I simply learned to try and accept it.

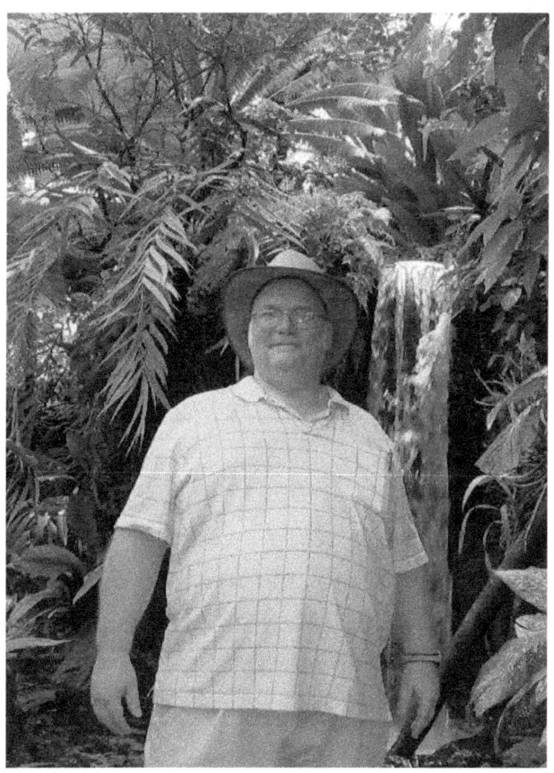

Chase Von: OK, just wanted readers to know that when we

thought the war was over and were shipping and flying things back is when I met you. Fortunately you and I are still in constant contact; unfortunately the war is still continuing as well and yes, expanding. I usually don`t ask tough one`s so soon or try not to, but since I did mention the war, do you see an end in sight personally regarding that? Because first it was Afghanistan, then Iraq and seems now it`s spreading over into Pakistan.

Not to mention the drums seem to be beating for Iran and there is the situation between North Korea and South Korea.

So in your opinion, are we in what George Orwell wrote about so long ago in 1984? I.e. "*Oceania* has always been at war *with East* Asia*."* Or do you personally see eventually, there being peace?

Ed Roberts: If you are asking if I think there ever will be an absence of war my answer is probably not. As you know I do believe however in "Mystigosia", a word that has fallen out of our vocabulary.

Simply put, it means the act of bringing Heaven to Earth. So many people have no problem envisioning that there can be Hell on Earth but far too few are able to grasp the concept that the other is just as easily possible. One of my goals is to bring back this word to our tongues and our hearts. We are poets; this is one of our many purposes.

Chase Von: Ok Ed and those are tough questions to ask up front, and honestly only time knows the answers but appreciate your sharing your thoughts on that and sure the readers do as well.

Switching gears, you were born and raised in Oklahoma! Over the years via you I`ve learned, (and I hope this doesn`t offend any Oklahoman natives), but is there a state you know of that has worse weather? (Smile.)

Fourteen tornado`s in one day? Hail the size of soft balls? Freezing winters that stranded someone else I interviewed there for a few days, (That being World Champion Boxer Hollie Hot Stuff: Dunaway) who went there and won her fight and then couldn`t leave due to an ice storm!

And you also have some horribly hot summers from what I gather and floods! Has the weather there influenced your poetry? (Smile.)

Ed: Only fourteen tornados in one day? ☺ I pulled this from the NCDC weather site
94 TORNADO(s) were reported in Oklahoma between 05/03/1999 and 05/04/1999.

Now that was a REALLY bad day.

It is hard not to be touched by the variance in the weather here brother. I always tell people we have tough trees here, they have to stand up against anything Mother Nature throws at them. I do feel it reflects in the people as well. You look at the

Murrah building bombing that happened in 1995. After the bombing, there was no looting, almost no crime at all for days.

People lined up to help those in need; something that happens here every time we are faced with a challenge. Several people have asked why I haven`t moved somewhere else where I might be able to get more exposure with my writing. My answer is simple, I am from Oklahoma, born and raised. I wouldn`t trade the people here for anywhere else in the world.

Chase Von: On a serious note, I`ve been literally blown away by some of the comments you have received on your poetry. Many have brought this two time war veteran to tears as well as some of your poetry itself. How do you--- And this is one of those comments, swallow that your words have this kind of an effect on someone? Knowing because someone found your words, there is an actual life that might not have had a chance to know life, had they not?

2005-11-03 00:29:42

~The Silent Voice~

I told one of my friends that i was going to weigh my options. Kate sent me here to read this. There are choices i have to make, thanks to these words abortion won`t be one of them. I guess this is what friends are for and poets as well. Thank you

Ed Roberts: The words other leave touch me in a way I don`t think too many can fully understand. I never planned any of this. There was a point where I actually walked away from poetry for almost 15 years. It took me almost dying to bring me back. I hope people understand I am no one special. I really am just a regular guy who makes his living working at a call center to buy groceries. When people ask how it makes me feel to receive some of the comments that I do I simply ask them what they would feel if these were being written to them? I really am no different but I know you understand this Chase and of course, with all of the good comments there are those who would much rather see me not writing at all. At first those did worry me a bit but it fell on the acceptance thing again. I am a man of faith. I simply asked myself why would I be afraid to die? Over my lifetime I have faced death on far too many occasions.

Threatening to kill someone who has faith is honestly not much of a threat if one looks at it in the perspective. It may seem odd but I look at it that I haven`t had someone threaten me in awhile. I am a little worried that maybe on one level I am simply not doing enough.

Chase Von: That`s truly as heavy as it gets brother. Tell our readers about your younger years, what life was like for you coming up in what I tend to think of as the Bad Lands after hearing about how swiftly and horribly the weather can be there. (Smile.) Though I do plan to leave the land of earth quakes and seasonal fires to visit one day. (Heh, Heh.)

Also, when did you first get into writing and when did you really start taking poetry seriously?

Because I`ve read so many comments that are similar to the one above and you truly do have a gift the world needs to see more of!

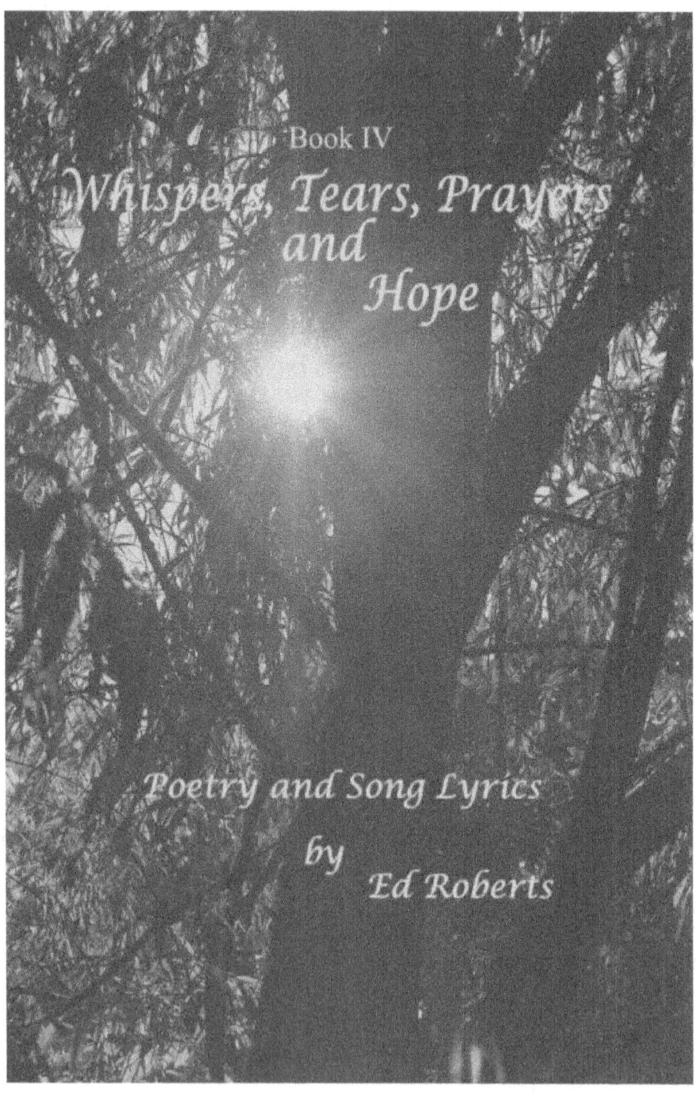

Ed Roberts: I literally have been writing almost my entire life. When I was nine I wrote my first short story "The House of Harnam." A man finds out the hard way his new bride comes from a family of vampires and in the end learns it is never easy to become part of the family. The story was 99 pages long. Unfortunately I have almost a photographic memory. I could probably sit down and rewrite this story in a few hours.

As far as poetry goes I wrote a poem when I was a junior in high school. I told my English teacher I would like to submit it for the High School anthology. (At this time this was only reserved for seniors.) He not only had it published in the anthology but submitted it to several magazines as well. The poem "In Silence" appears in my first book "A Poet`s Last Stand." I do keep praying for the day though that we will raise a generation that will not be able to understand it. Unfortunately it could have been written yesterday.

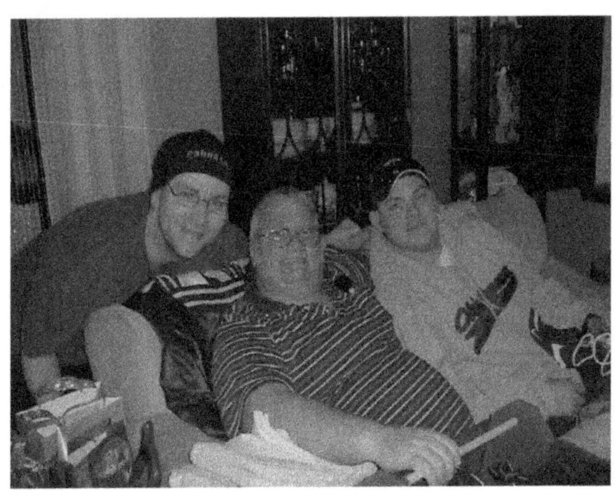

Ed Roberts and his sons

Chase Von: What are some of the web sites and other places where people can find out more about you? And also, since I published your last book, I know sales have been slow.

Poetry is a hard sell to begin with and I happen to know that also, because I too write poetry but I haven`t ever read the amount of comments on anyone else`s poetry that I`ve read on yours that literally save, and change lives! I know you`re a modest man, but how much does it hurt you to read people saying the following, knowing it deeply affected them and changed their lives, and then to think about how many lives aren`t being changed, because other people aren`t exposed to the chance to see your words?

2006-06-30 12:34:37
A poem written By the Man who left the Bar

My God this is so powerful. I lost my brother five years ago in a car accident. You`d think that would have reached me, huh? Let me assure this has! I will never be that man, with a single poem you sobered me up to try and be the man my brother would have been proud of.

2006-05-26 07:48:53
There was a Man

Tomorrow would have been my son Robert's thirteenth birthday. He was killed by a drunk driver March 28th. The saddest part of all is that the boy driving the car that struck him was only 17 himself.

I plan on getting involved with MADD to help try and keep more mothers from being in this position. My friend Betty gave me a list of your poems that she said I had to read. I know why she chose this one.

2006-05-22 22:06:53
Missing

Today marks the one year anniversary of my daughter Kimberly`s death. I was what was missing in her life, a life she took on her 16th birthday. Now she is missing in mine. Your words tear my heart apart like no other I have EVER read. You don`t know how hard I pray that I could have read them earlier. I have read several of your poems tonight. You helped me in more ways than I could ever say. Bless you and I hope these words find more dads that need them. Hopefully before it is too late for them.

2006-04-04 19:30:16
I Thought it Would be Harder

Doing 3rd year of 25 here in Calif. earned internet privileges today was surprised to see a poetry site on the list of sites GOD I wish i could`ve come here earlier. Things really might have been different. Will read more and let a few friends here know to come here as well. Dude, you are a light in a whole lot of darkness.

2006-02-21 13:14:36
Us vs. Them

This poem burns through you like the wind to your very bones. My cousin was killed in a bombing in Amman, they were 25 years old. These men would have called me brother and you the enemy. I will never be one of them and will stand by your side. They damn themselves to hell with their actions. You are a lamp sent to us by God to shed light on their evil.

Ed Roberts: It is a double-edged sword, brother. I have saved over 200 pages of comments I have been sent by people over the last eight years. For every comment I save there are usually five to ten I do not. What is hard for people to understand is I simply write the words. Once written I try to find a way for others to read them. What happens after that is out of my control. I cannot take credit for what I do not do. So many times a person`s comment starts out by saying they were sent to my site by a friend, a teachers, or a loved one. These are the ones who deserve the credit my friend. I have said all along I am simply a poet. I am not a businessman and I honestly cannot imagine myself trying to write for money. It has never and can never be like that. I do look at the sales of the book, or lack thereof, and feel that in some way I have failed in a lot of ways to accomplish what I started out to do. My goal all along has been to change the world with poetry and possibly the way the world looks at it as well.

A few years ago I started The Poetry for Life Project. It basically consisted of three small books I put together which contained some of the most powerful poems I have written. Each was aimed with a specific purpose in mind. Over a three year period I did ship copies of these to people in nine different countries but I was never able to get them established where they were used by schools here in the US, this was my original attention. I feel I have had some effect in many places of this planet but here at home there is so much more that needs to be done. At the end of June I am closing the PFL project and have built a new site to take its place.

Book sales have not been sufficient enough for me to continue to file a tax report out each month and I was advised that this would be classified more as a hobby than a business.

Again, I never thought of it that way to begin with.

Chase Von: Are there any projects you have in the works you, that you can give our readers a heads up about?

Ed Roberts: Though I am not operating the PFL project I do plan on continuing to write. It is how I breathe; I honestly do have no other choice.

I have a new web site in place www.edrobertspoetry.com I felt this had to be done before I closed the other one; far too many people and organizations send people to my poetry for help.

I could not and would not ever make it where they can`t do this.

Over this summer I plan on working with my Godson Rayce on finally putting the poem *There was a man* to video. This has been a goal of mine for some time now. I feel if we are able to do this and do it right it holds the potential to affect the lives of a lot of people. As you know, the poem itself already has.

I also haven`t ruled out doing another book but there are many arguments against this right now. I do have four books listed as e-books in the Sony E-book library and our book *Whispers, Tears, Prayers, and Hope* is listed on Amazon.com, as you stated earlier though sales of these have been almost non-existent. When people ask why I feel this is, I simply ask them when the last time was that they bought a poetry collection or even saw one in a bookstore. As you are aware, most bookstores refuse to carry a poetry section or if they do it usually is VERY small and hard to find. This is something I have tried to change for several years now. Unfortunately, I have not done a very good job at it.

Chase Von: Who are some of the other writers you admire, or just people in general?

Ed Roberts: There are so many people in this world I admire it would simply be impossible to even begin to try and list them here. I have read poets from Poe to Shelley, Frost to Emerson but also from George Manos to Chase Von and from Bamdev Sharma to Ursula T. Gibson. Far too few people realize how many great poets we have right now in this world. Unfortunately many of these may never be discovered, at least while they are living anyway.

My heroes range from Jesus to Ghandi but also from Nelson Mandela to Father Bao. In case you are wondering Father Bao has his own poem, it is *"A Lesson in Faith"* that appears in the latest book. There are so many people I have met I feel that need to have their story told. Poetry is how I try to accomplish this.

Chase Von: What would you say to the poets out there who are considering putting their work into print?

Ed Roberts: There are a lot of companies out there that seem to be VERY willing to help you get your writing into print, be it poetry, fiction, or almost anything else. Most of the time these companies promote several packages for their services, giving greater price levels for each.

I want people to understand there is a big difference from having something appear in print and having people actually buy a book. I feel far too many people learn this lesson the hard way. They spend hundreds and possibly thousands of dollars, believe me there is no limit to what some companies will charge, and they end up with either boxes of books they store in their garage or having total book sales of less than a dozen copies which were purchased by friends or family members at an outrageous price. (I have seen paperback books listed on certain sites that sold for $25.00 or more and had less than 100 pages.)

Chase Von: Pretty hard dose of reality, are there any suggestions you would offer here?

Ed Roberts: There are a lot of ways to share poetry, of course few that generate revenue I`m afraid. There are several online magazines one can submit their poetry to and a few legitimate web sites as well. One does need to investigate some of these because the site itself could be sponsored by a company who will try and get money through onsite contest and offering "awards" that come as long as you spend the money to receive a certificate of pay a large amount of money to attend an awards banquet. As far as agents I do not know any who represent poets at this time but there are a few legitimate publishers, including yourself, who are willing to work with poets.

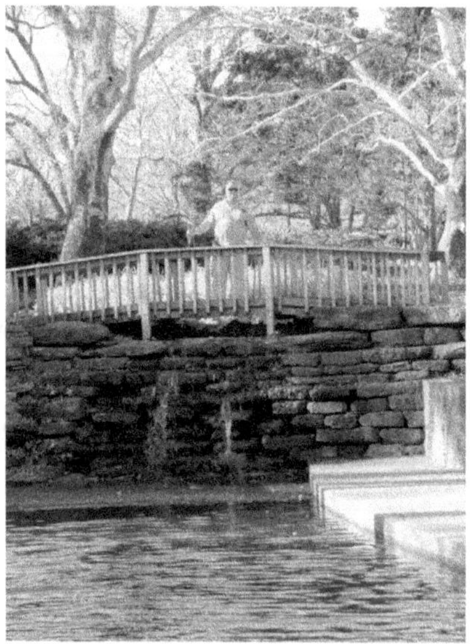

I guess the most important thing I can say here is one honestly needs to examine their goal before pursuing getting their work published. As for me, it has never been about book sales or money. I have said all along I can`t write for dollars, there are some things that one can not put a price tag on. In life though, these are usually the things that mean the most. I work at a call center here in Oklahoma to buy groceries. I write poetry to try and change the world. Believe me, as you know my brother, sometimes the world does listen.

Chase Von: What would you say if you were standing before a microphone that could be heard by every child on the planet, and regardless of what language they spoke, they would understand you?

What positive advice would you give the children, if that were possible?

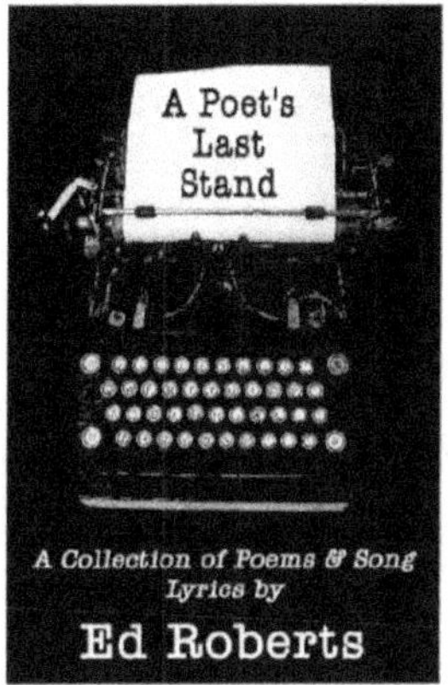

Ed Roberts: This is simple; "The biggest and most dangerous lie that you can tell yourself is that you are powerless to change the world around you. Each of us, in our own way, can change the world each day. If everyone on the planet moves a pebble just one inch that stone would travel 105,745 miles. Never look at anything as impossible but try to comprehend the possible instead."

Chase Von: What are some of the causes you either support or feel extremely strongly about?

Ed Roberts: We need to stop killing our planet. Going somewhere else isn`t a real alternative. If we could stop looking at are differences we could finally begin to understand it is how we are the same that brings us together. The world will be a much better place when this happens.

Chase Von: I also know you`re a strong animal lover. What are your thoughts on this and what do you think the impact will finally be when if ever it runs its course?

http://www.youtube.com/watch?v=vsiM-XjlcIc

Ed Roberts: What far too many people forget is that we ourselves are animals. When they are gone, so are we.

Chase Von: Quite frankly and sincerely, it is a huge mess, and my heart goes out to all those directly affected as well although in some way, it might very well just affect us all. Can you share one of your poems with us now?

Ed Roberts: There are honestly far too many I would love to share here. I want people to know they can always access my poetry from my poetry site if they need one or if they know someone who does. I don`t think this should ever require someone having to buy a book or should be determined by how much they can afford. I guess if I am to post a poem here it would be where it all started.

A Poet`s Last Stand

Be not so quick
To announce our death
Set aside your shovel and your spade
There will be no burial here
Not as long as these lips have words to form
Or there are tales to be spun
From these withered hands
Yes, we have been quiet
Overwhelmed by today`s clutter
You live too fast
We speak
But you have no time to hear
You cannot get culture
At your drive-through windows
Nor can we simply dish it out
For you to scan at will
Ours are words with meaning
They are to be savored for their value
They refuse to be simply devoured
Without leaving some taste behind
Please stop for just a moment
I promise to attempt to entertain you
Maybe it won`t hurt as much as you fear
You will not leave here untouched
For if I fail I will simply lie back
And let you cover my memory
To go about your life

As you began
In darkness
Poetry is not dead
As long as a single soul survives

Ed Roberts 5/14/91

Chase Von: Sure if the readers really meditate on your words here, they will see why your writings have affected so many lives for the good.

And now a really big question.

What is one dream you personally have that you would like to see take place in your life time?

Ed Roberts: I think it goes back to people being able to go into their bookstore and finding poetry there. There are so many writers that give life to such powerful words that have no means to get them to those who need them.

Poetry is not just about life, it is a part of it we all need. It honestly can accomplish far more than most can ever begin to imagine.

Chase Von: Well Ed, I want to thank you for taking the time to share yourself with our readers here. Something you also do on your own by sharing your works here on the SOP as well!

One love and I`ve been spoiled over the years because I`m

always one of the ones that gets to see what you have just created first. (Smile.)

Wishing you mountains more success and the best to you and yours and I know will stay in touch so keep writing!

Ed Roberts: I just want to say *Thank You* for making this possible brother and I hope more people discover how talented of a writer you are. I get to read your work as well. ☺

"We need to stop killing our planet.
Going somewhere else isn`t a real alternative."

---- Ed Roberts

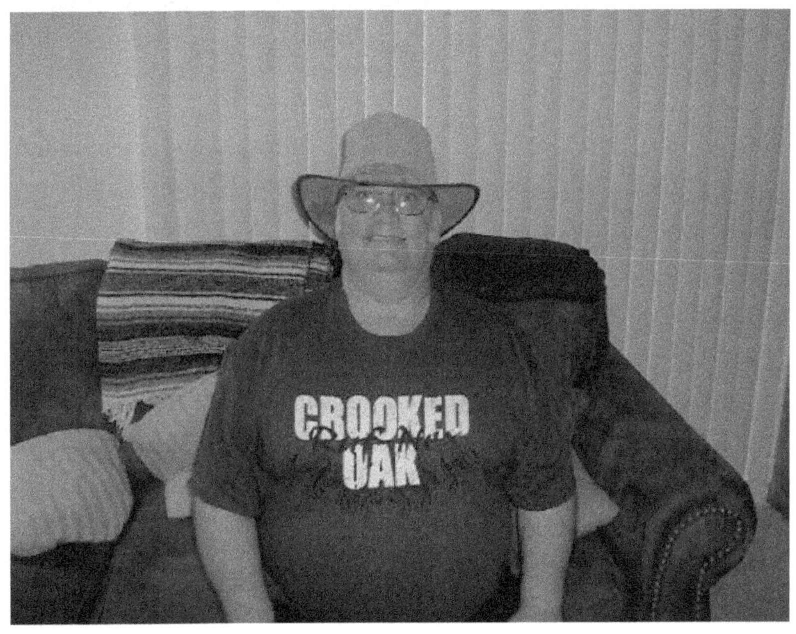

Interview with Elham "Elie" Madani

BREATH-TAKING BEAUTY,
ACTRESS, MODEL AND SINGER

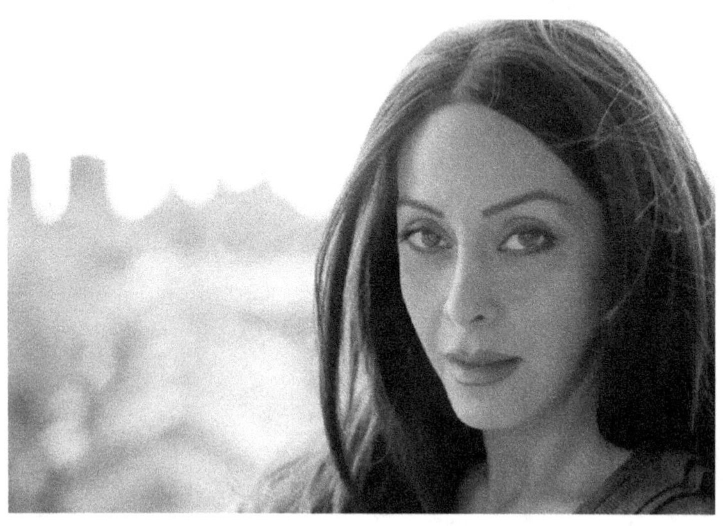

Chase Von: Hi Elie and on behalf of myself and the Student Operated Press, thanks so much for finding the time to squeeze this interview into your hectic schedule.

I personally think you have some of the most intriguing and beautiful eyes I have ever seen and I know I`m not the first to share that with you, but before we go into your natural beauty and your acting, singing and modeling endeavors, thanks again for sharing yourself with our readers here at the SOP!

Elham Madani: You are so welcome and it is also my pleasure to be interviewed by such a great person.

You are a very talented poet and writer--- And you also seem to be so gentle and brave from what I have discovered so far. (Smile.)

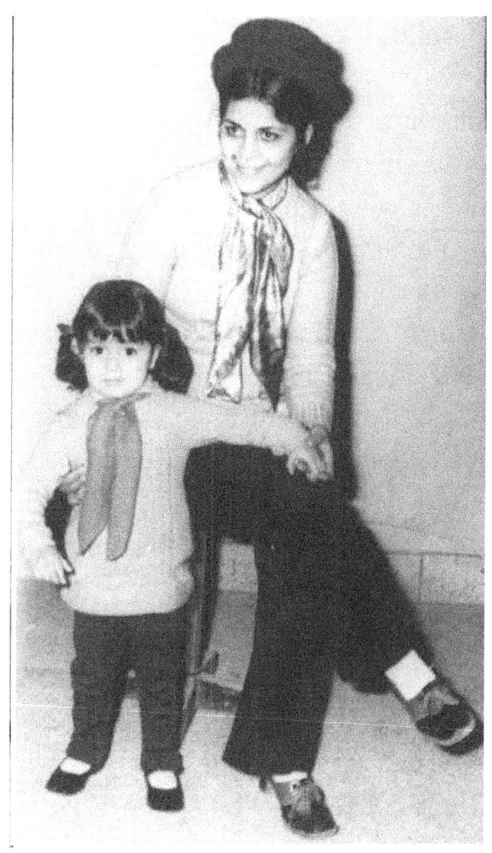

Elham (Elie) Madani when a child with her Mother

And about your beautiful eyes compliment? Yes, I have heard about my eyes almost from everyone during my life--- Mostly from men! (Ha, Ha!)

Chase Von: And thank you so much for the compliment yourself Elie! (Smile.) But getting back to this now, how about first if you tell our readers about your growing up years---Where did you grow up? Was it a happy childhood for you being the only child?

And when did you first become aware that acting was in your blood? Also was anyone in your family involved in acting or any other forms of entertainment? And lastly for this part, how supportive is your family of you pursuing your dreams?

Elham Madani: I grew up in Iran but in regards to my family background and history, I was raised mostly by my Mother because my Father was in a mission and progressing in his career in another country.

So I hardly saw my Father. In other words, I can say my Mother and my Grandmother and Aunts were the ones around me in my early childhood.

That`s also the reason my parents preferred to have only me of course, because it was and is still, very, very hard to raise a child when only one of your parents is present.

About my Mom, she was also doing her studies in another city and I can say I had a very independent but lonely time while growing up.

But being alone is like a tablet; it has both good effects and bad side effects yes? (Smile.)

To be alone, that pushed me to discover myself more than the other little kids around me and also be so curious and independent. I discovered literature and movies at an early age. I mean by the time I was 7 or 8 years of age, I had already read big novels by Charles Dickens, Emily Brontë, Fyodor Dostoyevsky and a few others--- That`s what made me aware of the beauty of literature, and to love the drama in movies by so many different personalities.

It was also a big help that I loved art, especially acting, modeling, dancing and singing but there is a reason why I did not pursue it sooner than I have--- And that`s because of the Islamic Revolution that first barred so many things in Iran and also none of the things I was interested in, interested family members. They were not into Acting or Singing or Modeling at all. Both my parents as you know Chase were professionals in the Medical Profession.

So it was a very brave revolutionary step for me to not study medicine and instead become a literature teacher. Even now I quit that job and now I am here to go after my heart`s desire but better late, than never--- Right Chase? (Ha, Ha.)

I wanted and still want all the time to be the top and first in everything I participate in because I put all my soul and energy into it! At that time, however, the only part of art I could take part in was reading the Holy Quran--- It was all we could do then--- Meaning around the early revolution, (Around 20 to 25 years ago). It did help however, that I`d had big success at

"Holy Quran" singing events in my native country!

It was really the only thing that I could do during those times and I won 18 times! I beat out all the people I competed against and got 1st Place Winner as the ***Best Holy Quran Singer*** according to my voice and manner of pronouncing Arabic and its accents. That is why I know the Arabic accent very well now. (Smile.)

But I should tell you, Mother passed away in a harsh accident some years ago, when she was still relatively young and too much beautiful. It was the biggest and worst shock ever in my life!

She never knew I loved acting this much because she passed away before I could share that with her, but I am sure she would be the best supporter for me as she was truly there for me as best as she could be, in everything else prior to her death.

She also may have had some idea though because at all the family parties and get togethers, I always got in trouble because I had a novel or a modeling, cinema magazines and not my class homework. (Ha, Ha.) Reading was my hobby instead of playing with other kids.

Chase Von: So sorry to hear of the passing of your Mother, Elie, and I know you`re making her soul proud!

And you do have quite an extensive education to fall back on with a Bachelor`s degree in Literature and a Master`s degree in Linguistics, not to mention you also speak Arabic, Hindi, Persian, (Farsi) as your my native language, Afghani and English but I really think with your beauty and talent, I don`t see you having to rely on those at all!

I do want to ask this though, since you were an only child, although you don`t have to be an only child to do this--- But did you have any imaginary friends? Or did being an only child make your imagination more active?

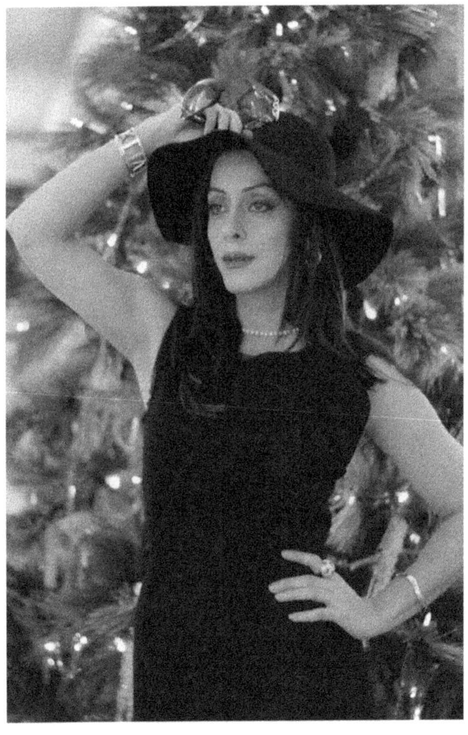

Elham Madani: Every child has imaginary friends I think and

I had them as well. But not any in particular that was always there. Mine were more so during the reading of books I was reading and I could communicate with them (Characters) very well--- Feel them ever but even more so with the movies. I mean even now, if I see a sad story, even if it is in a cartoon, I will cry or happy ending I will laugh out loud and recently I`ve discovered I can even smell things when watching some movies.

Can you believe that Chase? I mean I can smell hot chocolate or like fires burning etc... Strange or what? (Smile.)

Chase Von: Interesting Elie and that`s taking ***Empathy*** to a whole different level! If you haven`t seen it, please don`t watch ***Blazing Saddles!*** There`s one scene in there you would be better off not--- Smelling--- (Smile.)

Also, you`re very experienced at horseback riding, have some background in Martial Arts and are skilled in Belly, Hindi, Bollywood, Latin, Ballroom, Salsa, Meringue, Cha Cha, Persian, and Afghani dances as well! Are there any video`s of you dancing? Ah--- I believe there are some curious minds out there, which just might want to know--- (Heh, Heh). And also, if not now, is there a chance you could make a video with perhaps an introduction saying, this is Hindi, and do a sample of that dancing, and this is Cha Cha, and do a sample of that and so on?

And let me (I mean the world) know. (Smile.)

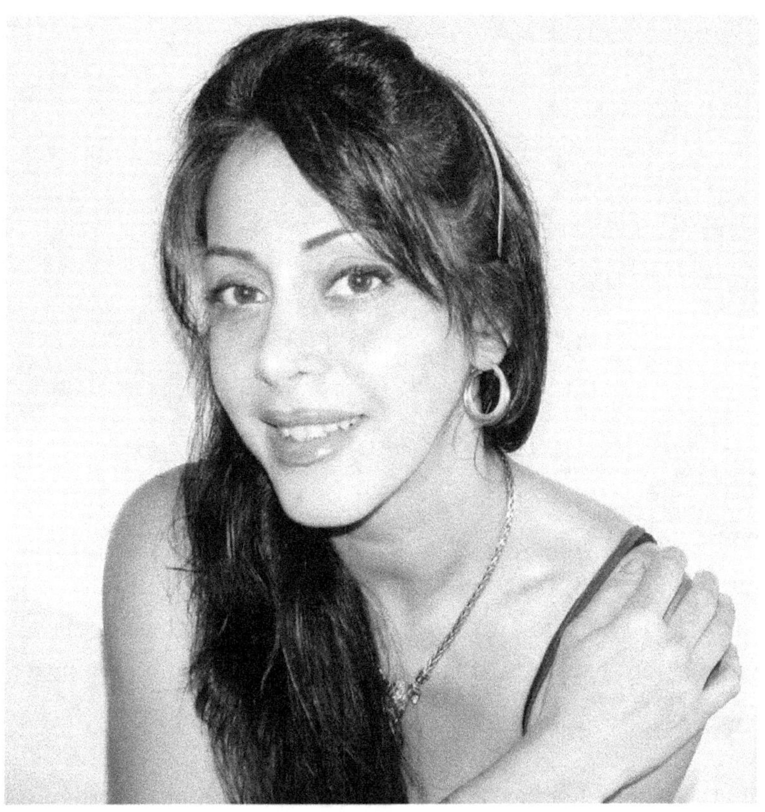

Elham Madani: (Ha, Ha.) Chase--- (Smile.) And of course I love to show case my talents! Especially if you`re asking me! Are there any directors out so we can make this happen? (Ha Ha.) If so, I will be there!

And I do have some homemade video`s that aren`t professionally recorded and unfortunately, I left them in my country while moving here but I would be very happy if I get a acting role and get to dance also during it!

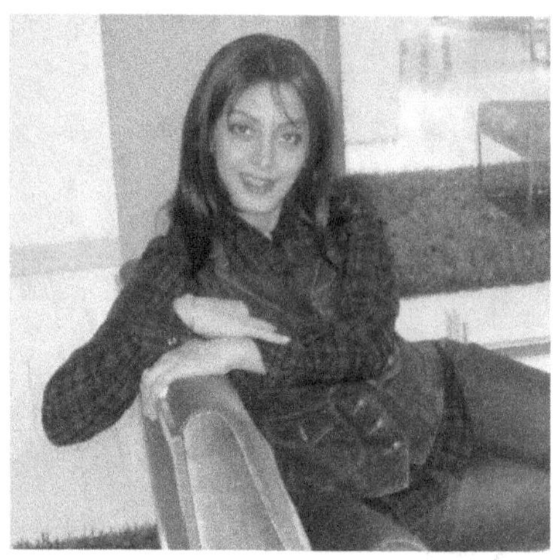

And Chase, I can say I was so scared at first to learn to ride a horse! I wanted to so badly though, I had to tell myself to get rid of this fear and I`m glad I decided to do it because I also wrote a script where I`d have to ride a horse and even jump on it later!

That happened when I took part in a 24 hour short movie making and I wrote this script were I acted as a paralyzed girl who has to ride the horse to escape the dark life she has.

I was doing all actors makeup as a makeup artist--- That is also another one of my skills --- So I had multiple jobs in that movie and yes, my good acting class mates and me made it within 18 hours only with the student facility and it won as best short movie and me best actress and director! But far as learning horseback riding? I had 6 month training prior to that and broke my finger as well but I did it! Scared but--- Yes I did!

Chase Von: I--- Ah, I mean the world will surely appreciate that dancing video Elie! (Clearing throat)--- (Smile.) And knowing how to ride a horse will probably help you a lot in your future roles--- And now on to your many accomplishments and I can`t list them all! You were voted the best actress for your role in ***I Know You Will Come*** and ***Search of Freedom***, The Best Player in the Theatrical Play ***Shahid***, Top Finalist Actress at the ***Universal Academy of Acting*** for 2010, 1st Place Singer in the Singing Competition, ***My Country***, and ***Miss Beauty/Most Photogenic*** in 2009 for ***Internet Votes*** and that`s just listing a few!

More recently you were cast in ***Killer`s Freedom*** with the extremely well known and accomplished actor Michael Madsen and talented actress Rachel Hunter, as well as Lazar Rockwood, Jennifer Dale and Tony Pearce! My friend Jenny McShane has worked with Michael Madsen in the past as well but what was your experience like working on that project, and who are some of the actors and actresses you admire most and would love to create with?

Elham Madani: Great question, all of them are great, because they are doing hard work but I would love to work with Robert De Niro, Al Pacino, Dustin Hoffman, Johnny Depp, Tom Hanks, and Keanu Reeves and may I add Bollywood actors too?

I`d also love to act with Amita Bachan, Salman Khan, Shahroukh Khan, Amir Khan as well and Meryl Streep, Jodie Foster, are two of my favorite actress. I dream to be in the next

James Cameron, Steven Spielberg movies too!

Chase Von: I know at present you are still in Canada Elie, but that you do want to come to the US and further pursue your dream in actual Hollywood! How do you like living there and how soon do you think you`ll be here in America?

And also, your parents obviously didn`t know, or weren`t very understanding of your chosen profession, but what advice would you give to people who know they want to pursue something that will make them happy, but aren`t getting the support from others or even worse, face ridicule for even thinking about it?

Elham Madani: Yes Chase, of course I moved to Canada only to pursue my deep long term desire to do my best and use this highest energy that is burning in me to cry out and say here it is!

There is a star who wants to be discovered in the galaxy! (Smile.)

And about your second question? Yes again, this is exactly my story! Not only did none of my family or friends support me---

But also tried to mock at me some in a way but I never gave up and I believed in my hidden desire and dreams and power!

So my advice is that people do what they want and not what they might think would please others. It OK however in this movie business to have other educations and job skills to run your life as well in the beginning until you truly establish yourself. But if you don`t ever try Chase, you won`t ever know!

And yes, some might think I am so crazy because I left my PHD and now I am here and ready to get a break and move to Hollywood! When? I should be ready after April 2011 when I finish my project here.

I`m working on a theatrical project and also different types of modeling projects like lingerie, classical looks, part modeling like hands, eyes and feet right now, but as I mentioned before, I`d love more camera work, so we`ll see what will be my gift from Santa Claus and hopefully it will be happy news for 2011 and 2012 in Hollywood! (Smile.)

Chase Von: Great answer Elie and often we see people who appear to be living their dreams, but having interviewed quite a number of people, I know quite a few who have not only had no support from those you would think would be close to them--- But who have strained relationships with parents, siblings and even supposed friends because they are pursuing what they themselves want in life! Granted, success is the best revenge but reaching that next level isn`t made any easier if you don`t have people supporting you.

I`m also interviewing the amazing Kimberlee Morton and her attitude has been to prove everyone that has anything negative to say about her pursuits--- Wrong! (Smile.)

Are there any projects you have in the works now, you can give are readers a heads up about? Or are you waiting to get to the States to really get going?

Elham Madani: Yes, I am working on a theatrical project named ***The Conference of the Birds*** by a very successful Canadian-Persian director, Dear Soheil Parsa and I have an attorney role and some commercials, however, my aim is to get leading roles in feature movies in Hollywood. You know, there are many good subjects around or about the Middle-East and USA--- And I will be a very good, strong choice for those kind of movies. As a person who lived over there and knows the cultures very well besides knowing the languages.

But about your other question, here I should add, beside all of those other elements, like unsupportive friends and family in my case Chase, there were also governmental issues, community and cultural points of view as well. As I mentioned before, I had big, big barriers!

Just thinking about that I left all my family members, friends, my permanent job--- Even my PHD just to get more opportunities to be seen universally!

Oh My! But success needs big sacrificing and lots of passion does it not? So it wouldn`t be fair if I do not have a big break! What do you think? (Ha Ha.)

But I do have one good supporter--- You know who? My big talented singing Parrot! She also loves the camera like me and starts making kissing poses when I turn it on and loves singing--- She even sings *Diamonds Are a Girl`s Best Friend* by Marilyn Monroe! (Smile.)

And most of the time when I wake up or come home; she is asking me what is your name Mama? And she answers it, "Superstar."

That of course makes me smile and more motivated when a bird can discover my talent--- Why not directors? (Ha, Ha!)

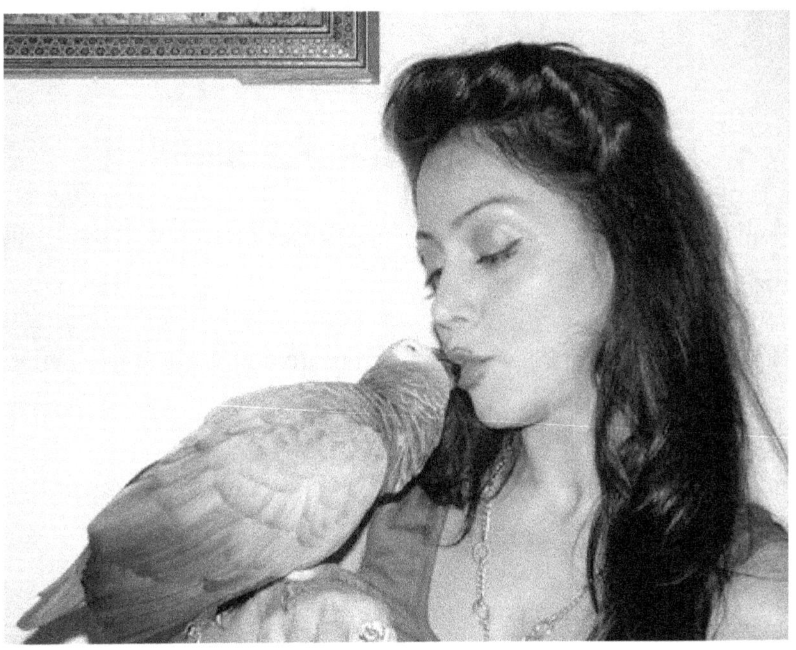

Chase Von: Lucky Bird! (Smile.) But you know you have me, my co author Betty Dravis and I can only see your fan base growing as more people see your exotic beauty Elie!

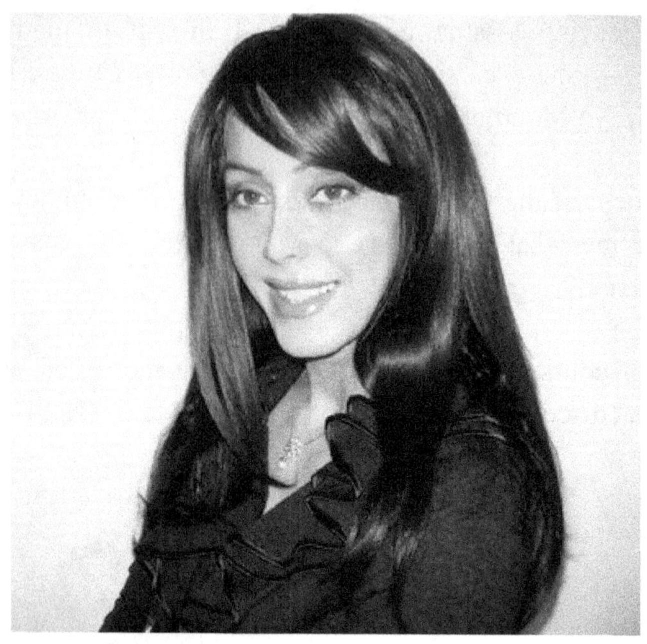

What are some of your links, or web sites where people can learn more about you Elie?

Elham Madani: People can learn more about me at my IMDb page here,

http://www.imdb.com/name/nm3354774/resume and also these as well Chase ---

http://www.youtube.com/user/souniama1?feature=mhum#p/u

http://elhammadani.workbooklive.com/Home.aspx

http://www.facebook.com/home.php?#!/elhammadani

Chase Von: I always try and ask a tough one Elie, so the one I have for you is the Ambassador of India, after her experience in an American Airport, said she would not ever visit the United States again!

I think we all understand the need for security in today`s age but I think that what is taking place is ridiculous! What are your thoughts on that and also, because beautiful women, children, elderly and those with physical disabilities etc seem to be being singled out, are you flying or driving when you make your move to the United States?

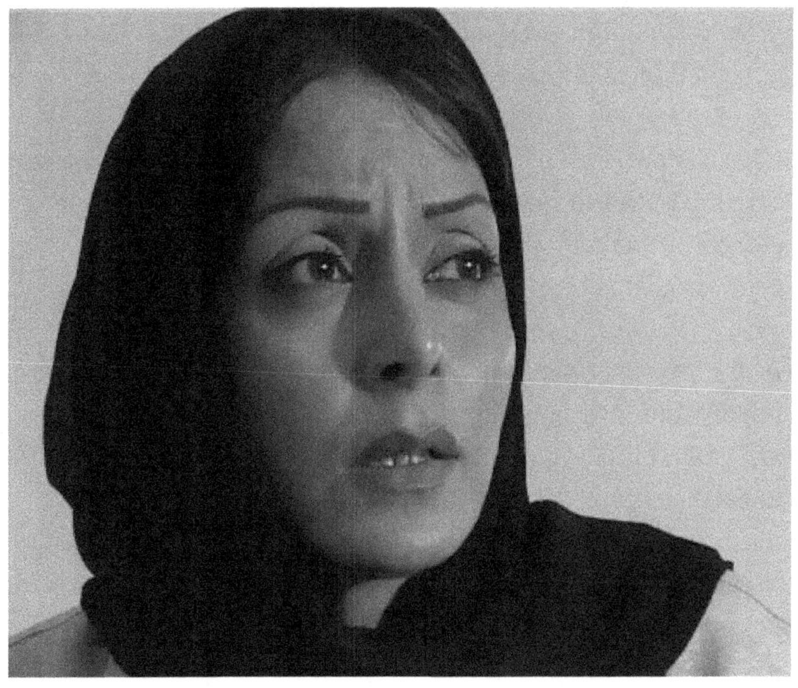

Actress Elham (Elie) Madani in *I Know You Will Come*

Elham Madani: As far as I know the reason was her "Traditional Dress"--- Meaning she was wearing a long dress named Sari. That seemed for the security people to make it look like she was kind of hiding something illegal or maybe some harmful things.

Of course it is not right for a respected Ambassador to be treated that way and I feel she has every reason to be upset about it! But in my case, I think I will have to fly otherwise I might not get there as soon as I would like. It would take weeks or more of driving.

What do you think? Or maybe I can borrow an invisible cloak or something and perhaps by pass the investigation? (Smile.)

Chase Von: I think in all honesty Elie, if they are in fact singling out beautiful women--- You are certainly going to get picked! Thanks for sharing your perspective on that very controversial subject.

And now, what would you say if you were standing before a microphone and could be heard by every child on the planet, and regardless of what language they spoke, they would understand you?

What positive advice would you give the children, if that were possible?

Elham Madani: This is my message and it is not only for kids--- That after any bitterness, there is better happiness and after any breakage, there is a big victory! After any closed door there is an opened door and just have hope and try to get to your goals in a way not to hurt yourself and anybody else!

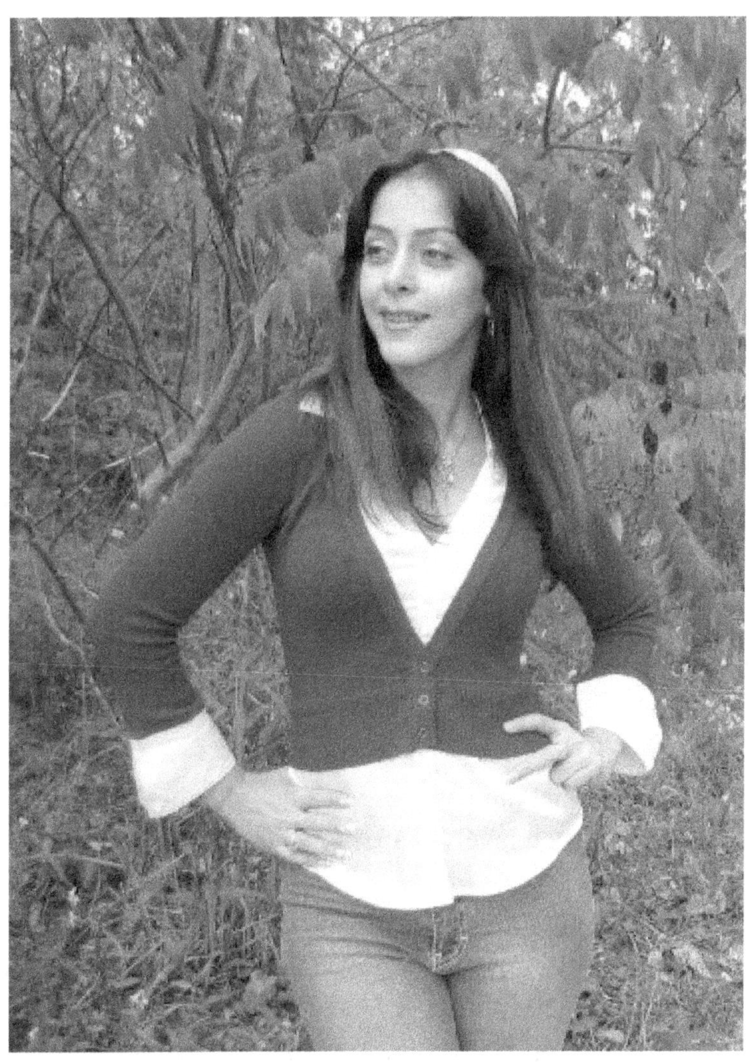

Meaning by hurting--- You don`t do drugs and no violent actions! Or anything that will take you away from who you really are is not good for you! Be yourself at all times because that is your success already because no one is you! And don`t use too much alcohol or any kind of drug that will take your real "Self" away from you!

Because if you do not like yourself--- Do you think drugs or abnormal things will help you or make you better or change you into something you do like? Not at all!

Only you and just you only can make YOU a better person! And one more thing, I hate this philosophy when the parents get old enough the children make an excuse and leave them in nursery homes! It is not right at all! They raised you when you were small and weak and unable to do anything for yourself! Is that OK now for you to leave them alone if they do not want it?

I will refer all to a movie that touched my heart a lot! Named ***Bagheban*** acted beautifully by Hema Malini and Amitabh Bachchan for you to watch!

Chase Von: What are some of your favorite meals? And how do you stay in such lovely shape? (Smile.)

Elham Madani: I do love "Spicy" foods Chase like Indian food (Cari-Tandoori) a lot! (Smile.) It is why I am spicy too! (Ha, Ha!) But seriously, I am in shape because of walking too much shopping for dresses, jewelry, that I love a lot! As I mentioned before, Diamonds Are a Girl`s Best Friend! (Smile.)

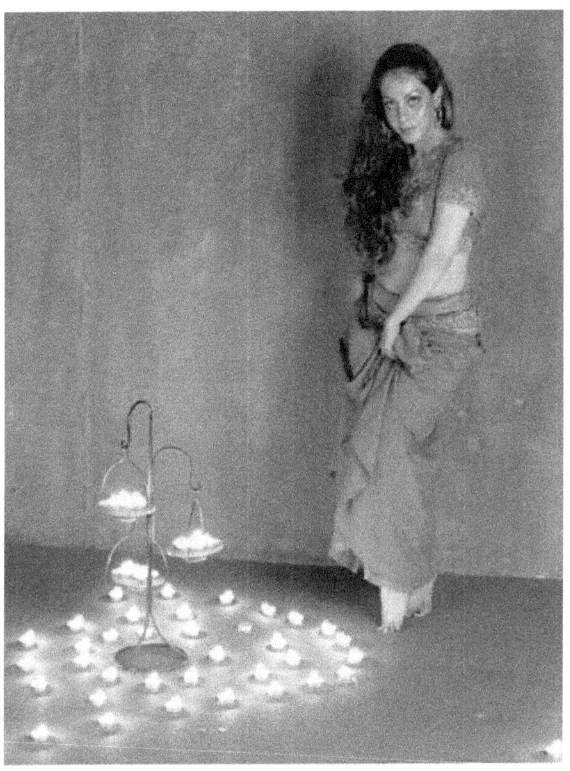

But acting classes and walking around the city just finding the places for auditioning in Toronto will help you lose all your fat as well! (Ironically!)

Chase Von: I know you`re a model and actress, but is there the possibility you might be putting out any music CD`s in the future Elie? And if so, what type of music do you think you will be recording to share with this world of ours?

Elham Madani: OH Yeah! I have very good vocal cords for singing! I am now learning how to sing and also different types of dancing. I do love Country Music and Pop Music and of course Bollywood music and dances a lot! I do think it depends on discovering what vein I can go the furthest in.

Maybe one style will work better for me than others since English is not my first language.

Chase Von: Looking forward to hearing that Elie and thank you so much for finding the time to share yourself with our readers. I`m truly wishing you continued success and also looking forward to seeing you in more movies here!

On behalf of myself and the ***SOP***, I truly appreciate you making time for this and don`t be a stranger Lady and wishing you a wonderful Holiday Season!

Elham Madani: I appreciate your time and you generously giving me a chance to say some parts of my story. And also share my ambitions and my looking forward to getting an opportunity to make a life in movies! Hopefully one day I will also be able to share a very hopeful and positive story of a girl who survived after many very hard times in her life.

Although most people would think of her as only a luxuriously spoiled girl Chase, but I know better because that girl is me. Thank you so much again for this opportunity and I thank the *Student Operated Press* as well and wish all Happy Holidays and you know I will stay in touch with you my friend! (Smile.)

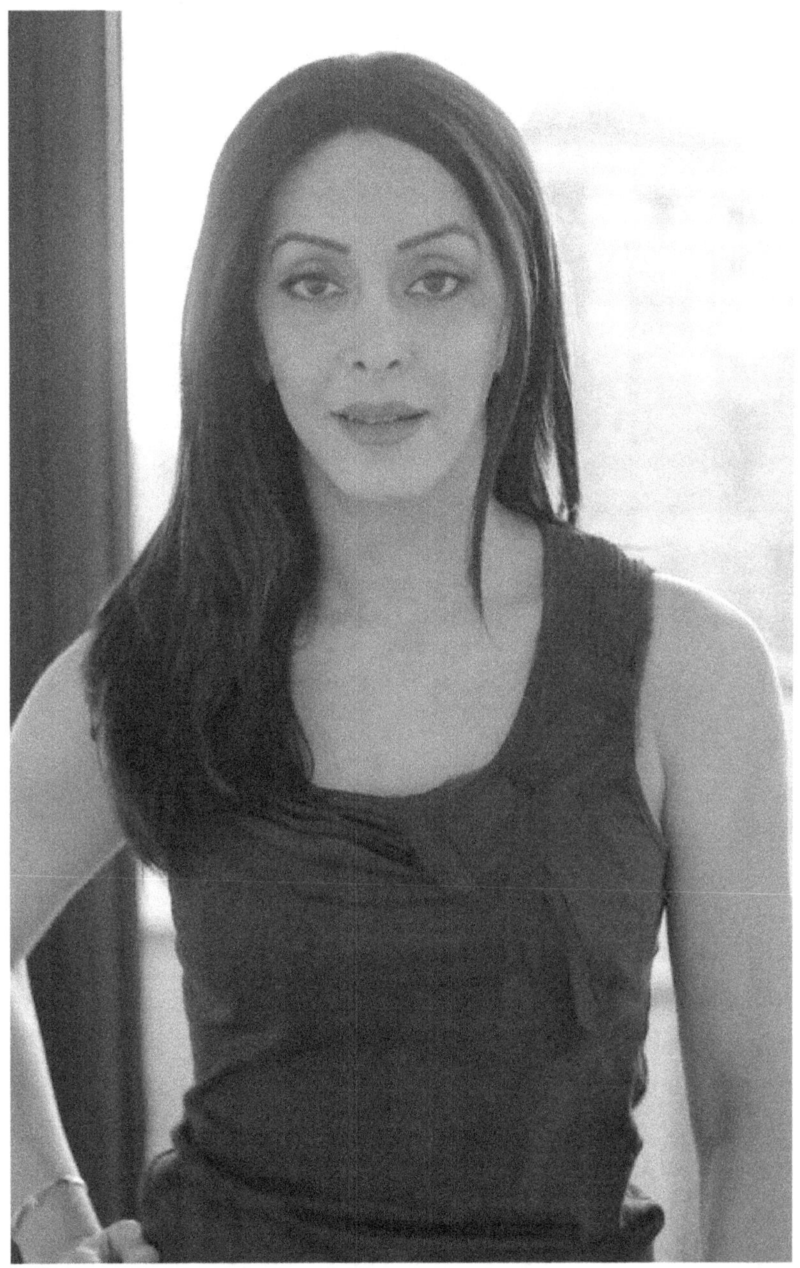

Interview with Gretchen Hirsch

AUTHOR OF *BACK AGAIN TO ME* AND MORE

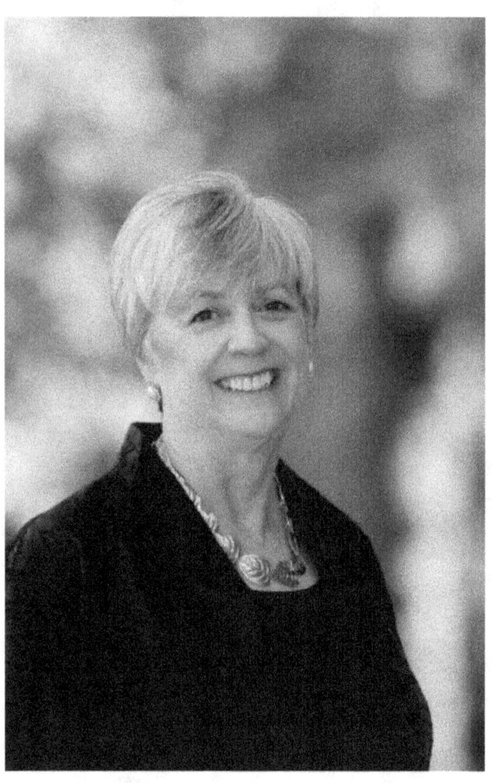

Chase Von: Hello Gretchen, on behalf of the Student Operated Press and myself, I want to thank you for fitting this into your hectic schedule and finding some time to share yourself with our readers. I know you`re really busy concentrating on your new release called *Back Again To Me* and how important this book, of the seven books you`ve written or collaborated on, is to you.

I also truly admire the choice you`re making with this book and the cause you wish to support with some of the proceeds from it, but before we discuss your latest work, can you tell our readers what your younger years were like growing up? Was that in the Midwest? And when did you know that writing was going to be such a major part of your life?

Gretchen Hirsch: I started writing in the third grade. I adored my teacher, Miss Martha Unkel, and in one of my report cards she mentioned to my parents that she wished she could get me to write because I loved to read so much. That`s all I needed to hear. Starting that day, I wrote a book, fourteen chapters, I believe, that had something to do with a girl and a horse. If you put me under hypnosis, I might be able to recall it, but otherwise, it`s a blank. Anyway, whenever I finished a chapter, Miss Unkel let me read it to the class, which was pretty heady stuff for an eight-year-old. After that, though, I didn`t write again, except for school and college papers, until I was in my thirties. I had other exceptional teachers, too, who taught me the mechanics of how sentences and paragraphs go together.

So while writing is never easy (I`ve always said it`s like digging a trench with a teaspoon) at least I don`t struggle with the basic elements.

I`d characterize my early childhood as idyllic. We lived on a street with lots of kids of all ages and both sexes, and we all did things together, especially in the summer. We ran the neighborhood streets from morning until night, perfectly safely. Our parents weren`t worried about where we were because we were on our street, in and out of everyone`s houses all day long. We spent hours playing kick the can and softball, riding our bikes (without helmets), and going to a place we called "the Hole," which really was just a big ravine, to explore. Reading, swimming pretty much all day every hot summer day, dance lessons (I thought I`d be a dancer for a while, and then I realized the sacrifices that would require and also realized I wasn`t willing to make them). Lots of time in our little library, which is still there, even though the town now has one of the top library systems in the state. And when I go into that tiny library today, it still smells exactly the same as it did when I was five. As I grew up, of course, there was all the angst that accompanies middle school and the ups and downs of high school, but it was a great place and time to be a young person. There was a tremendous amount of cooperation between home, school, church, and even the police department, and almost all my friends grew up well and have lived productive lives.

Chase Von: You`ve written or co-written seven books! I`ve interviewed my share of authors and I don`t think any of them has accomplished that yet! (Smile.) I know my co-author Betty Dravis wants to write at least six because she`s also had six children and like many authors, she feels like her books are children as well, and I`ve often told others when I write a poem, song lyrics, quotes or a story, or a book they do feel like my children, because they are creations that came from me.

But what I want to ask is, you`ve written *Woman Hours: A 21-Day Time Management Plan That Works; Talking Your*

Way To The Top, alone; *Helping Gifted Children Soar, A Practical Guide For Parents and Teachers* with co-author PH.D Carol Ann Strip, which is also available in Spanish (and Korean); *A Love for Learning: Motivation and the Gifted Child* with her as the co-author, as well (although she must have gotten married since her last name changed to Whitney); *Bud Wilkinson: An Intimate Portrait of an American Legend* with co-author Jay Wilkinson; *The Complete Idiot`s Guide to Difficult Conversations* and your latest, *Back Again To Me*, both solely by yourself.

But what was it like for you to hold your very first book in your hands? And do they feel like children to you also?

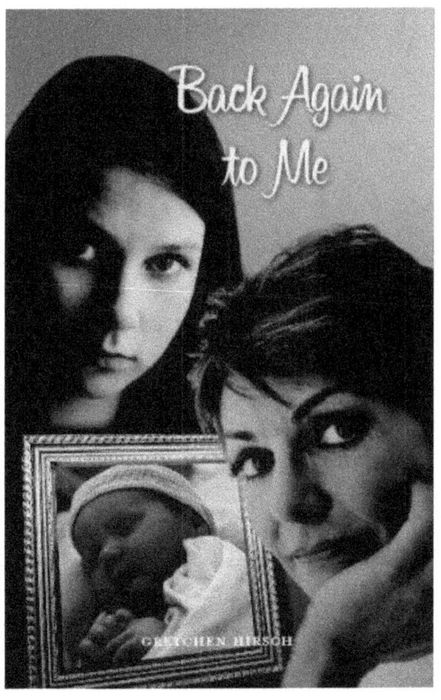

Gretchen Hirsch: Goodness, it was a long time ago, and it was such a freakish thing. I had developed a course in time management for women and someone said I should write a book about it. So I did. And then I sent it "the complete manuscript, not a proposal "to an old friend from high school who was working in publishing in New York. And I sent it to her house! Talk about doing everything wrong. After three months, she took it off her coffee table; gave it to a reader, who liked it, and then forwarded it to an agent friend. It took the agent eleven tries, but she got the job done and *Woman Hours* was published by St. Martin`s Press. I remember how much I loved my editor and going to New York to meet her and my agent (who I`d known only from the phone), seeing the cover design and loving it, touring a little, doing some speaking. It was a great experience.

I don`t think of my books as my children. They are my work and I love creating them and, yes, there is a long labor period, but holding a book, at least for me, is not like holding a child. (And that comes through very clearly in *Back Again to Me.*)

Chase Von: I couldn`t agree with you more Gretch, and considering your work for gifted children, it seems natural that your latest book is to help all children. Now back to *Back Again To Me* --- Karen Joan your niece who introduced us, told me she had read the manuscript draft for this roughly fifteen years ago and loved it then. But in order for it to be more with our current times, did you have to go in and modernize quite a bit of it? I`m thinking fifteen years ago people didn`t have computers, and family entertainment was everyone gathering around the radio in the living room. (Heh-Heh.) But seriously, a lot has changed in this world of ours from now to then, so did you have to alter it to be more receptive for today`s world?

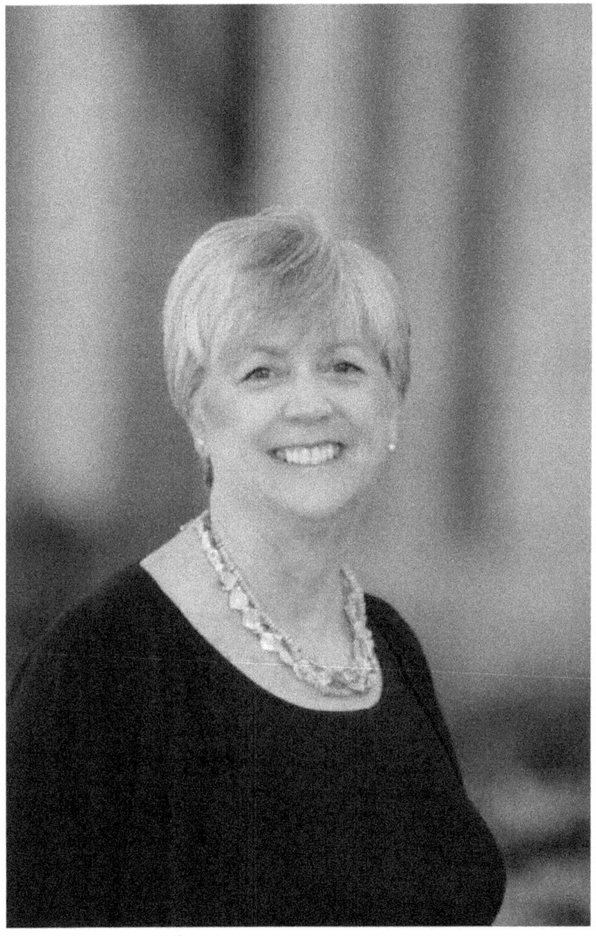

Gretchen Hirsch: This book was long in its gestation, that`s for sure. The book Karen saw was not the book I have now.

What she read all those years ago I now would characterize as a really, really long outline. In the intervening years, I`ve expanded and refined it as I had time, because in those years I also was writing all the nonfiction; working in hospital marketing; getting my own kids launched; welcoming all my grandchildren; going through some really horrendous times during my parents` illnesses and deaths (and without my sister, those days would pretty much have done me in); watching my husband survive a health crisis, and then having a period of illness of my own that took a couple of years to diagnose and a couple more to cure.

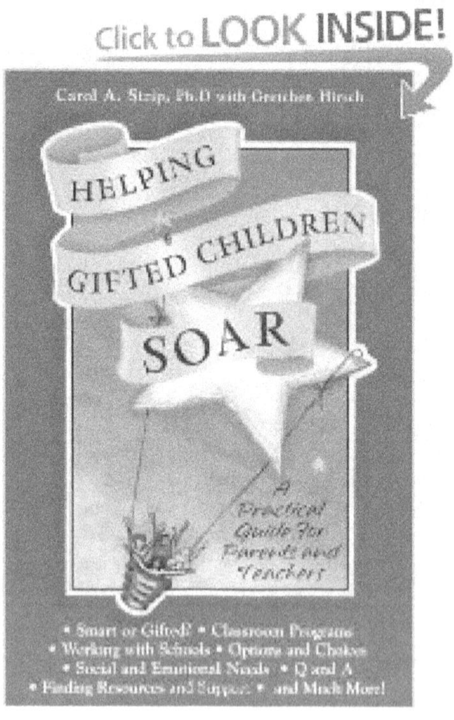

Actually, I didn`t have to change much of the manuscript at all because the action takes place in 1985, and events that happened then were set in stone. Interestingly, there have been some very large changes in the last two-three months about issues the book touches on, but they aren`t retroactive, so I didn`t have to rip the book off the press to address them.

Chase Von: Who are some the writers you truly admire and look up to? And for that matter, people in general that you feel have been mentors and positive influences in your life?

Gretchen Hirsch: Well, I`ve mentioned Miss Unkel, but there was also a high school teacher who had a big influence and who tried to get me to widen my literary horizons. My parents, who were the smartest and most loving people I`ve ever known, were hugely influential in every aspect of my life. As I said, they`re both gone now, but I still feel their presence every day of my life.

I loved Shakespeare in high school and college, and still do, but I haven`t read everything. A pivotal moment in literature for me was sitting down in college one afternoon to read "The Wasteland," with the references spread out all around me. It was eye-opening, mind-blowing, and all the other clichés. I loved it, but my favorite poem is "The Love Song of J. Alfred Prufrock." It`s the first poem I ever read that moved me to tears. So I`d say Eliot was an influence. My tastes are eclectic, from Ann Patchett to Pat Conroy to Sidney Sheldon. I like fiction and nonfiction; I`m currently reading Wally Lamb`s *The Hour I First Believed.* It`s harrowing, but very good. I`ve always liked Susan Isaacs` writing. I love David Sedaris, especially *Me Talk Pretty One Day*. I just finished his *When You Are Engulfed in Flames.* Humor writing is a mystery to me, and I`m entranced by someone who can do it well.

Chase Von: Without giving too much away, can you share with our readers the general premise? And why this book, unlike many books, incorporates so much more than just an unwed young mother, baby and adoption? Why is it of interest to all women and men, for that matter, and the variety of ways it touches on just about every aspect of all our lives?

Gretchen Hirsch: In essence, this book is about women and the ways we relate to each other as mothers and daughters, sisters, and friends, and also to the men in our lives. The story is simple: The narrator, Corrin, is a widowed working mom with a sixteen-year-old daughter, Shelley. Shelley is clearly a highly gifted child, but she becomes pregnant. The rest of the book is about the decision the family must make about keeping the child or surrendering him for adoption. It`s about hard choices and growing up. Shelley grows up but Corrin does also. It`s not a saga, but it covers a fairly wide sweep of time, from the Forties through the Sixties, into the Eighties to 2008.

It is most definitely *not* my own story, but it`s informed by what we talked about "what it was like to grow up in the suburban Midwest, then and now.

Chase Von: Just from my own life, I know " I have a son (Jamel) from my wife`s previous marriage, and two between us and still, he`s, in my opinion, my son. He`s also an honor-roll student and he`s been invited to be in *The United States Achievement Academy of Who`s Who`s In Foreign Language.* But what I`m getting at is that most the families you meet nowadays are pieces of families, in a sense. Rarely do you meet someone who is with his or her actual biological mother *and* father.

Do you think our society`s current system is largely to blame for this? I mean, there used to be a time when the man brought home the bacon, so to speak, and the woman maintained the home.

Nowadays both have to work, the children are often raised by schools and babysitters, and in reality, if you really think about it, both parents often spend more time with co-workers of the opposite sex than they do with their own spouses Or at least awake, quality times *Usually* when someone gets home from a long, hard day, the last thing they want is to be sociable. What are your thoughts on that?

Gretchen Hirsch: I`m not sure anything is to blame. Families are not necessarily "worse," but you`re right, families are different. By the time my husband and I had been married ten years, half the couples we knew who were married around the same time were divorced. Most of them went on to successful second marriages. I know many, many intact families who are very happy and into their second and third generation. I know intact families who are miserable. I know single moms and children who are doing fine and single moms and children who

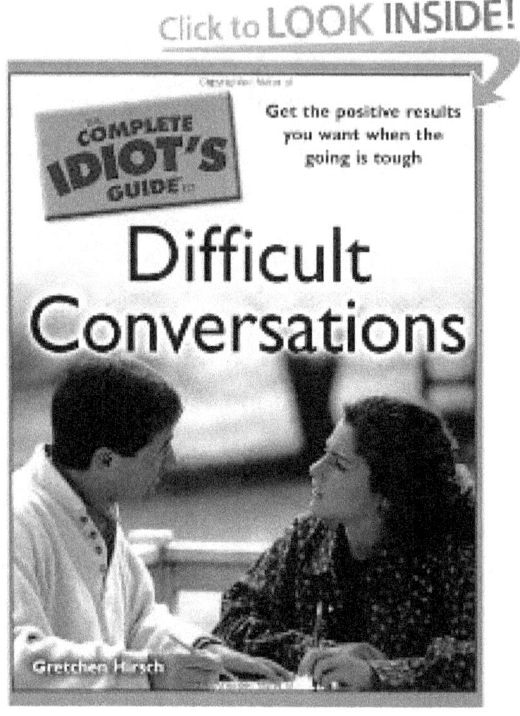

don`t get along at all. I know kids who have managed divorce well and kids who have been damaged. Were all the marriages that adhered to the role division you mention successful? I`m sure they weren`t, but it wasn`t discussed so freely. I do feel we have lost a sense of commitment to relationships, and I worry a little about the coming generation who do so well with cyberspace relationships, but often have difficulty navigating the world of real-time give-and-take with real people. Life is hard and commitment is hard, but many people today seem to want everything to be easy. I think the recession has in some ways pointed out that what really matters is not the stuff we acquire, but the quality of our relationships. It`s been a kick in the pants for a lot of people. Hard times can destroy, but they can also result in stronger families if people make a commitment to one another.

Chase Von: I think you will find this despicable, but I learned of this by listening to the Alex Jones Radio show.

DYFS or the Division of Youth and Family Services along with CPS have been accused of some horrendous things, which is why I think your book and the goal you have for helping children is so admirable. But what are your thoughts on this Gretchen?

http://www.youtube.com/watch?v=KrCWIcZbfUQ&feature=r elated

And this?
http://www.youtube.com/watch?v=Nub5R4LCio8&feature=rel ated

The reason I share this is because it pertains to children with their parents, but I also know that many of the children that are in CPS are given many of these drugs as well.

This is a more direct story:
http://www.youtube.com/watch?v=esfxq4vLxrw

And this:
http://www.youtube.com/watch?v=ekKSrJxYfNk

This too is horrible:
http://www.youtube.com/watch?v=hcgwHa1GPF0&feature=related

Gretchen Hirsch: I appreciate your sense of outrage about many of these issues. I share it. However, I number among my friends some foster parents who are wonderful, dedicated people, and I believe we can`t tar an entire group of people with the same brush, which is what is happening to American discourse today. We demonize and insult without regard for the exceptions.

It`s dangerous and frightening.

On the other hand, I`m always astonished when I read horror stories and find that those charged with the day-to-day management of child placements can be so oblivious to conditions. I wonder if they are even making the home visits.

Yet, on the third hand, I recently spoke with a young woman in a social service agency not related to foster care who now, because of budget cuts, has an enormous caseload scattered over a huge geographic area. So the problems are systemic as well as specific, and this country needs to figure out what its priorities are.

Chase Von: I don`t believe your book delves this deeply into the issues of adoption as listed above in some of the videos, but the flip side of that is your book and your contributions to the Dave Thomas Foundation for Adoption, which was founded by Dave Thomas, who founded the famous Wendy`s Restaurants is also going to be helping others so that they don`t have to endure the things some of these people above have had to endure. (One of the few fast food places I really like, mind you, and love the chili) (Smile.)

A best friend of mine from high school who is, unfortunately, no longer with us had a little brother that was picked up and taken by the Division of Youth and Family Services. He turned out okay and is now not only a school teacher but also a talented Christian rapper going by the stage name of *The Tcha.*

Well, he has absolutely nothing good to say about his experiences there.

This is a link to his MySpace page where our readers can find his song “Thankful”... http://www.myspace.com/thetcha --- He speaks candidly in one of his songs regarding it. But the reason I share this is the subject of your book truly does touch on so many things and just from learning of it, it has rekindled memories of things that need to be changed.

Have you always been someone who is unafraid to do something to make lives better for those whom you don`t even know, Gretchen?

Gretchen Hirsch: I`m afraid I`m not as brave as you make me out to be. *Back Again to Me* is about one child in one family "and there was no particular risk to me in writing it. It`s a novel that I hope people will enjoy reading; I hope it might make them think about the consequences of teen pregnancy, which is on the rise again after years of decline. Of all the developed nations, the U.S. has the highest rate of teen pregnancy, and statistics tell us that more than eighty percent of teen pregnancies are unintended. If a teen chooses not to terminate the pregnancy, different families make different decisions about what to do: raise the child in his or her family of origin, with help from the grandparents; open adoption; closed adoption; and some options in between. *Back Again to Me* is about one choice. Recently, there has been an MTV show called *16 and Pregnant* that provides a graphic glimpse about what happens when a baby has a baby. Some people say it glamorizes teen pregnancy, while others feel it`s a cautionary tale, but whatever the differing opinions, it`s pretty powerful stuff, as to-be moms and dads find out what this decision is all about.

Chase Von: Where can our readers learn more about you? You`re various links to your websites and do you have any future projects you are working on that you can share with our readers?

Gretchen Hirsch: I do. In addition to my day job in university communications, I`m also a book doctor, working with other authors to make their books as strong as possible for submission to agents or editors or even for self-publishing.

I have one of those projects now and am hoping for another one or two soon. In addition, I`m outlining a new book called *The Prayer Chain*, which is a novel about some women who belong to such a group. And that`s all I can say, except that it`s set in the same town and some of the same characters will be part of the story.

They won`t be the focus, but they`ll be around. I thought it would be only two, but another let me know yesterday that she expects to be in this book. Characters do that, and you generally have to let them have their way. My website and blog are at www.gretchenhirsch.com, and my business website is www.midwestbookdocs.com.

Chase Von: What are some of your favorite meals? And I know you mentioned the Midwest in your book trailer and how most people aren`t aware of its beauty and just see it as something to fly over to get from one place of importance to another.

But are there some meals that are common there as well to the natives? (Heh-Heh.)

Sounds like I`m making the Midwest akin to the Wastelands in Australia, huh?

But seriously, I know I think of my grandmother and Virginia when I think of batter bread or as she used to call it, "Spoon Bread" and salted fish --- I really miss her cooking.

Gretchen Hirsch: There is nothing better in the world than Ohio sweet corn and tomatoes, so I try to find as many uses for those as I can, in season. Heaven is a grilled cheese, fresh tomato, fresh basil, and bacon sandwich. Or rustic soup, made with bread and tomatoes. Sweet corn picked fresh in the morning and in the pot as soon as possible. Or cut off the cob and creamed or sautéed very simply. And in the winter, lovely, hearty beef stew with caramelized vegetables.

Or a great meatloaf with baked or roasted potatoes and green beans. Or a whole chicken in the rotisserie. Not too much tofu in our lives, although we`d probably be healthier if there were.

My daughter and son-in-law and their son lived with us for a while. My son-in-law is a culinary-school-trained chef, although that`s not what he does for a living, and he taught me a lot about eating first with the eyes (and the nose) and how taking the time makes even the simplest food a feast. I make a mean from-scratch brownie and my grandson`s favorite mac and cheese, which does not come from a blue box.

My son recently has gone into the dipping sauce/wing sauce/marinade business (www.mrstew.com), and though I, generally, am not crazy about spicy food, this stuff is terrific!

Flavor first and heat back instead of the other way around. I`m very impressed with his recipes and his resolve, so I`m learning how to incorporate the sauces.

Chase Von: What are some of the other causes you feel very strongly about and support? I know you are very involved with educating the public and parents on gifted children, and your recent book and proceeds from it going to the Dave

Thomas Foundation for Adoption is truly admirable. But are there any other causes that you plan to aid in the future?

Gretchen Hirsch: Not all the proceeds are going to the Foundation, just part of them from the opening week. I intend to share proceeds with organizations or charities for every live or online event I do. Sometime those charities will be chosen by those who invite me to speak, and sometimes I`ll select them. I`m partial to charities that do the hands-on work "food pantries", for example.

I am very concerned about gifted kids. We have a lot of them in our family, and much of the educational emphasis today is concerned with bringing underachieving kids to proficiency.

But children who already are past proficiency when they enter a grade level sometimes get very short shrift. Some educators believe that gifted kids will "get it on their own." Sometimes they do, but sometimes they lose their motivation to learn in school if they aren`t adequately challenged.

They can end up as classic underachievers and sometimes even in the justice system. That`s a terrible loss. So I hope the books I`ve written with Carol Strip Whitney raise some awareness of those issues.

Chase Von: How important is family to you, and what is your take on the state of our current world?

Gretchen Hirsch: My family is everything to me. I have been lucky enough to live in the same city, Columbus, Ohio, all my life, and my family here goes backward and forward for six generations.

For my entire life, I was surrounded by my parents, grandparents, even my great-grandmother, my sister and brother-in-law and their children, and then my kids and grandchildren. My husband`s family also goes back the same number of generations here. In fact, both families have been in Columbus since the 1850s. My son and daughter and their spouses and children all lived here for a time, but my son and his wife and kids moved south a few years ago. I`m happy to say they are back in Ohio, less than two hours away, so it`s almost as good as having them in the same city. I was really missing out on knowing my only granddaughter, and I`m thrilled to be able to see her and her brothers much more frequently. I used to take care of the boys a great deal, but my granddaughter was born in the South, and I knew her far less well. Now we`re making up for lost time. My daughter and her husband and son are ten minutes away. My sister and brother-in-law are even closer. At one time, we actually lived across the street from one another and still managed to give each other privacy.

My grandson attends the same school system that housed his mother and me and my mother. I`ve always said I`m Ohio born, Ohio bred, and when I`m gone, Ohio dead. Deep roots here.

My take on the world? Today is a frightening time. It`s also exhilarating. We have it within our power right now to cure diseases, promote justice, and save the planet. If we`re not stupid

Chase Von: What would you say if you were standing before a microphone that could be heard by every child on the planet, and regardless of what language they spoke, they would understand you?

What positive advice would you give the children, if that were possible?

Gretchen Hirsch: Education opens every door and is the key to a productive life. Respect the worth and dignity of every human being. We all have different talents, and we need to appreciate the gifts we see in others. Don`t be too concerned with material goods. They ebb and flow. Concentrate on what`s timeless "and beyond time.

Chase Von: I`ve slowed down on interviewing for personal reasons and to promote my latest book with my talented co-author Betty Dravis. Guess you could call it ME TIME but to be more specific, it`s a joint effort, so it`s more like WE TIME.

I don`t think it would be fair of me to have her doing all the marketing alone, and marketing a book as you certainly know, is where the work part comes into play for us writers.

But when your niece Karen Joan, who is a friend to both me and Betty, contacted me and told me about your book and what you were doing, I felt I had to make an exception and do my little part in this. I do hope it helps spread the word because I can think of nothing more important in our world than our children.

Gretch, which you gave me permission to call you the first day we met, on behalf of the Student Operated Press and myself, thanks for sharing yourself and your truly worthy mission with our readers. I wish you all the success the world can provide in this worthy endeavor you have taken on, and I hope many children benefit from your immense talent and truly charitable heart.

Gretchen Hirsch: Thank you, too. This has been a real pleasure. And I have some catching up to do on your work. I`ll look forward to it.

"--- writing is never easy--- I`ve always said it`s like digging a trench with a teaspoon---"

--- Gretchen Hirsch

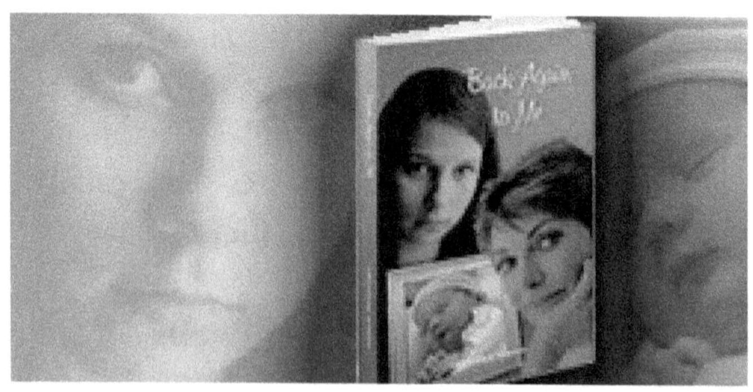

Interview with Alexa Dectis

BEAUTIFUL SINGER, ACTRESS AND MORE

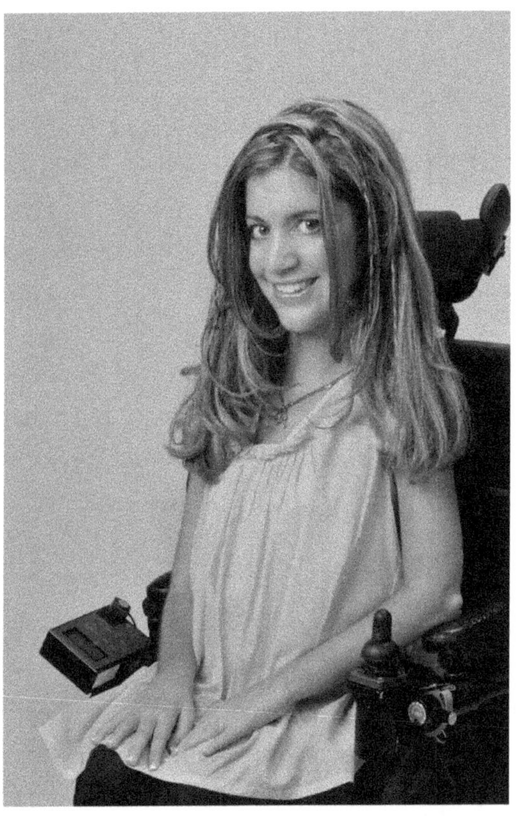

Chase Von: Hey there Alexa and on behalf of the Student Operated Press and myself, thanks so much for finding the time to share yourself with our readers! Our mutual friend Jessica Gilbert shared you with me, and when I first saw your picture I thought what a beauty! Sure you get that all the time though. (Smile.)

I also know you have so many different things you`re working on so again, thanks so much for finding the time to do this interview.

Alexa Dectis: Of course! Thank you! I am so happy to be here!

Chase Von: I have to tell you that when I first went to your my space page, Jessica didn`t tell me you were in a wheel chair. I also have to honestly admit that initially, I felt badly for you, but the more I`ve learned about you the less I feel that way.

Hope that didn`t come out the wrong way but what I`m trying to say is you are truly such an inspirational young woman, that people don`t feel sorry for you once they get to know you, they feel inspired!

I`ve also introduced you to my friend Poet Dawn Huffaker, author of Flights of Fancy and also Flower Escapes along with an incredibly gifted photographer named Michele Duncan. (I can honestly say, I`ve seen flowers all my life it seems, but the gift Michele has for taking pictures, coupled with the gift Dawn has for writing nature poetry, made me feel like I was seeing the beauty that flowers possess for the first time)! Like yourself, Dawn has been in a wheel chair the majority of her life but also like you, she hasn`t let that stop her from achieving and making this world a better more beautiful place! You sing, you act, you`re also an artist and you were so determined to raise the funds for your new CD that you even

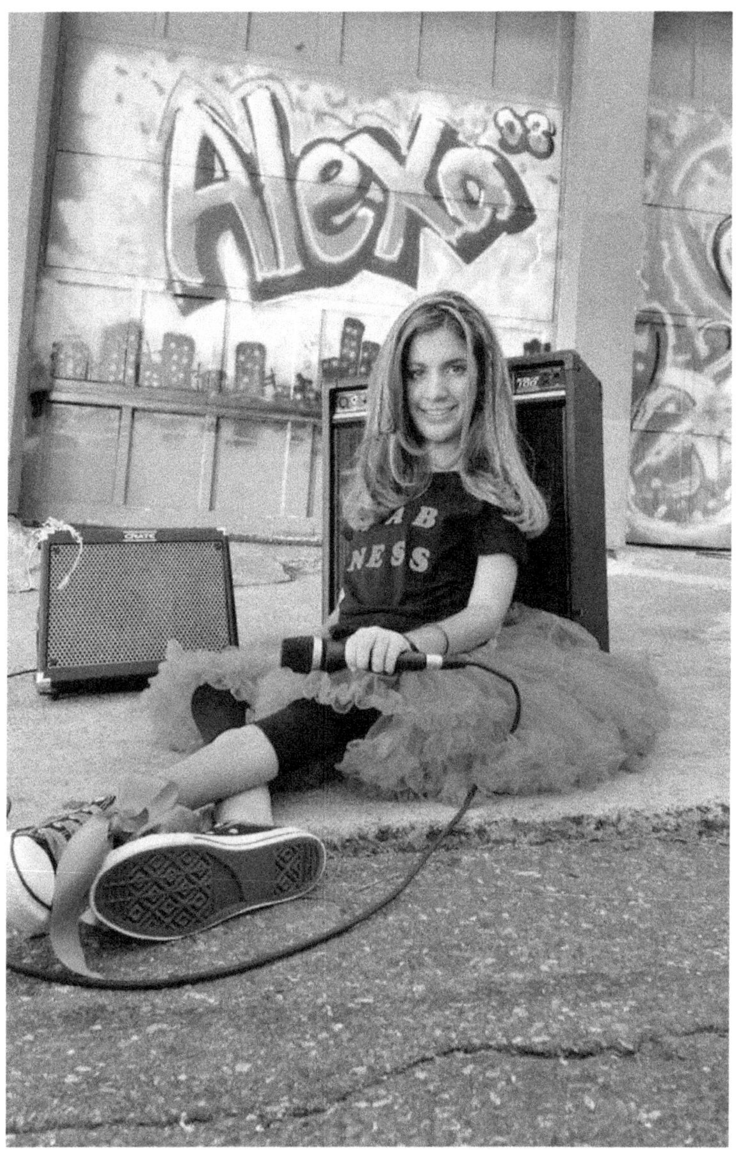

sang on the streets of Manhattan to raise money for it! Where does this incredible drive you have come from Alexa? And

I`ve read you decided to embrace your Spinal Muscular Atrophy when you were just five years old as a gift. Can you tell our readers more about what made you see it that way?

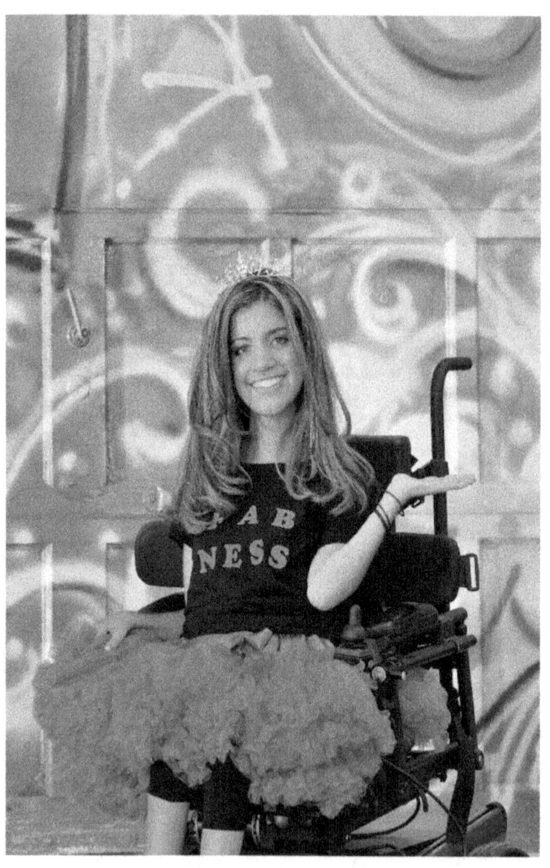

Alexa Dectis: Once I was old enough to understand what Spinal Muscular Atrophy was, I had a choice to make. I could either hate it or embrace it. I chose to embrace it. When I was five years old, I learned meditation. I also began to explore what my purpose in life was. I realized that my purpose in life was to inspire others. God did not put me in this chair because he wanted me to be sad. Before I was born, God helped me choose my life. This was the life I chose with God.

Once I realized what my purpose in life was, I made it my lifelong mission to inspire others. I am never going to stop until my mission is completed.

Chase Von: I have to tell you Alexa, in many ways you remind me of another young lady, and child prodigy by the name of Akiane Kramarik. She also has a deep love for God and you both have such beautiful and down to earth personalities that conflicting as this might sound, seem to have originated in Heaven!

I think it would be fantastic if you two did a show on Oprah with her showing her art and you singing!

I really believe the number of people you two would reach and inspire would be off the charts!

By the way, my boss here at the SOP goes by the name of *The Italian Oprah.* (Smile.) She`s also interviewed Maya Angelou who is someone that Oprah truly admires but I`m sure when she learns of you, you`re going to be on the list of people she admires as well! (Smile.) Who are some of the people you yourself admire? I know about Hillary Duff, but not only singers, but just people in general?

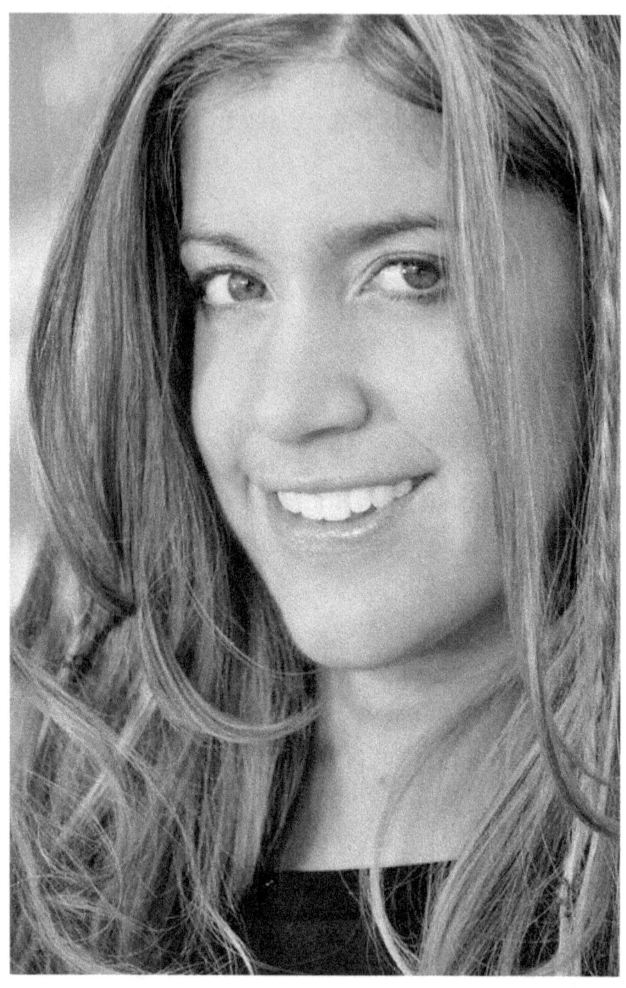

Alexa Dectix: Although Oprah greatly inspires me, God is my biggest role model. God always loves.

God is always humble. God is always calm. If we all try to emulate those behaviors, we can create a world overflowing with love.

Chase Von: You have your own new CD called *Fairy Tale* with the songs *Fairy Tale, It Girl, Your Reason* and *Progression.* My daughter who is nine really loves *Fairy Tale!* (Smile.)

What is the best place for people to buy your music? Also other links like to your My Space page or web pages and such, so those reading can learn more about you?

Also, a friend of mine, Kim Kline who won *Best Top 40 Artist of the Year in 2007* and beat out Amy Winehouse, Colbie Caillat and Daughtry also has her songs featured in the popular show on MTV called *The Hills*. Another friend and singer, Alina Smith, is scheduled to sing in the Olympics! The reason I bring this up though, is when I listen to your songs I can easily see them being featured as song tracks in movies and television programs as well! Is that something you`re also working on?

Alexa Dectis: If people are interested in buying my CD, *Fairy Tale*, they can go to http://www.alexadectis.com. It is also available on most digital music stores. A portion on the proceeds from all sales will go towards Spinal Muscular Atrophy Research. I want my music not only to inspire people, but also get others out of their wheelchairs.

I would really love to hear my music on a soundtrack or TV show. Right now, I am just trying to reach as many people as I can. If being on a soundtrack or TV show would help people realize their potential, I would love to be a part of it.

Chase Von: That`s wonderful Alexa! And also, you`ve been the State Ambassador for the Pennsylvania Muscular Dystrophy Association four times! And the local MDA Ambassador for eleven years! You also continuously get standing ovations when you perform for the Harley Davidson`s Ride for Life and the MDA Black and Blue Balls! Not only that, but you appeared in the MDA Jerry Lewis Telethon, you were the Amazing Kid of the month in January 2009 and you also appeared in the popular CBS soap opera, Guiding Light!

Do you have any plans on having your own television show? One where you could not only use one of your songs as the theme song, but feature your own original songs throughout the show?

Alexa Dectis: That would be really fun! Like I said before, I am just meeting as many people as I can and doing projects that will help me inspire others. If something like that would help me reach the world, I would love to participate in such a project.

Chase Von: You have a lovely voice. What is the song writing process like for you? And are there any duets that you can see in the future? And if so, who comes to mind for you if you were to sing a duet? (Smile.)

Alexa Dectis: Thank you! Songwriting is my favorite part of the musical process. It is so liberating. It is a way I can share my message of love, honest behavior, and fulfilling a purpose in life. As for collaborations, I have a lot of friends who also perform and write songs. I would love to work with any of them. A primary key to success is to learn from others. Surround yourself with people that have the ability to teach and inspire you.

Chase Von: Where can our readers learn more about where you`re going to be performing next?

And is there anything else your working on you can give our readers a heads up about?

Alexa Dectis: If anybody is interested in seeing me perform, they can check out my official website (http://www.alexadectis.com)

And my MySpace page (http://www.myspace.com/alexadectis) for updates.

Chase Von: What are your favorite meals? And I believe your sixteen yes? You`re also a rising star and a very lovely one at that!

Your fan base is growing larger every second! (One of the first things I thought when I saw your picture was, if Alexa said she used ***Head and Shoulders Shampoo***, the sales would go through the roof for it. (Smile.)

But how do you handle all the fan mail you get from your male admirers? And are your parents cool with that? Also, with all the publicity surrounding you, is that difficult at times to handle in regards to your classmates?

Alexa Dectis: One of my favorite meals is sushi. Living in New York, there is really no better sushi location. It is on every corner! Yes, I am sixteen. It is really incredible to have so many fans at such a young age. Online safety is very important. My parents have been wonderful in guiding me through my fan mail. I urge all children to be very careful online. Although I have received a generous amount of publicity, I am still a regular kid. When I go to school, my friends and I talk about fashion at the lunch table, not the latest commercial I filmed. I have been fortunate in being able to surround myself with really wonderful people.

Chase Von: Just thought I`d ask because being famous which you are becoming more every day now, is in itself, very difficult for some people to deal with. But you have shown you can handle just about anything! Did you design your CD cover?

Because it`s very eye catching and beautiful!

Alexa Dectis: Thank you so much! I made it very clear to my team that Fairy Tale was the theme of the record. I envisioned what I wanted, told my wonderful graphic artists, and watched it come to life.

Chase Von: I`ve of course heard of the Christopher & Dana Reeve Foundation and those who wish to learn more, here`s the link:

http://www.christopherreeve.org/site/c.ddJFKRNoFiG/b.4048063/k.BDDB/Home.htm

And I know you`re young, but you`re also not only very talented, but very intelligent as well, do you think there is a possibility that stem cell research might be the answer for you and those like you in similar circumstances?

Alexa Dectis: I do believe that stem cells could be an answer. However, I support sources other than fetal stem cells.

Although there is more research and money invested into fetal stem cells, it is my firm belief that adult stem cells will lead to the cure. Fetal stem cells are a risky experiment, because they are not fully developed. While they might cure an illness, they can still grow into nearly anything, even a dangerous disease.

I encourage researchers to explore adult stem cells.

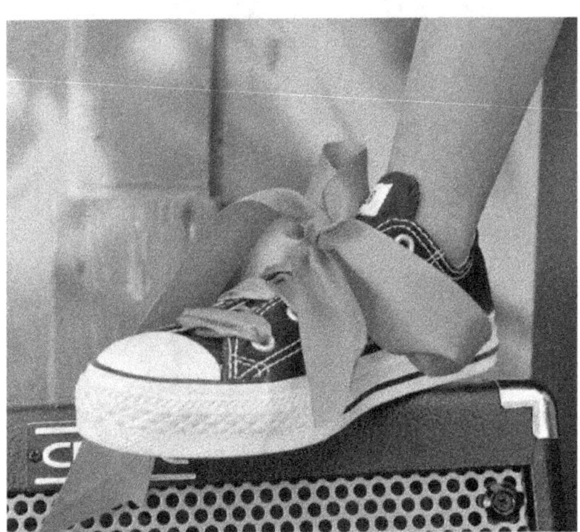

Chase Von: Your lovely voice is just one of your many gifts, like myself, you`re also a poet. (Smile.)

Can you share one of your shorter pieces with us here?

Alexa Dectis: Well my poetry is my lyrics. I sing these lines in my song *Make It Through.* I wrote this song for others who have my disease.

Every time we close our eyes
It`s Heaven that we see
Another life is lost
Another soul goes free
You`ve risen up above

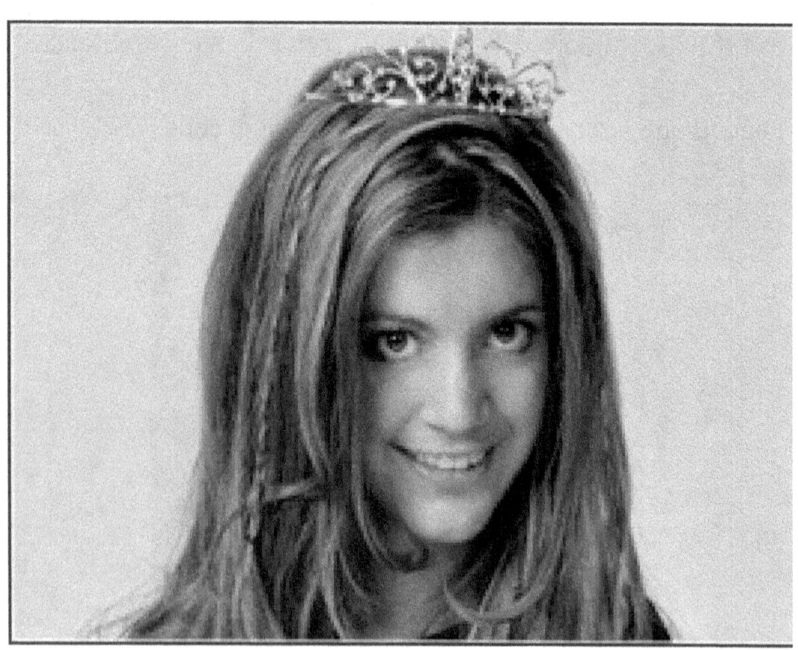

Chase Von: That`s lovely Alexa! What would you say if you were standing before a microphone that could be heard by every child on the planet, and regardless of what language they spoke, they would understand you?

What positive advice would you give the children, if that were possible?

Alexa Dectis: You are beautiful. You have the potential to change the world. You are an angel born to spread love. Never forget how much potential is inside your tiny little body. God gave you that gift so that you may teach others how to live their life for positivity... Today, embrace that.

Chase Von: This is a personal question Alexa. And since you`re not THAT many years removed from it, I figured you might know the answer. My daughter is in what I call the *Beanie Baby* phase. She has an army of them! Are there any things you collect or did collect?

Because when she says can I go over my friends house and play and packs these things up, it looks like she`s carrying a suitcase! (Heh, Heh.)

Will she ever out grow them? Apparently every hour they come out with a new one she has to have! (Smile.)

But when for yourself, did you really start taking music totally seriously instead of well, just girly stuff? Then again, maybe boys like Beanies too, but I`m just curious.

Alexa Dectis: Your daughter sounds adorable! I must admit, I did go through the Beanie Baby phase. (Laugh.)

I began taking music seriously when I was about thirteen. Before that, I always sang and wrote down lyrics. However, I did not begin the process of creating my CD until I was thirteen.

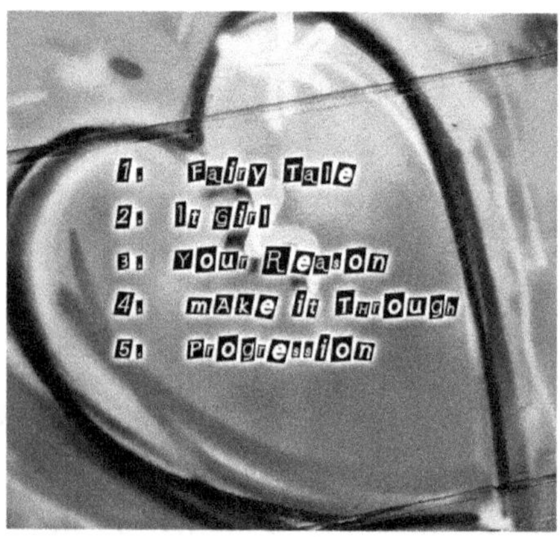

Chase Von: Thanks Alexa, I was just thinking we were going to have to add another room on the house and probably start claiming these little creatures on income taxes. (Smile.)

Thanks so much for sharing yourself with our readers and you are truly the definition of INSPIRING!

I`m wishing you mountains of more success and also you and yours, all things good! I`m certainly also looking forward to hearing about even more wonderful things I know you`re going to accomplish! PS, when you`re on Oprah, tell her I said READ MY BOOKS! (Heh, Heh.)

Seriously, I`m laughing but I`m ah, serious. (Smile.)

Alexa Dectis: Thank you so much for this opportunity! I really appreciate that you are helping me spread my message to the world. I can`t wait to have the opportunity to talk to Oprah. I don`t know how it will happen, but the how is not important.

The will is what leads us where we are meant to be. Being on Oprah would be the greatest gift in the world. When it happens, I can`t wait to share the experience with you and all of the readers. Remember, live to inspire.

"A primary key to success is to learn from others."

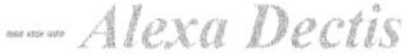

--- Alexa Dectis

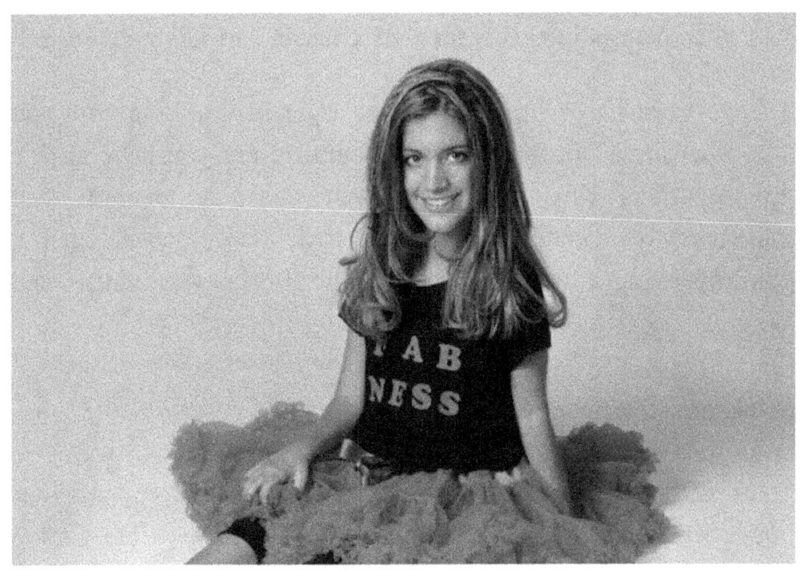

Interview with Claire Dodin

GORGEOUS ACTRESS, MODEL AND MORE

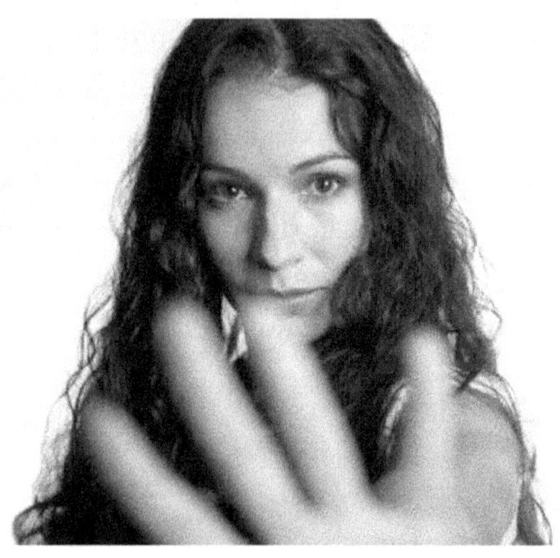

Photographs in this interview courtesy of Claire Dodin

Chase Von: Hey Claire and it was a pleasure talking with you the other day! Not only are you beautiful but you have such a lovely voice! I`m like most American men, meaning I`m blown away myself by a woman with a foreign accent, but your speaking voice is also as sought after as your acting and singing!

And you are extremely pretty as well so you`re also sought after as a model, though I know you prefer action! (Smile.) So thanks for finding the time to share yourself here with our readers. I have many questions I want to ask you but first, I want to know more about your childhood.

What would you say it was like growing up in France? My father was in the military so I was in other countries as well as a child and I know there`s a difference compared to those raised solely in the States.

And we spoke on both your parents being school teachers as well. How supportive have they been of you, their daughter who is making a serious mark in the world of entertainment, with your choosing that path in life as a career choice? We didn`t get to talk that long but I would think they were thinking you might pursue what they both do and I also imagine it wouldn`t be something that they would just easily accept. (Smile.)

Also I know you have siblings as well, are they supportive also?

Claire Dodin: Thank you Chase, you are very kind and I`m blushing!! ☺

I was told that as an artist we are supposed to have had a terrible childhood; humm " well mine was actually very happy, because my parents were teachers, they had lots of holidays so we would travel throughout Europe, visiting the many gorgeous cities and countryside. It was a blast! It`s probably the reason why I ended up moving to this country, I was raised with the desire to explore the world and its beauties.

My Mum built a theatre in the attic of our huge apartment when I was around seven. I remember putting on plays there with my sister for our friends.

It was such a happy time and when I decided I`d just have to play for the rest of my life! (LOL!)

It took a while for my family to accept what I do, as it was not exactly what they had in mind for me, (He, He!) This is simply because they worry about me and they know how hard it is to make a living in this profession. They hoped I would have a regular job and be safe, but now they are happy for me because they can see that everything is going well. When they saw me on TV the first time was probably the moment they started to believe that I could make a living at this. My grandmother was very excited when she first saw my face printed in big on a newspaper!

My sisters and brother have always been supportive, but they are a different generation, when you are young you believe in your dreams. It`s when we grow older that we lose the ability to believe, and we start to worry about money, stability etc, the truth is that life can be hard and it is not always easy to keep positive.

However, how can you achieve your dreams if you don`t take risks? I`ve always thought that I would rather try and fail than not try and settle for less than what I want. But like **everyone** I`ve had moments of doubts, moments that were so hard I nearly gave up. Somehow, I always managed to find a light of hope, and keep going. I now have no regrets, I`m really glad I went after my dreams because my life right now is amazing. It was all worth it! And I`ve still got many dreams to look forward to living! ☺

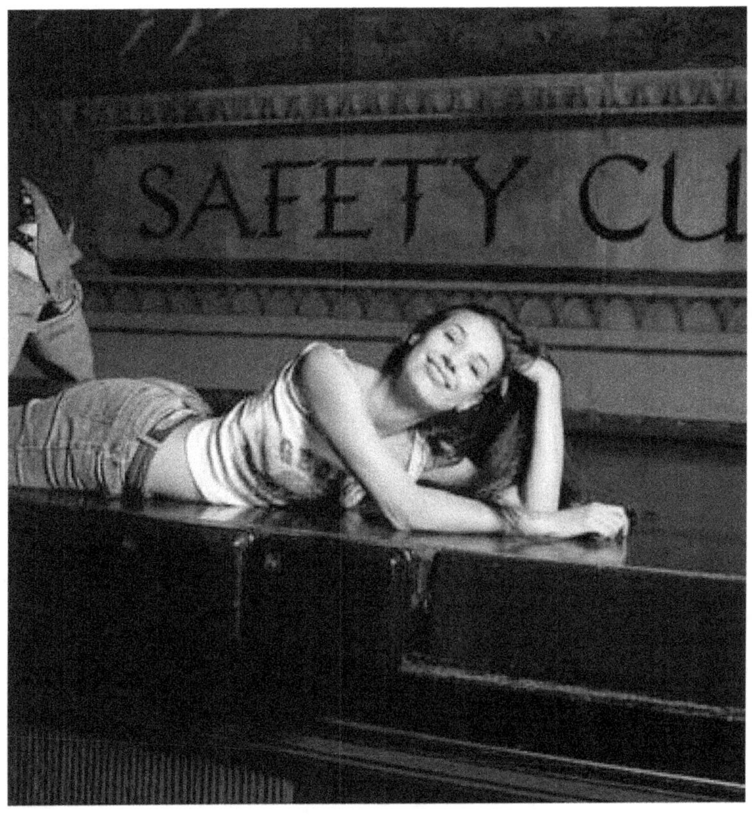

Chase Von: You speak not only French, but also English and can also converse in German! We spoke on how being able to speak another language basically opens up your world. I remember I gave you the example, that if you and I were walking down a street in France, you would be able to understand everything where as I, who can`t speak French, would be in a bubble so to speak.

Like being present, but still, not totally there because of my inability to understand the language. Bazhe, whom I`ve interviewed as well, is a writer, poet and artist and also the author of the acclaimed book ***Damages***, and he speaks seven languages! (Smile.)

But you also told me you can understand other languages like Spanish and Italian and such, and although you can`t converse freely in some of these languages, you still can communicate and get your point across! How important do you think it is for people to stretch their boundaries and learn other languages? And do you think your ability to grasp languages so quickly helps you in your work in entertainment?

Claire Dodin: I speak French and English fluently, which of course is a huge advantage in this world. If I didn`t speak English, I couldn`t work in English speaking countries. Whatever your profession is, speaking other languages allows you to expand both at work and on a personal level.

My German is unfortunately very basic, and I don`t speak Spanish or Italian, but when I am in a conversation, we can manage to understand each other because communication is not just about spoken language, it`s also about body language, facial expressions, body movements etc.

These languages, particularly French, Spanish and Italian, are very close; the words are similar, just pronounced differently, so we can get by and it can be a lot of fun too!

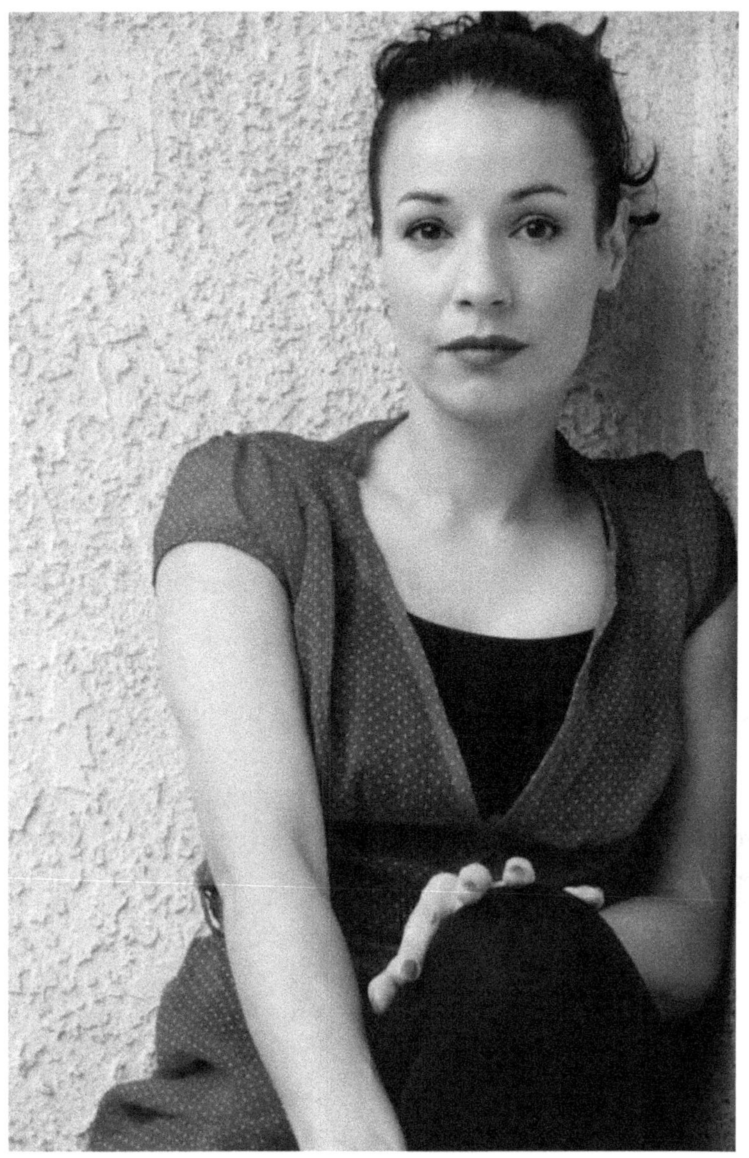

Photo by Karianne Flaathen

Chase Von: I know I told you I took three years of Spanish and it got me laughed at when I went to Mexico by people on a bus holding chickens. (Smile.) Still more to learn. But that brings me to your sought after voice! You`ve been runner up in the 2008 ***Best Foreign Voice*** for the ***Voicey Awards*** and 2009 and are a member of the ***Society of Accredited Voice Over Artist*** or **SAVOA**! You`re also the voice for a popular video game in France. ***Universe at War*** by ***SEGA*** and your character is ***Queen Masari Altea.*** Are there any other games you`re the voice for I`m missing?

And I have to tell you, what really threw me for a loop as well is when you told me you are also the voice in France for the French version of the ***Laugh and Learn Bear*** by ***Fisher Price!***

My kids like many children, have had toys that have voices but for the first time after speaking to you I thought, wow, what an awesome responsibility to have! How does it make you feel knowing that when kids are learning they are learning from your voice? And isn`t it ironic, that even though both your parents are teachers, and you`re in entertainment, you are still teaching? (Smile.)

That really has to be something they are extremely proud of!

Claire Dodin: I also recorded a video game for *Disney* called *La Maison de Mickey (Mickey`s funhouse)* and it was hilarious, so much fun! I love doing this kind of work!

I have voiced a few toys for *Fisher Price*, but my favorite one of all times was the bear. It actually is my favorite job ever.

When I was in studio recording it, I was picturing the kids playing with it and it made me so happy! I was on cloud nine for days after that, a smile would never leave my face!

Moments like these make me feel like the luckiest person on earth, because my job is awesome! ☺

It is true that I`ve recorded a lot of educational projects for children; soon you`ll be able to hear me on an iPod application that teaches animal names. Another very cute job! ☺

I love recording things for children, it is very rewarding.

I have also just recorded an audio book for children with extracts from very famous classic books/fairytales and French poetry. When I do this kind of work, I feel like I am contributing to passing on knowledge and it is wonderful.

Chase Von: You`ve worked extensively in France and in England, and now your here in the US!

I know I told you I myself lived in England for 4 years and you were there for ten, but how do you like the States? And will you be making this your home? Or do you plan on returning to France one day? Also, what would you say is the biggest difference between being in England and being in the U.S. now? I know you said you no longer have to ride the tube, but have to deal with the traffic here but I mean culturally speaking. Like are the people here as nice as in Europe?

Claire Dodin: I love the US and I am planning to stay here if I can; but I will also always go back regularly to England and France. I don`t think I`ll ever live over there for a long period of time, but I`d love to go back to shoot films. I will always be attached to Europe and the old buildings, the gorgeous architecture, the small cafes and of course my family and friends.

And yes, people in LA are as nice as the ones in Europe! It`s a myth that Americans don`t like the French; everyone is always lovely to me and loves my accent! ☺

I`m having a great time; people here have made me feel really welcome. When my Mum came to visit, she was surprised to see that everywhere we went Americans were smiling and helpful and chatty; it was not what she thought it would be like. Now she`s raving about America! ☺

Chase Von: I also know you have a background in ***Aïkido***, so they better be nice. (Smile.)

And you`re very skilled with the sword as well! You`ve also been very busy playing in ***2084*** as a French Newscaster, ***Rubicon, Diamond Ice`d, Face to Face, Murder Club, Grab One Thing***, and *also* ***5 episodes of Under the radar: "CMONS"*** which is on the French version of ***MTV!***

And I can`t possibly name all the things you`ve done but

you`ve also acted in quite a few stage plays such as, ***Footprints of the Giants of Musical Theatre*: *Sondheim,***

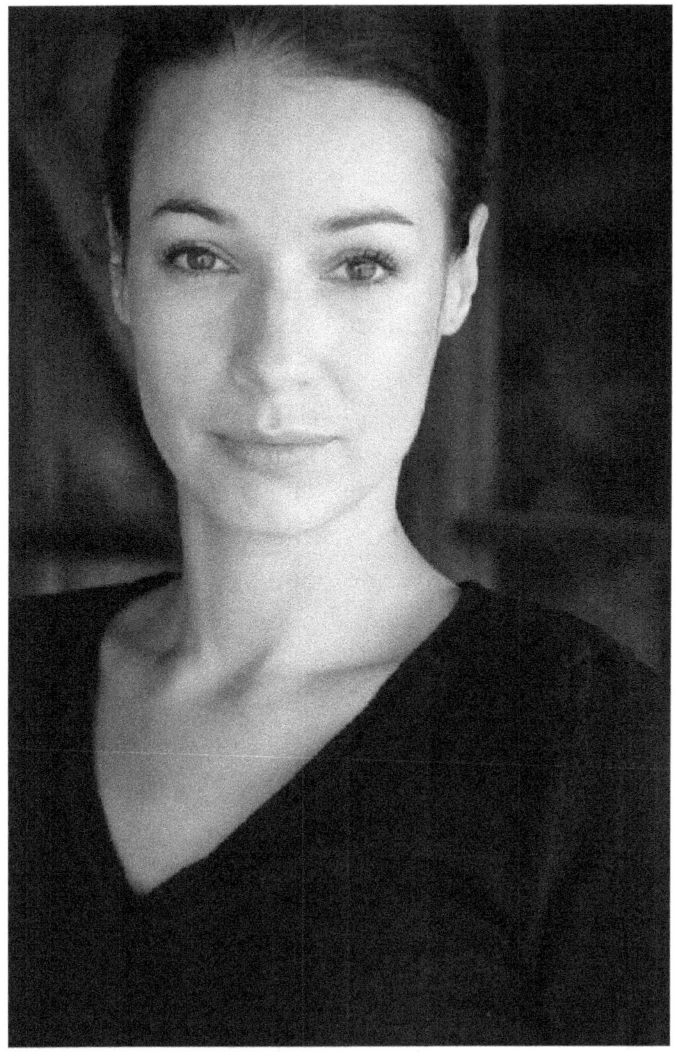

Photo by Karianne Flaathen

Notre Dame De Paris*, *The Man Who Knows*, *Café de Paris*, *Arabian Nights*, *Private Lives*, *Canterbury Tales and really again, too many things for me to mention here! (Smile.)

But by doing musicals and cabarets and singing and also by knowing so much about weapons, and martial arts do you think that enhances your chances above others when it comes to winning roles?

Claire Dodin: Absolutely, all extra skills make you more employable, and they are fun to learn!

Chase Von: How do you stay in such great shape and what are some of your favorite dishes to grub on? And although I don`t miss the fog in England, I do miss the Fish and Chips, do you?

And also, how supportive are your fans bases from Europe, now that you`re on this side of the pond? (Smile.)

Claire Dodin: I keep in shape by exercising when I can. dancing, (sword fighting, He, He)! And eating well. I`m not really a fish & chips girl, even though I`d eat it sometimes, I`m more a vegetable and whole grains person. A perfect meal would be for example poached salmon with brown rice, broccoli and salad.

I do have a vice though: chocolate. So I ask my boyfriend to hide it and only allow me one or two pieces a day. This way, I don`t do excess. Because otherwise, I`d eat everything there is in one go! (Smile.)

As for the fans, let`s just say that thanks to the internet, it doesn`t matter where you live! ☺

I am so grateful for their support and I feel very blessed that there are people I have never met who care about me.

Chase Von: That`s right; you did say you also dance as well! (Smile.)

Where can our readers get more information on you and the things you`re doing and have done?

You know like your various web site links, and web pages?

Claire Dodin: My acting website is: http://claire.dodin.net.

I post on it the latest news so you can easily keep up to date with what I am doing.

My voice over website is www.clairedodin.com

I also post videos of my work on YouTube when I can:
http://www.youtube.com/user/clairedodin

And there`s my IMDB page where you can see more details about the films and who is in them:
http://www.imdb.com/name/nm2749457/

And here`s my My Space page as well:
http://www.myspace.com/clairedodin

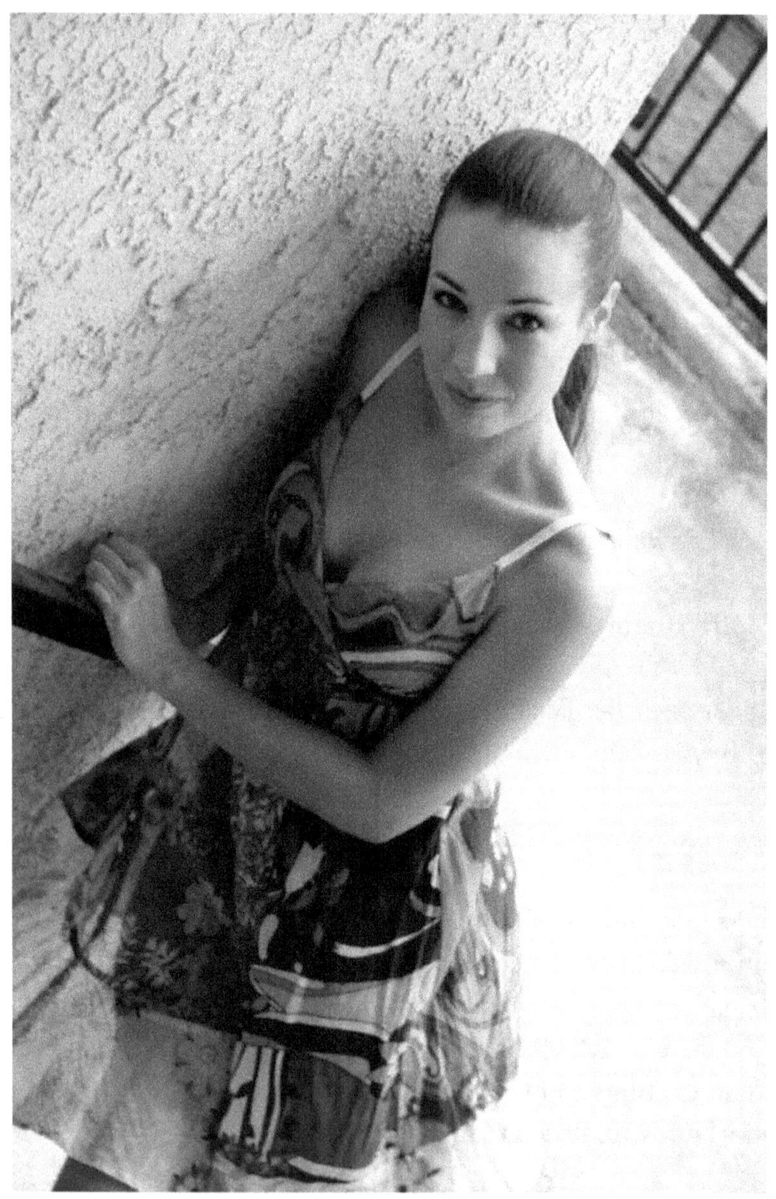

Photo by Karianne Flaathen

Chase Von: Are there any projects you have in the works now you can give our readers a heads up about?

Claire Dodin: Yes, I`m very busy right now, LA seems to like me ☺.

I have a small part in an exciting feature film which will come out in cinemas soon called 2084. It`s a film about a group of survivors following a virus outbreak. The official website is: http://www.2084movie.com

I`m also currently shooting a feature called *The Last Act*: A man diagnosed with cancer decides in a desperate moment to involve himself in a scheme to rob a Drug Lord. It`s going to

be both fun and touching. My character is called Paulene and lives in cozy gorgeous place in Ireland.

I`ll be playing Francine in the French film *La froideur de l`été,* an arty stylized film, very intense. This will be very visual, the director is super talented, the photography will amaze you!

http://lfdlfilm.weebly.com/index.html

Then I`ll be shooting another French film called *Marcel et le Petit Pois,* my character is called Magalie. It is going to be a beautiful poetic film in the style of *Amélie.* I can`t tell you more about this yet, but it will be really fabulous.

And after this one, another film in French language called

Women in which I play Delphine. It is a surreal and strange film; my character is pretty provocative which is going to be a change from the characters I usually play.

And I am a series regular on the radio play *We`re Alive* that you can listen to for free on iTunes or on the website: www.thezombiepodcast.com.

It`s a really fun story of survival against zombie with great music and sound effects. I highly recommend it, I`m super proud to be part of this!

I post info on my website when it is possible, so to know when they come out and what I`m doing next, just log onto http://claire.dodin.net

Chase Von: You also have a CD out! Can you tell us more about that? And where that can be purchased? Also, who are some of the people you`ve really enjoyed working with?

And who are some of the people you admire and look up to and would love to work with in the future here in the United States?

Claire Dodin: I sing the song *Goodnight, Miss Louise* on the *Solo Eclypse* album called *Artifacts.*

You can buy it on iTunes or Amazon, just enter my name in the search to find it or follow this link:

http://www.amazon.com/Goodnight-Louise-Vocals-Claire-Dodin/dp/B001AW0PS4/ref=sr_1_1?ie=UTF8&s=dmusic&qid=1262326341&sr=8-1

I collaborated with the amazing song writer Scott Pollak on this song. It is his album. I added lyrics to the song and started singing a melody; at first it was just for fun because I loved his music, and then we ended up keeping the song because everyone liked it.

I also sing the most gorgeous song on the soundtrack of *La Froideur de l`été.* It`s a French song with piano and cellos. The recording will be available soon to download. I`ll post the release date on my website as soon as I know.

I have been lucky to work with a lot of talented and inspiring

people on many projects; but working with Billy West on the film *2084* was without a doubt one of the highlights. I am such a fan of his, his voice work is just incredible and he is the kindest person you could meet.

A real sweetheart! I hope I get to work with him again.

Like probably every actor on this planet, I would give anything to work with talents like dame Judi Dench or Cate Blanchett.

There is so much to learn from incredible talents like them. But they are not the only ones; I could give you a really long list of hugely talented actors. This is part of the reasons why our job is so much fun; we constantly learn from others and get to meet amazing people.

Chase Von: What would you say if you were standing before a microphone that could be heard by every child on the planet, and regardless of what language they spoke, they would understand you?

What positive advice would you give the children, if that were possible?

Claire Dodin: Oh, I would most likely sing something instead of speaking. Something beautiful and fun. And I would say to them to always love one another and never forget to dream and go after their dreams. The secret to happiness is in the joy of the journey.

Chase Von: What are some of the causes you either support or feel extremely strongly about?

Claire Dodin: There are many causes close to my heart. One of them is the *Compassionate Eye Foundation*: http://www.compassionateeye.org.

It brings water, sanitation, schools etc to poor areas of Guatemala and Africa where conditions of living are extremely difficult. Our mission is to support, honor, and empower those in developing nations in order to expand educational opportunities, basic health services, and tools for sustainable economic development.

Once a year a group of actors and photographers get together to shoot pictures and sell them via *OJO* images and *Getty* Images. The proceeds go to the *Compassionate Eye Foundation.* I did this for the first time a couple of years ago and we managed to raise enough money to build a school in Guatemala with our London shoot. It made me so happy! This event happens every year in several countries. ☺

Here`s a link to see what we did (can you spot me in there? He, He!)

http://www.youtube.com/watch?v=DlgNMVFovGs

If you are an actor or a photographer and would like to donate your time and talent, please get in touch with the foundation via the website. You can also give donations. Thanks!

Also, because of the terrible recent events in Haiti, I strongly recommend to go to http://www.directrelief.org/ and show your support. I am so fortunate to be safe and well, and when I

see the suffering of the population over there it truly breaks my heart. We must do everything we can to ease their suffering. I believe that the Red Cross also does a terrific job helping in Haiti, it is also a great charity to be involved with.

Chase Von: I always try and ask what might be a tough one Claire. What are your personal feelings on all the hype about the H1N1 Flu Virus? And do you personally plan on taking the shot or have you?

This is a video of a girl that was going to be a Cheer Leader for the ***Washington Redskins*** football team. I think it`s very sad and those who have seen it will be using this to make their own choices as to whether they are going to take it or not.

UPDATE ON WASHINGTON REDSKINS CHEERLEADER CRIPPLED FOR LIFE AFTER BEING VACCINATED

The link in the event video doesn`t work:

http://www.youtube.com/watch?v=mh5F5wP8RdU

Claire Dodin: It is a terribly sad story, and it is very difficult to stay objective in our reasoning when we see such devastating stories; but the truth is that every medication we take has a possibility of serious side effects. What we need to do before taking any medication is weigh the benefits against the risks.

Look at what is written on your aspirin box, the possible side effects, yet most people still take it when they have a headache.

I`ve had the flu shot many years in a row, when I was at "risk" i.e.: working in close contact with the public, particularly in hospital. I personally have not had any side effects from it.

Some people should absolutely take the vaccine, because the flu kills, but only some people, the ones that are at risk.

Consulting your doctor about it is the best thing to do.

If you are young, in good health and not at risk, then really I don`t think it is worth getting the vaccine. But it is a decision that needs to be taken case by case with the help of your doctor.

I don`t think this year should be particularly different than other years, the flu kills every year, it`s just that this year it started in the summer before the vaccine was ready so many people started to panic.

I will not get the vaccine this year, I do not think that I am at risk; but I would encourage people to discuss it with their doctor before making a decision.

Chase Von: Thanks for sharing your thoughts on that Claire, and on behalf of the *Student Operated Press* and myself, I really want to thank you for finding the time to do this interview! After being overseas all that time, I know not only are you busy, but you must still be adjusting to life here. (Smile.)

So thanks again and I did have one more question. I know you`re still doing voice work in other countries but will your voice be in any American cartoons and video games here in the near future?

Claire Dodin: I very much hope so! My dream job would be to voice a cute character on a *Disney* or *Pixar* animated film. And you know that I go after my dreams! ☺

Chase Von: That`s wonderful, be sure and shoot me an email when that happens so I can check that out as well. And continued blessings and success to you!

Claire Dodin: Thank you Chase, it has been a real pleasure to meet you and get to know you. I wish you all the best for the future!

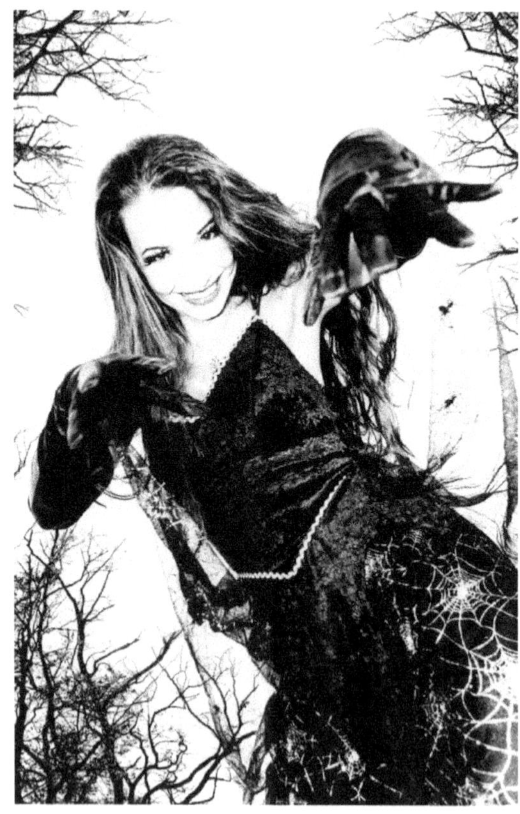

Interview with Jamie McCall

EXTREMELY TALENTED ACTRESS AND DANCER

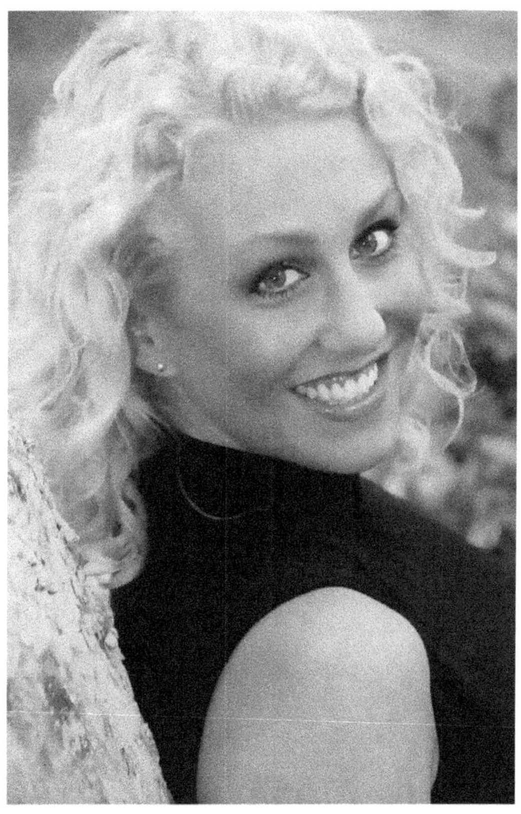

Chase Von: Hi Jamie and you`re like a magnet! (Smile.) Meaning when someone learns of you, they can`t wait to learn more. You`re an actress and a dancer and a rising star in Hollywood, so thanks so much for spending some time with me and sharing yourself with our readers here at the Student Operated Press!

Jamie McCall: Well thank you, Chase, and the SOP!

Chase Von: I have a lot of questions I want to ask, but before I do, can you tell our readers where you grew up? And also, what was your reason for going in the military and becoming an Officer?

Have you always been someone that loves entertaining others because I`ve seen your video of you "Belly Dancing" and quite frankly, if that was the last video left on the planet of someone doing that, I would still be happy! (Smile.)

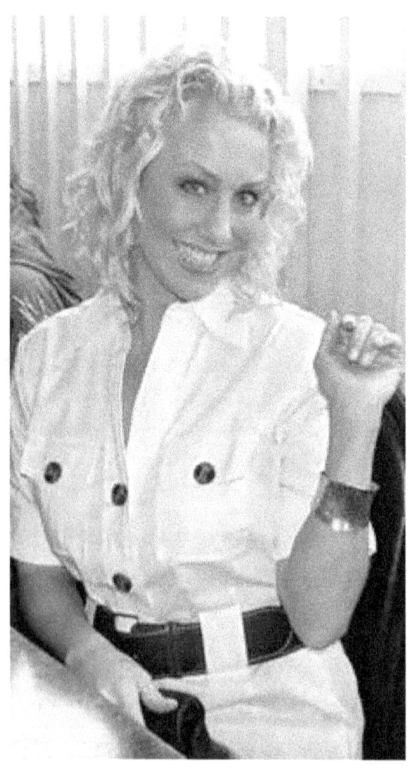

Jamie McCall: I was born in Portland, Oregon, lived there a few years, then moved to Galveston, Texas, and then finally settled in Idaho. I went back to Oregon for college. I spent most of my adult life back East before moving to LA. Washington DC, NYC and then Puerto Rico were all homes.

I have a long family history of Naval Service and wanted to continue in that vein, being the first female in my family to do so.

My Uncle is a retired Navy fighter pilot, the real TOP GUN, F-14 Tomcats, and was my mentor growing up. I`ve always kind of lived a dichotomy, though, as I`ve always been interested in the arts as well, starting with dance and stage production as a very young girl. I`ve been a performing artist since I could walk, basically. I also studied music - specifically the violin and piano.

Chase Von: Normally I ask tough questions a little while later, but I`m a former Marine and as you know, the Marines and the Navy work very closely together. But you share a picture on your my space and your Face book of you shaking hands with the highest ranking Navy Officer and yourself, not long before he committed suicide.

Your comments regarding him are quite respectful but I`m just wondering, is the family to your knowledge OK with that? And how did that affect you yourself when you heard it? After having so recently met him? I didn`t ever meet him but I thought it was truly sad when I heard it as well.

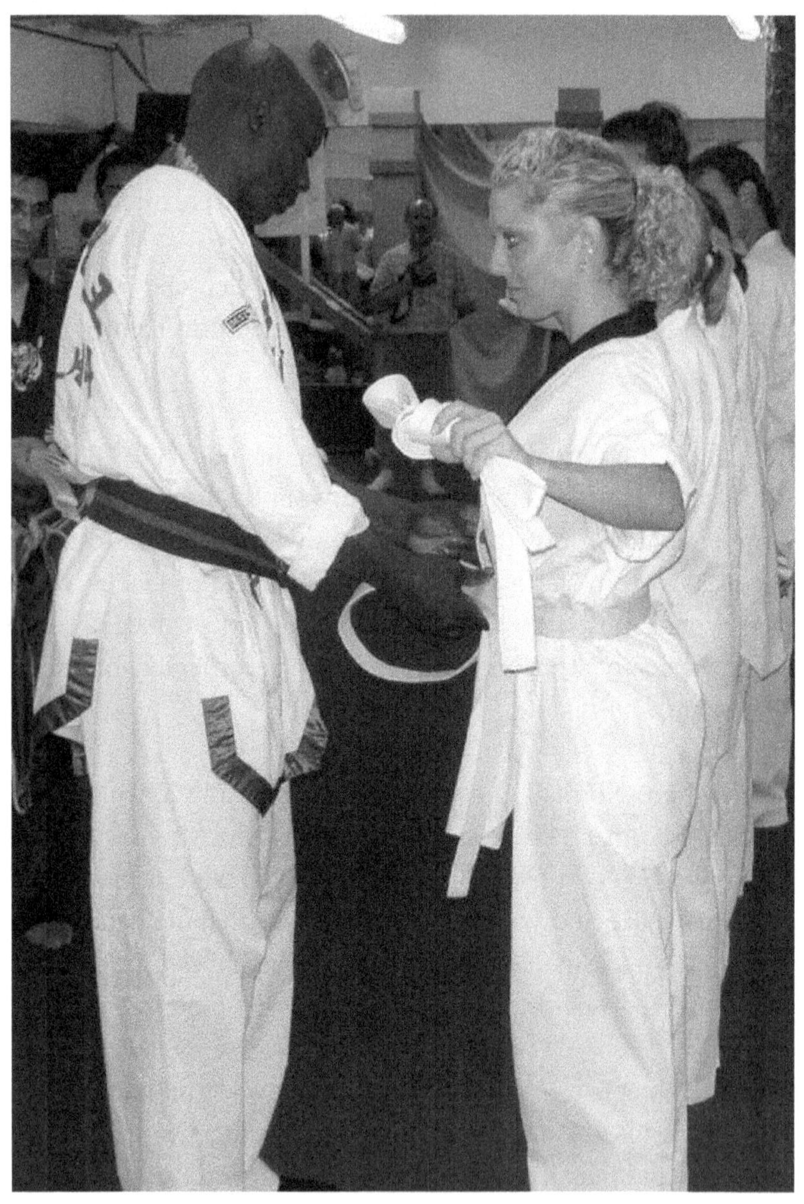

Billy Blanks giving Jamie McCall her yellow belt

Jamie McCall: I`m not sure how his family would feel about it. It was quite some time ago now, but I just recently found the photo, which is the reason for the recent blog. It`s a personal blog, not a formally published work, so I didn`t seek any clearance or approval from his family. It was very respectful, because I respected Admiral Boorda. It`s personal, because I worked for him. I was speaking from personal experience with my article on the subject.

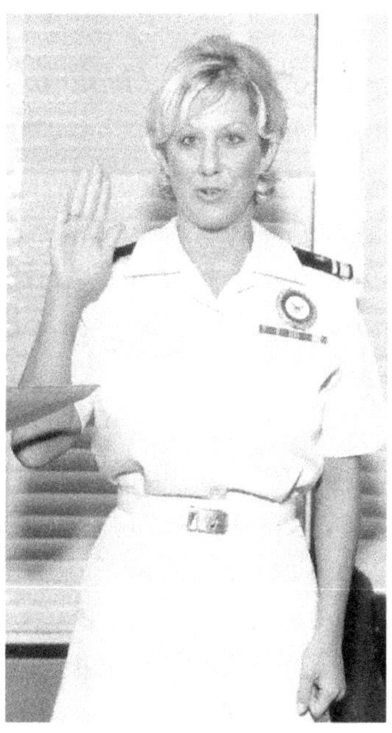

Chase Von: Thanks Jamie and of course, your perspective is valuable since you did in fact meet him. I myself had a troop show up looking like Chesty Puller one day (As many ribbons as me or more), when we had to wear Charlie`s. I was in a rush, but later I found out that the Sergeant Major had seen him as well, and ran a records check and low and behold, he didn`t rate a lot of what he was wearing. I`ve got friends that were shot in the face, people that worked for me, that have one leg now and people I`ve worked with that are no longer here.

In the case of Admiral Boorda, I`m sure it was just an honest mistake, but there are quite a few people that are pretending these days and yes, he was punished for that and rightfully so, but enough on that.

You`re also writing a book titled, *Living the High Life without Drinking the Champagne.* And also have another book out of poetry called *Renaissance Girl,* and I`ve seen you reciting some of your poetry and I also have to say, you excel there as well! Can you tell our readers a little more about what *Living the High Life without Drinking the Champagne* is about, and why you titled it that?

Jamie McCall: ***High Life*** is an inspirational memoir telling of my time in the Navy and the transition to Hollywood. I basically lost my Navy career to alcoholism. I`m sober now 8 1/2 years, but it was quite a struggle. I was dying in hospitals, rehabs & emergency rooms for two years. I nearly lost my life.

It was humiliating, extremely painful and shameful. I had to start over from scratch, having lost everything I ever wanted & fought for. This is where the title comes from. I`m living "the dream", hob-nobbing with the stars, following adventure without the drugs & alcohol. It can be done!

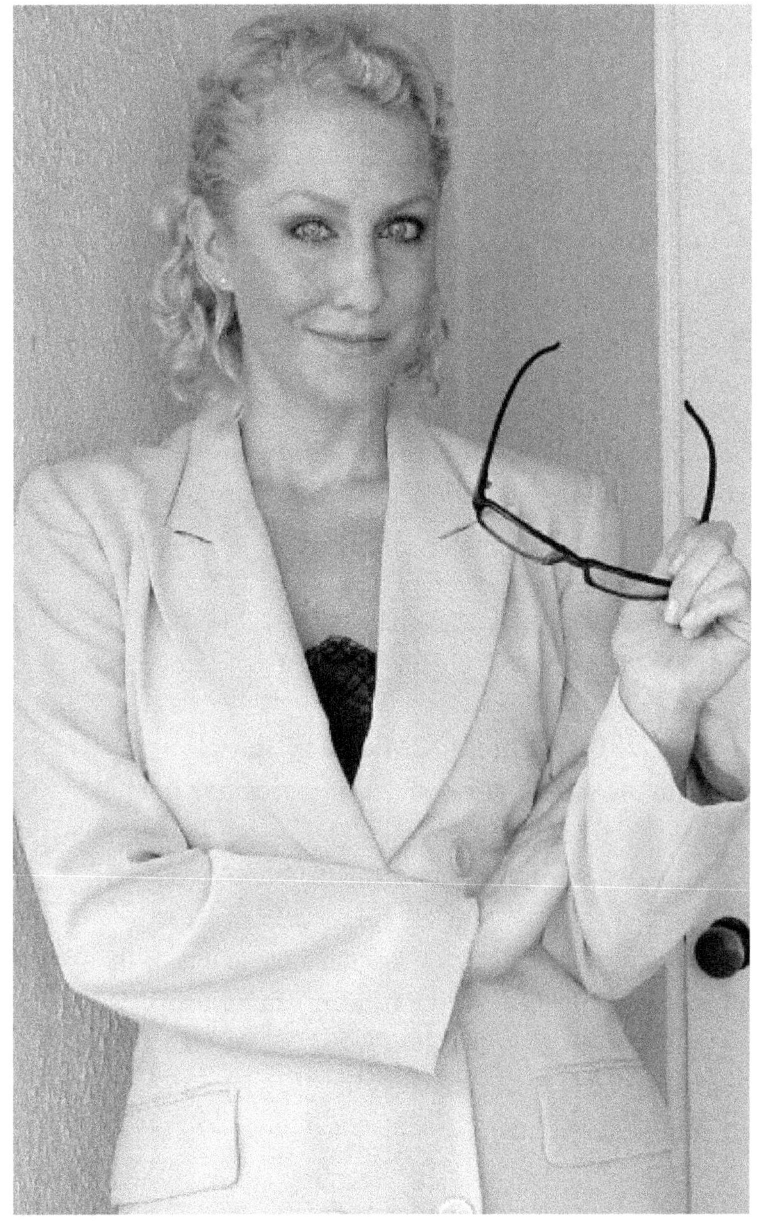

Chase Von: I`m probably going to take some heat for this, (Smile.)

But when I saw your video of you Belly Dancing I was amazed! I even showed it to my wife and asked if she could dance like that. (She is a natural when it comes to dancing as well). I already told you, Shakira herself has some legit competition now!

But what I wanted to say is, some folks are born with two left feet it seems, and have no rhythm. Have you been able to dance like that all your life because I`ve also seen videos of you doing other dances and you`re remarkable in those also!

And gifted as you are in so many areas, why aren`t you on *Dancing with the Stars*? Or do they just not know about you yet?

Direct link to JMac Sexy Back -

In the event the video doesn`t work, the link:

http://www.youtube.com/watch?v=CkAct_l3WQs

Jamie McCall: Yes, I often joke that I came out of the womb dancing! I love Shakira, she`s one of my favorite artists.

Here`s a quote I love, "I get up, I walk, I fall down... meanwhile, I keep dancin!"

I`ve actually started a campaign to get cast on the next season of DWTS! I`ve met many people from the show already - the word is getting out. Contact ABC & let them know you want me to represent veterans & the military on the show!

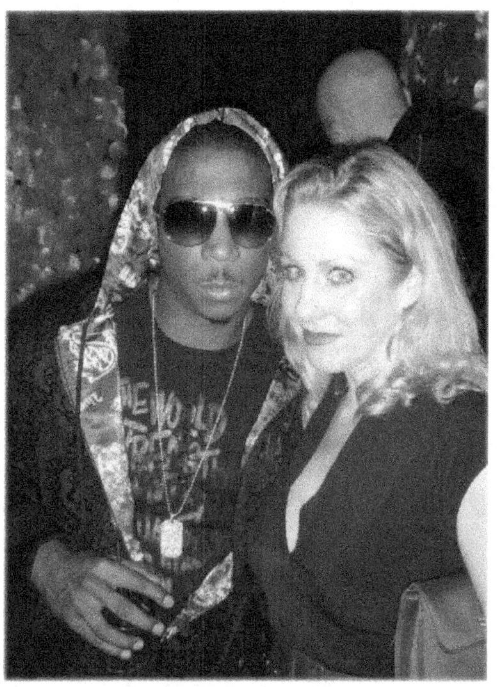

Ja Rule and Jamie McCall

Chase Von: You`re just making your start really in Hollywood, but a great start it is! You`re going to be in *The Reapers,* still in pre production, but you`ve already been featured in *God Complex, Pushing Daisies, Private Practice, Grey`s Anatomy, Splitting Hairs, Ascension Day, Back in the Day, Bravo`s Shear Genius,* and various other projects! Are you living your dreams Jamie? Also, how important do you think it is that people do try and live their dreams?

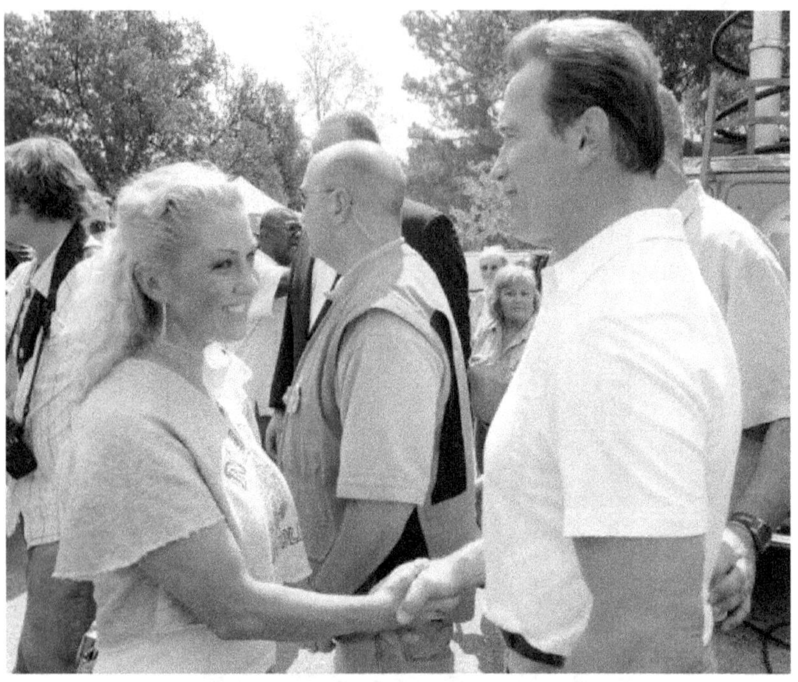

Jamie McCall: It`s not only important, it`s the purpose! It`s the whole reason we`re here in this life experience, in my opinion, to find our joys and our passions. It takes courage, but yes I`ve always lived that way. I`d be more mad at myself for not trying, than if I tried and failed.

Chase Von: You`re a fantastic dancer and actress but also a great at poetry and as well! Which you know is very dear to my heart as well because I think I`m a poet first.

But do you think in the future you will be also writing scripts since you also have that in your background from being in Public Relations while you were in the military?

Jamie McCall: Yes, that`s part of the Master Plan. I`ve already written the treatment. I love writing, whether it be poetry, or editorial articles, blogging or just journaling for myself at home.

Chase Von: I also told you, that in some ways, you remind me of the phenomenal actress Brittany Murphy! I got the chance to meet her when I was in the last war I was in. She was part of the USO tour that came to entertain the troops, and unless you meet her in person, this won`t make sense. But Brittany Murphy seems to be able to say complete sentences just with her eyes!

I know that sounds silly, but it`s true to me because I`ve met her.

But what I want to ask you next, is one, do you consider that a compliment? And two, do you think the military time you spent is also helping you with what you learned, to be successful in Hollywood?

And also three, it looks like we`re going to be there for a while, so is that something you would consider doing as well? Entertaining our warriors?

Jamie McCall: Sure, I`ll take that as a compliment. She`s a fine actress. I`d love to meet her myself! I`ve not met her yet.

And yes I absolutely believe my military service has given me the edge to make it in showbiz! The self-discipline, character, leadership skills, courage and sense of adventure I developed have been crucial to my progress! I`m very excited about doing a USO tour and am working with some folks to make that happen when the time is right, hopefully early 2010! It is absolutely one of my goals on the top of my priority list, and

I`d be honored and thrilled to do it!

Chase Von: Who are some of the people you have really enjoyed working with in your acting career? And also who are some of the people you consider mentors? And lastly, who have you not worked with yet, but would love to in the future?

Jamie McCall: Ving Rhames was the first I worked with who became a mentor. He`s been in the game so long and is always working, which is a feat in & of itself in this business! We met on my first professional acting gig down in Puerto Rico and became friends, and stayed good friends for my first three years in LA.

I`ve worked with Kristin Chenowith a couple of times and she is adorable and so talented.

There are so many people who I want to work with - Clint Eastwood, whom I`ve met a couple of times, Jamie Foxx, Susan Sarandon, Ron Howard, Quentin Tarantino, Daniel Day Lewis, Meryl Streep, just too many on my list...

Chase Von: Are there any future projects you`re working on you can give our readers a heads up about?

Jamie McCall: I`ve recently started hosting a couple of web series, “Hollywood Minute” and one that has a good shot at turning into a TV pilot, “Lifestyles of Celebrity Pets.”. “The Reapers” is set to start filming early spring 2010 to hopefully be on the big screen by Halloween! There`s a few other tricks up my sleeves as well...

Chase Von: Can you give our readers some links to your various web pages so they can learn more about you?

Jamie McCall: Certainly, I`m all over the place! You can`t miss me! Pick your platform:

www.JamieMcCall.com
www.IMDb.com/name/nm2210588
www.youtube.com/OfficialJamieMcCall
www.myspace.com/OfficialJamieMcCall
www.facebook.com/OfficialJamieMcCall
www.Twitter.com/JamieMcCall

Chase Von: What would you say if you were standing before a microphone that could be heard by every child on the planet, and regardless of what language they spoke, they would understand you?

What positive advice would you give the children, if that were possible?

Jamie McCall: Love yourself! It sounds so simple and cliche, but I really think we have an epidemic of low self -esteem in this country & the world over, which is the root cause of so many problems.

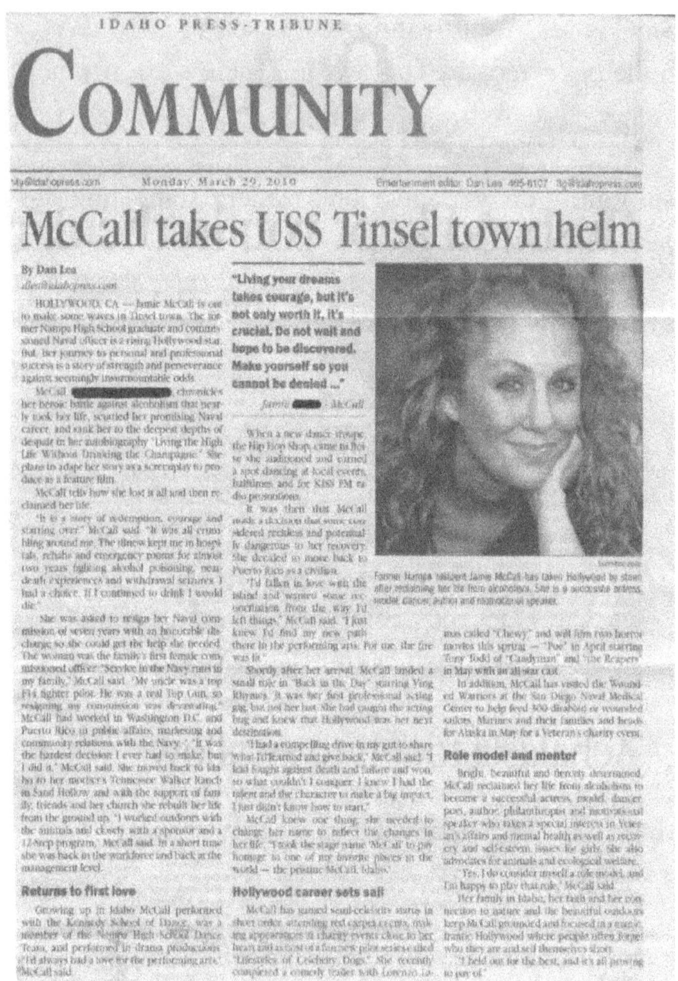

IDAHO PRESS-TRIBUNE

COMMUNITY

[illegible]@idahopress.com Monday, March 29, 2010 Entertainment editor: Dan Lea 465-8107 [illegible]@idahopress.com

McCall takes USS Tinsel town helm

By Dan Lea
[illegible]@idahopress.com

HOLLYWOOD, CA — Jamie McCall is out to make some waves in Tinsel town. The former Nampa High School graduate and commissioned Naval officer is a rising Hollywood star. But her journey to personal and professional success is a story of strength and perseverance against seemingly insurmountable odds.

McCall [illegible], chronicles her heroic battle against alcoholism that nearly took her life, scuttled her promising Naval career, and sank her to the deepest depths of despair in her autobiography "Living the High Life Without Drinking the Champagne." She plans to adapt her story as a screenplay to produce as a feature film.

McCall tells how she lost it all and then reclaimed her life.

"It is a story of redemption, courage and starting over," McCall said. "It was all crumbling around me. The illness kept me in hospitals, rehabs and emergency rooms for almost two years fighting alcohol poisoning, near-death experiences and withdrawal seizures. I had a choice. If I continued to drink I would die."

She was asked to resign her Naval commission of seven years with an honorable discharge so she could get the help she needed. The woman was the family's first female commissioned officer. "Service in the Navy runs in my family," McCall said. "My uncle was a top F14 fighter pilot. He was a real Top Gun, so resigning my commission was devastating." McCall had worked in Washington D.C. and Puerto Rico in public affairs, marketing and community relations with the Navy. "It was the hardest decision I ever had to make, but I did it," McCall said. She moved back to Idaho to her mother's Tennessee Walker Ranch in Sand Hollow and with the support of family, friends and her church she rebuilt her life from the ground up. "I worked outdoors with the animals and closely with a sponsor and a 12-step program," McCall said. In a short time she was back in the workforce and back at the management level.

Returns to first love

Growing up in Idaho McCall performed with the Kennedy School of Dance, was a member of the Nampa High School Dance Team, and performed in drama productions. "I'd always had a love for the performing arts," McCall said.

"Living your dreams takes courage, but it's not only worth it, it's crucial. Do not wait and hope to be discovered. Make yourself so you cannot be denied ..."

Jamie [illegible] McCall

When a new dance troupe, the Hip Hop Shop, came to Boise she auditioned and earned a spot dancing at local events, halftimes and for KISS FM radio promotions.

It was then that McCall made a decision that some considered reckless and potentially dangerous to her recovery. She decided to move back to Puerto Rico as a civilian.

"I'd fallen in love with the island and wanted some reconciliation from the way I'd left things," McCall said. "I just knew I'd find my new path there in the performing arts. For me, the fire was lit."

Shortly after her arrival, McCall landed a small role in "Back in the Day" starring Ving Rhames. It was her first professional acting gig, but not her last. She had caught the acting bug and knew that Hollywood was her next destination.

"I had a compelling drive in my gut to share what I'd learned and give back," McCall said. "I had fought against death and failure and won, so what couldn't I conquer. I knew I had the talent and the character to make a big impact. I just didn't know how to start."

McCall knew one thing: she needed to change her name to reflect the changes in her life. "I took the stage name 'McCall' to pay homage to one of my favorite places in the world — the pristine McCall, Idaho."

Hollywood career sets sail

McCall has gained semi-celebrity status in short order attending red carpet events, making appearances at charity events close to her heart and as host of a [illegible] pilot series titled "Lifestyles of Celebrity Dogs." She recently completed a comedy trailer with Lorenzo Lamas called "Chewy" and will film two horror movies this spring — "Poe" in April starring Tony Todd of "Candyman" and "The Reapers" in May with an all-star cast.

In addition, McCall has visited the Wounded Warriors at the San Diego Naval Medical Center to help feed 300 disabled or wounded sailors, Marines and their families and heads for Alaska in May for a Veteran's charity event.

Role model and mentor

Bright, beautiful and fiercely determined, McCall reclaimed her life from alcoholism to become a successful actress, model, dancer, poet, author, philanthropist and motivational speaker who takes a special interest in Veteran's affairs and mental health as well as recovery and self-esteem issues for girls. She also advocates for animals and ecological welfare.

"Yes, I do consider myself a role model, and I'm happy to play that role," McCall said.

Her family in Idaho, her faith and her connection to nature and the beautiful outdoors keep McCall grounded and focused in a manic, frantic Hollywood where people often forget who they are and sell themselves short.

"I held out for the best, and it's all proving to pay off."

Former Nampa resident Jamie McCall has taken Hollywood by storm after reclaiming her life from alcoholism. She is a successful actress, model, dancer, author and motivational speaker.

Chase Von: What are some of the causes you either support or feel extremely strongly about?

Jamie McCall: Of course the USO and all the veterans organizations out there, animal shelters and the protection of endangered species & prevention of abuse & rescues, sober living, recovery and rehabilitation advocacy and education! Keeping music & the arts in schools! We short-change the future of our nation when we short-change our school system. It`s atrocious what`s happened to it.

Chase Von: Besides dancing, how do you stay in such fantastic shape? And what are some of your favorite meals?

Jamie McCall: I`ve always been an athlete. I`ve always been very active, both in the gym and outdoors! I like to switch it up & try new things. I was also a competetive swimmer for years, all the way through college and swam in the Navy. Martial arts, horseback riding, downhill skiing, jogging, hiking, you name it, I`ll do it. On diet - balance. That`s it. Just try to have balance and moderation of all things. Eat smaller portions more frequently. It really works.

Chase Von: Personally, I don`t think I could get tired of watching you dance. (Smile.)

But you`re also learning Martial Arts from the legend Billy Blanks himself! My Sifu and friend, nickname *Scrappy* and I won`t say his real name because I`m going to share some more and I have to ask him if he`s OK with that, fought Billy Blanks three times. He won once, lost once, and drew once back in the day in competition.

He also just recently got inducted into the Martial Arts Hall of Fame and I`ve learned, the same people that make the rings for the Super Bowl winners, also make their rings as well.

Taimak *The Last Dragon* and quite a few other notables got inducted the same time he did, but I will only mention one of those others for now, and that was David Carradine, post humously.

But are you studying Martial Arts because you think it will benefit you in acting? And also, is it also benefiting you just in life in general based on your view?

By the way, he (Scrappy), was also shot in the face his last time to the war, and obviously survived and is still recuperating. Bottom line, is, he`s going to have to deal with this injury for life. But he has also got certified to be a referee for Mixed Martial Arts even despite all that, since because of his own injuries, (He`s won two purple hearts mind you), it`s doubtful he will be able to compete himself any more. But then again, neither he nor I believe in saying the word never. (Smile.)

Jamie McCall: I love the Martial Arts! Billy`s the best.

There`s a reason why it`s called an "Art" and not "Martial Sports", because it is a performing art as well, and with all the different styles, everything is up for personal interpretation and expression. That`s another thing that I love about it. I`ve studied TKD and Karate, and want to get into the Chinese styles next - Kung Fu. Yes, it`s good for career, but it`s something I`ve always wanted to do on a personal level as well.

I get so much more out of it than just physical fitness. Self confidence, spiritual inspiration, clarity & balance, discipline...the list goes on.

Chase Von: Can you share one of your shorter poetry pieces, so our readers can get a glimpse of that side of you? And you have so many sides Lady! (Smile.)

Jamie McCall: Hmm, Ok, a short piece:

Cracker Jack Love

Back & forth, forth & back.
Say goodbye then take it back.
Take it slow. Take it fast.
Desperate to make it last.
Hanging on with all your might...
Ten knuckles turning white.
Fighting panic. Feeling frantic.
Panting, manic from the chase - WAIT! Don`t go!
Ebb & flow. NO! Tug-of-war.
Who`s in control? Think you are?
Then you`re a fool.
Addiction`s the Star.

Like a sugar high eatin` Cracker Jacks
Snackin` late at night, feeding only fat
Packin` that crap deep into cavities in your teeth
Pains sharp and wrenching yet you continue stuffing
Your mouth gluttonously with the candy-coated popcorn
Wedging itself deep in the crevices causing discomfort
The sugar feeding the black hole that`s now embedded deep
Rotting its way from your teeth down into your soul...
You need a root canal - a deep cleaning
Yet you can`t stop!
You keep munching `till you finish the box.
It`s empty...now what?
Change your diet? Self-discipline?
Or try it YET again with another box
Of Cracker Jack snack addict love...

~jMc 2006 copyright

Chase Von: Thanks so much and talented oozes from you! I`m wishing you all the success life has to offer Jamie! And I do have a request. Because the only complaint as I`ve told you before, about your Belly Dancing video I had, was it wasn`t long enough! (Smile.)

You have a plethora of talents and I`m so glad you are sharing them with the world and also that you took the time to share yourself with us here, at the Student Operated Press! Love and light and don`t be a stranger OK? And wishing you and yours, a wonderful Holiday Season!

Jamie McCall: Thanks so much, Happy Holidays to you & all the readers as well! I`ll leave you with my mantra:

"Do not wait and hope to be discovered...
make yourself so you cannot be denied!"

--- Jamie McCall

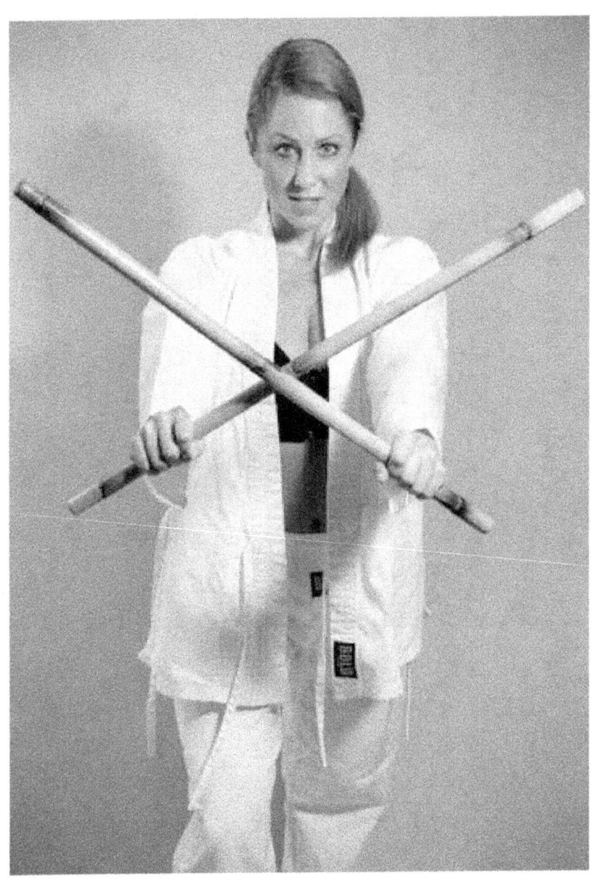

Interview with Yolanda "Yo" Jackson, AKA "Poetic Flow"

TALENTED WORDSMITH

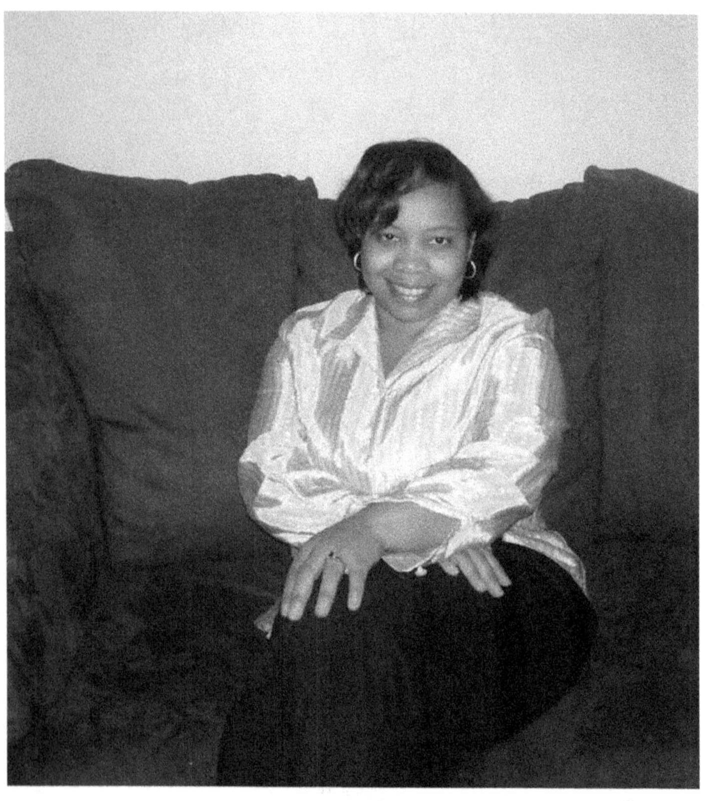

Chase Von: Hey Poetic Flow and on behalf of the Student Operated Press and myself, thanks for finding the time to share yourself with our readers! I know we were supposed to do this what? Years ago now? So I appreciate your patience with me but like yourself, have had a lot on my plate and things still keep popping up!

But also, the New Year is upon us so maybe we were supposed to do this to kick off 2010! (Smile.) Again, glad you`re making time for this to share yourself with our readers and we`re getting to this!

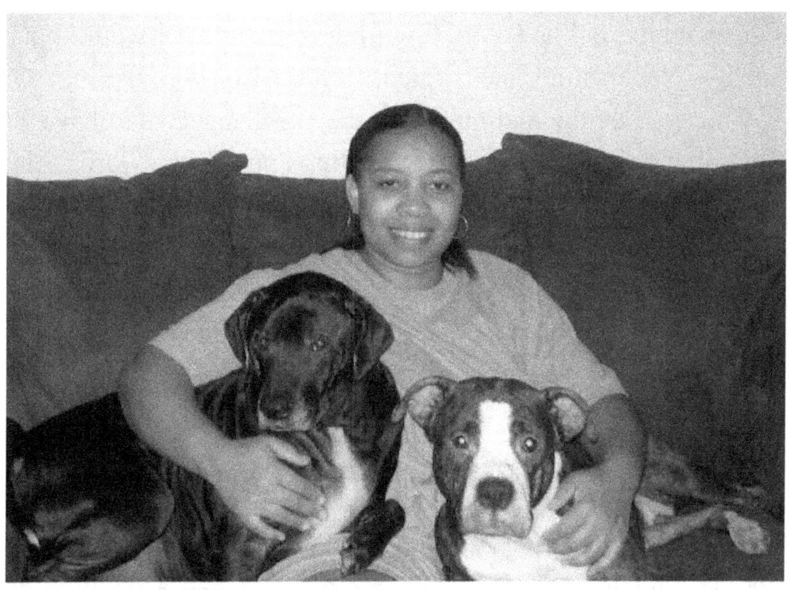

Poetic Flow: Hey Chase! Thank you for the opportunity to interview with you. I`m avid believer things happen in their appointed time, so this was the time for the interview instead of a year ago or so (Smile.) We all get busy and it`s understandable, but I`m glad we are having the chance to do it now, in a brand new year, wow 2010, I remember when we went into 2000, 10 yrs have flown by! WOW!

Chase Von: What were your younger years like? Are you a native of Chicago? And was writing something you knew you wanted to do at a very young age or is it something that came to you later in life? (I`ve read your web page mind you, and it says you began in 1985 but I don`t know how old you are.) (Smile.)

For example, if I had started writing in that year I would have been--- Never mind, next! (Heh, Heh.) Also, is it just me? Or is Chicago one the main cities in the US that seems to have an over abundance of love for the written and spoken word? And if you agree with my belief that it certainly is one, is it harder to stand out there for what you do considering there are so many that truly appreciate poetry there? Or is it just the opposite of that, because there are so many that are truly and sincerely into it there?

Poetic Flow: Hmmm, my younger years, (LOL.) Well I`m the oldest of four children and the only girl. My grandmother was a HUGE influence on my life, she taught me a lot about life, people, GOD, spirituality, education, etc. I had a really good childhood into teenage life and transformed into adulthood very smoothly. I am born and raised Chicago, IL.

I always had the gift of writing, it wasn`t what I thought I`d be doing, my profession is in the legal world, I`m a Paralegal, my career goal is to become an attorney. In 1985 I was 12 years old, my grandmother and I use to have conversations about so many different things and she had seen some of my poetry because we use to have to do poetry/prose in grammar school.

She told me I had a gift and I should use that gift.

I begin to write more and more thereafter and my poetry just piled up one after another after another. One night we were talking about life and how unfortunate it is for some people and she told me I should write a poem about Street People, hence my poem "Street People." In my freshman year of HS, my black history teacher wanted us to write about black history, so I figured I`d write a poem using the letters of the alphabet.

My father helped me out a little and I ultimately wrote "The A-Z Black American Poem" which followed me throughout HS (i.e. recited it at assemblies, was published in the HS paper, etc).

Chicago most definitely is a city full of talent and love of poetry; there are many, many places in Chicago that host open mic/spoken word events. Kind of like New York, which is also a good place that has talented poets with a true love for this art.

I believe that each poet/spoken word artist is different in their own right. We stand out on our own accord based upon the audience and who likes to hear what type of poetry or spoken word pieces; you know the genre of it like music. My style of poetry is free-style, I don`t conform to specific ways poetry can be written, and I write it the way I feel like writing it (Smile.)

As you`ve seen and read before, my motto is "Inspiring, Motivating & Encouraging the World One Poem at a Time" - Each time I write something, it`s meant to reach someone in a positive way. I write my poetry based upon conversations, thoughts, feelings (not necessarily of my own), the universe, etc.

Chase Von: I have out three books, two of them being mostly poetry. I also know as a poet there are a myriad of subjects people can address and I like to think of myself as eclectic in that regard. But if someone was to ask me, what the overall theme of my books regarding poetry are about, I would have to say relational ship kind of things mostly. What do you say is the overall theme you believe your book addresses or what readers can expect from reading it?

Poetic Flow: Well Chase, as I stated above my motto is "*Inspiring, Motivating & Encouraging the World - One Poem at a Time*" - My poetry focuses on Life, *Love, Feelings, Thoughts, Situations, Circumstances, Spirituality.* My 1st book published in May 2008 through Author House Publishing (self publishing company) is entitled *`Poetic Flow Poetry for Your Soul`* all of what I mentioned above is reflective in my book. It is a collaboration of poems from 1985 through 2008. It encompasses 127 pages of poetry.

If people want to be inspired, motivated or encouraged, they will find a poem in my book to help them. I believe in being a positive being and I put out positive vibes in all I do, it is reflective in my book, my words, and my poetry.

Chase Von: We just opened up a Spoken Word portion here at the SOP! (Smile). So one, can you add some of you work here for our readers and two, when I did mine it was just beginning and I taped it in a closet. (Heh, Heh.)

I know, ghetto, but the first one I did in my recording studio---OK, my BATHROOM and it had too much of an echo effect I was told. (Smile.)

Everyone I know thinks that bathrooms have the best acoustics for whatever reason so any way--- I wasn`t trying to be professional, just to share.

But you also have hit the stage and I for one, admire anyone with the guts to stand up in front of
a room full of people and do their thing! (I`m a shy person). (Smile.)

What was it like for you, your first time? And do you enjoy it or is it something you have to mentally prepare yourself for each time you do it?

Poetic Flow: (LOL), you are funny.

The first time I ever read my poetry I was a senior in high school (1991), my teacher wanted me to read my "A-Z Black American Poem"; the second time I ever read my poetry before a large crowd was in 2007 at Navy Pier "A Celebration of Jazz" during Black History Month. A long time friend of mine Dee Yelvington invited me out because she put the event together. I`ve performed at various churches and some other open mic events. I was nervous the first time, the second time, the third time, lol...I don`t get the chance to go out much due to my work schedule (most events are held during the week at 9pm or later). I`ve gotten better, my knees don`t shake anymore, my hand doesn`t tremble anymore, lol. I enjoy it. I do prepare mentally, I read over my work (I`m a Poet, not a Spoken Word Artist) although I`m working on transitioning over (Smile.) - So I practice memorizing my poetry so I can perform it w/o the book or paper in front of me, but that`s still a work in progress (Smile.)

Chase Von: Thanks for sharing that Poetic Flow. I`m also interviewing Taalam Acey if he gets the chance to get to the questions I sent. (He`s a busy man, so I ain`t rushing the brother). (Smile.)

But he`s so good at the Spoken Word Living Legend Stevie Wonder himself interviewed him on his radio show! But who are some of the poets you yourself admire, spoken word artist you look up to? And just people you admire in general?

Poetic Flow: I`m probably one of the few poets who really didn`t know lots of poets. I enjoyed reading poetry by Gwendolyn Brooks and later on Maya Angelou; I`ve read some Nikki Giovanni. New school poets I`ve read some Taalam Acey, Donna Solitario, Tren, Poetic J, Joanne Stephens (who I did a collab with), Makeda (who I also did a collab with), Malik Yusef, Donique, Poet Janet Dawson, Poetic Central, Poetic1, GPA, Emmanuel Louis...just to name a few. Now when you talk about admiration in general, I admire my mother, my late grandmother (Verena), my late cousin (Centerius) and many other women, men in my family along with friends.

I`ve learned so much from people who have come into my life and impacted me, spit knowledge on me, opened my eyes to other ways of doing things, it`s just amazing! I am a very humble person and I know factually if not for the grace & mercy of GOD and people he has put in my life to help me along my journey, where would I be? I give thanks and honor and all glory to the Almighty Father for any and every blessing that has come into my path to walk in this life with me.

Chase Von: I see some of the folks you admire are on my list as well! (Smile.) Now I`m also waiting on someone else to get back to me if she can. And that`s phenomenal actress Christine Elise McCarthy!

She`s been on 90210, The Heat of the Night, movies with Chucky, (Yes, that doll that comes alive) and really, I think she needs no introduction and it would take up pages to list all her credits but that wasn`t why I was bringing her up any way. The reason I am bringing her up is she is an avid dog lover! And you are as well! (Smile.)

How many dogs do you have? Why do you love dogs so much and is there a particular breed you`re most fond of? Also, what are some of the causes you yourself support or feel extremely strong about? Because I also mentioned in another interview I did with Jenny McShane, about the former Governor of Alaska and her campaign against wolves. Something Ashley Judd made it her business to get involved in as well. But what are your feelings in general regarding that?

Poetic Flow: I had 3 dogs, but one of my dogs recently died (sad face). I am now down to 2 (A black lab mix -boy, and a pit bull- girl). I love dogs because I was raised around them; there hasn`t been a time in my life, except for when I was married, that I didn`t have a dog.

They are so loving, I mean we as humans can really learn

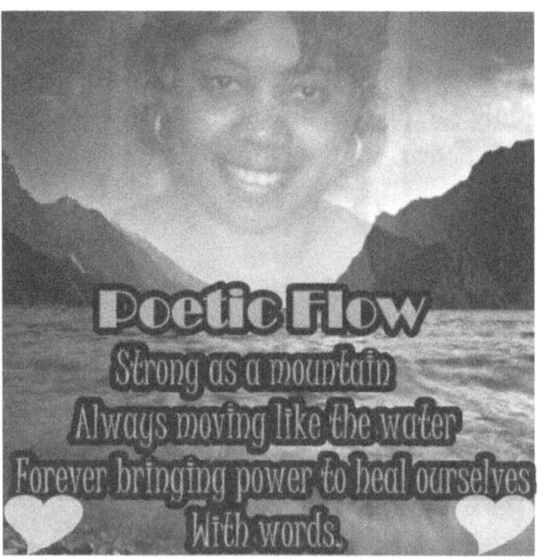

a LOT from dogs, they love unconditionally and they bring a sense of joy to your heart when you walk through the door. I grew up with all breeds of dogs (German Sheperds, Dobermans, Pit Bulls, Collies, etc. all big dogs, (LOL.)

I support the cause for homeless animals by donating money when I shop for my doggies. I feel horrible when I watch the commercials of all the abandoned and abused animals. I rescued my black lab from a humane society, my dog who died of illness; I rescued her from the streets. I put up signs to see if anyone would claim her and no one did. She was a Rhodesian ridgeback, AWESOME, AWESOME DOG!!!! - When it comes to wolves, ummmm yeah I don`t know. A wolf is not a domesticated animal, it`s a wild animal.

They are beauuuuutiful, but I wouldn`t trust one as a pet.

Chase Von: I`m a dog lover myself Poetic Flow, we have a Shepherd. One Shepherd. (Smile.)

And I still don`t think wolves should be shot from planes and have their front legs cut off wild or not.

Where can our readers learn more about you and where you`re going to be doing your next appearances? Also can you share your web sites and give our readers any inside scoop on any future projects you have in the works?

Poetic Flow: Great! Readers can learn and follow me on my website TRUE DAT THURSDAY www.yolandajackson.bravehost.com - I created this website in 2007 through the idea of my friend Shari. I used to send out my poetry every week (Thursday) to a list of readers which grew from 40 in 2007 to almost 1800 today. Last year in 2009

I opted to send my poetry out only once a month on 3RD Thursdays and I incorporate guest poets on my page also.

Within my TRUE DAT THURSDAY website I have links to connect people to me on myspace, face book and twitter. Also whenever I do performances, they can get that info from my website as well, there is a link regarding my upcoming performances on the page, just click and it`ll have all the info.

I am currently working on my 2nd book of poetry entitled "Love~N~Life Poetry" it encompasses 20 Love poems and the rest is about Life, hence the title :-) ... I am also going to simultaneously release a book of positive quotes for my readers so I`m hoping that goes over really well :-)

Both are scheduled for release this summer 2010, so stay tuned...

Chase Von: What are your favorite meals? Also when I lived in Jersey one thing that was almost like a piece of Heaven was a hoagie from Wawa`s. (Smile.) We also weren`t far from Philly, so of course Philly Cheese Steaks were another slice of Heaven when it came to getting one`s grub on! (Heh, Heh.)

But since I haven`t too my knowledge been there, what is a trade mark thing in Chicago that falls into that kind of a category? (Just in case I show up there, I will know what to get if I`m a bit famished. (Heh, Heh.) Also what do you do to remain in shape or is that something taking care of your dogs takes care of for you? (Smile.)

Poetic Flow: My favorite meal is at Thanksgiving, love turkey, dressing, potato salad, rolls, greens, cranberry sauce, yuuum yuuum!

My favorite food is chicken (grilled, baked, fried, broiled, boiled...) it doesn`t matter, I just love chicken. Chicago is known for #1 its Pizza (the deep dish from Giordano`s) and #2 it`s Maxwell Polishes down by the University of Illinois, delicious!!!! - I walk A LOT! Especially working in downtown Chicago, I think that keeps me in shape :-) ... I use my treadmill at times and I just let the dogs out in the back yard of the house, (LOL.)

Chase Von: On to something truly more serious now Poetic Flow. When we first met, I became aware of the loss you suffered of your brother. I also know something like that is painful to address, but address it you do in your poetry. Can you share one of your pieces that were inspired by that senseless loss and also, is that something that sparked your interest in working in the legal profession? Or were you already doing that?

Poetic Flow: I`ve been a Paralegal for almost 11 years now, so way before the killing of my brother I was doing that work. I have a passion for helping others and my ultimate goal is to become an attorney. The piece I wrote after my brother was killed was called *THE STAIN OF PAIN* written in 2007 (the year he was killed). I`ll share it with you now...

The Stain of Pain

Life is too short
This we know
Never knowing
When it`s our time to go

I woke up one morning (5/8/07)
Went on to work
Got a phone call
That could have given someone a stroke

My mother on the other line
Telling me my 22 year old brother was shot
This is just something
I would have never thought about

I left work
Got on the bus
Prayed to God
Didn`t make a fuss

Two stops before I got to my car
A few short blocks until I got in my ride
Another phone call from mom
Cinque has died!

My face is stunned
My heart confused
Not understanding
Why this happened to you

I called the family
Called some friends
Informing them
My brother`s life had come to an end

Still frozen in time
My mind working overload
Just saw my brother
A few days ago

We were talking about GOD
Talking about Life
Talking about the future
Man, this can`t be right

Someone took his life
They had no regard
Could care less
About our stress

As he stood and talked with friends
Laughing and talking smack
The gunman
Shot my brother in the back

He fled the scene
Still at large
I pray everyday
Knowing he has to answer to GOD

Now we`ve lost our brother
Mom and Dad, their son
His five children, their father
His life gone at the hand of a gun

Someone pulled the trigger
Never did they figure
The ripple effect it would have
Senseless Crime, it`s so sad

I thank God
For the 22 years
He gave me with my brother
Although I still shed tears

We conversated a lot
We had a real connection
I now think of Q as my guardian angel
My protection

I love you Q
Just the same
We`ll see you again, but until then
We live with the stain of pain

Written By: Yolanda Jackson

My brother lived his life knowing Christ died for our sins and he lived his life by giving love, which is why I know, he`s with the Father Above.

Chase Von: Thanks for sharing that Lady, and old as it is, it still rings true, an ounce of prevention is worth a pound of cure. So hopefully someone will read that and be influenced by it so they won`t cause someone else, undue pain.

What would you say if you were standing before a microphone that could be heard by every child on the planet, and regardless of what language they spoke, they would understand you?

What positive advice would you give the children, if that were possible?

Poetic Flow: I would quote one of my poems A QUICK LESSON ABOUT LIFE "Life is a big ball of experiences, in order to experience it you must Live Life, in order to Live Life you must Love Life, in order to Love Life, you must Love Thyself, Once this is done, Your possibilities are Limitless." (c) 2007 by Poetic Flow...I would let them know that I understand it can be hard, life is hard, people are not always nice, but continue to stay true to self, don`t fall by the wayside of crime and carelessness. I would tell them that they each hold the key to happiness, success, power and positivity because it all is a blend of one who loves themselves enough to know that GOD makes a way when there is no way, that despite all we see around us, the killings, gangs, homelessness, poverty and the list goes on and on, that even still we serve a POWERFUL AND MIGHTY GOD and sometimes we have to go through some things before we are presented with our blessing, but that comes with Life and Lessons to be learned to make us better and stronger people. So no matter what it is that they may ever go through in life, just remember to keep a Positive frame of mind because there is a positive in every negative.

Chase Von: How important is family to you, and what is your take on the state of our current world?

Poetic Flow: Family means everything to me. It is the hierarchy organizational system of the world. There is suppose to a MOM & DAD, but more commonly we see just MOM handling the business and she has done so very well. Lately I`ve seen more men step up to the plate and be single parents and I think that is Awesome since there is such a lack of that (definitely in the black community, but throughout all races as well). The state of our current world keeps me shaking my head. There is SO MUCH I don`t understand, but I have to refer back to Proverbs 3:5 "Trust in the Lord with all thine hearts and lean not unto thine own understanding." That scripture helps me get through so much!

The current world is full of greed, heartlessness, carelessness, and the list goes on and on. It`s so bad that you can`t even say HI to someone without being looked at all cross eyed and evil.

Have we really succumbed to a world where courteousness is a crime? Also, when did it become popular to carry a gun and shot people just because!? Why are these young kids, older kids and adults hiding behind guns to show their toughness?!!

Why do the police feel the need to harass people instead of

taking care of true crime?? Why are mothers and fathers stealing their own kids toys and selling them on the streets for drugs or to obtain drug money?

Why are we fighting a war we should have never even started!!? These are my thoughts on the world, I have many, many, many more, but I`ll stop with this... It`s just craziness to me!

Chase Von: Donna Solitario the author of *Embracing the Light* and more recently, *Coming Home to My Heart* introduced us, and I`m glad she did as you are a truly wonderful soul! But what I`m finding out as I get older is the more people I meet, the more people I meet that know someone else I`ve met or have had dealings with.

For example, I met, and it breaks my heart to say it and now even to write it, the now late, Brittany Murphy. I also interviewed actress, model and musician Jenny McShane and she too had met and worked with, not on a movie but a project with Brittany Murphy. So she was crushed by the news as well.

I also just interviewed Voiceover Extraordinaire Joan Baker. And I was looking through her pictures on my space (After), I had interviewed her and lo and behold, she`s in a few pictures with actress and model Shawn Richardz, who I`ve also interviewed! She told me, (Joan), that she and Shawn have known each other for, if memory serves me correctly, about ten years).

But what I`m getting at is the world just seems to be getting smaller for me in that regard. So I`m looking at your page to prepare for this interview, and I see one of your all time favorite movies is The Last Dragon.

I`ve communicated a few times with Taimak, who is an outstanding human being I might add, My friend just recently got inducted into the Martial Arts Hall of fame and lo and behold, there he is standing in a picture with Taimak who also got inducted at the same time! I could go on but what are your feelings on that?

Is the world getting smaller or what? Or is the communication such as the internet making these things possible? And for me, it`s a good thing but do you think it can be used for an even greater good also?

Poetic Flow: Well Chase, I`m a firm believer in there truly being 6 degrees of separation (for every 6th person you know they know someone mutually and the cycle continues). People think our world is SO HUGE, it`s really not, that`s why things like this happen (people meeting people who meet people that other people know, etc). As for the internet, it is a MONSTER!

People use it so much that they don`t even communicate verbally sometimes, it`s all via email, face book, myspace, twitter, text messages, etc. The internet is a BEAST! It can definitely be used for a LOT of good! So many people from kids to elders are on the internet, it is a great place for Positive Vibes, indeed!

Chase Von: Thanks not only for that, but for taking all the time you have to share yourself with our readers Poetic Flow!

I`m calling you that instead of Yolanda because I`m respecting your wishes! (Smile.) I`m also hoping you and yours had a wonderful Christmas and we and I say that as a collective we, have had a lot of bad news in 2009.

The loss of the lovely Farrah Fawcett, incredible actor and man Patrick Swayze, Brittany Murphy who I can personally attest to was so bubbly and so full of life. And the one and only Michael Jackson who I know the impact of that, was felt all around the globe. And I also wish I could list them all, who have positively affected so many of us with their gifts. But are you thinking what I`m thinking? 2010 can`t get here soon enough?

Poetic Flow: You are very welcome Chase and thank you for giving me this opportunity to share some of me with your viewers/readers, it is truly appreciated. Yes indeed we lost lots of celebrities (musicians, actors, actresses, etc). We also lost many unknowns (everyday people who don`t get the media coverage because they are in a different socio-economic level) - We lost many soldiers to the war also. With each year we face devastation of this magnitude and we look forward to the following year so we can leave behind the hurts, pain, disappointments, etc of the year before. I`m glad we are in a fresh and brand new year of a brand new decade of the new millennium!

Chase Von: Thanks again Poetic Flow and also looking forward to your audio interview with Judy. And also the very best of everything in 2010 and beyond to you and KIT!

Poetic Flow: Thank you Chase for this opportunity, it is truly appreciated and I appreciate you Love. I`m looking forward to the audio interview as well. Here`s to wishing you a Prosperous, Powerful & Positive 2K10! Peace & Blessings, Much Love ~ Poetic Flow

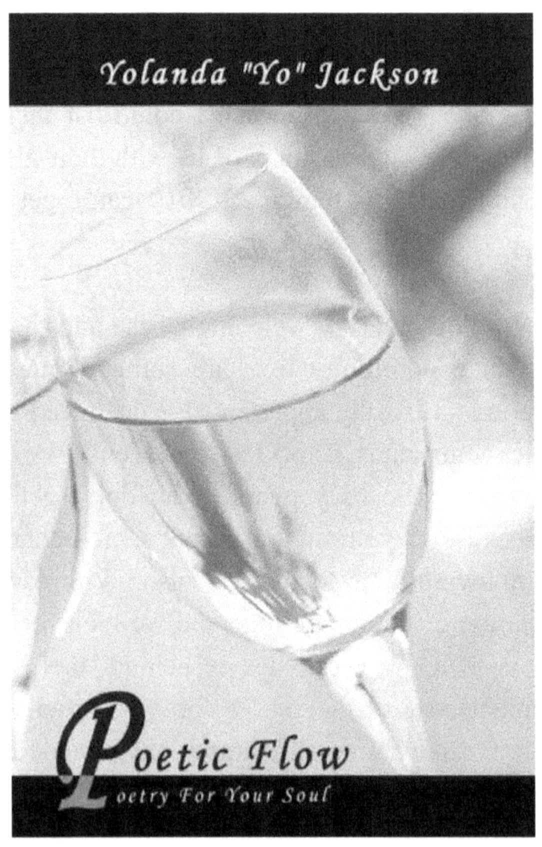

Interview with Diane Wayne

THE LOVELY AND MULTI-TALENTED DIANE WAYNE

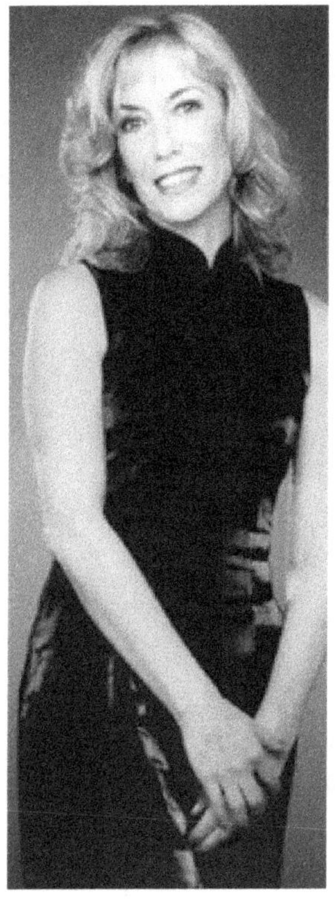

Chase Von: Hey Diane and on behalf of myself and the Student Operated Press, thanks for agreeing to share a bit about yourself here at the SOP. I learned of you through our mutual friend the lovely and amazing actress, model and soul Kitania (Kitty) Kavey, and I`m not surprised you two are friends as you`ve each had what I consider some very similar trials and predicaments in your lives.

We`ll get into that a little later, but for now, my thanks again for taking the time to share yourself with our readers.

Diane Wayne: Hello Chase, you`re very welcome. My thanks to you and the Student Operated Press for this lovely opportunity. Yes, Kitty Kavey and I are very close friends, sharing not only some similar life experiences, but some artistic ones, as well. In fact, at the moment, we`re working on a film together.

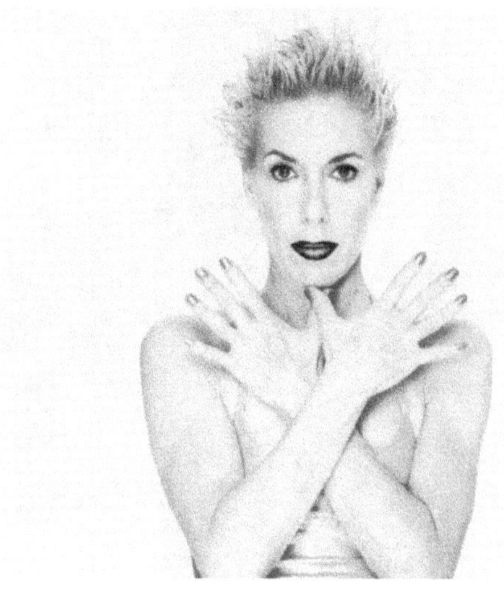

Chase Von: Let`s begin, as they say, at the very beginning. (Smile.) Where did you grow up? How would you describe your childhood? And the things you do now, such as singing, acting, dancing and writing song lyrics and poetry--- Are those things that you also did in your younger years because you loved them and that carried over into adulthood--- Or did you discover your love for them much later?

As for myself, I was writing poetry from the age of twelve or thirteen, so sometimes things we gravitate towards show themselves early on in life. Also, if there were artistic things you did even in your formative years, how supportive were your parents and teachers of those talents?

Diane Wayne: I grew up in Burbank, California, in what could easily be called "a war zone in the home." I truly know what it is to be terrorized, and it`s something I was not completely free of until my dad passed away in 2008. Being battered and sexually abused was not an ideal childhood. And running away from home before I was in kindergarten proved unsuccessful.

So with reserve at that time, I surrendered to my predicament and became a dutiful child. I decided then that God had given me "non-parents" for parents, so I could learn from my experiences. I didn`t know it then, but I believe being an abused and unwanted child is what led me, since 2002, to create "A Music Mission", my global charity for abused, homeless, and underprivileged children. Those times also taught me to look for what I could learn from difficult situations. I did my best to make my childhood an adventure. I had to survive. I had to grow-up. And I had to help my slower twin sister.

I did everything I could to create harmony in a hostile environment. I`m so grateful God gave me some brains, some talents, a good sense of humor, and a great imagination that allowed me to find something good in a horrific situation.

One of my earliest childhood memories is making music when I was about three years old. I used to wake up in the wee hours of the morning, crawl out of my bed, and wander through the dark house in my robe and slippers, pulling my xylophone-playing bear-on-a-string behind me, while making up words and melodies for songs.

I could also sit down at the piano and find all the notes to any song I heard before I could even write my name. And I would break into dance whenever I heard music playing (I still do!) Around that time there were violent episodes that were so traumatic that I became separated from my original songwriting connection until some years after I was out of the house and on my own.

What happened inside the house was seemingly unnoticed by the world outside. At age 3 1/2, I was co-starring in a television movie, and made two national commercials by the time I was 7.

But again, with the violence increasing inside the home and sexual abuse put a stop to my acting career at that time.

When I was around age ten, after my grandpa died, I got a guitar and taught myself how to play from the chord charts in music books. I played rhythms with music I heard on the radio and TV, and performed at retirement homes, hospices and the local Veteran`s Hospital.

Singing lead and close harmonies was also something that

came very naturally for me from a young age. In fact, some producers I later worked with here in Holland at Orange, Byte, and Restless Records, told me I was "inhuman" because I "phased in the computer," I sang so closely with myself doubling lead lines and harmonies.

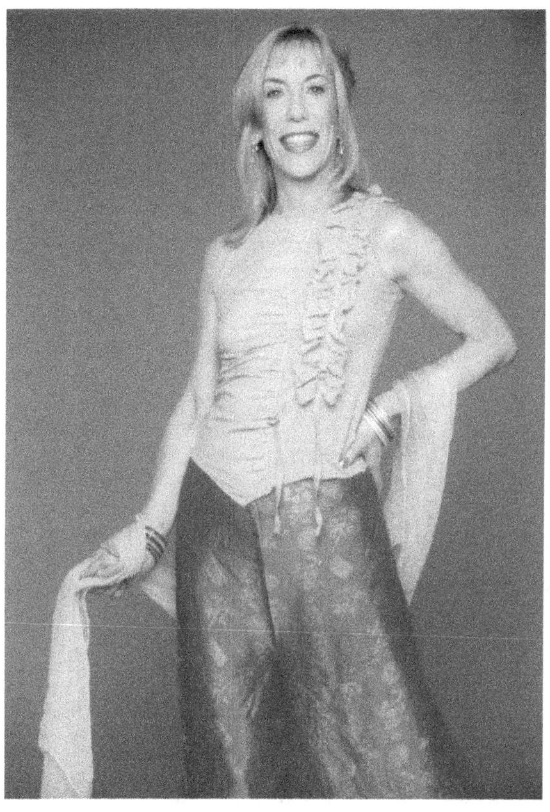

My poetry seemed to evolve along with my songwriting. (And Chase, not only have I enjoyed very much, the poems from you I have read, I also read you`re a Pulitzer Prize-winning poet. Congratulations!)

I`m a published poet too, and winner of an Editor`s Choice Award and Outstanding Achievement in Poetry Award. Here`s one of those poems, and again, one of my first poems, called, "Thoughts of You," published on the first page of the poetry compilation book, “Invoking the Muse.”

“Thoughts of You” (c) Diane Wayne (all rights reserved)

In the morning
at the piano playing
with thoughts of you
I am lost.
Then thrilled
until
I have to laugh out loud
a long time after
there stays a smile.

While I didn`t grow up in any kind of supportive atmosphere, I somehow felt music and singing and acting would always be a part of my life. And it continues to be true.

Chase Von: Pulitzer Prize winning poet? No Diane, I wish! (Smile.) You`re probably referring to the phenomenal life-saving and changing Poet Ed Roberts. I published his book ***Whispers, Tears, Prayers and Hope*** and we did submit it for that award.

And that`s right Diane, I do remember seeing something about your parent`s lack of support when I was reading up on you. In fact, them kicking you out the house was the inspiration for your song, ***"Don`t Give It Up Girl."*** So they were supportive only up until the point where you decided to choose your own road in life.

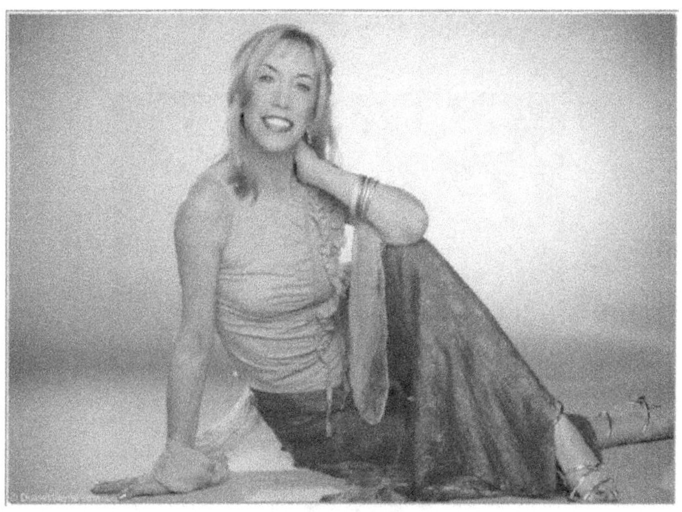

Diane Wayne: Parental support was feigned publicly. My parents were vehemently, adamantly, and violently opposed to my artistic aspirations in private. And yes, that`s why I was ultimately, forcibly ejected from their house, simply for announcing "I`m going to be a singer," when I was 17.

Don`t Give It Up, Girl, is one of the first songs I wrote once out on my own. I was sitting at a piano playing early one morning, just practicing some chord progressions when inspiration struck. The words and melody started flowing out together, which is often how my song writing happens. When I finished the song, I looked down at my heart, and asked "inspiration," "are you coming back?" I was so filled with passion and feelings, in what felt like timeless space; a space that felt so safe to express myself so freely. Inspiration seemed then, and still does, a very solid, yet fragile, intimate connection with my heart and soul, and God, and the whole world at once, as creation flows.

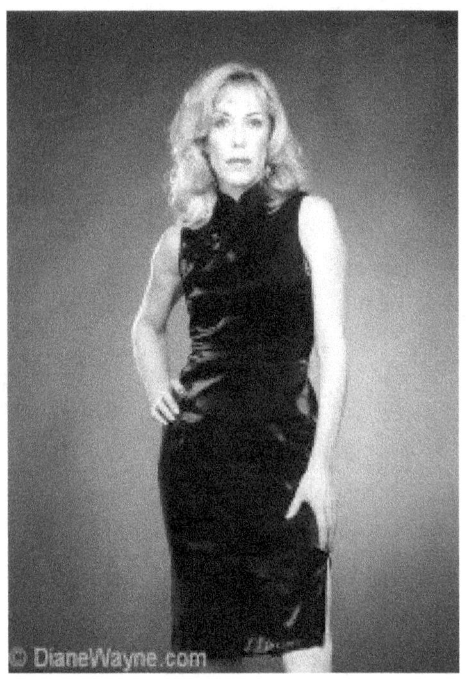

As I continue writing I`m always struck with a feeling and a place I can almost see to step into openly, where I find myself in a stream of consciousness where expression flows, almost effortlessly, until it is exhausted and feels complete. I call these moments my most beautiful obsessions, as they are truly the most intimate, exhilarating, satisfying moments of my life.

Chase Von: That must have been a very difficult thing to deal with, particularly at the tender age of seventeen! Talk about taking the lonely road of an artist who listens to the beat of their own drum---Have things in that department improved over the years with your successes in following your heart?

Diane Wayne: Most definitely yes! I`d been told from the beginning of my artistic career that I had to "pay my dues." So I just accepted the early days of homelessness and poverty as a struggling artist out on my own. It seemed a small price to pay for the experiences I was getting. I joined a show band, playing soul music and jazz fusion that toured on and off the road throughout the United States and Canada for about 4 years. We played all kinds of venues from tiny bars and county fairs to 5 star hotels and upscale nightclubs during that time.

But after those first few years I felt I`d gone as far as I could go on that level, so I took myself off the road, and really got back to writing my own variety of original songs again. I also wrote 1 minute promotional spots for local charity events in San Diego County on Radio Station KyXy, 96.5FM.

Within a few years I was showcasing my songs at singer-songwriter venues in Los Angeles.

Things were going well and I decided to take myself to Europe to expand my horizons. There were some very successful performances at the Buddha Bar Nightclub and The Tribarin in Paris, France, as well as clubs like The Alto, and the Paradiso in Amsterdam, Holland. But then an unexpected car accident left me with a serious whiplash and partial paralysis for a number of years. Still, I kept writing songs.

Finally my first label song release as a songwriter, came in the summer of 2005 with a pop-reggae tune I wrote titled *Run Away From Love*. It was performed and released on Tango Digital Productions by award winning Pacific Rim artist Daniel Rae Costello on his *The Beach Party Re-mix Collection* CD in Australia, New Zealand, and the Fiji Islands.

He re-released *Runaway From Love* again in 2008.

In 2007-2008 the New Zealand record label Mod Romantics globally released *Runaway from Love* a third time along with three other singles of mine; (with me singing) *Dusk*, *The Mist*, and *Colored Sky* from the first compilation of my solo CD, "D`Experience."

In 2005 I started doing two hour live performance radio shows and interviews on the radio here in Holland; first on Radio Miranda, 105.2FM and then on the biggest FM radio/television station in Holland: RTV-Alkmaar, 105.3FM. I continued doing shows throughout 2007, 2008, and 2009.

Chase Von: Kitty ran away and you were kicked out. You both were on your own at very young ages as attractive young ladies trying to make it in a very, at times, harsh world!

Because your life is in ways, so filled with complications forgive me if I jump around a bit.

Kitty`s motorcycle accident that almost killed her and left her with lasting physical affects that persist even to this day, also changed her life and in many ways for the better.

You had your own horrible accident as well. And like her, had to "Come Back" from serious injuries also that could very well, just as easily, prevented you from doing what you so love to do. And also, because you do so many things, I didn`t squeeze *dancer* and *photographer* into the interview`s title but has being paralyzed affected your abilities to dance?

Diane Wayne: I was definitely not dancing after the accident, nor was I singing or playing music. The paralysis affected my neck to my mid-back, so I had to use my whole body from the top of my head to my waist then to look to one side or behind me. Sometimes it affected one or both arms, as well. There were times my arms were so weak and painful I couldn`t use them at all. There was a period of time where my legs twisted inwards so I could barely walk, and a dancer`s turnout was impossible. I couldn`t lift my head by my neck alone, but had to use my hand to get my head in an upright position. I was pretty stunned at first. But I searched out every way possible to recover my original strength and mobility. Even though it took a total of 8 years, I refused to give up until I was healed and could continue singing, dancing, and playing music again.

Photography is something I started just a few years ago for fun, and the gratification I feel when I catch what I see in the world in a photo. It has also garnished me Editor`s Choice Awards, as well as an award for "Asymmetric Composition and Light Mix Throughout" for one of my photos titled "Keep Climbing," published in 2006 in the photography book, "Endless Journeys."

Chase Von: Can you tell our readers more specific details about your accident and how you mentally dealt with being paralyzed? Additionally, how difficult was it for you to adjust or even stand the drastic drop in your standard of living that you were once so accustomed to?

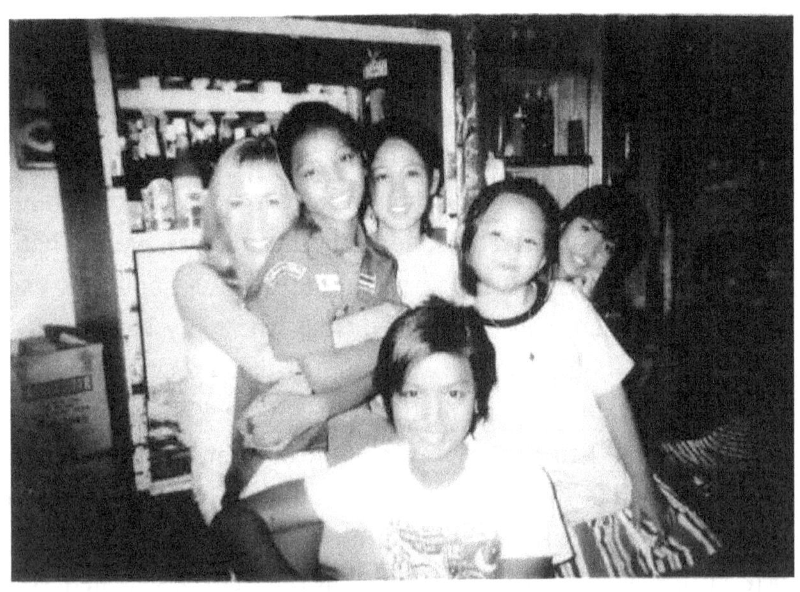

Diane on "A Music Mission" in Bangkok, Thailand

Diane Wayne: Firstly, I was determined to win over my situation. I just couldn`t believe God had taken me this far as an artist and that it was to be the end of my journey. I prayed a lot. Sometimes I cried. But I told God, "I`ll be so glad when these tears turn into laughter," as I truly believed that would come to be. I knew that painful repetitions would be part of my physical recovery, so being a musician and a dancer; I just took the pain with me, and persevered.

When every element of your being is struggling, it`s extremely challenging. You have to find the balance in surrendering yourself to your circumstances, and willing yourself to get through and overcome them, as I believed I would. And I did.

I believe we`ve all got to ride the waves of life. Part of that, for me, has been going through what I call "hell`s gauntlet" a number of times. I just kept telling myself, "this is food for songs." I was inspired by the worst times to write the songs "I Surrender," "Hold On," "Til I See the Sun," and more.

Yes, there was a drastic change in my standard of living from the chic, artistic area of Los Angeles, near Rodeo Drive in Beverly Hills, before I moved to Europe, and the tiny, concrete, attic room I ended up in after the accident in Amsterdam.

I was not only partially paralyzed, but also living alone, in that tiny 5` x 8`, 4th floor walk-up room, without heating or plumbing. I didn`t know anyone, and not being fluent in Dutch made my isolation even more trying. The freezing endless winter months dragged on for what seemed an eternity.

For those first two years I couldn`t even lift my head to look up the stairs while I struggled to make my climb up to my room. With each step I took I said, "yes" out loud until I made it up to the top to my room, just under the roof of that partially demolished building.

Chase Von: And lastly for this portion, how important to you was your faith during this dark time of your life?

Diane Wayne: My faith is truly what got me through it all. God was with me every second of every night and day. I just knew this wasn`t going to be the end. God gave me strength and hope and comfort to fathom the depths of my experiences.

And as I mentioned before, God gave me a good sense of humor. You can cry until you laugh sometimes, and laugh until you cry sometimes too.

I also took the opportunity to read healing books like "Women Who Run With the Wolves," "Feel the Fear and Do It Anyway," and "Conversations With God." I continued song writing and my own soul searching.

Chase Von: That`s wonderful that you were able to maintain that mind set and get back in the game! Now you`re also on a ***Music Mission*** that is helping orphans and underprivileged children all across the globe! Normally I ask those I interview what causes or charities they admire and/or support -- Can you tell our readers a little bit more about that and the various countries you have traveled to because of it?

Diane Wayne: Yes. My awareness for the concept for "A Music Mission" came to me initially in 2000 while traveling in Indonesia, and began to develop more while traveling in Vietnam in 2001 & 2002. I had become acquainted with some children from the streets in Saigon (Ho Chi Mihn City). After hearing from them about the streets gangs there, and the problems these children were having as they were struggling to survive, I started considering more about the reasons there is so much violence in the streets, there, and all over the world.

A lot of this seemed to me to stem from lack of safe outlets for expressionism for these children and the lack of protection available to them. I started envisioning centers that would provide self-esteem building creative development for them, and how I would ultimately like to provide that for these impoverished, abandoned, and abused children, globally.

I am in the process of creating a presentation for the United Nations, the World Children`s Organization, and Queen Beatrix of Holland. I am hoping to stimulate governmental co-operation in association with local corporations and businesses to contribute, provide, and support centers that will offer safe havens, with all tools and music equipment, as well as instruction and supervision for children in impoverished neighborhoods all over the world.

These centers will also provide job opportunities for care giving mothers and/or fathers. Instead of having to work demeaning or sexually oriented jobs to provide for their children`s welfare, the centers will provide proper wages and the job opportunities for those parents and care-givers to be with their children.

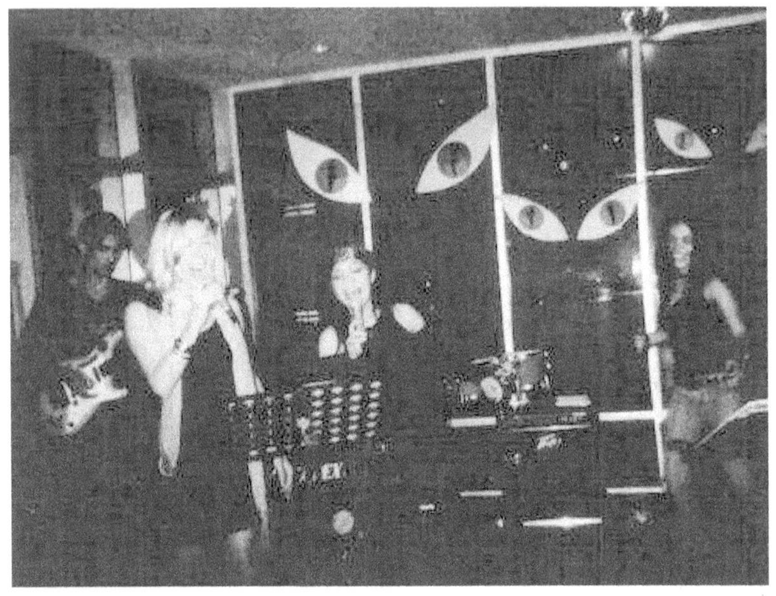

Diane singing in Baiyoke Sky Hotel, Bangkok, Thailand

Since 2002, and nearly every year following, I have traveled to 3rd world countries, including Vietnam and Thailand, doing what I can personally to brighten lives with music.

This has included free concert performances in their neighborhoods, and teaching the children singing, and playing keyboard and guitar. I`ve also brought good quality used clothing into these impoverished areas, donating it along with musical instruments to orphanages and other organizations.

I`ve really enjoyed spending time with these children, singing for them and with them, talking with them, and the parents and elders of these impoverished communities, and bringing in a healing friend to give free healing treatments for the ailing children and adults there as well. I was in Thailand doing this work at the time of the tsunami in 2004, and continued my time there providing aid and comfort.

In 2007 I was received by the Royal Offices of the King of Thailand and had the opportunity to deliver a presentation about A Music Mission as well as my newly released CDs.

A Music Mission has also inspired the Pacific Rim artist Danny Rae, who recorded and released my song, *Runaway From Love* in 2005 and 2008, to establish his new charity for children this year, 2010, that is to be funded by the Fiji Islands Entertainment Association, to provide opportunities for children of the Fiji Islands in the arts, as well.

I produced a film project for A Music Mission in 2009. And as I mentioned earlier, I`m preparing a presentation to the world organizations and the Heads of States that will receive me.

For me, it is a lifetime project and something that I feel passionately about.

For the rest, I do what I can to contribute clean water for children, plant trees, etc. via the Care2.com site of which I am a member.

I have great respect for the works of Angelina Jolie, Matt Damon, Oprah Winfrey, Alicia Keyes, U2`s Bono, and all celebrities who are using their affluence and influence to further the many causes that support the less fortunate in this world.

Chase Von: In your childhood, you appeared in the movie ***Parents of A Stranger*** with your twin sister. Which brings up another question I`d like to ask but will do that later as well. But initially after leaving home, you toured the States and Canada with several bands before eventually settling in Amsterdam.

And over the years you`ve penned popular favorites *Dusk, Timeless in Thailand, It`s Your Birthday, The Nights* and various other songs and are a recognized ASCAP songwriter as well as a professional SAG, (Screen Actors Guild) actress.

With all your various accomplishments Diane, particularly with the many obstacles and trials you`ve had to face, how important do you think it is that people actively pursue their dreams?

Diane Wayne: One of the most important things in this world anyone can do is follow their heart and pursue their dreams. It`s the most authentic life any of us can ever experience. A quote that inspires me to keep going in the face of adversity is from the film Seabiscuit: You know, you "don`t throw a whole life away just `cause he`s banged up a little." It`s referring to the "horse" but one can keep on pursuing the dream throughout life. There will always be obstacles for us, but that`s our opportunity for our greatest growth and transformation. Often during life`s most frustrating moments is when you`ll find a breakthrough.

God will send you the key you need to unlock the door of opportunity.

Chase Von: Who are some of the people in life you admire and or look up to in the music field, as well as just life in general?

Diane Wayne: As a professional singer and songwriter, I am greatly inspired by original soul artists from Smokey Robinson and Marvin Gaye to Alicia Keyes, as well as the eclecticism of the Beatles. Billie Holiday, Chet Baker, Tina Turner, Prince, Sting, and Pink, are some of my favorite artists, too.

I`ve been greatly inspired by Jesus Christ, Mother Teresa, Princess Diana, Gandhi, Dr. Sandjay Gupta, Angelina Jolie, Oprah Winfrey, U2`s Bono, Matt Damon, Leonardo Di Caprio, and the Jonas Brothers.

Chase Von: Can you share your web sites and links so our readers can learn more about you?

Diane Wayne: Yes, I`d love to! My new website is www.dianewayne.com, and I`ve got webpages on MySpace.com, Facebook.com, Care2.com, as well as a presence on Twitter.

Chase Von: What are some things you`re currently working on that you think our readers might be interested in hearing about?

Diane Wayne: At the moment, as I mentioned earlier, I`m working on a film with Kitania Kavey which I hope will bring more opportunities for my music to be in films.

I`m still working on my own film and music project for "A Music Mission", including the presentations for Queen Beatrix of the Netherlands, as well as the United Nations and the World Children`s Organization. I`m always writing new songs, and I`m putting together my own book of poetry.

I`ve written two other books, as well. One is a book of soul questions, called "Consider This", and the other is a collection of healing stories with and about Universal Healer Albertus Antonius Poland, titled, "Another Way of Healing", that also includes some stories about A Music Mission -- So I`m looking for a book publisher.

I have recently completed three CDs of my original songs, `D`Experience, `D` Atmosphere, and Special `D`, so I`m in the process of looking for a new label and I`m looking for artist management who is familiar with global artist representation.

Chase Von: What would you say if you were standing before a microphone and could be heard by every child on the planet, and regardless of what language they spoke, they would understand you?

What positive advice would you give the children, if that were possible?

Diane Wayne: Listen to your heart. Trust God. Believe in yourself. You are meant to be here. Do dare to be who you truly wish to be. Be honest. Be true. Keep your focus and your balance as you live and explore. Enjoy the process and the journey, and demonstrate respect and appreciation for everything.

Chase Von: What are some of your favorite meals and living in Amsterdam, have you added any new favorites because of your current living location? (Smile).

Diane Wayne: There are 143 different cultures living just in Amsterdam alone so food choices are very international here. I really love soups and curries from Thailand, Vietnam and India--some of which I actually make myself from scratch--and authentically, my Thai and Vietnamese friends tell me. I love Italian pastas, Spanish tapas, Greek salads and the decadent French pastries so plentiful around here.

Chase Von: I`ve traveled to quite a few countries in my time, but you have been so very many places Diane, I think you have me beat in that department! What are some of the places you really loved? And do you want to return to them some time in the future?

Also, when will you be returning to the states to entertain your fans on this side of the ocean?

Diane Wayne: There are things I love about all 16 countries where I have traveled and sung, so far, that could cause me to return. I`ve written about some of my experiences in my songs "Timeless in Thailand" and "The Bikini Song" (Brazil). Paris, France will always have my heart. I truly enjoy the eclectic variety of peoples, cultures, nature, spirituality, food, and art and music everywhere I`ve been. And I believe my art and A Music Mission, will continue to take me all over this world.

I don`t have a tour for America scheduled just yet--- "I don`t plan on returning until at least 2011-2012" because of my current projects here in Europe, unless a really lucrative opportunity presents itself!

Chase Von: I always try and ask a tough one Diane, something to give a broader scope of the thinking processes to our readers on those I interview on subjects in general that are disturbing or getting attention in the news media.

I asked "Voiceover Queen" Joan Baker about her thoughts on Tiger Woods, I asked Lovely Actress Claire Dodin her thoughts on a Washington Redskin Cheerleader hopeful that was struck with a debilitating disease after taking the Swine Flu shot. I`ve also asked various others difficult questions but yours is going to be two-parted.

First, since you are a twin, wasn`t it difficult to get kicked out for your dreams especially since you do have a twin? And twins are known to be extremely close to one another and often we`ve all heard have a psychic connection of sorts.

Also, and not numbering this one because you don`t have to answer this if you don`t wish to, but how ironic is it to you that you would act in a movie as a child called ***Parents of A Stranger*** and then later become estranged from your own parents who, must have thought since you were so determined to do your own thing, that they really didn`t know you?

And two, I don`t care what anyone`s religious beliefs are, but there seems to be a wave of demonic things happening and if you wish to describe them another way, so be it, but what are your thoughts on this recent story?

Twins Slay Mother

http://www.youtube.com/watch?v=gJpzL19xHP0

Diane Wayne: Regarding the "news story" unfortunately this kind of violence is common place in a great percentage of homes in America. I know I suffered countless beatings behind closed doors, and in those times I just took my punishments silently. Still I used to wonder why nobody saved me. And who knows, maybe it was a Godsend that I was forced out of that house, rather than being killed myself. It`s sad that these two young ladies are in this situation. My heart goes out to them.

You`re right, Chase, it is ironic. My character in "Parents of A Stranger" was a deaf child whose handicap my actor parents were unaware of in the beginning, and had difficulty communicating with, until the disability was discovered.

My real parents were blessed with a gifted child they had no desire to communicate with, and refused to acknowledge or support, or love, on any real terms.

Yes, there were times that my twin sister and I were blessed with synchronistic thought. However, her unfortunate chosen path of a life-long addiction to drugs and alcohol created a separation between us that is unfortunate due to her tenacity to continue her own destructive life-style, even though I`ve spent decades working to help her accept and overcome her disease.

There are many evils in this world: greed, dishonesty, violence and oppression, racism, prejudice, and the lack of global unity, freedom, and equality. I do what I can to make a positive difference, and make this earth a brighter place for all. I agree with you in not judging others because of their religious beliefs. I personally don`t really believe in organized religions, as I feel they create too much separatism in this world. I call myself a Universal Spirit Child, and have great respect for God, and the wisdoms available in a variety of religious dogmas.

Chase Von: Sorry to ask such a tough question of you Diane but like myself, I`m sure others are wondering what the H E double hockey sticks is going on in the world when something like this occurs, so thanks for giving our readers your perspective on it.

Now something much lighter; how do you go about staying in

shape and are there any specific things you do not only to stay in shape physically, but to keep your voice in prime condition so you can continue to be referred to as, “The Voice!” (Smile.)

Diane Wayne: Being referred to as “The Voice” is truly humbling, and fills me with gratitude for God, who gifts me with so much inspiration, sensitivity, and abilities to create and express.

As far as keeping my voice in shape, I sing all the time. I do believe it`s very important to warm up your voice before recording and performing, so you can sing for hours--and I`ve developed a series of exercises that accomplish this with ease, in a very natural way.

I demonstrated these exercises in a vocal workshop on a DVD titled "The Singing Studios Vocal Workshops." I`d love to have that out on the market in 2011, and need a producer/studio for part two “How to Learn and Perform Any Song in 30 Minutes.”

Physically I stay in shape by doing a dance stretch/combination for about 20-30 minutes every morning that I learned from my favorite dance teachers, Hama, and the late Tanis Michaels.

I gave up my car when I moved to Europe (although I am an excellent driver), so I ride my bicycle in all kinds of weather or walk everywhere. It`s also better for the environment!

When it comes to food, I have a huge appetite but I eat healthfully; California-style with lots of fresh fruits and nuts in the mornings, two balanced meals during the day and dinners are usually fish or kidney beans and rice with vegetables, Asian soups and curries and salads. I also drink 2 liters of spring water every day.

And I make sure I get enough sleep. The body and the voice need the proper amount of rest for optimum performance.

Chase Von: I want to thank you so much for finding the time to share yourself with our readers Diane and I`m wishing you continued success in all the various things you do!

So on behalf of myself and the ***SOP***, I want to say it`s very much appreciated and when you get a chance because I`m here and your there, give Kitty a hug for me and tell her to give one from me, from her to you, new friend. (I almost confused myself there). (Heh, Heh.)

And do K.I.T. And looking forward to hearing your audio with Judy! (Smile.)

Diane Wayne: Thank you, Chase. I`ll give Kitty the message, and the hugs. And we both send hugs back to you.

I always enjoy doing interviews, and sharing what I can about myself, my creative works, and A Music Mission.

It`s a great pleasure to meet you, Chase, and to do this

interview with you and the Student Operated Press. And I`m looking forward to the audio interview with Judyth Piazza, too!

"Listen to your heart. Trust God. Believe in yourself. You are meant to be here. Do dare to be who you truly wish to be. Be honest. Be true. Keep your focus and your balance as you live and explore. Enjoy the process and the journey, and demonstrate respect and appreciation for everything."

--- Diane Wayne

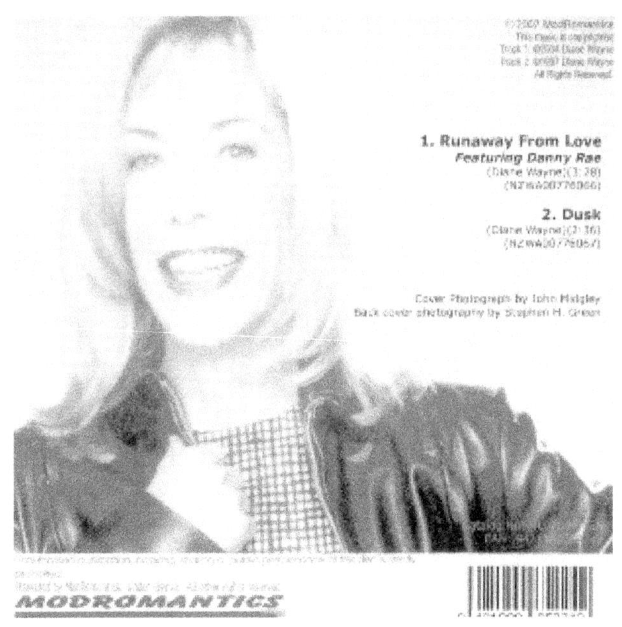

Diane`s CD *Runaway From Love*

Interview with Nicollette Varanelli

TALENTED SINGER AND SONGWRITER

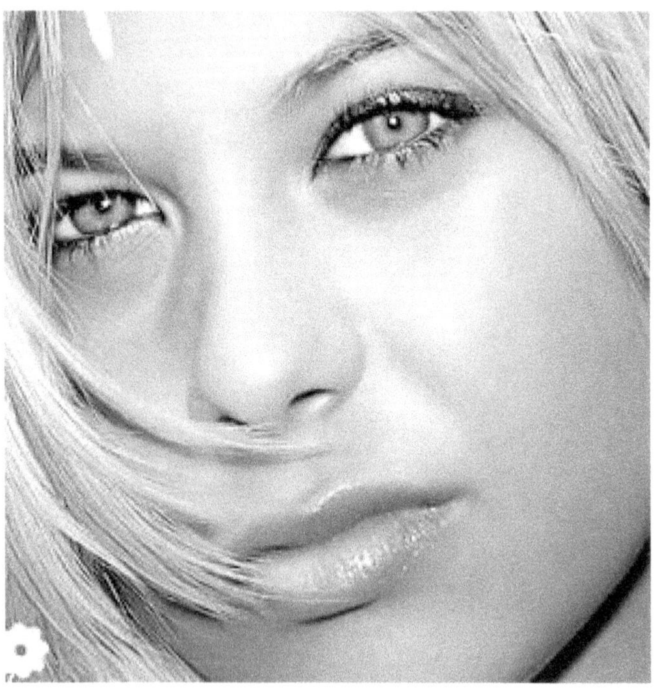

Chase Von: Hey Nicollette and on behalf of the *Student Operated Press* and myself, I want to thank you for finding the time to share yourself with our readers.

You`re a rising singer and also a model and I was on my friend Actress/Model/Musician Jenny McShane`s My Space page when I noticed you left her a comment.

I requested your friendship because based on your page, you looked really interesting!

And low and behold not only did you accept, you sent me a video of you singing one of my favorite songs! Etta James` *At Last* and you did a wonderful job which I`ve already told you.

But for now, thanks again so much for finding the time to share yourself with our readers!

Nicollette Varanelli: Well Chase Von, I appreciate that your allowing me the opportunity to have more people get to know me and hear my music. So I`m really happy to share my thoughts with you and your readers.

Chase Von: From reading up on you, it appears you were born to sing! We`ll definitely get to that, but before we do, what were your younger years like growing up in New York?

Nicollette Varanelli: I guess New York sounds intimidating if you didn`t grow up here but it`s kind of all I know. It has everything anyone wants. Entertainment, restaurants, clubs, ect. So it`s a great place, just extremely expensive!

Chase Von: And normally I wait a bit to ask a tough one, but since you are from New York, what were your feelings when 9/11 took place?

Nicollette Varanelli: Well I think 9/11 changed everything. I was in school and everyone got sent home.

Many of my friends parents worked in the the towers. So I was like soothing them telling them that they`ll be OK only later to find out that several kids parents never made it out of the building. I grew up a lot at age 11.

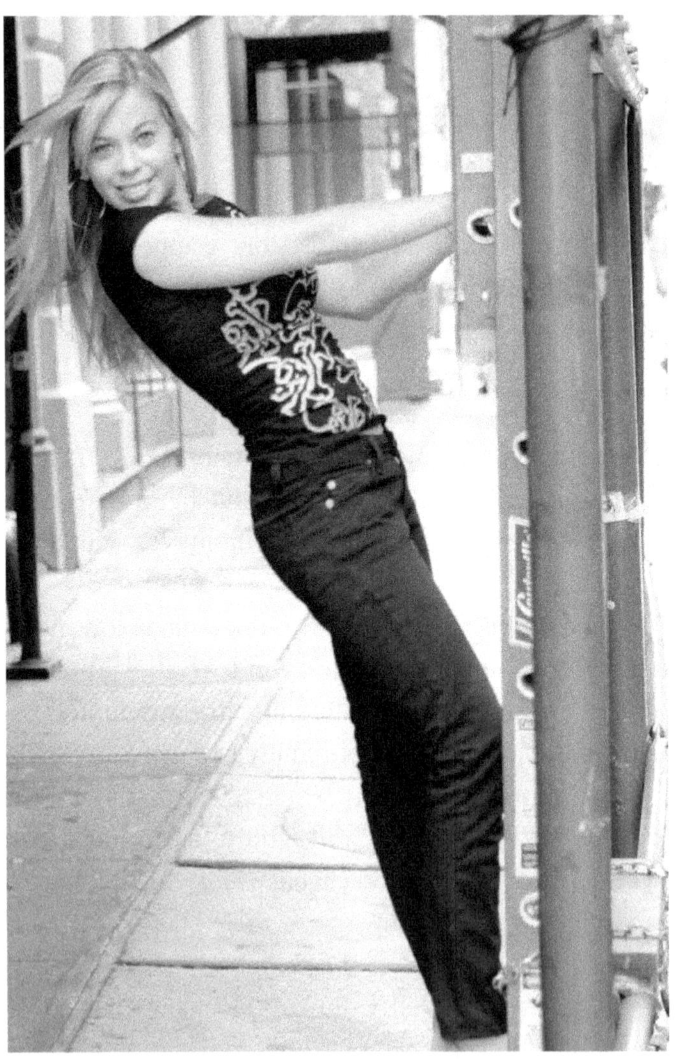

Chase Von: Actress and Model Shawn Richardz is someone else I`ve interviewed who is also from New York and I`m sure she totally relates to your feelings--- Now onto your singing. You were singing using a hair brush when you were two? (Smile.)

In a way that is unbelievable but then again, my three year old is completely nuts about the late Michael Jackson! Who are some of the people that you admire besides Brittany Spears, Mariah Carey, Jessica Simpson and Christina Aguilera in the music industry and is the late Michael Jackson one of them? I also would like to know what your reaction was when you learned of his untimely death?

Nicollette Varanelli: Besides the few you have mentioned (you`ve done your homework) which definitely have influenced my life, I do love the Kardashian`s.

Mostly because of their strong family connection and Kim`s mom manages her just like my dad manages me.

I love Katie Price just because she`s beautiful and a hard worker and always in the European spotlight, a role I`d like to have in the near future. The passing of Michael Jackson was a terrible waste.

I truly believe he was the greatest entertainer that ever lived! I am working with Jean-Marie Horvat who is a Grammy winning mixer of several of Michael`s albums and he shares many stories of how kind he was to everyone.

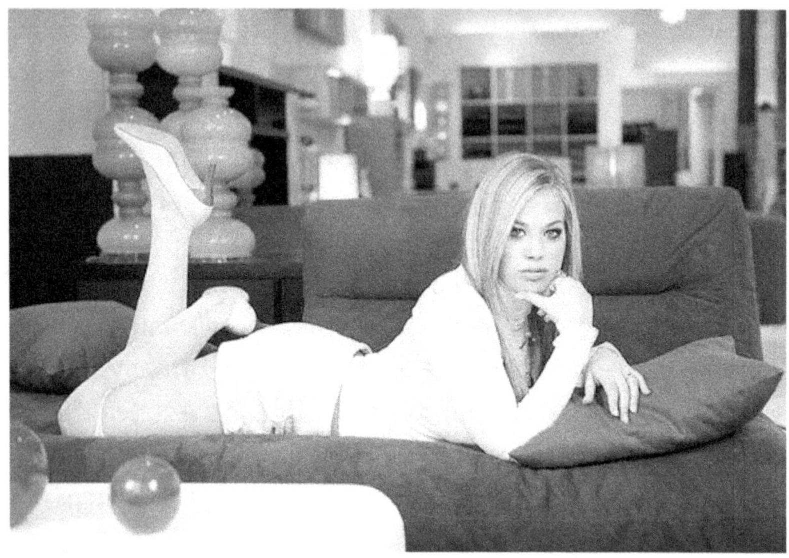

Chase Von: We`ve been watching the DVD "This Is It" and he truly was amazing Nicollette, nor did it look like he was anywhere near death. But like Michael, you also have a soft spot in your heart for children. Can you tell us more about St Jude`s Children`s Hospital and your inspiration for donating all the proceeds of your first CD to it? And not to sound corny but I happen to agree with the Beatles. I.e. What the world needs now, is love, sweet love.

Don`t you think if more thought as you did, the world would be a better place?

Nicollette Varanelli: Well I do believe that if everyone can do even small acts of kindness every day the world would definitely be a better place. If it`s just opening the door for someone or helping a senior citizen get into a car, everyone can do something to help someone. One of the reasons I want to achieve stardom is to use my platform to make the world a better place.

St Jude`s Children`s Hospital in Memphis is a special place.

It`s a place that treats children with cancer. This was one of the things I had a hard time accepting, why some children are stricken with this disease and especially at such a young age?

When I put my 1st CD out for sale, I decided I wanted to take my portion of dollars and also sales of photos and give it to St Jude`s so hopefully through research and development they can come up with a cure. I love children so much and felt why not do something?

Chase Von: Couldn`t agree with you more Nicollette and that reminds me of Brian O`Neal and his amazing song who also gave me and my co author Betty Dravis a blurb for our book Dream Reachers--- For those that haven`t heard it, here`s a link to the video:

Dreams in Color - Brian O`Neal

In the event the video doesn`t work, link is below:

http://www.youtube.com/watch?v=7h3SvpbQAHQ

Another thing that comes to mind is an Italian quote I read recently in a miniature book someone gave me as a gift. It says simply, *After the game, the king and pawn go into the same box.*

Now on to your many accomplishments!

You were part of a pilot girl band funded by *Universal Records* when you were just 14!

You`ve also performed the National Anthem at *Shea Stadium, Madison Square Garden* and the *Raymond James Stadium* in Tampa Florida before thousands! You`ve performed in 100`s of clubs and also appeared in *Connecticut Post*, *Planet Magazine* as well as the popular United Kingdom`s Magazine *Street Voice* and on top of that are appearing in a major motion picture as yourself!

Your Vocal Coach Don Lawrence has also worked with the likes of Mic Jagger and Lady Gaga!

And I also saw you sold out the *Fairfield Theatre*! And you have performed live with guitarist Al Ferante who taught Jon Mayer the guitar!

And this isn`t even touching on your successful modeling career!

Your star is definitely on the rise Girl! (Smile.)

What are some of the links to your various web sites so our readers can learn more about you?

And links where they can purchase your CD`s *Free Myself, Nicollette* and *I Don`t Wanna*?

IF YOU CAN SEE ME - NICOLLETTE VARANELLI

In the event the video doesn`t work, link is below:

http://www.youtube.com/watch?v=sY9CgXr07ak&feature=related

Nicollette Varanelli: Wow! I`m honored you did your research on me, that`s awesome and thank you so much for your compliments, I truly do appreciate them.

Someone can hear my music/pics live performances ect: www.myspace.com/nicollettesings
www.youtube.com/nicollettesings

Chase Von: Since you write or co-write all your own songs, how much of your actual life is being shared in your music and as a writer myself and also a retired Marine with PTSD, for me writing is something that helps me process life in general--- Is that true for you also?

Nicollette Varanelli: I love writing music! Music and writing have gotten me through every difficult situation I`ve experienced.

I always said without my 1st album, I wouldn`t be able to get through the breakup of my 1st boyfriend.

As I look back now I realize I`ll encounter tougher things but at the time, I was devastated.

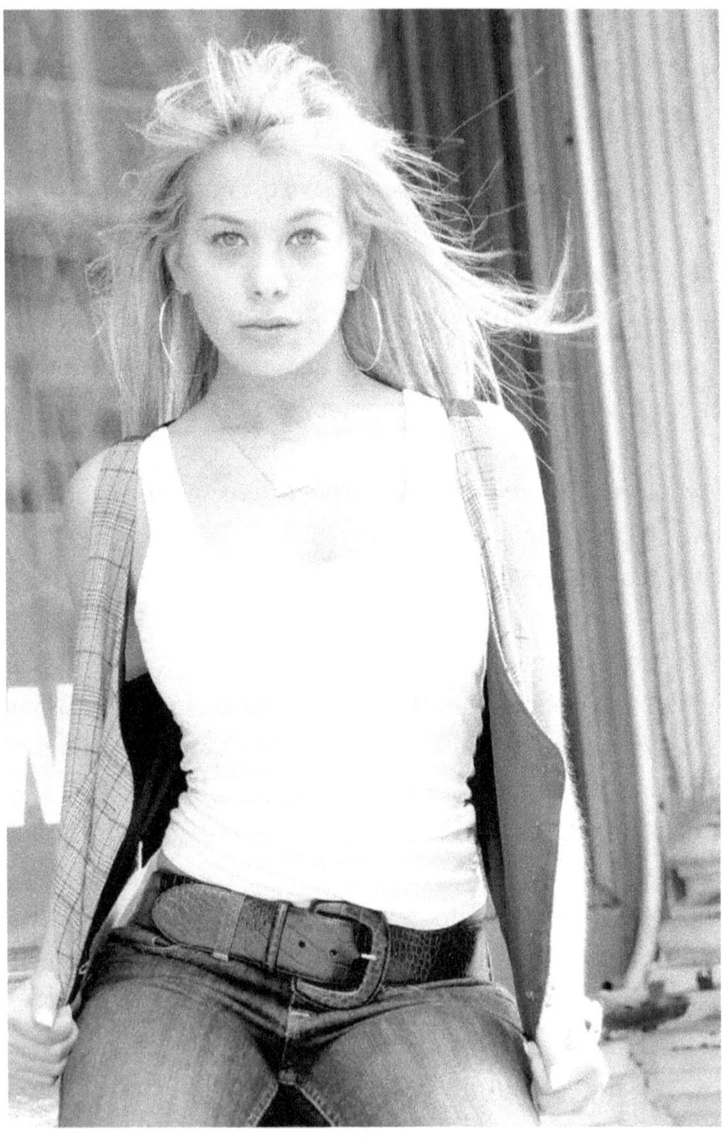

Chase Von: In another interview I saw where Paris Hilton was mentioned and you said you both were animal lovers nor did you utter an unkind word. It was addressing role models for young girls though, something you are more than willing to be and I have to say, I often feel sorry for Paris Hilton because she`s a beautiful girl, but a role model she certainly is not. Nor is it an armor I myself would like to don.

Why are you willing to take on such a huge responsibility and do you think there should be more in the entertainment industry who should do so as well?

Nicollette Varanelli: Well, I do feel comfortable being a role model because I am aware of my responsibility as a singer/performer and I think I`m a good person. So more importantly, I don`t have to do something that foreign to me, just be myself!

Besides as my dad/manager reminds me, if I`m going to---
"Talk the talk, I have to walk the walk."

But on that note, I`m not a role model to replace kid`s parents, just make it easier for them.

Chase Von: Well, you are very easy on the eyes Nicollette! (Smile.) How do you stay in such great shape considering how busy you are with singing and modeling?

Nicollette Varanelli: Well thank you! I work out every day, (there are gyms in every hotel) and eat right.

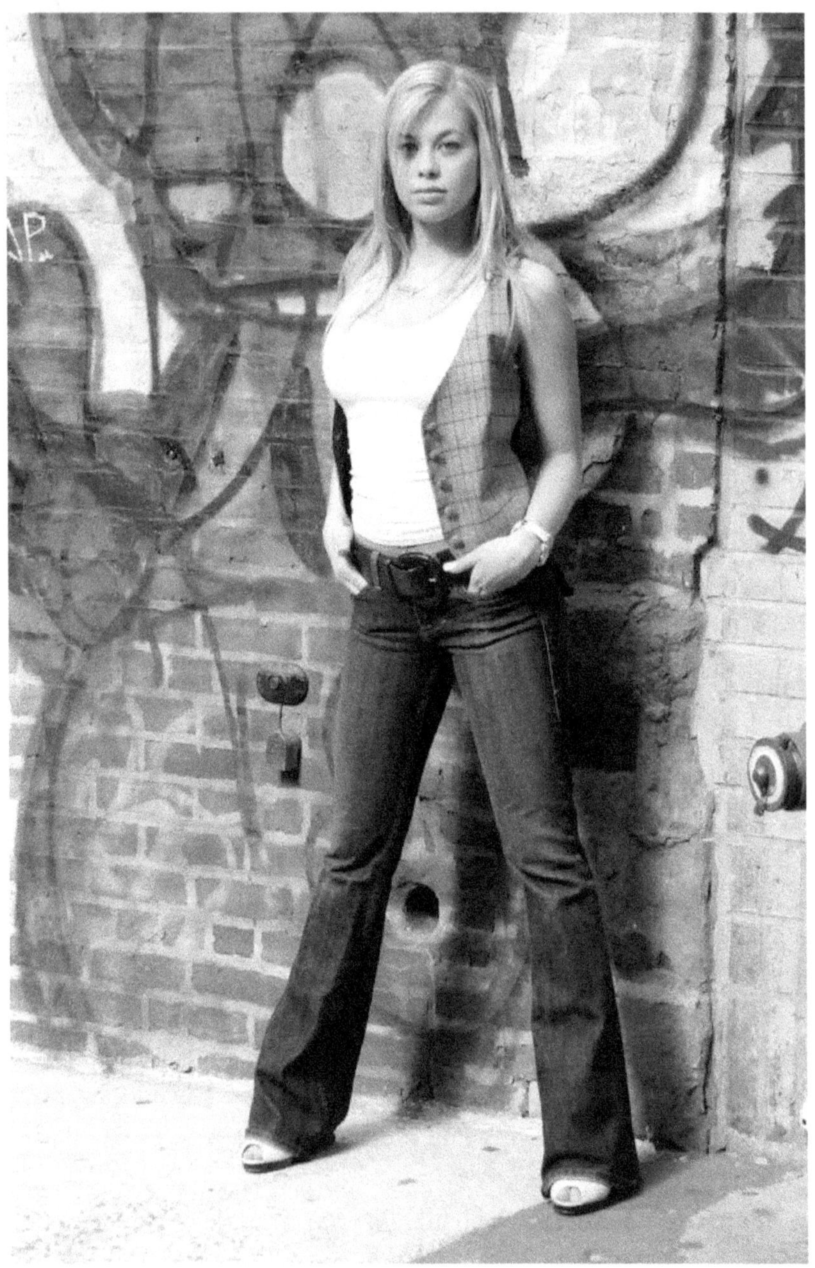

Chase Von: What are some your favorite meals?

Nicollette Varanelli: Coming from my Italian background I love pasta (any kind), meatballs, New York pizza, (there is a difference)!

Love sushi and Carvel no fat chocolate ice cream!

Chase Von: How important is family to you and what is your take on the state of our current world?

Nicollette Varanelli: I love family and miss having a big family. When I was little, we would have my great grandma (since passed away), grandparents and uncle and family`s, (they then moved to Florida), cousin`s come over every Sunday for an Italian festival (LOL.)

I miss all of that! But on that note after I achieve my goals my parents and sister are coming with me wherever I go.

I think the state of our current world without rambling, needs to grasp the importance of family.

Chase Von: What would you say if you were standing before a microphone that could be heard by every child on the planet and regardless of what language they spoke, they would understand you?

What positive advice would you give the children, if that were possible?

Nicollette Varanelli: Well what I would say to them is to believe in yourself. You can accomplish anything with desire, with hard work and believing in yourself and God.

Surround yourself with positive people and family!

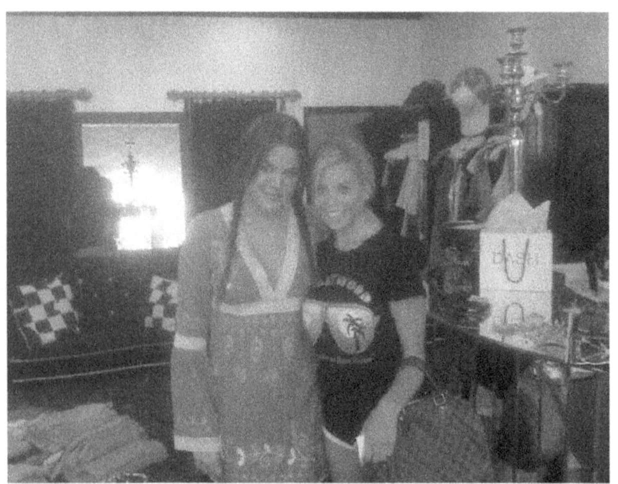

Nicollette sharing time with her friend Khloe Kardashian

When you fail and we all will fail at certain things, use that as a learning experience to achieve the next even better things the next time!

Chase Von: Is there anything you have on the horizon you want to give our readers and your fans a heads up about?

Nicollette Varanelli: I have so many exciting things happening in my life! I have a meeting with a famous movie producer/best-selling author this week.

I`m making new music as I type and about to work with a Grammy winning producer on 7 songs that will hopefully initiate me into getting signed to a major label (with a release album date).

I`ll be performing live this spring/summer in the NY/tri-state area, for dates and times visit my My Space.

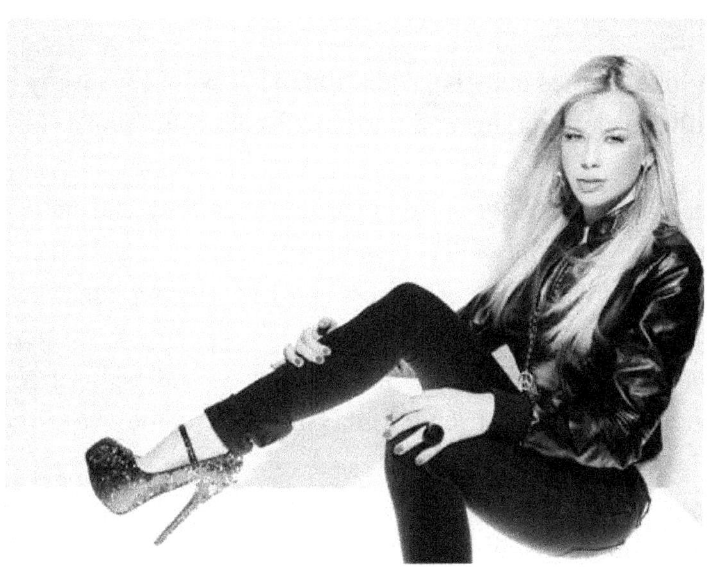

Chase Von: I know singing is a huge part of your life Nicollette. But I`ve seen you pictured with Khloe Kardashian and that you`ve also teamed up with Major League Baseball`s pitcher Craig Breslow on the Strike 3 Foundation raising funding for childhood cancer research.

But who are some of the other well known people you have met because you are following your dreams?

And of those, who has left the biggest impression on you to date?

Nicollette Varanelli: I have met Jessica and Ashley Simpson and Hillary Duff. I think all 3 are really awesome! But again I would have to say that Jessica has influenced me the most because she is so sweet and always is surrounded by family and close friends.

I do love clothes and shoes and like her I would want my own Nicollette clothing line and perfume; I guess stay tuned (lol.)

Chase Von: It`s been a true pleasure Nicollette and on behalf of myself and the *SOP*, I want to thank you so much for sharing yourself with our readers and I`m wishing you

mountains more of success and think it would be cool if you hooked up with my friend Alina Smith for some shows when you`re on the West Coast!

That would really give the audiences something great and for more on her, here`s her My Space Link:

http://www.myspace.com/alinamusic

Her and her band just recently won the KTLA Morning News Battle of the Bands.

And I know you`re spinning multiple plates but don`t be a stranger Lady!

Nicollette Varanelli: As a kid I always loved to entertain people. I loved being the center of attention, making people happy while I performed.

I have been blessed with supportive parents who have helped develop the gift God gave me. I want to use my stardom to be a positive role model especially for young girls.

I especially want to thank you Chase Von and the Student Operated Press for having me and having an opportunity for your readers to get to know me while I get ready to achieve "Super Star Status" (my 1st single, check it out on myspace)!

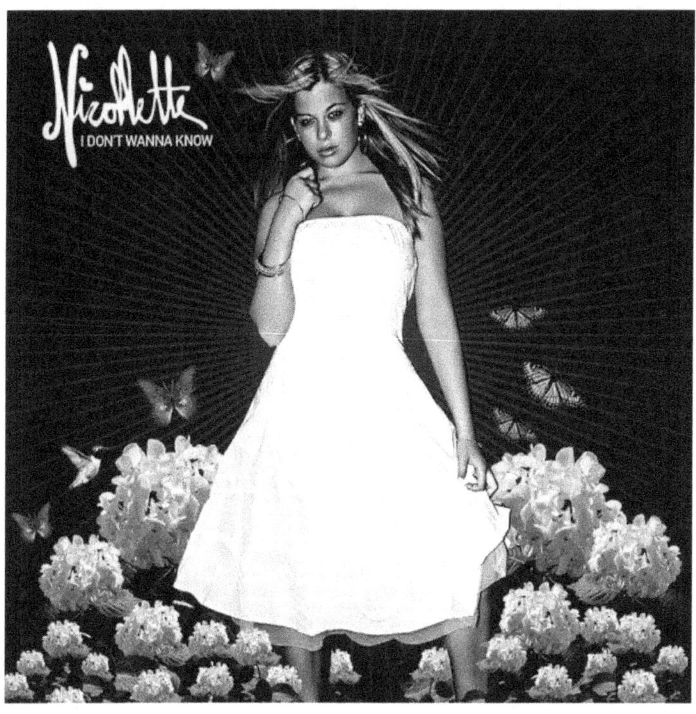

Interview with Wodige Wehali, AKA Reggie Solomon

TALENTED MUSICIAN, SINGER AND SONGWRITER

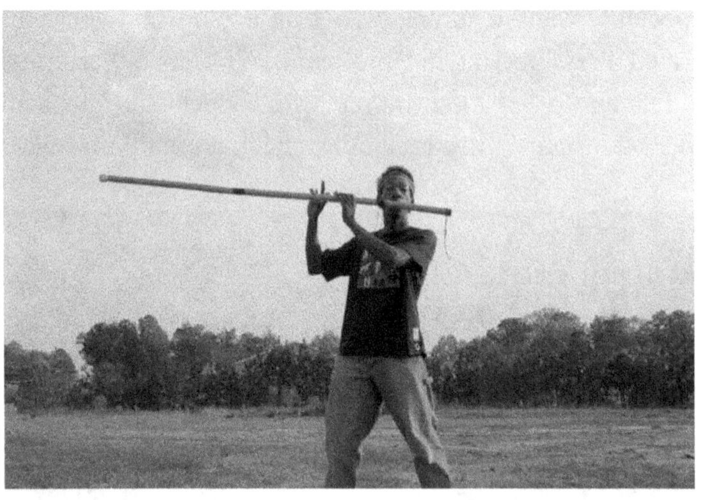

Chase Von: “Siyo,unali-i, Wodige!” (Smile.)

Have to be honest though, I believe that means “Greetings” in Cherokee and I wouldn`t know that if I hadn`t looked at your website.

Can you tell me what it really means? And also, on behalf of the Student Operated Press and myself, I thank you for finding time for this interview.

I learned of you through a mutual friend, (Adrian) and she is truly a wonderful, kind-hearted spirit who thinks the world of you. And just from listening to your music, I can see why.

So again, how I greeted you? What does that translate to best in English?

How important is your heritage to you? Oh, and for the rest of this interview would you prefer I refer to you as Reggie or Wodige Wehali a.k.a. Brown Eagle?

Reggie Solomon: It translates as "Greetings, my friend." You did very well. Whichever name you wish to use is fine, but for the sake of simplicity, Reggie is "Osda" (good).

My heritage is very, very important to me. For years I have celebrated my African-ness, and continue to do so, and now I have added my Native heritage to my self-expression. I have been doing much research on my Cherokee ancestry after an illuminating conversation with my now deceased maternal great-grandfather, who was Cherokee. I also discovered through genealogy that my paternal great-grandmother was also Cherokee.

Chase Von: Thanks for making it easy on a brother! Before we get into your music, which to me really touches the core of a person`s spirit, I want to ask some other questions to bring our readers from where you`ve been to where you are now.

So that said, where did you grow up?

What was your childhood like? And was music something you were exposed to early in life or was it something you were drawn to on your own?

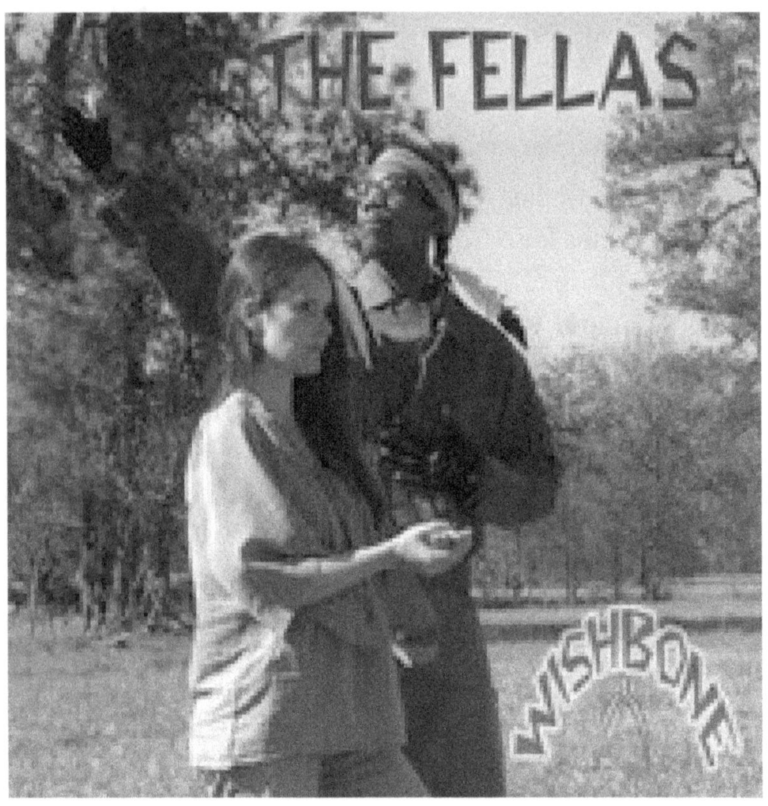

Kimberly Shaw Hayes (Vendettra) and Reggie (Wodige Wehali) Solomon

Reggie Solomon: I was born and raised in Macon, Georgia, a small town in the heart of the Peach State, just an hour south of Atlanta. I would say that my childhood was normal. I was blessed to have two wonderful, devoted parents and a caring older sister. I had a few close friends but preferred to keep to myself.

I could keep myself pretty entertained; I was always writing something, whether it was music, short stories or poems. I was at the top of my class throughout school. I wouldn`t have considered myself popular, though. I was pretty conservative back then "until college at least." (LOL!)

Music was always in the home: gospel, blues, R&B. The Jackson 5 started it all for me.

I loved that group! Then in the 80`s, Prince came along and totally blew me away.

Music chose me from an early age, guitar being my first instrument. I taught myself several different instruments and drew from a variety of different styles.

I listen to a little bit of everything.

Chase Von: I write so like a lot of authors and prefer not to use my birth name.

You`ll understand that better after this statement, though, I think: If I was a movie director and was doing a movie of Jimi Hendrix and I wanted someone who not only physically resembled him but also had the skills to play various instruments and a voice to match, I would be calling you!

How often do people say you remind them of Jimi Hendrix? And although I`m what I call an "Asphalt Indian,"

I still believe my totems are the panther, the hawk and the wolf. (I`m just sharing that because if this observation offends you, well, you could beat me up later or try to.

(Heh-Heh.) A Last Panther against a Brown Eagle? Wait! Do you have any other totems? (I might have spoken too soon.)

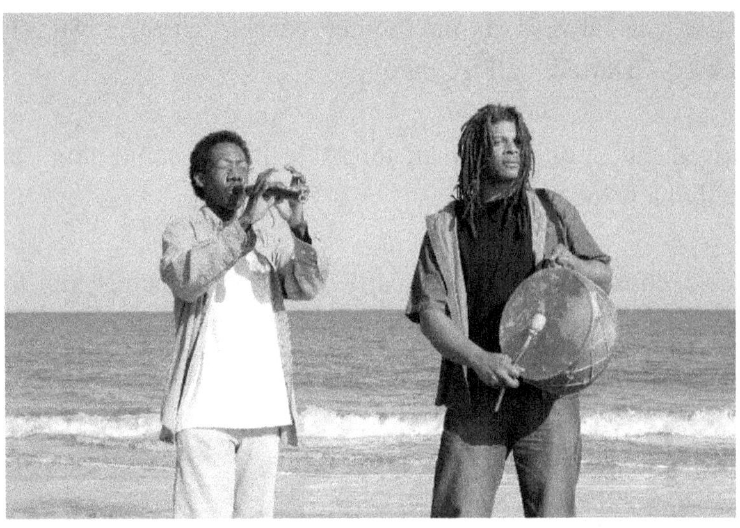

Reggie Solomon: (Ha-Ha.) I get the "Jimi" comparisons all the time!

I didn`t notice it until I started wearing the Native American headbands. My friends noticed before I did, and now when I see a picture of Jimi, it`s like: WOW! That looks like one of my poses!

And the fact that Jimi had Cherokee heritage must be more than just a coincidence (his grandmother was a full-blood).

Your totem observation is not offensive in the least. I believe we all have several totems, just some that stand out more than others. "Waya" (the wolf) is my birth totem and it fits me to a tee.

I am very independent and I am a loner.

My eagle totem is what I aspire to be, having the ability to soar above things and grasp the bigger picture.

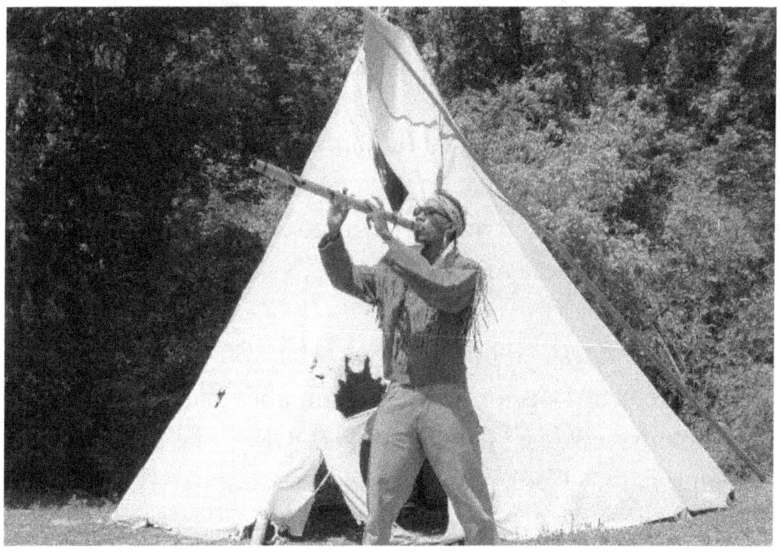

Chase Von: Great answer and "We Be Cool." Now I don`t have to reach out to some of my adopted tribal members that are in the book *Dream Reachers* that I recently did with my incredible co-author, the very talented and wise Betty Dravis.

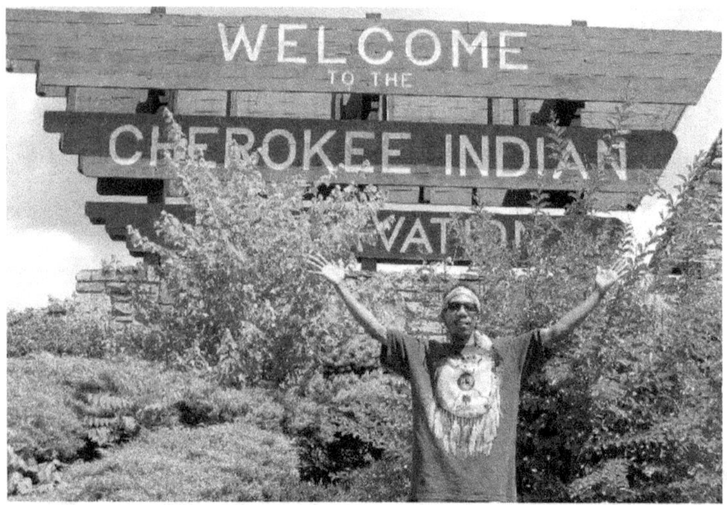

Actress/pop singer Kiara Hunter thinks of herself as a futuristic Bounty Hunter at times, actress/rapper Darcy Donavan believes she is Wonder Woman, and actress/model Shawn Richardz has a super-hero costume too!

But to be honest, I don`t know what Shawn's super-hero powers are, but I do know before she goes out to fight `Evil` she has to have some "Cool Whip." (OOPS! She's well-known for being in the "Cool Whip" commericial...)

(She`s also in the commercial as well)...

(Heh-Heh.) So... Sorry. Shawn! (That`s like telling the world, Superman`s weakness is kryptonite.)

You`re still cool though, Shawn, --- Cause no one knows who you are when you get into your secret identity.

(Maybe she`ll be too busy to see this). In case I lost you there, Reggie, those people are all in the book, but now on to something more serious.

Who are some of the people in music you truly admire and that you look up to? And not only in music, but in life, as well?

Reggie Solomon: The Jackson 5, Prince, Jimi Hendrix, Bob Dylan, R. Carlos Nakai (Native flautist), Michael Hedges (guitarist), Pierre Bensusan (guitarist) are but a few of my musical inspirations. The Great Spirit, Jesus Christ, my parents, Mother Nature, Martin Luther King, Jr. are some of the entities and people I look up to in life in general.

Chase Von: What is the process for you when it comes to writing your amazing songs? With me, because I write (create) also, I don`t sit around and think, OK, going to write something today. I just get hit with thoughts I feel like I have to catch before they get away. But again, what`s it like for you?

Reggie Solomon: Wado (Thank you) for the compliment. The process is very much the same as with you; it just happens.

Sometimes I may go for months without any substantial ideas and then suddenly "BAM!" A full-term baby is born! There are times that I dream of songs. Others, I have only words, or only music, and the rest comes much later.

Chase Von: I know you can be a one-man band, which is why if anyone does a movie about Hendrix I think you`re the one to

play him. But how much do your fellow musicians contribute to your music, i.e. with ideas?

And what are some of their names, so the world and our readers can learn more about them as well?

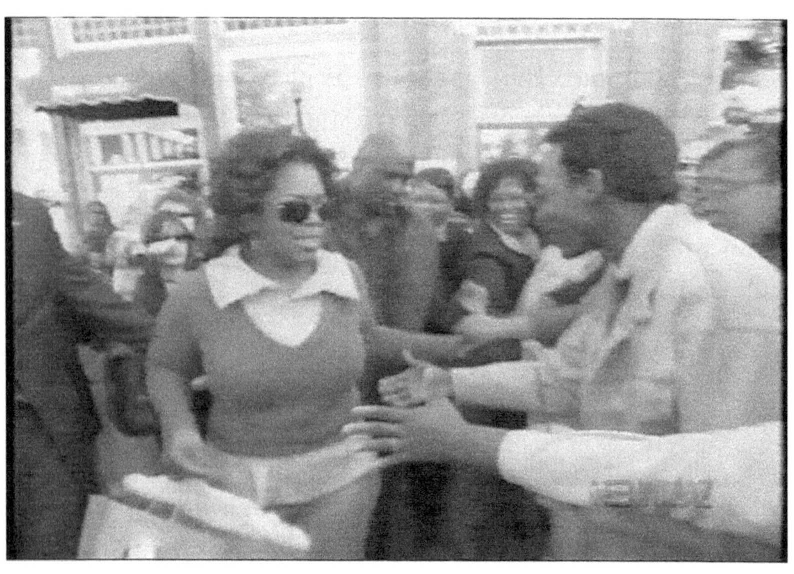

Reggie (Brown Eagle) greeting Oprah Winfrey

Reggie Solomon: Honestly, when it comes to my own music, I`m pretty much isolated, by choice. That`s my independent, waya nature shining though.

I may ask my musical friends to contribute parts, but usually, I just do it all myself. When I`m collaborating with others on a mutual project, it`s much more democratic.

My best friend Dean Brown (myspace.com/dushakband.com), who is a singer/songwriter in his own right, is a regular songwriting companion and occasional band-mate (in my group *The Fellas*). Some other fellow musicians that I have worked with include John Parks (myspace.com/john parks_19), Roger Hill (myspace.com/pleasantburg),

Vendettra (myspace.com/vendettra), Marcus Henderson (myspace.com/donian), Ted Katner (myspace.78094483), Skeebo Knight (myspace.com/skeeboknight), and Sister Virginia (myspace.com/sistervirginia), to name a few.

Chase Von: This is something Nhojj and I discussed in the interview I did with him--- How much of your music do you think is influenced by the experiences you`ve had in your own life?

Reggie Solomon: Actually, I think everything I have experienced is reflected in my music, but not always literally. My values, my biases, my sense of humor, it`s all in there. But you can`t take everything I write as a direct personal experience. It may have happened to someone else, or it may

have happened in a dream or fantasy, or it may be something I want to "happen" or not! (Heh-Heh.)

Chase Von: I`m Black, Blackfoot and Cherokee Indian, and from what family rumors say, also a little French. I think it would be hypocritical of me to NOT accept others regardless of their race, and I also like to look at the world myself as Good People, Bad People. And personally, I think you can find loads of each in any race. There are even those that would say I shouldn`t identify myself as black, because all blacks originated from Africa so I should say I am African.

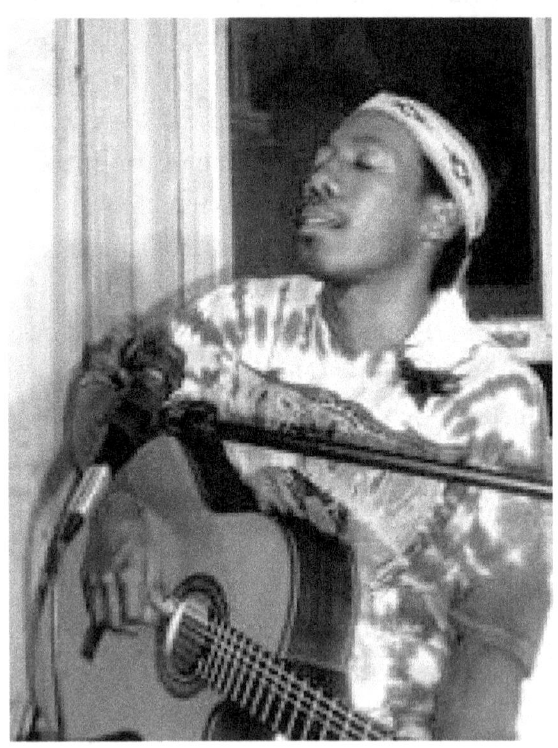

To me it`s semantics. And I really believe at the bottom of it all, we are all really one race. *The Human race* because when you get right down to it, we all require the same things: food, water, shelter and, of course, love.

But what are your views on the racial tensions that still exist, even despite the fact that in today`s world we have the opportunity via the Internet to learn and to meet and understand those all across the globe? And do you think that is bringing the world closer together because we can in fact have friends of all nationalities?

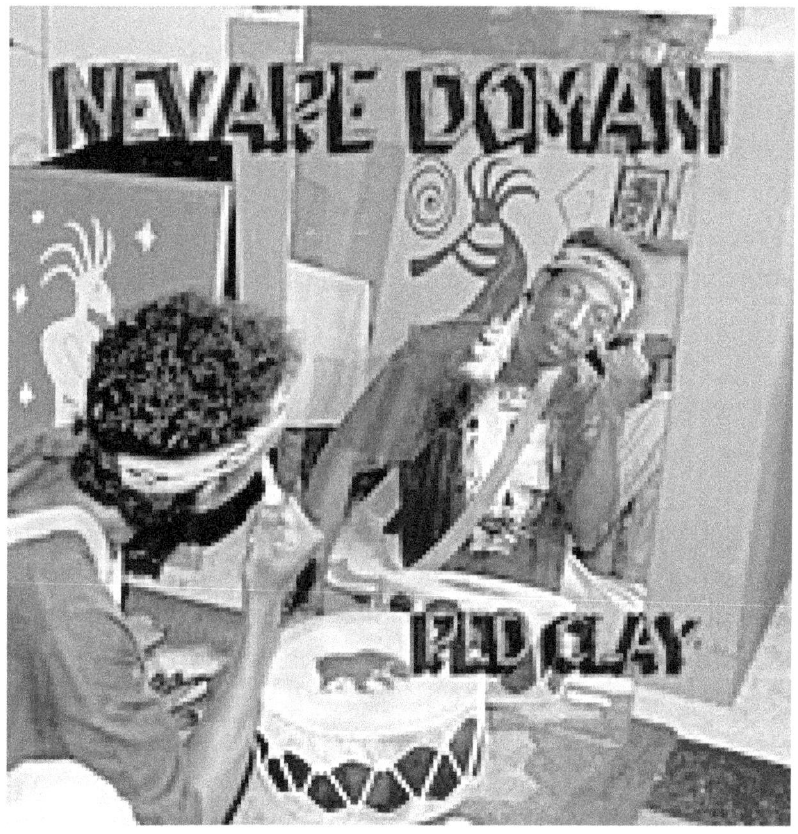

Reggie Solomon: I feel like you, that there is only one race, with many different flavors. It saddens me that in this day and age there is so much strife because of race, creed, and national origin.

Heritage should be a source of pride and respect, a grounding force. The Internet can be a wonderful unifier, allowing you to reach out to the world from your home computer. The same can be said about music, a very powerful and influential source.

Chase Von: Ditto, because I`ve been to Russia, I`ve been to Korea; I`ve been to more places than I care to name here. The common man and common woman of each country I`ve been to don`t seem to hate me because I might be different; they seem to be more curious than anything, so I think it`s hearts really.

But what is your view on the state or condition of our current world?

Reggie Solomon: Simply stated, we still have a long way to go, but I believe that things have gotten better and will continue to do so. We are becoming increasingly multicultural and influencing one another. Pretty soon, we`ll all be the same color anyway! (BIG SMILE.)

Chase Von: I often didn`t share this because I thought it would be silly to most folks, but I did share it with another outstanding poet and writer who calls himself The Chief. I had already included him in the acknowledgements in my book before he responded to it, that book being "Your Chance To

Hear The Last Panther Speak."

He wrote me back with his thoughts on what I`d shared and it brought tears to my eyes, I`m not ashamed to say. And that was this --- Every time I see a Hawk. I say "God Bless God." It might seem pretty silly or childish but I think the majority of people who pray are asking God for blessings.

And it`s my way of continuously reminding myself that to bless is to show thanks and what better way to say thank you than to bless the one that made it all possible to begin with? Silly or what?

Reggie Solomon: That`s not silly at all; I think that`s absolutely beautiful. It makes perfect sense.

Chase Von: What are some of the causes you feel very strongly about and support?

Reggie Solomon: Anything that brings people closer together and encourages healthy curiosity, education and hard work.

Chase Von: How important is family to you, and what is your take on the state of our current world?

Reggie Solomon: Family is of the utmost importance. It is the setting in which we develop into who we will become. The Cherokee value family over the self. The well being of the tribe is first and foremost. In the United States, the dominant culture values self over family.

This is echoing across the globe, it seems. Only indigenous cultures seem to know the real score.

Chase Von: What would you say if you were standing before a microphone that could be heard by every child on the planet, and regardless of what language they spoke, they would understand you?

What positive advice would you give the children, if that were possible?

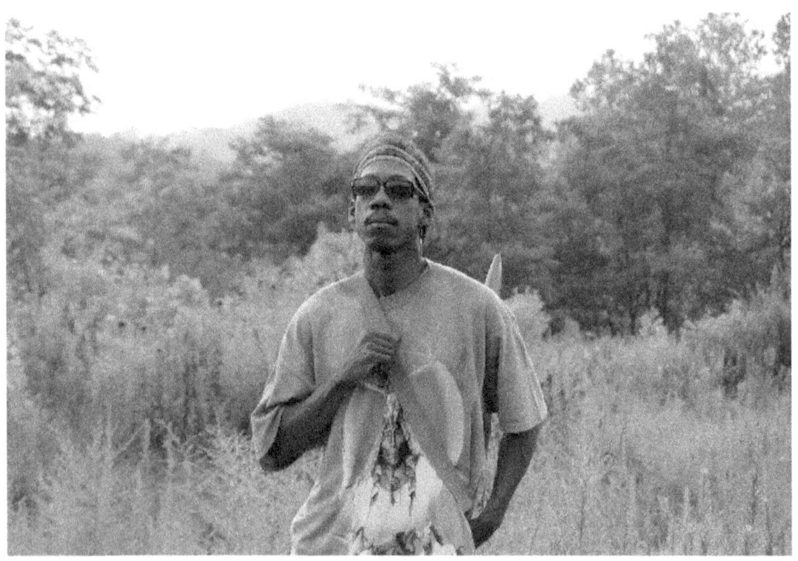

Reggie Solomon: Always remember to give thanks to The Creator.

Keep loving. Keep living. Keep learning. Keep asking. Keep working hard.

Chase Von: Where can our readers find out more about you, and purchase your music? Various links where it is available? And also do you have any websites that list your next performances?

Reggie Solomon: The portal into my little world exists at myspace.com/thefellasmusic. It has all the latest information on my CD/MP3 releases, gigs and Native American lore. For music videos, you can check out youtube.com/thefellasmusic.

Yes, I got videos too!

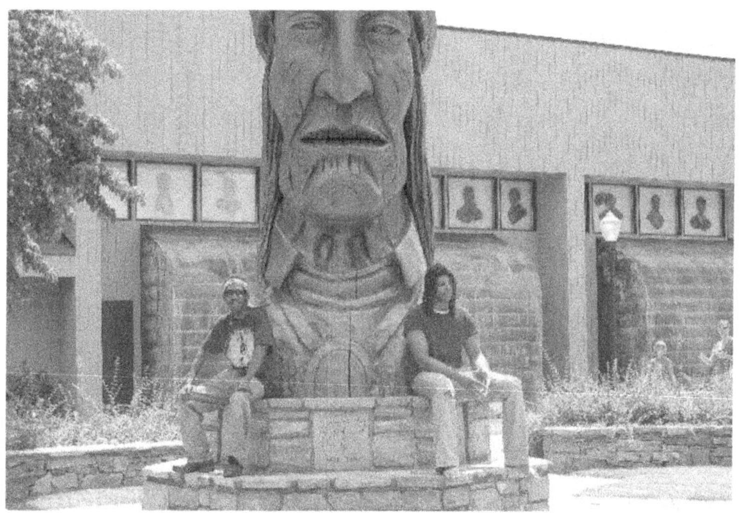

Chase Von: I want to thank you again for finding the time for this, and I also want to say, one thing that surprised me about your latest release, in addition to your amazing voice, is that you have so many things on your CD that are totally instrumental.

You truly made me remember my love of the flute. Sadly, I like a lot of other folks, equate the flute to the very popular character that David Carradine played in Kung Fu. Sadly, he is no longer with us.

My friend, the truly lovely Mary Christina Brown, recently did a movie with him, so I know, personally, how much the loss affected those who worked with him.

I also noticed in some of your songs that even when you got funky you still included the flute.

On the one I would call a dance track (Wish Bone), I think it sounded similar to Prince, who is a legend, as well. Incidentally, I shared some communications with Prince`s sister Tyka Nelson.

She has a CD out called *A Brand New Me* and just like you said above, experience can be the best teacher--- Even bad ones and she`s had a lot of them.

Hope she doesn`t mind me saying that but I just finished her book *Mama Never Taught Me How To Sing* and she writes about them. One last question, and I`m really serious on this one since I can be silly at times. I admit it because I think life is too short to be serious all the time but... For you--- What is the meaning of life?

And I`m asking you this question because it is undeniable to anyone that has heard your soul-touching music that you have spent a lot of time pondering that question.

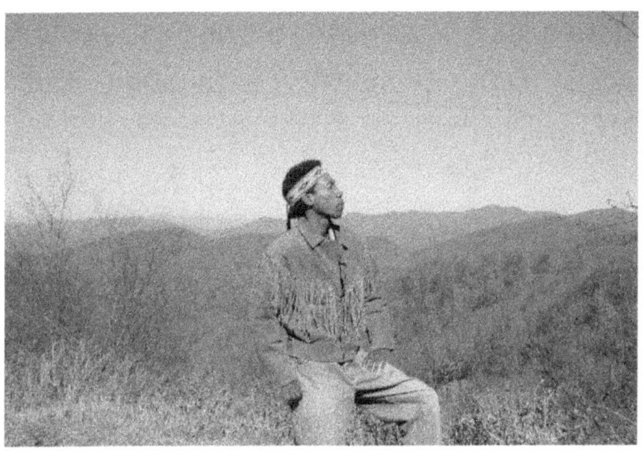

Reggie Solomon: For me the meaning of life is love. Love is truly the most powerful force in the cosmos. It can make you do things you never dreamed of. It can make you feel the strongest of emotions. It can change hearts. Without it, life is meaningless. I believe that what gives us meaning is our relationship to others, not just people but all sentient beings and the forces of nature. It`s a harmony. It`s a balance. Mitakuye Oyasin (we are all connected, from Lakota).

Chase Von: On behalf of the Student Operated Press and myself, thanks again, Reggie, for sharing some of your time, and continued success to you always.

I`m so glad Adrian shared a truly remarkable spirit such as yourself with me, and I`m grateful I can do my little part here to share you and your soul-lifting music with this world of ours. One love to you, Brown Eagle, and again continued success from The Last Panther...(Smile.)

Reggie Solomon: Wado for your time and consideration, my brother Panther. Your light shines brightly. One love to you, and may the Great Spirit bless you and protect you on your path. Namaste! Dohiyi, unali-i! (With honor and blessings, dear friend.)

"For me the meaning of life is love.
Love is truly the most powerful force in the cosmos.
It can make you do things you never dreamed of."

--- Reggie Solomon AKA Wodige Wehali

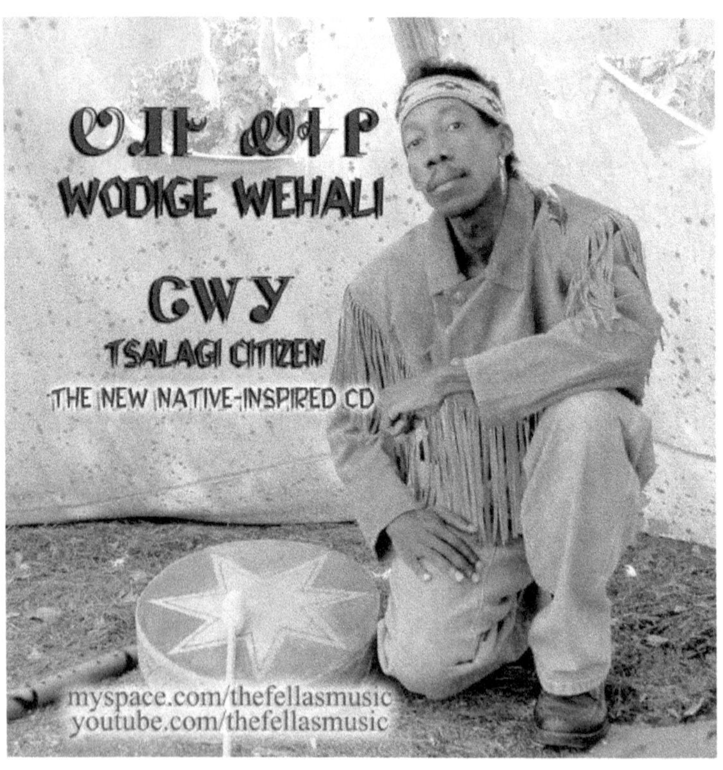

Interview with Joan Baker

THE QUEEN OF VOICEOVER

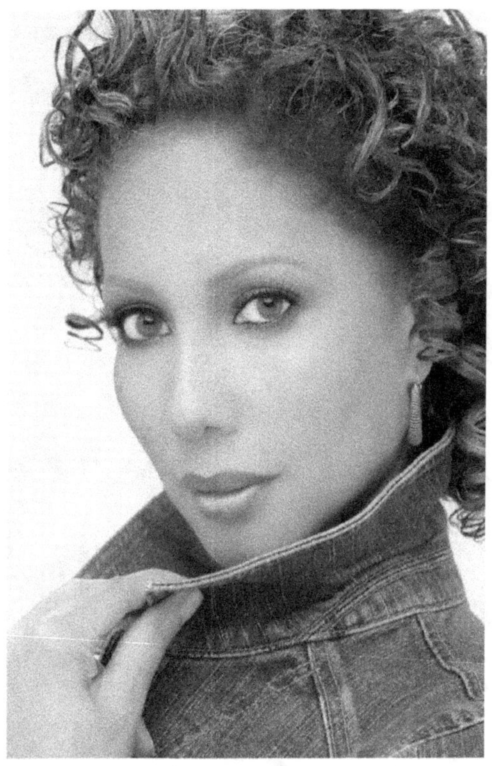

Chase Von: Hey Joan and talk about the entire package! You are beautiful; you`re an accomplished business woman. You love sports and you are also athletic and you are as comfortable in front of a camera as you are behind a microphone. Plus your accomplishments are incredible but we`ll get to all of that!

So on behalf of myself and *The Student Operated Press*, thanks so much for finding the time to share yourself with our readers and they wouldn`t know this if I didn`t share it, but you`re by your own choice, on a six day work schedule and still squeezing this in!

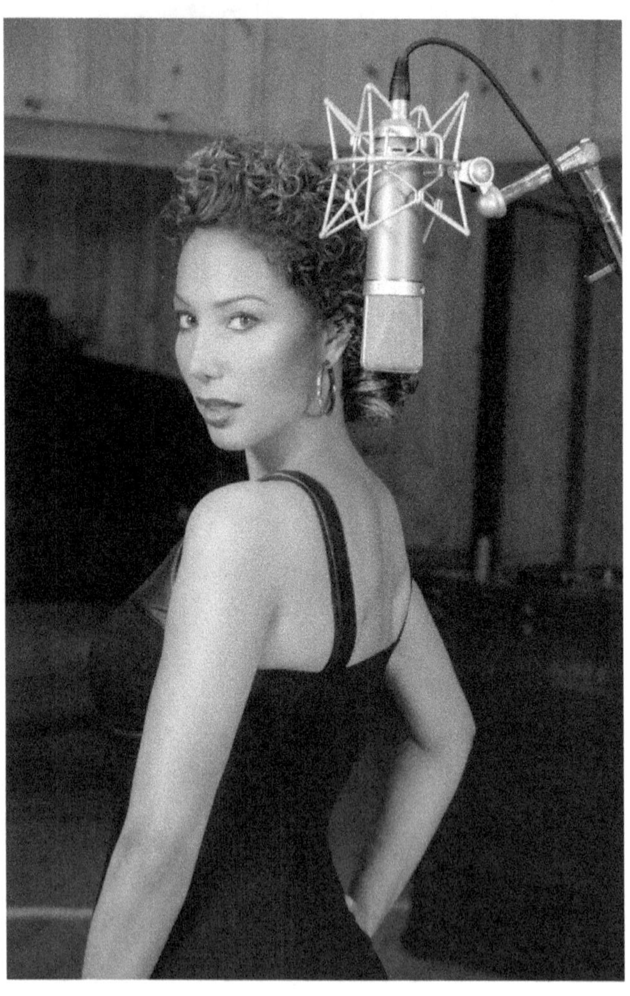

Joan Baker: It`s my pleasure Chase. Athleticism extends through all aspects of life and that includes making time for fun stuff like this.

Chase Von: Just from reading up on you a bit, I`m amazed! I`ve totally enjoyed learning more about you and I know that I`ve only scratched the surface but the one thing that comes through in everything I`ve seen and read is your wonderful personality!

Joan Baker: Oh, please stop, (don`t) stop! (Smile.)

Chase Von: You have this down to earth aura about you that really resonates with me, and I`m sure must resonate with all the others that come in contact with you! How different are you now, from the way you were as a child of say 8 or 9 years of age? (I use that age because that`s my daughter`s age and it is really much easier to see now, her personality taking shape).

And do you believe as I`ve read before, that our basic personalities are formed around that period, and then we just build on it? And also, can you tell us about your younger years and who was most influential in your opinion, of blessing you with such an incredibly positive and loving outlook on life?

Joan Baker: I think I`m very much like my personality of 8 or 9 years of age. I`d say the essence of my sensibilities was formed by then and I was on an inevitable path to become the more fully developed personality that I am now. For the most part I get a lot of positive feedback on my personality. It`s one of the few things I don`t really have to think about. I love, love, love people and when I`m with them I can`t help but engage

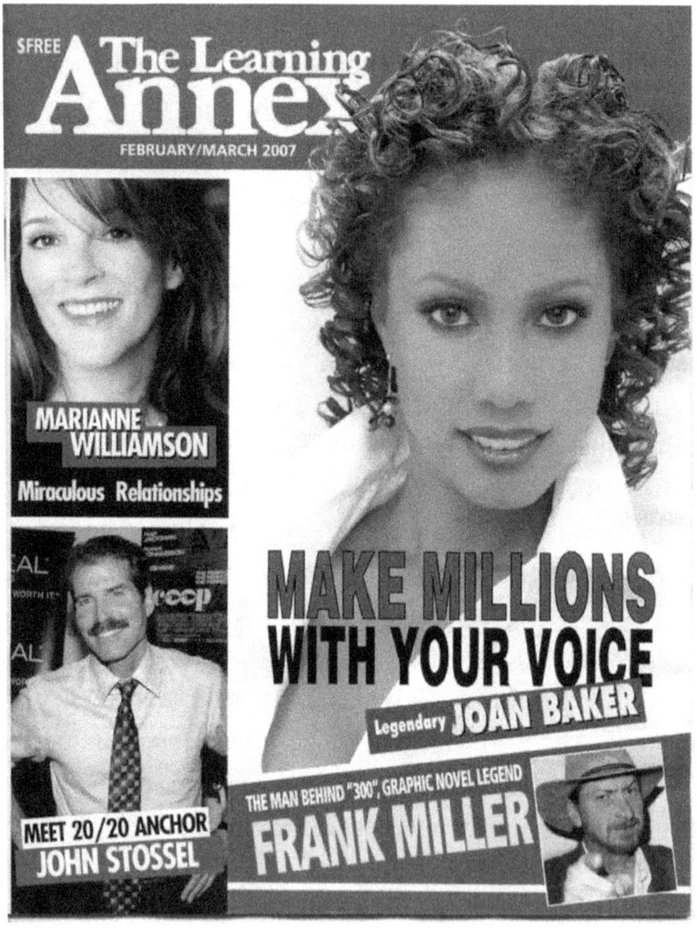

and take an interest in what they do and how they arrived at where they are in life. I also don`t mind sharing intimate truths about my own life, which I think gives each person the permission to open up.

I think the bulk of one`s personality is definitely formed at a young age but I also believe that there`s plenty of room to cultivate one`s personality through self-investigation and a desire to evolve one`s life and spirit. We all have our issues to bear, personality and otherwise, but that doesn`t mean we`re stuck with it. Clearly, we can take action to transform that which we don`t appreciate about ourselves, especially if it negatively impacts others, but there are also good things that we can elevate to higher plains and that`s as much an opportunity as fixing whatever we think is broken.

Chase Von: Like my boss and mentor here Judyth Piazza, you are really going after your dreams! I`m pretty sure she won`t mind me sharing this, but she always wanted to be a reporter but didn`t pursue it until much later in life after a failed marriage. Since then she has created the *Student Operated Press* and is blazing trails each day like you, in what she feels she was born to do! So she`s a business owner and it isn`t uncommon for her to work schedules like you yourself do also.

But the reason I bring this up is, she says all the time, when you`re doing what you love, it isn`t work. It`s something you can`t wait to get back to! Is that also your perspective? And why you are able to keep such long hours acting, doing voice over`s and coaching others in your craft which it is safe to say, you`re at the top of the class in?

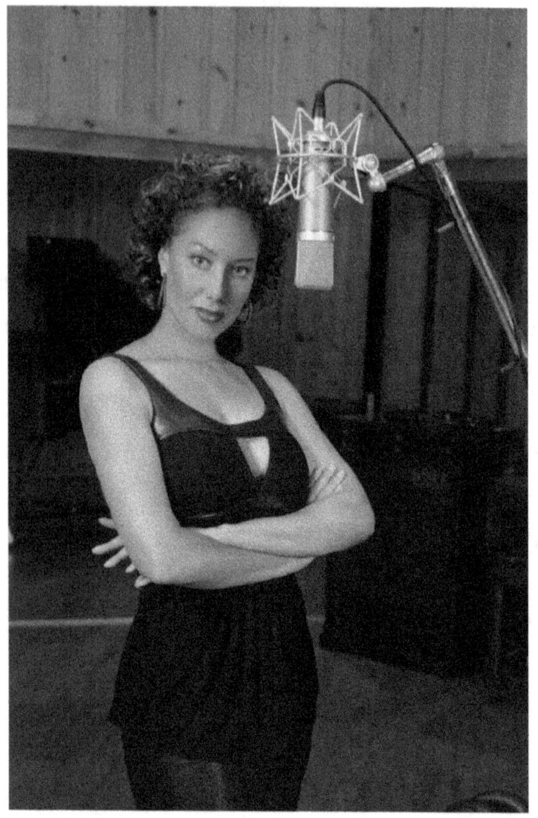

Joan Baker endorses Neumann USA World Class microphones

Joan Baker: Doing what you love is an interesting idea. I can`t say that I always love what I do, to be honest, but I am totally committed to doing it at the highest level I can. What often motivates me is the goal of delivering a voiceover performance that does everything my client`s desires. When I work with students, it`s their goals and dreams that I focus on, which means I dig deep within myself to bring 100% of my ability to the teacher/student experience. I guess what I`m saying is that my love is more for doing my best than it is doing my best at a particular thing. For example, I love the kind of challenges, interaction and admiration that comes from being a performer, but most of the work of being a performer is practice, marketing, networking, auditioning and, of course, hearing lots of saying "No" on your way to hearing "yes." There`s also the business side of being a performer, which is quite a slippery slope. I don`t love all these very real aspects of being a performer and yet they represent the majority of the doing.

If you want to be successful, you have to access a personal appreciation for more than just the stuff you love.

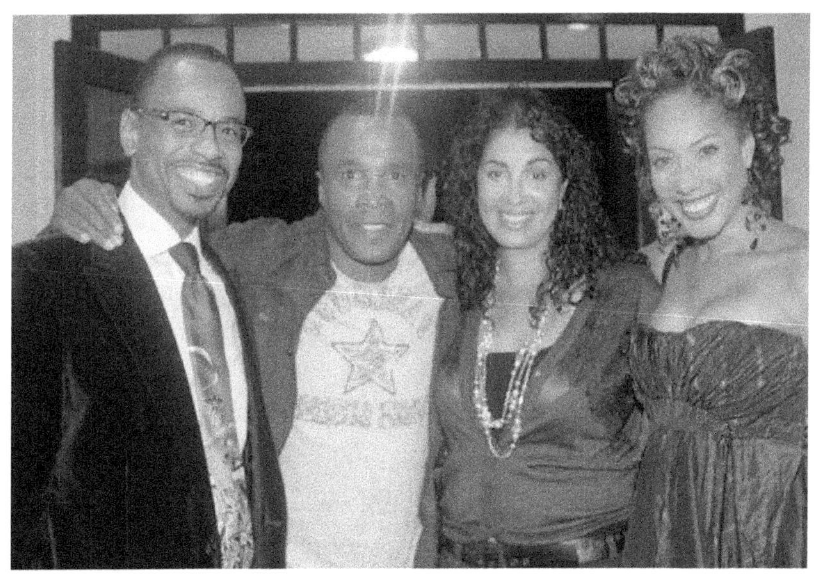

Joan Baker & her husband Rudy Gaskins pose with Mr. and Mrs. Sugar Ray Leonard

Chase Von: Also, I have another question that comes to me because of your interview with Maureen Anderson, but before I ask that, do you think it`s ever too late for someone to pursue their dreams?

Joan Baker: Arriving at Mount Everest is probably the least exciting part of the journey to get there. If you measure your dreams only by achieving a certain end result, you may find yourself trying to calculate when it`s time to give up your dream due to age or degree of difficulty or negative feedback from others. If instead you focus on the "process" that is the task of climbing the mountain, and if the process is the part you love, you will see that there is never a time to give up on your dreams.

Chase Von: One of the reason`s I asked that last question Joan is in your interview with Maureen Anderson, of the popular radio show, *The Career Clinic*, you guys touched on something I feel really passionate about, and as you`ll remember I`m sure,

I also shared something with you I had written on the subject from my book years before I heard you two addressing it.

But again, it struck a nerve. You were speaking about how as children, we believe in the impossible, then we become adults and the dreams we had as children have been all but squashed out of us in most cases. But what got me is that you both were saying to become a real "Adult", you had to get back to the mind set of the "Child" and go for your dreams! I could write novels on it myself because I think most adults are hating life!

And doing something they don`t enjoy but convincing themselves that they have to do it because it is the "Adult" thing to do. Can you give our readers your philosophy on that? And why you also think, so many people give up on their dreams and settle and why they shouldn`t?

Joan Baker: I wish I could give you a definitive answer that would free every reader to go for their wildest dreams with complete abandon. The fact of the matter is that we each have to start from where we are emotionally and intellectually as individuals.

Looking at the behavior of children will offer incredible insight, especially when it comes to the unbridled enthusiasm. That kind of enthusiasm can have you leaping over tall buildings before you realize it`s supposed to be a hard thing to do. Obviously, this kind of inner excitement doesn`t just happen because you happen to have a certain result in mind.

As adults we have to reach out for help and make time to reopen the windows to our youthful souls. Prayer, meditation, healthy living, giving back and honesty are some of the practices I believe will help anyone get to where they want to be. And honesty includes one`s self as much as it does others.

Hundreds of great thinkers over the centuries have pointed to the innocence of children as an access point for adults to reconnect with their most creative selves. In some ways, this reconnecting is a means for reinvention and transformation or even reincarnation.

Chase Von: Wonderful answer Joan and I couldn`t agree more! Unless you believe in reincarnation we only have one life to live!

Personally I think people have to add at least an extra hour to their days and make that ME time.

More if circumstances permit or less if that`s the case but some time where they do what they really feel they were meant to do! And even if it doesn`t pan out into something like stardom or wealth, they are still not neglecting that inner child that loves something and believes, and that part of themselves that knows there is more to them than their nine to five or what have you.

Might not happen in every case, but they are still doing what they love and who knows? Then they might be able to transition to it full time! Now something I had to think about whether I should ask you.

You couldn`t articulate it as a child, but you KNEW you wanted to help people and heal people and for people to feel better about themselves! One of your dreams as just a child, was to be someone that could go to a war zone and have your presence heal those who had been affected by all the violence and hardship. Tell your husband not to get mad at me mind you, but I`ve been to two of them and I KNOW if you had stepped off a plane, I would have felt better instantly! (Smile).

You truly are gorgeous!

But they have folks that go entertain the troops and I`ve met Brittany Murphy, Kidd Rock, Lee Anne Womack and Chely Wright and others when I was deployed. Also I`ve interviewed the Lovely Singer and Model "Leah DeVon" and she`s a veteran of USO tours and openly says that military audiences have been some of the most supportive and appreciative people she`s ever entertained in her life! So, my question is this, unfortunately it looks like for now, the wars are going to continue. So is that something you might consider doing? And if so would you bring your husband so he could also entertain and support our warriors as well?

Joan Baker: Thank you for the compliment. First of all, you don`t have to ask me twice to step into a spotlight. I have to admit that performing just sets me on fire. My husband also sets me on fire, so he can definitely come along. I would love to entertain our soldiers over seas. They need every comfort and inspiration they can get to do the work of protecting our nation and our freedom.

Entertainment is cathartic.

Even entertainers crave the experience of enjoying other entertainers. It would be my absolute pleasure to fulfill what must be an even deeper need for soldiers who are facing the very worst kind of scenario while being far away from the people they love and the culture they know. But entertainment is short lived. The show does come to an end and the curtain closes. I would also like to be a part of ensuring the soldiers get the kind of ongoing emotional and military support they need to complete their tasks and come home healthy.

Chase Von: Going back to you being beautiful! You were also a stand out in basketball but when it came to making it in the movies; you had to suffer some disappointments not because you weren`t lovely enough to be in any movie as the leading lady, but because they didn`t know what to make of your mixed racial heritage!

This sort of led you in the direction of voiceover and becoming for all practical purposes, the reigning QUEEN!

Now I might get beat up for this some, but there are those that think that the one`s that do voice over aren`t perhaps attractive enough to be standing on stage or in front of a camera but have the voices for it. That`s not to say I don`t know that there are many popular actors etc that lend their voices to movies and animations etc.

But seeing pictures of you? I think when you get around to it, you`re going to conquer Hollywood as well if you choose too! (Smile.)

But one of the most beautiful women to ever live in my opinion was Dorothy Dandridge! Halle Berry has also broke through and been very successful but I had to think when I heard you say that. Because a girl I went to junior high with who is also an actress, (Angela Meryl), but also an incredibly successful stunt woman is someone I can`t understand why, she isn`t getting more face time as an actual actress.

She`s won many awards and accolades for her stunt work and has been Beyonce`s stunt double and most notably at least to me, Vivica Fox`s stunt double in Kill Bill one! (That`s really her in all the fight scenes you see in the beginning of the movie getting thrown around and smashing tables).

Nothing against Vivica or Beyonce but she`s just as lovely as they are and in my opinion, so are you. But she`s also fair skinned like yourself.

This is Angela`s web site: http://www.angelameryl.com/

And I`ve interviewed a few actors and actresses but I don`t know if the scripts say, Asian woman says this, the White woman says that, then Black woman says this... Hey! We need a Black woman! Well, she`s been Miss America and is also an incredibly successful singer! Vanessa who? Vanessa Williams? Oh Yes! We`ll make an exception! (Smile.)

I`m mixed too, Black, Blackfoot and Cherokee Indian and rumored in family lore, a little French, but you also made the statement on Maureen`s show that now that we have our first time ever, Black President, (Who is really mixed), you think things will get better. Can you expound on that?

Joan Baker: Being of mixed race is not as simple as it seems.

It really comes down to an unspoken rule about the precise shade of your skin. Barack Obama, for example, is dark enough that America sees him and accepts him as black. He, himself, declares his race as African American. But the hard core truth of the matter is that self-selecting himself as African-American is just as arbitrary as self-selecting himself as white American.

Of course, he would never have become President had he run on the declaration that he was white.

Unlike Barack, my lighter skin shade makes it difficult for people to determine my racial heritage.

This is a difficult thing when it comes to the business of "entertainment" which operates on reaching and impressing audiences according to demographic criteria. An audience can`t follow a movie`s storyline or fully absorb a product advertisement if they are busy wondering about the nationality of the actor.

And that`s before we look at the movies and commercials that go out of their way to target a specific ethnic group. So yes, I lost many job opportunities because of what producers described as a nondescript racial heritage. And along with this attitude I was more readily described as exotic than beautiful. So as far as the "business" was concerned I had a face for radio.

I think things are definitely improving. Race is becoming less the criteria by which intelligent and enlightened people chose to make decisions and in the end, the market place will always bend to the will of the consumer`s decisions.

Chase Von: I don`t do the race thing myself, to me, it`s good people, bad people, which side of the line do you fall on? In the Marines it was... Was it a dark green Marine? Or a light green Marine?

(Meaning still a Marine, just like we are all still people. (Smile).

Now to your many accomplishments!

You`ve been the voice for the NCAA men`s basketball tournament! You`re voice over career has spanned over two decades! You`ve done hundreds of promos, programs; commercials and your list of clients include *ABC News, American Express, and ESPN*!

You`re also featured in Maureen Anderson`s book, *The Career Clinic, 8 Simple Rules for Finding Work You Love* which is available on Amazon! You`re also the author of *Secrets of Voice Over Success and Creative solutions: husband and wife combine talents to deliver award-winning ad campaigns.* And you`ve also worked with popular radio host Don Imus of *Imus in the Morning*, and your other clients are or have been, *King World, BLOOMBERG TV* and radio, *SHOWTIME, HBO, NBA Entertainment, COURT TV, Olay, Lens Express, Sony Music, JP Morgan Chase, Costco,* and the *New York Times* classified calls regularly to have you represent numerous clients!

You`ve voiced the TV campaign for *The Muhammad Ali Center* and narrated the documentary about the founding of the *William Jefferson Clinton Library*! Not to mention you`ve provided live announcements for the *Museum of the Moving Image Salutes Will Smith* " which aired on *Bravo TV*!

Sorry Joan, fingers are getting tired, so can you share some links and websites for our readers so they can learn more about you and your various other accomplishments?

Also for those that are interested in learning how to get involved and be successful in what you do?

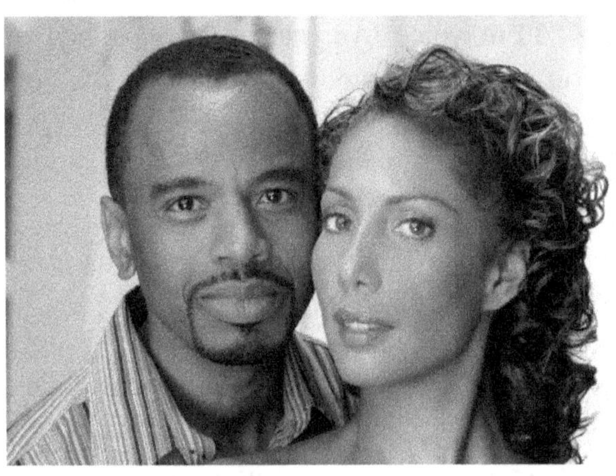

Rudy Gaskins with wife Joan Baker

Joan Baker: Two web sites cover the highlights of my career. First there`s my personal web site: **www.joanthevoice.com** Second, there`s my company web site that features the advertising and marketing work that my husband Rudy and I do as an ad agency. **www.pushcreative.tv**. I`m very proud of both.

Chase Von: Well Joan, I always try and ask a tough one. I don`t even want to weigh in myself, but I know you and your husband Rudy Gaskins believe in working together and it looks like you have a truly wonderful relationship!

So what are your feelings on the Tiger Woods thing?

And do you think if he had included his wife more in what he was doing, he wouldn`t have been as likely to have been tempted if that is indeed the case?

Personally I don`t like kicking people when they`re down.

I myself occasionally flirt but man; I wouldn`t wish what he is now going through on an enemy!

And although my wife doesn`t write, I do try to include her in what I`m doing. Do you think, as I think, that with most situations, people often end up spending more "Awake" time with others of the opposite sex than they do with their spouses?

And how would you handle damage control for him? Or would you if he asked?

And do you think by working with your husband or others working with their significant others, they limit the chances of that happening? Because let`s face it, in most situations, both have to work to make it and that leads to people being around others instead of the one`s they made a commitment to, in most people`s circumstances in this country.

Joan Baker: Tiger Woods would appear to be suffering some very severe emotional problems, not to mention delusional issues that are not uncommon to children who grow up in celebrity bubbles.

Obviously, had he been with his wife day in and day out, he would have had far less opportunity for being with other women. But that does not mean that he wouldn`t have manifested an equally adulterous mindset.

One could almost feel sorry for Tiger if not for the obvious fraud he knowingly perpetrated while looking down his nose at the rest of us. His arrogance knows no bounds and he doesn`t appear to have a decent bone in his body. He`s getting his just deserts now.

Perhaps the one good thing that may come out of Woods` disgrace is that women will wake up to a new understanding of our value as human beings and a common intolerance for being objectified by men.

No, there`s a second thing: Men too now have the space to revisit who they are in the matter of human regard for one another, especially when it comes to male behavior toward women. If we chose, the Tiger debacle could be a departure point for an evolved common respect.

Chase Von: Is there anything else you`re doing that we might see in the future you can give our readers a heads up about Joan?

Joan Baker: Many things are on the horizon-I`ll know better in 2010- “To be continued.”

Chase Von: Who are some of the people you yourself, truly look up to and admire? And people you`ve loved working with, and also people you haven`t worked with yet, but would want to?

Joan Baker: The late Don LaFontaine is the first person to come to mind as he was a personal friend who gave a great deal of himself to support my career and my dreams.

Don was a man who walked through many storms, some of his on doing, to emerge as a loving humanitarian and a talent of great humility. I love him dearly. Barack Obama is another person I admire a great deal because he has dared to put front and center, the shared ideals of the public`s most romantic soul.

He has challenged the world with what the world says it wants most of itself. He is championing a cause that is hard for us to accept, much like the way many of us dream of big things but dare not go after them. Obama was given a mandate to hold high our dreams and ideals and he has not stepped away from his promise to do so.

And on the most personal and profound level, I have to acknowledge my husband Rudy. He has always been in my corner, even when he`s had to get out of his own way to do so.

He does everything in his power to lift me up so I can better see the way, to clear a path so that I can better find my way, and to soften the ground so that can fall without fear. I give him the same support and we respect the power of being in accord with one another.

Video of Joan Baker with Don Lafontaine

The link in the event the video doesn`t work:
http://www.youtube.com/watch?v=vzZcdCma9AU

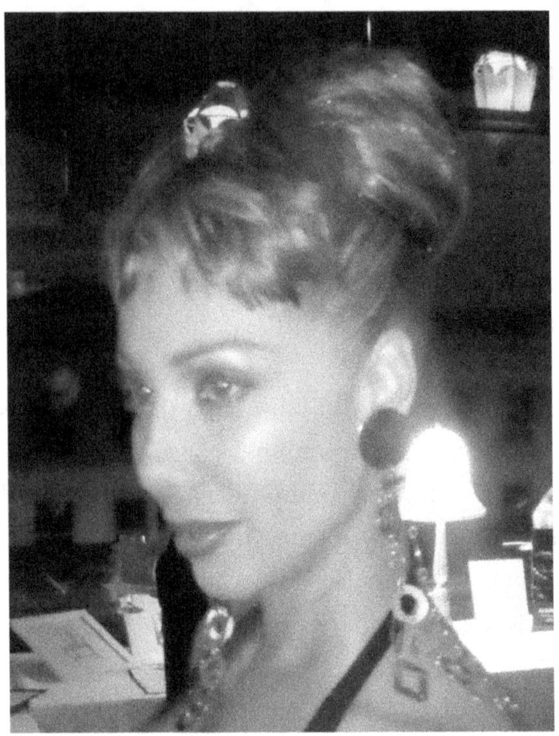

Chase Von: What would you say if you were standing before a microphone that could be heard by every child on the planet, and regardless of what language they spoke, they would understand you?

What positive advice would you give the children, if that were possible?

Joan Baker: I would share a quote from my husband: "You have everything you need to be everything you want to be."

Chase Von: Busy as you are, how do you maintain your fantastic figure?

And what are some of the meals you and that lucky man that get`s to call himself your husband truly enjoy? (Smile.)

Joan Baker: This is a very basic thing for me and it`s far from perfect, but I exercise, eat healthily and work with a spiritual healer on a regular basis. You could say that`s the trinity of my life and all things fall somewhere within that triangle. Rudy and I love Japanese, Indian and Soul Food cuisine. Oh, and don`t let me leave out our Mexican which I love also. Of course, moderation is important regardless of the cuisine. Rudy is also a great cook so we enjoy many of his home made dishes. And while we`re talking about food, some of my favorite shows are Top Chef and Iron Chef.

I can`t get enough of these shows because they are so incredibly inspiring.

Chase Von: How important is family to you? Also, I know you support the cause of Alzheimer`s and are also heavily involved with *Voices Echo an Alzheimer`s Cure.* Can you share with our readers your reason for believing so much in this cause?

And also more about it and some of the others that are also involved in this with you?

Joan Baker: I am very connected to my family. My mom and I have had quite a journey as mother and daughter and it wasn`t always easy by any stretch of the imagination.

In the end, however, our relationship has resolved to be the kind of relationship I couldn`t have dreamed up.

We are fast friends and share everything with each other. And she and Rudy enjoy each other as well. My father, who passed away 7 years ago from complications of Alzheimer`s, was a rock in my life.

He was always there, rain or shine, ready and willing to support my "wildest dreams" as willing to be by my side whether I was winning or losing.

My dad was also a great male role model who gave me something powerful to shoot for when I was finally ready to choose a mate in my life.

Rudy and my dad have very similar ethics. They got along instantly.

I also have 3 brothers who I love dearly.

We don`t get together for family reunions or anything like that but we are aware of the bond that ties us together and somehow there is a respect and a love that we feed from. We continue to share our lives with each other, something that has become a great deal easier with social networking.

Voices Remember

In the event this video doesn`t work, the link:

http://www.youtube.com/watch?v=j6Jmf8D96xQ

Chase Von: I also want to ask this Joan, recently I read something that was sent to me in email by best selling New York Times author, Janet Bray Attwood, I`m sure it was sent to many others as well, but it had my name at the top to make it seem personal. (Smile.)

But it said and this is directly from the message;

Chris and I often say; "Passion is what connects individual intelligence with universal intelligence"

That means when you are clear about your passions, you tap into the power that is organizing all the planets to circle around the sun, that organizes all the stars in all the galaxies, down to the smallest, finest particle of life on earth.

That`s a lot of power.

I think I told you before I think everything happens for a reason, and sometimes there are some "strange" things that happen as well that have led me to believe there is no such thing as coincidence.

Prior to you writing me back and saying you wanted to do the interview, I also got a confirmation from four time World Champion boxer Hollie (Hot Stuff), Dunaway saying she`d like to do an interview with me as well! But then I`m looking at your webpage, I click on you, and what do I see is the title of one of your pages? Hot Stuff! (Smile.)

Here`s her link and like you, she is quite hot! (Smile.)

http://www.hotstuffhollie.com/

But to me that sort of lets me know I`m going in the right direction when things seem to synchronize like that!

Do you often think, your passion opens doors for you and guides you in the right direction, even when what you may have (Thought) you wanted to do might fall off the radar, it is for a reason and for something else that will get you where you truly want to be, (perhaps faster), even though it doesn`t seem like it at the time, to take its place?

I.e., you could still be a movie star if you wanted to, but being in voice over as predominantly you are, has for all practical purposes, allowed you to become a living legend in that field, and it has helped you bridge voice over and the power of that community with aiding those affected by Alzheimer`s which was one of your goals, even as a small child, and that was to be a Humanitarian.

Because that might not have worked out so perfectly or quite the way it has, if you were a successful and always on call movie actress.

Seems to me like your life is indeed being guided by a higher power and it just occurred to me, that the higher power might even possibly be the spirit of your late father. Your thoughts on that?

Joan Baker: Passion is the catalyst for unbridled enthusiasm and hard work.

Passion lives in the realm of faith so that you`re willing to taken on the greatest odds, sometimes unable to see practicalities that might otherwise stop you in your tracks. Passion is your willingness to put everything on the line to achieve your heart`s desire.

Passion, however, is not about pushing blindly on the hope for divine intervention. My life has not always followed the path of my dreams but it has always followed my passions. It has led me to amazing opportunities and people I never dreamed I would encounter. It has also led me to learning experiences marked by disappointment and despair.

My dad is in everything I do and everything I have become. Being a movie star is a dream that carries with it certain criteria. Movie stars, for example, usually start rather young and grow up with a generation of moviegoers who come to know them as much for their longevity as their many memorable movies.

On that level, becoming the traditional movie star is no longer my goal. However, I fully intend to be in movies and enjoy the excitement of bringing my talent and craft to bear on the artistry of filmmaking.

Chase Von: Joan, you are such a wonderful and talented soul and certainly one that once met, can`t be forgotten. I`ve seen you in pictures with popular Talk Show Host Bill O`Reilly,

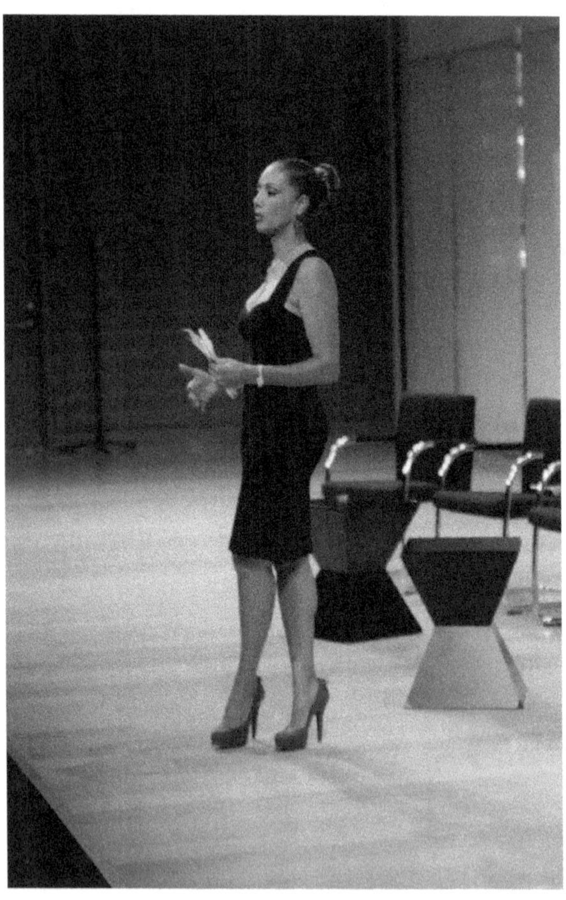

music sensation Wyclef once of the *Fugee`s*, former President Bill Clinton, comediene and actor Bill Murray, Senator John McCain, former boxer and promoter Leland Hardy, the Legendary Sugar Ray Leonard, tennis and super star tennis icon Serena Williams, lovely actress and model Shawn Richardz who I`ve also interviewed, and numerous other extremely well known, and easily recognized personalities!

I also think I would be remiss if I didn`t also mention this as well though, and that is all the other totally amazing voice over artist you`re pictured with who could also just as easily be in front of a camera! (Smile.)

Like your voiceover agent, Shari Hoffman, Marice Tobias, your husband, Rudy Gaskins, Valerie Smaldone, Bill Ratner, Joe Cipriano, Les Marshak, who introduces NBC News, Don LaFontaine, the voice for *Termitor 2, Judgment Day,* Rodd Houston, Cede ring Fox and so many others, but what I think is so truly amazing about you is how you are so sweet and again, time worn phrase, so down to earth!

So I truly want to wish you and your husband Rudy a wonderful Holiday Season and on behalf of myself and the *Student Operated Press,* my sincere thanks for sharing yourself with us here!

And saved round, I`m still going to introduce you to Claire Dodin! She hasn`t been in touch lately but I definitely want you two to meet! So Love and Light and continued blessings and success to you and your husband!

Joan Baker: You are so very kind Chase. You have a wonderful passion for life and people and a keen and sharp mind. It`s inspiring. I very much enjoyed the interview and I wish you the very, very best kind of success in your life.

"Arriving at Mount Everest is probably the least exciting part of the journey to get there."

--- Joan Baker

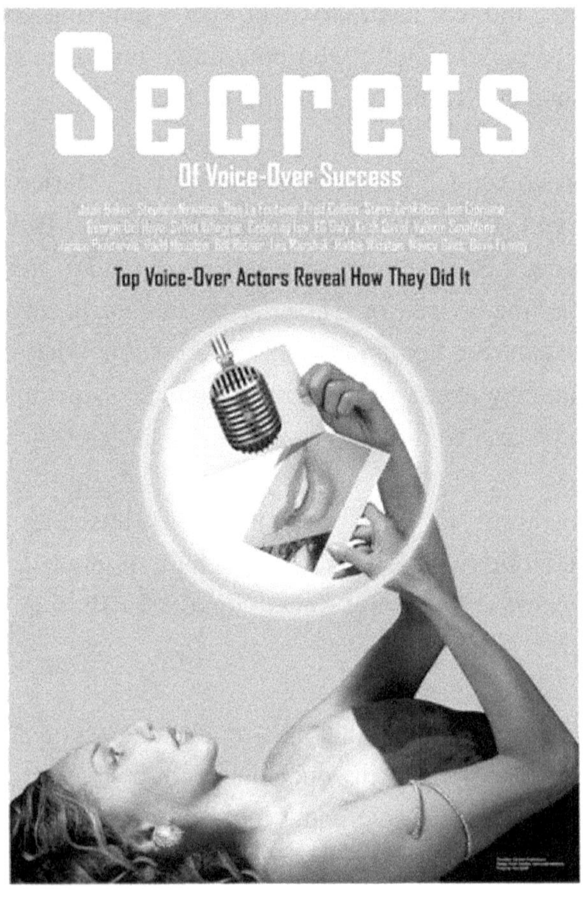

Interview with Judyth Piazza

DYNAMIC JOURNALIST IS "THE ITALIAN-AMERICAN OPRAH"

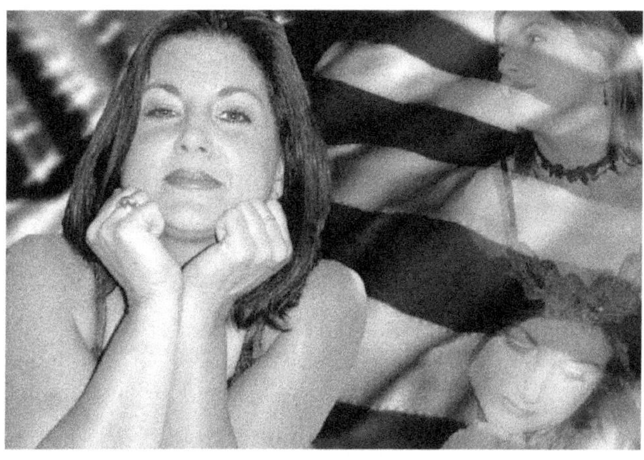

Chase Von: Looks like the tables have turned a wee bit huh MJ? (Smile.)

For the remainder of this interview I will refer to you as Judy or Judyth because MJ is my nick name for you and that might throw some people off. For the record, those that do know you or have worked with you will totally understand why I call you that. It stands for "Mighty Judy" and I began calling you that ages ago!

But back to business, years ago now our mutual friend, the incredible Inspirational Singer, Song Writer, Speaker and Life Coach Willard Barth introduced us and after the interview you did with me, you asked me to write for you and I accepted.

And wouldn't you agree it has been quite an interesting ride Lady? (Smile.)

However before we begin, since I personally know how busy you always are, thanks for finding the time to fit in this interview.

Judyth Piazza: I really thought you had already interviewed me Chase but let's do it!

Chase Von: No better time than the present so what I would like to ask first, is where did you grow up? How was your childhood? And in your case, you are doing exactly what you wanted to do as a child now but can you share the "Barbie Doll" story with our readers? (Smile.)

Judyth Piazza: I was born in Patchogue, New York to the parents of Joseph and Joan Piazza, a sister Lori 10 years old and brother Glen 6 years old. After 5 short years the family packed up and moved to Fort Pierce, Florida to be closer to grandparents and so that my dad could follow his dream of owning his own business. My parents enrolled me in St. Anastasia's Catholic School where I spent the next 3 years until we moved to Vero Beach, Florida when I was 8 years old and was transferred to St. Helen's Catholic School where I continued my education through High School. In the early 70's there was a TV series that came on every Friday night about a gritty reporter that investigated strange and somewhat paranormal crimes called "Kolchak: The Night Stalker." That is where I got the idea to wear an old fedora hat that belonged to my father. I wanted to wear it everywhere and once it started getting old and dirty and somewhat torn my mother started trying to bribe with other things so that I would get rid of the hat. One of the bribes was a Malibu Barbie doll with the corvette no less. I reluctantly took the Barbie doll but it couldn't have been more than ten minutes before I went to grab the hat out of the trash and place it back on my head. So, I guess you could say that is where the saying came from, *"When most little girls were asking their parents for Barbie and Ken dolls for Christmas, I was asking my parents for Peter Parker and Clarke Kent dolls. Even as a little girl I knew super heroes and Barbies were not real, but super writers were."*

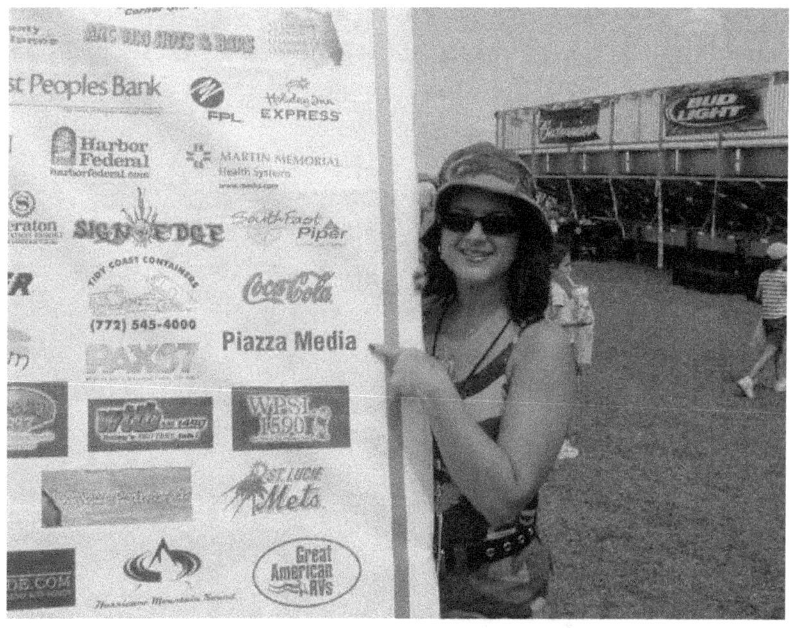

Chase Von: That's really cute Judy and I'm going to have to pay closer attention to my own children because like I discussed in my interview with Voice Extraordinaire Joan

Baker, I believe our basic personalities are formed when we are around 12 or 13 and from that point we just build on them.

And ironically, I was around that age when I wrote my first real poem. (Heh, Heh.)

Was there anyone in particular at that time that peaked your interest in being a news reporter?

To be honest, when I wrote my first poem, I didn't even know that is what it was at the time and I hadn't paid any serious attention to poetry. In fact, for quite a long time after that, I wouldn't even read any poetry by anyone else because when people found out I wrote, they would inevitably mention someone else who wrote that was famous--- But I didn't want my style influenced. (Smile.)

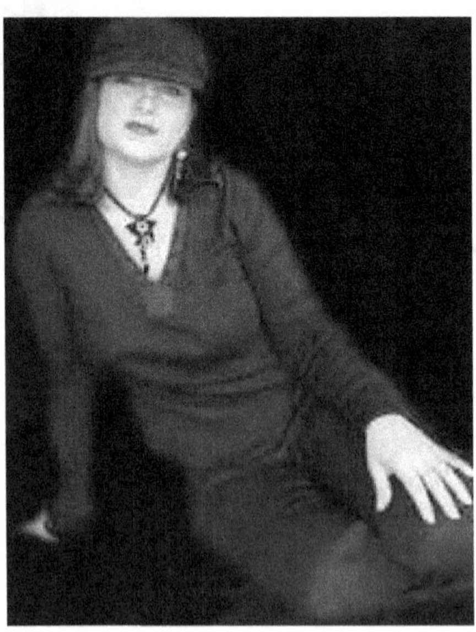

Judyth Piazza: Once again this all stems back to the TV shows that I was interested in. Kolchak was one of them but I absolutely loved Nancy Drew and The Hardy Boys. I couldn't get my hands on enough of those books and of course, the icing on the cake, TV.

Chase Von: Personally, I've always had what some would call an inquisitive mind.

In addition to Batman, Superman, Conan, Luke Cage, Spiderman, Submariner, Ta Challa, "The Black Panther", Bruce Lee, Muhammad Ali, Sugar Ray Leonard, Julius Erving, "Dr. J", The Jackson Five and later, just Michael Jackson, Encyclopedia Brown, Daredevil, Electra, (I know, she's a woman but she's bad A--! (Heh, Heh.)

One of my other hero's was Curious George! (Smile.)

As you know, I'm now retired military--- But in the military you're often too busy to follow the news and if you have down time, unless it pertains to you, the LAST thing you want to do with your free time (Or should I say in my case as not to generalize), is look at or read news!

Alright, you got me, I still read comic books but I'm still growing OK? Yes! I did watch the Curious George movie--- Yes! We own it! (Clearing throat). I've got small kids you know! (Heh, Heh.)

Now back to you--- Since I've been writing here at the SOP, I've also begun reading more and more things pertaining to news. What is it you learned when you were working as a reporter before going your own way, that still remains with you in the present?

Judyth Piazza: The one thing that I noticed as a street reporter was the necessity to write in 3rd person and covering both sides of a story. The biggest challenge for me as far as owning my online newspaper, The SOP is getting new media journalists to follow traditional newspaper guidelines.

This is important for website credibility and for the writers to land really good jobs by building an online portfolio. Speaking of Bruce Lee, I have been watching some of his films to grasp some his movements to use in boxing, which I recently became interested in. There is not another work-out like it.

Chase Von: When did you decide you wanted to fly? And how much did you have to go through before you could pilot that thing solo? And as a former Air Traffic Controller I know a little bit about the subject but what is that called? (Smile.)

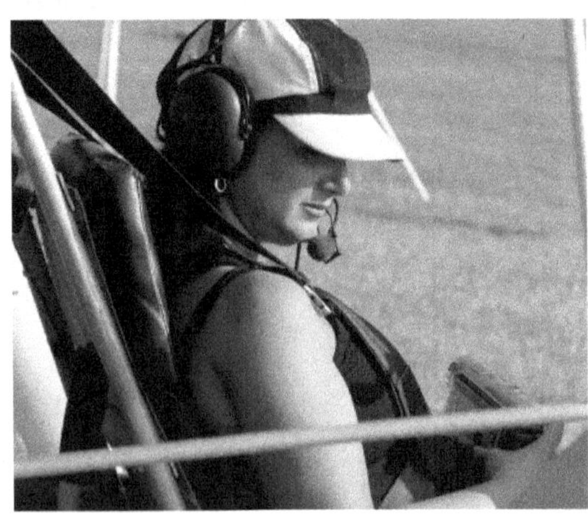

Judyth Piazza: I first became interested in flying when I had a guest on my program, Wesley Frieson. He is one of the inventors of the ultralight. Flying ultralights is a little different as far as FAA regulations go. You only need to be 14 to get what is called a sports license. I solo took off and landed after my first eight hours of training. As of now, I have logged around 240 hours. Also, I had a chance recently to take flying lessons in a Sesna 172 and I need around 30 more hours before I will feel comfortable soloing but again I believe that you can solo after 8 hours. I guess one of the reasons that I love flying is that believe it or not journalism has turned me into a bit of an adrenaline junkie so that probably explains that boxing as well.

Chase Von: I've interviewed Four Time World Champion Hollie (Hot Stuff) Dunaway, Top Contender Stacey (sta lo) Riele and as I type this, am working on an interview with Ada (Ace) Velez who has held numerous belts and was the first Puerto Rican woman to win a World Championship! Ahh... I was just visiting your Face book page now but what is this?

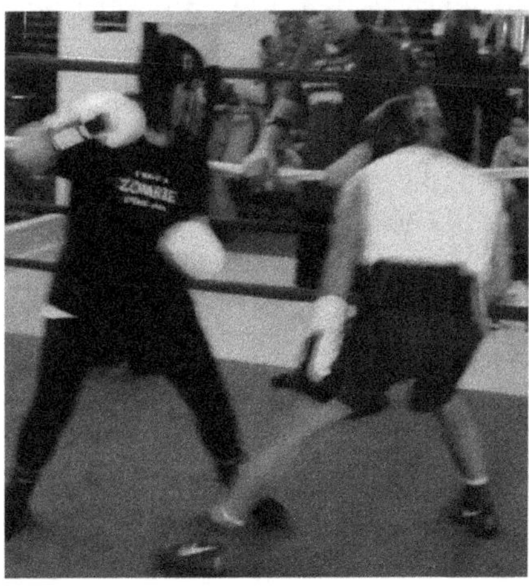

And are you planning to step in the ring with any of the above mentioned? And did any of those interviews in any way lead to you stepping into the ring? (Smile.)

Judyth Piazza: You know… I wouldn't mind getting in the ring with the Hawaiian Mongoose to see what I am made of (LOL.)

However, I will admit after I began boxing I went back and reread your interviews several times for motivation as well as checked out a few YouTube videos of the women boxers that you met.

Chase Von: There are a lot of people that want to write news or be reporters Judy, however there are NOT a lot of people that start their own online newspapers and host their own radio shows! Obviously you are going for your dreams Lady!

What was it like in the beginning when you first started? Also, you endured a painful divorce prior to doing any of this, went back to school to learn your trade and were older than most of the other students. Despite that, you've been very successful and are encouraging so many student writers and just writers in general that are in fact building resume's from their contributions here at the SOP!

So again, can you share what it was like starting out? And also what would you say to someone who has something they really want to do but think the ship for that happening, has already sailed due to their age?

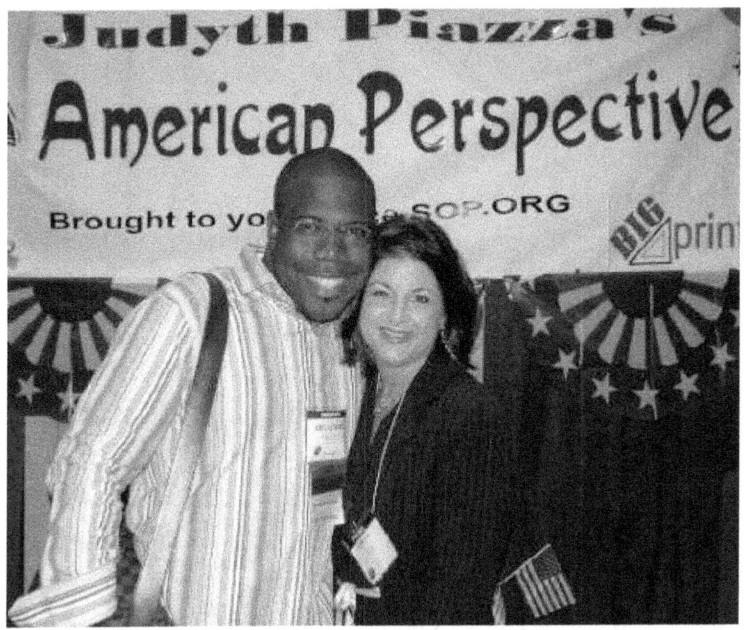

Judyth Piazza: First of all, no one's ship has sailed forever.

Anyone with the survival instinct would chop down a few trees and build their own boat. I have to say that I have been very fortunate to have some very good mentors the whole time and along my whole journey starting with one of my college professors at IRCC who encouraged me to become a writer because otherwise, I hadn't thought of it since I was a kid. My first editor at the Sebastian Sun Newspaper had a huge influence on me as well. She gave me a chance to write for the printed newspaper in Florida with very little experience.

She worked with me until I found my writing style and didn't discourage me from keeping on keeping on.

I also met another friend, Daren Copley at the College Press, which was an online student newspaper. Daren's vision was very similar to my vision and as I helped him with his paper it motivated me to start my own, The Student Operated Press, which today we call The SOP because we now work with more than just students. I was anchoring the TV news at WWCI TV 10 for a bit and asked them to give Daren a try. Not only was I writing for the college press while I was in college in my mid 30's, I was writing for The Calder Gazette and that is where I met Bruce Calder who noticed something in me that no one else did, Bruce helped me to develop my craft as well as teach me the ins and outs of online news. We worked well together so I asked him to build The SOP for me and work with me as my mentor. I had to figure out a way to fund the operation so that is where the radio show came in.

I started an online show to host on The College Press and after 12 weeks we took the show to a couple of local radio stations and they loved it. My producer and I started selling advertising for the show and in the first year we had enough money to keep the show on air as well as promote The SOP on air for 6 months prior to launching The SOP. This is one of the reasons that The SOP did so well from the start. Not many people are able to afford advertising on three radio stations where the show played a total of 6 times a week.

Chase Von: I know you have told me you wake up early and go to bed late, but that you can't wait to get back to work because when you love what you do, it isn't work, it is a pleasure!

Can you share what a typical day is like in the life of Judyth (Mighty J) Piazza?

Judyth Piazza: I have changed a bit since I started The SOP. I now go to bed early and wake up early. I really try my best to get 8 hours of sleep a day because I know it will make me feel better and live longer. I am usually in bed by 10 p.m. and up by 7 a.m. Coffee is the first thing I must get as soon as I roll out of bed. For Christmas I got a pull up bar so now in the mornings I do pull-ups first thing to get my blood pumping. I then turn on my computer and round up my immediate staff and then start going through mounds of emails. I have four people that help me first thing in the morning. I edit Newsblaze, The SOP as well as several other online papers until 10 a.m. as well as my new website, the official Judyth Piazza home page www.judythpiazza.com.

I usually start interviewing for the radio show at 11 a.m. and interview each hour until 3 p.m. In between interviews I edit, publish news, watch the networks and assign stories for writers to cover as well as help with the production of new programs on The SOP Radio Network. I usually eat lunch between 12 and 1 p.m. and take a stroll around the block to stretch or get in the car and head to the beach for some inspiration. If you can't find me at the studio I always tell people I am at the beach.

Everyone that is close to me knows that I am a beach bum. At 3 p.m. I usually help my daughter with her homework; Hillary is a senior in high school so we are hoping to get her into a good college. At 5 p.m. I box for 1 to 1 ½ hours 6 days a week.

After working out, I eat dinner, work for a couple more hours and then head to bed by 10 p.m. – 11 p.m.

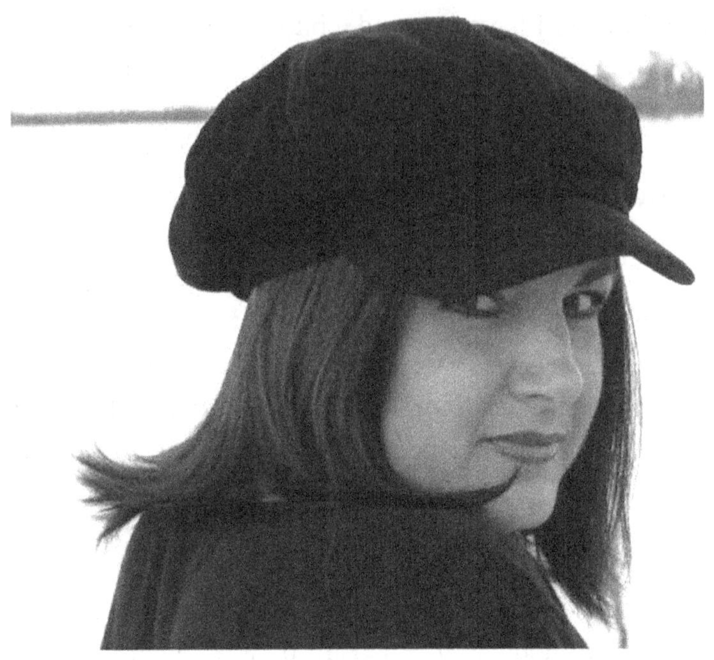

Chase Von: Changing gears, can you tell me and our readers a bit about this fitness program you are now doing and is your buddy John Basedow someone that helped you with it?

Judyth Piazza: John has been a regular on my show since 2005. I have always struggled with fitness because I work so much and always felt like I never had enough time.

One of the best things he ever told me was to take baby steps. Miracles don't happen overnight so when he mentioned baby steps this made sense. I now I have two different types of workout routines.

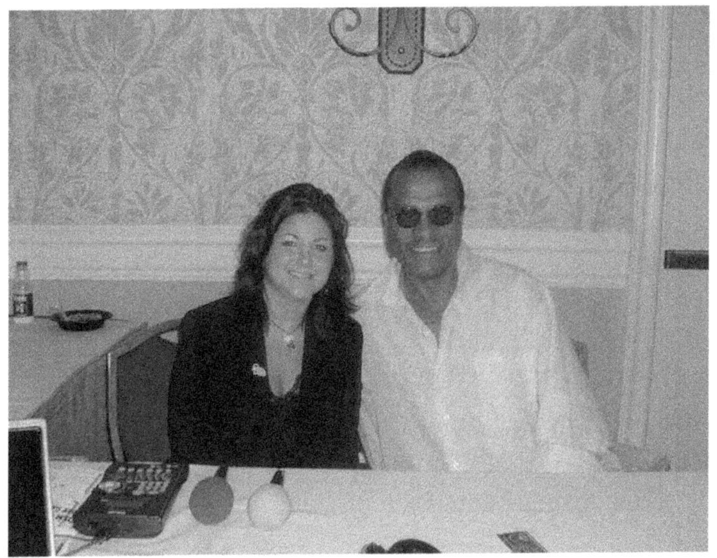

Judyth Piazza and Billy Dee Williams

The first one of course is boxing and the other is strength training that I do in the mornings before I start work 3 days a week. On day one of the 3 day work out I do 4 sets of seated dumbbell curls, 4 sets of standing curls, 4 sets of tricep extensions, 4 sets of calf raises, 4 sets of dumbbell reverse flies and 4 sets of pull ups. On the 2nd day of my 3 day workout I do 4 sets of pushups using a push up stand, 4 sets of pushups with the exercise ball, 4 sets of calf extensions and stretching. On the 3rd day we focus strictly on different type of leg exercises.

For my boxing workout I start out with 10 minutes of stretching, then 30 minutes of jump rope. Next, I put on my wraps and shadow box three 2 minute rounds. Then I put on my boxing gloves and work on the heavy bag, the reflex bag, and mitt training usually 3 two minute rounds. Then it is time for my favorite part, full contact sparring. I don't know if I mentioned it but my daughter and my niece also box with me.

Needless-to-say, this is a great way to work out family differences or a sassy mouthed teenager (LOL.)

Eating the right food is also very important to your fitness routine.

Chase Von: You have interviewed so many famous people in different areas it would take up I don't know how many pages to mention them all! But who are some of the people that have really left a lasting impression on you?

Judyth Piazza: In the past this is where I would take the opportunity to start name dropping some of the great people that have been on my show, great people like yourself. But I guess if I really thought about it and had to pick one or two, I think they would be Sean Stephenson, Author and Speaker and Robin Meade, CNN. Sean was a guest that personifies and embodies the true soul of my program. Sean was expected to die at birth due to Ostegenesis Imperfacta or the glass bone disease. Sean has proven that giving up is not the answer. He is one of the most remarkable guys that I have ever met. Sean has worked on Capitol Hill as Legislative Affairs Support Staff for Congressman William O. Lipinski and in the White House as a Presidential Liaison for the Office of Cabinet Affairs with President Bill Clinton.

Another person that had a very huge impact on me was Robin Meade. Robin Meade was the first person to give me a chance and my very first interview. When I started my radio show, The American Perspective in 2005 I had to figure out who would be my first guest. I wanted to choose someone that inspired me and that I knew that I could learn something from to help me in my journalism career. I had watched Robin almost every morning before leaving for class so I just decided to reach out to her and ask her for an interview. A smart person told me that all I had to do was ask. If she said no, life would go on. So that's what I did. I found her contact information and just asked. During the interview Robin told me, "Judy, someone has to do this job and it might as well be you."

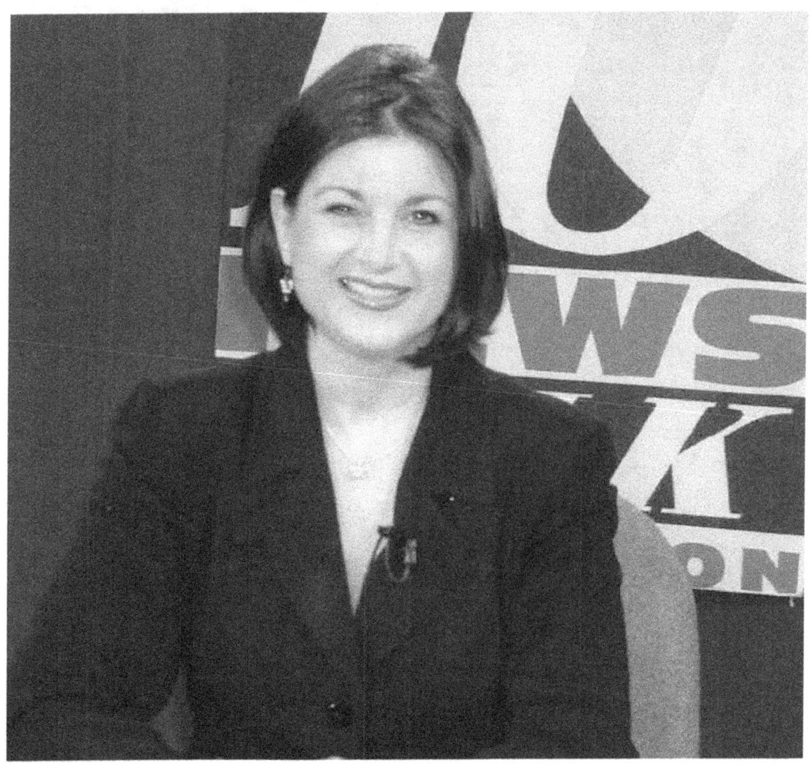

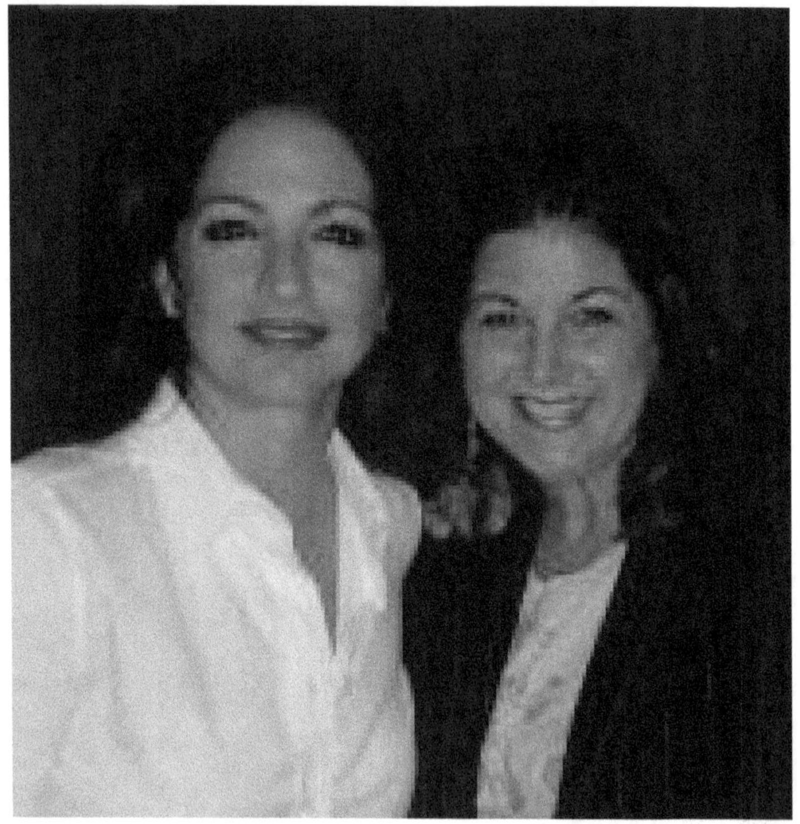

Gloria Estefan and Judyth Piazza

Chase Von: You're an award winning journalist and you also use to be a News Anchor/Reporter on WWCI TV 10 News.

You've also been a Freelance Correspondent for *Sebastian Sun Newspaper* Sebastian Florida, *Fort Pierce Tribune*, Pt. St. Lucie News and Women's Independent Press, Pittsburg, PA and are also the two time winner of the Italian America Civic

Association Scholarship and also won the American Association of University Women Scholarship!

You were also the Executive Editor of *Florida People Magazine*, a Freelance Writer for SOTAC Magazine out of Charlotte North Carolina and the Editor and Chief and Content News Manager for *NewBlaze* in Folsom California where you add more than 200 stories a day! And your radio show can of course be heard on The SOP Radio Network.

You're a member of the Florida Press, the Committee of Concerned Journalist, The National Press Photographers Association and the Association of Women in Communications. Might I also mention you're a graduate of the University of Central Florida with a degree in Organizational Communication!

I'm sure there is more but getting tired of typing all your credits. (Smile.) What can you tell our readers about on top of all that, you are also acting in movies as well?

Judyth Piazza: Another thing that I am really proud of is that I received a planning grant from the University of Central Florida to come up with better ways to use the Internet for information dissemination. Yes, I am toying around with a few acting roles that have been coming my way. The most recent movie that I was in and completed was "Blood Moon." Producer Chuck Williams recently asked me to be in one of his up and coming movies.

Chase Von: What are some of your favorite meals Judy? And since you have begun this exercise program, are there things you use to eat you are staying away from now?

Judyth Piazza: I live in South Florida so I am partial to Cuban food. The best way that I can describe the cuisine is it is kind of like American soul food meets the tropics. I also eat a lot of Medditerrian food and of course my all time favorite is PIZZA.

The workouts that I do involve a lot of sweating so I can pretty much eat what I want.

Chase Von: I know you are not only a dreamer, but a doer---What would you tell people that do have dreams that haven't acted on them yet?

Also, what would you say if you were standing before a microphone that could be heard by every child on the planet, and regardless of what language they spoke, they would understand you?

What positive advice would you give the children, if that were possible?

Judyth Piazza: I would tell people that have a dream and have not yet acted on them simply this: The very moment that you take the first physical, tangible step towards a goal or a dream it has already begun to come true.

All you have to do now if forge ahead, break your dream or goal into little baby steps and complete them one at a time then the only possible outcome is success.

If I could talk to every child in the world at one time, I would say love your neighbor, learn to read and speak as many foreign languages as you can, find a problem in the world that needs to be solved and go fix it.

Chase Von: How important is family to you, and what is your take on the state of our current world?

Judyth Piazza: I have two wonderful children, Tucker 20, and Hillary 17. Family is very important to me but at the same time my family can be my biggest critics and obstacles sometimes. However, being Italian I am very close with my family and I am glad that we can all be close together during these exciting times that I am currently living in.

I am very concerned about the state of the world right now. The Middle East has always been an important part of the world, long before our dependency on oil came along. So, I believe that we need to keep a very vigilant eye on the violence that is taking place over there. One thing that bothers me is that we went to war in Iraq to eliminate Saddam Hussein's chemical weapons stockpile but we found nothing. Today on the news I heard a reporter talking about Kaddafi's chemical weapons program. So, my problem is, if we were willing to go to war over a weapons program that did not exist why are we not willing to go to war over a chemical weapons program that everyone knows exists and will probably be used on the people of Libya at every moment.

I also think that we will soon have to make a choice when democracy rears its head in Saudi Arabia. Will the US protect our friends and oil interests and turn our backs on democracy or will we risk democracy and a free market economy in Saudi Arabia which will lead to astronomical oil prices. Because in a free market economy, need dictates price.

Chase Von: Who are some of the people in life that you truly admire and look up to?

Judyth Piazza: One of my biggest mentors in journalism is Djelloul Marbrook. I met Djelloul as a guest of my radio show in 2006 and asked him to be a part of The SOP. Djelloul is always available to mentor our writers and goes out of his way to support The SOP. Also, I met Alan Gray at Newsblaze in 2006.

Alan saw what I was doing with the SOP and knew that I needed an income while developing our business model.

I started editing for him as a contractor and never looked back.

I have also became very good friends with Joe Estevez, uncle of Charlie Sheen and brother of Martin Sheen.

He has been the person that has encouraged me the most when it comes to acting and Hollywood. Joe is a great guy and willing to help anyone that asks.

Chase Von: Do you have any projects your working on you can give the readers here a heads up about?

Judyth Piazza: I am currently working on my first book, which you are working on as well.

The book is a collection of some of my most memorable interviews as well as a few other special features such as my fitness routines, lots of photos and a few surprises. A neat feature of the book is that readers can visit TheSOP.org and search our archives to listen to the original audio interviews from the book.

Chase Von: Well Judy, (Mighty J) before we close, is there anything you would like to tell possible writers or those interested in writing for the SOP? I.e. What kind of credentials you are looking for, what they can expect because speaking from my own experience, I've met so many fantastic people through writing here and in so many ways, it has broadened my world.

So I thank you for that so very much and again, if someone is interested, how should they go about contacting you to get started?

Judyth Piazza: Well, we are currently looking for new writers, broadcasters, cartoonists and up and coming musicians to submit their work. The best thing that someone could do if they would like to work with us is email a short bio and a brief summary of why they would like to be a part of the SOP team to judy@thesop.org and I will get back to everyone personally.

Chase Von: Going to let you get back to that busy schedule of yours now, Lady, and WBIT.

(Will be in touch) but that is something we always are any way huh? (Smile.)

Judyth Piazza: Thank you, Chase, for believing in me as an author and being a mentor at The SOP.

"The very moment that you take the first physical, tangible step towards a goal or a dream it has already begun to come true."

--- Judyth Piazza

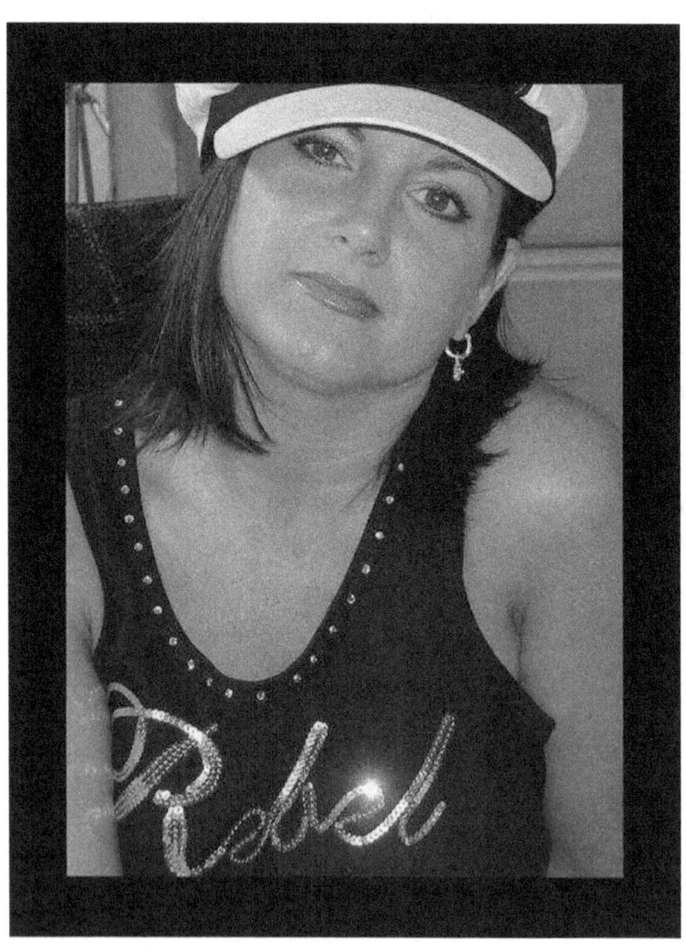

Interview with Ada "Ace" Velez

SIX TIME FEMALE WORLD BOXING CHAMPION

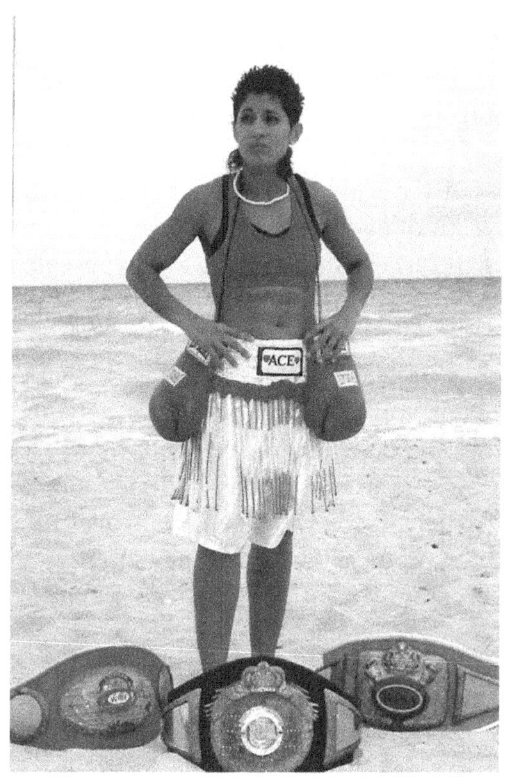

Chase Von: Hey Ada and it was great talking with you! On behalf of the *Student Operated Press* and myself, thanks so much for finding the time to do this interview with me and sharing yourself with our readers here at the SOP! I know you're in training now for yet another *Championship Belt,* so really appreciate you squeezing this in!

Ada Velez: Thanks Chase, the SOP and it's my pleasure!

Chase Von: I have a myriad of questions I want to ask you but before we get to all those--- Where were you born, where did you grow up and how was your childhood? Also, have you always been so athletic?

Ada Velez: I was born in Hollywood, Florida but we moved back to Puerto Rico when I was still a baby and lived there until I was about 12. We then moved back to Dania, Florida.

And yes Chase, I have always been athletic! In High School I ran track, played Volley Ball and Basketball and for three years straight I was the MVP in Softball. I played catcher and my nickname then was "The Wall!" (Smile.)

But over all my childhood was horrible Chase and I'm so glad I was able to reach you to up date and correct this part of the interview before the book went live. Yes, I still participated in sports but I was raised in the "Hood" in a very bad neighborhood where there were gangs all over and yes, I was part of one (You sprout, where you are planted), but I also want to say that if I can make it, coming from where I did, anyone can make it! And I hope not only to be an inspiration to women fighters, but also to the people who find themselves in the same "Sitch" I was once in.

Our track team won second in the District Nationals two times and I ran the 100 relay and the four hundred relay.

Unfortunately I didn't complete High School but I did eventually get my GED. I didn't get into boxing until I met Bonnie Canino and it's a good thing I did, because it got me out of the streets.

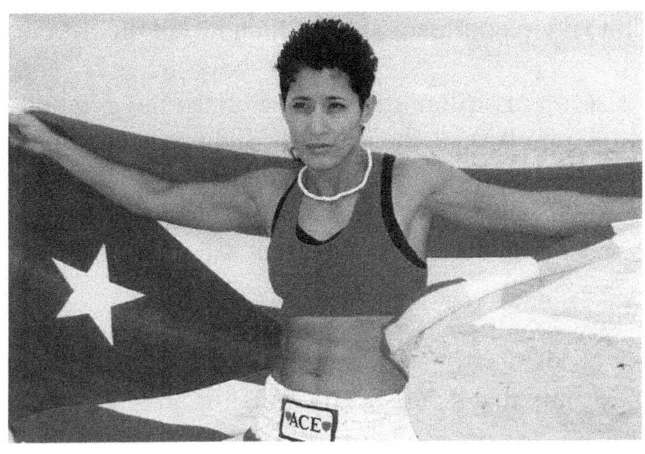

Chase Von: Now before we get into the boxing questions, one thing I want to point out as a heterosexual male to our male readers is that some of the loveliest women in the world are also into the sweet science.

To be honest, prior to interviewing Hollie (Hot Stuff) Dunaway I really hadn't paid too much attention to that. Sure, I knew of Laila Ali and Christy Martin and they are both attractive, but then there is yourself, Hollie, Krisztina (Baby Girl) Belinszky, Stacey (stalo) Riele, Mia St. John, Susianna "Susi" (Killer Queen) Levonovna Kentikian, Ina Menzer, Melinda Cooper, Holly Holm, Ana Julaton, Ria Ramnarine, Elena "Baby Doll" Reid, Chantel Cordova, Jennifer Salinas and really too many for me to list.

As I've said before many times, I'm married (Happily I might add), but not yet visually impaired. (Smile.)

But I also happen to think companies and advertisers etc are really making a huge mistake in not supporting you all more and using you in commercials and such to sell their products.

And it also seems to me like other countries as a whole, are a lot more supportive of their female fighters in comparison to America--- In particular, Mexico and Germany.

Would you agree or disagree with that statement Ace?

Ada Velez: Well first of all thanks Sweetie! And I do think there are a lot of attractive women in Boxing as well as hot men but I think that is an added bonus for all who are active in sports.

When your profession is something you have to be physically fit in order to be competitive in it, it not only makes you healthier but also allows you to look as good as you perhaps can. I don't think that way myself because I'm a humble woman but a little exercise for anyone will not only make them look better, but feel better also. Though sometimes I work so hard it is more pain than feeling good. But you want to work hard in training so when you are in the ring you're just having fun. (Smile.)

And yes Chase, I do agree with you that other countries are more supportive of their female fighters. In the state of Florida alone, it is obvious they support more male fighters than women and I think that is how it is over all in America as a whole. I can tell you this, when I fight out of country, I make a lot more money than I do here in the US.

Another thing that annoys me to no end is in most commercials they use real male boxers but in other commercials, they put up women that aren't really boxers and make it look like they are.

I'm always like--- "Who is that?" When I see things like that Chase it is so very unfair.

In Tennis for example and a few, very few might I add other sports, they use people like Venus and I'm always happy to see that because she is a champion and she earned it! Why isn't it the same way for us Female Boxing Champions?

And not only that, we really risk injury a lot more and we aren't respected in the main stream for our efforts or at least as it stands now.

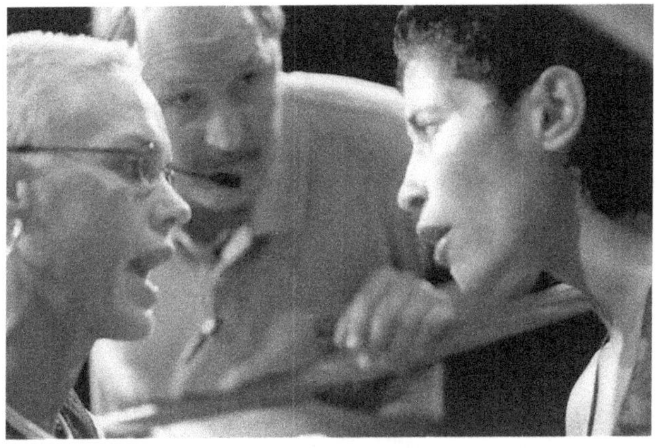

Bonnie Canino and Ada Velez between rounds

Chase Von: Now on to boxing questions Ace. Prior to revisiting women's boxing I was use to seeing what looked like cat fights. But in all honesty, when I watch fights now I am amazed at how technically proficient you women all are in the ring. In fact, some of you are so good that I find myself comparing the styles some of you employ to males I've seen in the past.

Hollie (Hot Stuff) Dunaway and I've told her this, reminds me a bit of Sugar Ray Leonard minus all the show boating he sometimes did. You remind me a bit of Hector (Macho) Camacho at certain times when I watch you fight.

The incredible Ann Wolfe who I've communicated with a few brief times and is truly a sweet heart, reminds me a bit of the equally impressive Joe Frazier and of course, Laila Ali reminds me of her father.

In short, the bar has definitely been raised and in my view, women (many of them) are just as good in the ring as men now.

Do you think in the not too distant future, that there will come a time when perhaps HBO, Show Time or another huge organization will feature as the main event an all women card for Championship bouts? And just being honest, I personally think if they did and it was marketed correctly, it could perhaps be the biggest pay day for them in recent memory.

Ada Velez: That would be a dream comes true! And it would inspire a lot of women to push even harder to become the best fighters that they can. Women fight really because they love the sport. Not for the money so our fights are always for real.

Chase Von: Speaking of pay days, you've held at one time or another four World Championships belts and one International belt. You told me and I have to agree, if a male had even half the accomplishments that you have already achieved, they would be millionaires!

Our mutual friend and "*Photographer Extraordinaire* and Author of "*Extraordinary Women of the Ring*", Mary Ann

Lurie Owen shared with me recently, they are possibly going to make Female Boxing one of the events in the next Olympics. One, would you be eligible for that because I know professional basketball players have played in the Olympics and two, do you think if it is included, that it might lead to a more equitable pay for female fighters after that kind of world wide exposure?

Because right now, women fighters aren't fighting for money or not much in comparison--- They are fighting because they love the sport and they aren't getting hardly anything although they are doing the same thing and taking the same risks as their male counter parts.

Ada Velez: That would be a God send! And I would be eligible and I would love to compete for the United States.

Maybe that would even the playing field a bit and women could seriously box as a career and get adequate pay instead of, fighting now and many of them or us, having to work at another job just to make ends meet.

Right now, there are men that are not at the top in various categories or weight classes that can still make a comfortable living where as there are "Champions" in women's boxing, that still have to do other things to survive.

Chase Von: I think another thing Ada that would improve purses is if more women supported female boxers as well. I don't know if you'll agree with this but there seems to me, to be a mindset--- Among many women where they will watch men fight but aren't interested in watching women fight.

I personally don't have to clock when and where Manny "Pac

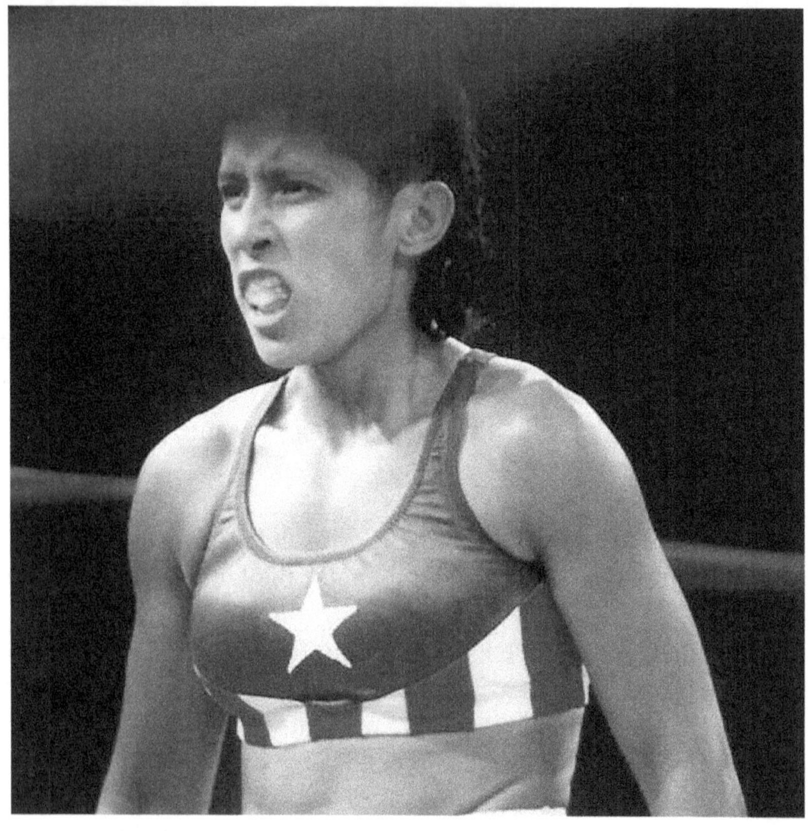

Man" Pacquiao is going to fight next because my wife will tell me. (Smile).

But she also doesn't seem to be very interested in watching women fights. This is probably out dated, but I recall hearing years ago women out numbered men three to one. But from what I can see, mostly men support women boxers by and large although there are a few women but both men and women seem to support male boxing.

Personally now, I enjoy a good women's boxing match or MMA match as much as I enjoy watching the male ones.

But if more women, just by mere numbers alone supported females I think purses would change overnight. Your thoughts on that? Or do you think most women are too lost in the belief it is OK for men to fight but don't like seeing women battle it out?

Ada Velez: I have to correct you a little bit Chase, there are actually a lot of men as well, that don't like seeing women fight. So on top of a lot of women not being supportive, that factors in as well. I do think that if it were included in the Olympics like you mentioned in the question above, it might help things in that regard.

But I've been fighting for about 13 years and you know how many titles and Championships I have won. I haven't gotten paid throughout that entire time more than a few thousand dollars a fight. After this coming fight I have been told, that if I win, I will then start making some real money.

I've been pretty sad over the years about that--- To accomplish all the things I have and to not get credit for it. But it looks like that might change. I also want to add that it isn't just boxing, but all female sports whether it be WNBA, Professional Soccer players, Professional women Softball players etc that get the short end of the stick.

I really believe we should all be getting equal rewards, but even in the year 2011, across the board except perhaps in Tennis, women athletes are still treated monetarily as if what they do is not as important as their male counter parts. Not to sound too melodramatic but once upon a time, slavery was accepted in America and it took years to change. And even though women have progressed in many areas where they once couldn't just like slaves eventually earned equal rights--- In women's sports over all, it seems like we are still treated as second class citizens. I do hope that changes soon and that I am a part of it!

Here's something else I think is really encouraging Chase! It boiled down to a "Woman" and an "African American man" this last election. Something that hasn't ever happened!

So that encourages to me also to continue to be "The Change" in boxing and in women's sports in general!

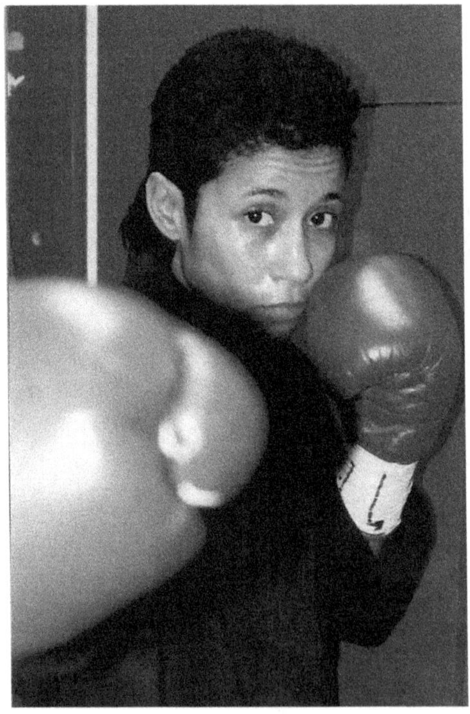

Chase Von: I have to ask this before I move on. In all sports one risk injury, but in boxing the purpose is to punch and not get punched and if you are great at it, you knock out your opponent and the sooner, the better. (Smile.)

But there's a lot more that goes on than just hitting. It's physical, it's mental, and there is the use of the ring to your advantage and also points scored for the most landed punches.

But what I want to ask you about is the things that often aren't seen--- I.e. like elbows and head butts. Are there some fighters who do it intentionally to throw other fighters off their game plan?

Also are their fighters that are behind that resort to that in order to injure an opponent because they aren't being affective in other areas?

Because I saw you get head butted in your fight against Rolanda Andrews and I was surprised they didn't take any points from her when she threw you down.

Ada Velez: When it comes to the head butts, throwing you to the floor or elbowing--- They're just showing that they are frustrated because you have already beaten them, mentally and physically.

Think about it Chase--- If they are doing that even after they KNOW the rules, which are explained to them, then they are showing that they are giving up and have already lost and lost heart to still fight like the rules say they should.

When someone starts doing that to me, I know I have already defeated them.

Chase Von: Speaking of Rolanda Andrews and might I add I have nothing but respect for anyone who steps in the ring and lays it all on the line--- She knocked out Mia St. John yet when she faced you, you literally destroyed her!

I think men or women could view that fight and use it as a learning tool to show fighters how they should fight. You in my opinion fought a perfect fight! You worked the body so hard she was gasping for breath between rounds and again, this is someone that knocked out Mia St. John!

But what I want to ask is do you look at fighters before you fight them and formulate a game plan along with your trainer?

Or do you just bring your game? My father, now deceased loved boxing and one of his favorite sayings was, "Kill the body and the head will die." You decimated her with body shots and that's not to say you didn't also go to the head but again, I'm wondering do you view fighters and train for how they fight or do you just feel them out and go to work?

Ada Velez: For me it starts at the weigh in--- When we make initial eye contact. The next phase for me is the first round. I KNOW from then on what will more than likely happen. I personally don't watch other fighters previous fights or hardly ever.

That's not how I prepare. I train and my trainers do that, and then without telling me, add in what they believe will get me the victory. So for me, it is more instinctive. I don't look at someone's fights and think... "They do this, so I think I better do that to counter it." I train--- And my trainers train me in such a way that I'm doing it without "Thinking" about it...

So big PROPS to my trainers and sparring partners! When I step in the ring you are seeing all their hard work and preparation in action as well and Chase, in Martial Arts they call it I believe, muscle memory. If you HAVE to think about what you are doing you lose valuable time. They prepare me in such a way that I am SO prepared I don't have to think, my body instinctively does that for me. (Smile.)

Chase Von: I always try and ask a tough one Ada and normally I refer to something in the news that is catching attention but in this case, I want to ask you something personal.

You don't have to answer this if you don't wish to but you were arrested for giving out vouchers at a Casino you worked at. You're also a former gang member but from everything I can see you had turned your life around for the good. It also looks to me like you were just being friendly and in my opinion, America has the largest number of inmates in the world and that alone says there is something wrong with the system.

I've been a Correctional Officer in a jail and I too have been arrested. (I also got tazered and the charges were later dropped but back to you.)

I personally think you were dealt with too harshly. In my opinion violent criminals and sex offenders should be kept away from the general population but people that aren't violent or a threat to human life who commit a wrong or a perceived wrong I think should be dealt with in a different manner. I also know from talking with you, they wanted you to tell on others which you refused to do and that too ended up increasing the time you had to serve.

One of my favorite poets is Kahlil Gibran and now that I know you love poetry as well from speaking to you, thought I would share this with you--- Kahlil wrote this many years ago and I think there is much wisdom in this and Poets---- And I'm sure my friend and fellow phenomenal Poet Ed Roberts would agree, often don't get the recognition they deserve either in most cases so Poets and most female fighters have much in common in that department...

Of the Martyrs to Man's Law

Are you one who was born in the cradle of sorrow,
reared in the lap of
misfortune and in the house of oppression?

Do you sup on a dry crust moistened
with tears?

Are you partaking of turbid water in which are
mingled sweat and blood?

Are you a soldier compelled by the harsh law of man to
forsake wife and children, and go forth into the field of battle
for the sake of Greed, which your leaders miss-call Duty?

Are you a poet content with your crumbs of life, happy in
the possession of parchment and ink, and sojourning in
your land as a stranger, unknown to your fellow men?

Are you a prisoner, pent up in a dark dungeon for some petty
offense and condemned by those who seek to reform man by
corrupting him?

Are you a young woman on whom God has bestowed beauty,
but who has fallen prey to the base lust of the rich, who
deceived you and bought your body but not your heart, and
abandons you to misery and distress?

If you are one of these, you are a martyr to man's law.

You are wretched, and your wretchedness is the fruit of the iniquity of the strong and the injustice of the tyrant, the brutality of the rich, and the selfishness of the lewd and the covetous.

Comfort ye, my beloved weak ones, for there is a Great Power behind and beyond this world of Matter, a Power that is all Justice, Mercy, Pity and Love.

You are like a flower that grows in the shade; the gentle breeze comes and bears your seed into sunlight, where you will live again in beauty.

You are like the bare tree bowed with winter's snow; Spring shall come and spread her garments of green over you; and Truth shall rend the veil of tears that hides your laughter.

I take you unto me, my afflicted brothers, I love you, and I condemn your oppressors.

Kahlil Gibran

--Kahlil Gibran, The Voice of The Master, Ch. 2 "Of the Martyrs to Man's Law"

So my question for you Ada is now you are back on your path

and shooting for yet another *World Title*, but did that experience make you wiser and even stronger? Or did it make you bitter?

Because that kind of time away, regardless of how good someone is can't be good for their progress and especially in an environment where you can't really train like you could on the outside. And also, you're fortunate to be able to fight and have that to rely on but if you weren't a fighter that really would have set you back not only in time, but in career choices.

Also which I found truly touching, can you tell our readers what you shared with me about the lasting friendship you made in there and how no matter where we find ourselves, God is looking out for us?

Ada Velez: First Chase, I love that poem and Kahlil Gibran's writings as well as the one's you yourself have wrote and shared with me! (You know I do love my poetry). And second, it was SO hard!

It also definitely made me bitter because I can't tell you how much it hurt me to be away from my son for that long which hurt me more than the embarrassment.

What I did, a LOT of people were doing Chase and my main goal--- Because I loved working there, was to keep the customers happy. Call me naive but it's just like the Bible says, money is the root of all evil and there's a lot of it floating around Casino's. And I figured since there were so many people doing it, why not? I wasn't trying to rob anyone, just keep the people that came to the Casino, coming back and happy. But yes, it did make me wiser and definitely stronger spiritually.

What a lot of people don't know is that I could have received a lesser sentence and I could have done that by telling them the others--- That were also guilty of what they came after me for but I wouldn't do that!

(I didn't know it was wrong and I wasn't going to tell on others and mess up their lives that were just as naive as I was.)

At least six others however, were also found guilty without me telling on anyone.

And yes, boxing saved me from the streets and I once was in a gang but keep in mind Chase, I didn't think it was wrong to please our customers and prior to this happening; I still had no record what's so ever and hadn't even gotten a traffic ticket!

And I'm not sharing this because I'm looking for sympathy Chase--- But when I was in I was so depressed that I couldn't train, I didn't eat and my weight dropped to well under a ninety pounds.

That brings me to this; God was DEFINTELY looking out for me, even in prison. There was a girl there that is now my friend for life and I can't wait till she gets out although I am not allowed to contact her or visit her. She saw me withering away and instead of hurting me or taking advantage of me in my weakened state--- She made it her DUTY in life to make me eat, to raise my spirits from the depression I was in and yes, I got me to even start training again.

Let me say this Chase and to all the readers--- No matter what state you find yourself in, God can send you an Angel. Believe me, I've been told I should write a book about my life many times and one day I might, but that is something that I don't think I could ever articulate to anyone on how much it increased my faith in the Almighty!

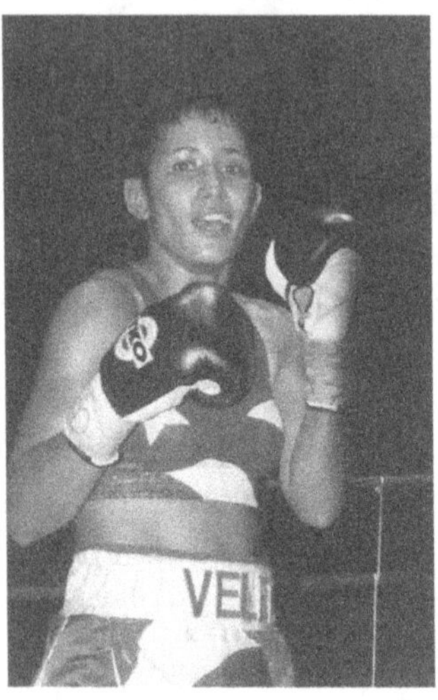

Chase Von: Now onto something lighter and I sincerely thank you for sharing your thoughts on the above and I'm sure your fans are more the wiser now from hearing your side of things.

Your accomplishments are off the charts!

In your amateur career you were undefeated and you also won a *National Title!* You are also the first Puerto Rican woman to win a women's *World Boxing Championship!*

This makes you a FOREVER part of lasting history!

As a professional you have an impressive record of 18 wins, 3 losses, 3 draws and 6 KO's! And I understand one of those losses was very controversial and many thought you won your fight in Denmark with Anita Christensen and even the Danish press strongly criticized the decision, saying on record you were robbed of your title.

You have won the WIBA (in different weight classes) and the IBA belts and are going to be battling undefeated, Melinda Cooper who has a stellar record of 20 wins, 0 losses and 11 KO's for the IBF Feather Weight World Title on March 31/2011!

What is it you want to achieve in boxing now considering you have already achieved so much?

And in the future do you see yourself bringing back some of those belts that are over in Germany? (Smile.)

And also so our readers in the area can check it out, where is your up and coming fight going to be held?

Ada Velez: Answering your last question first Chase it will be held in Costa Rica and secondly--- I will go "Where Ever" and fight "Whom Ever" so if Germany is where I can get another belt, just let me know when! (Smile.)

And you are right, I have achieved so very much in boxing but it isn't over yet. It is my ultimate goal to encourage women fighters that they too can be rewarded for their efforts and be rewarded the same way men fighters are.

I want to be the best pound for pound and also prove that women fighters can draw millions to watch their events the same as men. We discussed this above but can you imagine a male fighter who has achieved what I have, working a second job to make ends meet?

I don't want freebies, I want just dues and I also want to be so good, I get that and inspire all the female fighters that come after me.

Chase Von: I think it is obvious how you stay in such fantastic shape--- And you have not only some of the quickest hands in the game, but also some of the most powerful legs.

Sorry, have to admit, some men are taken in with the upstairs package but I've always been an admirer of nice legs. (Smile.)

So do you do a lot of road work or are you just genetically gifted in that department?

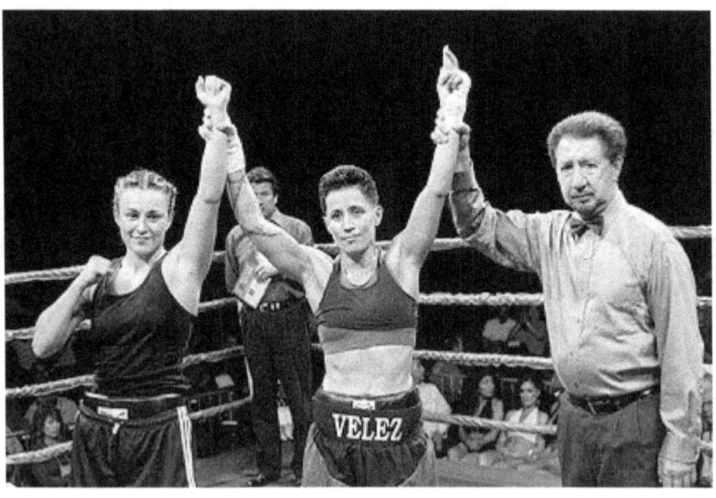

Ada Velez: That's my number one thing--- I love running my eight miles or more and doing my sprints! There are so many elements involved when it comes to winning and 'Endurance' is definitely a big one in boxing. Oh and sorry--- You just complimented me didn't you? Thank you Sweetie! (Smile.)

Chase Von: What are some of your favorite meals? I imagine as a fighter, you have to abstain from those a lot of the times to prepare but when you can really throw down, what is it you dig grubbing on?

Ada Velez: Well, I do love my *Puerto Rican* rice and beans Chase with chicken, (That's part of the dish) and has been around for many generations! But when training I try to eat a lot of fish, potato's and also chicken and stay away from too many red meats. My favorite meals vary with the moods I'm in and change often because I also love trying out different foods when I visit different places--- AFTER the fight. (Smile.)

When you go to other places and countries, you have to be careful you don't eat anything your body isn't use to or that might affect you in ways you wouldn't want it to before a bout. And my two weaknesses Chase are coffee and yes, potato chips. Coffee dehydrates you though so I really have to stay away from *Starbucks* unless I had a REALLY good day of training.

Then I can drive home a normal way vice changing my route home from the gym so I won't see one. (Smile.)

Chase Von: How important are dreams to you? And what would you say if you were standing before a microphone that could be heard by every child on the planet, and regardless of what language they spoke, they would understand you? What positive advice would you give the children, if that were possible?

Ada Velez: Dreams are everything! And I would tell children they can do anything they set their minds too; but to be persistent and not to give up when things don't seem to be working out. That's part of it meaning, you have to sometimes go through some 'Down Times' but instead of letting that stop you, you have to use that to make you stronger! And also this Chase, surround yourself with people that will lift you up when you are down. Or let God send you someone when things are bad.

People see my accomplishments and think WOW, but if they only knew how many times I have had to "Let go and let God..." Maybe when if I write a book, they'll know then. (Smile.)

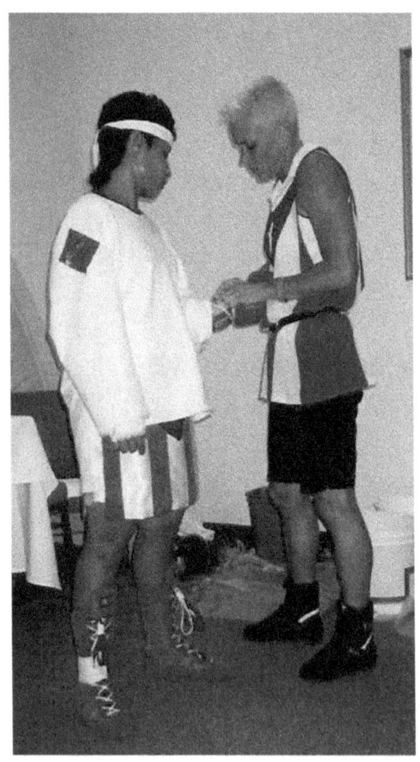

Ada and Bonnie Canino

Chase Von: How important is family to you, and what is your take on the state of our current world?

Ada Velez: Only everything Chase. I still get teary eyed when I think of not being with my son for so long but thank God that has passed! And the world? My heart breaks when I think of those in Japan and all those who are suffering. The state of our world is horrible but I think optimistically--- So I also think if man "Wakes Up"... things can change.

Natural disasters aside--- I do think there are a LOT of things we as people could be doing to make this world better and it is high time we do that! This is the only "Home" after all, any of us really have.

Chase Von: Who are some of the people, not just in boxing, but in life in general that you truly admire and look up to?

Ada Velez: First and foremost--- God! Then Michele Ponales who has been my backbone, my strength and too many things for me to share here. And of course my son who is my right arm and so much more! And I also look up to the rest of my family and friends, trainers, sparring partners, FANS and people like you Chase, who are taking an interest in 'Women's Boxing' and also sharing it more with the world.

Chase Von: Can you share any of your web pages or places where people can find you to learn more about you? And also, I know you're looking for a new sponsor. Would your face book page be the best place for people interested in doing that, to connect with you?

Ada Velez: Sponsors are definitely welcome and I am trying to figure out a connection between *Starbucks* and boxing---

Because considering how much business I give them, they should be sponsoring me! (Smile.)

But yes, people interested in that can hit me up on my face book page...

http://www.facebook.com/profile.php?id=100001119920721

And if they want to learn more about me and my career they can check that out here: http://www.wban.org/biog/avelez.htm

Chase Von: When I was in my last war, they had a USO tour come over to entertain the troops and lift spirits.

I met a lot of famous performers that cared enough to take out some of their time to come and visit us.

But the reason I bring that up is if the opportunity presented itself, would you be willing to go where many people are in harm's way, to give them a bit of entertainment?

I.e. like fight there because I know many of the troops would enjoy that!

Ada Velez: I love that idea! And I would also love to show those that protect our country how fantastic us professional women boxers are! Where do I sign up?

Chase Von: I could keep on asking you questions till time ends Ada, (Smile.)

But I'm already infringing on your time as is, since I know you are training for your next Championship belt.

So I want to thank you "Ace" for spending time with me and our readers and I'm wishing you continued success not only in boxing--- But in all you do and don't be a stranger OK?

Perhaps the next time we chat you can tell me the inside story on your winning this Championship. (That story you told me which shall remain between us about that one fight though is hilarious). (Heh, Heh.)

And going to close this for now with my minimal Spanish, (I had three years in school but like I told you, when I tried to use it in Mexico, I got laughed at on a bus by people holding live chickens)--- Maybe as time goes by you can teach me more, so that doesn't happen again?

So Va Con Dios Lady... (Smile.)

Ada Velez: You do need a LOT of help with your Spanish Chase. If I was on that bus I would have been laughing at you too! (Smile.) But then I would and will help you with it when I can.

So "Thank You" Sweetie and The SOP for having me! And you "Go With God" also. You actually got that one right... For a change. (Smile.)

Ada Velez | Rolanda Andrews 1/2

Link below in the event video does not work:

http://www.youtube.com/watch?v=-q3KoktecWY

Ada Velez | Rolanda Andrews 2/2

Link below in the event video does not work:

http://www.youtube.com/watch?v=7qOqEWHfrPE&NR=1

End of interview...

Chase Von Update:

On March 31st 2011, Ada "Ace" Velez stepped in the ring in Costa Rica in Central America or *República de Costa Rica* with Melinda Cooper for the vacant IBF Jr. Featherweight World Championship.

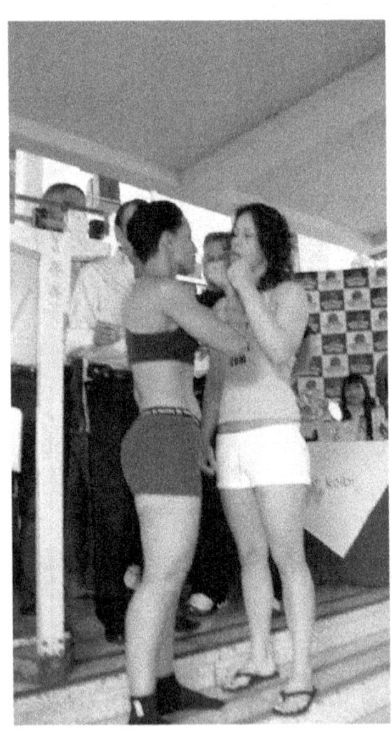

Ada "Ace" Velez and Melinda "La Maravilla" Cooper at weigh in

During Ada's absence from the boxing world which the reasons for are stated above, Melinda Cooper was such a dominant force in the sport she had difficulty even finding any opponents willing to face her. Melinda's impressive record of 21 Wins, 11 KO's, O losses remains one of the best records the world of women's boxing has ever seen.

She also made history as the youngest woman to enter professional boxing under the age of 18, to be granted a boxing license by the state of Nevada. In short, Melinda Cooper has already left a legacy that will be difficult for anyone to follow and has a VERY promising future ahead.

Due to her long absence and Melinda's dominance, despite all Ada's previous accomplishments--- This was not only one of Ada's most challenging moments but one where she was, (Which hasn't happened often), not the favored to win in this bout--- And considered the underdog with six to one odds against her--- Facing a younger, undefeated and very talented fighter who as mentioned above, couldn't find anyone willing to face her and who was destroying the competition that was---'Willing" to step before her.

Ada "Ace" Velez handed Melinda Cooper her first professional loss on 31 March 2011, shocking the boxing world in the process and claimed her 6th Professional World Title! And considering all that Ada has been through, I think and hopefully you will agree, that not only has she shown her heart in the ring as a Champion--- But as a Champion when it comes to all life's adversities... Congratulations P P! (Our little secret Ace)... And keep achieving your dreams "Warrior" and don't change!

Just talking to you and learning about you makes it clear why you are a "Champion" and although people at large admire you as a fighter, if more knew the "You" outside the ring, they too would do what I can't help but doing--- And that is admiring you as a very special soul as well.

Va Con Dios Ace!

Chase ☺

"People see my accomplishments and think WOW, but if they only knew how many times I have had to 'Let go and let God.'"

--- Ada "Ace" Velez

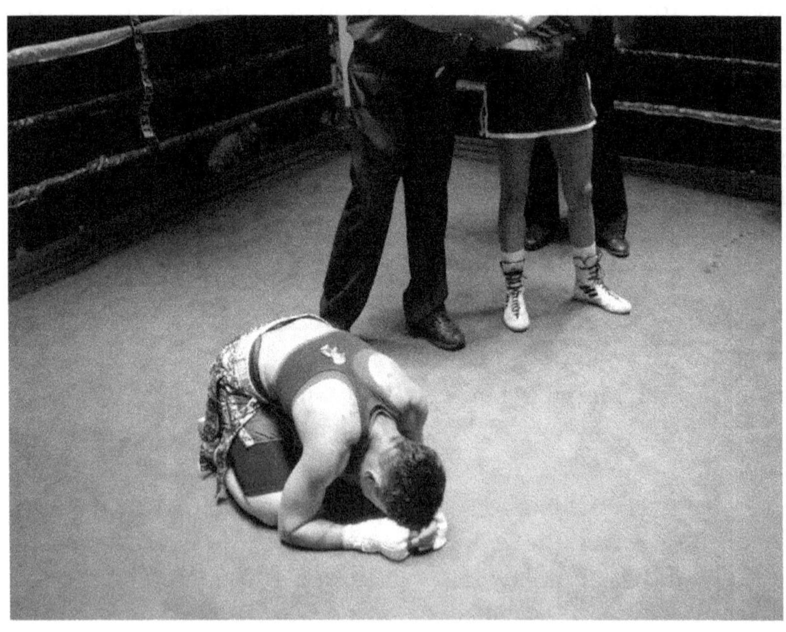

Ada "Ace" Velez giving thanks to God for another victory

About Author Betty Dravis

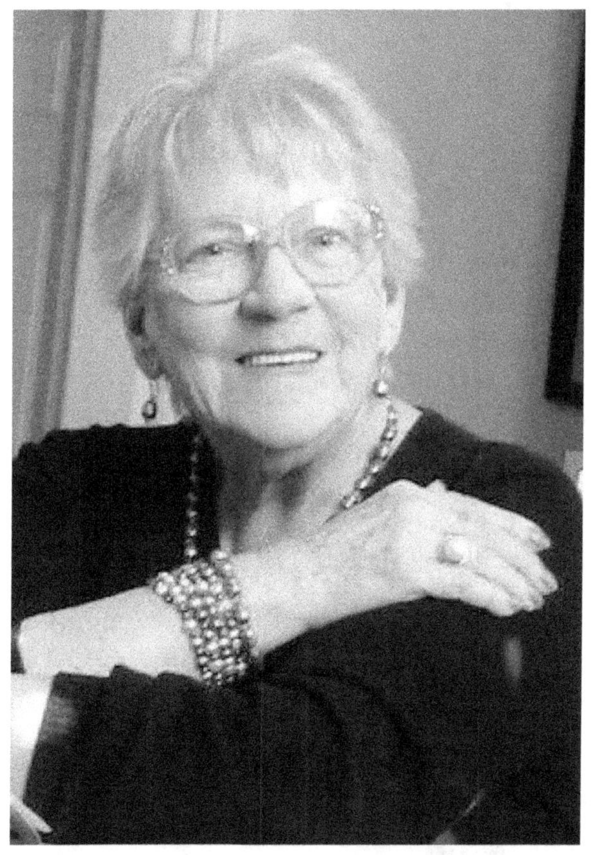

The multi-talented Betty Dravis

Betty Dravis is a retired, award-winning California journalist and newspaper publisher who also hosted a Cable TV talk show.

She was listed in several *Who's Who* books, is an honorary Kentucky Colonel, an esteemed "Dame of Dialogue," a member of American Author's Association, former member of Sigma Delta Chi and San Jose Newspaper Guild. She is the recipient of many California awards, including city, county and state and was a San Jose Woman of Achievement.

In addition to co-authoring this book, Dravis also co-authored the award-winning *Dream Reachers* (with Chase Von). This talented woman is also the author of three novels: *1106 Grand Boulevard,* an epic romantic thriller; *The Toonies Invade Silicon Valley,* a young adult fantasy adventure; and *Millennium Babe: The Prophecy,* a supernatural mystery adventure. She also has a number of published short stories and is an Amazon top reviewer.

Canterbury House Publishing will release two of the above books in eBook format in May 2011: *1106 Grand Boulevard* and *The Toonies Invade Silicon Valley.*

Dravis was born in Ohio, but is a long-time California resident. She has four surviving children, two angels in Heaven, nine grandchildren, four "greats" and a great-great granddaughter. The author now lives in Central California where she's working on her first serial-killer thriller. For more info, visit her website: http://www.bettydravis.com

Betty is also working to promote Stem Cell Research, along with her daughter Mindy James whose son Seth suffered a spinal cord injury in a motocross practice race. Read Seth's story on the Internet at Bridgestohope.com.

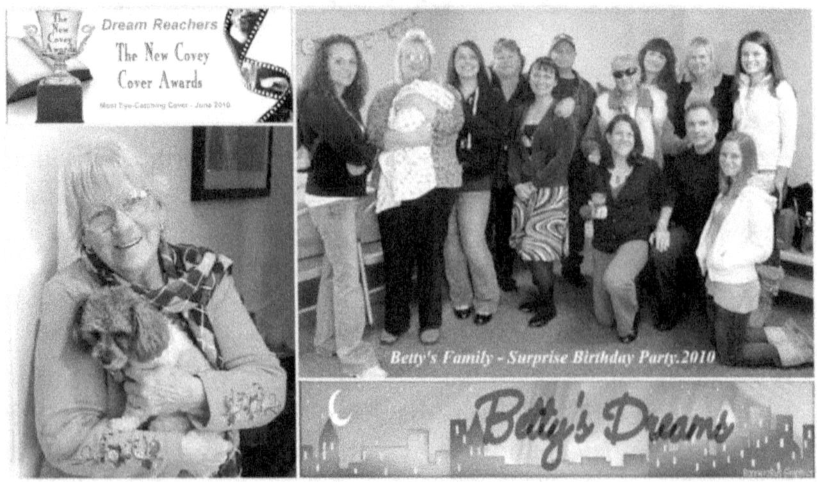

About Author Chase Von

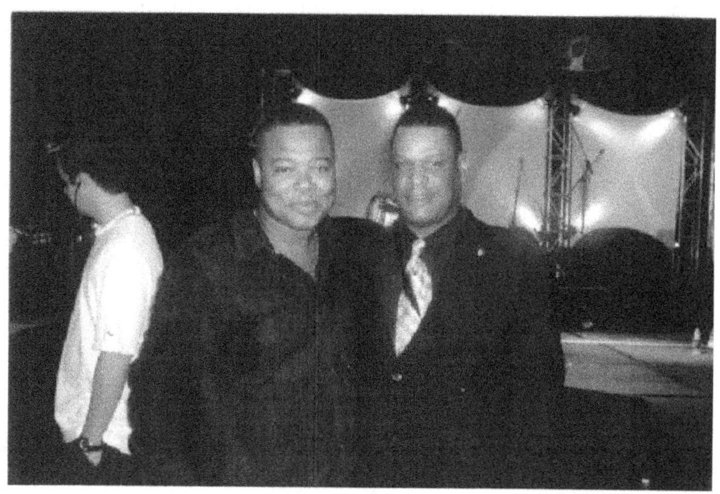

Acclaimed Gospel, Jazz and R&B Guitarist
A. Ray Fuller "*The Weeper*" and Chase Von

Chase Von was born in Japan to a military family. He is a retired United States Marine and also served in the US Army as an air traffic control tower operator. He has also been a county correctional officer, a human services assistant in a mental health facility and is a veteran of Desert Shield and Desert Storm, as well as OIF one and two.

In addition to co-authoring this book, Von also co-authored the award-winning *Dream Reachers* (with Betty Dravis). Von is also the author of *Pink, Blue and Green, Your Chance To Hear The Last Panther* Speak and also continues to contribute and mentor student writers at the Student Operated Press.

Additionally, one of his short stories is included in the 2007 *American Review Literary Journal* Vol. One, created by Bryant H. McGill, world-famous author, poet and consultant to the stars who is also featured in this publication. Pieces of his work have also been included in *Songs of Hope*, a compilation by Sachel.

Von currently resides in California with his beautiful wife and three lovely children. For more info, visit Chase at: http://www.nextcat.com/ChasevonTheLastPanther

"Moments pass
Commit them to memory
Tears fall
Understand
What they mean
Happy times drift up
From the depths
Of sub-consciousness
Think of them
And you might
Save a dream"

Excerpt from poem "You and Me"
by Chase Von
tlp
The Last Panther

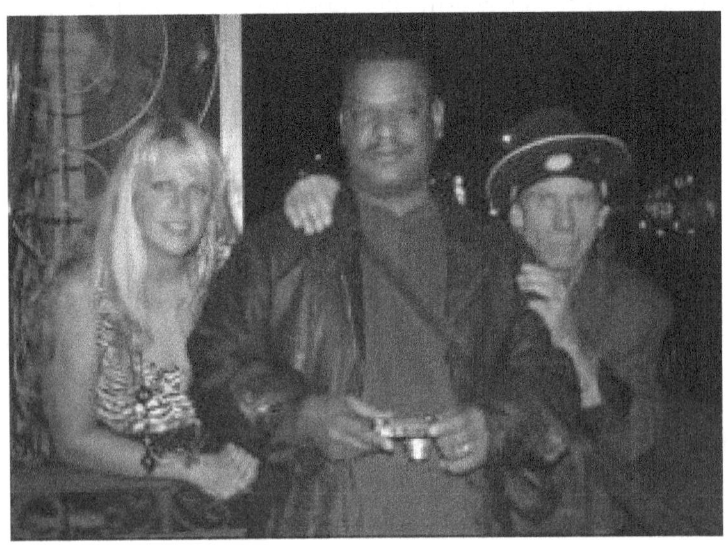

Chase joins MT of "*MT Robison and the Messengers*" and the lovely Linda Shrader, band manager, at an L.A. gig.

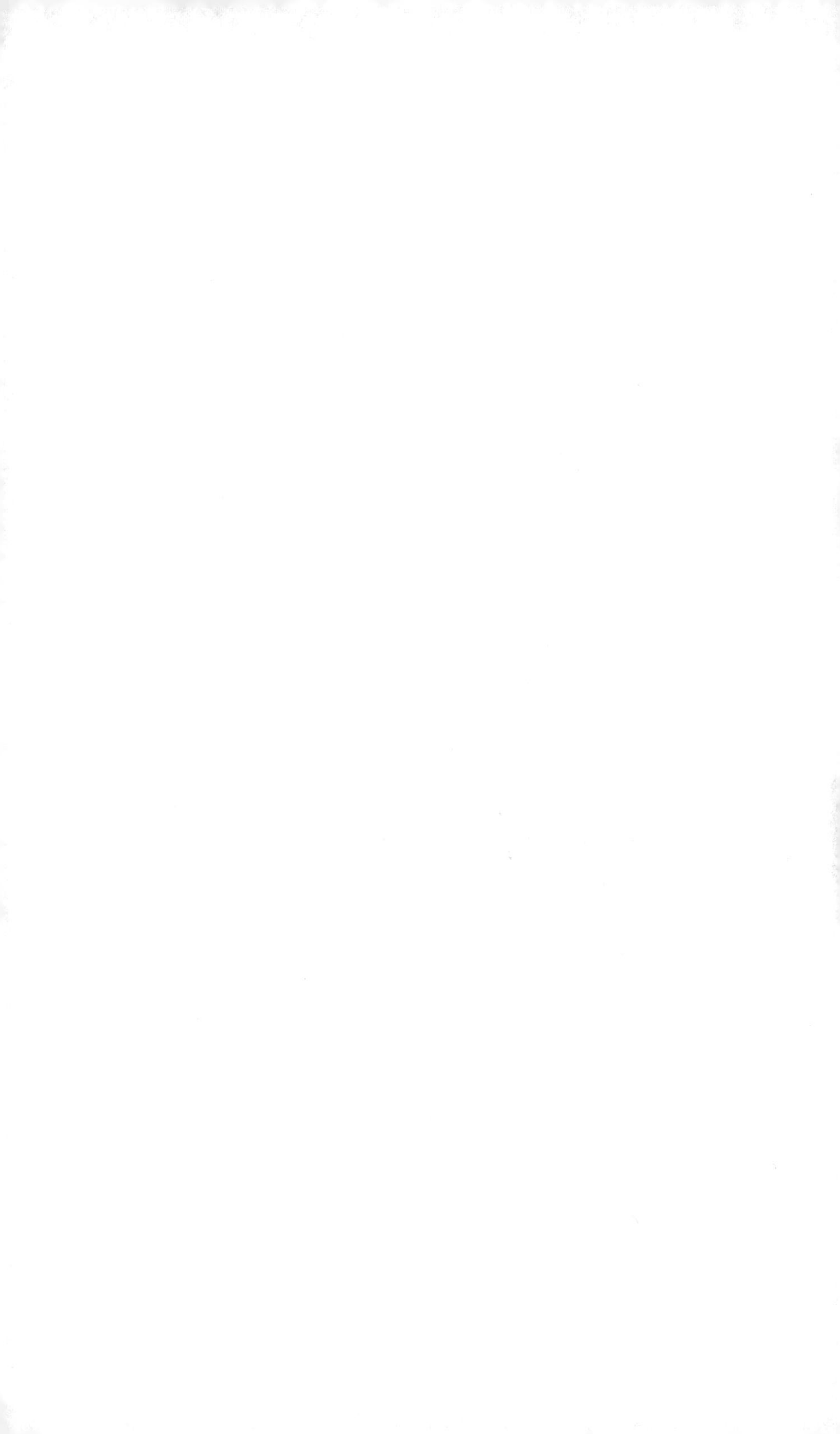